More Tomboy, More Bakla Than We Admit

INSIGHTS INTO SEXUAL AND GENDER DIVERSITY
IN PHILIPPINE CULTURE, HISTORY, AND POLITICS

1521~2021

ACADEMICA
FILIPINA+

More Tomboy,
More Bakla
Than We Admit

*INSIGHTS INTO SEXUAL AND GENDER DIVERSITY
IN PHILIPPINE CULTURE, HISTORY, AND POLITICS*

EDITED BY

MARK BLASIUS
AND
RICHARD T. CHU

vibal
FOUNDATION

MORE TOMBOY, MORE BAKLA THAN WE ADMIT

INSIGHTS INTO SEXUAL AND GENDER DIVERSITY IN PHILIPPINE CULTURE, HISTORY, AND POLITICS

On the cover: Filipino LGBTIA+ emerge from the closet of historical and cultural invisibility to step into the spotlight of Philippine studies. Photography by Patrick P. Olayta.

Executive Director: Gaspar A. Vibal
Program Director: Kristine E. Mandigma
Executive Managing Editor: Christopher A. Datol
Managing Editor: Kate E. Villaflor
Senior Acquisitions Editor: Rosalia E. Eugenio
Development Editor: Andrea L. Peterson
Production Editor: Bernadette M. Antonio
Editorial Assistants: John Nathaniel B. Berbon and Shiloah Grace M. Torrechiva
Indexers: Kim A. Broso and Andrea L. Peterson
Book Design: Francisco dC. Mendoza
Cover Design: Ryan T. dela Cruz
Layout: Patricia Ann G. Chan and Ryan T. dela Cruz
Photo Editing: Ryan T. dela Cruz and Ramcel S. Pon-an
Press Manager: Margaret B. Bacunawa
Print Coordinator: Alex T. Biñas

Published by Vibal Foundation, Inc.
1253 G. Araneta Avenue, Quezon City, 1104 Philippines
Tel. No. +632 85807400
Visit http://www.vibalgroup.com
Shop https://shop.vibalgroup.com

THE NATIONAL LIBRARY OF THE PHILIPPINES CATALOGUING-IN-PUBLICATION DATA

Recommended entry:

    More tomboy, more bakla than we admit: Insights into
      sexual and gender diversity in Philippine culture,
      history, and politics / edited by Mark Blasius and Richard T. Chu—
      Quezon City: Vibal Foundation, [2021], ©2021.
      488 pages, 15.24 x 22.86 cm.

      ISBN 978-971-97-0714-1 (Softbound)
      ISBN 978-971-97-0715-8 (Hardbound)
      ISBN 978-971-97-0737-0 (e-book)

      1. Gays – Identity – Philippines. 2. Lesbians – Identity –
    Philippines. 3. Gender identity – History – Philippines.
    4. Transexuals identity. 5. Gender identity – Social aspects.
    I. Blasius, Mark. II. Chu, Richard T. III. Title.

    306.766   HQ75.5   P020200132

CONTENTS

MINA ROCES
University of New South Wales

Foreword

THIS BOOK IS ESSENTIAL READING for all gender scholars and Filipino specialists as it navigates very well the complex meanings behind the terms used to describe the sexual identities of non-heteronormative individuals in the Philippines and in the diaspora. Among the anthology's main contributions is the way authors have demonstrated brilliantly that the Filipino cultural context does not necessarily conform to Western models used in LGBTIQ studies. Even if Western labels such as gay and lesbian have been appropriated, they are indigenized in ways that in some ways changed the Western-ascribed meanings. For example, Garcia discusses the debate about whether or not to use the word 'queer' or gay among scholars. Men who are sex workers servicing male clients may also perceive themselves to be straight men and not gay (Tolentino). Should the term lesbian be used or is tomboy more appropriate given that in the Philippines, the former implies a feminist identity as well as a sexual identity (Josef)? Pushing the current conceptual barriers in Western sexuality studies, Fajardo reveals how male seafarers have been able to have "meaningful friendships and kinship ties with bio-boys and bio-men," and Alburo's study of gay men in the New People's Army "destabilizes a heterosexualized military masculinity which brings forth the heteronormative image of the soldier as a real man patterned on being strong, aggressive, and skilled in the art of war."

Even indigenous terms such as *bakla* are also problematic. Garcia's astute analysis reveals that a theoretical distinction needs to be made between a *bakla* which is a gender term denoting effeminate or cross-dressing male, and a homosexual which refers to sexual choice. Filipino stereotypes of the '*bakla*' locate them in lower class jobs such as beauty parlours, exhibiting behaviour that is loud and flamboyant. A consequence of this pejorative representation is that Filipino men who have sex with men have internalized this discrimination and deliberately dissociate themselves with *baklas* (Baytan). Thus, as Baytan concludes, gay men and *bakla* prefer to use the term bisexual (BI) "to name themselves when in fact they know themselves to be gay or *bakla*." Tan's insightful research reveals that "it would be useful to remember that a 'bisexual' is often perceived as a "straight-looking gay male." Thus, those who label themselves as bisexual men in the Philippines do not fit the Western definition of bisexual (Baytan and Tan).

Filipino concepts of sexuality which see men as naturally lustful and women as incapable of sexual desire have meant that lesbianism is unfathomable. A consequence of this is that lesbians and tomboys have been invisible, making "outing" such a dangerous act (Pineda). Organizing them into activists also presents practical obstacles. Lesbians continue to be divided by political ideologies (Josef), and still have to gain a mass following in order to become a movement (Pineda). Even in organizations that have sanctioned same-sex relations, such as in the military arm of the Communist Party, ideological positions place issues of sexuality in lower priorities as "heterosexism for that matter, is framed within a totalizing discourse of 'class struggle.' Thus, addressing homosexuality as merely an issue of class oppression obscures the specific experiences of homosexuality in the Philippines" (Alburo).

Finally, the book challenges gender scholars to continue the project of rethinking these non-heteronormative concepts in the Filipino cultural matrix. As Baytan exhorts us in his exceptional chapter: "deconstruct the Kabaklaan from within. Indeed, questions of who is BI (and who is GAY) in the Philippines eventually lead us to the question of who is *bakla*?" After all, the semiotics of sexual identities are never static and continue to change.

Filipino culture's marriage imperative (Boellstorff 2005) and compulsory heterosexuality, legitimized by the strong Roman Catholic beliefs, have marginalized and discriminated against those who do not fit into these cultural norms. Filipino culture sees heterosexual marriage as the rite of passage to adulthood. Those who do not marry heterosexually are imagined to have failed to achieve adult status and suffer terrible social discrimination. Saskia Wieringa's model of heteronormativity and passionate aesthetics includes in this group of marginalized individuals not just those with non-heteronormative sexualities but also single women, single men, widows, separated men and women as absolute divorce is still not legal in the Philippines, and sex workers (Wieringa 2015). Should activists then attack the marriage imperative? Deconstructing conceptual categories, critical evaluations of the lived experiences of these actors, and the sophisticated nuanced interpretations of alternative sexualities in books such as this one, are essential to the mission of breaking the taboos surrounding the topic in Filipino culture, and replacing it with new norms that embrace sexual difference.

BIBLIOGRAPHY

Boellstorff, Tom. *The Gay Archipelago: Sexuality and Nation in Indonesia*. Princeton: Princeton University Press, 2005.
Wieringa, Saskia E. *Heteronormativity, Passionate Aesthetics and Symbolic Subversion in Asia*. Brighton: Sussex Academic Press, 2015.

More Tomboy, More Bakla Than We Admit

INSIGHTS INTO SEXUAL AND GENDER DIVERSITY
IN PHILIPPINE CULTURE, HISTORY, AND POLITICS

Top, Filipino, Nepalese, and Southeast Asian communities came together to celebrate, be seen, and fight for their rights as LGBTQ people in Hong Kong, a city that does not protect the rights of same-sex couples, trans and genderqueer individuals, or migrant workers. Photo courtesy of Athena Lam. *Above*, A March 2018 rally at the People Power Monument by supporters of the SOGIE Equality Bill. Photo courtesy of Gil Calinga for the Philippine News Agency.

The Sexual Orientation and Gender Identity Expression (SOGIE) Equality Bill, also known as the Anti-Discrimination Bill (ADB), was first proposed in 2000 and was passed by the House of Representatives in 2017, but to this day has yet to be approved by the Senate. It seeks to provide equal rights—such as the right to access public services and establishments, among others—to LGBTI individuals in the Philippines who continue to experience discrimination based on their sexual orientation, gender identity, or expression.

MARK BLASIUS AND RICHARD T. CHU

Introduction to LGBTI(Q)A+ Studies in the Philippines—A State of the Field Primer[1]

T HIS VOLUME OF THE ACADEMICA FILIPINA IMPRINT brings to fruition ten years of planning, research, and writing, as well as editorial selection, commissioning, and work of the editors of this volume with the publisher of the series. This work has been done with humility in order to contribute to an ongoing tradition of writing and to make a "textbook" for students and scholars of Philippine studies that is accessible in content as well as in financial cost to the reader. Our aim has been to build one "state of the field" milestone around which discussion and research agendas might continue in the Philippines and its diaspora, in regional and in global LGBTIQ studies.

1   In determining an appropriate "umbrella" term with reference to the diverse populace of those who are sexually marginalized—usually but not necessarily non-heterosexual, and those of non-normative genders as well as their allied individuals and groups in the Philippines that may find kindred identities and practices in the essays we publish here—the editors grappled with a few acronyms. LGBT and LGBTQ (lesbian, gay, bisexual, transgender, queer) appeared to be currently used in many Anglophone contexts. Use of "Q" supposedly appropriates, detoxifies, and resists a term of historical opprobrium despite opposition by some elder LGBTs and others who claim continuing toxicity, especially depending upon its context and subject of use (see, e.g., Pineda, *infra.* p. 99, 103–4). However, within the Philippines (and international contexts) "queer" as a nomenclature has not (yet) gained much traction, except among Filipino academics who read and use "queer theory" in their works (beyond its distinctive methodology, conceived as having a progressive critique of theories prioritizing assimilation of LGBTs into heteronormative societies). It may also be used, as we use it here, due to observation that local practices (see Alcedo's discussion of "sacred camp" herein) or fluidity of gender and sexual identities may have some resonance-in-translation with queer (as a relevant noun, adjective, or verb) in those parts of the world where the term *is* more frequently used. Similarly, SOGIESC (sexual orientation, gender identity and expression, and sex characteristics) has become an international legal- and social science-based encompassing nomenclature initially developed in 2007 by an international group of human rights experts that drafted "The Yogyakarta Principles on the Application of International Human Rights Law in Relation to Sexual Orientation and Gender Identity." These principles were updated in 2017 and nicknamed "The Yogyakarta Principles Plus

Both editors of the anthology have been reared on the recent historiography of Philippine studies of sexual and gender non-normativity, particularly a trajectory beginning with the trilogy of *Ladlad: An anthology of Philippine gay writing* (3 vols.) edited by J. Neil C. Garcia and Danton Remoto from 1994 to 2007; including writings of psychological knowledge toward an "LGBT Philippine Psychology" that are collected in two issues of the *Philippine Journal of Psychology* in 2013 and 2016, guest edited by Eric Manalastas, Mira

10," with the descriptive subtitle "Additional Principles and State Obligations on the Application of International Human Rights Law in Relation to Sexual Orientation, Gender Identity, Gender Expression and Sex Characteristics to Complement the Yogyakarta Principles." Now inclusive of "gender expression and sex characteristics" (beyond simple dimorphism of male and female—as with those who are intersex), the 2007 and 2017 framers were explicitly "[a]cknowledging that this articulation must rely on the current state of international human rights law and will require revision on a regular basis in order to take account of developments in . . . law and its application to the particular lives and experiences of persons of diverse sexual orientations and gender identities over time and in diverse regions and countries" (cf. note 18 below). Over the intervening ten years SOGI became widely used by global international organizations such as the United Nations and its agencies, as well as regional ones, and by national governments, nongovernmental organizations (NGOs) such as charitable and religious foundations, public policy "think tanks," allied social movement-based groups, and those dealing with human rights and health issues. For example, the year 2010 in the Philippines saw the founding of the Bahaghari Center for SOGIE Research, Education, and Advocacy, Inc. In surveying recent academic and popular literature in the Philippines, we observed that LGBT and LGBTIA or LGBTIA+ (lesbian, gay, bisexual, transgender, intersex, asexual or allied, with a "plus" indicating further *elective* inclusivity)—despite their Anglicism in the Philippines—are still widely used or are becoming widely used in popular and media representations although missing the nuanced research-based specificity of SOGIESC. While none of these nomenclatures roll off the tongue, for consistency and *inclusivity*, we decided to use LGBTIA+ whenever specifically referring to the Philippine context, unless other contexts are being referred to, or in citing works in which a different acronym is used; but we tentatively suggest "Q" when observational study or self-identification warrants its use due to (conceptual) *translatability* rather than *application due to equivalence*. Of equal importance for our project is the varied and fascinating use in Philippine contexts of multiply-derivative linguistic referents of self and "community" membership—such as *swardspeak*—especially as they express sexual, gender, geographic, and situational diversity that our authors analyze. Finally, we decided to place "Q" after "I" because in the history of LGBT activism both abroad and in the Philippines, the intersex community has been collaborating and organizing with the LGBT communities in fighting for common rights and against stigmatization and underrepresentation within a dominant heteronormative society (see Kaggwa 1997). Hence we have chosen LGBTI(Q)A+ which, at the time of publication, seems most forward looking both in the Philippine context and in trends of supportive transnational organizations.

Alexis P. Ofreneo, and Beatriz Torre; and most recently in the anthology, primarily written by Filipino youth and students and edited by Eva Callueng, *Buhay Bahaghari: The Filipino LGBT Chronicles* published in 2014, to mention other milestones.[2] We have been so inspired by this relatively recent continuing outpouring of literature that when our editor at Vibal asked us to begin with "the classics" we did not know where to begin—not because there are none but because there is no framework except perhaps chronology for conceiving what they could be. This is probably a good thing for Philippine literary and political culture since aside from a few singular landmarks such as Neil Garcia's *Philippine Gay Culture* (1996) and others in cinema and literature (some not necessarily LGBTIA+-authored), the Philippine canon appears to consist of the voices of a collective chorus rather than of a few cultural or academic celebrities. By itself, the latter's significance is often exaggerated in terms of uplift for LGBTIA+ people as compared with so-called grassroots democratic activism despite the contribution of scholarship and education to support and inform the claims of those activists.

It is somewhat ironic that among Southeast Asian countries, the Philippines is sometimes considered less gay-friendly—at least as a tourist destination and in terms of Planet Romeo's "Gay Happiness Index"—than some others (Thailand immediately comes to mind), and yet the popular and literary culture, if not the legal acceptance of LGBTIQ people in the Philippines, seems to belie this (cf. Mosbergen 2015). For example, country-based studies as well as examples in regional studies of same-sex love and gender transitivity have included Thailand, Indonesia, Singapore, and recently Vietnam, but it appears that the development of an English-speaking literary culture and extensive cinematic popular culture in the Philippines has spurred the development of an LGBT (if not fully "I," "Q," or "A") literary and artistic tradition that intellectual historians could argue constitute a "canon" more than in any other country in the region. That's one other reason, besides humility, why we hesitate to identify our goal here as more than a guide post. In retrospect, we recommend that students of Philippine and LGBTIQ studies develop the intellectual history of the islands (outside of the cosmopolitan centers of Manila and Cebu) while challenging intellectual constraints of heteronormativity to demonstrate this advanced canon as compared to the country's Southeast Asian neighbors, making it a kind of "oasis" within the political constraints of so-called "Asian values" (including Islam) on the one hand but existing despite the other constraints of Roman Catholicism (and Christian fundamentalism) on the other.

---

2   For other milestones in the Philippine LGBTIA+ movement, see Works Cited and Recommended.

II

The actual research, compilation, and writing for this volume of the Academica Filipina series during the ten years that were needed to bring it to fruition took a circuitous route amongst its editors, publisher, and writers. During a short-term Fulbright at the University of the Philippines (UP) Diliman in 2008, Mark Blasius spent many hours with editor-in-chief Gaspar (Gus) Vibal discussing his writing and teaching about the politics of sexuality across cultures and his particular interest in the Philippines sparked by his Filipino partner Rico Barbosa, whom he met at the first Asian conference of ILGA (International Lesbian, Gay, Bisexual, Trans, and Intersex Association) in Manila several years earlier and with whom he was then living in New York. Gus asked Mark to begin working with him collecting essays "that you will be reading anyway" and to select the best ones to gather into an anthology of scholarly but readerly essays on issues of diversity in gender and sexuality in the Philippines. Mark agreed and his interest was piqued enough to organize a paper presentation and discussion about the topic at a sexualities studies conference in Hanoi the following year and to pick the brains of some thinkers about the Philippines around his home university, the City University of New York (CUNY), such as Vince Boudreau, Martin Manalansan IV, Kevin Nadal, Dulce Natividad, and other Filipino scholars and activists passing through his university's Center for LGBTQ Studies (then Center for Lesbian and Gay Studies—CLAGS).

Early on, Mark realized he needed the assistance of another editor in addition to Gus who was becoming more and more involved in the daily operations of Vibal Publishing in Manila. Mark requested that he be allowed to invite as co-editor someone whom he met at a CLAGS conference and who was one of his hosts during his Fulbright at UP Diliman, Eufracio "Boi" Abaya, and Gus agreed. This appointment drew together a wondrous multi-year relationship that unfortunately ended when Boi, for personal reasons, had to withdraw from working on the book project. During this period of in-person, Skype, and telephone discussions Mark began to learn the humility of attempting first-hand and primary scholarship about another culture—made all the more fraught because that culture was simultaneously so far (even putting aside geographic and "neocolonial" considerations with the Philippines as a former US colony) and yet so near to Mark's own household sense of dual-nationality, seeing the political within the personal through sexuality. These few years of collaboration with Professor

Abaya, then of the UP Diliman Anthropology Department, have served as continuing inspiration to complete this project.

In addition to this early editorial collaboration, Professor Abaya wrote up an ethnographic study for the aforementioned conference in Hanoi titled "Ethic of Care: Growing Older as *Bakla* ('Gay') in a Philippine Locale," which inspires Mark to cite as formative to his own thinking and writing about whether a distinctive "ethos" arises from living a life marginalized with respect to normative relations of sexuality and gender. As such, *malasakit*—a Philippine ethos of sharing with another, especially when it involves that other's personal suffering, by *making the condition of the other one's own condition*, as lived by rural gender-transitive men (*bakla*) in the Philippines and the object of Professor Abaya's study—became the *object-lesson* of Mark's collaboration with him (Blasius 2013). Mark appeals to any interested reader of *this* anthology to help see Professor Abaya's still incomplete study to completion, as its world-making potential in Philippine as well as LGBTIQ studies deserves publication and, quite literally, a global audience (Abaya 2009).

Filipino historian Richard T. Chu and editor of another book in the Academica Filipina series took over from Professor Abaya in 2014. Having been born and raised in the Philippines, Richard had also experienced the stigmatization of being *bakla* from early childhood onward, and had witnessed the changes in the gay scene in Manila from the 1970s to the 1990s. Though he has lived in the US for the past two decades, he returns to the Philippines at least twice yearly, and thus maintains close ties with his home country, with Philippine scholarship, and with the LGBTIA+ movements developing there.

The Academica Filipina series addresses aspects of Philippine culture, history, and politics, for example, that have been central to Philippine nationality and identity but are often overlooked if not invisibilized by mainstream scholarship and even popular writing. Given this, Vibal's recommendation to this volume's editors from our beginning discussions was that this book within the series should have as a goal to demonstrate both the diversity and unique strivings and forms for inclusiveness within Philippine life. Indeed, early on one editor noted that implicit in the "we" of the book titles within the series (*More Tomboy, More Bakla Than We Admit*) is a sense of *denial*: Do Filipinos really have the tendency to deny Hispanic-ness, Pinay-ness, Tsinoy-ness, Islamic-ness, or American-ness, etc.; or if not really "deny" per se then neglect or marginalize these "sides" of what constitute "Filipino" or "Philippine" in local academic (and even popular) discourse?

In other words, "Filipino-ness" has been over-emphasized by nationalistic or heterosexist or heteronormative or male-"oriented" writing, to the exclusion or neglect of what makes "Filipino" also partly "Hispanic," "Chinese," "female," "queer," "Islamic," "American," and so on. While it could be argued that queer theory has seduced Asian subjects through a promise to universalize them, this volume, while speaking to both current transnational and more local theoretical debates in gender and sexuality studies, fundamentally tries to interrogate the applicability of "universalist" frames (including those pertaining to Filipino nationhood and identity) by using data and constructs analyzed in nested social, political, economic, and cultural practices. This approach could really make a difference, for example, in the ethics of research, through linking concepts of sexuality and gender identity (and the hierarchies they invoke) *strategically* to Filipino locales and language practices encouraging tomboys, *baklas*, lesbos, transpinays, bisexuals or "bi's," and other same-sex loving and gender non-normative Filipinos to author their own lives and thereby increase public understandings of the varied dimensions of Filipino identity, while also yielding a broader significance to the politics of gender and sexuality in the Philippines without unnecessary reliance upon "western" concepts.

Similarly, although much had (and has) been written, sometimes haltingly, sometimes confidently, about (what has come to be called) sexual orientation and gender identity and expression or "LGBTIA+" in the Philippines both by Filipino and non-Filipino scholars, Vibal suggested that we editors begin with some framework for publishing exemplary and enduring literature about our subject matter, and only where absolutely necessary supplement this with commissioned writings. This was intended to be a first volume, hopefully stimulating enough interest so that a burgeoning literature of the field would develop, especially from Filipino and local scholars that, as in Abaya's use of *malasakit*, enable the *translocal* to arise from the local(e), perhaps more than vice versa. It is ironic now that one of the two editors divides his time between the US and the Philippines (originally one of us lived and worked full-time in the Philippines), but from the beginning we have situated our conceptual perspectives in the interactions between "local knowledges," their intercultural translatability, and transnational circulation of knowledges: Richard writes of the history of the Tsinoy experience in the Philippines and its diaspora as a Chinese Filipino; Mark was originally attracted to what could be Philippine "queer" theory through a 1993 essay he reprinted in his historiography of "LGBT" movements, informed globally by its Filipino author-activist Jomar Fleras, which seemed at the time what political theorists would come to term "intersectional" analysis (Blasius and Phelan 1997).

III

So, our selection criteria of the essays contained herein began with a recommendation from the publisher to begin with what were considered to be classic writings about "non-normative sexualities and genders" firstly, and then secondly, add commissioned writings where we felt absences existed and gaps needed to be filled in. To address the former, we consulted colleagues both in the Philippines and abroad, sorting through what they thought should be written (or should have been written) as well as actual completed manuscripts or previously published articles. The second criterion is obviously extremely subjective and reliant on notions of "absent" or "must include" topics that are usually informed by preexisting disciplinary hegemonies and hierarchies dependent upon the Anglo-American academic system. For example, even considering the emerging field of "LGBTIQ" or simply "queer" studies, it was only during the ten-year germination period of our volume that the hegemony of cultural and literary studies in that interdisciplinary field began to gain recognition and subside, giving way to studies in the social sciences, biomedicine and so-called STEM fields (science, technology, engineering, mathematics) and more often originating in the "global south." Regarding the second equally problematic criterion for selection, in addition to "wish lists," our academic and political and community-based colleagues gave us suggestions resulting in long lists of previously published studies and others who might write to fill in the gaps; most of these, however, turned out to be previously published outside the Philippines or by diasporic Filipino scholars writing primarily about Filipinos in the diaspora.

Indeed, an original rigid framework where half the chapters would be written by self-identified *baklas* and half by "everybody else" morphed into a perhaps equally problematic, editorial debate about the extent to which the voices in the book should be in-country writers as opposed to *diasporic* writers. To be sure, one apposite case could be made that in the Philippine context of global householding and care chains, the boundaries and conceptual intention of *diasporic* have become increasingly blurred and complicated by class, gender, sex, geography, age, and other intersecting vectors.[3] For example, diasporic writers—by virtue of simple personal networking through conferences, invitational talks, and informal interactions—often have a better chance of getting published in international forums than

3   See Martin F. Manalansan IV's profound analyses of both Philippine state-sponsored export of female domestic labor and of the concept of diaspora by comparing his 2008 and 2010 texts, respectively on "queering" the chain of care and "servicing the world," referenced below.

scholars who both work and live in the Philippines. One of the editors here was made acutely aware of this when organizing the paper-presentation session devoted to the Philippines at the 2009 conference in Hanoi of an international sexuality studies organization. Filipino scholars living and working within the Philippines had extraordinary difficulty getting financial support to attend the conference (which could have been an hour flight from Manila except there were no direct flights during that year). Of four Filipino scholars, only one tenured faculty member received a travel-only grant from UP's flagship campus in Diliman, within Metro Manila. Another senior faculty member from the same campus was denied support because she was too close to her (mandatory) retirement, and graciously bowed out of the session so as not to jeopardize financial support and participation for the others. A third Filipino scholar, a graduate student at the same UP campus, found support only through the international organization sponsoring the conference and dormitory-style housing with the tenured travel-only awardee. The fourth Filipino scholar received full support from the US university at which she was ABD (all but dissertation); nevertheless, she and all the others had to apply for and receive scholarship awards from the sponsoring organization to pay for the expensive conference registration fee (covering importantly, official events and meals where much professional networking takes place, and very modest per diem expenses). Later, serving on the board of directors of such an organization, this editor saw similar scenarios play out between diasporic and non-diasporic scholars many times; even with well-meaning foundation-funded attempts to "spread the wealth around," scholars from areas of the world with the scarcest financial resources to support scholarship and professional travel had to take multiple intercontinental flights with uncertain accommodations and low per diems in order to get their work known and discussed by others in their own fields—internet camaraderie and "cultural globalization" aside. As a result, in choosing writings for this volume whenever possible we have prioritized (sometimes even already-privileged) scholars who both live and work in the Philippines with the model of "growing the field" from within, as Eric Manalastas, Mira Ofreneo, and Beatriz Torre have done through their own academic discipline, developing what they have called "LGBT Philippine Psychology" (see below).

In the end and sometimes in spite of ourselves, we editors have tried to find and publish studies of solid scholarship that can engage interculturally with same-sex loving, gender diverse people and their allies both within and outside the Philippines and across academic disciplines and to address both specialist and non-specialist readers. Even while focusing on this somewhat lofty motive, the forces of circumstance limited what we were able to publish and especially commission. One of our completed essays was written in the context of weekly 8-hour (each way) round-trip bus journeys between a university teaching job and studying for a PhD "at home" in Metro Manila while caring for two elderly aunts with medical problems and having poor or no internet access; another essay was not completed due to a heavy teaching (over)load and the expectation, for a single unmarried male in the Philippines, to financially support his partner's siblings who are married and have children; neither of these circumstantial forces overtly included disallowance of the subject matter of non-normative gender and sexuality itself through a potential author's lack of institutional support or fear of stigmatization, as self-reported by them to us. (Nevertheless, see the report on discrimination against LGBT students in the Philippines, Human Rights Watch 2017.) Other forces of circumstance resulted in no essay devoted completely to the contemporary transpinay movement in the Philippines; we asked two separate authors each to consider completing such an essay, then asked them to complete one together which they agreed to do, and despite repeated pleas from the editors it never materialized. (Fortunately, another author incorporated the early history of recent transgender identity and organizing in the Philippines into her own essay.) As we write this, new and exciting LGBTIA+ studies in the Philippines are appearing and we and our authors refer to them in the text and in our bibliographic recommendations.

The force of circumstance does not explain all the absences in our volume. Detailing the effect of HIV/AIDS on our subject is a prominent absence and although one of our authors promised early on to include this topic in a broader one, it never came to pass and given the exponential increase in seropositivity in the Philippines that recently became a highly-debated public issue internationally, its absence is our regret.[4] The early years of Philippine government strategies regarding the epidemic, partnering with local organizations and international NGOs during the early 1990s, were considered to be highly successful according to a December 2016 report of NGO Human Rights Watch (HRW). In those days, the prevalence and spread of the disease in the country was described as low and slow by informed local commentators. However, by the early 2000s there was a dramatic increase in country-wide prevalence and new reported cases between 2008 and 2015 as presented by HRW, especially among MSM

---

4   We laud, however, the landmark publication of Louie Mar A. Gangcuangco's *Orosa-Nakpil, Malate* (2006), which is a fictionalized account of a young medical student named John David de Jesus, and his sexual and love life, and of young gay men like Ross living with HIV. A study made by Jan Padios (2018) looks into the the rising incidence of HIV infection among call center workers in Metro Manila.

(men who have sex with men whether or not they have sex with women). Again citing HRW, this increase made the Philippine HIV prevalence rate by 2015 one of the highest for the Asia-Pacific region and higher even than Sub-Saharan Africa which at that time had "the most serious HIV epidemic in the world." This development is borne out by more recent statistics published by Manila-based LGBTQIA+ publication *Outrage Magazine* (www.outrage.com). On 8 March 2019, citing Philippine government official sources and breaking the information down by the country's regions, *Outrage* reported that there were 1249 newly confirmed HIV cases in January 2019 (approximately 41 new cases daily, 10 more cases per day than in 2018), and that these were mostly among Filipino males—roughly half being 25–34 years years of age and 32% being 15–24 years of age, with sexual contact the overwhelming mode of transmission (98–99%). (Lest this be considered as anomalous, 1272 new cases were later reported by the same sources as occurring during March 2019.) *Outrage* charts the total reported cases in the Philippines over the five years from January 2014 to January 2019 as 46,802 as compared to 63,278 total cases over the thirty-five years between January 1984 to January 2019. What happened? Recent efforts to address this question, particularly among younger MSM and transgender populations most relevant to this book, point to failures to implement relevant sections of the country's so-called "AIDS Law" of 1998 mandating "age- and development-appropriate" sexuality education for adolescent children, and the Reproductive Health (RH) Law of 2012. According to HRW, the RH Law "specifically provides for 'comprehensive sexuality education' that includes sexual health, children's rights, and values formation. However, in practice the majority of public and private schools provide no sex education classes or instruction on methods to prevent sexually transmitted infections." The HRW report continues that while Philippine President Duterte during his 2016 election campaign "spoke in favor of improving the rights of LGBT people [and] . . . Duterte has also committed his government to full implementation of the RH Law . . . [a]t the same time, Duterte has engaged in vitriolic and anti-gay rhetoric, which may indicate a different path than the one suggested by his more positive public pronouncements." The World Health Organization (WHO) advocated a "national condom strategy" in the Philippines, as simple access to condoms without stigma and misinformation about their use and effectiveness would have saved many Filipino lives during the period of the epidemic's recent expansion; but condom distribution and use was opposed by the Roman Catholic bishops, by politicians who fear them, and presumably by the citizens who support those politicians.

The HRW report also cites Philippine municipalities that have ironically declared themselves "pro-life" to avoid implementing the aforementioned laws and the expansive distribution of condoms. Of course, HIV/AIDS is not the only significant component of LGBTIA+ healthcare in the Philippines. According to "Being LGBT in Asia: The Philippine Country Study" (UNDP and USAID 2014), lesbians and trans men cite a lack of information about and how to use hormone replacement therapy and others cite the general absence of psychosocial health providers respectful of LGBT concerns, even despite the initiatives toward LGBT inclusion by the Psychological Association of the Philippines chronicled in this book, and the historic model the Philippines provided for self-care of elder *bakla* chronicled by the worldwide success of the indie film *The Home for the Golden Gays* notwithstanding. One of the very promising trajectories of the mutual translation process of community-based research and knowledge production with community development in the Philippines has been the growth since 2010 of the Bahaghari Center for SOGIE Research, Education, and Advocacy, Inc. (www.bahagharicenter.org). In the tried and true tradition of LGBTIA+ community centers around the world, the Bahaghari Center is led by a team that stresses the inclusivity of diverse members of the LGBTIQA+ community, such as deaf and HIV-positive people, with campaigns around SOGIE well-being, visibility and public education, the development of livelihood skills (such as journalism) of its constituents, and liaisons with local and transnational LGBTIA+ and other civic and human rights organizations. Especially in the context of the COVID-19 pandemic, we point to the needs being recognized and addressed by the Bahaghari Center to respond in an evidence-based and public way as well as for research studies and advocacy around the *sustainability* and *resilience* of LGBTIA+ community-based institutions and supportive programs by the Philippine government that are documented through local, international, and transnational auspices especially in coordination with the United Nations Sustainable Development Goals (see UNDP 2015) and the UN Human Rights Council's Independent Expert on Protection against Violence and Discrimination based on Sexual Orientation and Gender Identity. The establishment of the Independent Expert in 2016 unfortunately did not receive the support of the Philippine UN delegation which it claimed "would pursue a set of standards applied to a specific sector when there is no consensus on a set of universally-accepted human rights standards." Fortunately, the Philippine delegation voted with the majority of other member states at the UN Human Rights Council in July 2019 supporting a three-year extension of the Independent Expert's mandate. (See, for example: Badgett and Sell 2018 and Commission on Human Rights of the Philippines 2019.)

During this time of President Duterte, it has been difficult to find, in time for our publication, up-to-date and detailed scholarly work on the topics of LGBTIA+ legislative activism toward non-discrimination and positive dimensions of well-being from a human rights perspective, but its relevance is discussed briefly in some essays here. Nevertheless, there has been recent excellent scholarship on the Philippines' first LGBT political party Ang Ladlad but no analysis feasible timewise for inclusion or suitable for excerption here; but we refer readers to the master's thesis of Bradley Cardozo, and the publications of Roland Sintos Coloma and Cheryll Ruth Reyes Soriano cited here among our bibliographic references. A chapter on aging among Filipino *baklas* was unexpectedly pulled from the volume at the last minute. However, the two LGBT-devoted issues of the *Philippine Journal of Psychology* have published excellent specialized studies and abundant bibliographic references exploring many subtopics and contributing to the field as as a whole from a social science and human rights perspective.

The role of Roman Catholicism and religion in general (again, especially for the Philippine context including Islam and Christian fundamentalism) in relation to sexual orientation, particularly as it pertains to political oppression and institutionalized or casual homophobia, is not extensively dealt with in our book. Except perhaps in psychological science, Roman Catholicism is often taken as a given of Philippine subjectivity and nationalism in this as well as other LGBTIA+-oriented scholarly and activist writings, rather than as an historically residual cultural imperialism shaping scholarly research and debate and political agenda-setting as in other parts of the world. For example, as recently as 2009, the executive director of the Philippine-American Education Foundation (PAEF), which administers the US-initiated Fulbright exchange program of mutual support for research and teaching in both countries, plaintively but pre-emptively told the senior editor of this book that his application for a research-oriented Fulbright in the Philippines would not be approved if "homosexuality" was mentioned in it as a topic of research due to the presence on PAEF's board of directors of members of the clergy whose opposition to the topic negatively influences the other board members. (To be sure, the use of colonizers' religious beliefs to indigenize homophobia as a "cultural tradition" in postcolonial societies is not unique to the Philippines.) A more critical attitude than we were able to find—though focusing on the status of women's rights and their sexuality in the birth and evolution of the Philippine feminist organization Likhaan—may be found in Junice L. Demeterio-Melgar's "Raising Sexuality as a Political Issue in the Catholic Philippines" (2005).

The literature on LGBTIA+-themed popular culture in the Philippines is vast and our anthology has included a couple of these studies (see Baytan and Tolentino). One promising area for scholarly research is the media genre of boy's love (BL), as seen in many web series that have exploded in popularity in the last few years among millennials and Gen Z. Coming out of the Japanese genre of fictional media called *yaoi*, which features homoerotic stories between male characters, BL dramas began to be produced by Thai, Chinese, and Taiwanese television stations in the 2010s and their popularity quickly spread throughout Southeast Asia, including the Philippines. The first Filipino BL drama called *Gameboys*—about two young gay men, one a livestream gamer and the other his fan—was filmed and released during the COVID-19 pandemic lockdown. Other BL series shot during the lockdown, such as *Hello Stranger*, have since been released on YouTube and other streaming platforms, with higher-than-expected numbers of viewers. A dimension of scholarly research can focus on how members of the LGBTIA+ community deal with issues of coming out, romantic relationships, hooking up, illness, and death—and even social issues facing the country—at a time when face-to-face interactions are extremely limited. Another focus of research can be on how these series are able to include characters from a diverse background of gender and sexual identities not commonly seen in commercial television shows or movies. *Balangaw*, for example, features a group of eight friends, including one who identifies as lesbian, two as gay, one as bisexual, one as bi-curious, one as transgender, one as cisgender male in a relationship with a transgender woman, and one as asexual. This series has characters not only navigating issues of coming out, same-sex parenting, and exploring new sexual-relational forms, but also discussing the increasing curtailment of press freedom in the country. Finally, an area of scholarship can examine how these web series are akin to what other LGBTIQ communities in the world have done even before the onset of the pandemic—when aspiring actors, directors, and producers (even of erotica) as well as individuals and groups of friends shoot themselves or chronicle their lives as LGBTIQA+ by using mobile phones and uploading their videos to YouTube or other video sharing sites such as Vimeo; thereby visibilizing further the extraordinarily diverse and resilient community to which they and we belong. This is perhaps a fundable project for UNDP's sustainable development goals.

Lastly, while there are writings and illustrations in our book focusing on locales outside of the metropolitan areas of Manila and Cebu, much more research is needed for highlighting the numerous ethnolinguistic and regional life experiences of same-sex loving and gender diverse people in the Cordillera, Mindanao, Bikol, just for example, and elsewhere in the archipelago (see Sumayao and Jacobo 2019). That's why we hope this book will at least provide a stimulus for further scholarly and evidence-based readerly studies to come.

IV

The first two essays provide a historical and theoretical framing for the book as a whole. In order to facilitate reading the essays, the editors decided to divide them into five sections to reflect not so much their disciplinary backgrounds as the themes these works share.

The first set of essays frame, in the most general terms, the theoretical and historical perspective of the totality of essays contained in the book. One editor suggested placing Neil Garcia's as a lead-off essay, both for its broad and theoretically rich analysis of the notion of the *bakla* and for the author's name recognition in LGBTIQA+ studies within and outside the Philippines. In the end, the editors feel that, while Garcia's essay brings up epistemological and ideological questions for studies of gays, lesbians, and transgenders in the Philippines, Roselle Pineda's essay at least complements Garcia's in providing an equally rich historical analysis of developing lesbian identities and their social and political struggles, and in this specificity, the framework with which to more deeply appreciate the other studies included here on women-loving-women throughout Philippine cultures and histories.

The next unit contains three histories of sexual diversity and gender non-normativity in pre-colonial or pre-Spanish as well as during early Spanish and modern times. As studying the "past" is a way of rendering the "present" more understandable this section is placed next. Finding historical studies on this proved to be challenging, and the editor who is also a historian laments the dearth and the lack of such studies. Undoubtedly, this reflects not so much the *absence* of sexual diversity and gender non-normativity as the neglect or difficulty of undertaking this kind of research within the field. For instance, the reader would notice that all three works focus on the precolonial/early colonial period, i.e., prior to the eighteenth century. The editors had a difficult time finding studies focusing on the eighteenth, nineteenth, and early twentieth centuries. However, while researching through late nineteenth-century newspapers, the same historian-editor found the word *mababakla* used by Emilio Aguinaldo to rally Filipinos into resisting American colonization.[5] Furthermore, a case

5   Aguinaldo wrote: "Kaya, manga kababayan, pagtibayin ang pagasa, pakatiningin ang puso at atiming magaan sa loob na lakbaing pagsikapan, at huag mababakla muntik man, iyang landas na tadhana niyang lakarin natin, at sa dulo'y asahang matatagpuan ang maganda nating palad" [Thus, fellow countrymen, strengthen your faith, make your heart stout and do not be afraid of the journey ahead of us, and expect that in the end

has been recorded and found in the nineteenth century from the "Asuntos Criminales" files at the Philippine National Archives. This particular case in 1867 involved a certain Chinese named Tan Yuan who was accused of committing the "crime of sodomy" (*delito de sodomia*) with a younger male named Cipriano Tiongson.[6] Lastly, Rafael Comenge, a Spanish journalist in Manila, wrote in 1894 of the practices of sodomy among the Chinese in the Philippines.[7] This underscores the title of the anthology that expresses the need for more study of sexual diversity and gender non-normativity in Philippine society, particularly in the modern period.

The next three essays are placed within the unit titled "Filipino Sexual and Gender Identities" as each introduces to readers how terms such as "gay" and "*bakla*" (Tan); "lesbian" and "trans man" (Josef); or "bisexual" (Tan; Baytan) are currently used in an LGBTIA+ context in the Philippines. This section emphasizes the importance of naming ourselves (subjectivity) in the context of communicating with others as part of a diverse (intersectional) community.

We have entitled the fourth unit "Negotiating Sexual and Gender Diversity in Recent Philippine Culture" because the essays of Alcedo, Alburo, Tolentino, and Fajardo look into specificities of the lived gendered and sexual identities of certain individuals or groups of people associated with LGBTIA+ communities of the Philippines. These essays examine how people challenge the limitations imposed by heteropatriarchy and Filipinoness, sex-gender dualism, Catholicism-suffused cultural formations, and global capitalism, as well as provide examples of how to survive and thrive with our community-based identities.

The final unit deals with self-reflective or personal and intimate relations and individuals' subjective experience of them and how these are shaped by the "political," overlapping *structural* power relations of society—for example, those of families, institutionalized religion, public and

we will achieve our good fortune]. "Manga Cababayan," *Suplemento al Heraldo Filipino*, 7 February 1899, 3.

6   Joaine Jan A. Marquez, email communication, 13 June 2020. See also opener of Marquez essay in this volume.

7   Comenge wrote, "Son los chinos avecindados en Filipinas, dados á la sodomía y a los gustos griegos . . . . Hallándose los chinos sin mujeres en Filipinas, agrupándose por docenas en pequeñísimas casas, trayendo como equipaje de su deshonra el vicio nefando á cuestas, que crece con el contacto y la ocasión, las princesas nacen expontáneas y la sodomía se impone" (166–69) [The Chinese who live in the Philippines engage in sodomy and have Greek tastes. . . . [and] being without women in the Philippines, grouped by the dozens in tiny houses, they bring as a load on their backs their dishonorable nefarious vice, that grows with contact and the occasion, leads to the practice of prostitution and the prevalence of sodomy]. Cf. Jely Galang 2019.

private education, biomedicine, state and economic governance, and *practices* (e.g., therapeutic, activist, etc.) by which Filipinos negotiate, resist, adapt, or conform to a heteronormative identity and thereby reinforce or problematize and transform these larger structures of power and and how they shape selfhood. We want to show how the personal and the political mutually interpenetrate each other subjectively and through structures of intersectionality.

Theoretical and historical framings

We begin with two texts that share pride of place: J. Neil Garcia's 2009 "update" of his book *Philippine Gay Culture: Binabae to Bakla, Silahis to MSM* (1996) and Roselle Pineda's history of lesbian struggle in the Philippines published in 2001 in *Kasarinlan: Philippine Journal of Third World Studies*. Each opened up contemporary scholarly Philippine discourse about sexual diversity and gender non-normativity using the activist and scholarly language of "lesbian" and "gay" in an interdisciplinary framework that invites further study. Of course, both are time-bound in the sense that they were first published ten years before this volume was conceived and arguably could be updated based on activist practice and terminology (e.g., the Yogyakarta Principles and gains in international recognition of SOGIESC began in 2007, just before Garcia's and after Pineda's essays were published). However, to suggest intervening historical developments limit either's relevance as guideposts to the present as well as to the future is to do their perspectives a disservice based on their age; instead, let's examine briefly what's at stake in their discursivity.

First, there has been an expansion beyond "gay and lesbian" (and even the Anglophonic "queer") toward new sources of subjectivity that include gender fluidity and cisgender, trans-and inter-sexed and nonbinary bodies, "bi" and polyamory and asexuality, as well as relations—to oneself as self-identity and to others—of sexuality far in excess of what, for example, either German sexual scientist Magnus Hirschfeld in the early twentieth century and later global sexology or medical anthropology have catalogued. Indeed, these erotic, gendered, and embodied non-binary subjectivities have yielded a growing literature for reference and a research agenda for Philippine studies of gender and sexuality, the surface of which has only been scratched here by the essays of Baytan, Josef, Ofreneo, Alburo, and Fajardo, and elsewhere, in *Buhay Bahaghari*'s autobiographical essays. Nevertheless, by their inclusion within the canons of their fields through research and teaching, Pineda and Garcia *provided a platform* that enabled the study of sexual diversity and gender non-normativity (or non-*conformity* to be more practical) to advance within Philippine educational and research institutions, developing historically- and theoretically-based expertise that barely or only anecdotally existed before or was suppressed.

Second, the challenge of recognizing diverse sexual and gender identities and ways of living them inevitably raises questions of their inclusion within Philippine society. In Pineda's essay, inclusion involves recognition of female same-sex erotic love through lesbian visibility, cultural retrieval, and the empowerment of women; for Garcia it is inclusion within Philippine projects of national identity, state power, and political participation—as with the political party of Ang Ladlad. For both writers, inclusion is double-edged as it involves both "coming out" as well as "fitting into" existing structures of intersecting power relations in the Philippines. These societal power relations may have appeared "back then" as inequalities in nominally patriarchal, heterosexual institutions such as marriage, family relations, and their reflection in mass media and how these "western" sexual identities fit into Filipinoness.

As gay and lesbian visibility becomes more widespread and claims for sociocultural and political inclusion grow stronger, so does the recognition of multiple and differently-affecting forms of power and privilege shaping the life chances of gay and lesbian Filipino/as (what came to be termed "heteronormativity" throughout the fabric of life). This has meant taking into account *the intersection* of sexual diversity and gender non-conformity with, for example: socioeconomic class determining one's level of education, including sex education and a corresponding sense of self-respect; sociocultural stigma and marginalization on the one hand or invisibility on the other, thereby limiting one's ability to choose and then access the skills for a livelihood (and especially for people with non-normative sexualities and genders) that enable enough economic independence to "exit" abusive living situations or otherwise live with dignity; embeddedness in religious and ethnic traditions that often interact with class and economic opportunity to implicate those with non-normative sexual and gender identities in certain power relations (including but not limited to forms of sexual silence) differently than others within those same traditions as exemplified by diverse LGBTI support groups found in regional Philippine pride marches; non-normative variations in personal sex characteristics, gender identity, and erotic expression affecting physical and psychosocial development, aging, and particularized but overall health also affect one's ability to both "come out" into self-respect and dignity and to "fit into" a (nominally, at least) inclusive nation; and even the epistemology for comprehending these dynamics in the Philippines as compared with other parts of the world—all comprise just a few dimensions of Philippine LGBTIQ studies today.

The historical destinies of Philippine lesbian and gay citizens have been shaped by these (and more) intersectional power relations that still privilege some and marginalize other non-normative sexual and gendered subjects who claim continuing *exclusion.* This has meant transforming relations of exclusion both underpinning and extending beyond heteronormativity in order to address those sexed, gendered, and sexualized others—by recognizing their distinct subjectivities through, ultimately, a notion of gender and sexual rights and justice that both draws from and expands the perspective framed here by Pineda and Garcia. In this sense, their platform of visibility, its historical narratives, and theorization of membership in an ongoing social movement for (or "community" of) diverse sexualities and genders still offers us visions of the future which scholars, writers, and activists that follow them have taken up in the Philippines and elsewhere.

J. Neil Garcia's contribution to what he terms in his essay printed here as "Philippine-specific 'LGBT studies'" is at least germinal if not foundational, given the articulate and politically-committed postmodernist that he is. As a literary theorist-scholar, and with fellow creative writing teacher and political activist Danton Remoto as co-editor, he collected and perhaps commissioned during the years 1994–2007 three volumes of *Ladlad: An Anthology of Philippine Gay Writing* consisting of poetry, prose, non-fiction journalism, social science, bio- and autobiography, and erotica. (In this editor's edition, Vol. 1—purchased in 2003—was already in its fifth printing.) Among Garcia's other academic and non-academic writings, the *Ladlad* series especially represented, for a generation of gay men (and some non-"gays") a rallying cry for a nationwide movement. Thanks to its writers' personal and political commitments and their texts' readerly qualities through studies of personal development of gay self-consciousness (*ladlad* = to unfurl one's cape, akin to "coming out" in Tagalog gay jargon or swardspeak), through manners of sharing both sexual experiences and events of homophobic abuse and their public repudiation, and through acts of writing as education, mourning, and celebrating life in the context of *Tita Aida* (vernacular of that time for AIDS), this rallying cry echoed globally.

It is not the goal of an introduction to summarize blandly, or even uncritically, what it introduces so we conclude by suggesting that Neil Garcia's "update" of his landmark *Philippine Gay Culture* is a *manifesto* in the best sense of that word. Writing in 2007, the author grappled with Filipinoness by narrating the paradox between that latest shiny object of globalization—"global queering"—and the local lived experience of a Filipino *bakla* symbolized in the public death-by-electrocution (due to equipment failure) of twenty-something Joana Montegracia, a subaltern transgender performer, while trying to earn money in a Metro Manila beauty contest. In doing so, Garcia focuses our attention on the irony of universalizing the LGBT struggle in his "unfree nation's life . . . whose sovereignty is an egregious lie . . . whose justice is shackled and unenforceable." In our present time when "nation first" conservative authoritarianism is more obviously on the rise than ever on the international stage, J. Neil Garcia's prescient text appreciates the challenge and avoids extreme racial "nativism" while honing a politicized localism as a critical perspective for comparatively studying non-normative gender and sexuality—as a method, a field, and an incitement for Filipino LGBTIA+ scholars in the Philippines and all others elsewhere who may recognize a scholar-activist calling as their own.

Roselle Pineda's perspective may draw greater sustenance from the legacy of global feminist (often not specifically "lesbian") organizations, such as Isis International (based in Quezon City, Metro Manila, http://isiswomen.org), that serves as an archival repository for the history of feminism and for global networking and advocacy among feminists—linking local schools and universities, government gender offices, and NGOs—to inform her perspective. While there has been a history of writing and activism around women's sexuality and reproductive health issues in organizations such as Likhaan and through the politically left and social-justice oriented women's political party Gabriela, Pineda frames the history of Philippine lesbianism beginning with its sociocultural invisibility (including invisibility within intuitively supportive organizational environments) through a trajectory of challenge to heteronormativity with the promise of Philippine women's aesthetic agency. Indeed, if the *Ladlad* trilogy and the theoretical tradition and readership it represents also overshadows lesbian existence and culture through the volumes' focus on male same-sex relations, it is arguably more recently that even feminist-identified lesbians have taken the interrelations of socioeconomic inequalities, political disavowal in governing policies, corporeal and emotional "lived experience" concerns—including those surfacing through the inter-class erotic relationships expressed throughout *Ladlad* and by J. Josef's discussion of GALANG in this volume—into account beyond visibility and coming-out narratives. In this, her early work, Pineda sees the use of "lesbian" as both a historically constructed identity working to undermine gender stereotyping of women (herself citing Josef) *and* an inflection of *women's* agency working, despite historically profound constraints of centuries of colonialism and cultural imperialism, to transform Philippine culture in fundamental ways. Indeed, the class dimension of intersectional analysis and cultural politics was reinforced by one editor's interviews in Tatalon, a district of Metro Manila characterized by extreme poverty and squatters living on landfills, where most of his same-sex-loving female informants were tomboy couples, some of whom lived together in the home of the birth family of one, where one was (or both were) the breadwinners of the family unit—the price of familial acceptance of their relationship (perhaps)—and sometimes engaged in sex work with men for their income. Similarly, writing at the millennium Pineda sees lesbian visibility and unleashing women's agency as integral to both lesbian (and Philippine) history and to a differently-nuanced not-quite-queer (LGBTIA+) agenda locating "the political" within "the personal."

To be sure, Pineda's alternate framing of militancy to that of Garcia is both classic and, being replete with Philippine examples, not reductionist as she focuses upon the influence of art on politics as transforming one's lived existence in coming out, or lesbianism as a becoming, rather than as an endpoint of selfhood. Artistic expression provides two avenues to social change for Pineda: Lesbian art is creative praxis, proposing alternative ways of living and loving as a woman; this works together with the recovery of "lesbians"—women-loving-women—in art history which have been invisibilized by male-dominated historical documentation and professional status. In studying Philippine art, Pineda has discovered thematic "homoeroticism" in women's friendships and women's group activities such as bathing, in allegory, in female masculinity (cross-dressing), and in autoeroticism—what she terms "proto-lesbian" art. Pineda is hereby constructing (somewhat parallel to Garcia's *Philippine Gay Culture*), a history of lesbianism in the Philippines that is ongoing and has been taken up by other scholars and written about by Pineda herself as part of a developing intellectual movement toward original scholarship of the indigeneity of women's homoeroticism and sex-gender transitivity in Philippine culture, irregardless of exogenous western constructs of understanding.

Histories of sexuality in precolonial and colonial Philippines

This next section introduces three historical studies that focus on how—before the spread of Islamic faith in various parts of the Philippines, and during the colonization by the Spaniards and Americans—gender relations could be understood in relation to sexual behavior and identities (Brewer), and more specifically, how, in their contact with one another, the Spanish colonizers and the Chinese among their subjects negotiated their differing gender and sexual norms (Reyes and Marquez). With the exception of Malacca,

the Philippines is unique when compared to other Southeast Asian states because of its history of conquest by not just one but two (Spanish and American) western colonial powers that changed and reconfigured the gender and
sexual relations of its indigenous society.

In today's Philippine society, partly due to the influence and imposition of western—namely Spanish and American—gender norms, men are
regarded as the "stronger" sex, and occupy positions of powers especially in
the public realm. For instance, in the Roman Catholic church and Islamic
societies, those who hold the highest positions are men. Men are also viewed
as more likely to commit "adultery" and are forgiven for it (see for example,
the case of Philippine President Rodrigo Duterte) and women could be ex-
coriated simply by having a relationship with a married man (see the case of
Duterte critic and Philippine Senator Leila de Lima). However, it has also
been pointed out that even as men are privileged in Philippine society, Filipino women are able to exercise some power or authority deemed as belonging to men's domain. For instance, women held the presidency twice (under Corazon Aquino and Gloria Macapagal-Arroyo), a phenomenon which
might be difficult to find in other societies.[8] Sixteenth- to eighteenth-century
Spanish missionary accounts described how, in many indigenous societies,
women seemed to enjoy equal if not superior status to men. They actively participated in the economic realm, did not have to remain virgins before marriage, and could possess several lovers. Their societies also observed
a bilateral kinship system, in which, as an example, inheritance was parti-
tioned equally between men and women in the family. However, in some
areas women were sold to fetch a good price in marriage or to pay off debts.
Hence, in precolonial Philippine society, gender hierarchy and differentiation existed but were more customary and not codified into law, and even
so, male dominance varied among communities and among social classes. It
was Spanish colonization that transformed and reinforced gender differences among men and women that placed men above women (Eviota, 36–37).

One area where women predominated over men was the spiritual realm.
However, there also existed men who performed religious rituals while wearing female clothing to placate some evil spirit or to cure certain illnesses.
These men also behaved "femininely" according to those societies' norms of
a biologically-based sex binary. In today's English-language parlance, these
men could be called transvestites. In studying these "men," the first essay in
this section, Carolyn Brewer's "*Baylan, Asog*, Transvestism, and Sodomy:
Gender, Sexuality and the Sacred in Early Colonial Philippines," challenges the approach used by many western scholars studying Southeast Asian

8   The World Economic Forum's "The Global Gender Gap Report" of 2018 places
the Philippines as the 8th most gender-equal country.

societies that "links sex with sexuality, sex with nature, and nature with both woman and nurture, and therefore gender" to understand why these men were accorded a high status in their societies. According to Brewer, this approach led scholars to conclude that the spiritual potency—and hence, respect—held by these shamans arose from their identification with a "neuter 'third' sex/gender." But she argues that, in the Philippine case, "it was the male shaman's identification with the feminine, either as temporary transvestism or as a more permanent lifestyle choice, that reinforced the normative situation of female as shaman, and femininity as the vehicle to the spirit world."

Her point is that in Southeast Asian societies under colonial rule, "gendered categories were differently constituted within discrete cultural settings, which did not necessarily result in the advantage to the male." In particular, in most of Southeast Asia, one's sexual identity was not linked to one's biology, but rather to gender. In other words, while individuals may engage in same-sex acts, these were better understood as "hetero-gendered erotic acts" (Loos, 1320). In her examination of sexualities in Asia, Tamara Loos writes that

> studies of the erotic in Asian history reveal that gender played, and arguably still plays, a more significant role in determining sexual morality than the sex of participants… (it) was primary in determining normative heterosexual and same-sex erotic relations …. In other words, individuals' gender rather than their genitalia determined their sexual object choice (1320).

The next two essays demonstrate the kind of "discrete cultural settings" in the Philippines that would provide us with a better understanding of how gendered categories were not only differently constituted but also contested and negotiated. Raquel Reyes's "Sodomy in Seventeenth-Century Manila: The Luck of a Mandarin from Taiwan" gives us a glimpse of the clash that occurred between the Spanish colonizers and the Chinese community in Manila over the case of Lousu, who was accused of committing "sodomy" (*sodomia* or *pecado nefando contra natura*) and was to be punished. From the perspective of the Chinese, however, such an act—especially by an older, wealthy, or well-connected Chinese—did not constitute a crime under Qing dynasty imperial law. Eventually, through the negotiations made between a Chinese official Pangsebuan and the Spanish Dominican friar Alberto Collares, Lousu was allowed to return to Taiwan unpunished. Aside from demonstrating how notions of gender and sexuality differed between the Spanish colonizers, the natives, and the Chinese, this essay also exposes the limits of colonial rule in Spanish Philippines. In much of that history, Spanish efforts to regulate the minds and bodies of its colonial subjects often required adaptations and even leniency, as one of the editors' work has demonstrated in relation to the Chinese.[9] Reyes's study also provides a transnational perspective to the study of sexual and gender identities in colonial Philippines. By investigating how gender and sexual norms were understood and lived out not only in the Philippines but also in Europe and Spanish America, her essay provides us with a more nuanced, complex, and rich understanding of how individuals lived out their lives within the specificity of their historical contexts (Loos, 1324).

Joaine Marquez's essay "*Pecado Nefando* and the Chinese in Early Spanish Philippines: Hispano-Asian Encounters and Ethnosexual Discourses" also utilizes a similar approach. However, he expands on Reyes's essay by also investigating the "plurality of gender and sexual practices in late imperial China" to better understand how the Chinese in the Philippines, whom the Spaniards blamed for introducing the "abominable practice of sodomy" to the natives of the Philippines, negotiated their own gender and sexual identity roles. As a social history that looks intimately into the behavior of individuals such as Lousu, and as a transnational history that considers in more detail the contextual nature of the institutional responses of the Spaniards toward the question of sodomy and the Chinese, Marquez's study historically documents the agency of the Chinese and traces how ideas were translated across cultural and national boundaries.

All three essays in this section point us to some gaps in our historical knowledge of gender and sexual norms in precolonial and Spanish colonial Philippines and future directions for historical research, such as a history of intraregional Asian sexualities, especially one that deals with female same-sex erotics—if historical evidence could be found—and more studies that focus, as the other essays in this anthology do, on the specific local cultural and social milieus of these non-heterosexual and non-binary gendered historical actors.

Filipino sexual and gender identities

In October 2018, netizens of Philippine pop culture were witnesses to a word-war between two young Filipino singers, Darren Espanto and Juan Karlos "JK" Labajo. The firestorm arose when Labajo one day tweeted "@Espanto2001 gayness at its finest." The tweet was quickly deleted, but not before many followers of both singers had already read it. Labajo claimed that he did not write the tweet and that his account had been hacked. In reply, Espanto tweeted: "*Timing 'no? Dinelete ng "hacker" mo yung tweet na 'to after kang kausapin ng management. Pag nahanap mo yung hacker mo puntahan*

9   See Richard T. Chu, *Chinese and Chinese Mestizos of Manila: Family, Identity, and Culture, 1860s–1930s* (Leiden and Boston: Brill, 2010), 167–78.

niyo ako para malaman niyo kung sino yung totoong BAKLA."[10] (What great timing. The "hacker" deleted this tweet after your management had spoken to you. If you find the hacker, let him come to me so that you will find out who really is *bakla*.) A Twitter user then responded *"Eh bakla k naman talaga diba?* (But you're really *bakla* anyway, aren't you?). To which Espanto replied *"May gender identity issues ka diba? Wag mo akong itulad sa'yo"* (You have gender identity issues, don't you? Do not compare me to yourself).

The vitriol that Espanto exhibited in responding to tweets alluding that he was "gay" or *bakla* was understandable, for *bakla* is a Tagalog term to refer to someone who is deemed effeminate, and "gay" is often equated with the term. Both terms, especially the former, can be used derisively to insult someone.

Some netizens called Espanto out for using "bakla" as an insult to get back at Labajo. For instance, "Beachinera" wrote "All I know is, REAL MEN doesn't [sic] give a shit if they are judge [sic] as a 'Gay'. Let's stop using the BEKIs as an insulting term and respect LGBT. Cause you know what, sometimes Gays are more MEN than straight. Right?"[11] Espanto eventually apologized for using the term and tried to justify what he did. "I didn't mean to use the word 'bakla' as a derogatory term. I'm sorry if this has offended anyone and to the people who say I have 'fragile masculinity'? I've been bashed with this since I was in *The Voice Kids* (I was 12) *pero wala kayong narinig* (but you didn't hear anything from me). I'm 17 now, *kakapagod na rin* (it's also become tiring)."

Bakla is a gendered identity associated with femininity. In the context of Labajo's first tweet that set up this controversy, *gay* was used interchangeably with *bakla*. However, the term is not equivalent with *gay*, which, in the western sense, refers to someone who has sexual relations with people of the same sex. What does *bakla* really mean? How is it, along with other terms to refer to "gay" individuals, understood and used within the Philippine context, and how is it different from words used in the western world to refer to non-heteronormative identities and behavior? The editors of this volume decided to place the next three essays in succession as they help dissect the meanings of English-language terms that have been introduced into the Philippine lexicon since the United States colonized the Philippines in 1898 and made English an official language. More particularly, these essays discuss how LGBTIA+ terms such as *gay, bisexual,* or *lesbian* have been appropriated

---

10   According to Espanto, their record label MCA Music (Universal Music Philippines) had approached Labajo regarding the tweet.

11   "Beki" is another colloquial term for *bakla*.

and redefined by members of the LGBTIA+ community in the Philippines, and how such terms are used vis-a-vis local words such as *bakla*.

In his essay "From *Bakla* to Gay: Shifting Gender Identities and Sexual Behaviors in the Philippines," Michael Tan points out that *bakla*, unlike *gay*, was originally a term that connotes effeminacy, and not sexual orientation. In other words, it was linked with a gender identity (see Brewer in this volume). When the term *homosexual* was introduced into the Philippine lexicon, and then used interchangeably with *bakla*, the latter term began to be associated also with sexual identity and practice. But even with such association, the term *bakla* continues to be identified with effeminacy. Hence, even the word *bisexual* is used not as a "sexual identity" but as a gendered identity. "Bisexuals" in the Philippine context are popularly believed to be closeted *baklas*, i.e., men who act or believe themselves to be heterosexual but are secretly otherwise. Tan highlights these usages in a study he conducted involving participants of an HIV awareness and prevention workshop. The participants were mostly under the age of thirty, highly educated, Catholic, Manila-based, and from the middle- to upper-class spectrum of Philippine society. When asked how they self-identified, many chose *gay* instead of *bakla* as the latter term was associated with not only effeminacy but also as belonging to the lower-class *parlorista* (those who work in beauty salons or parlors). Hence, *bakla* connotes both effeminacy and class. These baklas are seen as pursuing "straight" men and paying or otherwise supporting them for sex. Filipino men who engage in sex with other men are considered "straight" to the extent they are not the ones who initiate sex or play an active role in soliciting it, except for proffering financial or similar gain. What his study shows is that the existence of "strong patron-client relationships" in the country—even among Filipino "gays"—and the rise of HIV/AIDS in the country, along with xenophobia, misogyny, and class discrimination, will continue to influence how the boundaries of gender and sexual identities are shaped and reshaped. Tan's essay raises provocative questions such as what middle- and upper-class members of Philippine gay society used to refer to themselves before the introduction of *gay*. One editor of this volume recalls not being spared from being called *bakla*—and consequently recoiling at the term—while growing up as a middle-class Filipino. Did the introduction of *gay* provide Filipino "gays" with a space to be dissociated from the negatively identified *bakla*? If so, what happens when, as seems to be occurring today, the term *gay* has also become identified with effeminacy? (See Baytan below.) Another question Tan's essays raises is how sexual and even simple friendships between older gay men and younger gay men in the Philippines are to be understood, i.e., whether there is a prevalence of "daddy-boy" relationships as there are in other societies and in what way these are "unique" among Filipino gay men.

Ronald Baytan's essay "Crazy Planets: Notes on Filipino 'Bisexuals'" delves deeper into the question of "bisexuality" in the Philippines. Baytan's essay gives readers an understanding of what "bi" or "bisexual" stands for within the self-authored profiles of users of an online sexual hook-up site called Planet Romeo (PR). While "bisexual" in the western world means someone who is sexually oriented to both male and female, among users of PR the word has come to mean someone who is sexually attracted to men—hence gay or *bakla* —but different from both because being "bi" also means being "masculine" or straight-acting, whereas "gay" and *bakla* have become associated with being effeminate. The reason for this dissonance from the western sense of the word is the absence of an alternative term when western colonizers conflated *lalake* or "men" with masculinity and Philippine society *bakla* (and eventually "gay") with effeminacy. Baytan points out that men who identify themselves as being masculine could not even use the term "gay" anymore to identify themselves, since "gay" has been appropriated by Philippine society currently to also mean "bakla," i.e., men who are effeminate. Without any other recourse, these men use "bi" to describe themselves in their online profiles.

In this context, an explanatory methodological and conceptual note needs to be added. Baytan's "scrubbing" of his data (note 8 in his text), apparently to protect the privacy of his research subjects, involved removing *any and all identifiers* that could possibly relate the essay's exemplary profiles to existing profiles on PR. As a result, there is no way to independently verify the author's data or to evaluate the theoretical conclusions he draws from this avowed evidence-based research study. The essay then has to be read as a more *speculative* one where the author's extrapolation— from Filipinos actually identifying their sexual identities as "bi" on PR into the "strategic fiction" of what Baytan terms the "Pinoy BI"—indicates, in the author's words, "what the subjects say they are and who they are, are two different things." Ironically, after Baytan's strong criticism of their sexism (effemophobic masculinity), their classism and stated rejection of luring any kind of "money boys," and their internalized homophobia (despite plausible deniability about wanting the perceived privileges "a global gay culture" could afford based on *who they say they are*), Baytan seems to heroize this Pinoy BI as "one of the excesses in the very rigid sex-gender system in the country. Morphing into a ticking time bomb, it only needed modern technology to explode" leaving the reader to anxiously await the author's next iteration of "this peculiar yet very important lot in Philippine LGBTQI culture."[12]

Finally, what these two essays reveal, again, is the need for more studies investigating further the association of "bakla" with someone who pays money or supports another person, in exchange for companionship and sex. More studies are also needed to investigate the role of religion, especially Roman Catholicism, in the way "baklas" are construed in society, on how "baklas," "bi's," and "gays" in the Philippines deal with the conflict between their sexual orientation, religious beliefs, and Baytan's professed, and hopefully shared, will "to pursue 'a liberatory body of thought about sexuality."

The next essay offers us a glimpse into the world of transgender and lesbian or tomboy individuals. Jennifer Josef's "Pinoy Tomboys, Lesbians, and Transgenders: Their Gender and Sexual Identities and Activism since the 1980s" focuses on the formation and framing of these sexual and gender identities based in part on her own experience as an activist up to the present. The essay also discusses factors such as Catholicism and the advent of hormone therapy that have shaped these identities, and the political activism of these individuals. In drawing from her own experiences as well as her involvement in lesbian and transgender social movements, Josef invites us to view these identities through the lens of intersectionality in order to understand why, for example, the LGBTIA+ community in the Philippines is "factious and deeply divided."[13] Though Baytan's and now Josef's studies combine both empirical and experience-based theorization, understanding Philippine factiousness may not come from comparing these two studies alone, however nominally complementary they appear to be. Notably, to do their theorizing in the context of academic specialization, Baytan focuses *solely* on "bi"-identified same-sex seeking Filipinos and Josef

12   Here, Baytan's aspiration may parallel that of queer intersectional theorist Cathy Cohen (see note 15) who wrote: "What I and others are calling for is the destabilization, not the destruction or abandonment of identity categories. We must reject a queer politics that seems to ignore, in its analysis . . . the usefulness of traditionally named categories . . . Instead, I would suggest that it is the multiplicity and interconnectedness of our identities that provide the most promising avenue for the *destabilization and radical politicization* of these same categories."

13   This may help explain why the first LGBT political party Ang Ladlad failed to gain enough votes (2%) to win a seat in the Philippine Congress. Although the first transgender congresswoman Geraldine Roman won a seat in the 2016 elections, her priorities have often been more aligned with the agenda of traditional politics (which can be misogynistic and homophobic) rather than primarily toward LGBT rights. However, she continues to be active in supporting the SOGIE Anti-Discrimination bill.

focuses primarily on Filipino non-normative gendered sexual subjectivities *except* those of Filipino gay men. To be sure, both invoke overcoming divisiveness and evoke conditions cited either by queer theorists' critique of identity politics (Baytan) or by postcolonial democratic and coalition politics (Josef), fostering broad-based sociocultural change arising from sexual and gender subjectivities. The final writings collected in this volume suggest one such holistic direction through LGBTIA+-inclusive Philippine psychological science and practice collaboratively developed across academic specializations within that discipline. (See below.)

Returning to Josef's "sequel" to her highly regarded earlier study about the mutation of a distinctively lesbian movement out of Philippine feminist theory and activism, her chapter here completes the move into and even a little beyond feminism-inspired lesbian specificity to account for trans men in the Philippine transgender movement. Interestingly in the Philippines, "lesbian" is a word that is used to refer to, or is used by those from a middle-class background, while "tomboy" is associated, similarly with *bakla*, with those of lower socioeconomic status. However, it is not clear whether the term "tomboy" is also identified more with gender than sexual identity, as *bakla* is. Furthermore, "lesbian" has been divided into either "butch" or "femme" and Josef traces the historical development of "trans men," thereby complicating those stereotypes accorded to separatist lesbians. Her contribution aspires to work in the interface between intersectionality and subjectivity as a political methodology, using the Philippine working class lesbian-transgender movement GALANG and interviews of its constituents as a case study. (See also UNPD, ODI, and GALANG 2020.)

Even with the history of men cross-dressing in early Philippine society, the status of transgender individuals remains uncertain. While the last two decades saw the creation of a number of transgender, transsexual, and "transpinay" organizations, the country's laws (in 2020) still do not recognize the rights of these individuals because the country's legislators do not consider gender realignment a reason to create new laws protecting transgender individuals, since Philippine courts only protect the rights of cisgender people, i.e., following "natural" law that one's biological or birth sex determines one's identity.[14]

---

14   In a slap to transgender people in the Philippines, in 2020 Duterte pardoned US marine Lance Corporal Joseph Scott Pemberton who had only served a little over half of his ten-year sentence for the killing of transgender woman Jennifer Laude in 2014. Duterte's action drew condemnation from Laude's family, human rights advocates, and members of the local LGBTIA+ community. Duterte justified his pardon by saying that he wanted to be "fair" to Pemberton.

In searching for a theoretical framework to understand the variances in the application and understanding of terms such as "bakla," "gay," "tomboy," and "lesbian" in the Philippine context, we can cite the work of Vicente Rafael that demonstrates how in colonial society those who were colonized appropriated foreign terms into the local vernacular in order to deflect the violence of colonization. In the case of middle- to upper-class Filipinos using "gay" to distinguish themselves from the derogatory "bakla," the same reason could be applied, though this "translation" is a distancing from the violence inflicted from a *local* term. The propensity of the LGBTIA+ community, especially the "gay" community, to come up with new terms under the rubric of what is called "swardspeak" can also be explained by Filipinos attempting to deal with the current displacements brought by neoliberal policies inflicted upon countries in the global south (see Tolentino in this anthology). From the three aforementioned essays, Pinoy LGBTIA+s constantly deflect or evade the negative associations of certain local words that others use to categorize them by appropriating terms found in the lexicon of western sexology to identify themselves, and by hybridizing both the local and the foreign.

Negotiating sexual and gender diversity in recent Philippine culture
The next set of essays examines what it means to be be LGBTIA+ in Philippine society in specific contexts. The first of these, Patrick Alcedo's "Sacred Camp: Transgendering Faith in a Philippine Festival," adds to our knowledge of LGBTI(Q)A+ studies in the Philippines in at least two areas—in its focus on 1) a non-Manila centered transgender individual and LGBT(Q) community in Kalibo, Aklan; and 2) the way LGBTIA+ individuals negotiate the hegemonic control of the Catholic Church and its teachings on homosexuality. In Aklan, the operative word for being gay is *agi*, which the author differentiates from *bakla*. As mentioned earlier, *bakla* is associated with not only effeminacy but also with being part of an uneducated and lower class. On the other hand, the word *agi* takes more of the playful quality of camp, as well as perhaps, the fluidity of gender and sexual identities that "queer" connotes in its usage as either noun, adjective, adverb, or verb.

Alcedo's essay also examines the intersection or juxtaposition of the "sacred" and the "profane," and how a provincial resident—Tay Augus— was able to appropriate gender, race, and religious norms in Kalibo society to find a "space" for oneself in the Ati-Atihan festival. It analyzes how LGBTIA+ individuals negotiate societal and religious norms and gives us an understanding of why such "ambiguities" actually make sense to Tay Augus and the people participating in the festival, which also points to the either more "flexible" or maybe just different attitudes that both secular and religious people in Aklan have toward sexuality, and to allow individuals to express their sexuality and gender identity, that may seem transgressive against but are still within the limits of church norms. Tay Augus's participation in the annual Ati-Atihan festival is seen as a *panaad* (penitential act) and his transgendering as a way to please the mischievous, equally androgynous, and powerful Holy Child, the Santo Niño.

Another study focusing on LGBTIA+ individuals outside of the capital city of Manila is Kaira Alburo's "Brother, Lovers, and Revolution: Negotiating Military Masculinity and Homosexual Identity in a Revolutionary Movement in the Philippines." Alburo's study about same-sex erotic love within a radical movement provides us with some insight on how such a movement, as a counterpoint to the conservative Catholic Church, might serve as a venue for "gay liberation," tolerance, or acceptance. In 1998, the Communist Party of the Philippines recognized same-sex relations and in 2005, the first same-sex marriage was performed as a ceremony, but not as a "legal" act. Based on her informants' accounts, Alburo shows how homosexuality is "negotiated in the context of ... masculinity" within the military arm of the movement, known as the New People's Army (NPA). Interestingly, but probably not surprisingly, while same-sex relations and marriages have been allowed, heteronormativity and the traditional concept of "bakla" still dictated the views of their cadres toward human sexuality and gender relations. Hence, gay as well as lesbian revolutionaries continued to experience discrimination or ridicule despite the changes in the movement's policies. "Straight" cadres also consistently felt confused about how "bakla" comrades could inhabit physically strong bodies and exhibit masculine behavior while being emotionally and mentally "female." Both Alcedo's and Alburo's studies demonstrate the prevalence of heteronormative institutions and values affecting the LGBTI(Q)A+ communities in the Philippines. Be that as it may, both studies also show the social identities and forms of love and of living that LGBTIA+-identified Filipinos manage to carve out to express their senses of self and personal ethics within their specific sociocultural, economic, and political contexts. We recommend that our readers consider the problematic use of "queer" for a Philippine context in comparison between the two chapters here. Alcedo's description lends itself toward a tentative approximation of *agi* as reflecting a queer sensibility in the Anglophonic sense of that term and its possible comparative analytic use for describing a collectivity of people. However, these excellent essays also suggest the limits of this term since there is no indication that either Tay Augus or other *agi* possessed a personal identity akin to "queer" (nor did the study's author suggest parallels of "camp" with "queer" in framing the essay's title) and we do not know from Alburo's study how heteronormative incoherencies between gender roles and sexual practices might be reconciled among avowed revolutionaries (revolutionary brothers), as "queering" the relationships between personal subjectivity and political mobilization might propose.

The next two essays in this section focus on the lives of men and women with whom Filipino LGBTIA+s interact and how their lives are implicated by globalizing forces that have led to the "feminization" of Filipino male labor and the reconfiguration and renegotiation of Filipino male masculinities in the diaspora. Rolando Tolentino's "Macho Dancing, the Feminization of Labor, and Neoliberalism in the Philippines" gives us a glimpse of the world of solicitous macho dancers whom gay men and straight women ogle and pay for sex. Tolentino explains how the neoliberal policies implemented under the Marcos government had created increased foreign investment in the country that promoted the export of labor. Many Filipino men found a niche in other countries as seamen and construction workers. However, not every Filipino man could afford or had the right connections to work abroad. Some of those who stayed took on more such feminized labor as domestic help and so-called macho dancing. The rise of macho dancing gay bars in the 1970s helped create in the public sphere a dominant gay identity closely identified with a "commercialized nature of sexual exchange."

The continuing neoliberal policies in succeeding governments in the country have produced a fantasy of being able to achieve economic mobility through the use of one's body (especially if young, sexy, or virile) that find expression in venues such as "beauty pageants [male, female, gay, or transgender], modeling and bikini searches, talent and game shows, and reality television." The Filipino gay community is known to be among the most ardent fans of beauty pageants. Could it be possible then that their identification with the country's delegates to international beauty pageants and winning is a gay man's fantasy of upward mobility in a country that is perennially in economic crisis, as in the case of Joana Montegracia in Garcia's essay?

Apart from the fetishization and commercialization of male bodies in service industries, the neoliberal policies pushed by the US and other industrialized countries, coupled with the policies of the Philippine governments, have resulted in the creation of a human export economy in the Philippines which has seen, as of 2019, the migration of more than 10 million Filipinos around the world. A large portion of this labor market consists of Filipinos working as seamen whom Kale Fajardo in his essay "Transportation: Translating Filipino and Filipino American Tomboy Masculinities through Global Migration and Seafaring" describes in what is part ethnography, part travelogue, part autobiography. Spending eight months with workers on a container ship and writing about his interaction with Filipino seaman, Fajardo, a transgender man (or trans man), contests statist narratives of these men as heterosexual, heroic, "macho," etc. by arguing that "Filipino masculinities—heterosexual male and tomboy—must be understood in relation to, *not* apart from, each other." He shows that tomboy can also be used to "signify FTM transgenderism." When Fajardo emphasized his working class background, the seamen would see him as a tomboy, but when he introduced himself as a *balikbayan* (a Filipino living abroad returning home), he was seen as a "lesbian." Hence, Filipino tomboy masculinities are better understood in relation to Filipino heterosexual male masculinities, instead of studied separate from each other as what, in Fajardo's words, "frequently happens in feminist accounts."

Moreover, he points out that there is some "emotional intimacy" between Filipino men, suggestive of more "fluid, contingent gender identities." He attributes this to *pakikiisa* which he defines as a "cultural concept (that) stresses the goal of creating 'emotional oneness' through the group, *not* through masculinist individualism, intragroup hierarchies, social competition, and violence that patriarchal . . . masculinities and 'male social bonding' have historically reinforced." Just like the indigenous concept of *malasakit*, *pakikiisa* could be a useful concept to help explain, for instance, why there seems to be in the local context more "acceptance" of gays and of individuals with a more fluid gender and sexual identity, and for social activists to utilize it in advocating for such acceptance.

Between the personal and the political

Sexual diversity and gender non-normativity have often been, if not the central features, at least hallmarks of progressivist social movements both within the Philippines and in many other parts of the world at least since the early twentieth century (for the latter) and into the present. These hallmarks are more apparent under conditions, for example, when individuals experience incommensurabilities within or between their own cultural forms and those of nearby co-existent others, when economic inequalities become intolerable, and within palimpsest legal systems expressing contradictions among their indigenous, colonial and postcolonial, and international components. (An example of the latter condition today might include sites of mutual support between local and transnational movements to decriminalize homosexuality.) Such sociocultural conditions as the above are sometimes broadly characterized through dichotomies of the west and the rest, north and south, globalization and localism or nativism. Several recent essays here take their perspective as "intersectional"—a term that characterizes the multiple identities of individuals derived from cross-cutting socioeconomically-based and culturally-inflected *power relations* (of class, "race" and skin color, gender, sex characteristics, ethnicity, sexual identity, age, physical challenge, religious belief, and others) that *simultaneously* privilege or disadvantage them in sometimes incongruous ways *and* provide opportunities for shared experience, for destabilization of pre-existing or "taken-for-granted" identities, and for collective political action with others.[15] Intersectionality's focus on *subjectivity* as a significant wellspring for political awareness and coalitional political mobilization is conceived in various ways through the progressivist advocacy motto "the personal is political," or sometimes as an individual's "right to privacy" within assumptions of liberal and libertarian theories ranging from the limits of state power regarding personal autonomy and responsibility to a defense against social or political persecution. This relation between the personal and the political even extends to cultural inventiveness and socio-economic development often beginning with coming-out narratives that may result in legal recognition of same-sex intimate erotic relationships toward marriage equality (and the redefinition in conceptualization and practice of both—same-sex intimacies and marriage—through their reinscription and adaptation within those relationships) resulting in new forms of care, "family," and child-bearing and -rearing. Further, intersectional analysis relating the personal (subjectivity) to the political (power) shows them as interpenetrating each other rather than as fixed positions, thereby raising fundamental questions about identity and becoming, such as "how can we say we?"[16]

In our book's essays, for example, such a "politics of ourselves," as mutable positions on a multi-temporal or -situational continuum (rather than an abolition of all distinctions) between the personal and the political may be seen in Garcia's *metaphoric* cautionary tale of the *actual* tragic performance of a transpinay on "the murderous stage that is her country's unremitting helplessness" and in Pineda's reflections about lesbian erotic art as both cultural retrieval and personal becoming which, beginning with implicit self-creation and -reinvention, potentially transforms Philippine social and

---

15   A recently-becoming "classic" analysis of this may be found in Cathy J. Cohen's "Punks, Bulldaggers, and Welfare Queens: The Radical Potential of Queer Politics?" in *Sexual Identities, Queer Politics*, ed. Mark Blasius (Princeton and Oxford: Princeton University Press, 2001), 200–27.

16   A germinal account of this politics of ourselves is Michel Foucault's "The Subject and Power," *Critical Inquiry* 8, no. 4 (1982): 777–95. For a discussion of the interrelation of the personal and the political through social media in the Philippines see Larissa Hjorth and Michael Arnold's "The Personal and the Political: Social Networking in Manila," *International Journal of Learning and Media* 3, no. 1 (2011): 29–39; the closing passages of Baytan (*infra*); and in the prevention and treatment of HIV/AIDS using ICT in Southeast Asia (Hankel, et al. 2015). Examples of new relational forms within LGBTIA+ pandemic-affected life abound in the web series mentioned above.

political institutions through women's relationships with themselves and all Filipinos. We can find similar continua between personal and political, for example, in Alcedo's depiction of personal agency for a provincial *bakla* by religious narrative and ultimate sociocultural toleration through communal performance of penitential subjectivity in a public festival; in Alburo's view of a communist military masculinity purportedly supplanting a recruit's subjective one in order to rationalize male same-sex marriage within a political movement privileging "political" class love over "personal" sexual love; in Fajardo's personal, intimate, but (even) as FTM (female-to-male) non-sexual, "emotional oneness" with Filipino seafarers on a containership that opens up the possibility for more "fluid contingent gender identities" and their implications for heteronormative regimes of sexuality (i.e., "the political"); and in Josef's outright use of the concepts of subjectivity and intersectionality by sourcing local, national, and transnational "political" advocacy for policy and structural change of a state's governing regime in the "personal" gender identities of tomboys, transgenders, and lesbians in the Philippines. Even in some of the historical studies published here, we may compare premodern gendered *roles* in Philippine social structure (Brewer) with later classification by colonial and ecclesiastical authorities of permitted or forbidden erotic *acts*—a classification that was dependent upon circumstances (including the socially-assigned status of the *individual actor* without regard to any psychic interiority or personal "authenticity")— and accordingly a classification that highlighted the *circumstances* under which these individual erotic acts would result in widely divergent political consequences (Marquez and Reyes), which we could then, in turn, contrast with those "new" situational considerations subsuming the historically-later concept of "intimate" relationships between the emergent "private" personages of "homosexual" subjects or even, recalling Brewer's critique of "modern" feminist interpretations of the "premodern," a later "third-gendered" sense of selfhood.

Calling something personal *or* political today evokes a perennial theme of human understanding and action to characterize the fate of individual existence in relation to the social relations and political order in which it resides. In modern European thought—a context in which the contemporary nation-state and international order arose, developed, and was rationalized—this characterization often involved a separation between *private* relationships among individuals in a "civil society" and those individuals' *public* relationships as citizens of "the state" that supposedly guaranteed their inherent freedom and equality as human beings. In such a framework, the state makes certain distinctively *political* claims (as differentiated from familial, religious, "natural," or other possible claims) on behalf of a common good of those within its dominion, that is, on behalf of *justice*.

This very schematic framework with some slippage in terminology has been adapted to be more specific to our own time and global space through the United Nations' practice and language of international law.[17] In other words, the powers or capacities that individuals exercise in their relations with each other—their freedoms stipulated as human rights and as equality with respect to each other—are supposedly guaranteed through their governments by national and international law, as both an enabling and limiting (counter) *power generated simply by their own collectivity* but stipulating more locally and historically specific conditions for realizing their common good. Accordingly, the provenance of *politics*, in that interface or shared space of interrelationships between an individual and both national and international societies—where various powers are exercised and resisted, where they are argued, agreed to, and fought about, where powers are introduced or reproduced or rearranged—*politics* happens in that space of power where conditions for living together toward a common good are conceived and enacted as justice. Thus, a call for sexual and gender justice may be understood as a call to address "politically" in a public language and in a shared space accessible to all, discovery of commonality through recognition of diversity in sexual relations and gender identities, and to redress what is conceived there as injustice. One template from LGBTIA+ politics has provided some guidance, that of a continuum of coming out (or in feminist terms "calling out") where the personal becomes political not as simply a one-time event but as an event on a continuum of "politicization," as mentioned earlier: between *private* individual and interpersonal relations of intimacy and their location within more expansive networks of power relations that constitute a *public* ordering of society devoted to realizing justice, or not—with injustice being characterized by systemic inequalities corresponding to an organization of powers denying those freedoms of human rights and maintaining those inequalities, for example.

17   See Office of the United Nations High Commissioner for Human Rights (OHCHR), "Born Free and Equal: Sexual Orientation, Gender Identity, and Sex Characteristics in International Human Rights Law, Second Edition" and "Living Free and Equal: What States are Doing to Tackle Violence and Discrimination Against Lesbian, Gay, Bisexual, Transgender, and Intersex People" (New York and Geneva: United Nations, 2019, 2016 respectively).

This can be a recognizable framework for contemporary democracies as well as for their challengers, and a test of how our understandings and actions about politics and justice can function in global as well as local arenas. However, the framework can also show the negative possibility of thinking about our political lives through an abstract dualism of public *versus* private that hides important features of the way power is exercised today and how injustice prevails, in particular with regard to sexuality and gender. One by now perhaps commonplace example is what happens when something considered private within a particular culture and historical context—even something seemingly as personal as sexual orientation—becomes politicized through challenging large-scale power structures. In this example, something becomes politicized when people challenge how overlapping systems of power shape relationships in their everyday lives by privileging the sense of selfhood for some with a sanctioned sexual and gender identity and disallowing that sense of selfhood for others. This happens through the coercive power of formal laws such as nation-state regulation, educational credentials and their institutions, strong norms such as religious doctrine and practice, as well as through more informal customary norms of fashion and advertising, mass media coverage, and access to less socially visible forms of power. Politicization within this framework has taken as its object the prohibition of civil marriage between persons of the same sex through calls that "the personal is political" and that prohibition of marriage equality is unjust domination of all through the system—or regime—of power called heteronormativity that privileges both formally and informally those heterosexually-identified and disallows others and their intimate relationships (and is a component of a broader regime of male domination over women called heteropatriarchy). Similar calls that sexual harassment of individuals in their workplaces is unjust have also demonstrated how dichotomizing between private and public can camouflage what is actually a political issue by treating unequal relations of power as if they were consensual. Other examples of "what counts" as political and how terms such as public, private, and intimate are historically, culturally, and situationally variable may be found in some of the essays that follow from Philippine autobiography and psychology that politicize, through a human rights framework, psychic concepts such as subjectivity and consent as well as psychology's own research methodologies.

These political aspirations and struggles are described in our final essays using concepts such as relational intimacy and authenticity to describe how selfhood or personal identity is constructed and inflected through relations with (or in fantasy about) others—in relations of friendship, love, familial closeness, communicative and affective transparency, but particularly in connection with both *sexuality* (a concept also largely modern and western according to Josef and Ofreneo citing Tan) and with *gender*. To historicize a little bit more, gender, as the culturally constructed and culturally variable behaviors expected of women and men—and traditionally viewed according to a now mostly outmoded notion of dimorphic *sex* (bodily attributes such as genitals, chromosomes, genes, hormones, and other physical markers many of which are mutable, subject to change)—became reconceptualized as independent not only of biological sex but also of sexuality (the motivation for and behaviors associated with obtaining erotic pleasure) by the end of the twentieth century through research into transsexual and intersexual phenomena as well as into erotic behavior across cultures. Today, sex, gender, and sexuality are no longer scientifically conflated with each other (Meyrowitz 2002). Their interrelationships as personal instances of a "human nature" and grounded in some kind of transcultural realness reflecting "natural law" have therefore become interrogatory points of departure, "question marks" for the work of our writers here. Their writing reflects how powers exercised through laws, norms, and everyday attitudes pertaining to sex, gender, and sexuality affect their manner of living in the (Catholic) Philippines, thereby making these public *political* issues. Indeed, popular psychological concepts such as authenticity and intimacy, like privacy, may be all the more controversial because they have become central to understanding the historical transformation of sex, gender, and sexuality as key ingredients of the personal; they can be seen to roughly parallel freedom and equality in states' obligations to promote LGBTI "living free and equal" in the UN's political thinking (note 17), on the one hand. On the other hand, these psychological concepts of human personhood denote democratically contested political issues such as limits of both state and non-state power in how we live *ourselves* using our sex, gender, and sexuality in pursuit of happiness, wealth, power, or other ideals. To recognize rights of authenticity-in-relationship (or intimacy), of personhood, and to protect from discrimination and violence based on sexuality or gender expression; to protect children from parent-authorized genital surgery or psychological coercion in the form of conversion "therapy" intended to fit them into normative dimorphic sex classification, stereotypes about psychosexual development, or "appropriate" gender identity; to simultaneously provide familial or pedagogical and social support for gay, lesbian, bisexual, transgender, intersex or asexual youth and everyone throughout the course of life—all these efforts at "calling something political" have been at the forefront of the politics of sexuality as it is supported by advances in psychological knowledge in the Philippines as chronicled here.

Finally, the writers herein often needed to question how sexuality and gender rights and justice have sometimes, in diverse parts of the world, been termed "icing on the cake" when so many people are deprived of other pressing human needs such as having adequate nutrition, shelter, healthcare, and safety, participating in the biological and cultural continuity of human life, having *access* to equal justice within publicly-known systems of law and their non-arbitrary application, and other publicly acknowledged needs. (See the Yogyakarta Principles' elaboration of these needs-as-rights in relation to SOGIESC through international law.) While the trivialization of gender and sexuality as "icing" as well as the prioritization this implies is so flawed (as though LGBTI people do not also suffer from food insecurity, homelessness, lack of access to healthcare and reproductive justice, and the infliction of violence upon them) this also distracts from what is important, which is how the boundaries between erotic, gendered, embodied subjectivity, our personal and private "intimacies," and the public or political "common good" are so permeable that aspects of our everyday lives either feel to us like, or become labelled as, a power struggle—a conflict between the personal and political. What might happen when male bonding or friendship becomes sexual erotic love (i.e., what is ironic about "bromance" is that it desensitizes a threatening contradiction of incest and romance in an English-language neologism for simple friendship)? How do women's erotic relationships with each other bring about generalized gender equality and even more generalized social justice as some have suggested herein? Why should parents or the state (or religious proxies) be allowed to shape a child's or any person's autonomous development of gender or sexual identity through coercive means such as conversion therapy (from lesbian or gay to straight or celibate, from gender "dysphoric" to gender normative, and through the use of genital mutilation on intersex children)? Thus, not only in the Philippines but throughout the world, this power struggle over "what counts" as personal autonomy, as intimate (or private) relations, and as the common good (involving the political relations of power, rights and obligations, and justice with regard to sexual diversity and gender non-normativity) has become central to our governing institutions, to our subjectivities or sense of autonomous selfhood, and to questioning knowledges about sex characteristics, gendered identities, and sexual-erotic practices. To sum up, what we have termed the politics of ourselves is about how we act and relate to others on an equilibrating or balancing continuum between private and public that usually involves not just a semantic (re)definition or fluidity of terms but a political "struggle" and a "settlement" or temporary working framework for living together amidst ongoing claims for changes in that framework based on recognitions of personal authenticity and diversity in the context of sexual or gender hegemonies that shape them, for example.

How LGBTIA+ Filipinos think through and navigate between the personal and the political in their lives is the focus of these final three essays. They do so from very different "writerly" perspectives but together illuminate this theme that importantly takes us full circle through the book. Richard T. Chu writes taking "an autobiographical approach to raise certain questions about a 'public' issue . . . a largely unexplored topic: that of the intersection of religious, ethnic, and sexual identities of the diasporic Chinese." In so positioning himself, Chu paves the way conceptually and implicitly suggests the challenging lived domain of an LGBT-inclusive Philippine psychology. The essay that follows, by Eric Julian Manalastas and Beatriz Torre, explicates politically this domain of interrelated psychic and sociocultural challenge, tracing how it has been taken up professionally in the Philippines through 2016, and catalyzed in a landmark 2011 public statement of the Psychological Association of the Philippines (PAP) about non-discrimination based on sexual orientation and gender identity and expression. That statement is reprinted next after their essay referencing it. Finally, Mira Alexis P. Ofreneo vernacularizes the scope and methods of psychological science in order to develop the outline of a distinctive theory and practice of Philippine LGBT psychology for transformative ends.

Richard T. Chu's essay explicitly begins with the themes mentioned above, providing both engaging content and unique methodology. Citing Ien Ang, he uses autobiography "as a more or less deliberate, rhetorical construction of a 'self' for *public*, not private purposes: the displayed self is a strategically fabricated performance, one which stages a *useful* identity, an identity which can be put to work. [Chu's quotation stops here but we continue with Ang.] It is the quality of that usefulness which determines the politics of autobiographical discourse. In other words, what is the identity being put forward *for?*" Richard Chu's autobiographical "usefulness" is its interventions into politics by means of unfurling a self-exposition (again, *ladlad*, or "coming out") and gift to the reader of how his Roman Catholic, Confucian, Filipino-Chinese diasporic, and gay male identities reflect the political through the personal. The essay discusses his role as a young sexually-aware male in a predominantly female household in Manila, as a student and an adult living between the United States and the Philippines, the reproduction of patriarchy through Catholicism and Confucianism as a family heritage, and his ongoing practice of "becoming" himself in this context. Whether through his experience of gender hierarchy and male privilege or the family's invisibilizing discriminatory treatment of his silent sisters, the non-ideological writing shows a teenager observing how gender stereotypes are learned as his sisters work dual shifts at school and the family business, preparing themselves for marriage, while the author's male privilege lets him off the hook to live away from home and pursue his own interests. To be sure, this self-described escape from the responsibilities of being "man of the house" by becoming gay was at the expense of his sisters and is starkly and honestly written. In a certain sense, the title of this chapter emblematizes through homage both the subject's relationship with his mother and with the Philippines: After his father's untimely death, it was his mother's "gift" of male privilege that enabled the subject of the narrative to become gay; it was his education in the US and return to the Philippines that strengthened his resolve to make the islands and their cultures an accepting place where LGBTIQA+ people want to stay rather than leave for better economic or more hospitable conditions.

Since so few can leave, the prospect of choice is introduced, through whatever means available. Far beyond a typical coming-out story (and through difficult cultural translation of it) this autobiography's *usefulness, the politics of it as autobiographical discourse, involves the question of where do values come from?*—whether Confucian, Buddhist, Roman Catholic, or those self-analytical ones of psychology guiding intimacy—that help some to slip through the routines by which these moral systems and institutions enable heteronormativity (but not others in Chu's intersectional perspective). The identity being put to work here is one searching for intimacy rather than orthodoxy and thus is in search of those private and public *conditions of choice*—as a value that we express toward each other, discoverable in Filipino autobiography that a diasporic subject is translating and thereby hoping to teach (as he was taught, i.e., for robust citizenship). The essay is grasping to recognize those different *conditions of choice* about our sexual well-being, bodily type or sex characteristics, as well as gender's roles, powers, and identities that are also where our values come from.

With this seeding of the field, our chapter sequence strives to show a politics of LGBTIA+ psychological knowledge being introduced in the Philippines as chronicled by Eric Manalastas and Beatriz Torre in their essay about the political struggle to guide psychological science along epistemological and moral-ethical standards informed by cross-national comparisons of psychological studies of LGBT populations, regional and global international agencies' standards of human health and well-being, international human rights, and Filipino psychologists' professional norms pertaining to gender and sexuality.[18] From a brief background on the status of LGBT people in the Philippines contextualized both within the rest of Southeast Asia and with domestic political achievements and obstacles to LGBTIA+ equality and well-being, the essay presents a detailed history and exposition of the strategy—spurred on by certain "critical events" ranging from the mediascape to political defeats in contemporary LGBTIA+ Filipino life—to recognize the political components of psychological science, its organization, and its practice in order to transform them into an "LGBT-inclusive Philippine Psychology."

Making "science" a political issue is always a tricky proposition as extreme problematic examples pertaining simply to the social sciences in other contexts demonstrate: the "science" of eugenics; twentieth-century ethnographic studies positing an "African Sexuality" (Arnfred 2004); and recent revelations of, denials about, and calls for professional sanctions against psychologists contracted by the US government to assist in "enhanced interrogation" (torture) at sites of "extraordinary rendition" (secret prisons) of suspected terrorists. Indeed, we can recognize how fraught has been the politics of science throughout the partisan politicization of the global HIV/AIDS pandemic (Seckinelgin 2017) as well as the partisan politics of public health during the COVID-19 pandemic. In the most general terms used here, a politics of knowledge could involve: (1) how something—some aspect of reality, here, that of personal well-being and relationships—becomes an object for psychological science; (2) how that psychological knowledge becomes *institutionalized* as a tradition or a discipline for teaching and justifying laws and norms governing human behavior; and (3) *who can*

18   Sources include: reports by the World Health Organization on sexual health encompassing psychological well-being; the World Bank-commissioned studies on LGBT contributions to national economies and development (see Badgett and Sell 2018); the ASEAN SOGIE Caucus and Regional Union of Psychological Societies; the Hong Kong Psychological Society; UNDP [with USAID], "Being LGBT in Asia: The Philippines Country Report" (2015); Psychological Association of the Philippines Scientific and Professional Ethics Committee, "Code of Ethics for Philippine Psychologists" (2010); "The Yogyakarta Principles on the Application of International Human Rights Law in Relation to Sexual Orientation and Gender Identity" (2007), updated to "YP Plus 10: Additional Principles and State Obligations on the Application of International Human Rights Law in Relation to Sexual Orientation, Gender Identity, Gender Expression and Sex Characteristics to Complement the Yogyakarta Principles" (2017). See also Eric Julian Manalastas, et al., "Homonegativity in Southeast Asia: Attitudes toward Lesbians and Gay Men in Indonesia, Malaysia, the Philippines, Singapore, Thailand, and Vietnam," *Asia-Pacific Social Science Review* 17, no. 1 (2017): 25–33.

exercise power through these human relations of psychology's organization: as the power relation that inheres in counselling ostensibly exercised by psychotherapist over the client; as the power exercised as expertise by someone trained in psychological science and contracted to solve problems of governing—such as employee management, public health, the conduct of war or peace through national security; or the power we obey when subjecting ourselves to psychological techniques of so-called self-help, just to give a few examples.

Obviously, this is but one analytic framework for thinking about the politics of knowledge. However, even by this very basic one, each of these components of a politics of knowledge is addressed in first-hand and trailblazing detail by the Manalastas and Torre essay about the transformation of psychological theory and practice that is both culturally-specific and LGBTIA+ sensitive, through themselves, their colleagues, and outreach to others in health- and care-related professions. For example, first, for "LGBT-inclusion" to become an object for psychological knowledge, LGBT psychological pathologization, social marginalization, and the harms these have inflicted had to be demonstrated through criteria of psychological knowledge itself, showing as well how the silence of the profession amounted to complicity in this harm. Manalastas and Torre emphasize the democratic processes of visibility and mainstreaming of LGBT psychologists and their allies both in research relevance and validity and in the historical practices of psychology. All three authors (including Ofreneo) demonstrate the wide range of new psychological and methodological issues "LGBT-inclusion" allowed to emerge and their spill-over effects into various subfields of psychological knowledge.

Second, in order to transform the power relations that the discipline of psychology enables in society, Manalastas, Torre, and Ofreneo had to change the discipline's institutional and collegial organization by getting the PAP to establish an "LGBT Psychology Special Interest Group" to monitor and expand the profession's research (mainly through publication), education (training teachers of psychology), advocacy (the profession's stated mission of "psychology in the public interest" through legislative advocacy and media outreach), practice (primarily counseling, assessment, and therapy), and (not least, given continuing stigma) recruitment of members for the special interest group. The direct causes and effects of these changes in psychology-as-an-institution are written in a nuanced, programmatic, and interesting narrative.

Thirdly, these changes in "what counts" as psychology and how the doors to the profession's institutions were opened to LGBTIAs and their concerns, affected who can exercise power through psychological expertise or on behalf of psychology's truth claims. Consequently, homophobic counseling, discriminatory employee assessment, and conversion therapy were challenged. Teachers and their students began to see sexual and gender diversity as positive human variabilities contributing to Philippine society, as well as to recognize the difficulties imposed on those who possess them. "Homonegative" social attitudes presented by political or other demagogues through the mass media as "truth" (supposedly backed by psychological science or other belief systems) were powerfully countered with reference to the PAP's Statement on Non-Discrimination Based on Sexual Orientation, Gender Identity and Expression (SOGIE) and developing research agendas informed by it. By chronicling the politics of Philippine knowledge, this essay, combined with our concluding one by Mira Ofreneo, demonstrates both the use and abuse of the politics of knowledge and how, through democratic action, knowledge can be produced and used for the common good. This "democratic science" (Epstein 1991) of Philippine LGBT psychology is made explicit through these two final essays as psychology in the public interest, aiming to, in their words, "give psychology away" not only through a profit-making enterprise or academic specialization but through public education, community practice, and generally "making psychology useful to people" through social change, recognizing the human rights of and working toward well-being for all LGBT Filipinos.

This work of LGBT theorization and political advocacy both within the discipline and in alliance with community-based organizations and the national and local governments is described by the leaders themselves of this project, a first stage of which culminated in two special issues (2013 and 2016) devoted to "Lesbian, Gay, Bisexual, and Transgender Philippine Psychology" of the profession's flagship journal, the *Philippine Journal of Psychology*.

We write "first stage" because one of the articles in these issues is that of Mira Ofreneo, as mentioned, another leader with Manalastas and Torre in establishing "LGBT Philippine Psychology." While writers on politics often prefer to begin with a "theory" and demonstrate how "political practice" realizes the theory, here we have deliberately begun with how the "politics of the personal" led to broader transformation. Ofreneo's essay is one of the inaugural theoretical studies resulting from this politics of knowledge's first stage, albeit a most comprehensive report on the human condition using the languages of psychology and human rights and the local experience of LGBTIA+ Filipinos. Its inclusion here seems a fitting temporary conclusion to the work-in-progress this book also aspires to be.

WORKS CITED AND RECOMMENDED

Abaya, Eufracio. "Ethic of Care: Growing Older as *Bakla* (Gay) in a Philippine Locale." Abstract. *Culture, Health & Sexuality* 11 (2009): 11–12.

Aishite Imasu 1941: Mahal Kita. Directed by Joel Lamangan. Performances by Judy Ann Santos, Raymart Santiago, Dennis Trillo, and Jay Manalo. Regal Entertainment Inc., 2005.

Arnfred, Signe, ed. *Rethinking Sexualities in Africa.* Uppsala: Nordic Africa Institute, 2004.

Badgett, M. V. Lee and Randall Sell. *A Set of Proposed Indicators for the LGBTI Inclusion Index (English).* Washington, DC: World Bank Group, 2018. Accessed 22 October 2019. http://documents.worldbank.org/curated/en/608921536847788293/A-Set-of-Proposed-Indicators-for-the-LGBTI-Inclusion-Index.

Baka Bukas (Maybe Tomorrow). Directed by Samantha Lee. Performances by Jasmin Curtis Smith, Louise de los Reyes, and Kate Alejandrino. Star Cinema, 2016.

Balangaw. Directed by Jay Altarejos. Performances by Jay Altarejos, Karen Toyoshima, Jal Galang, Tadsky Obach, Rap Robes, CJ Barinaga, Mela Habijan, and Mac Mendoza. Produced by 2076Kolektib, Edith Fider, and Pete Mariano. 2020.

Blasius, Mark. "Theorizing the Politics of (Homo)Sexuality across Cultures." In *Global Homophobia: States, Movements, and the Politics of Oppression,* edited by Meredith L. Weiss and Michael J. Bosia, 218–45. Chicago and Urbana-Champaign: University of Illinois Press, 2013.

Blasius, Mark and Shane Phelan, eds. *We are Everywhere: A Historical Sourcebook of Gay and Lesbian Politics.* New York: Routledge, 1997.

The Blossoming of Maximo Oliveros (Ang Pagdadalaga ni Maximo Oliveros). Directed by Auraeus Solito. Screenplay by Michiko Yamamoto. Performances by Nathan Lopez, Soliman Cruz, and J. R. Valentin. Cinemalaya Foundation, 2005.

Burlesk King. Directed by Mel Chionglo. Performances by Rodel Velayo, Leonardo Litton, and Elizabeth Oropesa. Produced by Robbie Tan. Seiko Films, 1999.

Cannell, Fenella. *Power and Intimacy in the Christian Philippines.* Cambridge: Cambridge University Press, 1999.

Cardozo, Bradley. " A 'Coming Out' Party in Congress? LGBT Advocacy and Party-List Politics in the Philippines." Master's thesis, University of California, Los Angeles, 2014.

Callueng, Eva. *Buhay Bahaghari: The Filipino LGBT Chronicles.* Diliman, Quezon City: University of the Philippines Center for Women's Studies, 2014.

Chu, Richard T. *Chinese and Chinese Mestizos of Manila: Family, Identity, and Culture, 1860s–1930s.* Boston and Leiden: Brill, 2010.

Cohen, Cathy J. "Punks, Bulldaggers, and Welfare Queens: The Radical Potential of Queer Politics?" In *Sexual Identities, Queer Politics,* edited by Mark Blasius, 200–27. Princeton and Oxford: Princeton University Press, 2001.

Coloma, Roland Sintos. "*Ladlad* and Parrhesiastic Pedagogy: Unfurling LGBT Politics and Education in the Global South." *Curriculum Inquiry* 43, no. 4 (2013): 483–511.

Comenge y Dalmau, Rafael. *Cuestiones Filipinas (estudio social y político). 1a. parte. Los chinos.* Manila: Tipolitografía de Chofré y compa., 1894.

Commission on Human Rights of the Philippines. *Inputs on Protection Against Violence and Discrimination Based on Sexual Orientation and Gender Identity with Focus on*

Data Collection. 31 March 2019. Accessed 23 October 2019. https://www.ohchr.
    org/EN/Issues/SexualOrientationGender/Pages/SubmissionsReportOnData.aspx.

Darna, Kuno? (Darna, For Real?). Directed by Luciano B. Carlos. Performance by Dolphy.
    Regal Films, 1979.

Demeterio-Melgar, Junice L. "Raising Sexuality as a Political Issue in the Catholic
    Philippines." In *Sexuality, Gender, and Rights: Exploring Theory and Practice in South
    and Southeast Asia,* edited by Geetanjali Misra and Radhika Chandiramani, 150–68.
    New Delhi: Sage, 2005.

Epstein, Steven G. "Democratic Science? AIDS Activism and the Contested Construction
    of Knowledge." *Socialist Review* 91 (1991): 35–64.

Evasco Eugene, Y., Roselle V. Pineda, and Rommel B. Rodriguez, eds. *Tabi-Tabi sa
    Pagsasantabi: Kritikal na mga Tala ng mga Lesbiana at Bakla sa Sining, Kultura, at
    Wika* [Excuse the Slight: Critical Notes by Lesbians and Gays on Art, Culture, and
    Language]. Quezon City: University of the Philippines Press, 2003.

Eviota, Elizabeth U. *The Political Economy of Gender: Women and the Sexual Division of
    Labour in the Philippines.* London: Zed Books, 1992.

My Father, My Mother (*Ang Tatay Kong Nanay*). Directed by Lino Brocka. Performances
    by Dolphy, Niño Muhlach, Phillip Salvador, and Marissa Delgado. Lotus Films, Inc.,
    1978.

Fefita Fofonggay viuda de Falayfay. Directed by Armando Garces. Performances by Dolphy,
    Rosanna Ortiz, and Rod Navarro. RVQ Productions, 1973.

Fleras, Jomar. "Reclaiming our Historic Rights: Gays and Lesbians in the Philippines
    (1993)." In Blasius and Phelan, *We Are Everywhere,* 823–33.

Foucault, Michel. "The Subject and Power." *Critical Inquiry* 8, no. 4 (1982): 777–95.

Galang, Jely Agamao. "Vagrants and Outcasts: Chinese Labouring Classes, Criminality,
    and the State in the Philippines, 1831–1898." PhD thesis, Murdoch University, 2019.

Gameboys. Directed by Ivan Andrew Payawal. Performances by Kokoy De Santos and
    Elijah Canlas. The IdeaFirst Company, 2020.

Gangcuangco, Louie Mar A. *Orosa-Nakpil, Malate.* Mandaluyong City: Louie Mar's
    Publications, 2006.

Garcia, J. Neil C. *Philippine Gay Culture: Binabae to Bakla, Silahis to MSM.* Diliman,
    Quezon City: University of the Philippines Press, 1996.

Garcia, J. Neil C. and Danton Remoto, eds. *Ladlad: An Anthology of Philippine Gay Writing.*
    3 vols. Manila: Anvil, 1994–2007.

Girl, Boy, Bakla, Tomboy (Female, Male, Gay, Lesbian). Directed by Wenn V. Deramas.
    Performances by Vice Ganda, Maricel Soriano, and Joey Marque. ABS-CBN Film
    Productions and Viva Films, 2013.

Hanckel, Benjamin, Laurindo Garcia, Glenn-Milo Santos, and Eric Julian Manalastas.
    "Assessing Needs and Capabilities: Towards an ICT Resource to Support HIV-Positive
    Gay Men and Other MSM in Southeast Asia." In *Transforming HIV Prevention and
    Care for Marginalized Populations: Using Information and Communication Technologies
    in Community-Based and LED Approaches,* edited by Christopher S. Walsh, 231–
    45. Digital Culture & Education e-book, 2015. Accessed 22 October 2019.
    http://www.digitalcultureandeducation.com.

Hart, Donn V. "Homosexuality and Transvestism in the Philippines: The Cebuan Filipino
    Bayot and Laki-on." *Behavior Science Notes* 3 1968 (4): 211–48.

Hello Stranger. Directed by Petersen Vargas. Performances by Tony Labrusca and JC Alcantara. Black Sheep, 2020.

Hjorth, Larissa, and Michael Arnold. "The Personal and the Political: Social Networking in Manila." *International Journal of Learning and Media* 3, no. 1 (2011): 29–39.

Home for the Golden Gays. Cinematography by Dennis Lehmann. Featuring Frederica Ramasamy, Leony C. Abada, and Semmy Baisa. Produced by Nola Grace Gaardmand and Timothy Ahrensbach. 2010.

Human Rights Watch. "Fueling the Philippines' HIV Epidemic: Government Barriers to Condom Use by Men Who Have Sex with Men." December 2016. Accessed 3 September 2020. ISBN: 978-1-6231-34303.

———. "Just Let Us Be: Discrimination Against LGBT Students in the Philippines." 21 June 2017. Accessed 23 January 2020. https://www.hrw.org/report/2017/06/21/just-let-us-be discrimination-against-lgbt-students-philippines.

ISIS International. http://isiswomen.org.

Johnson, Mark. *Beauty and Power: Transgendering and Cultural Transformation in the Southern Philippines*. Sydney: Bloomsbury Academic, 1997.

Kaggwa, Julius. *From Juliet to Julius: In Search of My True Gender Identity*. Kampala: Fountain Publishers, 1997.

Lim, Anne. *GALANG: A Movement in the Making for the Rights of Poor LBTs in the Philippines*. Toronto: Association for Women's Rights in Development, 2011.

Lizada, M. Antonio. "Liminality—So Happy Together … Too: Contemporary Philippine Gay Comedy and the Queering of Chinese-Filipino Liminality." In *Keywords in Queer Sinophone Studies*, edited by Howard Chiang and Alvin K. Wong, 103–31. London and New York: Routledge, 2020.

Loos, Tamara. "Transnational Histories of Sexualities in Asia." *The American Historical Review* 114, no. 5 (December 2009): 1309–24.

Macho Dancer. Directed by Lino Brocka. Screenplay by Amado Lacuesta and Ricardo Lee. Performances by Daniel Fernando, Jaclyn Jose, and Allan Paule. Produced by Boy C. De Guia. Viva Films, 1988.

Manalansan, Martin F. "Queering the Chain of Care Paradigm." *Scholar & Feminist Online* 6, no. 3 (2008): 10.

———. "Servicing the World: Flexible Filipinos and the Unsecured Life." In *Political Emotions*, edited by Janet Staiger, Anne Cvetkovich, and Ann Reynolds, 215–28. New York: Routledge, 2010.

Manalastas, Eric, ed. "LGBT Psychology." Special issue, *Philippine Journal of Psychology* 46, no. 1 (2013).

Manalastas, Eric, Mira Alexis P. Ofreneo, and Beatriz Torre, eds. "LGBT Psychology." Special issue, *Philippine Journal of Psychology* 49, no. 2 (2016).

Manalastas, Eric, T. T. Ojanen, B. A. Torre, R. Ratanashevorn, B. C. C. Hong, V. Kumaresan, and V. Veeramuthu. "Homonegativity in Southeast Asia: Attitudes Toward Lesbians and Gay Men in Indonesia, Malaysia, the Philippines, Singapore, Thailand, and Vietnam." *Asia-Pacific Social Science Review* 17, no. 1 (2017): 25–33.

"Manga Cababayan," *Suplemento al Heraldo Filipino*, 7 February 1899.

Markova: Comfort Gay. Directed by Gil Portes. Performances by Dolphy, Eric Quizon, and Jeffrey Quizon. RVQ Productions, 2000.

McSherry, Alice, Eric Julian Manalastas, J. C. Gaillard, and Soledad Natalia M. Dalisay. "From Deviant to *Bakla*, Strong to Stronger: Mainstreaming Sexual and Gender Minorities into Disaster Risk Reduction in the Philippines." *Forum for Development Studies* 42, no. 1 (2015): 27–40.

My Husband's Lover. Directed by Dominic Zapata, Gil Tejada Jr. Performances by Dennis Trillo, Tom Rodriguez, and Carla Abellana. GMA Entertainment TV, 2013.

Meyrowitz, Joanne. *How Sex Changed: A History of Transsexuality in the United States*. Cambridge, MA: Harvard University Press, 2002.

Mosbergen, Dominique. "Being LGBT in Southeast Asia: Stories of Abuse, Survival, and Tremendous Courage." *Huffington Post*, 11 October 2015, updated 20 October 2015. Accessed 22 October 2020. http://huffpost.com/entry/lgbt-in-southeast-asia_n_55e406e1e4b0c818f6185151.

Office of the United Nations High Commissioner for Human Rights (OHCHR). "Born Free and Equal: Sexual Orientation, Gender Identity, and Sex Characteristics in International Human Rights Law." 2nd ed. New York and Geneva: United Nations, 2019. HR/PUB/12/06/Rev.1.

———. "Living Free and Equal: What States are Doing to Tackle Violence and Discrimination Against Lesbian, Gay, Bisexual, Transgender, and Intersex People." New York and Geneva: United Nations, 2016. HR/PUB/16/3.

Outrage Magazine. http://www.outragemag.com.

Padios, Jan. *A Nation on the Line: Call Centers as Postcolonial Predicaments in the Philippines*. Durham, North Carolina: Duke University Press, 2018.

Peletz, Michael. *Gender Pluralism: Southeast Asia since Early Modern Times*. New York: Routledge, 2009.

Perez, Tony. *Cubao Midnight Express: Mga Pusong Nadiskaril sa Mahabang Riles ng Pag-ibig* (Cubao Midnight Express: Hearts Derailed along the Long Rails of Love). Mandaluyong City, Philippines: Cacho Publishing House, 1994.

Petrang Kabayo (Petra the Horse). Directed by Wenn V. Deramas. Performances by Vice Ganda, Luis Manzano, and Gloria Romero. Viva Films, 2010.

Plummer, Ken. *Intimate Citizenship: Private Decisions and Public Dialogues*. Seattle and London: University of Washington Press, 2003.

Psychological Association of the Philippines Scientific and Professional Ethics Committee. "*Code of Ethics for Philippine Psychologists*." 2010.

Rafael, Vicente. *Contracting Colonialism: Translation and Christian Conversion in Tagalog Society Under Early Spanish Rule*. Durham, North Carolina: Duke University Press, 1993.

Rainbow's Sunset. Directed by Joel Lamangan. Performances by Eddie Garcia, Tony Mabasa, and Gloria Romero. Solar Pictures, 2018.

The Rich Man's Daughter. Directed by Dominic Zapata. Performances by Jade Tanchingco and Althea Guevarra. GMA Entertainment TV, 2015.

Seckinelgin, Hakan. *The Politics of Global AIDS: Institutionalization of Solidarity, Exclusion of Context*. Cham, Switzerland: Springer International, 2017.

Sibak: Midnight Dancers. Directed by Mel Chionglo. Screenplay by Ricky Lee. Performances by Noni Buencamino, Lawrence David, and Gandong Cervantes. Tangent Films International, 1994.

Soriano, Cheryll Ruth Reyes. "Constructing Collectivity in Diversity: Online Political Mobilization of a National LGBT Political Party." *Media, Culture & Society* 36, no. 1 (2014): 20–36.

Sumayao, Ryen Paul and Jaya Jacobo, eds. *BKL/Bikol Bakla: Anthology of Bikolnon Gay Trans Queer Writing*. Naga City, Philippines: Naga Goldprint Inc., 2019.

Tan, Michael L. *Sex and Sexuality*. Policy Research Briefs Series 2. Quezon City: University Center for Women's Studies, 1998.

T-Bird at Ako (T-Bird and I). Directed by Danny Zialcita. Performances by Nora Aunor and Vilma Santos. Film Ventures, Inc., 1982.

Thoreson, Ryan. "Capably Queer: Exploring the Intersections of Queerness and Poverty in the Urban Philippines." *Journal of Human Development and Capabilities* 12, no. 11 (2011): 493–510.

Twilight Dancers. Directed by Mel Chionglo. Screenplay by Ricardo Lee. Performances by Tyron Perez, Cherry Pie Picache, and Allen Dizon. Produced by Ferdinand Lapuz. Centerstage Productions, 2006.

United Nations Development Programme (UNDP). "Leave No One Behind: Advancing Social, Economic, Cultural and Political Inclusion of LGBTI People in Asia and the Pacific—Summary." 13 October 2015. Accessed 15 October 2020. https://www.asia-pacific.undp.org/content/rbap/en/home/library/democratic_governance/hiv_aids/leave-no-one-behind--advancing-social--economic--cultural-and-po.html.

United Nations Development Programme (UNDP) and United States Agency for International Development (USAID). "Being LGBT in Asia: the Philippines Country Report." 4 December 2015. Accessed 23 January 2020. https://www.undp.org/content/undp/en/home/librarypage/hiv-aids/being-lgbt-in-asia--the-philippine-country-report.html.

United Nations Development Programme (UNDP), Overseas Development Institute (ODI), and GALANG. "Making it Work: Lesbian, Bisexual and Transgender Women's Economic Empowerment in the Philippines." Accessed 17 October 2020. https://philippines.un.org/en/42377-making-it-work-lesbian-bisexual-and-transgender-womens-economic-empowerment-philippines.

Wieringa, Saskia, and Horacio Sivori, eds. *The Sexual History of the Global South: Sexual Politics in Africa, Asia, and Latin America*. London: Zed Books, 2013.

Winter, Sam, Sass Rogando-Sasot, and Mark King. "Transgender Women of the Philippines." *International Journal of Transgenderism* 10, no. 2 (2007): 79–90.

World Economic Forum. "The Global Gender Gap Report 2018." Accessed 21 June 2019. http://www3.weforum.org/docs/WEF_GGGR_2018.pdf.

"Yogyakarta Principles on the Application of International Human Rights Law in Relation to Sexual Orientation and Gender Identity." Yogyakarta, Indonesia, November 2006. Accessed 15 September 2020. http://yogyakartaprinciples.org/principles-en/.

"Yogyakarta Principles Plus 10: Additional and State Obligations on the Application of International Human Rights Law in Relation to Sexual Orientaion, Gender Identity, Gender Expression and Sex Characteristics to Complement the Yogyakarta Principles." Geneva, November 2017. Accessed 15 September 2020. http://yogyakartaprinciples.org/principles-en/yp10/.

Zsa Zsa Zaturnnah, ze Moveeh. Directed by Joel C. Lamangan. Performances by Rustom Padilla and Zsa Zsa Padilla. Regal Enterntainment, 2006.

UNIT I

THEORETICAL
AND HISTORICAL FRAMINGS

LGBTindig

LGBT rights advocacy groups hold placards under a rainbow flag to fight for equal rights during a "Pride Parade" in June 2016. Photo courtesy of Reuters News Agency.

The first Pride March in the Philippines was held on 26 June 1994 at the Quezon City Memorial Circle through the efforts of ProGay Philippines (est. 1993) and the Metropolitan Community Church (est. 1992). More than a Stonewall remembrance, the march was a protest against the imposition of the value added tax (VAT). Thus, the Philippines was recognized as the first country in Asia and the Pacific to host a Pride-related parade. In 1999, Task Force Pride (TFP) was established as the official convenor of the annual community-driven Metro Manila Pride March.

This essay was previously published in *Philippine Gay Culture* (Hong Kong: Hong Kong University Press, 2009), 420–56.

J. NEIL C. GARCIA

Philippine Gay Culture:
An Update and a Postcolonial Autocritique[1]

A DECADE HAS PASSED since the publication of my historical and analytic survey of the discursive self-expressions and social ascriptions that constituted, from the 1960s to the 1990s, significant aspects of urban gay (*bakla* and "male homosexual") culture in Metropolitan Manila.[2] In the meantime, exigencies have forced me to revisit and reconsider some of the basic assumptions, concepts, and allegiances of this work, even as they have also affirmed and validated my faith in others (in particular, the chiefly deconstructionist procedure of its decidedly oppositional thrust).

In this paper, I wish to bring the concerns of this project to the immediate present, primarily by providing an updated empirical survey of events that have since then continued to animate and impinge on the lived dailiness of Filipino gays. Perhaps, it is inevitable that with the heightened sexualization of urban consciousness in the Philippines—courtesy of, among other things, the unstoppable march of cultural and economic globalization, the massive revolutions in information technology, and the local resistance to these various and related processes—such events would need to take on an increasingly political and indeed "national" character (and as the following update will demonstrate, indeed these events have).

The task of characterizing the "national moment" in Philippine gay culture over the last decade also presents me with an opportunity to argue for the importance of the postcolonial perspective on the issue of sexual politics in this corner of the Third World. Nonetheless, it is a postcolonial perspective that, first of all, does not neglect to acknowledge the material

---

1   This chapter was read by the author at the "Queer Asian Sites: An International Conference of Asian Queer Studies," convened by the AsiaPacifiQueer Network at University of Technology, Sydney City Campus, Sydney, Australia, 23 February 2007.

2   See my *Philippine Gay Culture: The Last Thirty Years* (Quezon City: University of the Philippines Press, 1996).

raison d'etre of colonialism: capitalist expansionism.[3] Moreover, it is a perspective that does not perfunctorily jettison the national question in favor of the typically class-bereft and migratory criticism to be evidenced in many examples of diasporic and poststructuralist-inflected "postcolonial" deployments of American antihomophobic and/or queer theory. On the contrary, the kind of postcolonialism that will be advanced here is one that seeks a renewed and critical remaking of the concept of the nation—a remaking that distinguishes oppositional nationalisms from mainstream ones, and that returns to, examines, and mines the great diversity and wisdom of anticolonial and national liberation theories and practices. Finally, the anti-heteronormative appropriation of postcolonial critique that I shall be proposing here is one that situates discursive and cultural struggles involving sexual and gender dissidence alongside and within the complex and neocolonially imbricated political economies of the many nation-states comprising the increasingly immiserated regions of the global South.

Just to be reflexive about things, let me begin with the writings. The past decade saw the appearance of not only limited-circulation newsletters and "zines" but also a string of nationally circulated publications: a regular gay and lesbian section in a nationally circulated broadsheet, a slew of "soft porny" gay magazines, a full-fledged gay newspaper, and more recently, lesbian and gay lifestyle glossies.[4] Moreover, openly gay newspaper columnists started making their opinions known in nationally distributed publications.[5] A case in point would be Manuel L. Quezon III, a strapping young writer who comes from one of the Philippines' oldest and most

---

3   Benita Parry, "The Institutionalization of Postcolonial Studies," in *The Cambridge Companion to Postcolonial Literary Studies*, ed. Neil Lazarus (New York: Cambridge University Press, 2004), 70.

4   From 1996 to 1997, *The Evening Paper* carried the weekly gay and lesbian section "Gayzette," which I edited. The same paper carried a weekly feminist (sometimes lesbian) section, "Kawomenan." The most popular soft-porn magazine of the period was undoubtedly *Valentino*. The first commercially available gay newspaper, *ManilaOut*, also came out in the late 1990s. The past five years saw the appearance of gay lifestyle glossies, foremost of which are *GPQ, Icon,* and *L Magazine*. For a short survey of the "Filipino gay magazine phenomenon" and a history of *Valentino* in particular, see Michael Kho Lim, "When the Politics of Desire Meets the Economics of Skin: The History and Phenomenon of a Filipino Gay Magazine," accessed 14 September 2007, http://bangkok2005.anu.edu.au/papers/Lim.pdf.

5   These publications included *Mr. and Ms. Magazine, Philippines Free Press, Evening Paper, Manila Standard, Philippine Daily Inquirer,* and *Philippine Star*—all of them nationally distributed. Some of these avowedly gay and lesbian opinion-writers are Oscar Atadero, Malu Marin, Ana Leah Sarabia, Danton Remoto, Michael Tan, John Silva, Jose Javier Reyes, and most recently Manuel Quezon III.

respected political clans (his late grandfather, Manuel Sr., was the president of the Philippine Commonwealth during the final years of the American occupation).

In the middle of 2006, Quezon engaged in an acrimonious debate with Isagani Cruz, a former chief justice of the Supreme Court and Quezon's fellow columnist in the *Philippine Daily Inquirer*, the Philippines' leading broadsheet.[6] As is typical of Cruz's weekly rants, the particular column that started it all expressed the venerable writer's irritation at the way local gay men have seemingly taken over his once-polite, genteel, and respectable city. In particular, Cruz waxes poetic about the bygone years in his old high school, in which the one or two gay students obviously knew their place, and conducted themselves accordingly. It is with a note of unfathomable sadness that Cruz remarks how this is no longer the case in a garish and "faggotified" Manila.

Quezon dared to challenge the septuagenarian Cruz, by taking exception to the latter's damning stereotype of the gay community, his elitist machismo, and shameless homophobia. It's important to note that by the same eloquent and passionate gesture, Quezon finally and definitively "outed" himself as a gay man—to the surprise of many of his devoted readers. This published debate dragged on for almost two months, with four or more vitriolic columns seemingly being hurled contrapuntally from both sides of the newspaper's "Op-Ed page." According to the readers' advocate, this debate generated the most number of letters ever received by the newspaper at any one time, and nearly all of them expressed support for the courageous Quezon, and anger at the former chief justice's blatant display of bigotry and injustice.

On the the other hand, it's interesting to note that the second most number of "letters to the editor" the *PDI* has thus far received were probably letters of protest against the series of commercial television advertisements sponsored by the Philippines' biggest telephone company.[7] These ads had aired around 2001, and what many individuals found objectionable about them then was that they depicted the best friend of the series' central male character as an embittered, jealous, and misogynistic sissy gay man who's out to ruin the romance between his friend and this friend's pretty bride-to-be.

---

6   The particular column by Isagani Cruz that started it all was titled "Don We Now Our Gay Apparel," and it came out in the 12 August 2006 issue of the *Philippine Daily Inquirer*. Quezon's subsequent responses took such bitchy and sarcastic titles as "Oblivious in Cloud-Cuckoo Land" and "The Grand Inquisitor."

7   Michael Tan, an outspoken gay columnist in the *Philippine Daily Inquirer*, devoted a column critiquing these homophobic ads. See Michael Tan, "Goodbye Billy," *Philippine Daily Inquirer*, 23 October 2001.

In the last decade, more and more gay- and lesbian-themed feature articles, interviews, reviews, columns, and news stories came out with increasing regularity in the Philippines' most popular broadsheets and magazines. As in the previous decades, their topic included such "lifestyle" concerns as romance, fashion, parenting, childhood, and that ever-present staple, the curious and altogether fascinating "subcultural lingo" of urban gay men (variably called *swardspeak, gayspeak,* and now *baklese*).[8] The difference here is the commentators' greater and more "colorful" degree of candor, especially as far as "sensitive" issue like safe sex, prostitution, alternative family arrangements, and promiscuity are concerned.[9] Interviews with well-known lesbian and gay artists—as well as memoirs and autobiographical

8   Some of the more memorable lesbian and gay celebrities interviewed during this period were Repertory Philippines' Zenaida "Bibot" Amador, cultural scholar and academic Nicanor "Nick" Tiongson, AM radio commentator Tita Swarding, hairstylist and makeup artist James Cooper, socialite and newspaper columnist Louie Cruz, television and film director Jose Javier "Joey" Reyes, transsexual beautician-turned-millionaire Ian Valdez, lesbian musician DJ Alvaro, and former matinee idol Rustom Padilla, who dramatically outed himself on a reality TV show that aired on Channel 2. See, respectively, the following: Ara Abad Santos-Bitong, "Bibot Diaries," *Philippine Daily Inquirer,* 11 December 2004, C4; "St. Nick Against the Moral Terrorist," Interview with Nicanor Tiongson, *Philippine Daily Inquirer,* 1 April 2001, D1; Pennie Azarcon de la Cruz, "When Machismo Gets Machismis," *Sunday Inquirer Magazine,* 11 February 2001, 6; Joy Rojas, "Taking it Like a Man," *Sunday Inquirer Magazine,* 24 February 2002, Q2; Wilhelmina Paras, "Dancing Out of the Closet," *Asiaweek,* 7 August 1998, 36; Oliver M. Pulumbarit "How Joey Reyes Stays Forever Young as He Turns 50," *Philippine Daily Inquirer,* 22 August 2004, A34; Patrick Magalona, "Ian Valdez: Baklang Palaboy na Milyonarya na Ngayon," *ManilaOut,* issue no. 2, 2000, 20; Eric S. Caruncho, "Music Makers: Life is Queer," *Sunday Inquirer Magazine,* 27 June 2006, Q8; and Alwin M. Ignacio, "This Beautiful Man," *L Magazine,* vol. 2, no. 1 2006, 68–69.

9   Examples of such frank discussions of the gay sexual subculture, promiscuity, prostitution, gayspeak, "rave parties," sexually transmitted diseases, and family-related issues are the following: Blue Arden, "How Fathers Cope with Gay Sons," *Philippine Daily Inquirer,* 13 June 2001, F1; Jose Javier Reyes, "In the Company of Fairies," *Philippine Daily Inquirer,* 15 June 2001, G1; Edwin Valdez Vinarao and Michael Remir H. Macatangay, "The Other Goods in the Mall," *Philippine Daily Inquirer,* 15 August 2001, C2; Ramon Tulfo, "On Target: Beaten Up by a Faggot," *Philippine Daily Inquirer,* 28 September 2002, A36; Miguel Garcia, "Learning a Lesson the Hard Way," *Philippine Daily Inquirer,* 6 November 2002, F3; Rina Jimenez David, "At Large: Can You Tell Who's Gay?" *Philippine Daily Inquirer,* 22 August 2004, A16; 2BU! Correspondents, "Chuva Chuk Chak Chenelyn Chenelyn Chika," *Philippine Daily Inquirer,* 6 November 2002, D3; Desiree Caluza, "It's the First Gay Outing Saturday in Chilly Baguio," *Philippine Daily Inquirer,* 10 November 2004, A1; and Michael L. Tan, "Pinoy Kasi: Save the Filipino Family," *Philippine Daily Inquirer,* 15 June 2000, A16.

pieces by lesser known contributors[10]—continued to grace the pages of national periodicals in the late 1990s and early 2000s. So did a number of mostly appreciative movie, book, theater, and music reviews of gay- and lesbian-identified works.

Gay and lesbian anthologies came out relatively frequently. The *Ladlad* series, of which the recently released *Ladlad 3* is the latest, gather together gay-themed works in fiction, poetry, and creative nonfiction from openly gay writers. *Rice!*, a gay-themed illustrated series, was launched in the late 1990s, but after just two installments its editors weren't able to sustain the publication. Sadly, *Tibok,* a lesbian collection from 1998, has not been followed up, as well. On the other hand, a number of books by openly lesbian and gay authors also saw print in the last decade.[11] These books range across the genres, and their authors include a number of "diasporic" artists—for example the novelist Bino Realuyo and R. Zamora Linmark. Like other Filipino American writers, Realuyo and Linmark continue to maintain ties with the country of their affection, chiefly through the themes and subjects of their works. Moreover, these writers keep the Philippines close by occasionally visiting, doing research, and giving readings with their appreciative readers, in Manila.

In the theater scene, a number of important gay plays were staged by theater groups based in various schools and institutions across Metro Manila. The most important of these were the following: *A Portrait of the Artist as Filipino,* a new and "deconstructionist" stage version of a well-known and critically acclaimed masterpiece; *Temptation Island... Live!,* a "camped up" theatrical adaption of an uproariously funny "heterosexual"

---

10   Examples of "confessional" articles that treat the question of gay and lesbian outing during the period are the following: "Lea and Amy: Love Conquers Homophobia," *ManilaOut,* issue no. 1, 2000, 28; Mark Peter Zamora, "Anticipating Gay Fatherhood," *Philippine Daily Inquirer,* 13 June 2001, F2; Bino A. Realuyo, "Dear Country," *Sunday Inquirer Magazine,* 11 June 2000, E1; Mozart A. T. Pastrano, "The Rite of Manhood Called Boy Bayot," *Philippine Daily Inquirer,* 28 February 2001, E4; John L. Silva, "End Page: The Origins of my Dress Code," *Sunday Inquirer Magazine,* 24 February 2002, 7; and Jade Lopez, L. J. Palma, Sam Tongson, and Gina Ramos, "Homo... What?" *Philippine Free Press,* 13 July 1996, 18.

11   Among the many gay authors whose books appeared in this decade we can include: essayists Louie Cano, Danton Remoto, and Jose Javier Reyes; fictionists Ernesto Carandang II, Ian Casocot, Vicente Groyon III and Gerardo Torres; poets Romulo Baquiran Jr., Ronald Baytan, Carlomar Daoana, Jaime Doble, Eugene Evasco, Alex Gregorio, Nestor De Guzman, Ralph Semino Galan, and Lawrence Ypil; and playwrights Ed Cabagnot, Nicolas Pichay, Rody Vera, and Rene Villanueva.

skin flick from the 1970s;[12] and *Zsazsa Zaturnnah: Ze Muzikal*, a musical based on a recent best-selling comic book about a gay-beautician-turned-Wonder-Woman. All these productions played to full houses, and enjoyed immense critical acclaim. In the restaging of National Artist Nick Joaquin's famous full-length drama, *A Portrait of the Artist as a Filipino*, Behn Cervanes and Anton Juan, two of the Philippines' best theater artists, essayed the roles of shrewish and pitiable aging gay brothers—a blatantly "queer" recasting of the original play's allegorical story of Old Manila's legendary spinster sisters (and their obsolescent father), helplessly caught in the cusp of violent vicissitudes during the American and Japanese occupations.[13] On the other hand, following the enormous success of the graphic novel that occasioned it, *Zsazsa Zaturnnah: Ze Muzikal* proved to be such a hit when it ran for a couple of months in 2006[14] that it was later turned into feature film produced by Regal Films and megged by gay director Joel Lamangan, which unfortunately showed to less enthusiastic audiences during that year's Christmas time citywide film festival.

Turning then to cinema, the first of several "Pink Film Festivals" of local and international gay and lesbian films was held in several big malls in Metro Manila in the middle of 1999.[15] Over the last decade, at least a dozen Filipino gay and lesbian films of varying genres have been produced and screened, to varying critical and commercial successes. The more remarkable of these films are those that locate themselves firmly in the national social context, and force a rethinking of so-called traditional Filipino values, gender and

12   *Temptation Island ... Live* was put up by Madiraka Events and Services and ran for the whole month of May in 2004 at the Republic of Malate. It was adapted by Chris Martinez from the original screenplay by Joey Gosiengfiao, and its cast included the following: Tuxqs Rutaquio, John Lapus, Peter Serrano, Raymond Sydney, Face Sales, Romnick Sarmenta, Floy Quintos, Johnny Ramos, and Christian Vasquez.

13   See the related articles on this queer restaging of Nick Joaquin's famous play: Cora Llamas, "New Musical Blurs Gender Lines," *Philippine Daily Inquirer*, 6 August 2001, E3; and Alex Vergara, "Portrait as Sisters' Act," *Philippine Daily Inquirer*, 25 February 2002, E1.

14   For some of the better-written reviews of *Zsazsa Zaturnnah Ze Muzikal*, see Roel Hoang Manipon, "Zsazsa Zaturnnah Zings," *L Magazine*, vol. 2, no. 1, 2006, 49; Francis Martinez, "Zsazsa Zaturnnah Inside Out," *L Magazine*, vol. 2, no. 1, 2006, 50–51; and Francezca C. Kwe, "Zsazsa Zaturnnah Off the Page," *L Magazine*, vol. 2, no . 1, 2006, 52–53.

15   For news coverage on this pioneering film festival, see the following related articles: "Pink Festival Celebrates Gay Pride," *Inquirer Libre*, 28 May 2004, 8; Vives Anunciacion, "Festival Queens: Second International Gay and Lesbian Film and Video Festival," *Inquirer Libre*, 5 July 2004, 8; and "Gay Films: UP Seeing Pink," *Inquirer Libre*, 5 July 2004, 13.

sexual identities, heroism, and the political and imaginative act of "telling history" itself. These outstanding films, which were invariably written and/or directed by openly gay individuals, include a couple of interesting war films, a few melodramas, some romantic comedies, and of course, a handful of skin flicks.[16]

Perhaps the most exciting development in local Filipino filmmaking is the increasing popularity and availability of the digital format, and gay and lesbian films have certainly explored this new technology's liberating possibilities. Spurred by the moribundity of commercial Philippine cinema, these gay and lesbian digital films have dared to engage with the controversial issues of gay and lesbian promiscuity, alternative domestic partnerships, and prepubescent desire, all within the purview of the extended Filipino family and the depressed national situation.[17]

Turning to television, the loud and shrieking faggot is not the only identifiably gay image to grace the small screen in the last ten years, although as with previous decades, this stereotype has certainly endured and proven indispensable to the concept of what is funny in Filipino entertainment. By contrast, a number of serious and even "sentimental" portrayals of Filipino gays and lesbians showed on Philippine television,[18] usually in documentary or "TV magazine" programs, and in any of the numerous "telenovelas" and melodramas that air during primetime on the country's two biggest TV networks, GMA and ABS-CBN. In both cases, these portrayals typically flesh out the narrative of a supposedly "true-to-life confession" from a letter-sender. In the end, the show's wise-woman narrator and host gets to extract nuggets of didactic wisdom from the exemplar-setting and tearfully reenacted tale.

Admittedly, however, the most groundbreaking television event of the last decade took place in the last quarter of 2004. Beginning in the middle

16   Some of these outstanding films were the following: *Markova: Comfort Gay, Aishite Imasu, Ang Lalaki sa Buhay ni Selya, Miguel/Michelle, Paraiso ni Efren, Pusong Mamon, Happy Together Forever, Sibak, Burlesk King,* and *Twilight Dancers.*

17   These digital-format indie films include the stylistically erotic *Duda, Bathhouse, Masahista,* and *Ang Lalake sa Parola;* the lesbian family drama *Kaleldo;* and the wonderful and internationally acclaimed *Ang Pagdadalaga ni Maximo Oliveros,* which, among other things, tackles the controversial issue of pubescent gay sexuality. For reviews of *Ang Pagdadalaga…,* see: Marcus Iñigo Laurel, " Budding But Not Yet Blooming," *L Magazine,* vol. 2, no.1 2006, 8–10; and J. Neil C. Garcia, "Paradoxical Philippines: On *Ang Pagdadalaga ni Maximo Oliveros,*" *L Magazine,* vol. 2, no. 1 2006, 13–14.

18   For commentaries on the changing attitudes toward gay and lesbian representations on Philippine television, see Nestor U. Torre, "Gays on TV," *Philippine Daily Inquirer,* 25 June 2005, A31; and Arvin Adina, "Boob Tube Reflects Changing Gay Image," *Philippine Daily Inquirer,* 6 November 2002, D2.

of September, *Out!*, the first lesbian and gay lifestyle TV show, ran for two months on GMA Channel 7, a national network owned and managed, in large part, by a famously evangelical family of telecommunications tycoons. This show's hosts were a young lesbian and two rather charming and twinky-looking gay men, and even though it did well in the ratings, it was cancelled after around a dozen episodes.[19] Apparently, the advertisers, probably heeding the moral call of the Manila Archbishop, pulled out their product placements for the show's post-primetime slot.[20]

On the academic front, the main campus of the University of the Philippines in Diliman, Quezon City, offered in 1994 the first "gay literature" elective in the country.[21] Initially a "directed readings" or "special topics" class, in 1996 the subject became a regular offering both on the graduate and undergraduate levels of the Comparative Literature program of the UP's College of Arts and Letters. UP Diliman would continue to lead the way in lending academic legitimacy to gender and sexuality concerns, housing and funding a research-oriented Center for Women's Studies, and a more student-friendly and service-oriented Gender Office, which its administrators inaugurated sometime in 2004.

Suffice it to say that the academic freedom and secularism of UP have proven germane to feminist as well as LGBT advocacy. In 1997, UP became the venue of the first National LGBT Youth Congress. This activity was organized and sponsored by the UP Babaylan, the university's first and most active LGBT organization. Later that year, a convention of gay and lesbian leaders was held as a follow-up to this students' congress. Percival Cendaña, the outgoing president of UP Babaylan at that time, ran for the presidency of the UP Diliman Student Council, and won. He was the first openly gay leader of the most important student organization of the Philippines' premiere state university. In the early part of 1998, UP also served as the venue for the first Asian Lesbian Network Conference. Organized by the country's

---

19   For GMA 7's press release on this show, see: "Out," *iGMA.tv* (*News and Public Affairs*), accessed 15 September 2007, http://64.41.100.97/npa.html.

20   That the reason for the show's cancellation was not that it was rating poorly (it was the best performing program in its time slot) but that the advertisers all decided to mysteriously pull out was among the insights shared in a candid interview with Jigz Mayuga, who hosted *Out!* together with JM Cobarrubias and Awi Siwa. For a text of the interview, see: Diana A. Uy, "The Colorful Life of an Ex-TV Host," *Manila Bulletin Online,* 18 April 2005, accessed 14 September 2007, http://www.mb.com.ph/issues/2005/04/18/SCTY2005041832950.html.

21   "Controversies: Out of the Closet," *Asiaweek,* 5 October 1994, 33.

leading lesbian advocacy organizations, the conference brought together participants from nine Asian countries. Two years previously, the first national Lesbian Rights Conference had successfully taken place in Silang, Cavite.[22]

On the other hand, toward the middle of 1995, a religious and elite school in downtown Manila, the De La Salle University, opened its own gay literature course. As with UP, this prestigious Catholic university continues to offer this undergraduate subject in the present time, which students may take as an elective under the gender and sexuality "area" of the undergraduate literature curriculum.

We can add to this little survey of academic developments the fact that the 1990s also bore witness to the birth and emergence of a Philippine-specific "LGBT studies." We may provisionally define Filipino LGBT studies as a method, field, and perspective of academic inquiry into gender and sexuality, as these relate to, inform and challenge the question of lesbian, gay, bisexual, and transgender politics and identities among Filipinos in the Philippines.

While not quite institutionally organized in any one discipline or site, LGBT studies is intermittently being carried out by Filipino scholars, not just in UP and DLSU, but also in other major universities of the country. Such studies may be said to be distinguished by their critical perspective, which evinces an avowedly political and politicized interest in the question of non-heteronormative identities and desires. Central to its project is a theoretical inquiry into epistemology: Just how exactly does one determine who gays, lesbians, transgenders, and bisexuals are?

We might say that it is the recognition of this "definitional crisis" that qualifies a work as a valid example of "LGBT studies," and distinguishes it from the naively positivist and often patently homophobic and/or effeminophobic researches that were carried out by students in psychology, guidance and counseling, sociology, anthropology, and the humanities in the bigger Philippine colleges and universities for at least three decades after the Second World War. Because they did not critically examine the concepts they employed, and because they failed to inquire into the colonial history of the Philippines, these early studies merely reproduced versions of the same hegemonic, Western knowledge.

22   See "Statement of the First National Lesbian Rights Conference, 7–9 December 1996," accessed 3 February 1998, http://hain.org/badaf6/lesbian-rights.html.

By contrast, in the 1990s, the inquiry LGBT studies has come to require is one which seeks to *problematize* the issues of gender and sexuality, first and foremost; and second, given the postcolonial context of the Philippines, this same inquiry into sexual and gender definitions is necessarily reflexively located in the particular "historical" moment at which it is initiated. Even as most of the scholars doing LGBT work write bilingually, their studies tend to be written in English, although as a recently published anthology of critical LGBT essays exemplifies, more and more researches are indeed being written in Filipino.[23]

In the meantime, in many schools in Metro Manila, increasingly "enlightened" though less conceptually sophisticated undergraduate theses are also being regularly carried out. The good thing is, these admittedly amateurish studies on literary and cultural production and reception, the media, theater, and linguistics, are now beginning to refer to the works of Filipino LGBT scholars. All together, these studies do paint a possibly brightening picture for Filipino LGBT scholarship in the future.

Perhaps the most significant development in the last decade is the emergence of the LGBT issue and of LGBT activism in the national political scene. From the available accounts, lesbian activism in the 1990s antedates the gay. In 1992, during the celebration of International Women's Day, a group calling itself The Lesbian Collective unobtrusively participated in the women's march. Two years later, in time with the anniversary of the Stonewall riots, a small but spirited contingent, composed primarily of members of the newly formed Manila chapter of the Metropolitan Community Church and the leftist collective, PRO-Gay Philippines, held a march around the Quezon Memorial Circle in Quezon City.[24] This march has been held yearly since then, although its participants have come to include not just gays but more and more varied representatives from the LGBT spectrum itself, and its venue has been transferred from Quezon City to Manila to Quezon City, and in the last two years, back to Manila.

In 1996, spearheaded by the AIDS-education NGO ReachOut Foundation, the "Solidarity" Pride March enjoyed the support of even more LGBT individuals and collectives.[25] ReachOut would continue to

23   See *Tabi-tabi sa Pagsasantabi: Kritikal na mga Tala ng mga Lesbiana at Bakla sa Sining, Kultura, at Wika*, eds. Eugene Y. Evasco, Roselle V. Pineda, and Rommel B. Rodriguez (Quezon City: University of the Philippines Press, 2003).

24   For an analysis of this march's significance, especially in relation to the framework of "gay rights," see my "Philippine Gay Rights," in *Slip/pages: Essays in Philippine Gay Criticism* (Manila: De La Salle University of the Philippines Press, 1998), 60–64.

25   This march received much media attention. The newspaper and magazine articles that covered it include the following: Nati Naguid, "All About Rights," *Philippine*

organize the pride march until 1998, the year when the march took part in the "grand procession" commemorating the Centennial of the Philippine Revolution against Spain, in the historic Rizal Park, only to break off into its own separate march towards the traditionally gay-identified district of Malate. A year later, the newly declared president—the former actor and mayor Joseph Estrada—became the target of mass protests, and various LGBT groups joined the noisy street rallies during his State of the Nation Address. Come 1999, with ReachOut backing out of its customary role, the pride march was organized by several LGBT organizations, and it served as the culmination of a month-long series of pride activities that revolved around the theme "LGBT Human Rights in the New Millennium."

Since 2003, in an effort to avoid the likelihood of inclement weather, the LGBT pride march has not been held in June but in December. Its participants have included an ever-growing number of LGBT organizations, representing interests as diverse as spirituality and sexual health, as well as specific regions, provinces, and cities outside the national capital.

Turning now to institutional politics, the LGBT legislative agenda was initiated in 1995 in the House of Representatives by Renaldo Calalay, a congressman from Quezon City, who filed a bill that sought to include the LGBT sector in the party-list elections.[26] A "citizens' alliance" of various LGBT organizations was mulled for this purpose, but like this initiative, it never prospered. Three years later, however, the Akbayan Citizens Action Party, a party-list organization that ran for (and won in) the 1998 national elections, sought the help of the several LGBT organizations in developing its agenda for the community, which it decided to include in its platform for governance. Obviously, this was a milestone. The groups that were consulted later constituted the "lobby" that would push for the passage of the antidiscrimination bill. A year later, after extensive discussion and planning among around a dozen LGBT organizations from some of the major cities and provinces in the country, the Lesbian and Gay Legislative Advocacy Network (or LAGABLAB) was formed.

In the lower house of Congress, Atty. Bellaflor Angara-Castillo, the lone representative from Aurora [Isabela in original—Ed.], a poor province northeast of Manila, filed the Lesbian and Gay Rights Act of 1999. This was a rather comprehensive proposal that included provisions for gay and lesbian

Free Press, 13 July 1996, 16; Choong Tin Sieu, "Revolution by Stages," *Asiaweek*, 7 August 1998, 38; Nati Nuguid, "Acceptance, Not Just Tolerance," *Philippines Free Press*, 13 July 1996, 14; and Anna Leah Sarabia, "Filipino Lesbians and Gays Make History," Gayzette, *The Evening Paper*, 8–10 March 1996, 29.

26   See "Encounter: Rep. Reynaldo A. Calalay, A Champion of Gay Rights," *Sunday Inquirer Magazine*, 24 September 1995.

domestic partnerships. This was the first bill of its kind ever to be filed in the Philippine Congress.[27] Its draft was promptly critiqued by LAGABLAB and other LGBT organizations, simply because it didn't emerge out of any kind of consultative process with the LGBT community itself.

In 2001, after several months of consultation and discussion with members of LAGABLAB, the antidiscrimination bill was filed in both houses of Congress. This bill was a watered-down version of the earlier bill, and its chief provision was to penalize those who would discriminate against any Filipino citizen by virtue of his or her sexual orientation. To promote passage of this bill in both houses, as well as to raise awareness in the country on the LGBT antidiscrimination cause, LAGABLAB launched a popular campaign, which it called "Stop Discrimination Now." This campaign was supported by the Philippine arm of Amnesty International, as well as by the International Gay and Lesbian Human Rights Commission, the Lesbian Advocates of the Philippines, and by other progressive civic organizations and individuals. House of Bill 6416, or the Antidiscrimination Bill, was passed in 2004 by the House of Representative, but the Senate failed to approve it before it adjourned its eleventh session.

Two years later, during the twelfth session of Congress, three antidiscrimination bills and three anti-same-sex-marriage bills were filed in the Senate and in the House of Representatives. These bills have since been referred to the pertinent committees. One of the senate bills, filed by Senator Ramon Revilla Jr., is pretty comprehensive, being the counterpart of the house bill that was sponsored by party-list representatives Etta Rosales, Mario Aguja, and Risa Hontiveros-Baraquel, and that had already approved by the House Committee on Civil, Political, and Human Rights. On the other hand, the other two bills pending in the upper house seek to prevent Philippine recognition of marriages contracted by Filipino transgenders and/or gay men in the Philippines or in countries which legally recognize such unions. Their primary provision is to amend the Family Code, by confining the definition of marriage to "natural-born males and females only." They were filed in reaction to recent court rulings that have allowed Filipino male-to-female transgenders to change their legal sex.

On the other hand, not to be caught napping, and eager to prove its concern and possibly win support from the obviously burgeoning and

27   See the related articles: Dinah Macatiis, "Lesbian and Gay Rights Act of 1999 Languishes in Congress," *ManilaOut*, no. 2, 2000, 12; "Prohibiting Discrimination on the Basis of Sexual Orientation (On Senate 18631 and House Bill 9095)," *ManilaOut*, no. 2, 2000, 38.

politicized urban LGBT community, the National Democratic Front, which continues to wage its Maoist-style revolution in the Philippine countryside, issued reports to the mainstream Philippine press that its leaders had already allowed gay and lesbian marriages among revolutionary fighters and *kadres*, up in the mountainous fastnesses of the archipelago.[28]

In the area of local jurisprudence, a nationally significant event occurred in 2006, when Ruvic Rea, a transgender captain of a local government unit in the southern Luzon municipality of Tayabas, Quezon, filed and won a sexual assault case against two councilors from a neighboring town. This legal battle was supported by several LGBT groups, and it is considered by many as a landmark case in the country.[29]

As a final note to this brief update, in early May of 2007, the Philippines held its local and national elections for the bicameral Congress. After the LGBT political party, Ang Ladlad, was denied accreditation to run for the party-list elections by the Commission on Elections,[30] its leader, Danton Remoto, decided to run for the Senate and later on the Lower House instead—"to offer," in Remoto's own words, "Filipino voters a choice." Remoto is a noted writer and professor of English and literature at the Jesuit-run Ateneo de Manila University. Had his party been allowed to run, and had it won (a likely eventuality, if the surveys from late last year were to be believed), it would have been the first explicitly LGBT political party to enjoy a congressional seat in this corner of the world. Needless to say, without the requisite party machinery, Remoto predictably lost in his bid to win a seat in the House of Representatives.

As this survey makes unmistakably clear, the last decade has seen ever-increasing kinds and degrees of public visibility, media astuteness, social organization, and politicization among Filipino LGBT groups and individuals. This has resulted in a viable though beleaguered "reformist social movement"—one that is not necessarily fully formed and organizationally coherent, although from all indications it seems to be firmly located in the

28   See Ross von Metze, "Gay Communist Rebels Marry in Philippines," *Gmax*, 28 February 2005, accessed 14 September 2007, http://www.gmax.co.za/look05//02/08-philippines.html.

29   For an overview of the last decade's worth of accomplishments on the Filipino LGBT rights movement, see: "LGBT Rights in the Philippines," *Wikipedia*, accessed 12 January 2007, http://en.wikipedia.org/wiki/LGBT_rights_in_the_Philippines.

30   The reason given by the Commission of Elections is that Ang Ladlad lacked a truly national constituency, and that Remoto, who heads it, and many other well-educated and middle-class gays like him, do not comprise an oppressed sector at all.

national political arena, even as it attends to a variety of LGBT localities and needs. This advocacy work has tended to engage in the struggle for institutional reforms, and has tended to see itself in the context of state structures and ideologies. Needless to say, the struggle is far from finished, and it has not been easy—*not in the least*—despite the celebratory and admittedly triumphalist tone with which I rattled off this short inventory of significant Filipino LGBT accomplishments.

It's important to note that while more and more LGBT self-representations are making it to the public sphere, primarily and even if only in Metro Manila, many of the aforementioned interventions and "lobbyings"—in the mass media, for example—have not been seriously followed through. Even LGBT legislative agenda has enjoyed more lip service than real and actual support from the supposedly sympathetic members of the Philippine Congress who have sponsored it. If anything, the past decades' socio-civic efforts by the Filipino LGBT community have generated not so much compassion as hostility from a number of powerful lobbies in the "high places" of national governance—such as, for example, the influential leaders of the Catholic Church, an institution which, in the morally medieval Philippines, continues to have the last say on many matters, both public and private.

In any case, this new and compelling importance of the national level of culture in the lives of Filipino sexual minorities provides me now with an opportunity to locate the LGBT question within narratives of Filipino nationness, and by the same token, to perform a postcolonial critique of official and state-sponsored discourses of Filipino nationalism, but still from a self-reflexive and politically "gay" perspective. Among other things, this task entails examining and seriously considering parallelisms and "contact zones" between postcolonial and anti-heteronormative theories. Finally, my hope here is that this theoretical reorientation will resituate LGBT activism and theorizing within the bigger framework of transnational capitalist imperialism, and the popular national struggles against it—in the Philippines, certainly, but also, arguably, in other comparably abject and paupered locations in the global South.

This is not to say that only insular or country-based LGBT political theorizing in what is now embarrassingly, belatedly, but still meaningfully called the "Third World," needs to be conscious of national realities when it carries out its social agenda. Astonishingly enough, the careful consideration of the national (and therefore, the colonial, neocolonial, and postcolonial) question proves equally if not more pressingly crucial in "cross-border" and international gatherings, as well—for instance, of the sort that we have been having in this lovely city for the past two days.

A couple of years ago, in Bangkok, during a plenary session of the First International Conference on Asian Queer Studies, a warm and wonderful colleague from the United States, a diasporic Asian queer theorist, very easily elided the nationally endowed specificities of the various but related discourses which we, the participants in that selfsame conference, sought to bring to light, scrutinize, and celebrate. In preferring and championing the diaspora-friendly, migratory, culturally ambivalent, poststructurally appropriable, and liberative label "queer" over the inalienably monocultural, predominantly WASPy, binarizing, middle-class, and residually medicalizing label "gay," she effectively and ruinously forgot the national contexts within which this preference and championing, in the case even of ethnic minorities in the multicultural United States, must take place. The profundity of this forgetting was such that she seemed unexpectedly surprised at the suggestion from someone in the gallery that in many parts of Asia, the term "gay" might have possibly been refunctioned or "indigenized" to mean many different things—things that are altogether remote from the racial supremacist and bourgeois realities for which she so vehemently upbraided it.

Looking at things from the perspective of anti-imperialist discourse, we can see that this tendency to speak in the "universals" of humanism is simply a function of globalization's asymmetrical flows of knowledge. We can look at these flows as constituting an economy of ideas, an "ideoscape" in which, following the norm-setting architectonics laid down during imperialism's Golden Age, the global North may be expected to supply the philosophy or the theory, while the global South is invariably called upon to supply the relevant and useful information—the multitudinous minutiae of ethnographic data. Given the terrifying global ascendancy of the US nation-state—an ascendancy that oppresses ethnic and sexual "Others" both inside and outside its borders—it was indeed rather unfortunate although finally understandable that such a tremendously damaging oversight was committed at that Asian conference by an American minority intellectual of Asian ethnic and affectional roots.

On the other hand, we also need to understand that the disappearance of the national question in much of American—and, increasingly, in global—queer discourse is simply consistent with the generalized "invalidation," particularly among Western knowledge systems, of nationalist struggles in the Third World. As with other similar invalidations, we need to see this in relation to the unstoppable march, in the last quarter of the previous century, of an invigorated and newly globalized Western imperialism.

Neil Lazarus's short account puts it rather plainly:

> At the level of political economy we can speak ... of the reassertion of imperial dominance beginning in the 1970s, that is, of the global reimposition and reconsolidation both—economically—of what Samir Amin has called the logic of unilateral capital and—politically—of an actively interventionist "New World Order," headquartered in Washington, DC. One of the fundamental preconditions of this re-imposition and re-consolidation was the containment and recuperation of the historical challenge from the third world that had been expressed in the struggle for decolonization in the post-1945 period ... The demise of the bipolar world, which had been based around Cold War political ideologies, shifted the emphasis to the variations of political economy within the world system. After 1975, as many commentators have observed, political sentiment in the West tended to turn against nationalist insurgency and revolutionary anti-capitalism ... [31]

In addition, the unquestioned and spectral presence of American queer theory at that Asia-Pacific Conference in Bangkok may also need to be seen in light of the fact that, from the 1980s onward, postcolonial studies itself has been most vigorously and profitably espoused by economically mobile "diasporic" intellectuals from the global South who have come to hold tenured positions in academic institutions in the North. Such scholars have generally not inquired into the profound political and ethical implications of this fact. Indeed, as Arif Dirlik memorably put it,[32] many of them have seemingly forgotten that the imperialism they routinely critique in their erudite and difficult commentaries is precisely the global capitalist condition that, to begin with, makes their institutional work possible.

It's interesting, really, but in their critical productions quite a few diasporic postcolonial critics generally do not examine their own positions in the global order, and instead compulsively romanticize and extol the "contradiction," "detachment," and "distancing" effect of migration. One way to explain this curious fixation—and its attendant amnesia—is by

31   Neil Lazarus, "Introducing Postcolonial Studies," in Lazarus, *The Cambridge Companion to Postcolonial Literary Studies*, 5.

32   Arif Dirlik, "The Postcolonial Aura: Third World Criticism in the Age of Global Capitalism," *Critical Inquiry* 20, no. 2 (1994): 328–56.

recalling that, as with Europe's idyllic Romantics and alienated modernists, "exilic" postcolonial critics, being intellectuals, must simply spurn the "profane" and pragmatic world of economic relationships in favor of the vast repositories of "sacred" cultural capital that they both symbolically and actually possess.[33] In regard to this we must also remember that for every diasporic postcolonial critic who chooses to reside and teach in the First World, there are countless others in the Third World who have no power to migrate into the West—or choose not to. It becomes obvious, then, that we as post- and anticolonial thinkers who remain resolutely located in the global South cannot peremptorily apotheosize the migrant's flight away from the predicament and strife of daily political struggle in our respective countries without at the same time rendering our own brutishly lived—and endured—realities an unspeakably terrible disservice.

And yet, these interesting explanations and painfully honest attestations notwithstanding, what likely happened then in Bangkok is infinitely simpler: out of a powerful and ebullient sense of solidarity with her *ex-centric* colleagues in sexuality and gender studies in various sites across Asia and the Pacific, our "queerist" immigrant friend simply forgot the nationally complicit dimension of her and indeed all our theorizings. It's quite possible that, as with many of us —American-residing or otherwise— who went to Bangkok to share our work in anti-heteronormative and/or antihomophobic activism and discourse-formation, back in 2004, the single-minded allure and urgency of the local caught inside the dizzyingly pleasurable and promising wefts and woofs of the global simply "eased out" from her consciousness the determinate role of the national, even or especially where questions of marginal genders and sexualities are concerned.

I certainly have not been very forthcoming in addressing this nexus myself. The neglect of the national in my book from 1996 is announced in its very title: the study's declared intention to refuse engaging with the fraught question of "nationness" is blindingly clear in the use of the geopolitical locator Philippine, instead of the identity denominating term, Filipino.

Other that registering a demurral against the machismo that characterizes official nationalist discourses in the Philippines, my reason then for deciding to willfully bracket out "Filipinoness" in my work was that I wanted to avoid lapsing into the ethnic essentialisms as well as the gender and sexual normativities that inescapably attend such a discussion.

33   Andrew Smith, "Migrancy, Hybridity, and Postcolonial Literary Studies," in Lazarus, *The Cambridge Companion to Postcolonial Literary Studies*, 260.

Moreover, skipping over the national meant I could link myself *somewhat seamlessly* with the global. This way, I could argue for conceptual and ethical alliances with a panoply of contemporary gay, lesbian, LGBT, and/or queer(ist) theories and movements, whose poststructuralist leanings routinely reject foundationalist fictions—especially the improbable, ethno-nationalist kind. And then again, my study is certainly not exceptional in this regard. The relative absence of critical discussions of the enduring import of nationness in the papers delivered at the Bangkok conference prove that as far as research on sexuality in the greater part of Asia is concerned, not engaging with the national question seems a most logical thing to do, given the conservatism and erotophobia endemic to the cultural traditions of many of the nation-states that comprise this immense and diverse continent.

As I envisioned it, my study would propose not only an empirical but also a conceptual history—the former being a descriptive survey of popular and academic writings on and by Filipino male homosexuals, and the latter being a genealogy of discourses and performativities of homosexuality—and the bakla and/or gay identity that they effectively materialized—in urban Philippines from 1960s to the 1990s. In order to properly contextualize its questions, this conceptual history would engage with significant recent events in the Philippines' sexually self-aware present, but would also hark back to the colonial past. This shuttling between the "now" and the "then" was meant to uncover the process of sexualization, in and through the discursive enforcements of the allied institutions of colonial modernity, that implanted the new sexual order of "homo/hetero," and further minoritized what had already been an undesirable, because effeminate, local identity: the bakla.

While the terms bakla and homosexual are far from perfectly congruent, the reason they are taken as interchangeable by many Filipinos is that the social effect they entail, as far as the persons who bear their names are concerned, is the same: stigmatization. It is my study's considered opinion that the current-day bakla is burdened not only by his gender self-presentation, but also, and more tragically, by his "sexual orientation"—an attribute capable of defining who he is, as a matter of deep psychological being, as an innermost question of *self*. Nonetheless, as the literary texts the study critiques demonstrate, there do exist encouraging narratives that the pathologizing of the bakla into and *as* a homosexual has made available—and these are the narratives of hybridity, appropriation, and postcolonial resistance, which may be seen in the works of many "politicized" Filipino gay writers and artists.

As can only be expected, these different "gay texts" demonstrate how despite or precisely because of the sexualizing "modernization" of local gender relations, the very people who have been pathologized by the American sexological regime are ironically "enabled" by this very stigma, which they subsequently appropriate in projects of reverse discourse, to serve various self-affirming ends. Thus, it is my study's conclusion that the discourses of homosexuality, gayness, and gay identity, as Filipino gays currently understand, live, and champion them, are as much the ascriptions of the Philippines' colonial and postcolonial histories of gender and sexuality, as the expressions of the various freedoms and desires that these selfsame histories have paradoxically conferred.

In order to carry out these distinct but related projects, in the book I therefore needed to inquire into the various published and documented representations of the bakla and/or the gay, as well as into the various self-representational tropes that may be found in the literary works of the Philippines' earliest openly gay writers. The overriding motive of this study was to trace the beginnings of a politically gay consciousness—and thus, the beginnings of a gay movement—in Metro Manila, the biggest urban center of the Philippines. More important, I wanted to be able to offer a plausible account for why this political movement had seemingly stayed inchoate or "emergent," despite its intermittent activity and obvious and all-too-urgent necessity, and to argue for a more constructionist or "universalizing" perspective on the entire issue of gender and sexual oppression, so that any future imaginings of a movement that will oppose it can be better informed of the irreducible differences that only "constitute" it.

In pursuing these objectives, I was forced to reconsider the "gender divide" between "effeminate" and "masculine gays"—a division which I took as analogous to a kind of class antagonism between the "respectable" and the "vulgar" ascriptions and self-expressions of the bakla and/or gay identity, as the semifeudal and neocolonial culture had continued to simultaneously constrict and enable them. It's interesting that while this divide persists up to now, the last decade's worth of activism has shown us that the movement is, indeed, possible, to the degree that it isn't anymore predicated on just the Gay but rather on a coalition among the Gay, Lesbian, Bisexual, and Transgender identity formations that have taken root in urban Filipino cultures across the past three decades. While the fear of ghettoizing or minoritizing the gay question—which I expressed over and again in the book—still persists and remains with me to this day, the precarious existence of a coalition across the gender and sexual lines as far as Filipino LGBT activism is concerned does betoken a more revolutionary and universalizing moment in the foreseeable future, especially when this moment takes place, as I will argue in the proceeding paragraphs, within the purview of an effectively anticolonial "national liberation."

As was heartily predicted in that study, looking at the last ten years we can clearly see that, in fact, more effeminate- than masculine-identified gay men have been willing to come out and risk themselves for the cause. And this isn't such a bad thing, after all, even as gay masculine performativities are currently enjoying a renewed currency and becoming more and more aggressively visible, prodded on as they would appear to be by the numerous internet chat rooms and "hook-up sites" that offer digital evidence of the idealized male embodiments many web-surfing Filipino gay men prefer to "have" and "be." (And yes, even here, the salience of the national remains particularly pointed: for example, the heaviest traffic and the most number of subscriptions in "Guys 4 Men"—one of the most popular of such web sites frequented by Filipinos nowadays—may be found when clicking on the "Philippine" button.)

And yet, much as I desired my study to escape the mystical and sticky nets of national/ist determination, at this point I simply can't deny that as I wrote it then, and as I look back on it now, the entire project was and is itself allegorical of the larger Filipino collectivity. That is to say, no matter how "local" I wished to ground and delimit my work, more often than not I in fact ended up implicating Filipino nationness—even conjuring forth a specter of the national body, in and through the act of neglecting or even perhaps "repudiating" it. This is clear to me now in the silences and assumptions of the book's chronologically arranged chapters—especially in regard to specific linguistic categories that I couldn't help taking as indicative of abstractions that were supposed to be concrete and local, but were really more imaginary and national than I was willing to admit.

This is clear to me now when I think of my interpretive forays into and rereadings of the Spanish and American colonial archives, and in the faith-bidden simplifications they inevitably committed in regard to the fundamentally unreadable past. And finally, national allegorizing is clear to me in the motivation to offer up my study, written in an internationally accessible English, as a nationally relevant and representative commentary on the forms of discursive resistance a politically motivated reading of Philippine gay texts might reveal. This, despite the tortuous and complicated qualifications in the study's painstakingly self-reflexive introduction; despite the study's declared careful attention to micro- rather than macro-exercises of power; and yes, despite the overall deconstructive concern for "constitutive difference" that underwrites the entire project.

The decision to not seriously include the issue of nationness in that critical work resulted in its inability to more intimately link up its theoretical and methodological concerns with postcolonialism. Because postcolonialism denotes an interdisciplinary field that examines the global impact of Euro-American colonialism in the modern era, it aims to describe the mechanisms of colonial power, recover marginalized voices, and theorize the complexities of resistance, identity, nationness, hybridity, and other such important and related concerns.[34] In other words, postcolonial studies seeks to inquire into the complex political relationships between culture and history in the (neo)colonized spaces of the world, and this enormous task typically involves the assiduous critique of European representations of the colonies, the study of resistant texts and cultural practices coming from among the ranks of the colonized, and lastly—nowadays, most crucially— the sustained interrogation of transnational neoliberal globalization,[35] which pursues, in a new and exponentially more lethal form, the imperial project to exploit and immiserate vaster and vaster regions of the already immiserated Third World.

None of these goals are, per se, inimical to the study of complex non-heteronormative identities and desires in geopolitical sites like the Philippines, in which the national, relative to the increasingly homogenizing narratives of the colonial and the global, in fact functions as a localizer, and in which colonial power has established an increasingly sexologizing, capitalist social order. Needless to say, the 500-year-old expansionary dynamic of capitalism-as-imperialism is the "big picture" within which to properly see colonialism, neocolonialism, and the various postcolonialist discourses of resistance[36]—including, let me now insist, the anti-heteronormative—that seek to dismantle the annihilating legacies of these unfinished historical passages.

Indeed, the various postcolonial "debates"—for, as I like to tell my students, postcolonial discourse is really postcolonial *discord*—can and do illuminate the different nationally circumscribed LGBT projects

34   Vincent B. Leitch, general ed., "Introduction to Theory and Criticism," in *The Norton Anthology of Theory and Criticism* (New York: W. W. Norton & Company, 2001), 25–26.

35   John McLeod, "Introduction," in *The Routledge Companion to Postcolonial Studies*, ed. John McLeod (London: Routledge, 2007), 7.

36   Peter Childs and Patrick Williams, *An Introduction to Postcolonial Theory* (Hertfordshire: Prentice Hall, 1997), 17.

we undertake. For example, using the concepts commonly used in postcolonialism, we can see how our appropriation, localization, and transformation of the sexological discourses that were colonially implanted in our societies possibly reflect the processes of identification, counter-identification, and finally, dis-identification, that the colonial and/or postcolonial subject, as she has often been described by this critical discourse, typically undergoes.[37]

Postcolonial theory tells us that with identification, the colonized subject uncritically accepts the labels given her by colonialism. The early kinds of empirical studies on homosexuality written by Filipino social scientists from the 1940s to the 1970s all adopted this strategy, which remained naively and damagingly trapped in the positivist fantasies of the colonial biomedical discourse. With counter-identification, the subject rejects the terms of the debate and denies its basis. This is the path taken by many nationalisms, which embrace nativity. And yet, very clearly, this position also remains trapped in a binary opposition to the relationally dependent and equally *fanstasmatic* category of the "foreign." In the Philippines, counter-identification is evident in nativistic studies that are invariably written in a triumphalist version of Tagalog, and extol the "indigenous" gender-crossing tradition as well as the irreducible uniqueness of the Filipino bakla.

Finally, what dis-identification implies is that the subject unapologetically accepts and yet critically transforms, hybridizes, and/or appropriates the concept provided by colonialism. This process only affirms the fact that meaning doesn't reside in ideas or in languages per se, but is rather always a social event—a "situated accomplishment"—and as such is eminently open to resignification and recontextualization. Needless to say, this is the strategy employed by many Filipino LGBT scholars nowadays, who painstakingly situate the Western-derived but locally appropriated terms they seek to deploy, explain, and critique.

Aside from these "identificatory" categories, another interesting overlap between postcolonial and anti-heteronormative discourses is the theoretical parallelism between the notion of the subject implicit in the former's theory of hybridity, and the latter's phenomenally generative and much-celebrated concept of performativity. The overlap is clear when we consider how both theoretical accounts posit the self—be it a

---

37   This threefold model was first proposed by Michel Pecheux in relation to the "collusion/resistance" question of language and ideology. See Michel Pêcheux, *Language, Semantics and Ideology*, trans. Harbans Nagpal (London: Macmillan, 1982).

gendered, sexual, or indeed national self—as the mimetic, citational, and repeatedly performed approximation of an unrealizable norm. Employing a novel cross-hatching of these two theories, we can therefore infer that because national identity, like maleness or femaleness, is a kind of compulsory "performativity," then it only follows that one's Filipinoness—or Americanness—is not what one is, but what one does. Following the performative thesis of gender identity, we can say that there is no simple and singular performance of one's national identity, for it is a norm that can never be fully inhabited, only cited repetitively in a lifelong process of actualization.[38]

There is no essentially Filipino subjectivity, only its performative production as the effect of acts and discourses that do not simply characterize but actually constitute it. Agency, or the possibility of subverting the Filipino norm, therefore lies not in a presocial realm of any purely experienced "synthetically unifying" Filipino freedom, nativity, or selfhood, but in the *variation* between the ideal and its performance—in this case, between the essential fiction of Filipinoness itself, and its particular enactments by discursively *animated* Filipino subjects—as forms of negotiation with normative, "national" power. Thus, from the perspective of performative theory, it's conceivable that the farther from the norm one's performance of one's nationness goes—in other words, using the terminology of postcolonial theory, the more "hybrid" one is—then the stronger one's exercise of negotiated agency paradoxically becomes.

Needless to say, the narratives of sexuality and nationality interimplicate in many ways. We must remember that in various regions in the global South, the nation is not a critically mooted or exhausted concept. Rather, it continues to wield enormous political force that inspires devotion, and is still seen by many democratic and popular struggles as the most potent and poignant battle cry for anti-imperialist resistance. As in many other underdeveloped countries, nationalism in the Philippines isn't a singular or a unified discourse. Rather, there currently exist Philippine "nationalisms" of varying sorts—from the institutional to the counter-institutional, from the official to the grassroots and communitarian, from the top-down to the bottom-up, from the millenarian to the secularist, and yes, from the reformist to the more militant and peasant-revolutionary. What is common to all of them, however, is that they

---

38   For more on this "national" deployment of Butlerian performativity in relation to the question of national identity, see my essay "Sexuality, Knowledge and the Nation-State," in *Performing the Self: Occasional Prose* (Quezon City: University of the Philippines Press, 2003), 3–15.

are fundamentally riven between nationalism's arguably modern project of emancipating all its diverse members, and the admittedly *retardataire*, nativist reaffirmation of communitarian—and thus, largely imaginary—customs, practices, and identities.

Experience tells me that nativist nationalism tends to nest most blissfully—and profitably—in institutional discourses in the Philippines, where it routinely essentializes "Filipinoness" into a pure and transcendental "unity" that unproblematically existed before the *Conquista*, was suppressed by colonization, and persists preternaturally up to now. Needless to say, this rhetorical move towards metaphysical "sameness" only serves to overshadow and discount the historical and all-too-harrowing fact that, if anything, Filipinos are becoming more and more socially divided, mainly under ideological duress and by virtue of the ruthless enforcements of social and economic abjection, sheer state indifference, and brutality. In the face of the stark and increasingly maddening images of systematic government corruption, patronage politics, grinding poverty, neocolonialism, multinational capitalism, economic and environmental plunder, gender violence, and all the terrible rest, institutional nationalists working in the arts and the social sciences—and the corrupt neocolonial state whose interest they are often "contracted" to serve—enjoin the Filipino people to avert their eyes, and dream themselves into a fabled nativity's mist-draped and simply recoverable past, for this is where their redemption *truly lies*.

It is thus at once the enticement and the claim of this kind of state-sponsored nationalism that the authentically Filipino *essence*, once restored to its rightful owners, will henceforth resolve all their present-day contradictions, and harmonize, and bind them under the aegis of all-inclusive "being" or "nature"—just like the good old days, well before the Hispanic deluge. Because what it's all about, despite appearances, is the imposition of fascistic sameness on the intractable hordes and legions of the nationally circumscribed "real," nativist nationalism reduces the differences and complexities of both the present and the past, and makes both plainly accessible to one another.

Even as nativism is highly suspect as a nationalist activity, we must however recognize that in many post- and neocolonies, it has been far from useless, inasmuch as it performed the all-too-crucial reversal of the order of privilegings colonialism had set in place. However, this initial inversion of colonialism's violent hierarchies—the unavoidable first step many decolonizing movements had to take—needs to give way to a reflexive examination of epistemologies, to an increasingly reflexive responsiveness to contexts, and for an even longer time after that, to a constant complication of the interpretive task.[39] As has been the compelling insight offered by anti-heteronormative theories, the purpose of transgressive knowledge isn't, after all, merely to overturn oppressive norms. The goal of radical knowledge is to undermine the very terms by which normative power defines the subjects it simultaneously subjugates and hails into being.

In the Philippines, it is difficult to resist the mystique of nativist nationalism, not the least because its simplistic Self/Other logic is being continually endorsed by practically all religious and educational dispensations. And because to a large part our anti-heteronormative work has no choice but to be nationally allegorical, if we must traffic in this kind of discourse at all then I submit that rather than participate in institutional nationalist and nativist discourses, we must instead endeavor to generate and offer more and more complicated forms of "critical nationalist knowledge."

This task bids us to be wary of institutional or cultural nationalism's many "excesses." Just what are these? First, while purporting to speak for the collective, this kind of nationalism is in fact produced and championed by the elite class, whose interests it serves. Second, institutional nationalism is itself an offshoot of imperialism, against which it emerged as a response, and on which it relies in order to conceptually exist. Third, cultural nationalism is an "Orientalism in reverse," inasmuch as its struggle to recuperate a lost precolonial identity is in fact premised upon the struggle for independence, and thus is underwritten by a desire to be affirmed and acknowledged by the colonizer, whose imprimatur it seeks. And lastly, this species of nationalisms constructs a bourgeois narrative of anticolonial resistance, and in doing so, suppresses alternative narratives from abject and marginal subjects.[40]

Clearly, insofar as the discourse of homosexuality itself is a colonial endowment (and a postcolonial appropriation) that has tended to settle in wealthier, more Westernized nooks in any colonized country, our secretly nationalizing and anti-heteronormative counter-discourse—a discourse that is typically spoken in the registers and languages of colonization—can likewise be readily critiqued for comparable forms of such "excesses." In our disavowed but nonetheless inescapable allegorizing of the nation—despite or precisely because of our localizing and specifying imperatives—do we not in fact exclude rather than include? Do we not elide and dismiss,

39   Even the early and possibly most eloquent champion of anticolonial nationalism declares that a national culture is not and should not be seen as a folklore, nor as an "abstract populism," but as something that belongs to the present as well as to the future. See Franz Fanon, *The Wretched of the Earth*, trans. Constance Farrington (New York: Grove Press, 1968), 43.

40   Childs and Williams, *Introduction to Postcolonial Theory*, 197.

for the sake of convenience, questions of class in our own bitterly divided societies, thereby privileging the realities, ideas, and experiences of one class over those of the others?

And finally, do we not now and then also engage in a kind of "self-exoticizing" Orientalism, for even as we offer up our local and national narratives in international "story-telling events" (such as this one), we somehow know that these narratives must simply be meaningful only insofar as they are recognized as different (that is to say, Other) by the Western Self, that must simply remain the implicit and immoveable norm? Indeed, thinking critically about the historical and cultural specificities that nationness implies can help us perceive and critique the devastating notional "oversight" common to the now-routinary "ethicizing of queer sexualities" across cultures, nations, and worlds—an oversight that emanates out of the need to supplant the "diversifying of queernesses" across the globe, whose end goal is still, despite claims to the contrary, the academically profitable production of the contrastive identities to the Western queer.

In an ironic reversal, the Western queer subject, in many of the recent studies on global and/or "glocal" homoeroticisms and/or homosexualities, becomes the Self against which numerous Others continue to be counterposed. The terrible thing here is that, in the end, the discourse all this serves to legitimize and propagate is, still and all—and despite token appearances to the contrary—the *same* and sameness-making discourse of Western (sometimes called "postcolonial")queerness itself.[41]

41   An example of the elision of cultural—and indeed, national—localities under the convenient and homogenizing description of "queer postcolonial theory" may be seen in the work of Martin F. Manalansan IV, whose study of the "global gay modernity" of Filipino gay men living in New York City conflates the experiences of Filipino immigrants to America with the cultures and socialities of Filipinos living in the Philippines. His queer postcolonial ethnocentrism is such that, in his book, *Global Divas: Filipino Gay Men in the Diaspora*, Manalansan haphazardly surveys the various Filipino efforts at theorizing kabaklaan in the Philippines, and faults them for their essentialist presuppositions that do not take into account the diasporic issues that beset Filipino American bakla queers like himself. This is a disingenuous move, for it neglects to register the fact that these local theorizings of Philippine-specific kabaklaan do not even pretend to pertain to the diasporic question; moreover, while it condemns local Filipino scholarship for its naive and "essentialist" presuppositions, by positing a sameness across the transnational divide between Filipinos in the Philippines and Filipino immigrants to the United States it is in fact promoting its own devious—and neocolonial—essentialism. For an interesting review of Manalansan's book, see Peter A. Jackson, review of *Global Divas: Filipino Gay Men in the Diaspora* by Martin F. Manalansan IV, in *Journal of Southeast Asian Studies* 36, no. 2 (2005): 328–30.

This is not, of course, to say that only wide-eyed and delusional engagements with American queer theory are guilty of oversights such as these. In a cogent appraisal of the inadequacies of certain varieties of postcolonial criticism, Benita Parry urges us to be ever mindful of the fact that colonialism is nothing if not a modality of expansionist capitalism, whose relentless pursuit of profit, markets, and cheaper labor motivated the European imperial project in the first place. To Parry, a postcolonial discourse that is exclusively devoted to culturalist questions of textual and intertextual resistance, and of otherness and difference, runs the horrific risk of devaluing the material and social dimensions of the imperial annexation of territories, on the one hand, and the abuse of human labor in the colonies on the other, as well as neglecting the dissident practices of and by the colonized in response to these depredations. Needless to say, one of the greatest shortcomings of this kind of postcolonial discourse is that its culturalist orientation serves to highlight only discursive or "epistemic" modes of resistance, ignoring altogether collective political actions and initiatives that are not so much ambivalent as downright oppositional.[42] Further, the issue of class tends to be absent in this variety of postcolonial discourse, alongside the consideration of how contemporary postcolonialities are effectively overdetermined and situated by late capitalist imperialism within the increasingly globalized scheme of socioeconomic things.

In the Philippines, postcolonial and critical nationalist knowledges must necessarily be more supple and capacious than what official or institutional discourses have thus far written and propagated about Filipino "nationness," for ultimately, their objective is to understand, address, and improve the condition of all the different communities and individuals that constitute the lived realities of the Philippines' national becoming, even or especially when it means questioning and challenging the normative grounds of its existence. Following the admonition of Franz Fanon (the famous early champion of anticolonial nationalism), these knowledge-formations must not speak of the national in folkloric terms. For Fanon (and for us), the nation is as much located in the past of a people struggling to bring itself into and keep itself in existence, as it is in their present and, certainly, their future.

We need to see that Fanon's critical and activist strivings for popular national liberation remain as valid today as they were half a century ago. Rather than dismiss them outright as utopian aspirations, as postcolonial critics we need to remember and relate them to the harrowingly inequitable "global" circumstances of the present. Moreover, our postcolonial

---

42   Parry, "The Institutionalization of Postcolonial Studies," 75, 78.

interventions must never forget that the subaltern struggle and resistance against both colonial and postcolonial elite domination—the collective, anticolonial, popular, and liberation movements that would erupt every so often in the past—courageously persist to this day in the many beleaguered and downtrodden nations of the impoverished Third World, whose common referent is nothing if not the jaggedly uneven institutional distribution of resource—of "wealth and illth"—on a planetary scale.[43]

As I can only briefly argue here, while it is clear that nationness in these globalizing times remains both a necessary and desirable paradigm within which to carry out our creative and critical projects in the global South, this in itself does not mean that we may not interrogate the ways the concept and historical fact of the nation—especially in relation to its intrinsically problematic ethnic, gender, sexual, linguistic, religious, and generally "cultural" claims—serve to construct, include, and exclude the different realities that attend both our different experiences of nationness, and our studied considerations and/or artful representations of it. Even as they must recognize their strategic uses, Filipino LGBT scholars also need to revaluate and appraise just what these nationalistic projects achieve or don't achieve—what they exclude, what they unfairly and untenably assume, what effects they produce in the knowledge systems of the various disciplines, and, as is often the case in the Philippines, what "complicities" and roles they may wittingly or unwittingly play in the legitimation of abusive state authority.

Nevertheless, we must always be mindful of the fact that evil effects of globalization on the plundered masses of the plundered earth cannot all be peremptorily blamed on the failures and abuses of the nationalisms therein. On the one hand, the thwarting of many national liberation movements in the global South has irrefutably been the masterful handiwork of aggregations and complexes of insuperable translocal and global forces.[44] On the other hand, nationalism is rarely an unproblematic and coherent discourse or ideology in these regions, in which national bourgeoisies acting as and through state agents typically deploy the passionate mystique of a myth-making nationalist rhetoric to justify their pecuniary enterprises and selfish political agendas. Obviously, we need to remember that the everyday practice, idea, and ideal of the de facto nations of the world necessarily

43   Tamara Sivanandan, "Anticolonialism, National Liberation, and Postcolonial Nation Formation," in Lazarus, *The Cambridge Companion to Postcolonial Literary Studies*, 64.

44   Laura Chrisman, "Nationalism and Postcolonial Studies," in Lazarus, *The Cambridge Companion to Postcolonial Literary Studies*, 196.

exceed the abuses which official nationalist discourses typically legislate and enact. As postcolonial critics of gender/sexuality, we would do well not to surrender the myth and reality of the Filipino nation to its exploiters; instead, we should recuperate it and acquaint it with more locally rooted alternative and radical performativities and conceptualizations.

Other than inviting us to attend more forcefully to the continuing urgency and significance of the national, in our part of the troubled world the postcolonial imperative also urges a rethinking of theories and methodologies. Recognizing the Eurocentricity of much of modern history, postcolonial discourse enjoins us to ask ourselves whether an overreliance on Western poststructuralist theory, while initially enabling of minoritized positions in the West, necessarily has to be the situation everywhere else.

It's true that poststructuralist Western theories provide us a virtual arsenal of conceptual and lexical means by which to describe the complexity of our "postcolonial" conditions. One of the more recent and interesting genealogies of postcolonialism has been offered by the cultural critic and historian Robert J. C. Young, who has declared that deconstruction is, contrary to conventional wisdom, one of the tricontinental anticolonial traditions whose terms provided for the transformation of Marxism in postcolonial discourse. In other words, inasmuch as he counts Third World expropriations of class-inflected Marxist critique among the theoretical progenitors of postcolonialism, Young sees the latter as a "form of activist writing that looks back to the political commitment of the anticolonial liberation movements and draws its inspiration from them."[45] Young further explains that poststructuralist theory is a major wellspring of postcolonial thought for, as he contends, its well-known deconstruction of totality is nothing if not the dismantling and rejection of the imperial structure itself. Thus, the decolonization movements in Europe's former colonies—Young maintains—were in fact the historical referents of the poststructuralist moment in cosmopolitan philosophy.[46] Doubtless, deconstructionism and poststructuralist critique in general have supplied postcolonialism with the requisite concepts and methods with which to challenge, undermine, and dismantle Western imperialist forms of knowledge, as they are institutionalized in the colonial archives.

And yet, while it's true that Fanonian anticolonial nationalistic discourse didn't directly influence the deconstructionist moment in postcolonial

---

45   Robert J. C. Young, *Postcolonialism: An Historical Introduction* (Oxford: Blackwell, 2001), 6.

46   Parry, "The Institutionalization of Postcolonial Studies," 78–79.

criticism, as Young points out the latter nonetheless was an offshoot of postwar decolonization in such Francophone territories as Algeria. Recent postcolonial accounts now tell us that conceptual compatibilities or analogies do exist between them—for example, Third World or Fanonian humanism is, in many important ways, performatively similar to the poststructuralist critique of Western civilization's self-determining subject.[47] In the end, while we must strive to engage with a poststructuralist critique of Western philosophy and its complicities with colonialism, we must not abandon the undeniable and *untranscendable* distinctions between the global North and the global South. Nor should we situate *all* the debates of colonialism within the terms and genealogies of Western thought, and sacrifice the study of *all* history to a theory of language or discourse alone. Not everything "poststructural" or "postfoundational" can be seriously entertained by us, to be sure. Simply put: we must recognize that the deconstructive decentering of *all* categories of thought can often be inimical to the assertion of the very concepts that prove vital to the struggle of many of the world's countless disenfranchised and (neo)colonized peoples.[48]

The incongruence between our locations is clear, after all: in the global North, postmodernism decenters liberal humanism's individual subject and deems it incoherent, while in the global South postcolonial discourses (chiefest of which continues to be nationalism) still must affirm an alienated subjectivity—an identity that postfoundational and anti-essentialist theories inevitably precludes. We can, I believe, rightfully insist that poststructuralism, a highly elitist and "parochial" development in relation to the rest of the world, need not be seen as the standard for all kinds of theorizing, after all. While oppositional intellectual work in the global South must remain wary of essentialism, especially as it is invoked by neocolonially complicit institutional discourses, and as it pertains to accounts of the pure and native past, we nevertheless must not let this concern deter us from allowing more and more localities, individualities, and collectivities in our societies to speak and carry out their own representational projects, to declare their own "lived experiences," in the furiously unraveling interstices of the here and now.

In America—I must mention—the lost cause of identity has seemingly been picked up once more, and a number of critics have arrived at what they

47   Stephen Morton, "Poststructuralist Formulations," in McLeod, *The Routledge Companion to Postcolonial Studies*, 172.

48   This has been the point of many of the critics of the postmodern-inflected varieties of postcolonial discourse. See Aijaz Ahmad, *In Theory: Classes, Nations, Literatures* (London: Verso, 1992), 43; and Kumkum Sangari, "The Politics of the Possible," *Cultural Critique* 7 (Fall 1987): 157–86.

believe to be a philosophically and politically acceptable theory, by which they can once again respect and accept the experiential self-understandings of the oppressed individuals and groups in their midst, as these strive to come to terms with and articulate their "sense of self" within the social forces that shape it. This new theory is called "postpositivist realism," and it looks at identity as being both constructed and real, in the sense that it is experienced as real by individuals whose sense of self unfolds within the meditations of the social and cognitive processes.[49] This theory makes it possible to argue that, first, certain social concepts are better than others, for they generate experiences and self-identifications that liberate rather than oppress, and second, even the most naive "experiential" knowledges deserve to be given an "epistemic status," for even they represent a quest for what may possibly be revealed as ultimately universally real—a continuing quest that, as such, must pass through error, rectification, and enhancement.

It's interesting that some American critics would seem to need a new constructionist theory of "the real" just to allow themselves to speak, as though they haven't already *really* been doing this, all the while that they have been generating the "subject-effects" of postmodernist theory, which shut out considerations of the totalizing effects of capitalism while at the same time continuing to offer narratives of subjectivity that are necessary for this rapacious capitalism to proceed unperturbed. Little wonder that all these difficult theories of the "incoherent subject" have thrived most luxuriantly in the richest and most capital-endowed countries of the world! I find it supremely ironic that many in American academe seem to always need more and more "convincing" theories to justify taking an interest in life and its welfare. On the other hand, in the various national spaces we inhabit—inside the massive gashes that rive the surface of the unfree world—when we encourage ourselves and one another to speak, it is both partially and painfully because we know that speech, theory, or discourse can scarcely even approach the unspeakable privation, hardship, and abjection of our people's increasingly impossible lives. Suffice it to say that while our theorizing must keep its oppositional moorings, it nonetheless has no choice but to take cognizance of the silenced, marginal, and subaltern among us, whose "lived experiences" certainly deserve representational, discursive, epistemic—not to mention simple, actual, and livable—space.

And yet, we must speak in this theory-laden language that is the burden of our time and circumstance—the onus of our inescapable colonial

---

49   See one of this new "philosophy's" most important books: Paula M. L. Moya and Michael R. Hames-Garcia, eds., *Reclaiming Identity: Realist Theory and the Predicament of Postmodernism* (Los Angeles: University of California Press, 2000).

inheritance. This means that in the process of engaging in representational and self-representational work, we must try to reclaim the many pasts occluded by imperialism, primarily by engaging our history in a meaningful conversation—a dialogue that will negotiate a path between the annihilating extremes of nostalgia and cynicism. For many of us, this conceivably might mean describing if not documenting the coping mechanisms and survival strategies of our nation's oppressed cultures and peoples. Analyzing these processes of adaptation and survival means moving away from a wistful meditation on past origins, toward a recognition of how the present uses narratives of the past in order to enable itself. Here, I must insist that this self-ironic historiographic undertaking is not the same as nativism, which we must remember mystifies rather than illuminates the relationship between the nation's "now" and its necessarily fictional "then."

We can also attempt to negotiate between the essentialist and constructionist positions by looking for traces of split, hybridized, syncretic, double (or even multiple) consciousness in our own intellectual traditions, and for "antecedents" to poststructuralist theories in our own local and/or national texts.

In my book, a preliminary and tentative attempt to deploy a more local theory of "constitutive otherness"—which is to say, deconstructionism— may be seen in my radicalizing of the Tagalog-Filipino binary for "depth/ surface": *loob/labas*. This binary has been repeatedly explained, commented upon, and thereby "colonized" by a variety of religious and positivist thinkers, who have pointed to the lexical richness of *loob*, and have mined it for its various metaphysical and psycholinguistic implications. As I see it, the corporeal associations implicit in the *loob/labas* binary can certainly be claimed and deployed for its transgressive and reinscriptive potentials by Filipino LGBT thinkers, who can always overturn the "violent hierarchy" to which this conceptual opposition has traditionally been subjected. Indeed, this "reversal" is what I attempted to perform in my work when I argued for a perversely "somatizing" reading of this popular national idiom of gendered subjectivity, in my discussion of the "psychospiritual inversion" evident in the self-representations of the effeminate bakla in urban gay cultures of the Philippines.

Those doing postcolonial and LGBT work in the Philippines may also want to locate early examples, in local critical and creative discourses, of what postmodern theory commonly refers to as "complicitous critique." This critical procedure describes a form of transgressive irony that reinscribes difference right at the heart of the Same.[50] Astonishingly enough, evidence of it may be found in the writings of many of the early Filipino nationalists. Just now I'm thinking of the Philippines' foremost hero—the writer-martyr and revered "Father of the Filipino Nation," Jose Rizal. In the preface to his edition of a seventeenth-century Spanish book about *Las Islas de Filipinas*, Rizal laid down an essentialist claim to an ancient "racial singularity"[51]—an awareness of whose "yesterday" he sought to rectify for and to restore to his people, with which they could begin their work of "charting out their future."

Constructed by Spanish colonial discourses, both in the Philippines and in Europe, as a civilizational "Other," Rizal decided in this book to fervently embrace this powerful social fiction, and to champion it against the odds. What's supremely interesting is that in his other writings (for example, his correspondences to friends and former mentors),[52] Rizal reveals to us that he clearly understood just how fictitious, improbable, altogether risky, and ultimately provisional this entire "racial" and/or "civilizational" enterprise was. And so, we can plausibly argue that, even then, Rizal provided us a local model for the transgressive and complicitous use of irony—as a "double-talking, forked-tongued mode of address" that *knowingly* participates in colonialism's oppressive discourse, in order to subvert and transvalue it, *from within.*

More recently, sometime in the 1960s, Jaime Bulatao, a Jesuit anthropologist from the Ateneo de Manila University, articulated his theory of "split-level Christianity."[53] Putting aside this clergyman's missionary zeal—a zeal that caused him to bemoan the woeful coexistence of contradictory "cognitive" and "philosophical" systems in the lives of Filipino "folk Catholics" who are given to preaching one thing, and yet practicing another—his social theory in fact anticipates, rather interestingly, the postcolonial notion of hybridity. As commentators like Homi Bhabha

50   Linda Hutcheon, "Circling the Downspout of Empire: Postcolonialism and Postmodernism," *ARIEL: A Review of International English Literature* 20, no. 4 (1989): 149–75.

51   Antonio de Morga, *Sucesos de las Islas Filipinas*, vol. 16 of *The Philippine Islands, 1493–1898*, ed. Emma Blair and James Robertson (Cleveland: Arthus H. Clark, 1903–1909), 130.

52   *The Rizal–Blumentritt Correspondence* (Manila: Jose Rizal Centennial Commission, 1961), 120.

53   Jaime Bulatao, SJ, "Split-Level Christianity," in *Brown Heritage*, ed. Antonio Manuud (Quezon City: Ateneo de Manila University Press, 1971), 16–33.

would later on explain, hybridity or transcultural "mixedness" derives mainly from the ambivalence of colonial power itself [54]—an ambivalence that is evidenced by and results in the lack of fit between colonial norms and their affective performances by the subjects they simultaneously determine and animate. The imagery of a "split-level" colonial personality itself repeats the eminently deconstructible "depth/surface" dualism—a dualism that, as my book from 1996 attempted so painstakingly to illustrate, functions as a particularly cogent trope for gendered and sexual subjectivity in many different locations in the Philippines.

And so, again, why must we take special cognizance of the nation when we perform our anti-heteronormative work?

First, because nationness is implicit and inescapable even or especially when we traverse the confusing networks and tortuous defiles of the local-global interface. National formations, national histories, national performativities in fact constitute localities in the 500-year-old cartography of capitalist imperialism. Certainly, it would be much better if we were to render conscious and *visibilize* one of the grounding assumptions of our studies, rather than delude ourselves into thinking that this grounding no longer exists, or that it longer has any bearing on our findings at all. This caveat is especially significant in the case of a cultural site like the Philippines, in which the increasing visibility of LGBT political activism, and the increasing cultural productions by LGBT artists and writers who now possess a more political consciousness, find their greatest urgency and relevance within the framework of the Filipino people's continuing national struggle to free themselves from poverty's steady and annihilating grip.

It's all too clear that in the last fifteen years, Filipino LGBT political practice has been inexorably shuttling between the local and the national (and, now and then, when the opportunity permits, the international) fronts. I guess what I'm saying here is that Filipino LGBT studies needs to catch up with these praxiological movements, and the first step it must take is not to dismiss considerations of nationness in favor of an unproblematized deconstructionist, thoroughly Westernized (and probably middle-class-friendly) framework that so expediently moots it. Second, consciously implicating the national in one's study links it up to the question of colonialism and its unfinished aftermath, and thus makes available to one's repertoire of conceptual tools and critical methodologies

54   Homi K. Bhabha, *The Location of Culture* (London: Routledge, 1993), 45, 75, 86.

a more properly postcolonial paradigm concerning the matter of gender and sexuality. The materiality of the sexual and gender questions necessitates both an engagement with the material reality of the nation-state, and a critique of normative forms of nationalism that, in their obsession with the nativist past, colonize the nation's differences into a sameness. Our cultural struggles against heteronormativity, homophobia, effeminophobia, and other oppressive ideologies, need to be grounded in the historical reality of the nation, especially when the masses that constitute this nation continue to struggle daily and bitterly and fundamentally to survive. After all, the solipsistically minoritizing (and thus, self-defeatist) tendency of the LGBT paradigm becomes only all too apparent when it is positioned alongside a universalizing scheme that is by turns national and cross-national; which is to say, that is both postcolonially "resistant" and neocolonially "oppressive."

And yet, these discursive struggles also need to continuously complicate their languages and tools, for while every country needs not just one myth but rather many myths or enabling stories of its past, this past doesn't have be imagined and retold at the expense of the lived and suffered differences of selves and others that have most certainly comprised it, and that can only be made known to us through an openness to alternative forms, modes, and themes of representation, as well as a keen and unremitting critique of normative concepts like selfhood, nativity, identity, and the like. And while it's true that Filipino LGBTs, like all Filipinos, need and deserve to have a past, critical nationalist perspectives tell us that this past need not be any less complex, conflicted, difficult, fraught, riven, mixed, contradictory, "open," and unspeakable than our present—a present whose foundational stories should never be fashioned at the expense of what we know and are capable of knowing about ourselves. Suffice it to say that it is perfectly possible to put nationalism in the service of the specific and the local (and even the autocritical)—as, indeed, many oppositional Filipino artists and critics, LGBT or otherwise, are now beginning to do.

In all this, it's important that we keenly remember how colonialism—in all its geopolitical, cultural, and racial aspects—has not so much diminished as intensified in our presently globalized times. The continuing promise, however, of postcolonialism—both as an intellectual and an activist discourse—is that it can be harnessed toward the formation of new critical and even popular movements (sexual or otherwise) across the entire world, who all profess similar political and ethical commitments to oppose the neocolonial global Empire.[55] To my mind, the most pressing challenge that

---

55   McLeod, "Introduction," in *The Routledge Companion to Postcolonial Studies*, 6.

faces postcolonialist appropriations of anti-heteronormative theory today is finding creative ways to marshal the eloquent force of both postcolonial and queer theory's conceptual sophistication that has typically been used to deconstruct shibboleths of Western epistemology—toward the fashioning of an autocritique of their own important but dangerous premises. Among other things, this would necessitate an anti-heteronormative rethinking of all theoreticist and culturalist biases that cursorily dismiss expressions of communal political action as helplessly self-delusional, as well as a serious reconsideration of critical theory's complicity in the persistent imperialist subjugation of neocolonized peoples in the name of neoliberal globalization.[56]

In the end, the burning, all-important, and strategically "universalizing" question of national liberation can only inform and animate the Filipino LGBT struggle, when it is clear that the great majority of the people who repetitively "perform" and discursively materialize the Filipino nation continue to be erased, abjected, and subalternized by a global capitalist order whose iniquity and avarice, by all indications, know no bounds.

Allow me to conclude with a simple but hopefully instructive image.

It's the front page of a tabloid that comes free with every purchase of the *Manila Standard*, a nationally circulated broadsheet. This particular issue came out early in December of 2006. The picture in the lower half is that of US Marines Lance Corporal Daniel Smith, accompanied by his American legal counsel. They are facing the judge of a local regional trial court that has just found Smith guilty of raping a Filipina—codenamed Nicole—while he and his fellow marines were barhopping in the Subic free port back in 2005. On the left corner of the masthead is a graph that shows the continuing appreciation of the Philippine peso vis-à-vis the US dollar—the happy result, according to the government's giddy economic planners,

---

56   According to Benita Parry, it is imperative that postcolonialism perform the following critical tasks, if it is to become truly relevant in these neocolonial and globalized times:

> empirical investigations of economic migrants, ... the substantive and experiential situations of the majoritarian settled populations of the nation-states of Asia, Africa, and Latin America ... [of] the millions of people whose mobility is constrained; who are not part of the reservoir of cheap labor in either the home cities, the Gulf States, or the old and new metropolitan centers; who still engage in subsistence farming, or in extracting raw materials and producing goods for world markets.

See Parry, "The Institutionalization of Postcolonial Studies," 74.

of the Christmastime windfall of remittances coming from the millions of Filipinos who are working contractually overseas. Opposite the graph are the latest results of the weekly Lotto, an electronic game of chance overseen by the same government agency that handles the operation of casinos all across the country. To the right of the photograph are the headlines of stories of an undeniably national import: Canada is willing to employ 30,000 Filipinos in the next few years, and, on a slightly sour note, the Asian Games being held in Doha have yet to yield a single Filipino medal. The day's glaring headline, however, announces—rather, exclaims—in a bold sans serif font, the tragic and untimely death of a "gay beauty pageant contestant."

This story is certainly newsworthy, as tabloids in Manila go: a twenty- to twenty-five-year-old male-to-female transsexual, probably preoperative, who went by the stage name "Joana Montegracia," made it to the final round of one of the many bakla beauty pageants that commonly take place, late at night, during any of the various weekend fiesta celebrations of parishes in Metro Manila.[57] This particular pageant was held in Caloocan City, a district known for the density of its Chinese-owned factories and teeming slums. Sporting a "sexy costume," Joana walked up the stage to

57   Gigi M. David, "Gay Contestant Natigok sa Stage," *Standard Xpress*, 5 December 2006, 2.

showcase her talent—a dance number that would call to mind the sinuous curves and "sex-bomb moves" of a famous local television starlet with an American screen name, Aubrey Miles, whom Joana wishfully and arguably resembled. Joana walked to center stage, got a hold of the microphone, and promptly collapsed on the floor. The audience cheered and clapped at the unexpectedly dramatic performance. Only when Joana remained motionless despite the minutes-long accolade did it become apparent that her "fall" wasn't a performance at all. Standing barefoot on the stage's metal floor, Joana was doomed the moment she held the lethal and malfunctioning microphone in her nimble and perfectly manicured hand.

There are many interesting localities and translocalities in this story. For instance, Joana's transgenderal enactment is permeated by a fretwork of complex material desires: her chosen family name, "Montegracia," sounds vaguely Spanish, and in the unfinished saga that is the Philippine oligarchy, this choice of surname blatantly announces its user's wish for a genteel and elite genealogy. Her impersonation is audibly directed toward the bountiful opportunities offered by a welcoming and mythical America, not only because the fascination for beauty pageants—with their swimsuits, talent competitions, and interviews—was an endowment gratefully received by Filipinos from the American colonial dispensation, but also because the exemplary Filipino woman she is referencing and attempting to "become" bears a quaintly American name—a name that betokens ideas of unhampered outward mobility: the *miles* and *miles* of possibilities that begin from the tips of one's itchy and American-dreaming feet.

Certainly, there are "performativities," "normativities," "transcultura- tions," "hybridities," and "constructivities" that we may tease out, tropologi- cally or otherwise, from within the interstices of this sad and bizarre little narrative. But finally, such theorizing and textualizing, such allegorizing and semiotizing, such overreading and underreading must simply confront the final and irrefutable reality that she, whatever her legal name was, the sexily clad, smiling, winsome and womanish *byukonera* who, like countless oth- ers in her mean and tightfisted city, must've entered this pageant to experi- ence the joyful headiness of competition (and possibly earn a living on the side), *Joana Montegracia*, beauteous grace of the windswept mountain—as the banner story banners it—she, this transgendered subaltern, is now *tigok*, which is gayspeak for "kaput," finished," "no more."

We can say that when Joana died that night, she died on the vile and murderous stage that is her country's unremitting helplessness.

As laid out on this tabloid's front page, the irredeemable bathos of this newsy but finally insignificant death is iconically hemmed in by the multiple realities framing the dailiness of an unfree nation's life. It is a nation whose economy rests squarely on the shoulders of its singularly productive and competitive global export—its overseas-bound people, who were trained to be doctors but work as nurses, trained to be engineers but work as foremen, trained to be teachers but work as maids: men and women of substance who are routinely ravished, beaten up, kidnapped, maimed, and returned to their families inside sealed boxes, which, for a few years now, have been arriving at the Manila International Airport sometimes five or six times a day.

It is a nation that is always on the lookout for good news, of athletes or beauty queens or singers making it big in the big and better world out there; a nation whose national pastime is also its national daydream: striking it rich at "Mega-Lotto" (national gambling which the big fish run) or the jueteng (national gambling which the small fish protected by the big fish run), for out in the streets of the woebegone nation there are no real jobs to be found, no real incomes to be made, nothing real to be expected other than the promise of a lucky combination of lucky numbers, all printed on a lucky card purchased on just that lucky day.

It is a nation whose sovereignty is an egregious lie, for the former colonial master never really left for good, and returns and returns as a visiting and unstoppable force that expects to be accorded all the privileges he had once arrogated unto himself through the sheer brutality of conquest, but now fully knows will be served amicably to him on a silver platter, by the sad and culturally damaged people whose natural patrimony he has pillaged, whose brain he has washed, whose soul he has bleached, whose dreams he has invaded, whose children, grandchildren, and great-grandchildren he has enslaved with all the generous loans and aid packages that will take lifetimes to disown, and whose women he can devour anytime the urge to feed his inner beast comes.

Why, again, did Joana die? She died because she is as benighted and ill-fated as her nation.

Meanwhile the Philippine government, bowing to American pressure (and taking advantage of the New Year's Eve frenzy), handed over custody of Smith to the cushy and well-appointed US embassy, barely a month after he had been convicted as a rapist by a Filipino court—whose justice is shackled and unenforceable.

Love in Old Manila (2017) by Felix d'Eon. Watercolor and ink on paper with antique paper border. An original drawing depicting lesbian love and romance. Photo courtesy of the artist. Felix d'Eon is a Mexican artist specializing in the art of queer love, romance, and sensuality.

This essay was previously published in *Kasarinlan* 16, no. 1 (2001): 131–62.

ROSELLE V. PINEDA

Bridging Gaps, Marking a Struggle: The History of the Filipina Lesbian Struggle in the Philippines

The beginnings of a journey: Remembering a lost past

> They published your diary, that's how I got to know you
> key to the rooms of your own and a mind without end
> here's a young girl, in a kind of a telephone line through time
> and the voice at the other end comes like a long lost friend... [1]
> — from the song "Virginia Woolf" by Indigo Girls

JUST LIKE A "TELEPHONE LINE THROUGH TIME and the voice at the other end comes like a long lost friend." These words play in my head over and over like an auto-reverse tape on deck. Ultimately, it was the drive to bridge gaps that brought me to this study. It was the desire to unravel that compelled me to write this. It was the desire and the last attempt to wail out and reclaim a past that was so violently taken from our hands. Somewhere along the way we allowed this past to slip away from us, so that, now, today, when we look in the mirror, we recall nothing that brought us here. Now, here, in front of the mirror, we could not retrace the steps that we took that made us this way. All we are left with is this presence that we try so hard to crush away from our skin because we don't recall any of this before. And we are left to think that we are alone in this process. That we have no past, that we have no memory, that we have no history. [2]

I am very young in this community, the lesbian community, and I admit that there were things I was not able to experience, especially in the beginnings of our struggle in this country. Somehow, this aspect of lesbian

---

1   Indigo Girls, "Virginia Woolf," from the album *Rites of Passage* (New York: Epic Records, 1992).

2   Excerpts from this paragraph were directly taken from my #96 journal entry written in August of this year.

activism was taken for granted along the way. Somehow, it was no longer important for some lesbian feminists today to look back at the things that our foremothers accomplished, or even the reasons why we are here in the first place. I feel that there is a great need to write our past, and this is why almost all my life as a lesbian activist, I have been looking for that chance to trace the history of lesbian struggle in the country. To take an initiative to know and learn about the things that I had no chance to experience when I entered the community. I feel that it is time that I pick up the phone and dial the numbers that would give me a chance to take a look at things that happened in and with our community in the past. And maybe, just maybe, I could even write in here a fragment of that long lost past. There is a lot of catching up to do... and so, I write this.

The Filipino lesbian struggle and community have been in existence for almost a decade now, and yet, there is not enough comprehensive written history on where, when and how we started as an activist community. For us younger feminist and lesbian advocates, there has always been a feeling of dis-location from our origins. I have heard declarations and statements that the lesbian struggle came from the women's movement in the country, but there is still a great lack of understanding of what the relationship between the les-bian and women's struggle is all about. There is rapture somewhere between the birth and the present state of the struggle, and I think this rapture remains to be one of the reasons why our progress is still moving at a very slow pace today. This miscommunication or should I say, dislocation from our origins remains one of the major reasons why the lesbian struggle at present is still a struggle and not a movement. It is one of the reasons why the struggle is dis-organized in many ways. I am projecting this paper to be the primary answer to, (1) the problem of lesbian invisibility in Philippine history, and (2) the problem of the present lesbian struggle's dislocation from its roots.

For this paper, it is my intention to (1) trace the history of the Filipino lesbian struggle and try to re-tell its story, (2) lay bare the reasons for this seeming dislocation from our origins that most young, lesbian-feminists ex-perience at present, (3) bridge this gap that occurs between the present les-bian struggle and its origins from the women's and people's struggle back in the 1980s, and, (4) locate lesbian art history within the history of the lesbian struggle and community in the country.

Scope, methodology, and limitations

Before this study, fragments and bits, and pieces of events and people mark the lesbian struggle in our country. There was no attempt to write a compre-hensive story of our origins and our struggles as a community. Even in many scholarly papers, the emphasis or the information told about the history of

Filipino lesbianism is written in very vague phrases, or if not, a declaration that there was no origin of lesbianism in the country, for example:

> Walang nakitang dokumentong nakasulat kung kailan nag-umpisang pu-
> masok ang lesbianismo sa Pilipinas. May umiiral na same-sex behavior sa
> lipunan ngunit walang nakatala kung sino ang kauna-unahang Filipinang
> tomboy. Kinokonsidera sa papel na ito ang taong 1993 bilang umpisa ng
> panitikang lesbiana dahil sa taong ito unang nalimbag ang isang koleksiyon
> ng mga kuwentong lesbiana ng isang manunulat na lesbianang Filipino.[3]
> (There was no written document of how and when lesbianism started in the
> Philippines. There were various same-sex behavior and practices however,
> but there was no record of whoever was the first Filipina lesbian. For this
> paper, it is considered that 1993 marked the beginning of lesbian literature
> because it was during this year when the first collection of lesbian writings
> by self-identified Filipina lesbians was published.)

Up to the present, such vagueness about the history of the Filipina lesbian struggle, including advocacy through literature still characterizes lesbian scholarly writings. This study is an attempt to put an end to this vagueness, and retell our story in a more comprehensive manner. However, I do not particularly declare this study to be the most complete written history of our sector because of the following limitations:

1. I am limited to confine my study within the periphery of the visible. This is to say that the lesbian struggle that I am talking about here does not include the struggles of Filipina (lesbians) who consciously defied heterosexual norms in the Philippines society (although that would be another point of study). For this particular study I will only examine and write the history of lesbian activism covering the period when feminism already came to us, when the modern concept of lesbianism and homosexuality already came to us and when, consciousness about lesbian identity was already being discussed.

2. There were very few articles written about the development of the lesbian struggle in the country. Because of this, it became very hard for me to even start the research, as I was faced with an overwhelming un-

3   Minerva Lopez, "Si Nena, si Neneng at si Erlinda," in *Tabi-tabi sa Pagsasantabi: Mga Kritikal na Tala ng Lesbian at Bakla sa Sining, Kultura at Lipunan,* ed. Eugene Evasco, Roselle Pineda, and Rommel Rodriguez (Quezon City: University of the Philippines Press, 2003), 9.

certainty on where and when I would begin looking for our roots as a community. I had to rely on interviews with the people who were there from the start of the struggle, and the people who are most active at present. But even this posed a problem for me because the people operating in our community work in such secrecy, lesbian ethics as we call it, that most information were given in very vague terms, causing nuances in accounts from each of my sources.

3. The information given by my sources were not all complete because of the secrecy that I mentioned above. This secrecy, or lesbian ethics, is an unwritten agreement in the community that we protect each other's welfare through careful respect for the privacy of each and every one of us. Thus, preventing the disclosure of certain names, places, and time frames in the course of my research. "Outing"[4] is a very delicate process for lesbians because of the possible sanctions awaiting us if we identify ourselves as lesbians in the society. For example, in the course of my conversations with my sources, it was very rare that I heard names and places dropped. This is because some of the lesbians that we talked about were women in the so-called high society, and revealing them as lesbians would jeopardize their political and economic power in the society. We have to understand that the issue of lesbianism is a very delicate matter, and we as lesbians are faced with real dangers of harassment, social castration, even to the point of physical violence, just because of being lesbians, and so, "outing" is such a dangerous act.

4. To recreate the story of a sector that has been deemed invisible almost all its time of existence, and to retell a whole decade of lesbian struggle in the country is task too great, it cannot be completed within a few months of research.

Nevertheless, I will try to be as thorough as possible with this study. But given the major limitations that I mentioned above, I feel it is just right to admit the reality that this study has a lot of loopholes especially in terms of writing the history of the Filipino lesbian struggle in the country. For example, one of the limitations of this study is that, the events and the people accounted are only those which are visible and out as "lesbian" events and personalities. This is a limitation because, I know for a fact that there are

4   Being "out" means to admit one's lesbian sexual identity. "Outing" can be experienced in different levels and in different occasions. For example, a lesbian can be "out" with her friends but not with her family, or, there are some circumstances that a lesbian would deny sexual identity for protection from homophobia, or from further harassment.

still undocumented, unseen and unvoiced languages, events, people and happenings that all contributed to the formation of what we now call, the Filipino lesbian struggle. I know for a fact that more that half of our stories lie within the bounds of the closet or the invisible. This, however, does not change the fact, that I still project this paper as a primary and exploratory answer to the problem of lesbian invisibility in history. I say primary because to my knowledge, this maybe is the first comprehensive paper on this subject, and exploratory, because there are still a lot of things to be done for our struggle and community's history to be retold and retraced.

"Marking a struggle" is another driving force that compelled me to write this paper. Again, I will delve into the problem of lesbian invisibility, and for a sector and a struggle that has been initially marked as,

> (A) ghost, whose sexual activities cannot be defined, and yet she repeatedly reappears, haunting the heterosexual imaginary. This ghosting of lesbian desire has made Possible a denial of its reality for too long. Reader can learn from Castle that the 'apparitional lesbian' is not absent from history, but is to be found Everywhere.[5]

The push that our sector is and has always been a part of history is a crucial step in order to address our initial problem of lesbian invisibility. To come up with evidences that, yes, we have a history as a movement is an important part of advocacy. The idea that we are a sector marked in history is a significant ingredient in the foundation of any political movement. Thus, I am not only retelling a long lost history of lesbian struggle in the country; I am also marking it in the larger historical map of the Philippines, ultimately examining its location within the various political arenas in the country.

This paper is divided into three major parts exclusive of this introduction. These parts are: (1) The discussion of the problem of lesbian invisibility and how the lesbian has been invisible in many ways, specifically, in history as both a practice and a struggle, in the feminist movement and the gay movement. (2) The origins of our struggles from the late 1980s up to present. (3) The location of lesbian art in the larger lesbian struggle. (4) The conclusion, which I will formulate with the assumption that every struggle's dream and ultimate goal is to become a movement, and in which I will incorporate some prescriptions and methods, which we can use in order to achieve this goal.

---

5   Martha Vicinus, introduction to *Lesbian Subjects: A Feminist Studies Reader* (Indianapolis: Indiana University Press, 1996), 9.

Sin of omission and the problem of lesbian invisibility

I've seen that life touches us with pain
and we change, becoming strangers to ourselves
tell me what happened along the way
how did I lose me along the way?[6]

— from "Wall of Silence" by October Project

I recognize that I cannot begin to wail about invisibility without even explaining how we became invisible in the first place. For people who are not aware of the existence of lesbians, for people who trivialize our existence and continue to relegate our issues in the dark corners of history and politics as mere sentiments, I know it may be hard to comprehend that our struggles and resistance throughout history are very real and very radical. It was the responsibility to uncover this lost history that brought me to this. But again, how can I even begin to write about a lost history, when we don't have any recollection of when, where and how our history was taken away from us? And so, I decided to begin this paper of recollection by discussing the problem of lesbian invisibility, and how we were invisibled in the course of history, and in the long run, how we accepted the comforts of our dark corners.

Sinead O' Connor wails this misfortune in her song "Famine" by saying that "if there's going to be healing, there has to be remembering and then grieving, so that then, there can be forgiving, there has to be knowledge and understanding."[7] I think we, as lesbians, are in the state of grieving for our faceless presence. I think that we are starting to remember what happened to us along the way, no matter how much it hurts to retrace our steps, in order to reclaim this past that we were deprived of, that we are entitled to, and that we are uncovering now.

"Lesbian history has always been characterized by a 'not knowing' what could be its defining core."[8] This statement by Martha Vicinus largely describes the state of lesbians in history. Almost all my entire life as a lesbian, when I ask about lesbianism and our roots, it has always been that lesbians are, "entities lying neither in or out the locus," "something that's undefined," "neither heterosexual nor homosexual," and "outside any periphery." I think this high degree of uncertainty of

6   October Project, "Walls of Science," from the album *October Project* (New York: Epic Records, 1993).

7   Sinead O' Connor, "Famine," from the album *Universal Mother* (Canada: EMI Records, 1994).

8   Martha Vicinus, *Feminist Studies Reader*, 2.

our roots and our subjectivities are not only dependent on the resistance to define lesbian identity to give way to lesbian diversity. I think this uncertainty lies within the fact we are almost invisible in history and under the banner of other gender-oriented movements, like feminism and male homosexuality.

For this paper, I will discuss three levels of invisibility from which the "lesbian" suffered and is still suffering from: (1) history, (2) the feminist movement, and (3) the queer[9] movement. These three aspects contribute largely to the continuing invisibility of lesbians because these three aspects are the locations from which lesbians could be located as a legitimate entity in the society.

Lesbian invisibility in history as both subject and practitioner

In this section, I will examine how the lesbian existence was not only discouraged in previous societies, but practices of which, involved certain sanctions in the society. This violent erasure of our existence does not only erase lesbian existence in history but it also relegates us under other subjectivities that were seen as outcasts in society like witches, spinsters and prostitutes.

In Laura Weigert's study of images of witches and prostitues in sixteenth century in Western prints and painting, she concluded that sexual practices of women that exclude men, mainly through self-genital stimulation and genital stimulation with each other (lesbian sexual practice), are discouraged and sanctioned as a deviant behavior.[10] Not only were they called witches and prostitutes, but they were also legally punished and executed in the name of pagan and unchaste practices against Catholicism. In the final analysis, these sexual practices of women with the absence of men were deemed by the Catholic-patriarchal society of Europe as a threat to male dominance. Thus these women with these practices were either burned at the stakes, or forever branded as freaks of society, Adrienne Rich also took into account similar instances specifically in the fifteenth- and sixteenth-century Europe when many lesbians were tried and executed because of practices, sexual or not, that excluded men, for example, the refusal to

9   "Queer" is a Western term for various sexual identities and other "different" (not necessarily deviant) social practices such as lesbians, gays, transgenders, transvestites, and transsexuals.

10   Laura Weigert, "Autonomy as Deviance: Sixteenth-century Images of Witches and Prostitutes," in *Solitary Pleasures: The Historical, Literal and Artistic Discourses of Auto-eroticism*, ed. Paula Bennet and Vernon Rosario II (New York and London: Routledge, 1995), 21.

marry.[11] Punishment, she said, did not only promote compulsory heterosexuality in the society but also relegated lesbian practices and subjectivities into the darkest corner until they became invisible.

The whole point is that lesbian existence and practices were not only
discouraged but also punished. With this violence committed against lesbians, it is logical that, lesbianism would be relegated into the invisible.
Eventually, women and lesbians alike allowed this in the hope of a better
life, out of danger and out of economic impoverishment. In the Philippines, it is expected that this kind of invisibility would also be felt because
of certain economic and cultural conservatism that is expected of and imposed on women (lesbians) by the hetero-patriarchal society.

Despite this situation, some women chose not to give in to this oppression. They expressed their resistance through women bonding, or being solitary women. The cases of Paz Paterno and Adelaida Paterno who both died
unmarried,[12] and the many cases of witches, widows, unmarried women,
and spinsters in fifteenth- and sixteenth-century Europe, evidenced the resistance. [13] Thus, lesbianism and other women-oriented practices which can
also be read as 'lesbian,' using Rich's concept of lesbian continuum,[14] were
seen and should be seen as a resistance to patriarchal oppression. However,
this is another misconception of lesbianism that we should be wary about,
as Adrienne Rich says, that lesbianism is an expression of women who hates
men, or, "simply acting out of bitterness toward men."[15]

Feminism and compulsory heterosexuality
In the process of lesbian invisibility through violence and state sanctions,
it came to a point when even women no longer questioned or put into account that heterosexuality is an institution also imposed by patriarchy. In
Adrienne Rich's article, "Compulsory Heterosexuality and Lesbian Existence," she took into account with great detail the numerous assumptions

---

11   Adrienne Rich, "Compulsory Heterosexuality and Lesbian Existence," in *Powers of Desire: The Politics of Sexuality*, ed. Ann Snitow, Christine Stansell, and Sharon
Thompson (New York: Monthly Review Press, 1983), 180.

12   Raissa Claire Rivera, "Women Artists and Gender Issues in 19th Century Philippines," *Woman, Take Back History and...: Review of Women's Studies* 6, no. 2 (July–December 1998) Quezon City: Center for Women's Studies, University of the Philippines
Diliman, 93.

13   Rich, *Compulsory Heterosexuality*, 180.

14   Adrienne Rich's concept of lesbian continuum says that all women are potentially lesbians because of the primary bonds of women to each other, which started as far
back as mother to daughter relationship. Ibid., 192.

15   Ibid., 178.

of feminists in different fields and various levels about the innate hetero-sexuality of women. She also added the neglect of contemporary feminism with regard to the various histories of women who resisted institutional-ized patriarchal modes and systems such as marriage despite societal cas-tration. According to one assumption, "biologically men have only one in-nate orientation—a sexual one that draws them to women—while women have two innate orientations, sexual toward men and reproductive towards their young."[16]

To assume that women are innately sexually drawn towards men is to assume and promote heterosexuality as a whole and that women are only naturally attracted sexually to the opposite sex. This assumption of feminists is very much felt in various fields of study. In psychoanalysis for example, examination of motherhood by theorists like Nancy Chodorow, assumes that men and women are collaborators in upholding patriarchal ideologies. In these statements, Chodorow implicitly assumes that a society is pro-duced through the union and collaboration of men and women (hetero-sexual communion), thus, the only way to dislodge patriarchy is by equal caring emotionally, physically, and mentally, by both men and women in the name of parenthood.[17]

In the Philippines, this saddening but otherwise very real tendency is also felt. In the women's movement, for example, it was only in the ear-ly 1990s that the lesbian issue was explored. Before this time, issues that women discussed were always along the lines of heterosexual concerns in relation to socio-economic conditions.

In my own experience in asserting lesbian space in Philippine art, I have encountered much discrimination from both feminists and lesbians alike. In an art criticism workshop for example that was held in 1998 by the Na-tional Commission for Culture and the Arts, when I was presenting an argu-ment for a possible lesbian-oriented framework of criticism I was repeatedly asked why there is a need for such assertion. Precisely because it was never discussed at any place, at any corner, even the dark corners, of art history and criticism. I think there is not only a need but a great need to assert the lesbian position as a legitimate critical framework. In another internation-al conference catering to Southeast Asian women, I was surprised to find that there was no lesbian representation in the arguments presented in the panel. Luckily, I was there and the coordinator was open enough to let me

16   Adrienne Rich quoting Alice Rossi in the article "Children and Work in the Lives of Women," which is a paper delivered in the University of Arizona, Tucson, Feb-ruary 1976. Ibid., 177.
17   Ibid., 181.

read a lesbian art manifesto at the concluding part of the conference. The point is, that there is still a great need for lesbians to be "out" as art practitioners in order for this space to be reclaimed. This is a need because even such spaces, that claim to be women-oriented spaces, surprisingly leave out the lesbians, and are even filled with lesbophobia and aversions toward lesbians to a certain extent.

Thus, on the one hand, feminism poses itself as a women-oriented cause and yet imposes certain heterosexist patterns that relegate lesbians into the dark corner even more. On the other, feminism's assuming position as a mother loving a daughter (lesbian) can also be equally dangerous because of its desexualized notion of women's relationships to one another. Cheshire Calhoun in her study on why the lesbian disappears under the sign "women" tells us that:

> When feminist woman loving replaces lesbian genital sexuality, lesbian identity disappears into feminist identity, and the sexual difference between heterosexual women and lesbians cannot be effectively represented. Moreover, when lesbian cross-dressing and role-playing is denied, a distinctively lesbian relation to (and I will argue, outside of) gender disappears into a feminist relation to gender. The women-identifed-woman is incapable of either the femme's redeployment of femininity or butch's gender crossing. As a result, the gender difference between heterosexual women and lesbians cannot be effectively represented, indeed is repressed, under her image.[18]

It is an ambivalent feeling actually, that on the one hand, we need to connect and affirm sameness with our sisters in the feminist movement. Most of the time, this sameness means to change the language of our identities and conform to the conventional identity of women, such as essentially veering away from the idea of the mannish lesbian and promote feminine lesbianism as an empowering image of lesbianism. Moreover, hovering under the umbrella of women poses dangerous tendencies of denying lesbian sexuality, meaning, the body attraction, pleasure of the lesbian gaze, the breasts, the buttocks, etc. Lesbians are encouraged to be asexual under the feminist banner because feminism promotes the veering away from the conventional "male gaze." The male gaze, which compartmentalizes women's bodies as a site of pleasure, despite the fact that lesbians, or most lesbians, do take pleasure with the site of women's bodies. On the other hand,

18   Cheshire Calhoun, "The Gender Closet: Lesbian Disappearance under the Sign 'Women,'" in *Lesbian Subjects: A Feminist Studies Reader*, ed. Martha Vicinus (Bloomington and Indianapolis: Indiana University Press, 1996), 212.

we need to affirm our own sexualities as lesbians, which made us different from heterosexual women in order to preserve and reclaim our subjectivity, existence and lost history. However, as I have been saying, affirmation of our identities does not mean segregation. It should not be viewed as a move that as lesbians we are ultimately separating ourselves from the rest of the feminist community by affirming our differences. As Ani Difranco would say,

> The world song is a colorless dirge without the differences which distinguish us, and it is that difference which should be celebrated not condemned.[19]

We can, by means of sisterhood solidarity, still affirm our differences and work as one to emancipate women and lesbians from patriarchy and empower our ranks.

Gay movement and male homosexuality

When queer theory and the gay movement flourished in the early part of the 1990s in the West, lesbians were once again, subsumed under the banner of another gender-oriented cause. Adrienne Rich said,

> Lesbians have historically been deprived of a political existence through "inclusion" as female versions of male homosexuality. To equate lesbian existence with male homosexuality because each is stigmatized is to deny and erase female reality once again. To separate those women stigmatized as "homosexual" or "gay" from the complex continuum of female resistance to enslavement and attach them to a male pattern, is to falsify our history. Part of lesbian existence is, obviously, to be found where lesbians, lacking a coherent female community, have shared a kind of social life and common cause with homosexual men.[20]

In the Philippines, it was very recent that the lesbian struggle came to work in collaboration with the male gays. Historically, we (lesbians) owe the birth of our struggle to the women's movement, but we have come to affirm that we also have certain commonalities with our gay brothers. But as it happened, lesbians were once again relegated to the silent corners in this collaboration because gay males are more flamboyant and we are reduced to being their female counterparts. Once again, the only solution to this relegation is to assert and affirm our lesbian identity, so that even if we are

---

19   Ani Difranco, from her first album released in 1992 called *Ani Difranco*.
20   Adrienne Rich, *Compulsory Heterosexuality*, 193.

working in coalition and collaboration with other gender-oriented causes, we would not be invisible.

All the three aspects that I discussed above contribute to the continuing invisibility of lesbians in any society, and in the Philippines in particular. This discussion of lesbian invisibility will help explain the importance of marking the lesbian in history, whether in Philippine history or in the more specific context of Philippine art history, for lesbian art. I also hope that this section explains where I am coming from in this study. That, I am coming from a marginalized sector in search of a root that has been scrubbed away from our hands, our faces, our beings.

Bridging gaps: The history of lesbian struggle in the Philippines

I call it "bridging gaps," because along the way, we as young lesbian feminists were somehow snatched from our roots in this struggle. Without a mother or at least, a sense of that mother to guide through this struggle, but only with sisters to hold our hands, we search desperately for symptoms of our beginnings. We work in darkness. We work disjointed from a starting point, from a beginning that we can call our own. We were gapped. We were broken loose from that beginning, but now is the time to reconnect. Now is the time to bridge or tie the knots once more with that process, with that beginning... and this is an attempt to retrace that alignment.

Aida Santos was one, or probably the only one who came out as a lesbian in the mid-1980s. Back then, she was one of the most active players in the underground national democratic movement, battling with issues of dictatorship, foreign imperialism, feudalism and bureaucrat capitalism, which will eventually emancipate our countrymen from poverty toward national economic and democratic progress. She was also one of the pioneers of the women's movement in the Philippines.

It was the women's movement in the 1980s that conceived and reared the lesbian struggle even within the secret tresses of the national democratic movement.[21] This concern for the lesbian issue within the national democratic movement came into serious discussions within the ranks of feminists, when murmurings within the movement that there are discriminatory practices against the lesbians and lesbophobia started to accumulate. These murmurings and secret discussions went on for years until a position paper by the MAKIBAKA underground women's organization in the

21   Aida Santos, interview by the author, Pag-asa Village, Quezon City, 8 September 2000.

national democratic movement marked the formal inclusion of the issue of sexual orientation within the movement.[22] However, even if there was an incorporation of sexuality issues, it was very clear at that time that all issues were in line and should be analyzed within the socio-economic discourse.

During the 1990s the issue of dictatorship began to decline as a new brand of Catholic-bourgeois ideology took over, the issues on gender and sexuality also took on a different facade. Led by a few strong members of the women's movement, which came from the national democratic movement along with younger feminist lesbians, discussions about gender and sexuality became a major concern of the women's movement. Despite this seeming popularity of sexuality issues, the lesbian issue remained untouched. It remained peripheral and not part of the central issues of the women's movement. Despite this continuous marginalization, lesbians started to form clusters that started out as *barkada* within various women's organizations, since most of these lesbians are part of these organizations anyway. In 1992, the first formal lesbian organization was formed and centralized in urban Manila and was called The Lesbian Collective (TLC).

With the growing awareness towards sex and sexuality, the women's movement, piece by piece, slowly opened its system to other women's concerns and issues like prostitution and violence against women which were all analyzed in relation to socio-economic discourse. In the Women's March in March 1993, the women's movement carried the theme "Violence-Against-Women."[23] This was the first time that the women's movement carried an issue that was closer to women's rights, which was slightly apart from its former issues of anti-dictatorship and socio-economy. It was during this time that the newly formed TLC had the initiative to read a statement by lesbians to discuss issues of violence against lesbians. Lesbians after all are women, thus, the issue of violence against women also affects lesbians.

It was a breakthrough both personally and politically for the members of TLC to join the Women's March under the banner of lesbians, and to actually read a statement as lesbians in the program. Within the women's movement, the lesbians had to struggle for space.[24] To read the lesbian statement, members of TLC had to struggle for their place in the program when they were told they would be cut off from the program because of time constraints. They were even requested to just read the statement while

22   Ibid.
23   JJ Josef, interview by the author, UP Diliman, 25 August 2000.
24   This is yet another evidence of lesbian invisibility within the feminist/women's movement that I discussed in the second part of the paper.

marching to Mendiola, which was the final destination of the march. One marcher, JJ Josef, recalls:

> Tapos nung, hanggang nagma-martsa na, ipinarating sa amin na hindi raw puwedeng basahin yung statement namin, kasi daw walang time. So, kung gusto pa rin daw namin habang naglalakad mula Welcome Rotonda papuntang Mendiola, basahin habang naglalakad.[25]
> (When we were already marching, they (program committee) told us that we could not read our statement because there was no time. So, if we still want to read the statement, we will have to read it while walking from Welcome Rotonda to Mendiola.)

Finally, some of the older feminists voiced out their support for the younger lesbians who were finally allowed to read the statement in public as part of the program. And so, the then appointed TLC speaker Giney Villar publicly read the first lesbian statement at Mendiola.[26] It was a very heartwarming experience for everybody in TLC because it was the first time for most of them to march under the banner of lesbianism. It was the first time that something about lesbians was publicly read, listened to and applauded. Most of all, it was the fruit of a collective effort of lesbians who formed clusters and barkadas within the women's movement. From then on small lesbian formations started blossoming in and around urban Manila.

Outside Metro Manila, a number of small lesbian groups were also being formed. In Baguio, a number of professionals and young feminist activists formed Lesbians in Baguio for Nationalism and Democracy (LesBoND), which advocates the welfare of lesbian mining workers and lesbians working in the Baguio Export Processing Zone."[27] In Davao, a small sociocivic lesbian group headed by Andi Consunji called The Group was gaining recognition by participating in raising funds for schools, environmental activities, and other socio-civic concerns. Although these groups were not clear about the political lines of women's welfare and the particularity of the issue of lesbianism in the country, they had proven that lesbians can bond together to form a comprehensive collective nationwide.

In 1993 the controversial (but according to Aida Santos, very premeditated) interview article by Pennie Alarcon in the Valentine's issue of the

25   JJ Josef, interview, 25 August 2000.
26   Ibid.
27   JJ Josef, "Sexual Identities and Self-Images of Woman-Loving-Women: An Exploratory Study on the Realities of Woman-Loving-Women in the Philippine Context" (master's thesis, UP Diliman College of Social Science and Philosophy, October 1997), 11.

Sunday Inquirer Magazine called "When Aida Met Giney" was published. It was in this article that for the first time, lesbian love, lesbian sex, and the idea that lesbians are essentially ordinary people was discussed in a public venue, the media. A very important detail in the article was also given to the public, the contact number of Women's Education, Development, Productivity and Research Organization (WEDPRO) where Santos was a board member. This brought about an overwhelming response from lesbian readers from all walks of life who started calling WEDPRO for inquiries and counseling. To accommodate all the calls, it came to a point when the staff needed to spend half of their time at the office counseling over the phone.

The board of WEDPRO then formed a small cluster within the organization to provide, train and monitor lesbian counseling and the Womyn Supporting Womyn Committee (WSWC) was born. The committee served as a special committee directly under the executive board of WEDPRO. The organization managed to acquire funds for its phone counseling project and started training lesbian counselors to answer the callers. Fortunately, a substantial number of WEDPRO employees were also lesbians so the incorporation of the lesbian issue within the mandate of WEDPRO was an inevitable occurrence even without formalization. Most of all, it was in the project called the "Lesbian Hotline" managed by WSWC, that lesbian work was deemed as a profession, paid, monitored and assessed as part of the work load done in WEDPRO. For the first time, the lesbian clusters that do work voluntarily and out of the spirit of camaraderie are compensated for professional work.

Meanwhile, in the field of literature and publications, a joint project of Santos and Villar, in cooperation with Karina Bolasco of ANVIL was being negotiated. The lesbian anthology was projected to be the first Filipina lesbian literary anthology, way before *Ladlad* and *Tibok: The Heartbeat of the Filipino Lesbian* was published. However, because of time constraints, the lack of sources of lesbian literary production and the dominance of closet lesbian writers in the anthology, it was postponed indefinitely. In lieu of this, Santos, with the co-authorship of Villar, funded and published the first lesbian anthology in 1994 called *Woman-to-Woman: Prose and Essay* to serve as a testing ground in identifying the market for lesbian-oriented books. But a serious problem surfaced as the publisher suddenly disappeared and took with him thousands of copies of the book which were sold to various bookstores. It was a heartbreaking experience for the authors because even they do not have copies of their own book.

During this year TLC slowly faded from lesbian organizing and the former members started forming their own groups. What was a formalized "barkada" started to part ways because of conflicts in political beliefs. Since most of the members of TLC were also members of various feminist organizations with active roles in the larger national democratic movement, it was inevitable for the conflict within the national democratic movement to affect its followers and members in the women's organization. It is to be noted that during this time a faction within the national democratic movement, which actually started even in early 1992, emerged. A separation between what we call as "re-affirmists/RA"[28] and "rejectionists/RJ"[29] characterized one of the low points in the leftist movement. These political conflicts also brought about a division within the TLC as some members sided with the re-affirmists group and the others with the rejectionist group. It is believed that lesbian organizations, even up to now, are loose with regard to the imposition of political beliefs aside from lesbian politics. According to JJ Josef, one of the lesbian theorists in the country, this may also be one of the major reasons why most lesbian groups break up. She said,

> Sa umpisa, galing din yan sa iba-ibang political groupings, parang nag-agree kami noon na it did not matter kung RA ka, kung RJ ka, kasi madugong-madugo ang issue at that time. May effect rin yun sa organization. So ang naging agreement namin, eto yung issue natin lesbianism, women's issues pero andiyan din, hindi naman natin kinakalimutan yung political at class issues. Pero yung pagiging RA, RJ, third force, o kung ano mang klaseng may the force be with you ka, huwag mong dalhin yung agenda mong iyon sa grupo. Tingnan natin kung anong basis of unity natin yun ang i-push natin. Pero eventually siguro? Kasi nga ayaw naming mag-impose sa isa't isa. So parang hindi rin ganoon kahigpit yung pagkapit sa membership. Kasi yun din yung reason, kasi kumbaga yun yung nag-attract sa amin to form the group, dahil may freedom ka to express yourself, kahit anong political leanings mo puwede, and yet, yun din siguro naging rason kung bakit evetually nawala yung grupo.[30]

28   What we call RA or re-affirmists today in the leftist movement reaffirms the Maoist-Leninist model of Philippine Revolution concocted by Jose Ma. Sison, in which the peasants are seen as the revolutionary leaders in alliance with protetariat forces in various urban centers. This methodology was designed because of the recognition that the Philippines is still largely an agricultural and feudal society.

29   RJ or rejectionists, on the other hand, reject this Maoist-Leninist framework of analysis by Joma Sison. With the leadership of the late Ka Popoy Lagman, RJ took the revolution to the urban centers with the belief that the Philippines is now a socialist country because of the rapid growth of factories, urban centers, and other urban infrastructures. The proletariat forces became the crucial sector to push this kind of revolution towards victory.

30   JJ Josef, interview, 25 August 2000.

(In the beginning, we agreed that it did not matter if you're RA or RJ, or-whatever your political grouping is, because it [the break up of the National Democratic Movement] was really an issue during that time. We agreed that we should only concentrate on the issue of lesbianism and other women's issues, and although we always make it a point to include other political and class issues in the struggle, the individual's political leaning was not impor-tant, or rather, we agreed that we won't bring that into the lesbian organiza-tion. Eventually, it may be precisely because of this political slackness, we weren't able to hold on to the members. The reason why we were attracted to the group in the first place, that space for political freedom, is maybe the same reason that the group eventually faded away.)

After TLC's break up, there was a sudden yearning to continue what the organization started. There was still a struggle to insert the lesbian agenda within the women's agenda especially after the historic reading of the lesbi-an statement in the Women's March. The emotions were too overwhelming to be dismissed simply because TLC broke up. Because of this yearning to put the lesbian into the fore of political discussion and the sincere effort of the public to receive their agenda, members of TLC began forming various lesbian organizations with various lesbian agendas, issues, focus and meth-odologies in terms of breaking the problem of lesbian invisibility. Some of the members formalized the then WEDPRO sub-committee, WSWC, and formed the Womyn Supporting Womyn Center to continue the objectives of the committee. Other members formed the media advocacy oriented group Can't Live in the Closet (CLIC).

In the United States, it was during this time that the historic Stonewall Commemoration[31] took place. Gay and lesbian groups from different states marched in colorful outfits to celebrate this new gender freedom. This was the beginning of the traditional Gay and Lesbian Pride March, which is held every June of each year. In this march in the US, the first Filipino New York-based lesbian organization Kilawin Kolektibo took part in the march.

In the Philippines, it was not until 1996 that the Gay and Lesbian Pride March, which became the Lesbian, Gay, Bisexual, and Transgender Pride March, was adopted and celebrated.[32] But it was in 1994 when news about the growing population of "out" gays and lesbians in the North America and the growing awareness of queer theory, transgenderism, and the gay move-ment, that lesbians and gays in the Philippines started crossing boundaries.

31   Mary Ann Ubaldo, written interview, June 2000.
32   JJ Josef, interview, 25 August 2000.

In a small forum called "When Lesbians Meet Gays," the lesbians who were moving only within the periphery of the women's movement started seeing possibilities of collaboration and coalition with our gay brothers.[33] The forum, small as it was, was an eye-opener for both the lesbian and gay sectors because they were finally communicating and getting to know each other. Josef quotes Michael Tan of the Remedios Aids Foundation,

> Tapos I think si Mike Tan ang nagsabi noon na wala tayong choice. Kailangan at darating at darating ang panahon na kailangan nating mag-work together. Ngayon ia-avoid ba natin yon o kailangan nating paghandaan?[34]
> (I think it was Mike Tan who said that we have no choice because the time will eventually come that we will find it necessary to work together. The question is, are we going to avoid it or be prepared for it?)

This was the start of the lesbian collaboration with the local gay or *bakla* movement. It was June 1996 that the preliminary discussions and collaborations among the gays and lesbians culminated in the First Filipino Lesbian, Gay, Bisexual, and Transgender Pride March which was held in Remedios Circle, Malate.

The year 1996 was also very important for lesbian organizing because of the First National Lesbian Rights Conference (FNLRC), the first nationwide network conference of lesbians in the Philippines was held. The idea for the FNLRC was initiated by accident by two members of WEDPRO who attended the 3rd Asian Lesbian Network (ALN) Meeting in Taiwan in 1994.[35] The Filipino representatives in the said Asian wide networks meeting volunteered the Philippines as the site of the 4th Asian Lesbian Network meeting in 1998. The WSWC managed the conference with the help of other organizations like LesBoND, The Group in Davao, and CLIC in preparation for the 4th ALN. The vision of internal lesbian networking was to tap various regional and multi-sectoral lesbians in the country, ranging from peasant lesbians, butch,[36] femme,[37] factory workers, etc. The initial step for the group was to hold regional consultations in the provinces and sectoral consultations in the urban centers.

The conference was well attended by representatives of various sectors. Unfortunately, and as expected, the direction and discussion about lesbian

33   Ibid.
34   Ibid.
35   Aida Santos, interview, 8 September 2000.
36   Butch lesbians are masculine-looking lesbians.
37   Femme lesbians are feminine-looking.

issue were dominated by the more articulate and more feminist-educated lesbians from the middle class and the urban Manila sectors. This marked the beginnings of a transition period in the language and concern of the lesbian struggle in the Philippines.

The FNLRC played a crucial role in introducing and making the lesbian visible in Philippine society. It was the first time a press conference about lesbianism was held in Blue Café in Malate, a small café owned by John Glenn, one of the pioneer bar owners in the area and a gay icon. During the press conference, lesbian stereotyping was the foremost issue that was discussed. According to Josef, it was a concious effort for the group to present a variety of lesbian looks to the public, from the butch type lesbians or tomboy to the feminine-looking ones, to debunk the stereotype that all lesbians are masculine, "women wanting to be men," or tomboy-looking.

The press conference was covered by both tabloid and broadsheet newspapers. With the variety of the media coverage, a variety of issues and questions were also raised in the conference, from trivial questions on lesbian sex, relationships and lifestyle, to more political questions like lesbian rights, agenda, and identity. The discussion of these issues may have been limited by time and the public nature of a press conference, but the gains that this conference achieved were very crucial to the development of the Filipina lesbian struggle, even if it drew some scandalous tabloid headlines like "Mga Tomboy, Nag-alsa!" (Tomboys Revolt!) As Josef puts it, the radicalness of the idea that for the first time, lesbians were being heard and written about in a political manner, can never be erased. It was also during this conference that it was concluded that December 8 would be the official National Lesbian Day in accordance with the celebration of the Human Rights Day on December 10. It is at this point that we can say that we have marked a struggle.

Marking a struggle

I came into the lesbian struggle in 1997 when I attended the First Gay and Lesbian Leadership Conference in December of the same year. During this late part of the millennium there were changes that occurred in the direction and language of lesbian organizing in the country. I have observed four of these tendencies.

First, the premonitions of meetings and getting-to-know-you activities in 1994, then the beginnings of a collaboration and reaching out to our gay brothers in 1996 and finally the formal beginning of gay and lesbian collaboration in the "First Gay and Lesbian Leaders Conference" in 1997, a number of gay and lesbian organizations and alliances started initiating various activities especially in urban Manila. More often than not, the gay and lesbian issues were discussed at the same level as the encompassing issue of homosexuality.[38] The Task Force Pride March for example, is growing every year in terms of participation by gays and lesbians not only in the march itself, but also in the conceptualization of the whole activity.

Second, lesbian and gay organizing became more geared towards cultural venues and issues such as art and media, and as a result have produced more artistic, media and literary productions that discuss, cater to and produced by gays and lesbians. This change was brought about by the continuing popularity of western queer theory that emphasizes reading popular iconography and culture to root out lesbian, gay, bisexual, and transgender symptoms and language. Moreover, with the growing popularity of lesbian and gay visibility in the country, lesbian and gay theorists started to tap every possible niche they could find to assert queer issues and agendas. Culture and arts were recognized as relatively liberal venues and potentially queer-friendly and so a number of gay and lesbian academics, theorists, and cultural workers started focusing on these venues for asserting the homosexual agenda.

It was in 1996 when lesbian art was first exhibited when Maita Beltran and Irma Lacorte mounted their paintings as part of the cultural aspect of the FNLRC. The formation of the lesbian art community however was only formalized and truly felt when *The Purple Palette* art exhibition was held in UP Diliman in 1998 and *Lesbianarama* was concluded this year. In literature, *Tibok: The Heartbeat of the Filipina Lesbian* was published in 1998.[39]

Third, methodology has also shifted from small formations in various sectors to coalitions and alliances. For example, in 1998 LAGABLAB or Lesbian and Gay Legislative Advocacy Network was formed as an alliance that focuses on the lobbying and critiquing legislative bills and laws that pertain to gays and lesbians.

Fourth, in terms of the theme of advocacy, issues about lesbianism have shifted from the more socio-economic political concerns to that of the post-structuralist idea of diversity and identity politics.

Lesbian organizing

At present, the trend of lesbian advocacy and activism is still very much the same as in the late part of the 1990s. Pride March is on-going, art exhibits are

---

38   Another evidence that lesbians were invisible under the banner of gay male, as a female counterpart of homosexuality [*sic*].

39   Anna Leah Sarabia, ed., *Tibok: The Heartbeat of the Filipino Lesbian* (Manila: Anvil Publishing Co., 1998).

still being mounted and written about, media appearances are still being done, and lesbian literature both in the academic and creative aspects are still being negotiated. Finally, the marking of our struggle as a legitimate part of this political battlefield has been partially fulfilled as our issue is now being discussed, and to a certain extent, heard in various aspects of the society. More and more lesbian organizations, whether or not they have a conscious political or feminist inclination, are being formed in and out the urban centers of the country. Some of these organizations are: WSWC, CLIC, LesBoND, KAMPI, The Group, LINK (Davao), Lucky Guys of La Union (La Union), Bambang True Friends Association (Nueva Vizcaya), Lesbian Advocates of the Philippines (LEAP), UP Sappho Society, SOUL or Society of United Lesbians (Manila), Dykes of Manila (DYMLAS), Filipino Lesbians On-Line (FLO), INDIGO, and LESBIND (Zamboanga). These organizations have contributed to the growing visibility of lesbians in various society [*sic*], whether it be in grassroots organizing, socio-civic efforts, sports, arts, or in the youth sector.

In the regions, one of the strongest lesbian organizations since the formation of TLC in 1992 is LesBoND. This group was a well-known radical, left-leaning group working and organizing lesbians in the Export Processing Zone and various mining companies in the Mountain Province to protect their rights as lesbian workers and as members of the proletariat sector. Through the years, LesBoND experienced turmoil in politics, ideology and status of members, but somehow persevered. LesBoND's primary work is within this periphery of grassroots organizing. THE GROUP in Davao on the other hand, organizes various fund raising and socio-civic activities like workshops and health-oriented projects within Davao City to help the community and to debunk the stereotype that lesbians are liabilities to the society. Other groups like KAMPI, Bambang True Friends Association, and Lucky Guys of La Union hold yearly basketball tournaments for the locals in their respective communities.

In Manila, organizations like WSWC struggle to promote and propagate discussions on lesbian politics, identity, organizing and agenda while other organizations like CLIC and LEAP concentrate on media advocacy. The younger groups like UP Sappho Society, DYMLAS and SOUL, concentrate on gathering and organizing the lesbian youth sector, particularly the middle class students, and in the case of the Filipina Lesbians On-Line and DYMLAS, an internet-based network for young lesbians.

The fact that we are already out there and being talked about is already a big step towards legitimizing our position in this society. The fact that we are already out there and participating actively in the progression of the society whether in grassroots organizing, art, culture gathering, peer counseling, socio-civic activities and politics, it proves that lesbians are legitimate members of the society, worthy of recognition and respect. As Santos put it:

> Hindi naman na tayo kabataan, hindi rin naman tayo katandaan, pero tingin ko kumbaga dalaginding na tayo. Tapos na tayo doon sa paggapang. Naniniwala ako na nakalabas na tayo. Nakalabas na tayo.[40]
>
> (We are not so amateur anymore in this struggle, we may not be as mature though, but we are definitely not amateurs anymore. I believe that the hard ascend to start a movement is over.)

Breaking silence: The history (so far) of lesbian art in the Philippines
It was in 1996 when the first symptoms of lesbian art came into view. Almost simultaneously and in separate venues, Irma Lacorte and Maita Beltran, two of the most prominent lesbian artists in the country decided to become full-time artists. Without even being conscious about creating a category for lesbian art in the country, their works truly reflected bits and pieces of their sexuality. In almost parallel occasions, these two artists slowly entered the Philippine art world through the margins. Although Maita Beltran's exhibitions are widely written about in broadsheet papers and various art magazines, her shows were mostly held in cafes and restaurants only. She has not exhibited in an art gallery or museum. One show that Maita had already mounted is *Out of the Closet, Into the Canvas*, which was a coming out exhibition both of her sexuality and her artistry. While Lacorte has been working her way into lesbian advocacy as a member of WSWC through her art works, because whenever there are cultural nights that cater to gay and lesbian causes, her paintings have always been mounted. Some of the individual shows that Lacorte mounted during this time was the *Pagmumunimuni ng Isang Lesbiana* series which was exhibited at the Blue Café during the FNLRC cultural night.

When I came into the community in 1997, I envisioned to introduce art as a legitimate venue for lesbian advocacy. My vision was to create lesbian space within the art community and vice versa and to carve a space for art in the lesbian community. It was not easy. Given this invisible existence of lesbian artists in the country and the hetero-centric trend of women in the arts, to "break the silence" means to break the thick screen that hides lesbian artists and reveal their flesh, minds, and unheard voices. Breaking silence means to be recognized and say that, "yes, there is lesbian art in the Philippines."[41]

---

40   Aida Santos, interview, 8 September 2000.
41   Eloisa Hemandez, curator of *The Purple Palette*.

The first challenge is to search for "out" lesbian artists who are ready to face the discriminating eyes of the public, but there are very few of them. Luckily, I have discovered both in my lesbian and art journeys three brave women who were in the movement even before I accepted my own sexuality—Beltran, Lacorte, and Tata Lim. These three women paved the way for lesbian art through their numerous engagements in the art field, either by exhibitions or joining art discussions. In 1997, I tried to initiate discussion on the possibility of putting the lesbian as a legitimate category of visual arts when I curated and organized a joint gay and lesbian art and literary exhibition with participation by friends like Lacorte, Joaquin Hernandez, and Eugene Evasco called *Intimations of Desire* at Cafe Coribana in Malate.

The second challenge is to battle the discouragement that my lesbian cohorts and art practitioner colleagues gave me whenever I talked about the possibility of marking the lesbian as a category of Philippine art. As I wrote in one of my articles entitled, "Visualizing Lesbians: Lesbian Art as a Category of Philippine Art":

> When I started this project in 1997, I had only drew grins, negative questions and arched brows as a sign of doubt or even adversity for what I was doing. Surprisingly, even from my lesbian cohorts. More often than not, there is a lack of support from the community because "there are more things to be prioritized than art" by people who are involved in the struggle... and one of these priorities is the basic need to sustain day to day existence.[42]

The third challenge is to find financial support from agencies and institutions that are willing to shell out money for these kinds of themes and projects. Fortunately, in 1998 I found the opportunity to formally launch lesbian art in the Philippines when I was appointed as the Cultural Committee head of the 4th Asian Lesbian Network Conference held in the Philippines. It was this opportunity that paved the way for the possibility of launching the vision that I have been working on for some time. It was in this conference when the Steering Committee gave me funds and resources to come up with various cultural presentations in the course of the five-day conference. I used the funds to gather works by various lesbian artists in the country and organized the first lesbian group exhibition entitled *The Purple Palette*. It was originally envisioned to be a group exhibition of various Asian lesbian artists, but because of time and financial constraints the participation was reduced to the Philippine delegation only. *The Purple Palette* featured works by Lacorte, Beltran,

---

42   Roselle Pineda, "Visualizing Lesbians: Lesbian Art as a Category of Philippine Art," *Natives' Wish*, September 2000.

Ramilo, and Lim. It was also the first collaborative work from various lesbian art practitioners in the country. Curator Eloisa Hernandez volunteered to help me with the mounting of the show. It was also in this show that the academe started showing interest in lesbian art. Art critic Flaudette May Datuin voiced out her solidarity message for the rising lesbian artists from the point of view of feminist/women's art. Most of all, this was the first occasion when the phrase "lesbian art" was mouthed and used, both in the statements of the organizers and the critics, in the Philippines.

The Purple Palette was a turning point in the history of lesbian art in the country for it formally launched lesbians making art and art produced by lesbians as a category of Philippine art. The events after this were overwhelming in terms of response and stimulated fervor from various art practitioners in the country. Other art practitioners and enthusiasts started organizing lesbian art exhibitions of their own. The most recent of these exhibitions are JJ Josef's *Kasali Kaming Kasari Niyo* at the University of the Philippines Center for Women's Studies, featuring art works by Chigo, Briggy, Lacorte, Beltran, Bing Concepcion, and Lorna Ysrael. The others are Hernandez's *Lesbianarama* at Surrounded by Water, and works by Maita Beltran, Bing Concepcion, Lacorte, Ramilo, and Eloisa Hernandez exhibited at Jorge Vargas Museum. *Kasali Kaming Kasari Niyo* marked a very important factor in the development of lesbian art in the Philippines because it introduced several new names in the roster of lesbian artists, that is mostly dominated by Lacorte and Beltran. New names in art like Ysrael, Chigo, and Briggy prove that there is a growing interest in this field. *Lesbianarama* is also noted for its initiative to enter lesbian art in art institutions such as the museum. It was also the first one to initiate formal engagement with the academe as the last day of the exhibition was devoted to a forum between the artists and academics. This was arranged and co-sponsored by the Department of Art Studies of the University of the Philippines, Diliman.

Other venues such as the internet are presently being explored by lesbian art practitioners. In 1998, an e-mail-based Filipina lesbian artist network was established by Ramilo, a painter from New York, and myself. We called it "Pinay Dikya Art Link." We had 30 members from the Philippines and North America for the initial construction of our web site. Unfortunately the link was discarded because of maintenance problems. In the World Wide Web however, a web magazine called *Natives' Wish* has been a regular venue for articles on art and lesbianism. One of the producers, Libay Cantor,[43] is both an artist and editor of said site.

---

43   Libay Lisangan Cantor is a Filipino lesbian Palanca awardee writer and editor, filmmaker, and photographer, who co-produces and co-edits a web magazine *Natives' Wish*.

In the academe, aside from *Tibok: The Heartbeat of the Filipino Lesbian* which was published by Anna Leah Sarabia in 1998 and *Woman-to-Woman: Prose and Essay* which was published by Santos and Villar in 1994, there are a number of published papers on the subject of lesbianism and art. Some of these papers are my own studies on the various aspects of art and lesbianism such as "Breaking Silence" in *Diliman Review*, "Out of the Closet, Into the Dance" in *Philippine Humanities Review*, and "The Nativity of the Dyke" in the *Art Association of the Philippines Ginto Compendium*. *Tabi-tabi sa Pagsasantabi: Mga Kritikal na Tala ng mga Lesbiana at Bakla sa Sining, Kultura, at Wika* is an anthology of critical papers which is in the process of publication to be edited by Rommel Rodriguez, Eugene Evasco, and myself. Other academics who are starting to write on this subject include Flaudette May Datuin, and in literature, the pioneering undergraduate theses of Sharon Pangilinan and Minerva Lopez are very critical and well-written studies on lesbian literature in the Philippines.

Marking a category

The lesbian intervention in Philippine art history should be recognized long before the formalization of "lesbian art" in the country. In a research which I recently conducted regarding "proto-lesbian"[44] in various paintings and prints in late eighteenth- to early twentieth-century Philippine art, I have discovered that lesbian undertones are evident in works as early as this period. Some lesbian tendencies that I discovered in my findings are homoerotic tension in women's friendships, homoerotic tension in women's group activities such as bathing, homoerotic tension in women images as an allegory, cross-dressing, and autoeroticism.[45]

However, lesbian art as a category is fairly young in both the art and lesbian community, and it is true that even up to now this subject still draws negative grins and pessimistic laughter. Nonetheless, it is undeniable that our voices as lesbian art practitioners are slowly being heard and being taken seriously and that we have something to say on this matter. It is only very recently that supporters and enthusiasts, both in and outside the lesbian

44   Proto-lesbian images are images of lesbians before the modern concept of lesbianism came to the Philippines. The term is adapted from Minerva Lopez's conception in her article "Si Nena, si Neneng at si Erlinda: Ang Sex Variant sa Panitikang Pilipino," (Nena, Neneng, and Erlinda: The Sex Variant in Filipino Literature) but the concept was rehashed and revised into my own idea of "lesbian sexuality as lesbian textuality." In this light, proto-lesbian images are considered to be lesbian texts produced in the eyes of the lesbian subject.

45   Roselle Pineda, "Eloquent Crevices: Investigating Proto-lesbian Images in Prints and Paintings in the Late 18th to the Early 20th Century Philippine Art" (unpublished paper, September 2000), 32.

community, started to assert the voice of the most active lesbian art practitioners in the community. Such recognition is important, especially in a context which is bound by cultural conservatism, economic encumbrance, and lesbian invisibility and voicelessness. Art, and lesbian art in particular, is no doubt one of the venues and fields where discussion and assertion of the "different" is welcomed, allowed, and sometimes celebrated. Despite the danger of essentialism and tokenism, we need to assert our identification as lesbians regardless of subject, medium, and language, and despite the risks of appending the word "lesbian" to their art, we need to gather lesbian art practitioners and a body of work that will allow us to establish our own category of art as lesbians.

All these efforts indicate that, while we are at a young and amateurish stage, we as lesbian art practitioners are ready to go out, be visible, and assert and create our space in this field called art. I just hope people are ready for us.[46]

Bridging gaps, marking a struggle: The lesbian struggle and the formation of a movement

The lesbian struggle has existed for almost a decade now. It was in 1992 when we formally launched the struggle through the first reading of a lesbian statement on violence against lesbians in the Women's March. In 2002 we marked our first decade of lesbian advocacy. However, the struggle seems to be moving at a very slow pace and lesbian organizing seems to have stagnated at the small formations that have been there years ago. This is not to say that there were no changes at all in the struggle. In fact, there is a 100 percent growth in the number of lesbians who are out and into advocacy now since its beginnings in the 1980s. Moreover, there are some new groups also that were formed over the last year, like the UP Sappho Society in Diliman, which is the first lesbian organization catering to the youth lesbian sector, and LEAP which included former members of CLIC. However, this does not change the fact that organizing remains to be at a slow pace and centered on middle class and urban lesbian concerns.

This language of transition in the lesbian struggle happened and was marked in the late 1990s, so the direction of the lesbian struggle became more inclined towards urban gay and lesbian concerns. The bourgeois, who has very little, if not no inclination, for grass roots organizing, also dominated the leadership and activism during this time. During this shift

46   The last sentences are taken from my article entitled "Visualizing Lesbians: Lesbian Art as a Category of Philippine Art," *Natives' Wish*, September 2000.

in language and concern, the lesbian struggle seems to have created fissures and gaps between its present status and its origins in the women's movement and the national democratic struggle.

In order for any ideological movement to have a "movement," it is necessary to create a mass base. To create a mass base, one must recognize the mass of people and the concern of that mass in a given society. In the Philippines where poverty is an overwhelming phenomenon, it is inevitable to go back to the issue of socio-economic politics in order to emancipate other discriminations and oppressions. In this country where the majority lives below the poverty line, the lesbian mass must also be living in poverty. Because of these recognitions, the present lesbian struggle must re-think the course that it has been taking for some time now, which is basically urban-centric and bourgeois in nature. How can you organize a mass base when you do not even recognize your constituents? In order for the present lesbian struggle to do this there should be a looking back and a bridging of the gap with the origins of the struggle. It is to look back and recognize the ideology of the women's movement and the national democratic movement, which were the foremothers of the lesbian struggle. It is only through this bridging that we will be able to understand the need to look into the lesbian masses in the country, and to eventually come up with mechanisms to organize these lesbians. Only through the organizing of the lesbian mass can we create a mass base that is not only limited to the issue of sexuality and gender, but cuts across very specific post-colonial subjectivity of class and race. Eventually, this mass base will be the key to the movement that we have been dreaming of.

This "looking back" is not to deem the current lesbian struggle invalid. It is also important to recognize the power of the media, culture, and cross-sexual identity coalitions for the expansion of our ranks. However, there is a great need to recognize the original vision of our struggle. This vision is based on socio-economic conditions because our country is still largely arrested in this overwhelming poverty. We can only emancipate our sexual identities in accordance to the emancipation of our socio-economic condition into a level that would give us the luxury of time, space, and means to freely think about our diverse sexual identities.

It was Santos who pointed out that the key term here is "rights," and people's rights are always "lesbian rights." Until we are able to address the needs and discrimination against the lesbians who are deprived of their right to work freely, without the threat of being fired or being assaulted because of being lesbians, the dream of victory will remain far from reach. Until we learn to engage the mass of the lesbians who are the ones who do not have the choice and luxury of time and money, unlike the relatively privileged middle class and upper class lesbians, the dream of creating a lesbian mass base will remain unrealized. Until we are able to reach out and recognize who we should be tapping to improve and strengthen our ranks, the dream of a lesbian movement will remain to be a dream. Until that time, we will dream and hopefully, reorganize.

BIBLIOGRAPHY

Boniol, Leti. "Closets are Not for Us: Views from Five Lesbians." *Women and Sexuality: Women in Action* (ISIS International Manila) no. 1 (1999).

Calhoun, Cheshire. "The Gender Closet: Lesbian Disappearance under the Sign 'Women.'" In *Lesbian Subjects: A Feminist Studies Reader*, edited by Martha Vicinus. Bloomington and Indianapolis: Indiana University Press, 1996.

Josef, JJ. "Sexual Identities and Self-images of Woman-Loving-Women." Master's thesis, University of the Philippines, Diliman, 1998.

————. "Sexual Identities and Self-images of Women-Loving-Women." *Gender Construction: Review of Women's Studies* (edited by Albino Pecson Fernandez, UP Diliman Center for Women's Studies) 9, no. 1 and 2 (1998).

Lopez, Minerva. "Si Nena, si Neneng at si Erlinda: Ang Sex Variant sa Panitikang Pilipino." In *Tabi-tabi sa Pagsasantabi: Mga Kritikal na Tala ng Lesbiana at Bakla sa Sining, Kultura, at Wika*, edited by Eugene Evasco, Roselle Pineda, and Rommel Rodriguez. Quezon City: University of the Philippines Press, 2003.

Pineda, Roselle. "Working from the Margins, Reaching to the Lesbian Masses: Re-Orienting Lesbian Activism in the Philippines." Unpublished manuscript, 1999.

————. "From Here and Afar: Lesbian Organizations Here and Abroad." *Natives' Wish*, 2000.

————. "Visualizing Lesbians: Lesbian Art as a Category of Philippine Art." *Natives' Wish*, September 2000.

————. "Eloquent Crevices: Investigating Proto-lesbian Images in Prints and Paintings in the Late 18th to the Early 20th Century Philippine Art". Unpublished manuscript. 2000.

Rich, Adrienne. "Compulsory Heterosexuality and Lesbian Existence." In *Powers of Desire: The Politics of Sexuality*, edited by Ann Snitow, Christine Stansell, and Sharon Thompson. New York: Monthly Review Press, 1983.

Rivera, Raissa Claire. "Women Artists and Gender Issues in 19th Century Philippines." *Woman, Take Back History and…: Review of Women's Studies* 8, no. 2 (July–December 1998).

Vicinus, Martha. Introduction to *Lesbian Subjects: A Feminist Studies Reader*. Edited by Martha Vicinus. Indianapolis: Indiana University Press, 1996.

Weigert, Laura. "Autonomy as Deviance: Sixteenth-century Images of Witches and Prostitutes." In *Solitary Pleasures: The Historical, Literary and Artistic Discourses of Autoeroticism*, edited by Paula Bennett and Vernon Rosario. New York and London: Routledge, 1995.

UNIT II

HISTORIES OF SEXUALITY IN PRECOLONIAL PHILIPPINES

Top, *Sayang* ceremony among the Itnegs. Above, An Itneg shaman renewing an offering to the spirit shield (1922, Philippines). Reprinted from Fay-Cooper Cole, *The Tinguian: Social, Religious, and Economic Life of a Philippine Tribe* (Chicago: Field Museum of Natural History, 1922). *Background texture*, The "Bolinao Manuscript," which is a compilation of reports written between December 1679 and October 1685 by Dominican priests of Pangasinan and Zambales, collated on the order of Archbishop of Manila Felipe Pardo, OP, for the purpose of eliminating animist practice in Zambales. The manuscript suggested that male shamans dressed in women's clothes only when performing ceremonies, rather than assuming a transgender identity. Ministerio de Cultura y Deporte. Archivo General de Indias. Filipinas, 75, N.20.

Among various ethnic groups in precolonial Philippines, shamans known as *babaylan* were believed to have spirit guides and to be able to commune with the spirit world. This important religious position was held by women, as well as by men who assumed feminine identity.

This essay was previously published in *Intersections: Gender, History, and Culture in the Asian Context*, no. 2 (May 1999), http://intersections.anu.edu.au/issue2/carolyn2.html.

CAROLYN BREWER

Baylan, *Asog*, Transvestism, and Sodomy: Gender, Sexuality, and the Sacred in Early Colonial Philippines

This pagan priest, while offering his infamous sacrifices, was possessed by the Devil who caused him to make most ugly grimaces; and he braided his hair, which for his particular calling he wore long, like a woman.

– Chirino

The Devil… also chose some effeminate men that they called Asog in ancient times. Ordinarily they said of these Asog that they were impotent men and deficient for the practice of matrimony.

– Alcina

THE IMPORTANCE OF WOMEN to the spiritual wellbeing of the inhabitants of the Philippine archipelago was a recurrent theme in the reports emanating from the quills of missionaries, explorers, and administrators alike from the first European contact with Magellan in 1521 and subsequently during the decades following Legaspi's arrival in 1565.[1] However the reports contained references to some men who were also practitioners in the spiritual realm. Viewed through the sixteenth- and seventeenth-century Hispano/Catholic gaze various representations of these men emerge

---

1   Forty-four years to the day after Magellan's death, Governor Miguel Lopez de Legaspi arrived at the port of Cebu. From that moment, except for the brief British occupation in 1762–1764 [1763 in original—Ed.], the Philippines until 1898 [1895 in original—Ed.] was under the colonial rule of Spain. During this time the indigenous people were educated to Catholicism, but not to citizenship, as their legal status before the law was that of minors. See Edward Gaylord Bourne, Historical Introduction to *The Philippine Islands, 1493–1898*, 55 vols., ed. Emma Helen Blair and James Alexander Robertson, (Cleveland: Arthur H. Clarke Co., 1903–1909; Mandaluyong, Rizal: Cachos Hermanos, 1973, 1: 76. (Henceforth B&R).

in relation to their religious roles, linked as they were to cross-dressing, a more permanent effeminate lifestyle, and/or ambiguous sexuality.

I begin this paper with a discussion of the importance of gender analysis in understanding the role and status of these male/feminine shamans. I evaluate the sources we have about these men in the light of recent theorizing about non-conformist sex/gender roles,[2] and in relation to links between spiritual potency and a possible "third" sex/gender' as proposed by Leonard Andaya in his thought-provoking paper, "The Bissu: Study of a Third Gender in Indonesia,"[3] Ian Wilson, in "Reog Ponorogo: Spirituality, Sexuality, and Power in a Javanese Performance Tradition,"[4] Josko Petkovic's "Waiting for Karila: Bending Time, Theory and Gender in Java and Bali,"[5] and Ramón Gutiérrez in his exciting text, *When Jesus Came the Corn Mothers Went Away*.[6] I explore the potential of this "Indonesian" and Pueblo Indian model, that links sex/gender ambiguity or androgyny with spiritual prowess, in relation to examples of male transvestite shamans in the Philippine situation during the first century of Animist/Catholic confrontation.[7] An important aspect of my

---

2   Peter Jackson, "*Kathoey* -Gay-Man: The Historical Emergence of Gay Male Identity in Thailand," in *Sites of Desire/Economies of Pleasure: Sexualities in Asia and the Pacific*, ed. Lenore Manderson and Margaret Jolly (Chicago and London: University of Chicago Press, 1997), 166–90; Mark Johnson, *Beauty and Power: Transgendering and Cultural Transformation in the Southern Philippines* (Oxford and New York: Berg, 1997); and Sharyn Graham, "The Third and Fourth Genders of South Sulawesi, Indonesia" (Indonesian seminar, Murdoch University, Western Australia, 7 April, 1999); Dédé Oetomo, "Gender and Sexual Orientation in Indonesia," in *Fantasizing the Feminine in Indonesia*, ed. Laurie J. Sears (Durham, NC: Duke University Press, 1996), 259–69.

3   Leonard Y. Andaya, "The Bissu: Study of a Third Gender in Indonesia" (paper presented at the Engendering the History of Early Modern Southeast Asia Conference, University of Hawai'i, Honolulu, 20–22 March 1998).

4   Ian Wilson, "Reog Ponorogo: Spirituality, Sexuality, and Power in a Javanese Performance Tradition," *Intersections: Gender and Sexuality in Asia and the Pacific* 2 (May 1999). An interesting point made by Wilson is that the *warok* tradition was introduced so that men could, by abstaining from sexual intercourse with women, accumulate spiritual potency. In place of women, the warok form close relationships with feminized boys.

5   Josko Petkovic, "Waiting for Karila:Bending Time, Theory and Gender in Java and Bali," *Intersections* 2 (May 1999), http://intersections.anu.edu.au/issue2/Josko.html.

6   Ramón A. Gutiérrez, *When Jesus Came the Corn Mothers Went Away: Marriage, Sexuality and Power in New Mexico, 1500–1846* (Stanford: Stanford University Press, 1991).

7   Mark Johnson provides a brief overview of the historical roots of transvestism throughout the Southeast Asian region, and homosexuality in the Philippines. While his

argument is that I situate the male shamans in relation to their female counterparts and come to the conclusion that the model that creates a link between sex/gender ambiguity or androgyny and spiritual prowess does not fit
the Filipino case.

In discussing what the Spanish missionaries wrote about the male shamans of the Tagalog and Visayan areas in the Philippines, discourses of gender,
sex, and sexuality are blended together in a way that makes their reliance on
one another seem normal and "natural." For purposes of clarity in this paper
I wish to separate them. In the first instance, the focus on gender relations
strategically allows for the explicit demarcation between biological categories
based on genitalia and reproduction, and socially constructed categories imposed upon a sexed body[8] that are both historically and culturally contingent.
As far as analysis of any religious paradigm is concerned, as with all spheres
where men and women interact, I contend that it is essential to make gender
relationships a tool in the analytical basket to more clearly discern specific
links between the construction of gender and social status. However, one of
the pitfalls in discussing constructions of gender cross-culturally is that we are, as
Peter Jackson laments, limited by distinctions offered by "the English terms man/
woman (denoting sex and/or gender), male/female (denoting only biological
sex), and masculine/feminine (denoting only gender)."[9] Even though in the Philippine ethnic groups under discussion these clear-cut distinctions between

focus is mainly anthropological, he does borrow from Garcia to suggest that historically
"the sexuality of effeminate and gender-crossing men, such as the *bayoc* and *baybaylan* ...
was culturally un(re)marked." See Mark Johnson, *Beauty and Power*, 33. See also J. Neil
Garcia, *Philippine Gay Culture: The Last Thirty Years* (Quezon City: University of the
Philippines Press, 1996).

8   Joan W. Scott, "Gender: A Useful Category of Historical Analysis," *American
Historical Review* 91 no. 5 (December 1986): 1056. At this point I would like to acknowledge the contribution of feminist inspired anthropological research and insights on gender relations. For an overview of the evolution of theories of gender asymmetry see
Micaela di Leonardo, "Gender, Culture, and Political Economy: Feminist Anthropology
in Historical Perspective," in *Gender at the Crossroads of Knowledge: Feminist Anthropology in the Postmodern Era* , ed. Micaela Leonardo (Berkeley and Los Angeles: University
of California Press, 1991), 1–48.

9   Peter Jackson, "*Kathoey*-Gay-Man," 167–68.

Currently in the "west" these distinctions are made all the more pronounced by
medical intervention, which tends, by the use of surgery and/or hormonal treatment, to
alter the body, born ambiguously sexed, to conform to either male or female anatomical
norms—with the corollary societal expectation of sex/gender congruence.

sex and gender are not always perceived or apparent, because English is the language-tool of this paper, I use the words, male/female, man/woman, and masculine/feminine precisely as defined above so as not to confuse the issues under discussion. Whenever possible, indigenous terms are employed.

Within European, monotheistic societies, the dualism inherent in the male/female dichotomy spills over into an unequal gendered power relationship between men and women that Hélène Cixous illustrates as man over woman.[10] However, in Animist, precolonial Southeast Asia, gendered categories were differently constituted within discrete cultural settings, which did not necessarily result in the advantage[11] to the male that Cixous's model demonstrates. Indeed, in pre-contact Animist Philippines, there was a bilateral kinship system, women actively participated in the economic realm and maintained control over their earnings, virginity was not valued, "adultery" was not noteworthy, both women and men were 'chieftains,' and women predominated in the spiritual domain.[12]

While, theoretically, I distance the biologically sexed body from gender categories (feminine or masculine) or as Jolly and Manderson put it "natural essences" from "cultural constructs,"[13] the separation of biological sex (male/female) from sexuality is not so clear cut because of the ambiguity inherent in the term *sex*, and neither is sexuality so clearly delineated from gender—a distinction that Spanish colonizers of the Philippines failed to make. As far as sexuality is concerned, Pringle explains how the word sex can refer "both to an act and a category of person, male or female."[14] The ambiguity arises simply because sex can be used to dis-

---

10   Hélène Cixous, "Sorties," trans. Ann Liddle, in *New French Feminisms: An Anthology*, ed. Elaine Marks and Isabelle de Courtivron (New York: Schocken Books, 1981) 91.

11   Joan Eveline suggests that it is a political move to focus on men's advantage rather than woman's disadvantage. As she explains, "the discourse of women's disadvantage reinforces an assumption that processes advantaging men are immutable, indeed normative." She also argues that equal opportunity or "equal but different discourses tend to obscure rather than expose the ongoing production of gender." See Joan Eveline, "The Politics of Advantage," *Australian Feminist Studies* 19 (Autumn 1994): 129–30.

12   See Carolyn Brewer, "Holy Confrontation: Religion, Gender and Sexuality in the Philippines, 1521–1685" (PhD thesis, Murdoch University, May 1999).

13   Margaret Jolly and Leonore Manderson, Introduction to *Sites of Desire/Economies of Pleasure: Sexualities in Asia and the Pacific*, 5.

14   Rosemary Pringle, "Absolute Sex? Unpacking the Sexuality/Gender Relationship," in *Rethinking Sex: Social Theory and Sexuality Research*, ed. R. Connell and G. Dowsett (Melbourne: Melbourne University Press, 1992) 88.

cuss non-gender specific behaviour resulting from the urge to gratify the sexual instinct, or to delineate corporeal sexual difference. "In either case," argue Jolly and Manderson, "it denotes a refractory 'nature' which seems to resist or to escape cultural construction."[15] Foucault also discusses this problem by suggesting that in the socialization of procreative behavior, the notion of sex makes it possible "to group together, in an artificial unity, anatomical elements, biological functions, conducts, sensations, and plea-sures" and then "to make use of this fictitious unity as a causal principle, an omnipresent meaning."[16] While Foucault's comments are constrained by reference to the medicalization of "sex" from last century, it is my contention that the essentialist position which links sex with sexuality, sex with nature, and nature with both woman and nurture, and therefore gender, was imported into the Philippines by the Spanish missionaries in the sixteenth century, who themselves relied on the biologically deterministic philosophies and theolo-gies of Aristotle, Augustine, and Aquinas.

Indeed, the source materials provided by the Spaniards are sprinkled with examples of indigenous constructions of gender that departed sub-stantially from the patriarchal models with which they were familiar. The predominance of female shamans whose role was to propitiate the spiritual realms is one such example of the transgression of Hispano/Catholic sex/gender boundaries,[17] and the male shaman who dressed and "performed" as a woman is another.[18] While the Spaniards always linked the female sha-man with Satanism, they explained the identification of the "male" with the "feminine" with reference to either a supposed anatomical deficiency or what they labelled "the abominable sin against nature," or sodomy.[19] I deliberately avoid the use of "homosexuality" since this was a term intro-

15   Jolly and Manderson, Introduction to *Sites of Desire/Economies of Pleasure,* 2.

16   Michel Foucault, *La volonté de savoir,* 1976, trans. Robert Hurley as *The History of Sexuality, Volume One: An Introduction* (London: Penguin Books, 1978; repr., 1990), 154.

17   Gayle Rubin, "The Traffic of Women: Notes on the Political Economy of Sex," in *Toward an Anthropology of Women,* ed. Rayna Reiter (New York: Monthly Review Press, 1975), 157–210.

18   Judith Butler, in rethinking the boundaries between gender, sex, and desire, stresses the performative component of a gendered identity. See Judith Butler, *Gender Trouble: Feminism and the Subversion of Identity* (New York and London: Routledge, 1990).

19   For a discussion regarding the Spanish attitudes to "the abominable sin against nature" see Walter L. Williams, "The Abominable Sin: The Spanish Campaign Against 'Sodomy,' and Its Results in Modern Latin America," in *The Spirit and the Flesh: Sexual Diversity in American Indian Culture* (Boston: Beacon Press, 1988), 131–51.

duced into the language in the late nineteenth century to refer to people sexually attracted to persons of the same sex. To use "homosexuality" in this context would blur the gender issue, because the "sin against nature," in the source documents, refers equally to anal intercourse between two men, or a man and a woman.

In discussing male shamans in the Philippines who did not conform to normative (by Hispanic standards) masculine gender behavior, I rely largely on two sets of texts. The first group, written at the beginning of the Catholic/Animist interface, between 1590 and 1610, include the anonymous "Manila Manuscript," ca. 1590,[20] and Chirino's *Relación*, 1604.[21] I occasionally draw on material written by other writers of this very early colonial period, particularly the Dominican historian Diego Aduarte[22] and Juan de Plasencia,[23] for corroborative evidence. The second set of documents was written after Catholicism had been a presence in Zambales Province, Luzon, and the Visayan

20   "The Manners, Customs, and Beliefs of the Philippine Inhabitants of Long Ago, being Chapters of 'A Late 16th Century Manila Manuscript,'" transcribed, translated, and annotated by Quirino and Garcia, *The Philippine Journal of Science* 87 (4 December 1958): 430. Henceforth "Manila Manuscript." Because of the colored illustrations included in this manuscript, Charles Boxer suggests that the compiler must have been "a rich or influential man, as nobody else could have afforded to pay the high prices involved by such a lavish use of gold leaf in the illustrations and chapter headings." Boxer also suggests that a layman compiled the manuscript, "since there is a remarkable absence of any trace of missionary zeal, which it would have been very difficult for a friar or a priest to avoid displaying." Given these reasons, the probable owner of the manuscript was Governor Goméz Peréz Dasmariñas, or his son Luis Peréz, who arrived on a galleon in 1590. Luis succeeded his father as governor, after the elder's murder. See Charles R. Boxer, "A Late Sixteenth Century Manila Manuscript," *Journal of the Royal Asiatic Society of Great Britain and Ireland* (JRAS) (April 1950): 37–49, especially 47–48. For a discussion regarding the two Dasmariñases see Carlos Quirino and Mauro Garcia, Introduction to "Manila Manuscript," 330–33.

21   From 1590, the Jesuit father Pedro Chirino spent twelve years in missionary work mostly in Tagalog and Visayan regions where he was "charged with the uncompromising task of planting the cross of Christ where the conquistadors had unfurled the flag of Castile." See Ramon Echevarria, "Introduction," in *Relacion de las Islas Filipinas por Pedro Chirino*, trans. Ramon Echevarria (Manila: Historical Conservation Society, 1969), vii.

22   Diego Aduarte, *Historia de la provincia del sancto rosario de la orden de predicadores en Philipinas, Japon, y China*, Tomo I (Manila: Colegio de Santo Tomás, por Luis Beltran impressor de Libros, Manila, 1640), trans. Henry B. Lathrop, in B&R, 30.

23   Juan de Plasencia, "Relation of the Worship of the Tagalogs, their Gods, and their Burials and Superstitions, 1589," in B&R, 7: 185–96.

islands of Samar and Leyte, for upwards of three-quarters of a century. They include the Jesuit Alcina's 1668 *History of the Bisayan Islands,*[24] written during his thirty-five years of missionary activity during which he studied Visayan customs.[25] The other manuscript was compiled by various Dominican mis-

24   Francisco Ignacio Alcina, *The Muñoz Text of Alcina's History of the Bisayan Islands, 1668,* trans. P. S. Lietz (Chicago: Philippine Studies Program, Department of Anthropology, University of Chicago, 1962). Like Chirino, Francisco Ignacio Alcina was also a Jesuit brother. He arrived in Manila in 1632 and spent thirty-five years in the Visayan Islands, particularly Samar and Leyte. The Jesuits had set up mission stations on these islands during the last few years of the sixteenth century, so the influence of Catholicism had permeated throughout his "resource" area for about four decades before Alcina began the observations which lead to the completion, in 1668, of his remarkable manuscript. See Murillo Velarde, "Jesuit Missions in the Seventeenth Century," in B&R, 44:56.

25   In his manuscript, which provides the most detailed discussion of all the above-mentioned documents, Alcina gives a lengthy account of the male shaman, his non-conformance with masculine gender codes and hints at links with homosexuality. However, his research and observations were centred on his personal acquaintance with one "mute indian" from the pueblo of Sulat in Ibabao, who the people told him would have been a shaman in "ancient times." The name of the "mute indian" was never recorded. (See Alcina, *History of the Bisayan Islands,* 1, 3:214.) Alcina crosses temporal boundaries comparing this man with the male shaman of an earlier period, referring to the years before the arrival of the missionaries and Catholicism when the "guiding memory of the ancestors" (p. 215) would have enriched the lives of the people (p. 214). Nevertheless, Alcina's comments regarding this man are offered in the belief that he has located a genuine shaman as a research subject even though no evidence is provided to prove that the "mute indian" did practice as a shaman. Indeed, Alcina stresses his subject's observance of Catholic custom by stating that he had "heard" the man's confession at various times. Further, although many cultures associate a physical or mental disability as a sign from the Gods, given the importance to shamanism of the chants associated with appeasing the spirit world, it is difficult to imagine how a "mute indian" might have accomplished this ritual ceremonial aspect of the shaman's work.

In attempting to acquire ethnographic information, Alcina was faced with a predicament. For his project he needed access to the "idolatrous" memories that Catholicism had sought to exterminate, while at the same time his religion continued to heap scorn and derision on those memories. As he sought to clarify the sex/gender orientation of his "mute indian," Alcina lamented the resistance that he experienced from his informant and from the Visayan people who he complained revealed information sparingly, especially in matters of what he labelled the "occult." Their diffidence forced Alcina to glean evidence from what little they would divulge, to which he added speculation or guesswork based on assumption and preconception. This report, read across the grain of its ostensible meaning, is important in highlighting problems with crosscultural readings, representations, and practice. It is also useful in verifying perceptions of the gender nonconforming

sionaries stationed in the town of Bolinao, Zambales Province, between 1679 and 1685. This manuscript, the "Bolinao Manuscript,"[26] was collated on the orders of Archbishop Felipe Pardo with the express purpose of eliminating Animist practice from the Zambales district.

Texts that give some indication of the relationship between the female and male shamans are scarce, although the Manila and Bolinao Manuscripts, as well as Alcina do provide scanty observations—some of which are contradictory. When faced with these irregularities I have searched for corroborating evidence from the same era and area. Further, in analyzing the scraps of data regarding these peripheral male shaman figures, it is crucial to keep in mind Foucault's caution that "it would be a mistake to infer that the sexual morality of Christianity and that of paganism form a continuity. Several themes, principles, or notions may be found in the one and the other alike, true; but ... they do not have the same place or the same value within them."[27] Because, the male shaman's voice has been silenced, it is neither possible to discern how these men understood their own gendered subjectivity,[28] nor to understand how other Filipinos perceived them.

The male shamans were variously labelled: *bayog* or *bayoguin* by both Juan de Plasencia[29] and the anonymous author of the Manila Manuscript,[30] *bayoc*

male that are basically unchanged since they were first introduced during the Hispano/ Catholic colonization of the Philippines.

Some Filipino scholars are of the belief that Alcina's *History of the Bisayan Islands*, provides evidence for the existence of ambiguously sexed individuals (hermaphrodite) in the precolonial archipelago. Private conversation with Neil Garcia, University of the Philippines, Wednesday, 25 January 1995.

26   "En San Gabriel Extra Muros de Manila en primero de Septiembre de mil seiscientos y ochenta y cinco años, Bolinao, Zambales," AGI, Filipinas, 75, N.20, J, 1 September 1685. Henceforth "Bolinao Manuscript."

27   Michel Foucault, *Histoire de la sexualité* vol. 2, *L'Usage des plaisirs* (Paris: Éditions Gallimard, 1984); trans. Robert Hurley (Harmondsworth: Penguin, 1986), 20–21. While Foucault remains carefully "objective" in relation to matters of sexuality, it is significant that he unquestioningly used the term "pagan," which is indicative of one who works within a Darwinian evolutionary framework, in spite of the insights of postmodernity.

28   In this instance I imply Chris Weedon's definition. "'Subjectivity' is used to refer to the conscious and the unconscious thoughts and emotions of the individual, her sense of herself and her ways of understanding her relation to the world." See Chris Weedon, *Feminist Practice and Poststructuralist Theory* (Oxford: Basil Blackwell Ltd., 2000), 32.

29   Plasencia, "Relation of the Worship of the Tagalogs, their Gods, and their Burials and Superstitions, 1589," in B&R, 7: 195.

30   "Manila Manuscript," 430.

by Salazar,[31] and *asog* in Alcina's account from the Visayas.[32] Other writers used "priest" as distinct from "priestess" or alternatively they employed the indigenous word for 'priestess' (*baylan* or *catalonan*), discriminating the gender with the addition of a Spanish masculine suffix. They also used *anitero*. In labelling the male shamans I use *bayog* for examples from the Luzon area and *asog* for the Visayas. The most common indigenous referents for the women who performed the role of spirit medium and healer were *baylan* (Visayan), *catalonan* (Tagalog), and the more general *anitera*.[33]

A "third" sex/gender category?

In analyzing the position of the berdache, in sixteenth century New Mexico, or the present day role of the *bissu* in Bugis society, or the *warok* in Pongorogo (Indonesia), various theorists, particularly anthropologists, have explored the link between non-conforming gender behavior of the male and spiritual potency.[34] As Gutiérrez noted the *berdache,* known as a "third sex,"[35] were "biological males who had assumed the dress, occupations, mannerisms, and sexual comportment of females."[36] Andaya has provided a useful theoretical overview of examples from throughout the Asian region in which the male does not conform to "the more conventional sexual and gender dualism of society."[37] Borrowing Gayle Rubin's coinage of the compound

---

31   Vicente de Salazar, *Historia de la Provincia de el Santissimo Rosario de Philipinas, China, y Tunking, de el Sagrado Orden de Predicadores,* in B&R, 38:236.

32   Alcina, *History of the Bisayan Islands* 1, 3:213.

33   There were many other indigenous words to describe Animist religious practitioners. For a discussion on these words, and the changes wrought by Hispanic Catholicism, see Carolyn Brewer, "From 'Baylan' to 'Bruha': Hispanic Impact on the Animist Priestess in the Philippines," *Journal of South Asia Women* 2, no. 3 (December 1996): 99–118.

34   Graham alone mentions both the *calalai* (females who live like men) and *calabai* (hermaphrodites or males who live like women) of South Sulawesi, but in this situation she asserts that it is only the men who are seen to benefit spiritually from their ambiguous sex/gender identification. Sharyn Graham, "The Third and Fourth Genders of South Sulawesi, Indonesia" (Indonesian seminar, Murdoch University, Western Australia, 7 April 1999).

35   Gutiérrez, *When Jesus Came,* 33.

36   Ibid., 33–34.

37   See Andaya, "The Bissu," 10. While Andaya does briefly mention the reverse female situation (i.e., female/masculine), he does not elaborate, nor does he specifically suggest that these females have special access to spiritual power.

expression *sex/gender*,[38] Andaya states that "third" sex/gender groups who "function outside societal norms"[39] have suprahuman powers of intercession with the sacred.[40] He writes,

> The third sex/gender group is regarded as being neither male nor female or of being a composite of both. It is their ambiguous status which locates them beyond the more conventional sexual and gender dualism of society, and becomes a sign associated with the primal creative force.[41]

Andaya provides a list of perceived typical characteristics of such groups, which refers to non-conventional gender behaviour and some sort of anatomically and/or behaviourally inspired "lack." Citing Adriani and Kruijt's study of the shamans of Bare'e Toraja of Central Sulawesi, conducted at the beginning of the twentieth century, he writes,

> They were male priests characterised as being effeminate, uninterested in sex, and of never having participated in warfare. Their penis size, it was rumoured, was only half a finger long. Using a special language they could summon spirits to conduct them heavenward in order to recover the soulstuff which had fled an individual causing h/er [sic] to fall ill.[42]

It is this blend of biology being cheated both by biological "lack" and by identification with the opposing culturally ascribed gendered behavior that Andaya argues enables the priest to gain spiritual potency. As he surmises, the priests occupy a "third" neuter space, "not between a society's dominant paradigm of male/female sex, masculine/feminine gender, but outside it,"[43] to represent a supposedly ambiguous, androgynous or neu-

---

38   Rubin, "The Traffic of Women."

39   Andaya, "The Bissu," 4.

40   Ibid., 4–5.

41   Ibid., 10.

42   Ibid., 4–5. Andaya cites Adriani and Kruijt, *De Bare'e-Sprekende*, 1: 363, 364–65; 3: 38. He also cites other cases: the male Kodi from Sumba, the male basir of the Ngaju Dayak of Kalimantan, the male *manang bali* from the Iban in Borneo who are all empowered to perform the religious rituals by dressing in women's clothing. It is the male basir of the Ngaju Dayak who is said to be either hermaphroditic or impotent; the male, Iban *manang bali* must be "sexually disabled" before wearing women's clothes. See Andaya, "The Bissu," 4–7.

43   Andaya, "The Bissu," 4.

ter category.[44] It is this model of ambiguity between sex and gender that I examine in the Philippine context with reference to both female and male shamans who operated as Animist practitioners in the first century of the cultural encounter with Spain.

Spanish reports of the non-conforming gender behavior of Filipino male shamans focussed on their transvestism, non-conformist (according to Spanish codes) gender behaviour and/or gender identity, which occasioned speculation regarding their "defective" anatomy and possible links to sexual preference. The Manila Manuscript identified "old women or Indians [indigenous men] dressed as women" who perform the *maganitos*,[45] adding that many of these men "ordinarily act like prudes, and are so effeminate that one who does not know them would believe they are women."[46] As well as clothing and behaviour, the hair of the male shaman particularly caught the attention of the missionaries. Chirino noted the clear link between a feminine hairstyle and shamanism when he wrote that the "pagan priest... braided his hair, which for his particular calling, he wore long like that of a woman."[47] Rodriguez added that it was "filled... with a kind of resin or turpentine."[48]

When Alcina was writing half a century later, his understanding of the gendered subjectivity of the 'ancient' *asog* concurred with the sex gender non-conformity offered in the much earlier Manila Manuscript.[49]

44   Ibid.

45   "Manila Manuscript," 394.

46   Ibid., 430. In elaborating, this manuscript suggests that in their "going about " the women "walk very slowly, making a thousand movements with their body" (p. 398).

47   Pedro Chirino, *Relación de las Islas Filipinas y de lo que en ellas han trabajado los padres de la Compañía de Jesús* (Rome: Estevan Paulino, 1604); *Relación de las Islas Filipinas: The Philippines in 1600 por Pedro Chirino*, trans. Ramón Echevarria (Manila: Historical Conservation Society, 1969); also "Relation of the Filipinas Islands and of what has there been accomplished by the Fathers of the Society of Jesus," trans. Frederic W. Morrison and Emma Blair, in B&R, 12: 169–321, 13: 27–217. This quote Echevarria, 25; B&R, 12: 212.

48   W. C. Repetti, *History of the Society of Jesus in the Philippine Islands* (Manila: Manila Observatory, Cum Permissu Superiorum for Private Circulation, II, 1938) 241. This reference is in regard to an attack in 1602 on the Jesuit Father Alonso Rodriguez, the superior of Loboc. One of his priests had stolen an indigenous anito and one night, some men, including a "pagan priest," went to the convent to regain its possession, 12 June 1602.

49   Given the similarities between the Manila Manuscript and Alcina's account it is not beyond the realms of belief to suggest that Alcina had had access to a copy of the earlier document.

He wrote,

> The fact is the *Asog* considered themselves more like women than like men
> in their manner of living, or going about, or even in their occupations. Some
> of them applied themselves to women's tasks, like weaving and cultivating,
> etc. In dress, although they did not wear petticoats (these were not worn
> by women in ancient times either) they did wear some *Lambon*, as they are
> called here. This is a kind of long skirt down to the feet, so that they were
> recognized even by their dress.[50]

Alcina then moved his narrative from the "ancient times" (precolonial)
to the specific characteristics of a "mute indian" research subject who was
known to him. This "man," he wrote,

> was so effeminate that in every way he seemed more like a woman than
> a man.... His dress was even over the legs with a wide *Bahaque* which re-
> sembled, under the *Lambon*, the old time petticoats. All the things that the
> women did, he performed, such as weaving blankets, embroidering and
> sewing clothes, making pots, which is the work of [women]. He danced also
> like they did, never like a man whose dance is different. In all he appeared
> more a woman than a man.[51]

While Alcina's comments regarding this man are offered in the belief that he has located a genuine shaman as a research subject, no evidence is provided to prove that the "mute indian" did practice as a shaman. Indeed, the influence of Catholicism is abundantly apparent as Alcina
stresses his subject's observance of Catholic custom by stating that he had
"heard" the man's confession at various times. (See note 25.) While contemporary scholarship labels men like Alcina's "mute indian," "who have
bodies of one sex and who think of themselves either partially or fully as
members of the atypical gender," as transgendered,[52] the imposition of
Catholicism added a negative bias to their transgender performance.[53]
Therefore, shamans who attempted to live in both the "new world" of the

---

50   Alcina, *History of the Bisayan Islands* 1, 3: 214.

51   Ibid., 214–15.

52   Holly Devor, in her introduction to *FTM: Female to Male Transsexuals in Society*
(Bloomington and Indianapolis: Indiana University Press, 1997), xxv.

53   See note 7.

Spaniards as well as maintaining the links with their Animist roots modified their behavior accordingly.

The Bolinao Manuscript suggests that rather than a complete transgendered existence, the three identified male shamans dressed in women's clothes only when they performed the ceremonies for the *anitos*. These included the seventy-year-old Calimlim[54] (deceased at the time the manuscript was written and who would not have been born at the time of Catholicism's initial foray into Zambales), Calinog,[55] and Mamacuit.[56] The various co-authors of this document pointedly emphasize that these men dressed as women to perform the ceremonies of sacrifice and do not suggest that the transvestism was anything but a temporary "aberration."

Sexuality and the "third sex/gender" space

Thus far I have concentrated on defining sex/gender roles, or as Margaret Jolly and Lenore Manderson put it, separating "natural essences" from "cultural constructs."[57] However, the Spanish missionaries, as did Adriani and Kruijt three centuries later, confused the categories of sex, sexuality, and gender and introduced anatomical "deficiency," and/or "deviant" sexuality.[58] Neither Alcina nor the author of the earlier Manila Manuscript arrived at this latter point immediately, but it seemed to develop through a process of elimination, as they sought to discover any deficiencies or difference in the sexual anatomy of the *asog* that might explain why a male would voluntarily reject his masculinity (which in Spanish codes equated with privilege) and identify as a woman.[59] Alcina and the author of the Manila Manuscript were unanimous in their opinion that "almost all *asog* are impotent for the

---

54   "Bolinao Manuscript," f. 1b.

55   Ibid.

56   Ibid., f. 2a.

57   Jolly and Manderson, Introduction to *Sites of Desire/Economies of Pleasure,* 5.

58   For a discussion of the way these separate but overlapping categories have what Rosemary Pringle calls a "schizoid relationship" with each other, see her superb article, "Absolute Sex? Unpacking the Sexuality/Gender Relationship," in *Rethinking Sex: Social Theory and Sexuality Research,* ed. R. W. Connell and G. W. Dowsett (Melbourne: Melbourne University Press, 1992), 76–101.

59   In the same way, from his 1996 research in Indonesia, Dédé Oetomo argues that a common misapprehension that surrounds gender non-conforming men is that they "are sexually impotent and/or have abnormally small or shrivelled genitals." See Dédé Oetomo, "Gender and Sexual Orientation in Indonesia," in *Fantasizing the Feminine in Indonesia,* ed. Sears (Durham, NC: Duke University Press, 1996), 261.

reproductive act,"[60] and therefore "deficient for the practice of matrimony."[61] Alcina's curiosity regarding the "deficient" genitals of the *asog* remained unfulfilled, since he admitted that the "mute indian," "would never allow himself to be touched, nor would he ever bathe in front of others."[62]

However, presumably to satiate his curiosity, Alcina persisted in his search for an anatomical answer. He attempted to discover whether the asog constituted a third hermaphroditically-sexed group; that is, a group possessing both male and female reproductive organs. In this pursuit, he abandoned his efforts to surreptitiously view the genitals of his subject and turned instead for information to other members of the community who were surprisingly forthcoming in their disavowal of the existence of hermaphrodites. However, Alcina was reluctant to believe them, instead suggesting that "these matters ... are verified with difficulty"[63]—and verification was what he lacked. He pursued the matter by investigating his informant's

---

60   "Manila Manuscript," 430.

61   Alcina, *History of the Bisayan Islands* 1, 3: 213.

62   Ibid., 215.

It is worth noting that this behavior was altogether unusual or worthy of comment, since Chirino devoted several pages to the bathing habits of the inhabitants, in which he observed that throughout the archipelago modesty was the rule rather than the exception. Chirino writes,

> From the time when they are born, these islanders are brought up in water. Consequently both men and women swim like fish, even from childhood. They bathe themselves at all hours, for cleanliness and recreation; and even the women after childbirth do not refrain from the bath, and children just born are bathed in the rivers and springs of cold water.... Through modesty they bathe with their bodies drawn up and almost into a sitting position, with the water up to their necks: being most careful not to be seen, although no one was near to see them. (See Chirino, *Relacion*, trans. Echevarria, 25; B&R, 12: 212.)

It must also be noted that while the Spaniards were not in the habit of shedding their cassocks and taking a bath, they were not averse to enjoying the cool environs to be found at various springs of crystal clear waters where, it is said, they devoted their time to lectures and studying. One such pool was known as Pozo Nang Marunong [pool or well of the learned man/savant/scholar] near Antipolo. In an anonymous book about the Virgin of Antipolo, the author notes that the name of this pool originated from the habit that the original Jesuits had of frequenting the site to enjoy its coolness. See Seminario Central de San Francisco Xavier de Manila, *A La Madre de Dios en al Quincuagésimo Aniversario de la Definición Dogmática de su Inmaculada Concepcion* (n.p., n.d.), 51.

63   Alcina, *History of the Bisayan Islands* 1, 3: 213–14.

sexual preference. Alcina reported that he "heard his [the mute Indian's] confession various times with sufficient indication of his sins, but not a trace in the matter of the sixth commandment."[64] He further eliminated "the sin against nature" with the observation that his informant maintained his distance from men.[65] Given Alcina's "evidence" it would appear that the "mute indian" was, like Alcina himself, celibate.

The "sin against nature" was a topic of much interest to the first generation explorers, settlers, and historians and it was sometimes, but not exclusively, associated with male shamans. As early as 1588, just twenty-three years after Legaspi claimed the archipelago for Catholicism and Spain, the English explorer, Francis Pretty, suggested that Filipino men were so "given to the fowle sinne of Sodomie," that the "women of the countrey ... desired some remedie against that mischiefe."[66] It must be noted that Pretty's ref-

---

64   Alcina, *History of the Bisayan Islands* 1, 3: 215. From a twentieth-century perspective this action appears to be breaking the sanctity and confidentiality of the confessional. However, the privacy of an enclosed confessional was not afforded to the Filipinos in those relatively early years of the colonizing endeavour and it was normal for confession to be heard by the priest in the church—while others who were waiting for the sacrament could listen in. Catholicism and the Protestant Church define the Ten Commandments slightly differently. In Catholicism the first commandment is a conflation of the first two commandments of Protestantism,

> You shall have no other gods but me.
> You shall not make yourself idols;
> You shall not serve them or worship them.

This means that subsequent commandments are differently numbered with the sixth commandment of Catholicism, "You shall not commit adultery," being the seventh commandment in Protestantism. To bring the number of commandments up to ten the Catholic tradition has included at number nine the additional restriction on "coveting your neighbor's wife."

65   Alcina, *History of the Bisayan Islands* 1, 3: 215.

66   Francis Pretty, *The Admirable and Prosperous Voyage of the Worshipfull Master Thomas Candish of Trimley in the County of Suffolk Esquire, into the South Sea, and from thence round about the Circumference of the Whole Earth Begun in the Year of Our Lord 1586 and Finished 1588,* in Richard Hakluyt, *The Principal Navigations Voyages Traffiques and Discoveries of the English Nation* (Glasgow: James MacLehose and Sons,1904), 11: 33–34.

Pretty's construction of woman as the guardian of men's morals was a concept promoted by Rousseau a century and a half later. See Jean-Jacques Rousseau, "Dedicated to the Republic of Geneva," Chambéry, June 12, 1754, in Rousseau, *The Social Contract and Discourses* (London and Melbourne: Dent, 1973), 42.

Left to right, Ignacio de Santibáñez, second archbishop of Manila, 1595–1598, advised the king of widespread sodomy amongst the indigenous peoples; Miguel de Benavides, third archbishop of Manila, 1603–1605, conducted a further inquiry into sodomy amongst the indigenous peoples. Source: *Anales Ecclesiasticos de Philipinas, 1574–1682: Philippine Church History, A Summary Translation* (Manila: Roman Catholic Archbishop of Manila, 1994), 44 and 49.

erence to 'the fowle sin' is reflective of his observance of the Catholic "ancient civil or canonical codes [where] sodomy was a category of forbidden acts,"[67] rather than a criminal action. Contradicting Pretty's opinion that the women objected to "sodomie," in 1598, the second archbishop of Manila, Ignacio de Santibáñez, in a letter to Philip II, suggested that the practice of sodomy was widespread amongst both men and women, although it was not considered worthy of rebuke or censure. From his sinophobic perspective, Santibáñez wrote,

> The sin of Sodom is widespread among them [Chinese], and they have infected the natives with it, both men and women, for since the latter are a poor-spirited people who follow the line of least resistance, the Chinese make use of them for their corrupt pleasures; this curse though extensive attracts little public notice.[68]

67   Foucault, *The History of Sexuality*, 1: 43.

68   Archbishop Santibáñez, to Philip II, Manila, 24 June, 1598, cited in Horacio de la Costa, *The Jesuits in the Philippines 1581–1768* (Cambridge, Massachusetts: Harvard University Press, 1961), 207.

Subsequently, in 1605 when under oath, Father Pablo Ruiz de Talavera gave evidence on the subject to the third Archbishop of Manila, Miguel de Benavides—evidence which reiterated Santibáñez's contention that the act of sodomy was introduced to the "natives" by the Chinese.[69] These two

69   Talavera's case was based on the linguistic argument that there was "no word or name for it [sodomy], until these Chinese came to this country." (See Pablo Ruiz de Talavera in evidence to Archbishop Miguel de Benavides, 15 February 1605, in B&R, 13: 278.) On this point Phelan argues that "the absence of a word does not necessarily prove the nonexistence of this practice [sodomy] as the Spanish sources seem to imply." See John Leddy Phelan, *The Hispanization of the Philippines: Spanish Aims and Filipino Responses 1565–1700* (Madison, Milwaukee, and London: The University of Wisconsin Press, 1959), 186n24.

Similarly convinced, Morga was adamant that there was, in the archipelago, no record of the "natives practicing the depraved and sinful offense against nature or sodomy," although he added that both men and women had been contaminated with the "depravity" through their contact with both the Spaniards and the Sangleyes (Chinese). See Antonio de Morga, *Historical Events of the Philippine Islands* (Mexico: at the shop of Geronymo Balli, printed by Cornelio Adriano Cesar, 1609; José Rizal edition, Manila: José Rizal National Centennial Commission, 1962).

The sinophobia must be read in light of the continual friction and threat of rebellion of the Chinese immigrants. The residents of the burgeoning Spanish city of Manila were both afraid of the Chinese and reliant on them for their marketing and market gardening skills. Moreover, the blame attached to the Chinese can be accredited to the fact that "Spanish observers were," as Phelan succinctly wrote, "vituperative Sinophobes." See Phelan, *The Hispanization of the Philippines*, 186n24.

At the end of the sixteenth century, sodomy was considered to be a specific act, albeit contrary to "natural law." However, Rizal's 1887 commentary on Morga's text is consistent with Foucault's contention that the discursive explosion of sexuality in the eighteenth and nineteenth centuries, generated in large by medical discourse, moved the focus from sin to crime, from the act to the perpetrator of the act, and from sodomy to a specific criminal sodomist. See Foucault, *The History of Sexuality* 1: 38, 43, 101. St. Thomas Aquinas refers to the act as an "unnatural vice," and "against the ordinance of nature." *See Summa*, IIa IIae, 154, 11 and 12. Demonstrating his interpolation into the sexual discourse of his time, Dr. Rizal explicitly refers to "the abominable crime of sodomy." See Rizal's annotation in his translation of Morga, *Historical Events of the Philippine Islands*, 289, n2. Furthermore, Rizal exhibits both homophobia and sinophobia as he defends his male compatriots as well as an absolute disregard of the "indio women" and "vagabond children" whom he situates outside the category "Filipino." He writes,

> Despite what Morga says and despite the fact that almost three centuries have already elapsed since then, [1609] the Filipinos continue abhorring this crime

men along with the historian Antonio de Morga were in agreement that the "unnatural sin" was commonly practised with "facile and unchaste" Indian women who were bribed by the Chinese.[70]

However, in the missionary reports there was a persistent reference to sodomy amongst male shamans. The Dominican Aduarte claimed, from what today would be labelled his "homophobic perspective," that the male shamans were "a wretched class of people, and with some reason despised on account of their foul manner of life."[71] The author of the "Manila Manuscript," in a non-condemnatory tone, declared that *bayog* "marry other males and sleep with them as man and wife and have carnal knowledge"[72]—a statement which contradicts the suggestion that the genitals of these men were somehow malformed.[73] But, there were also examples from Bolinao of male shamans marrying women, which again confounds the "deficiency" theory. Their marriages did not of course preclude the men from having homosexual relationships—a point stressed by Dédé Oetomo in relation to the *reog* of Indonesia.[74] In the two instances in the Bolinao Manuscript

and they have been so little contaminated that in order to commit it the Chinese and other foreigners have to make use of their fellow countrymen, of the indio women who are their wives, or of some wretched vagabond children. (289, n2b.)

70   See B&R, 13:278. In the unlikely event that it could be proven that sodomy was introduced by the Chinese, it would counteract any suggestion that sodomy between males was an essential component of male shaman behavior.

71   Aduarte, *Historia*, in B&R, 30:286.

72   "Manila Manuscript," 430.

73   Reference to dictionaries confirms links between gender non-conforming men and either anatomical deficiency or homosexuality. Blumentritt, in his 1895 Bikol dictionary, provides the definition of *asog* as "name of a type of priest of the ancient Bikols. The *asog* dress as women and they imitate their flirtatiousness totally." He adds that the word *asog* is also the "name of the idolatrous priests of the Bisayas." He adds two references to sexual preference, suggesting "they were priests of a cult of pederasty" drawing similarities to "the camayoas, priests of the Indians of the Guarequa (Isthmuth of Panama) that appear like the asog of the ancient Bikols." See Fernando Blumentritt, *Diccionario Mitológico de Filipinas segunda edición* (Madrid: Corregida y Aumentada, Segunda edición, 1895), 359. Blumentritt's addition of a cult of pederasty, is pure speculation and I have found no supporting evidence in the early chronicles. In Father English's 1986 *Tagalog-English Dictionary*, the shamanistic association of *asog* has been lost. Retained instead are two short definitions, "sterile" and "asexual," which are both linked to some form of deficiency. See Leo James English, *Tagalog-English Dictionary* (Manila: National Book Store, Inc., 1986), 82.

74   Josko Petkovic, "Dédé Oetomo: Talks on Reyog Ponorogo," *Intersections: Gender and Sexuality in Asia and the Pacific*, no. 2 (May 1999), http://intersections.anu.edu.au/issue2/Oetomo.html.

where *bayog* were married to women who were also shamans, the *bayog* readily abandoned the religious tradition of their ancestors for the privilege of heterosexual Hispano/Catholic masculinity. So powerful was the hegemonic conditioning provided by the Spaniards, that these men became expert witnesses for the Spanish inquisitors,[75] giving evidence against their own wives.

To this point I have discussed what has been said, both in historical texts and contemporary analysis, about the transvestism, sexual anatomy, and sexuality of the Filipino male shaman, in an effort to come to some understanding of the sex/gender/sexuality of these men. While many theories were propounded by various Spanish or European writers in the late sixteenth- and seventeenth-centuries in the Philippines, contradictions, such as perceived links between non-conforming sex/gender behaviour, anatomical deficiency, and homosexuality, emerged throughout the documents to challenge the universality of their claims. It could be argued that these anomalies were the result of regional variation, but the author of the Manila Manuscript brings this suggestion into dispute by claiming that "although it is true that in these islands of Luzon, Panay and Cebu there is an infinity of languages, one different from the others and as a consequence different garbs—some very barbaric, others of medium and still others of very high conception—almost all agree as to pagan rites and ceremonies."[76]

Nevertheless, as Andaya put it, the missionaries were adept at enforcing "conformity of the population into… [a] two sex, two gender model,"[77] and it is undeniable that Catholicism itself had a huge impact in regendering the male to conform to Hispano/Catholic sex/gender congruence. There did, however, emerge one unchanging aspect of male shaman behavior. That is, that the minimum prerequisite for male entry into the ranks of shamanism was that he dress in feminine clothes for ritual purposes. Even after other permanent lifestyle choices that reflected a sex/gender ambiguity had been renounced, a form of male-feminine transvestism remained a prerequisite for Animist ritual—as in the case of Bolinao.

What is significant about the *reog* case is that the men seeking spiritual prowess limit their sexual activity to young "feminized" boys or *gemblak*—hence the reference to sex/gender ambiguity.

75   "Bolinao Manuscript," ff. 7b, 8b, 10a–14a, 17a–18a.

76   "Manila Manuscript," 428.

77   Andaya, "The Bissu," 2. While historians such as Costa and Phelan deal with the imposition of Hispanic/Catholic models of sexual morality (i.e., chastity, marriage, monogamy, heterosexuality), they do not explicitly deal with issues involving gender. Given that this area of scholarship is relatively new to the academic stage, perhaps this is not surprising.

The Filipino case

To this point, in investigating male shamans, it would appear that the Indonesian and Pueblo Indian model of sex/gender ambiguity leading to spiritual potency would fit the male shaman in the Philippine situation precisely. Nevertheless there is one other aspect to be considered—that of gender roles. In both the Pueblo Indian and Indonesian situations men were in control of the spiritual spheres. As Gutiérrez explained of sixteenth century New Mexico,

> In a largely horticultural society women asserted and could prove they had enormous control and power of seed production, child-rearing, household construction and the earth's fertility. Men admitted this. But they made the counterclaim that men's ability to communicate with the gods and to control life and death protected the precarious balance in the universe.... Because potent femininity polluted and rendered male magic impotent, men abstained from sex with women for a prescribed period before and after their rituals.[78]

This prevalence of the male in matters spiritual was not replicated in the Philippine case, where it was the female shamans who predominated in the religious realm. Therefore, for the model that proposes a link between sex/gender ambiguity and spiritual potency to be universal and relevant to the Philippine situation, it must also fit as far as the female shaman is concerned. In this case we could expect to find examples of female sex/male gender identification amongst women who exercised authority within the spiritual sphere. This is not the case.

Thus far, in investigating male shamans, it would appear that the Indonesian model of sex/gender ambiguity leading to spiritual potency, proposed by Andaya, Wilson and Petkovic would fit the male shaman in the Philippine situation precisely. But for the model to be applicable to the Philippine situation, it must also fit the experience of the female shamans who predominated in the religious realm. In other words, for the model to be relevant as far as the female shaman is concerned, these women would also have to fit the androgynous or ambiguous third sex/gender group. If this was the case we could expect to find examples of female sex/male gender identification amongst those women who exercised authority within the spiritual sphere. This is not the case.

Antonio Pigafetta, in writing about the ceremony of the "consecration of the boar" that he observed in 1521, during Magellan's fateful stopover

---

78   Gutiérrez, *When Jesus Came*, 3.

in Cebu, made plain the importance of women to religious ritual. Two "old women" were the ritual facilitators: dressing in specific clothes; chanting prayers and dancing; offering food thanksgiving to the gods; killing a pig; anointing the foreheads of the people present with fresh pig's blood (with the exception of the European observers); and then consuming the thank offering food by "inviting only the women to join them."[79] Stressing the ritual significance to this Cebuano Animist community of the old women's role, Pigafetta explained that only women were able to perform this ceremony and that the pig meat was never eaten unless it was consecrated and killed in this way by women.[80]

Indeed, the various accounts subsequent to Legaspi's arrival are quite specific about the fact that in the Philippines the majority of Animist shamans were women whose ranks were swelled by a few males who dressed as women.[81] While statistics were not normally given, the Bolinao Manuscript does provide some idea of the statistical imbalance involved in that community. During an inquisitorial-type investigation in and around the town of Bolinao between 1679 and 1685, the Catholic missionaries listed the names of those from whom they confiscated *instrumentos* used during Animist ritual. Named were 115 female shamans and three males who dressed as women to perform the rituals—a ratio of almost 50:1.[82] Further, both from the lists and the statements collected under oath and collated in the Bolinao Manuscript, it is made plain that the older female shamans passed on "the art of doing sacrifices to the anito or anitos" to the younger women only after they were married.[83]

Returning now to the hypothesis that it was identification with a "third" sex/gender space that gave Pueblo Indian and Indonesian men alike both

---

79   Antonio Pigafetta, "Primo Viaggio Intorno al Mondo," in B&R, 33:167–71. An earlier translation is Anthoyne Pigaphete, "Anthony Pigapheta, Patrician of Vicenza, and Knight of Rhodes, to the very illustrious and very excellent Lord Philip de Villers Lisleaden, the famous grand Master of Rhodes, his most respected Lord," trans. Lord Stanley of Alderley, in *The First Voyage Round the World by Magellan* (New York: Burt Franklin, originally published by the Hakluyt Society, 1874), 97–98. A paraphrased, more culturally sensitive version is offered by William Henry Scott, *Looking for the Prehistoric Filipino* (Quezon City: New Day Publishers, 1992), 126.

80   Pigafetta, "Primo Viaggio."

81   Alcina suggests that "what is generally accepted and least doubtful is that they were commonly women not men." See Alcina, *History of the Bisayan Islands* 1, 3: 212.

82   The Dominicans confiscated, from around 300 named women, the *instrumentos* used for the purpose of propitiating the spirits; mentioned also were three men, who dressed in women's clothes when they performed the ceremonies for the *anitos*. See "Bolinao Manuscript," ff. 1b-19b.

83   Vila, "Bolinao Manuscript," f. 9.

a vehicle into the sacred domain and special potency or agency within that domain, it is my contention that, in the Philippine context, this question cannot be resolved without taking into consideration the complex relationship between female and male shamans. Because of a paucity of data on this subject, and the contradictory nature of what is available, this relationship is difficult to reconstruct. Indeed two of the earliest reports, namely Plasencia and the Manila Manuscript, present conflicting evidence.

The Manila Manuscript emphasizes the auxiliary nature of the male shaman's position in relation to the "priestess." "The function of the priests," the anonymous author observed, "is to help [the priestesses] on all occasions; in general, to help the priestesses invoke the spirits."[84] In a conspicuous effort to elevate the *boyog* from his subordinate role, somewhat analogous to a curate in the Christian tradition, this author seemed impelled to add that in spite of their inferior status, the men who dressed as women "act[ed] with more pomp, ceremony and authority," than did their female counterparts.[85] In other words the Spaniard considered that even though the women were in charge, the men "executed" a more commanding performance of the ritual. This assertion was doubtless influenced by Spanish cultural norms of the day, which equated authority with a male rather than a female voice. Further, the double "performance" of the *boyog* who was required to perform as a woman at the same time as he dramatized the religious ritual, blatantly highlighted the "pomp and ceremony" of the ceremonial process, and, of course, parodied the "performance" of gender.[86] On the other hand, Plasencia introduced an ecclesiastical hierarchy, similar to that with which he was familiar, suggesting that the male *sonat* is "a sort of bishop who ordains the priestesses, for they knelt before him."[87] Plasencia, however, admitted that women were not represented in the sample from whom he obtained information. As he stated, he interviewed only "old men" from whom he "obtained the simple truth after weeding out much foolishness."[88]

84   "Manila Manuscript," 430.

85   Ibid.

86   See note 18.

87   Plasencia, "Relation," in B&R, 7:196. McCoy argues that Alcina "was the first to observe a hierarchy inspiritual powers," but, while Plasencia does not give the same amount of detail as does Alcina, he does note a series of hierarchical structures particularly between the *sonat* and the *catolonan*. Alfred McCoy, "Baylan: Animist Religion and Philippine Peasant Ideology," in *Moral Order and the Question of Change: Essays on Southeast Asian Thought*, ed. David W. Wyatt and Alexander Woodside (New Haven, Connecticut: Southeast Asian Studies, Yale University, 1982), 338–413, 361.

88   Plasencia, "Relation," in B&R, 7: 185.

In relation to documents written after decades of Catholic influence, Alcina is curiously silent. Only the Bolinao Manuscript hints that men were in control of the religious realm, but even then the evidence is contradictory. Written after the Augustinian Recollects and the Dominicans had maintained a continual presence in Zambales province for eighty years, this manuscript conferred the title "principal priest" on two different men, both of whom lived or had lived in the convent with the Dominicans. One of these men had been deceased for four years when the manuscript was collated.[89] The priest acknowledged, though, that this man's sister was in charge of the most powerful Anito. The other, Calinog, was variously labelled the "principal priest,"[90] "principal *anitero*,"[91] "Master of the *maganitos*,"[92] or "Master priest,"[93] by various male *principales*. However, Calinog himself was not so dogmatic and described himself merely as "one of the first [*primeros*] Ministers."[94] However, this evidence must be read in the light of the inquisition-type investigation that was being conducted at the time, when the two so-called "principal priests," along with the male *principales*, had turned prosecution witness for the Dominican inquisitors and were involved in giving evidence against female shamans. Further, according to details from the initial Bolinao Manifesto, many more instrumentos, used in ceremonies of spirit propitiation, were confiscated from some individual women shamans, than from the men who were supposedly the "principal priests."[95]

In spite of the inherent disagreement between these reports, it would be naïve to dismiss the suggestion of a principal male shaman out of hand since, given the relatively symmetrical gender relationships that existed in the Philippine archipelago prior to European contact, it would be hard to

89   "Bolinao Manuscript," f.1b.

90   Statement of D. Nicolas Baptista, "native," 1 October 1685, "Bolinao Manuscript," f. 34a.

91   Statement of Captain D. Gaspar Montoya, "native," 2 October 1685, "Bolinao Manuscript," f. 36a.

92   Statement of Captain D. Francisco Lubao, "native," 3 October 1685, "Bolinao Manuscript," f. 37b.

93   Statement of Captain D. Alonso Sorribuen, "native," 14 October 1685, "Bolinao Manuscript," f. 42b.

94   "Declaración de Joseph Calinog, citado arriba, hedad de 40 años por su aspecto," 14 October 1685, "Bolinao Manuscript," f. 43a.

95   For example, 67 items were confiscated from Da Ana Masanti, 61 from Michaela Samari, while only 26 were taken from Calinog. Of the other two named male shamans, the deceased Calimlim had 18 items confiscated, and Mamacuit 21 items. See "Bolinao Manuscript," ff. 1b and 2a.

believe that an occasional male did not gain spiritual potency equal to that of his female contemporaries. But I argue that in the precolonial period these cases were unusual, rather than the norm,[96] and that it was the influence of the male-centred Hispano/Catholicism that eventually tipped the balance in favour of the male shaman, so that by the late nineteenth to early twentieth centuries, as Evelyn Tan Cullamar suggests, all the *babaylan* on Negros were male.[97]

In the Philippine context at the beginning of the colonial endeavour, there is, moreover another aspect to highlight regarding the thesis that the occupation of a neutral "third" sex/gender space signals exceptional access to spiritual power. While there is no doubt that most of the religious facilitation was performed by women, there is no evidence that women's sacred potency was in any way dependent upon identification with a "third" sex/gender space (i.e., female body/masculine behavior). Indeed, both female and male shamans, for ritual purposes, dressed in clothing that was identified as belonging to women.[98] In the relative gender symmetry prevalent throughout the archipelago at this time, the temporary or permanent male/feminine inversion of the *boyog* served a threefold purpose. It gave the male shaman status and authority in a sphere that would otherwise have been denied to him. It reinforced the stereotypical boundaries of femininity, but in so doing it also, importantly, reinforced the normative situation of woman as shaman. Given this reality it must be argued that spiritual potency was dependent, not on identification with a neuter "'third" sex/gender space,' but rather on identification with the feminine—whether the biological sex was female or male.

---

96   In rare circumstances, even in Confucian China, an occasional woman managed to escape the normal confines of her gendered subordination and rise to a position of supreme power. The Empress Wu is one notable example. In the year 690 CE, the Empress Wu, tired of her position as empress dowager, defied the "natural order" and declared herself emperor of China. In so doing she claimed the title "Son of Heaven," which up until that time had been the monopoly of the *yang* or masculine cosmic factor.

97   See Evelyn Tan Cullamar, *Babaylanism in Negros: 1896–1907* (Quezon City: New Day Publishers, 1986).

98   It has been argued by Lenore Manderson, in relation to the contemporary Thai sex-trade industry, that male transvestites and cross-dressers "perform in ways that reflect their ... perceptions of the feminine," thereby reinforcing normative gender boundaries. These Thai performers are not required to live permanently within the boundaries of the femininity they parody and after the performance they have the option of reverting to their privileged masculinity. See Lenore Manderson "Parables of Imperialism and Fantasies of the Erotic: Western Representations of Thailand-Place and Sex," in *Sites of Desire/Economies of Pleasure*, 125.

Given the exclusion of women from Catholic priesthood, what is particularly noteworthy within the Animist tradition under discussion, is that while authority was normally vested in women, men were not eliminated from the priestly role of shaman, although they were expected to "vest" in the appropriate "feminine" ritual clothing. Indeed, while Catholicism maintained (then and now) an exclusively male/masculine priesthood, the women leaders of the Animist tradition did not feel the need to exercise total control and exclude men from their ranks. It could be argued that this situation highlights a typical tension between what is essentially a patriarchal system where women have to be confined and controlled, and a bilateral system that entertains a largely matrifocal religious system where the authority lies with and is exercised by the woman shaman, who does not have the need to constrain and control the men.[99]

With the arrival of the Spaniards the privilege and social status that accrued to shaman men from actively identifying with the feminine in Ani-

---

99   It can also be argued that an essential difference between the priesthoods of Catholicism and Animism arises from links that are made between the historical Jesus, who existed in a male body, and the iconic representation of Jesus that the male priest embodies—a point that is continually made in some quarters today. Indeed, during my research in Manila, I attended the 8 a.m. service at St. Francis of Assisi, on Shaw Avenue on Sunday, 23 July 1995. This iconic link between the priest and Jesus was made during the service, and used to give authority to a sermon on the Catholic position regarding the forthcoming Beijing Conference on Women. The priest informed the congregation that the words that came out of his mouth were not the words of an ordinary man, but that they were Jesus's words.

A dominant feature of the argument of some of those who seek the continued exclusion of women from the Catholic priesthood rests on the fact that women do not have all the anatomical features (male genitals) to fully represent the Christ. Representative of this position is John Saward who writes that "for a woman to be an icon of Christ is simply impossible and indeed the attempt to make her such would reduce the whole incarnational basis of the sacraments to what we have called docetic transvestism." See John Saward, "Icon of Christ," in *We Still Say NO to the "Ordination" of Women to the Priesthood*, ed. David Chislett (n.d., n.p.), 14. Docetae was the name attributed to those early Christians, labelled heretics, who believed that the body of Christ was not real and had no substance, rather it was phantom-like or apparent. To refer to the priesting of women as "docetic transvestism" is to suggest that while the cross-dressing of women into priestly garb makes them look like priests, it is merely a heretical illusion.

In the nature and/or ancestor based Animist religions in the archipelago, there was no founder of Animism to provide the biological sexual blueprint for future shamans. In this instance biology did not represent destiny, and it was sufficient for a male to outwardly replicate the look and behavior of the woman shaman by dressing up and performing the feminine.

mist society was stripped away. The Spaniards held the conviction that the Devil had, as Arcos explains, "fooled the Indians into worshipping him with *excrements* in place of the *sacraments* of the Church of God,"[100] but they also believed that the Devil was specifically attracted to women. As Sprenger and Kramer pontificate in their 1486 handbook on witchcraft, *Malleus Maleficarum*, "the greater number of witches is found in the fragile feminine sex than among men."[101] Their reasoning:

> Since women are feebler in both mind and body, it is not surprising that they should come under the spell of witchcraft. For as regards intellect, or the understanding of spiritual things, they seem to be of a different nature from men.... But the natural reason is that she is more carnal than a man, as is clear from her many carnal abominations. And it should be noted that there was a defect in the formation of the first woman, since she was formed from a bent rib, that is, a rib of the breast which is bent as it were in a contrary direction to a man. And since through this defect she is an imperfect animal, she always deceives.... And all this comes from the etymology of the word, for *Femina* comes from *Fe* and *Minus*, since she is ever weaker to hold and preserve the faith. Therefore a wicked woman is by her nature quicker to adjure the faith, which is the root of witchcraft.[102]

Sprenger and Kramer did not discriminate between sex and gender categories when constructing their links between what they perceived as the abominable corporeality of femaleness and the proclivity towards the *femina* of Satan. However, for Spanish missionaries, the non-conformist feminised gender identification of the male shamans of the Philippines confirmed that the Devil was attracted not only to the female body but also to the feminine. As Alcina explained, "although their priestesses were ordinarily women selected ...

---

100 Roberto Moreno de los Arcos, "New Spain's Inquisition for Indians from the Sixteenth to the Nineteenth Century," in *Cultural Encounters: The Impact of the Inquisition in Spain and the New World*, ed. Mary Elizabeth Perry and Anne J. Cruz (Berkeley: University of California Press, 1991), 28.

101 James Sprenger and Heinrich Kramer, *Malleus Maleficarum, 1486*, translated with introductions, bibliography, and notes by Rev. Montague Summers (London: Pushkin Press, 1948), pt. 1, q. 6.

102 With the reference to woman being an "imperfect animal" Sprenger and Kramer not only remove her from the category human by situating her in the animal world, but even in that state she is still "imperfect." See ibid.

by the Devil, he also chose some effeminate man [*sic*] that they called *asog* in ancient times."[103] Indeed, Alcina specifically linked the feminine with the devil and he was quite adamant in stating that it was the effeminacy of the *asog* men that attracted the satanic spirits who "chose them [*asog*] for this ministry."[104]

In summary then, I have discussed the gender non-conforming men who operated within the mainly female/feminine sphere of Animist ritual facilitation in sixteenth and seventeenth century Animist Philippines. I discussed what has been written about these men from various sources, highlighting the similarities and contradictions between reports and bringing into question the notion of a prerequisite anatomical "deficiency" and "the sin against nature" as defining factors for gaining spiritual potency. By using gender relationships between female and male shamans as an analytical category, I questioned, in relation to the Philippine situation, the model that claims that it is identification with an ambiguous "third" sex/gender space that provides shamans with spiritual potency. On the contrary, I conclude that in the Animist precolonial Philippine archipelago it was the male shaman's identification with the feminine, either as temporary transvestism or as a more permanent lifestyle choice, that reinforced the normative situation of female as shaman, and femininity as the vehicle to the spirit world.

103 Alcina, *History of the Bisayan Islands* 1, 3: 213.
104 Ibid., 215.

Sangleyes, ô Chinos.

Chriſtiano.   Gentil principal.   Pescadòr con chanchuy y salacot.   Cargador con pinga

Foreground, Sangleys of different social classes in the Spanish era, as depicted in the *Carta hydrográphica y chorográphica de las islas Filipinas* (1734) by Fr. Pedro Murillo Velarde. Illustrated by Nicolás dela Cruz Bagay and Francisco Suárez. Printed by Nicolás dela Cruz Bagay. Photo courtesy of Bahay Tsinoy Museum. *Background texture,* Map of Manila and its suburbs in 1898 by Francisco J. Gamoneda. Wikimedia Commons.

The majority of Chinese sojourners, traders, and settlers in the Philippines during the Spanish colonial period came from southern Fujian and spoke Hokkien, leaving their mark on many aspects of Filipino culture such as clothing and cuisine.

This essay was previously published in *Sexual Diversity in Asia, c. 600–1950*
(London, New York: Routledge, 2012), 127–40.

RAQUEL A. G. REYES[1]

Sodomy in Seventeenth-century Manila: The Luck of a Mandarin from Taiwan

Introduction

LOUSU WAS A CHINESE MANDARIN FROM TAIWAN who frequently visited Manila's Parián, the quarter designated by Spanish authorities for the Chinese. In 1670, the colony's Real Audiencia, or appellate court, found Lousu guilty of the crime of sodomy and condemned him to death. The record are not explicit about Lousu's transgressive activities, but he appears to have enjoyed sodomitical encounters with a number of Chinese males residing in the Parián, and with one favorite in particular. The records tell us nothing about Lousu's intimates, but their anonymity give us grounds to speculate that they were social inferiors and were most likely to have been younger than the statesman from Taiwan. Sodomy in this early modern Spanish documents is variously and vaguely termed as *sodomia*, or *pecado nefando contra natura*,[2] and, as in Europe, the term encompassed a range of pathologized acts that included male–male anal penetration, male–female anal intercourse and other heterosexual non-generative sex acts, masturbation, and sexual intercourse with an animal or a corpse—acts then regarded in Europe as crimes or sins against nature and punished with the utmost severity.[3]

1   I am grateful to Ana H. Callejas, archivist at the Archivo General de Indias, and William G. Clarence-Smith, Peter Boomgaard and Jim Richardson for all their help and encouragement.

2   This term derives from the strongly phrased Latin *peccatum nefandum contra naturam*, rendered commonly as "unspeakable sin against nature," although *peccatum*, derived from *pecco*, denoted illicit sex, rather than "sin." See J. N. Adams, *The Latin Sexual Vocabulary* (Baltimore, MD: Johns Hopkins University Press, 1982), 202.

3   The literature on sodomy in Europe prior to the modern period is vast. See for instance Mark D. Jordan, *The Invention of Sodomy in Christian Theology* (Chicago: Chicago Series on Sexuality, History, and Society, University of Chicago Press, 1997); Franz X. Eder,

Lousu faced execution for committing *pecado nefando* and would surely have been put to death had it not been for a timely confluence of factors:
protests from Manila's Chinese community against his incarceration; the
desire on the part of Spanish authorities in Manila to preserve good diplomatic relations with Taiwan; and the fact that Lousu was the mandarin of
an important man named Pangsebuan, a cousin to Zheng Jing, the "king"
of Taiwan. While Lousu languished in prison, Pangsebuan lobbied for his
release by writing a petition to Manila's governor general that succeeded
in getting his sentence suspended. Beyond these bare facts, little else is
known about Lousu other than he was evidently well-connected and was
well-regarded by his high-ranking and influential master.

This chapter examines Lousu's transgression—the earliest documented
instance yet located of a male–male sexual relationship in the Philippines –
in its transnational and local context.[4] It draws on letters from Pangsebuan;
petitions from non-Christian Chinese who lived in the Parián and feared
recriminations if the execution were to take place; and reports from a Spanish friar advising Spanish officials of Chinese reactions in Manila's Parián.
The data presented here sets sodomy within the wider sexual culture of early
modern Filipinos, within troubled and highly volatile relations between
Spanish and Chinese, within the fragile political relations between Taiwan
and Spanish Philippines, and as part of the record of male–male sexual encounters that crossed all these boundaries.

"Sodomy" in Mediterranean Europe and the Hispanic empire
Early modern Europeans imputed a range of meanings to sodomy—
from bestiality to anal intercourse with men, women, or children—
and much has been written on the repressive climate of Protestant and
Counter-Reformation Catholic Europe, where practitioners of sodomy
and other sex practices deemed aberrant faced punishments that were
typically harsh and severe, in some cases involving torture and death by
burning. Definitions and punishments usually rested on the judgement
of authorities, both secular and ecclesiastical, and in some areas of

Gert Hekma and Lesley Hall, eds., *Sexual Cultures in Europe: Themes in Sexuality* (Manchester University Press, 1999); Kent Gerard and Gert Hekma, eds., *The Pursuit of Sodomy: Male
Homosexuality in Renaissance and Enlightenment Europe* (New York: Haworth Press, 1989).

4   Although largely attentive to the modern period, recent work on transnation-
al approaches to histories of sexuality, in particular the "American Historical Review
Forum on Transnational Sexualities," has been helpful in thinking through Lousu's case.
Essays by Margot Canaday, Marc Epprecht, Joanne Meyerowitz, Dagmar Herzog, Tamara
Loos, Leslie Peirce and Pete Sigal in "AHR Forum Transnational Sexualities," *American His-
torical Review* 114, no. 5 (December, 2009), 1250–1353.

early modern Mediterranean Europe, definitions could be restrictive. Compared with Spanish Inquisitions, the inquisitorial courts of Portugal, for instance, tried "sodomy" along the stricter parameters of homosexual sex. Sodomy was the second leading inquisitorial capital crime in Portugal from late sixteenth to the mid-seventeenth century, during which time 4,500 denunciations were recorded, 450 men were tried, and 30 were put to death. Xenophopia seemed to seal the fate of foreigners in Portugal's courts since most of those tried were slaves, Moriscos, or immigrants.[5]

This attitude appeared to prevail elsewhere. The majority of prosecutions for sodomy and sodomical acts on board Spanish ships involved officers from the lower ranks and foreigners. Ferdinand Magellan, the first European to set foot on the Philippine islands, took a dim view of sodomy and showed little patience toward those who engaged in the nefarious sin during his circumnavigation of the world. In 1519, Salomon Antón, the Sicilian master of the *Victoria*, was found guilty of committing sodomy and, on Magellan's orders, was burned at sea near the coast of Brazil. The second man implicated in the case, and apprentice sailor from Geona, later drowned after being thrown overboard by his shipments.[6]

Mediterranean homosexual practices and ideas about sexuality inevitably shaped Iberian thinking and attitudes toward native sexuality and homosexual practices during the period contact and conquest. Sodomy was viewed as not only a sin and fundamentally evil, but evidence of native barbarism and an inferior level of civilization. Richard Trexler has argued that male transvestism, cross dressing, and effeminacy encountered in the Americas gave rise to a more specific attitude of disgust and condemnation toward passivity, sexual or otherwise, that infused Spanish discourses on conquest and accounts of native behaviors. The passive sodomite, especially one who dressed as a woman and exhibited womanish and effeminate ways, the *berdache*, was thought particularly detestable and abominable, deserving of ridicule and death by burning.[7] In practice, the enforcement of orthodoxy and morality in distant colonies fluctuated between stances of leniency and stringency; the desire to civilize and the compulsion to punish and abolish. Research on the Inquisition in Mexico and Peru, for example, has shown

5   William Monter, "The Mediterranean Inquisitions of Early Modern Europe," in *Reform and Expansion 1500–1600*, vol. 6 of *Cambridge History of Christianity*, ed. R. Po Chia Hsia (Cambridge: Cambridge University Press, 2007), 300–1.

6   Federico Garza Carvajal, *Butterflies Will Burn: Prosecuting Sodomites in Early Modern Spain and Mexico* (Austin: University of Texas Press, 2003), 91.

7   Richard C. Trexler, *Sex and Conquest: Gendered Violence, Political Order, and the European Conquest of the Americas* (Cambridge: Polity Press, 1995), 170.

the dilatory, cautious or confusing enforcement of orthodoxy and the jurisdiction of the Holy Office over an indigenous populace whose recent conversion to the Catholic faith, and comprehension of that faith, was continuously and fiercely debated.[8] Church morality and Spanish ideas of sex and
sexuality were often areas of unrelenting conflict and struggle between the
Spanish friar and his freshly baptized flock. The mid-sixteenth-century Yucatec Maya, for example, found ways of preserving long-standing beliefs and
practices by circumventing, or even undermining, missionary impositions
and deftly manipulating Church teaching to their own advantage.[9] Punishment, if enforced at all, might come only after a protracted trial fought by
religious and secular ambiguity and disorder.[10]

Naming, describing, denouncing

As in the Americas, Spanish ecclesiastics in the Philippines endeavoured
to root out the sin of non-procreative sex through conversion to Catholicism and within the confessional. According to Carolyn Brewer, the sacrament of confession enabled indigenous sexual practices and mores to be
clearly identified and demonized by the Spanish Catholic priest, who, in
assuming authority over sexual discourse, sought to eventually produce
the "self-policing subject"—whose conversion to the Catholic faith was
developed, sincere and absolute.[11] Vicente Rafael has drawn attention to
the relentlessly interrogative and often prurient of tone of confessional
questions related to illicit sex acts between men and women that would
have assailed the sensitivities of the native listener.[12] What is also to be

---

8   See for instance, Richard E. Greenleaf, "The Inquisition and the Indians of New
Spain: A Study in Jurisdictional Confusion," *The Americas* 22, no. 2 (October 1965): 138–
66; Richard E. Greenleaf, *The Mexican Inquisition of the Sixteenth Century* (Albuquerque:
University of New Mexico Press, 1969); Henry Charles Lea, *The Inquisition in the Spanish
Dependencies* (New York: Macmillan, 1908).

9   John F. Chuchiak IV, "The Sins of the Fathers: Franciscan Friars, Parish Priests,
and the Sexual Conquest of the Yucatec Maya, 1564–1808," *Ethnohistory* 54, no. 1 (Winter
2007): 69–129.

10   Zeb Tortorici, "'Heran Todos Putos': Sodomitical Subcultures and Disordered
Desire in Early Colonial Mexico," *Ethnohistory* 54, no. 1. (Winter 2007): 35–69. For a discussion on sodomy and the sexuality of native Americans at the time of conquest, see Francisco
M. Berroa Ubiera, "Los indios y el pecado nefando," *Boletín Museo del Hombre Dominicano*
28, no. 29 (2001): 103–18.

11   Carolyn Brewer, *Shamanism, Catholicism and Gender Relations in Colonial Philippines, 1521–1685* (Aldershot: Ashgate, 2004), 66–69.

12   Vicente L. Rafael's examination of eighteenth-century confessional manuals and,
more broadly, Manila's developing print culture, had laid emphasis on the role of language,

pointed out is the sheer range of sex acts, sexual behavior and play that came to be detailed as priests sought to name, describe, define and attach what they thought to be the vernacular equivalent to Western terms, given either in Castilian or Latin—a linguistic process that identified, specified, censured and denounced acts and behavior judged to be transgressive and immoral. The confessional manual and *Arte de la lengua tagala* by Fray Sebastian de Totanes, published in 1745, included lengthy questions on sex acts with animals,[13] the ingestion of aphrodisiacs and erotic gratification with "your fellow man, in the manner of a woman" (*capouamo lalaqui, cun babaye*).[14] It dwelt on such activities as bathing together, showing naked bodies, masturbation (described as touching *naghihipoan*), carnal play (*nagbibiroan* and *pinalaroan*) with one's own and each other's body parts, speaking lustfully and to arouse sexual desire, and ejaculation, literally rendered here as release of "filth" from the body to the "outside" (*labas*):

> Did filth come out of you? Did you perhaps draw it out from your playfellow? (*At nalabasan ca ng marumi? Cun pinalalabasanmo ang manga cabiroanmo?*)[15]

If ejaculate was translated by Totanes as "filth," Juan de Noceda and Pedro de Sanlucar, compilers of the *Vocabulario* of the Tagalog language, published in 1754, provided two Tagalog terms for male semen, *tubor* and *lamor* respectively, for the given Latin terms *semen naturae* and *semen*. "Sodomy," referred to as *peccatum nefandum*, was curiously translated using the rather coy term *socob*, rendered euphemistically in Castilian as *Poner una cosa debaxo* [sic] *de otra, dormir dos debaxo de una manta* ('Put one thing under another, two sleep under one blanket'); and *sobsob* translated in Castilian as *potrarse de hinojos*, which in English might be translated as

---

specifically linguistic difference and the working of linguistic translation in the process of Catholic conversion and the nature of Tagalog submission to Spanish colonialism. Vicente L. Rafael, *Contracting Colonialism: Translation and Christian Conversion in Tagalog Society under Early Spanish Rule* (Durham, NC: Duke University Press, 1993), 91–108.

13   A sample question concerning bestiality from Totanes's confessional manual is "At mey guinauaca caya anomang cahalayan sa alin mang hayop?" ("And did you do anything lewd to any kind of animal?"). Fray Sebastian de Totanes, *Arte de la lengua tagala y manual tagalog para la administración de los santos sacramentos* (Manila: Nra. Sra. De Loreto en el pueblo de Sampaloc, 1745), 147.

14   Ibid., 144.

15   Ibid., 143–46.

"prostrate on their knees."[16] Published a few decades earlier, the Visayan *vocabulario* by Matheo Sanchez directly associated the word *libug*, the term for "sexual lust" in both Tagalog and Visayan, with both adultery and copulation between native Visayan and Chinese *(Sangley)*, even indicating the resulting offspring *El mestizo de Sangley y Bisaya.*[17] Evidently, in the minds of priests at least, the sexual appetite of both Visayans and Chinese could be thought of as a synonym for *libug.*

The sexual preferences of "third sex/gender groups,"[18] individuals possessed of male genitalia and gendered female, aroused both the curious interest and ire of priests who described them as "effeminates" *(afeminado)* and understood them to be men who were treated as women and took on the appearance of women.[19] Known variously as *asog, bayog,* or *bayoguin* in the Visayas and the Tagalog-speaking areas of Luzon, third sex/gender individuals were typically native, male-bodied transvestite or transgendered ritual specialists once common in many parts of Southest Asia.[20] Indigenous male shamans–male animist ritual leaders who appropriated the dress and behavior of their spiritually powerful female counter-parts, the *baylan* and the *catalona*—it was thought, not only perpetuated heretical animist beliefs but also engaged in the heinous crime of sodomy. Male shamans, Spanish missionaries observed, were hermaphrodites and were believed by the natives to gain spiritual potency by assuming the clothing, mannerisms and occupations of women. Effeminate behavior and transvestism were not always

16   This is the first time a vernacular translation of *peccatum nefandum* has been given. Earlier translations and in other indigenous languages have yet to be found. Juan de Noceda and Pedro de Sancular, *Vocabulario de la lengua tagala* (Manila: Imprenta de la Compañia de Jesús por Nicolas de la Cruz Bagay, 1754), n.p.

17   Matheo Sanchez, *Vocabulario de la lengua bisaya* (Manila: Colegio de la sagrada Compañia de Jesús; por D. Gaspar Aquino de Belen, 1711), n.p.

18   The term is owed to Leonard Andaya, "The Bissu: A Study of a Third Gender in Indonesia," in *Other Pasts: Women, Gender, and History in Early Modern Southeast Asia* (Honolulu: Center for Southeast Asian Studies, University of Hawaii Press, 2000), 27–46 ; and also Christian Pelras, *The Bugis* (Oxford: Blackwell, 1996).

19   Matheo Sanchez, *Vocabulario de la lengua bisaya,* n.p.

20   For general discussion on gender and ritual specialists in Southeast Asia and the Philippines in early modern and contemporary times see Barbara Andaya, "The Change Religious Role of Women in Pre-Modern Southeast Asia," *South East Asia Research* 2, no. 2 (1994), 99–116; Neil Garcia, *Philippine Gay Culture: Binabae to Bakla, Silahis to MSM* (Quezon City: University of the Philippines Press,[1996] 2008); Mark Johnson, *Beauty and Power: Transgendering and Cultural Transformation in the Southern Philippines* (London: Berg, 1997); and Fenella Canell, *Power and Intimacy in the Christian Philippines* (Cambridge: Cambridge University Press, 1999).

adopted permanently; some shamans would not allow others to touch them, nor would they bathe in view of others.[21]

Another native sexual practice associated, though somewhat tenuously, with sodomy was penis piercing. Viewed by sixteenth-century Europeans as uniquely and spectacularly savage, piercing the penis and inserting into it a pin made from wood, ivory, gold or other metals, to which was appended a variety of star-shaped spiked cog-like wheels and spur-like protrusions, was common to the Tagalogs and the Visayans, who referred to the pins and wheels as *tugbuk* and *sakra*.[22] Ostensibly used for the purpose of giving women greater sexual stimulation and pleasure, penile inserts were judged by Spanish missioners to exceed even sodomy in depravity and wickedness. Some Europeans, however, linked penis piercing to the prevention of sodomy. The English corsair Thomas Cavendish, while stalking the coasts of Samar in 1588 on the look-out

21   Carolyn Brewer, "*Baylan, Asog*, Transvestism, and Sodomy: Gender, Sexuality, and the Sacred in Early Colonial Philippines," *Intersections: History and Culture in the Asian Context*, no. 2 (May 1999): 10, accessed 30 November 2009, http://intersections. anu.edu.au/issue2/carolyn2.html. Brewer dismisses any link between the ambiguous gender identity and homosexuality of the Filipino *asog* and *bayoguin* and their spiritual prowess, a connection which has often defined other transvestite male ritual practitioners of different societies, particularly the *berdache* of sixteenth-century New Mexico and the *bissu* of the Bugis peoples of south Sulawesi, Indonesia. Donn V. Hart makes a similar point in relation to contemporary homosexuality and transvestism amongst the effeminate male *bayot* and *lakin-on* of southern Negros in the Visayas. Interestingly, Hart writes that the local term for pederasty and homosexual anal intercourse practiced by the *bayot* is *oros* or "Chinese kick" in reference to the traditional understanding that the Chinese introduced sodomy to Filipinos. Donn V. Hart, "Homosexuality and Transvestism in the Philippines: The Cebuan Filipino Bayot and Lakin-on," *Behavioral Science Notes* 3, no. 4 (1969): 230–31. George Weightman, similarly, observe that the stereotyped views of Chinese as "licentious infidels" and "sodomists" continues to inform anti-Sinicism in the Philippines. George H. Weightman, "Anti-Sinicism in the Philippines," *Asian Studies* 5, no. 2 (1967): 228.

22   For secondary literature on the phenomenon see in particular William Henry Scott, *Barangay: Sixteenth-Century Philippines Culture and Society* (Manila: Ateneo de Manila University Press, 1994), 24. For other contemporary analyses of penis piercing see Donald E. Brown, James W. Edwards and Ruth P. Moore, eds., *The Penis Inserts of Southeast Asia: An Annotated Bibliography with an Overview and Comparative Perspectives*, Center for Southeast Asia Studies Occasional Papers Series 15 (Berkeley: University of California Press, c. 1988), 29–60. More recently, Linda Newson has discussed the practice in relation to fecundity and its negative impact on fertility in her book, *Conquest and Pestilence in the Early Spanish Philippines* (Honolulu: University of Hawai'i Press, 2009), 59–60.

for Spanish galleons,[23] spied the phenomenon in Capul Island amongst Visayan men and male children, motivating him to remark:

> This custome was granted at the request of the women of the country, who finding their men to be given to the fowle sinne of Sodomie, desired some remedie against that mischief.[24]

Late sixteenth- and early seventeenth-century records on the Inquisitions in the Philippines (which was established as a district of the Mexican Inquisition, itself a branch of the Spanish Inquisition) show that a wide range of people resident in the colony—Spaniards, the clergy, "mulattos" and Middle Easterners, most notably Armenians—were readily investigated for crimes against the faith: Protestantism, Judaism, other blasphemous and heretical practices, witchcraft, sorcery, and sexual immorality. However, *indios,* the designated term for native inhabitants of the Philippines, were specifically excluded from the inquisition's jurisdiction. This followed the policy of exemption applied to the Indians of Mexico.[25]

In the early decades of Spanish rule, official policy toward Manila's migrant and sojourning *Sangleys,* especially those suspected of engaging in *pecado nefando,* was not entirely clear. Melchor Dávalos, an *oidor* or judge assigned to Manila by Philip II, wrote in 1584 appealing to the king to issue guidelines as to the sort of punishment that should be meted out to those Chinese who, reportedly, committed sodomy on board their ships: "I am studying this topic in order to give notice to this Audiencia [Tribunal]," he reflected. He had also been disturbed by the complaint that the Chinese were insincere and opportunistic in their conversion to Catholicism: "Some [friars] tell me that they don't want to baptize [Chinese] because they are

---

23   William Lytle Schurz, *The Manila Galleon* (New York: Dutton, 1959), 310.

24   Thomas Cavendish in Francis Pretty, "The Admirable and Prosperous Voyage of the Worshipfull Master Thomas Candish [Cavendish] . . . Round about the Whole Earth, Begun in the Yeere of our Lord 1586, and Finished in 1588," in *The Principal Navigations Voyages Traffiques and Discoveries of the English Nation Made by Sea or Over-land to the Remote and Farthest Distant Quarters of the Earth at any Time within the Compasse of these 1600 Yeeres* by Richard Haklyut (Glasgow: James MacLehose and Son, 1904), 332–33.

25   F. Delor Angeles, "The Philippine Inquisition: A Survey," in *The Pacific World: Land, Peoples, and History of the Pacific, 1500–1900,* vol. 17 of *Religions and Missionaries around the Pacific, 1500–1900,* ed. Tanya Storch (Aldershot: Ashgate Variorum, 2006), 129–35. On the persecution of Armenians see F. Delor Angeles, "Armenians before the Philippine Inquisition," *Silliman Journal* 28, no. 3–4 (1981): 113–21.

certain to deny it when they return to their country."[26] By the following year, Dávalos was ready to adopt a firm stance concerning "gentiles, idolators, and sinners against the law of nature." In addition to writing a strongly worded recommendation to evict and expel all Muslims from the Philippine archipelago, or at least "subject them and make them pay tribute,"[27] Dávalos came up with a series of ordinances and prohibitions concerning "idolatry and sodomy," 36 points in all, that dealt with a host of offenses and were meant "to make said unbelievers and those who are converted to Catholicism understand that they are our vassals, and that we have spent our treasures for the salvation for their souls."[28] Point 15 stipulated that the "baptized *indio* or not baptized who eats humans flesh, or commits the sin of sodomy against nature, is to be arrested and sent to the royal prison."[29]

Three years later, persons found guilty of sodomy were being sentenced to death by fire. The fiscal of the Audiencia, Gaspar de Ayala, writing to King Philip II in 1588, reported that a group of Chinese, 14 or 15 in number, accused of "sodomy and much evil and corruption" were taken aback by the severity of the punishment to befall them and, pleading ignorance, claimed that the crime with which they were accused was far from serious in their own country. Spanish officials, however, would have none of it. Public notices in Chinese were put up throughout the Chinese quarter with the warning that the offense was punishable by death at the stake and confiscation of property. As Gaspar de Ayala related, two of the accused Chinese were burnt to death and the others flogged and thrown into the galleys.[30]

Pressure to punish crimes of sodomy continued unabated in ensuing years. In 1598, Fray Ignacio de Santibáñez, the first Archbishop of Manila, alarmed at the prevalence of sodomitical practices amongst Manila's Chinese, thought it necessary to establish the Inquisition for them.[31] The following year, a royal decree (*real cedula*) sought to regulate the resident *Sangleys* and to "do justice to *sangleyes* who committed sodomy." The Chinese (and any others) were forbidden to practice the "abominable sin

26   Letter from Melchor Dávalos to Philip II, Manila 3 July 1584. Archivo General de Indias (AGI), Filipinas, 18A, R.2, N.9, Fol. 10.

27   Melchor Dávalos cited in Geoffrey Parker, "David or Goliath?: Philip II and his World in the 1850s," in *Spain, Europe, and the Atlantic: Essays in Honour of John H. Elliot* ed. Richard L. Kagan and Geoffrey Parker (Cambridge: Cambridge University Press, 1995), 255.

28   Melchor Dávalos to Philip II, 20 June 1585. AGI Filipinas 18A, R.3, N.19. C.

29   Ibid.

30   Gaspar de Ayala to Philip II, 20 June 1588. AGI, Filipinas 18A, R.6, N.36.

31   Ignacio de Santebáñez to Philip II, 24 June 1598. AGI, Filipinas, 74, N.42.

against nature" or try to commit it on the penalty of being burned alive and the confiscation of property.[32] Neither could any *Sangley* cohabit with any Christian woman, the penalty for which was 200 lashes, 10 years in the galleys, and the confiscation of half of his property.[33] Spanish soldiers garrisoned in the Spanish fort at Terranate (Ternate) in the Maluku islands did not escape the judgement. An official holy edict condemning *el pecado nefando* provoked a riot amongst soldiers to the point of mutiny. On the advice of Pedro de Heredia, the Spanish governor stationed on the island, 120 rioting soldiers were imprisoned and the ringleaders, who confessed to conspiracy and sodomy, were garroted and burnt.[34]

Sodomy and Chinese–Spanish relations

The supposed Chinese penchant for sodomy joined a long litany of other allegations and accusations, from gambling to greed and gluttony, which Spaniards regularly leveled against a community they observed to be growing materially prosperous and procreating at an alarming rate, and upon which Europeans depended for even the most basic of necessities. Confidential correspondence between Philip II and Archbishop Santibáñez of Manila reveals a host of European impressions, perceptions and imaginings about the Chinese. Santibáñez accused the Chinese, and most especially the resident non-Christian Chinese, of both gluttony and sodomy.[35] Worse still, he informed the King, they were contaminating the native inhabitants with their infidel vices:

> It is great hindrance to the growth of the faith and morals of the natives that there is a continual communication with the infidel Chinese ... In the first place, on account of their greed, they have taken to the cultivation of gardens and other real estate; whence it follow that all the native Indians live idle and vicious lives without anyone urging them to labour ... besides being retailers and hucksters, one Chinaman uses more food and wine than

32   Real Cedula, 22 June 1599. AGI, Filipinas, 329, L, 1, F. 15v-16r.

33   Ibid.

34   11 October 1636. AGI, Filipinas, 330, L. 4, F. 16r–21v; 6 November 1636. AGI, Filipinas 330, L. 4., F. 21v–23r.

35   See for example Edgar Wickberg, *The Chinese in Philippine Life, 1850–1898* (Quezon City: Ateneo de Manila University Press, 2000 [1965]); Alfonso Felix Jr., *The Chinese in the Philippines*, 2 vols. (Manila: Solidaridad Publishing House, 1966–1969); Margaret Wyant Horsley, "Sangley: The Formation of Anti-Chinese Feeling in the Philippines—A Cultural Study of the Stereotypes of Prejudice" (PhD diss., Columbia University, 1950).

do four natives. What is worse than this is that the crime against nature is as prevalent among them as in Sodom; and they practice it with the natives, both men and women. As the latter are poor wretches and lovers of gain, and the Chinese are generous in paying for their pleasures, this calamity is spreading wide without any public manifestation.[36]

By the end of the sixteenth-century approximately 20,000 to 30,000 Chinese, mostly single males, lived in Manila, far outnumbering the 2,000 or 3,000 Spaniards.[37] On the one hand, the Spaniards recognized that the Chinese were indispensable to the economy of the colony, as farmers, unskilled laborers, craftsmen, storekeepers, cooks, and servants. On the other hand, they monopolized all manner of trades and occupations, and, it was thought, remitted the considerable wealth they had generated back to China. Most worryingly, their unwillingness, ambivalence or opportunistic attitude to Catholic conversion meant that their political loyalties would always remain suspect.

Fear of the numerical dominance of the Chinese and the possibility of an invasion assisted or even instigated by China greatly influenced Spanish attitudes, policies, and response to Manila's Chinese. Residential segregation and periodic expulsions—tactics and policies used in the Peninsula in relation to the Moors and Jews, who presented similarly intractable but economically necessary communities[38]—exacerbated the tensions between the authorities and the Chinese migrants. Backed by expulsion laws issued from Spain, secular officials were wont to act as they saw fit in curtailing the numbers of Chinese and their power in the cabildo, or municipal government. Writing to the king in 1597, Francisco Tello, the Spanish Governor General, reported:

> Considering the troubles that might result, and the large numbers of Sangleys here . . . I took away their power in the administration . . . I have expelled from this land a large number . . . and I shall soon order many

36   Letter of Archbishop Ignacio Santibáñez to Felipe II, 4 June 1598, in *The Philippine Islands, 1493–1898*, ed. Emma H. Blair and James A. Robertson (Cleveland: A. H. Clark, 1903–1907), 10: 149.

37   Edgar Wickberg, "Anti-Sinicism and Chinese Identity Options in the Philippines," in *Essential Outsiders: Chinese and Jews in the Modern Transformation of Southeast Asia and Central Europe,* ed. Daniel Chirot and Anthony Reid (Seattle: University of Washington Press, 1997), 155.

38   Anthony Reid, "Entrepreneurial Minorities, Nationalism and the State," in *Essential Outsiders,* 45–71.

others to go, leaving only three or four thousand men, who are necessary for the service of the land.[39]

By early August 1597 Tello had expelled over 8,000 Chinese "in order that those who are not needed may return to their own country, [because] they teach the natives very evil customs."[40] Antonio de Morga, lawyer and lieutenant governor of the Philippines, reinforced Tello's actions, remarking:

> It is necessary to rigorously restrict the Chinese from going about as they now do . . . and imparting many bad habits and sins to the natives. It would be very advantageous forcibly to eject all the Sangleys who are scattered throughout the islands.[41]

Later, after living in the country for almost a decade, Morga more explicitly voiced his disgust toward sodomy, which he regarded as a particularly reprehensible sexual habit and, interestingly, he attributed not only to the Chinese but also to his fellow Spaniards. In 1609 he observed:

> All the time that the natives lived in a heathen condition there is no record of their having fallen into the unmentionable sin against nature, but men and women alike have caught something of the disease through their contact with the Spaniards who have since come to their land and, still more, through contact with the Sangleyes who have come hither from China, and who are greatly given to this vice.[42]

One Spanish cleric, the Jesuit priest Ignacio Francisco Alcina, ventured to say that some Spaniards were not content with *Venus ordinaria*, that is, normative penile–vaginal sexual intercourse, but he appears to have been alone in this opinion.[43]

39   Letter of Francisco Tello to Felipe II, 29 April; 1597, in Blair and Robertson, *The Philippine Islands,* vol. 10, 42.

40   Ibid.

41   Report of Conditions in the Philippines by Antonio de Morga, 8 June 1598, in Blair and Robertson, *The Philippine Islands,* vol. 10, 81.

42   Antonio de Morga, *Sucesos de las Islas Filipinas* [1609], trans. and ed. J. S. Cummins (Cambridge: Hakluyt Society, 1971), 277.

43   The admission by the Jesuit priest, Ignacio Francisco Alcina, that a few Spaniards "ya no se contenta con la Venus ordinaria" is quoted by John Leddy Phelan, *The Hispanization of the Philippines* (Madison: University of Wisconsin Press, 1959), 186.

Manila's community of Armenian merchants, disgruntled by Chinese mercantile incursions and only too willing to support repressive measures against the Chinese, lent their voices to the denunciations, and confirmed the sexual promiscuity and immorality of the Chinese:

> And certainly few Sangleyes are married but there are many *indias* and *indios* with the "eye folds" [Mongolian fold?] . . . Regarding sodomy, we say and know what has been published and said by all, that it is a pest that clings to the *indios* as an illness which they do now grow out of . . . [the Chinese] go in one *banca* [boat] with an *indio* [and] mix in a clumsy and violent manner with him.[44]

Chinese attitudes toward Europeans were correspondingly marked by cautiousness, suspicion and distrustfulness. Spaniards were called *Fu-lang-chi*, meaning the "Franks," and were described by the Chinese as physically grotesque, in possession of giant bodies, skin the color of "white calcium," eyes like that of a cat and curly beards that covered the face as "black gauze." It was rumored that Spaniards ate babies and would pay 100 gold coins for an infant in order to consume it.[45] These legends aside, however, the Spanish policies of "taxation, control, and conversion" that were used to deal with the Chinese resulted in harshly oppressive or restrictive treatment and abuses of all kinds. Chinese uprisings, violent eruptions of hostilities, and sanguinary reprisals between Spaniards and the burgeoning Chinese populations were near-regular occurrences in Manila throughout the sixteenth and seventeenth centuries. Certain occupations, such as bakers and butchers, were thought to be more susceptible to anti-Spanish rebellion and revolt.

Chinese revolts were met with wholesale slaughter. Just to compare, in neighboring Dutch-controlled Batavia, an anti-Chinese pogrom took place once, in 1740, and claimed 10,000 lives. In Manila, massacres occurred in 1603, 1639, 1662, 1686 and 1762. The 1603 pogrom claimed approximately 20,000 lives; in 1639 the number of deaths was estimated to be between 22,000 and 24,000.[46] In Manila, as in Batavia, Europeans were

---

44   *Díalogo y conversacíon entre un español y un armenio contra los chinos sangleis (1686)*, MSS 11014 (H. 1R-25), Biblioteca Nacional de España.

45   Albert Chan, "Chinese-Philippine Relations in the Late Sixteenth Century and to 1603," *Philippine Studies* 26 (1978): 1–82.

46   Timothy Brook has most recently treated the 1639 massacre in relation to the Manila–Acapulco galleon trade and the temporary downturn in silver production in Potosí. Timothy Brook, *Vermeer's Hat: The Seventeenth Century and the Dawn of the Global World* (New York: Bloomsbury Press, 2008), especially 166–81.

aided and abetted by native inhabitants.[47] Reporting on the 1603 "*Sangley* Insurrection," ecclesiastics and secular officials alike viewed the massacre of so many Chinese as a significant and, indeed, a divinely endorsed step toward the extirpation of sodomy in the Philippines:

> It could be clearly seen that the Lord alone led the war for the destruction of this enemy—so pernicious for the spread of the gospel, and averse to natural law, for they were a very Sodom [sic]; and with their intercourse with the natives, their cancer was spreading.[48]

Pangsebuan's plea

By the time Spanish officials in Manila received a plea for clemency towards him, Lousu, the mandarin from Taiwan, had been in jail for several months charged with sodomy and condemned to die. The letter came from Pangsebuan, whom Lousu served as mandarin. Pangsebuan had every reason to think that his word carried weight. He was governor general of states and arms (*estados y armas*) of Taiwan and cousin to the "king" of Taiwan (*Rey de isla Hermossa*), Zheng Jing, known to the Spaniards as Sipuan, the eldest son and successor of the late Zheng Chenggong (Koxinga). It was, presumably, this status that gave authority and force to his message, rather than the vapid case he put forward in his brief, unctuously diplomatic words. For reasons he did not care to specify, Pangsebuan confirmed that his mandarin Lousu, as a foreigner in Manila "may have unknowingly broken the laws of the land for which he was imprisoned." However, confident in the Spanish authorities' spirit of good neighborliness and friendship, and in the justness of Spanish laws, he expected that this "serious business," and his mandarin, would be handled with mercy, fairness and justice.[49]

---

47   The Chinese massacre in Batavia is fairly well documented. See for instance, Mary Somers Heidhues, "1740 and the Chinese Massacre in Batavia: Some German Eyewitness Accounts," *Archipel* 77 (2009): 117–47; Claudine Salmon, "The Massacre of 1740 as Reflected in a Contemporary Chinese Narrative," *Archipel* 77 (2009): 149–54. Scholarly coverage of the Chinese massacres in Manila is poor. Only the 1603 massacre, the first to have occurred, has received attention, most notably by José Eugenio Borao, "The Massacre of 1603: Chinese Perception of the Spanish on the Philippines," *Itinerario* 22, no. 1 (1998): 22–39.

48   This and the following quotes are taken from Consulta de el Padre Fraile Aluertto Collares, ministro de el Parian de los Sangs [Sangleyes] extramuros de esta ciudad. Dated 17 September 1670. AGI, Flipinas 10 R. 1, N. 7.

49   "Letter from Ecclesiastics on the Sangley Insurrection (1603)," in Blair and Robertson, *The Philippine Islands*, vol. 12, 146–47.

In considering Pangsebuan's plea, the Audiencia sought the opinion of Padre Aluertto [Alberto] Collares, a prominent and learned Dominican friar who had been ministering to the Parián community for 24 years and was proficient in Chinese. A level-headed priest, Fray Collares urged the governor general not to act rashly. In a carefully worded letter, Collares proposed a tendentious compromise that reveals him to be shrewdly pragmatic, even Machiavellian. First, he impressed upon the governor the effect the case was having in the Parián. Leaders of the Chinese community, Collares related, had become upset and agitated by the death sentence handed to Lousu and had approached him to voice their concerns. These leaders were worried that Pangsebuan's letter had had little effect on the governor general, who, they thought, showed great offense by disregarding it; not to mention Pangsebuan himself, who would also be grievously offended: "I don't doubt [Pangsebuan] will be very offended that his plea has had no effect," Collares observed.[50] Alluding to events of previous times, Collares warned the governor that the case could give rise to new conflicts and counseled him not to take their protest lightly:

> The selection of the means to keep these provinces in good order is solely in your hands but I don't doubt, because of the resentment these Chinese feel, there will be some commotion which . . . has to cause us sufficient disquiet.

Second, Collares recalled the "good friendship" that currently defined the relationship between the "king" of Taiwan and Spanish Manila, one which should be preserved. Third, the traffic of goods and people between Manila and Taiwan, he reminded the governor, was neither infrequent nor insignificant. As Collares noted, visitors from Taiwan should not be ignorant of Spanish laws, given the ease with which people moved in both directions between the two borders.

His solution comes across as wily and unprincipled. Given that the criminal act in question involved two individuals, he suggested that justice and diplomacy could both be served if "One could be given to justice and the other to matters of the state and good governance." If Lousu was pardoned, Collares reasoned, "no-one can accuse your Grace of not serving your King well if you condescend to Pangsebuan's request . . . You might be attacked by the righteous who might find fault with you" but, ultimately, "Your Grace will gain more and counter misfortune." The consequences of

50   Letter of Pangsebuan. n.d., AGI, Filipinas, 10, R. 1, N. 7.

not taking this route, Collares darkly warned, were not to be borne. "The Chinese would be given to understand that we pay little heed to their leaders and there will be unrest" and, conversely, "it would set a bad example to neighboring kingdoms ... if petitions and supplications form their nobility made little impression on those of us who have to take decisions."

Did the good Dominican father accurately represent the fears of the Chinese in the Parián? It would seem so. The Audiencia was also compelled to consider a petition presented by a group of infidel (unbaptized) Chinese merchants and sampan captains. Despair and genuine fear animated their plea. Pangsebuan, their petition revealed, had not been content with merely writing to the governor general. According to the signatories of the Chinese petition, Pangsebuan had exerted pressure on the Chinese in the Parián to bring his wishes more forcefully to the governor's notice, exhorting them to expend every effort to release his mandarin with the threat of violent repercussions on their relatives in Taiwan should they fail to secure Lousu's freedom:

> On the order we ... received from Pangsebuan ... all of us solicit the freedom of Lousu infidel Chinese ... it was an infamy that he a man of quality was imprisoned in a public prison ... not only imprisoned but condemned to the death penalty ... If carried out it would lead, without any doubt, to great remonstrations from Pangsebuan and therefore also from Sipuan, our King, his cousin, [who] would manifest his fury against our fathers, sons, mothers, relatives, because as absolute and fearful King, he [Sipuan] would attribute it to our negligence and lack of care.[51]

The Chinese of the Parián, therefore had attempted to free both Lousu and his *compañero* and, having failed, feared for their persons, property and the lives of their loved ones. Their petition begged the governor general to pardon both of the accused and to return Lousu safely to Taiwan where he "may show himself to the King as proof of the good relationship [between Manila and Taiwan.]."[52]

Conclusion
On 21 September 1670, the death sentence that had been handed down by the Audiencia to "two Sangleyes for *pecado nefando*," Lousu the Chinese

---

51   Peticion de los Sangleyes capitanes que vinieron de China y demas mercaderes de este Parian, n.d., AGI, Filipinas, 331 L. 7., F. 12r–13v.

52   Ibid.

infidel and his companion, was suspended by Manuel de Leon, governor general of the Philippines. The decision, clearly much influenced by Fray Collares, was reached with the view of wishing to maintain "good relations with the neighboring kings" and acceded to the request made by the King of Taiwan's first cousin.[53] In general, Catholic priests were at the forefront in identifying, condemning and rooting out sexual and gender diversity wherever they found it, adopting more or less of a hard line stance to male–male sexual activities and practices, and buttressing laws promulgated by secular officials. In this instance, however, a priest, a decidedly emollient figure in the story, was quite prepared to bend religious principle in the interests of diplomacy. It is tempting to ask whether Manila was a destination for sexual encounters during this period, and to wonder just how exceptional Lousu's case was, but the evidence needed to settle such conjecture is not forthcoming.

---

53   Real cedula a Manuel de Leon, Gobernor de Filipinas [21 September 1670]. AGI, Filipinas, 329 L.1. F.15V–16R.

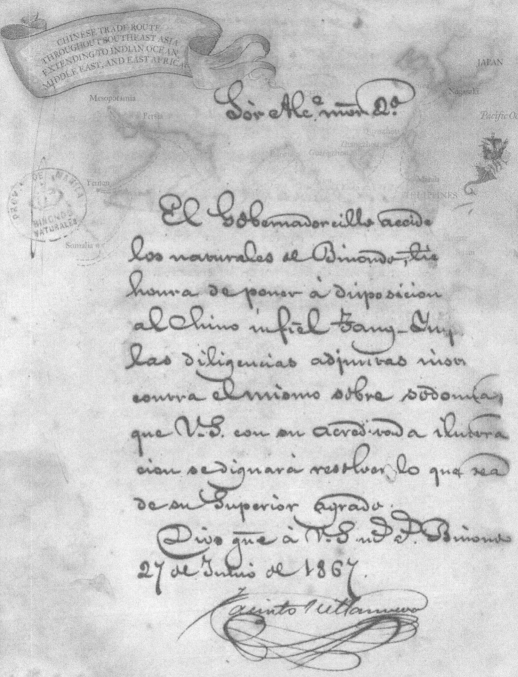

El Gobernadorcillo accide
los naturales el Binondo, tie
honra de poner á disposicion
al Chino infiel Tang-Cuy,
las diligencias adjuntas insw
contra el mismo sobre sodomia,
que V.S. con su acreditad a ilustra
cion se dignará resolver lo que sea
de su Superior agrado.

Dios gue á V.S m.s a.s Binondo
27 de Julio de 1867.

Foreground, Microform of an archival document describing an 1867 case against Tan Yuan who was accused of committing the "crime of sodomy" *(delito de sodomia)* with a younger male named Cipriano Tiongson. Asuntos Criminales collection, National Archives of the Philippines. Photo courtesy of Joaine Jan Marquez. *Background texture*, A map indicating the extensive Chinese trade routes, which extended throughout all of mainland and island Southeast Asia.

JOAINE JAN A. MARQUEZ

Pecado Nefando and the Chinese in Early Spanish Philippines: Hispano-Asian Encounters and Ethnosexual Discourses[i]

Introduction

WHILE CHINESE MERCHANTS had flourishing commercial ties with native inhabitants centuries before the arrival of the Spaniards, it was only when Spanish sovereignty was firmly consolidated in the Philippines that there was a great influx of Chinese migrants and traders. When the Spaniards first arrived in Manila in 1570, there were only about a hundred and fifty Chinese merchants, but less than fifty years after the establishment of colonial rule, the number of Chinese residents had dramatically increased to 15,000.[1] Over the course of the early years of Spanish rule, the *sangleyes*[2]

i   This study was originally a research paper written for the History 228.1 (Cultural History of the Philippines) course taught by Dr. Richard Chu at Ateneo de Manila University in the second semester of academic year 2015–2016. Many thanks are due to the editors, Dr. Chu (UMass) and Dr. Mark Blasius (CUNY), for their insightful and valuable comments, queries, leads, suggestions, and encouragement on various drafts for this paper's publication. I wish to thank Ms. Regina Carmeli Regala (Xavier School and Ateneo English Department) for her generous assistance in translating some Tagalog passages cited in the paper, and Mr. Timothy Ong (University of the Philippines Linguistics Department) for his valuable advice related to folk lexicons. Some sections of this study have been presented at the 14th Philippine-Spanish Friendship Day Conference: *Founders, Pioneers, and Builders: Understanding Interactions and Connections in Colonial Philippines* (5–6 October 2016, University of the Philippines Diliman), and at the conference *Chinese in the Philippines: New Studies, Current Issues, Future Directions* (12–13 January 2017, Ateneo de Manila University).

1   Edgar Wickberg, *The Chinese in Philippine Life, 1850–1898* (Quezon City: Ateneo de Manila University Press, 2000), 4; Milagros C. Guerrero, "Chinese in the Philippines, 1570–1770," in *More Tsinoy than We Admit: Chinese-Filipino Interactions over the Centuries*, ed. Richard T. Chu (Quezon City: Vibal Foundation, 2015), 64.

2   There are various explanations as to the provenance of the term. Edgar Wickberg (*Chinese in Philippine Life*, 9) traced the word's origin from the Mandarin word *shanglu* (商旅), which means "merchant traveler." On the other hand, both Filipino historian

(one of the official Spanish terms used to refer to Chinese immigrants) were able to establish and maintain a strong position in the colonial economy. At the same time, however, their increasing number and their seeming resistance to conversion and assimilation made the Chinese notoriously suspect in the eyes of Spanish authorities. A majority of the migrant Chinese remained as *sangleyes infieles* (Chinese infidels), while Christian converts were regarded as insincere since most conversions were viewed as economically motivated, and that the Chinese converts still continued to practice Chinese "religious" customs.[3] Writing in 1596, Antonio Morga warned Philip II that the Chinese were "a people with whom one must live with much watchfulness and caution."[4]

The sense of anxiety that the growth of Chinese presence posed to the colonial regime was aggravated by complaints of Spanish officials, both secular and ecclesiastical, of scandalous and serious offenses being committed by the Chinese against the Christian religion. Such practices frowned upon by Spanish officials included the "lawless carnal intercourse" between Chinese men and native Christian women, the cohabitation of Chinese men with local women, and the practice of bigamy or multiple marriages where Chinese men kept a wife in China and married another in the Philippines.[5] It appears, however, that the Spaniards were most concerned about the perceived widespread practice of *pecado nefando* or *sodomía* (sodomy) among Chinese men in the colony. Melchor Davalos, an *oidor* (civil judge) of the Real Audiencia, made one of the earliest references to the "nefarious sin" when he reported in 1584 that the Chinese were practicing sodomy on board

Richard Chu (*Chinese and Chinese Mestizos*, 69) and Spanish historian Antonio García-Abásolo (*La Imagen Española de los Chinos en Filipinas*, 2008, 69) believe that the word originated from *changlai* (常來) meaning, one who "comes often" or "people who come and go." As evidence, Chu based his explanation on the sixteenth-century Boxer Codex while Abásolo cited a letter of Governor-General Francisco de Sande to Philip II dated 7 June 1576.

3   Albert Chan, SJ, "Chinese-Philippine Relations in the Late Sixteenth Century to 1603," in *More Tsinoy than We Admit*, ed. Richard T. Chu (Quezon City: Vibal Foundation, 2015), 37; Richard T. Chu, *Chinese and Chinese Mestizos of Manila: Family, Identity and Culture, 1860s–1930s* (Mandaluyong: Anvil Publishing, 2012), 76; Wickberg, 8, 16; Gregorio F. Zaide, *The Pageant of Philippine History: Political, Economic and Socio-cultural* (Manila: Philippine Education Company, 1979), 1: 434.

4   Antonio de Morga, "Letter to Felipe II" (6 July 1596), in *The Philippine Islands, 1493–1898* (Ohio: Arthur H. Clark, Co., 1903–1909), 9: 266. Hereafter BR.

5   Chu, *Chinese and Chinese Mestizos*, 165; Dasmariñas, "Letter to Felipe II," 9: 319; Antonio García-Abásolo, "La Audiencia de Manila y los Chinos de Filipinas: Casos de Integracion en el Delito," in *Homenaje a Alberto de la Hera: Instituto de Investigaciones Jurídicas* (Mexico: Universidad Nacional Autónoma de México, 2008): 353.

their ship.[6] A scandalized Dominican Bishop Benavides complained in 1603 that the Chinese were a "very pernicious people" who seduced the natives into committing the "unnatural sin," clearly a reference to sodomy.[7]

"Unorthodox" desires and practices such as same-sex sexuality and transgenderism in the Philippines have been the subject of study over the past two decades. Such studies include J. Neil Garcia's *Philippine Gay Culture: Binabae to Bakla, Silahis to MSM* and Carolyn Brewer's *Baylan, Asog, Transvestism, and Sodomy: Gender, Sexuality and the Sacred in Early Colonial Philippines*, which explored various indigenous concepts of gender and sexuality to demonstrate the nuances of native gender cultures, and questioned the existence of a universal, essentialist gay or homosexual identity in the precolonial Philippine cultures. While such works have addressed aspects of precolonial and colonial same-sex desires and practices among the natives, there exist limited historical studies on same-sex sexual behaviors among "non-indigenous" members of Philippine society, such as the ethnic Chinese in the Philippines. Among the historical studies dealing with male-male sexual encounters involving Chinese in Spanish Philippines include Jesuit historian Albert Chan's *Chinese-Philippine Relations in the Late 16th-century to 1603*, and Raquel Reyes's *Sodomy in 17th-century Manila: the Luck of a Mandarin from Taiwan*.

One theme of this study is to attempt to situate local sodomy prosecutions against the Chinese in the early Spanish period in light of a transnational perspective, which is defined by Tamara Loos in her *Transnational Histories of Sexualities in Asia* as "history… centrally concerned with flows and circulation… among sites" rather than with events and developments that are geographically-bound.[8] Historical studies that focus on themes such as commerce, migration, gender and sexuality necessitate a closer examination of the interconnectedness of local narratives with global contexts. This study therefore attempts to understand the issue of sodomy in light of how local encounters mediated and connected trans-imperial contexts in early Spanish Philippines: the sodomy prosecutions in Spain and colonial Latin America, and the relative plurality of sexual cultures in late imperial China and the indigenous Philippine societies, in order to gain fuller appreciation of the exchanges, interaction, and movement of people and ideas in early Spanish Philippines. While *Sodomy in 17th-century Manila*

---

6   Melchor Davalos, "Letter to Felipe II" (3 July 1584), in BR, 6: 63.

7   Miguel de Benavides, "Complaints Against the Chinese" (3–9 February 1605), in BR, 13: 278.

8   Tamara Loos, "Transnational Histories of Sexualities in Asia," *American Historical Review* 115, no. 5 (2009): 1309.

by Reyes also discussed the sodomy prosecutions in Mediterranean Europe and the Spanish empire in relation to the developments in the Philippines, this paper endeavors to also take into account the plurality of gender and sexual practices in late imperial China to give voice to the viewpoint of the Chinese migrants, and it considers in more detail the contextual nature of the institutional responses of the Spaniards towards the question of sodomy and the Chinese.

Another theme that this historical investigation seeks to address is to examine how the trans-Pacific encounters between the *sangleyes*, the *indios* (Christian natives) and the Spaniards transformed "local" meanings attached to sex and gender practices. For instance, Joane Nagel in *Sex, Ethnicity, and Sexuality* conceived the term *ethnosexual constructs* to denote ideas or images that groups have about the sexuality of other ethnic groups who are then viewed as sexually *different* from, and usually inferior to their own normal and proper ways of being sexual.[9] Hence, Spanish colonialism seemed to involve the transformation from diversity in their sexual ethos amongst colonized peoples; here through the sexual "othering" of Chinese migrants. In a similar vein, Micheal Peletz in his work *Gender Pluralism: Southeast Asia Since Early Modern Times* discussed how the dynamics of colonial power insinuated itself into local regimes of gender and sexuality, and in the process *constricting* the plurality of sexual expressions and the hardening of gender and sexual lines.[10]

It is perhaps important to recognize that interracial unions and inter-cultural mixing were much more tolerated in Spanish Philippines compared to British and Dutch colonies in Southeast Asia, where racial segregation was more strictly observed and interracial mixing was viewed with stronger prejudice.[11] For instance, Western observers noted that Spaniards, mestizos, indios and Chinese mingled more easily in the Philippines than in other Asian colonies, and even as early as the sixteenth century, the Spanish crown already legitimized interethnic marriages under Catholic rites.[12] Nonetheless, while such relative tolerance existed in Hispanic territories such as the Philippines, what this historical study attempts to demonstrate are the *limits* of ethnosexual relations in Spanish Philippines, especially in relation to the question of same-sex desires and practices. Attention is devoted to examining

9   Joane Nagel, *Race, Ethnicity and Sexuality: Intimate Intersections, Forbidden Frontiers* (Oxford: Oxford University Press, 2003), 9.

10   Michael G. Peletz, *Gender Pluralism: Southeast Asia since Early Modern Times* (New York: Routledge, 2009), 119.

11   Fernando N. Zialcita, *Authentic Though Not Exotic: Essays on Filipino Identity* (Quezon City: Ateneo de Manila University Press, 2005), 221–23.

12   Ibid.

the conditions that led to the *constriction* of what was once a range of culturally permissible sexual and gender modalities among pre-Hispanic people and the migrant Chinese as a result of their encounters with early modern Spanish Christian universalism which was less receptive, if not overtly
opposed, to a plurality of sexual expressions. Ethnosexual frontiers such as
same-sex desires and relations were "patrolled and policed, regulated and
restricted… across ethnic borders."[13]

The final theme of this study is an examination of sodomy as a unit of
historical analysis to understand same-sex desires and practices in the early
colonial period. In his work *Sodomy, Local Sexual Economies, and Inquisitors
during Spain's Golden Age*, Cristian Berco contends that sodomy is a useful barometer for gauging the social and state perceptions of various social
groups in the early modern period.[14] Similarly, Peletz associated the "partial
silencing" of sodomy within the more encompassing "constriction and overall transformation of pluralistic sensibilities" of gender and sexual relations
in early modern Southeast Asian societies.[15]

Examined against the backdrop of the precarious and troubled interethnic relations between the Chinese and the Spaniards, this paper will attempt to show how sodomy, as a moral and criminal offense, was used by
the colonial regime to target "undesirable" social groups, such as the Chinese, who were deemed in need of regulation or even extirpation in the interest of local social order. The historical significance of Spanish responses
to the question of sodomy adds another dimension to understanding the
construction of the sangley as an "ethnic other." By studying what various
colonial accounts—taken from letters, ordinances, confessional manuals,
and codices—reveal about Spaniards' perceptions of indigenous and Chinese sexualities, and the institutional actions taken by the colonial regime
to denounce and purge the diversity of sexual desires and practices, this paper will endeavor to show how colonial discourses transformed the cultural
matrix through which gender and sexual practices were interpreted.

Sodomy in the early modern Spanish empire

In early modern Europe, sodomy was understood as a malleable and fluid
concept signifying various non-procreative sexual acts ranging from anal sex
to bestiality, and those who engaged in sodomy and other "unnatural" sex

13   Nagel, *Race, Ethnicity and Sexuality*, 14.
14   Cristian Berco, "Social Control and Its Limits: Sodomy, Local Sexual Economies and Inquisitors during Spain's Golden Age," *The Sixteenth Century Journal* 36, no. 2
(2005): 331.
15   Peletz, *Gender Pluralism*, 123.

practices were dealt with harshly and severely, with punishments involving torture and burning at the stake.[16]

Condemnation of sexual practices that were deemed "unnatural" or "against nature" was rooted in the institutionalized thinking going back to early Church fathers. St. Augustine declared sexual acts that did not take place in a "vessel fit for procreation" as sinful and aberrant, and medieval theologians like St. Thomas Aquinas included same-sex sexual activity, bestiality, masturbation and "unnatural" heterosexual sexual positions in the category of *luxuria* (lust).[17]

In various parts of the Spanish Empire, sodomy was referred to as *abominabale delito* (abominable crime), *pecado contra natura* (sin against nature), and *pecado nefando* (the nefarious or unspeakable sin).[18] Whereas the rest of early modern Europe was engulfed in witch-hunts, the Spanish tribunals became preoccupied with prosecuting Moors, Jews, and sodomy.[19] Definitions and punishments of, and jurisdiction over sodomy varied in Spain. In territories under the Crown of Aragon, sodomy covered the whole range of male homoerotic activities (i.e., from kissing and fondling to consummated anal sex) along with non-procreative heterosexual behaviors, and cases were brought before the Inquisition.[20] The Aragonese Inquisition prosecuted some 1,623 cases between 1540 and 1700.[21]

On the other hand, secular authorities in dominions under the Crown of Castile beginning 1509 were given authority to prosecute sodomy cases.[22] The legal code *Siete partidas* enshrined laws that punished individuals convicted of same-sex sexual acts to death by stoning, which was eventually replaced with death by burning.[23] Since territories in the

---

16   Federico Garza Carvajal, *Butterflies Will Burn: Prosecuting Sodomites in Early Modern Spain and Mexico* (Austin: University of Texas Press, 2003), 5; J. Neil Garcia, *Philippine Gay Culture: Binabae to Bakla, Silahis to MSM* (Quezon City: University of the Philippines Press, 2008), 17; David M. Halperin, "How to Do the History of Homosexuality," *GLQ: A Journal of Lesbian and Gay Studies* 6, no. 1 (2000): 92; Zeb Tortorici, "Against Nature: Sodomy and Homosexuality in Colonial Latin America," *History Compass* 10, no. 2 (2012): 162.

17   Tortorici, "Against Nature," 170.

18   Zeb Tortorici, "Heran Todos Putos: Sodomitical Subcultures and Disordered Desire in Early Colonial Mexico," *Ethnohistory* 54, no. 1 (2007): 45.

19   Garza Cravajal, *Butterflies Will Burn*, 40.

20   Cristian Berco, "Producing Patriarchy: Male Sodomy and Gender in Early Modern Spain," *Journal of the History of Sexuality* 17, no. 3 (September 2008): 357.

21   Garza Carvajal, *Butterflies Will Burn*, 77.

22   Tortorici, "Against Nature," 167.

23   Laura A. Lewis, "From Sodomy to Superstition: The Active Pathic and Bodily Transgressions in New Spain," *Ethnohistory* 54, no. 1 (2007): 130.

Spanish Indies, including the Philippines, were incorporated into the Castilian legal and administrative system, it was the secular authorities, not the Inquisition, which had jurisdiction over sodomy (unless the act directly involved heresy or blasphemy).[24]

In the case of both Spain and Spanish America, those who were mostly targeted and punished for sodomy prosecution were men who belonged to social groups judged as suspicious and undesirable by virtue of their social, ethnic and religious identifications. Most sodomy denunciations in Aragon were made against foreigners, but the heaviest, most extreme punishments, like elsewhere in the Iberian Peninsula, were inflicted on slaves, immigrants, and *moriscos* (descendants of Muslim converts to Christianity).[25] Sodomy prosecutions in the Spanish empire seem indicative of a deeply rooted pattern of xenophobia and ethnic discrimination.

While colonial records make it clear that some Spaniards were also denounced for sodomy, no trials were held in most cases. The only notable exemption was a 1771 case concerning Spanish friar Fray Agustín María who was banished for ten years as punishment for whipping, fondling, and committing other nefarious acts with four native men.[26] What stands out in the position of the ethnic Chinese in Spanish colonial society was the extent to which negative stereotypes and claims about their sexuality contributed to their creation as ethnic and sexual "others." The succeeding section will endeavor to describe how the practice of sodomy among the Chinese, and the hostile judgment and dim view of the Spaniards towards it, contributed to the development in the early centuries of Spanish colonization of a social climate propitious for discrimination, oppression, and at times violence against the Chinese.

Pecado nefando and the sangleyes

Various letters and memorials sent by Spanish officials to Madrid frequently mention accusations that the Chinese were corrupting native men and women into committing the "sin against nature." In two letters to Madrid in

---

24   Ibid. In practice, however, the Inquisition was given jurisdiction to sodomy cases with acts of heresy involved. This was seen in a 1640 Inquisition case of an unidentified Spanish man in Manila who was denounced for asserting that *pecado nefando* was not a sin (Archivo General de la Nación, Indiferente Virreinal 4128, exp. 13). In 1662, a certain Marcos Benitéz was denounced by his wife for committing male-female sodomy, and for making claims that "sodomy between husband and wife is not a sin." (Archivo General de la Nación, Inquisición 595, exp. 13, fols. 202-206). See Zeb Tortotici's NYU Archival Database (http://hdl.handle.net/2451/42172).

25   Berco, "Social Control and its Limits," 338.

26   See Zeb Tortotici's NYU Archival Database (http://hdl.handle.net/2451/42172).

1603 and 1605, Archbishop Benavides blamed the Chinese for introducing sodomy to the natives.[27] Governor Dasmariñas was particularly concerned about the proliferation of such "abominable" practices as a result of the unrestricted presence of Chinese who were able to live and mingle freely with the natives.[28] In particular, he described Tondo (then a suburban commercial district or *arrabal* located on the right bank of the Pasig River), where about 250 Chinese men lived among a large native population, as a place "full of sodomy."[29] Natives were accustomed to bathing and swimming naked in rivers and creeks near the Párian (segregated Chinese quarter in Manila), and to the chagrin of the Spaniards, the Chinese living nearby could easily see the exposed natives and lure them, especially boys, into committing the "nefarious sin."[30]

Spaniards regarded the Chinese as an obstacle and threat to the recently converted natives who were still viewed as highly susceptible to corrupt influences, especially from the Chinese. Bishop Salazar described the natives as a "poor spirited people" who were used by the Chinese "for their corrupt pleasures," and the bishop expressed unease at the apparent lack of public condemnation towards sodomy.[31] Archbishop Benavides blamed the warm and humid weather for making the natives liable to commit carnal sins.[32] He also condemned the Chinese for "generously" using bribes to entice natives to engage in sodomy "for the fulfillment of their desires."[33] Spanish authorities maintained that the natives were just recently converted and had the proclivity towards licentious and perverse sexual practices, and argued that exposure to the "corrupting" influences of the Chinese could easily lead the natives away from good morals and make them lose their Catholic faith.[34]

Spanish sources like Benavides's letters and Morga's *Sucesos* claimed that natives had no knowledge of sodomy because of the absence of an equivalent word for sodomy in the local languages.[35] John Leddy Phelan, in his work

27   Miguel de Benavides, "Letters to Felipe III" (5–6 July 1603), in BR, 12: 107; Benavides, "Complaints Against the Chinese," 13: 271.

28   Dasmariñas, "Letter to Felipe II," 9: 315.

29   Benavides, "Letters to Felipe III," 12: 107, 109.

30   Benavides, "Complaints Against the Chinese," 13: 274.

31   Domingo de Salazar, "Letter to Philip II, Manila" (24 June 1950), quoted in Horacio de la Costa, SJ, *The Jesuits in the Philippines, 1581–1768* (Quezon City: Ateneo de Manila University Press, 2014), 204.

32   Benavides, "Complaints Against the Chinese," 13: 271.

33   Ibid., 278.

34   Chan, "Chinese-Philippine Relations," 39.

35   Benavides, "Complaints Against the Chinese," 13: 278; Morga, *Sucesos de las Islas Filipinas* (1609) in BR, 16: 130.

Hispanization of the Philippines, contended that the Spaniards' claims were suspect since the lack of local terminology for sodomy did not necessarily prove the absence of sodomy among natives.[36] In discrediting the Spaniards' charge that the Chinese introduced sodomy to natives, Phelan explained that the practice of same-sex sodomy probably proliferated among the natives as a result of the increased presence of the Chinese.[37] In addition, if sodomy was to be defined not only as same-sex acts but also in the broader category of "unnatural" sexual acts, then the natives' use of penis inserts and their practice of non-missionary positions in heterosexual intercourse, as Spanish missionaries had noted, can also be considered "sodomitical" in nature.[38]

Most importantly, the linguistic argument of the Spaniards is problematic since certain entries in lexicographic texts written by Spaniards themselves already point to the act of sodomy. In Gaspar de San Agustin's confessional manual, *Confesionario copioso* (first published in 1713), native terms such as *nagpuit* and *nagpapuit* were listed as references to "active" and "passive" anal sex respectively (*puit* being the Tagalog term for buttocks).[39] In addition, Alonso de Mentrida's *Diccionario de la lengua bisaya hiligueina y haraya de la Isla de Panay* (first published in 1637) documented terms in Hiligaynon or Ilonggo, a Philippine language spoken mainly in the western Visayas region that may provide significant clues to the presence of sodomy in the indigenous lexicon. The *Diccionario* rendered *boli* as a local term for buttocks (*culo* in Castilian), and Mentrida included derivative terms such as *napaboli* ("*ser sodomitco activo*" or active sodomite) and *guin buri* ("*el pasivo*" or passive in Castilian) to refer to sodomy roles.[40] The insertions in *diccionarios* and *confesionarios* of such indigenous terms for acts otherwise regarded as "sodomitical" serve as counterpoints to Spanish claims that natives did not have knowledge of such acts.

Early modern Europeans viewed sodomy not only as "the ultimate sin" but it was also regarded as evidence of native barbarism and an inferior

36   John Leddy Phelan, *The Hispanization of the Philippines: Spanish Aims and Filipino Responses, 1565–1700* (Madison: University of Wisconsin Press), 186.d

37   Ibid.

38   Francisco Ignacio Alcina, SJ, *Historia de las islas e indios de Bisaya* (1668), trans. Cantius J. Kobak, OFM, and Lucio Gutiérrez, OP (Manila: UST Publishing House, 2005), 421; Morga, *Sucesos*, 16: 130; Garcia, *Philippine Gay Culture*, 163.d

39   Garcia, *Philippine Gay Culture*, 167.

40   Alfonso de Mentrida, *Diccionario de la lengua bisaya hiligueina y haraya de la isla de Panay* (Manila: Imp. de D. Manuel y de D. Felis S. Dayot, 1841), 81. I am grateful to Mr. Timothy Ong (UP Linguistics Department) for sharing valuable information regarding corporeal entries in the *Diccionario*.

level of civilization.[41] Hence, while European visitors in China expressed great admiration at the superior levels of advancement of the Chinese in government, the arts, and sciences, they were also scandalized at the level of tolerance for same-sex practices in late imperial China. The Italian Jesuit missionary Matteo Ricci was appalled at the social acceptance of male same-sex sexual practices in the China he visited.[42] Homoerotic references in writing and the arts flourished and enjoyed popularity among the elites since the Ming dynasty.[43] Vitellio explained that Westerners like Ricci encountered a Chinese society where male homoeroticism indeed reached a high level of popularity and had become fashionably widespread.[44]

In most of China's ancient history, same-sex desires and relations were not understood as perverted, sinful behaviors like in early modern Europe. Men, who had sexual relations with other men were not considered distinct, and it was only the penetrated male who, by virtue of his "emasculation" resulting from his penetration by another man, was perceived as "different."[45] In a society that was relatively tolerant of fluidity and diversity in sexual desires and practices, sexual mores in late imperial China allowed men to have sexual relations with both women and other men. For instance, most elite men who enjoyed sexual relations with other men were also married, and fulfilled familial responsibilities.[46] As long as one observed the Confucian moral order such as maintaining family obligations and other social expectations, sexual relations between men were permissible in most of ancient Chinese history. Although the Qing dynasty enacted laws prohibiting sodomy (ji jian), in practice, such official restrictions dealt almost exclusively with male rape or non-consensual sex between men, and functioned as a deterrent for men from engaging in sexual activities that may lower their social status (i.e., an elite male being penetrated by a male of inferior status).[47]

41   Richard C. Trexler, Sex and Conquest: Gendered Violence, Political Order and the European Conquest of the Americas (Cambridge: Polity Press, 1995), 170.

42   Bret Hinsch, Passions of the Cut Sleeve: The Male Homosexual Tradition in China (Berkeley: University of California Press, 1990), 137; Giovanni Vitellio, "Exemplary Sodomites: Chivalry and Love in Late Ming Culture," NAN NÜ 2, no. 2 (2000): 252.

43   Hinsch, Passions of the Cut Sleeve, 152; Wu Cuncun, Homoerotic Sensibilities in Late Imperial China (New York: Routledge, 2004), 3.

44   Vitellio, "Exemplary Sodomites," 250.

45   Matthew H. Sommer, "The Penetrated Male in Late Imperial China: Judicial Constructions and Social Stigma," Modern China 23, no. 2 (April 1997): 142.

46   Martin W. Huang, "Male-Male Sexual Bonding and Male Friendship in Late Imperial China," Journal of the History of Sexuality 22, no. 2 (May 2013): 328.

47   Matthew H. Sommer, "Dangerous Males, Vulnerable Males, and Polluted Males: The Regulation of Masculinity in Qing Dynasty Law," in Chinese Femininities/Chinese

It was in this encounter of differing views towards same-sex desires and behaviors that the Chinese in Spanish Philippines found themselves being targeted for sodomy prosecutions, and seen as a perverted and dangerous group. The arrest of fourteen Chinese men accused of committing sodomy in 1588 exemplifies such clashing sexual views. Although the Chinese protested that the practice of sodomy was common among men in China, two of them were condemned to die by fire, and the rest were flogged and sentenced to the galleys.[48]

Joane Nagel argued that despite the diversity of sexual desires and practices among individuals, in any historical period and society, there will always be a *hegemonic sexuality* that tends to "define socially approved men's and women's sexualized bodies, approved kinds sexual desires for approved numbers and types of partners," and in the process also subordinates other forms of sexual desires and practices.[49] As demonstrated by archival sources, the interethnic tensions between Spaniards and the Chinese during the early colonial period were accompanied by xenophobic belief that only *other* nationals and ethnicities, such as the Chinese, were naturally inclined to sodomy. The subsequent section will attempt to examine the role of key colonial institutions, such as the Church, the Inquisition, and the civil government, and how they were instrumental to shaping and controlling sodomy, and ultimately, to the construction and imposition of a certain kind of hegemonic sexuality structured around Spanish Christian universalism and European orthodox notions of gender and sexuality.

Early Spanish responses to *pecado nefando*

Finding themselves living with a population considered as the backbone of the colonial economy but whose sexual beliefs and practices the Catholic Church condemned, the Spaniards found it difficult to deal with the issue of sodomy. It appears that in the early decades of the Spanish colonization, the Spaniards had varied and uneven responses to the question of sodomy. There were initial indications that some Spanish ecclesiastical and civil authorities either reluctantly tolerated or blatantly ignored sodomy. High-ranking government officials like Melchor Davalos of the Audiencia Real hesitated to mete out punishment against Chinese culprits for fear of the detrimental effects to the colonial economy that harsh anti-Chinese measures might

Masculinities: A Reader, ed. Susan Brownell and Jeffrey N. Wasserstrom (Berkeley: University of California Press, 2002), 74.

48   Chan, "Chinese-Philippine Relations," 38.

49   Nagel, *Race, Ethnicity and Sexuality*, 8.

bring.[50] The Dominican Archbishop Miguel de Benavides complained that the Jesuits, who ran an estate and kept a successful poultry industry in Quiapo, protected the Chinese who lived there and turned a blind eye to sodomy and other "vices" being committed by the Chinese.[51]

Others, however, saw the need to take tougher courses of action. By making reference to China as a country of "vile" and "wicked" people who practiced sodomy among other negative stereotypes, Governor Francisco Sande urged Madrid in 1576 to send military expeditions to invade China.[52] In 1603, Benavides recommended the expulsion of most, and the restriction of immigration of the Chinese as solutions to address the "diabolical crime" of sodomy, and correct other "immoralities" being propagated by the Chinese.[53] Lastly, some Spanish officials viewed anti-Chinese pogroms as divinely sanctioned to cleanse the colony of the nefarious sin such as what this excerpt from a report on the 1603 massacre of the Parián suggests:

> It could be clearly seen that the *Lord alone led the war for the destruction of the enemy*—so pernicious for the spread of the gospel, and averse to the natural law, for there were *a very Sodom* [sic]; *and with their intercourse with the natives,* their cancer was spreading.[54] (Italics mine)

An examination of the Manila Synod of 1582 also reveals colonial discourses about sodomy and the Chinese. In formulating a legal theory justifying Spanish sovereignty in the Philippines, the Manila Synod concluded that even if the Spanish Catholic monarchs were only granted spiritual dominion over the archipelago, it was still necessary to establish military and political dominion over the islands in order to provide protection for missionaries and converts from attacks by "infidels."[55] Following such a legal framework, both the Church and the colonial state sought to exercise meas-

---

50   Davalos, "Letter to Felipe II," 6: 63.

51   Benavides, "Letter to Felipe III," 12: 109.

52   Francisco de Sande, *Relation of the Philippine Islands* (1576), in BR, 4: 51, 59.

53   Benavides, "Letter to Felipe III," 12: 111.

54   José Eugenio Borao, "Consulta de el Padre Fraile Aluertto Collares, Ministro de el Parián de los Sang [Sangleyes] Extramuros de Esta Ciudad" (17 September 1670), Archivo General de las Indias (AGI), Filipinas 10, R.1., N.7., quoted in Raquel Reyes, "Sodomy in Seventeenth-Century Manila: The Luck of a Mandarin from Taiwan," in *Sexual Diversity in Asia, c. 600–1950,* ed. Raquel Reyes and William G. Clarence-Smith (New York: Taylor and Francis, 2012), 134.

55   Greg Bankoff, *Crime, Society and the State in the Nineteenth Century Philippines* (Quezon City: Ateneo de Manila University Press, 1996), 6.

ures to restrain groups perceived as potential social and moral menace to the newly baptized such as the Chinese. This was expressed in a passage from the synod's documentation recommending the segregation of the Chinese from the natives:

> [The Chinese] are shameless and given to sodomy. Consequently, the governor should make sure that *they do not have male Indians* [natives] *for servants, especially boys,* nor female Indians… [and since the] Chinese are given to idolatry and other vices… these will catch easily among the Christians if they live with them.[56] (Italics mine)

Such provision in the Manila Synod not only reveals fears and anxieties about same-sex sexuality, but also how such discourses were used to rationalize, in the words of Micheal Peletz, "civilizing missions necessitating a colonial presence"[57] thereby legitimizing in this case the Spanish imperial ideology. The details from the synod's draft also reflect the general tendency of the Spaniards' to conflate the Chinese and the sin of sodomy. In the interest of "protecting" natives from the corrupting influences of the Chinese who practiced the abominable sin, the Chinese were to be controlled and regulated. Moreover, the document speaks of the need to subject the Chinese, by virtue of their being an ethnic "other," to strong moral judgment and strict social control for not conforming to the dominant group's definition of acceptable, *natural* sexuality. Popular conceptions of ethnic distinctions, therefore, were not only based on variations in language, religion, customs or "race," but these claims of differences also carry with them sexually loaded meanings that demarcate who is moral or immoral, and who is virtuous or polluted.

Institutional responses and sodomy prosecutions

At least for the first two centuries of Spanish colonization, the Church provided the ideological foundation and played the strategic role in the initial consolidation of colonial rule. Hence, the Spanish Crown depended on the Church for the maintenance of its sovereignty, and the enforcement of social control in Spain's only colonial outpost in Asia. In their efforts to achieve spiritual conquest of the islands by converting natives, the Spanish missionaries sought not only to teach catechism using translations in various indigenous languages, they also attempted to observe, document, and understand

---

56   *The Manila Synod of 1582: The Draft of its Handbook for Confessors*, trans. Paul A. Dumol (Quezon City: Ateneo de Manila University Press, 2014), 60.

57   Peletz, *Gender Pluralism*, 125.

the cultural practices of their new wards. As such, the friars produced the first ethnographies about the native inhabitants and what they discovered provoked fervent opposition to certain indigenous gender and sexual mores such as cross-dressing, premarital sex, polygamy, divorce, engaging in sexual coupling positions other than the missionary coital position, and the use of penis inserts.[58] According to J. Neil Garcia, some of these sexual practices of the natives technically fell under the wider conception of sodomy as "unnatural" sexual acts or any sexual position outside the "missionary," not just same-sex erotic activity.[59]

It was through the sacrament of confession that the Church was able to effectively enforce its orthodox standards for sexual morality. The idea of the Christian confessional as a sophisticated apparatus for social control was first articulated in Michel Foucault's landmark work *History of Sexuality (Volume 1: An Introduction)* which states that Western social institutions such as the Christian church have largely relied on the use of confession for the regulation and surveillance of bodies and populations.[60] Inspired by Foucault's analysis of the coercive capacity of the Christian confessional, historian Vicente Rafael in *Contracting Colonialism* discussed the value of confessional manuals to Spanish missionaries in monitoring and disciplining native bodies and desires during the early stages of Catholic conversion and Spanish colonial rule in the Philippines.[61] By asking all sorts of questions to reveal the natives' conduct and faith, Spanish missionaries were able to successfully indoctrinate and supervise indigenous converts thereby helping consolidate colonial rule in Spain's most distant colonial outpost.[62] Like in Latin America, Spanish missionaries in the Philippines published bilingual texts called *confesionarios* that served

58   Alcina, *Historia de las islas e indios de Bisaya* (1668), trans. Kobak and Gutiérrez, 257–59; Carolyn Brewer, "*Baylan, Asog*, Transvestism, and Sodomy: Gender, Sexuality and the Sacred in Early Colonial Philippines," *Intersections: Gender, History and Culture in the Asian Context* no. 2 (May 1999): 13; Garcia, 163–64, 168; Morga, 16: 130–31; Phelan, 61–64, 186; Juan de Plasencia, OSF, "Customs of the Tagalogs" (1589), in BR, 7: 194. Although Alcina placed the blame for the spread of sodomy on the "frequent dealings" between Chinese and natives, the Jesuit missionary mentioned that some Spaniards in the colony also engaged in sodomy but did not elaborate further (Alcina, *Islas e indios de bisaya*, 421).

59   Garcia, *Philippine Gay Culture*, 170.

60   Michel Foucault, *The History of Sexuality Volume 1: An Introduction* (New York: Vintage Books, 1978), 56.

61   Vicente Rafael, *Contracting Colonialism: Translation and Christian Conversion in Tagalog Society under Early Spanish Rule* (Quezon City: Ateneo de Manila University Press, 2000), 103.

62   Phelan, *Hispanization of the Philippines*, 65.

as guides for natives in examining their conscience prior to confession. These texts listed questions specific to each of the Ten Commandments, and were intended to elicit a truthful "narrative of sins," including sinful sexual practices, that probed into the most intimate details of a person's life.[63]

An excerpt from one of the earliest *confesionarios* published in the islands, Tomas Pinpin's *Librong Pagaaralan nang manga Tagalog nang Uicang Castila* [The Book for Tagalogs to Learn the Castilian Language] (published in 1610), is instructive of how Spanish missionaries monitored their native converts, and how colonial, hegemonic notions of sexuality reconfigured the cultural matrix by demonizing certain sexual desires and practices, which were otherwise neutral to the indigenous culture:

> 16. May doon ca cayang salang ano anoman sa capoua mo lalaqui, at sa ca-poua mo babayi caya? 17. Turan mo din con anong asal na calibugan ninyo, ninyong catongo mo, con nagsisiping cayo, at con nagdaramahan cayo, at con nagbabauan caya cayo...? 19. Pinababao mo caya ang asaua mo [*mujer*] sa yio? 20. Gongmaua ca caya nang anomang ycalabas niyon con ano yaong marumi [*polución*] sa cataoan mo...? 22. Pinagquiquimis mo, ó pinag dara-rama mo ó pinaglalamas mo ang cataoan mo nang malabasan nang tobod [*polución*]? 23. Binobotingting, tinitiltil mo ang quinalalaquinan mo nang domating yaong mahalay?
>
> [16. Did you commit carnal sin with another man or woman like yourself? 17. Also, tell me acts of carnal sinfulness that you and your companion en-deavored, whether you had intercourse, touched each other and lay atop each other...? 19. Did you make your wife position on top of you? 20. Have you done any acts to release that which is unclean from your body? 22. Were you rubbing, caressing or stroking your body when something unclean came out of your body? 23. Were you fondling, squeezing your manhood when you felt sinful desire?][64] (Translation, insets, and italics mine)

By the end of the seventeenth-century, similar *confesionarios* were circulated such as Fray Sebastian de Totanes's *Arte de la lengua tagala* published in 1745. The manual included questions covering sexual behaviors such as bestiality, ingestion of aphrodisiacs, bathing together in

63   See Ma. Mercedes G. Planta, "Prerequisites to a Civilized Life: The American Colonial Public Health System in the Philippines, 1901 to 1927" (PhD diss., National University of Singapore, 2008), 64; Rafael, *Contracting Colonialism*.

64   Tomas Pinpin, *Librong Pagaaralan nang mga Tagalog nang Uicang Castila* [The Book for Tagalogs to Learn the Castilian Language] (1610), ed. Damon L. Woods (Manila: UST Publishing House, 2011), 100–1.

the nude, and erotic gratification with a fellow male "in the manner of a woman" (*capouamo lalaqui, con babayi*).[65] In relation to judicial practices involving sodomy, confession as a means of obtaining narration of the "unnatural act" was regarded as *regina probationum* (the queen of evidence) when the accused himself would admit to committing the nefarious sin.[66] Through naming and describing a range of non-procreative sexual acts considered immoral and aberrant by the colonizers, confessional interrogations compelled natives to reveal intimate details of their lives, and allowed friars to censure and denounce the "unorthodox" and ultimately, to single out, problematize, and control specific aspects of natives' bodies, relationships with others, and desires.

While the Church's role was crucial in maintaining social control, the Spanish civil bureaucracy also participated in the enforcement of punishments against actions deemed as contraventions to Spanish Catholic moral sensibilities. At the center of the colonial power structure was the Real Audiencia de Manila, which in the early Spanish period dispensed justice, and assisted and checked the powers of the governor-general.[67] The Audiencia also exercised legislative powers by promulgating *autos acordados* (literally, "acts agreed upon"), which were regulations or local ordinances enacted by members of the tribunal.[68]

In 1599, the Real Audiencia enacted a legislative measure that formally sought to regulate the resident Chinese in the colony. After years during which sodomy was relatively disregarded, the royal ordinance was the first to legislate punishment for the nefarious sin and other sexual offences by the Chinese:

> First, we ordain and command that none of the said Sangleys [Chinese], or any other persons whatsoever, shall *commit or practice the said abominable sin against nature*, or try to commit it. Whoever shall do so shall incur the *penalty of being burned alive by fire*, besides having *all his goods confiscated* to the treasury of His Majesty.
>
> We ordain and command that none of the aforesaid [Chinese] *shall cohabit or have carnal intercourse with… Christian Indian woman,* under penalty that,

---

65   Reyes, "Sodomy in Seventeenth-Century Manila," 129; Sebastian de Totanes, *Arte de la lengua tagala y manual tagalog para la administración de los sacramentos* (Manila: Imprenta de Miguel Sanchez, 1865).

66   Alejandro Cañeque, "The Political and Institutional History of Colonial Spanish America," *History Compass* 11, no. 4 (2013): 285.

67   Nicholas P. Cushner, SJ, *Spain in the Philippines: From Conquest to Revolution* (Quezon City: Institute of Philippine Culture, 1971), 168.

68   Zaide, *Pageant of Philippine History*, 274.

in such case, he shall incur *punishment of two hundred lashes and ten years in the galleys*, as criminals sentenced to row, without pay, and of *confiscation of one-half his property*."[69] (Italics and insets mine)

Jurisdictional disputes between civil and ecclesiastical authorities characterized the early years of the Spanish bureaucracy, and the legislation of the 1599 anti-Chinese, anti-sodomy law was in itself an example. Cases involving the Chinese of the Parián, Binondo, and Santa Cruz should have been judged by the *gobernadorcillo de chinos* who was an official in the Manila area in charge of dealing with Chinese criminal cases and civil suits.[70] However, the Audiencia in this case demanded *exclusive* jurisdiction of sodomy litigation involving the Chinese.[71] It can be argued that by taking charge of sodomy cases, the Audiencia was seeking to justify its presence in the islands.[72] Since it was previously dissolved in 1589 mainly due to the financial constraints of operating a judiciary that handled few important cases, the Audiencia saw the opportunity to assert its importance by placing cases of sodomy involving the Chinese under its own jurisdiction. It can be reasonably surmised that given the prevalence of sodomy among Chinese in Manila, the Spaniards' penchant to control the Chinese, and the pressures in previous years to prosecute the nefarious sin, the Audiencia saw it as fitting and imperative to meddle on a matter prohibited to its jurisdiction. As such, this may well exemplify the uniquely Spanish concept of *obedezco pero no cumplo* (I obey but do not comply) where local colonial officials had very wide discretion in exercising legal powers emanating from Madrid, in this case pertaining to jurisdiction regarding Chinese affairs.

While there was a reference to the arrest and prosecution of fourteen Chinese in Manila for sodomy in 1588, the earliest detailed documented case after the enactment of the anti-sodomy law was in 1670 involving Lousu, a Chinese bureaucrat based in Taiwan (Formosa), who frequently visited the Parián.[73] According to Reyes's study, Lousu appeared to have enjoyed sexual encounters with a number of Chinese men in the Chinese enclave in Manila, and with one favorite in particular.[74] Lousu's intimates were most likely social inferiors and were younger, thus reflecting the pattern of hierarchized

---

69   Francisco Tello, et al., "Ordinances Enacted by the Audiencia de Manila, June 1598–July 1599)," in BR, 11: 56–58.

70   Wickberg, *Chinese in Philippine Life*, 37.

71   Juan Cerezo de Salamanca, "Letters from Juan Cerezo de Salamanca to Felipe IV" (10 August 1634), in BR, 23: 310.

72   Cushner, *Spain in the Philippines*, 173.

73   Reyes, "Sodomy in Seventeenth-Century Manila," 127.

74   Ibid.

roles based on age and social status in same-sex relationships in late imperial China. Pagsebuan, a cousin of the ruler of Taiwan (*Rey de Isla Hermossa*), pleaded to Spanish authorities for Lousu's clemency by saying that as a foreigner, Lousu "may have unknowingly broken the laws of the lands for which he was imprisoned."[75] Lousu expressed surprise and naiveté at the gravity of punishment being handed down for an act which was outright permissible in his society of origin.

Due to an opportune confluence of factors—protests by Manila's Chinese community for his release from prison; the desire on the part of authorities, especially the influential Fray Collares (prominent Dominican friar who ministered to the Parián), to preserve good relations with the Chinese; and the fact that Lousu was a bureaucrat of an important man named Pangsebuan who was related to Taiwan's ruler—Lousu and his companion were both acquitted by the Spanish governor-general from the crime of *pecado nefando*.[75] Lousu's case draws attention to the role played by the Catholic clerics, in the person of Fray Collares, in urging the Governor-General to pardon Lousu and his companion. While members of the clergy generally adopted a hardline stance to same-sex sexual acts by identifying and condemning sodomy, in Lousu's case, the friar showed flexibility and leniency in bending rigid religious and legal principles in the interest of diplomacy.

Conclusion

The Philippines, as the Spanish colonial outpost in Asia, occupies a unique position in the Spanish empire given the large and strong presence of ethnic Chinese. In the early years of Spanish rule, colonial officials sought to control and inculcate loyalty to the Chinese who were seen as resistant to assimilation and, given their numerical strength, potentially threatening to Spanish sovereignty. The study of early Spanish attempts to prosecute sodomy highlighted the relevance of examining themes like gender and ethnicity from a transnational perspective, that is, beyond the confines of a territorially bound historical narrative. The institutional actions and responses taken by the early colonial regime towards sodomy, particularly against the ethnic Chinese in the Philippines, can only be fully understood in the context of

75   Ibid., 127, 136. Although not as detailed as Lousu's, another documented case of sodomy dating back to 1890 was that of a certain Tingco who was imprisoned in Manila for the "unnatural crime" of sodomy. There were no details about his sexual offense but accordingly, after being released from prison, Tingco engaged in theft and vagabond activities and even attacked the house of a government official. He was later on captured and executed in Manila (See Casimiro Diaz, OSA, *Conquistas de las Islas Filipinas* (1890), in BR, 42: 248–50).

the prevailing notions and attitudes in early modern Spain towards what was regarded as *pecado nefando* or *pecado contra natura*. Similar to the Jews and the *moriscos* of early modern Spain, the sangleyes, who were an economically significant but culturally inassimilable people in early Spanish Philippines, became targets for sodomy denunciations. Additionally, understanding the behavior of Chinese men like Lousu necessitates a closer look at the details of the sociocultural milieu of late imperial China, where male same-sex desires were much more prevalent and accorded with a certain level of legitimacy compared to early modern Europe. In cultures such as the Ming and Qing societies with relatively pluralistic sensibilities with regard to gender and sexual acts, Lousu's case was therefore by no means an isolated one. Such insights would have been missed if complex historical developments outside the territorial confines of Philippines were not taken into account.

The second theme of the study focused on the "tensions between race and religion that ran through the whole of the Hispano-Asian Pacific"[76] as reflected in encounters such as sodomy prosecutions in early Spanish Philippines. Although same-sex sexual acts and other "unorthodox" sexual practices were punished harshly in early modern Spain and colonial Latin America, what made early Spanish Philippines a uniquely interesting case was the significant presence of Chinese migrants whose cultural views and practices towards same-sex relations were viewed as threats to the dominant, hegemonic Spanish and Catholic notions of gender and sexuality. The increased presence of the Chinese therefore has all the more complicated the already existing sociocultural and sexual diversity among the *indios*, which was taken by the Spaniards as a direct challenge to the political and universal moral order they were trying to impose in the colony, hence driving a "political strategy of difference" that classified early colonial society into "loyal" versus "dangerous" and "moral" versus "sinful" subjects.

It was in the presence of interethnic tensions between Spaniards and Chinese that sodomy was applied as an invidious stereotype, and a justification for the pattern of distrust and hostility against a despised ethnic "other." Negative images (i.e., "source of sodomy," "unchaste and abominable") about the sexuality of the Chinese contributed to their creation as disreputable and dangerous outgroups (i.e., to protect natives from corrupt influences), and at times were used to justify their exclusion, oppression, and even extermination. Even up to the early twentieth century, the association of sodomy

---

76   Ryan Crewe, "Transpacific Mestizo: Religion and Caste in the Worlds of a Moluccan Prisoner of the Mexican Inquisition," *Itinerario* 39, no. 3 (2015): 464.

with Chinese still existed in the local imaginary as reflected in the Cebuano term "Chinese kick" for male-male sexual intercourse. [77]

Finally, the last theme that this study sought to address was the utility and potential of sodomy as a unit of historical analysis to illuminate broader political and social developments through the lens of a marginalized social group like the Chinese. Examining the attempts of the Spanish regime to prosecute sodomy reveals much about the policy and practice of Spanish colonialism in the Philippines. The fact that there were conflicts between civil and ecclesiastical authorities, and between the gobernadorcillo de chinos and the Audiencia Real de Manila on jurisdiction over sodomy also shows the administrative issues and ambiguities in the early Spanish rule.

For the most part, the consolidation of colonial rule in the early stages of the Spanish regime relied heavily on the Church's task of religious conversion, and it was through the sacraments, particularly confession, that the Church was able to effectively enforce its orthodox standards for sexual morality. In general, while Church officials who assumed authority over sexual discourse were at the forefront of denouncing sodomy, there were certain instances when individuals exercised their agency through the flexibility and reluctant tolerance they showed in dealing with "illicit" sexual acts between men. The role of Fray Collares in the Lousu affair, in a way, challenges the popular image of the intolerant and unsympathetic Spanish friar in Philippine history. The hesitation of some civil officials to prosecute some Chinese for sodomy, and at times, the blatant disregard of some missionaries towards sodomitical activities were illustrative of Spain's policy of basic compromise between religious-cultural ideals and social and economic interests. The varied and uneven response of early Spanish civil and church authorities towards sodomy suggests some level of accommodation where "Spanish Christian expansionism had to coexist with a burgeoning trans-pacific trade."[78]

In closing, it has been demonstrated how Spanish anxieties about same-sex desires were heavily suffused with racial or ethnic fears. These attempts to silence "desires that dare not speak their names"[79] reflect tensions, conflicts, and negotiations that emerged from the sustained interactions between early modern Spanish empire and maritime Asia, or what this paper calls Hispano-Asian encounters. Using archival documents to understand

---

77   Donn V. Hart, "Homosexuality and Transvestism in the Philippines: The Cebuan Filipino Bayot and Lakin-on," *Behavioral Science Notes* 3, no. 4 (1969): 231.

78   Ryan Dominic Crewe, "Pacific Purgatory: Spanish Dominicans, Chinese Sangleys, and the Entanglement of Mission and Commerce in Manila, 1580–1620," *Journal of Early Modern History* 19, no. 4 (2015): 337.

79   Peletz, *Gender Pluralism*, 123.

how the early Spanish colonial society defined sodomy, and who committed sodomy and why, provides deeper insight into details about subjects considered "dangerous" by the colonial regime, and it also speaks about the workings of power in Spain's colonial outpost in Asia, which was also perhaps, to appropriate a phrase from a Spanish historian, Spain's *colonia más peculiar*[80]—the most queer colony.

80   Taken from the title of the book, *Filipinas, La colonia más peculiar: La hacienda pública en al definición de la política colonial* (Madrid: Consejo Superior de Investigaciones Científicas, 1999), written by Spanish historian Josep M. Fradera.

Bibliography

Primary sources

Alcina, Francisco Ignacio, SJ. *Historia de las islas e indios de Bisaya*. Part 1, Book 3: 1668. Translated by Cantius J. Kobak, OFM, and Lucio Gutiérrez, OP. Manila: University of Santo Tomas Publishing House, 2005.

Benavides, Miguel de. "Complaints against the Chinese" (3–9 February 1605). In *The Philippine Islands, 1493–1898*, edited by Emma H. Blair and James Robertson, 13: 271–86. Ohio: Arthur H. Clark, Co., 1903–1909. Hereafter BR.

———. "Letters to Felipe III, Manila" (5 and 6 July 1603). In BR, 12: 271–86.

Chirino, Pedro, SJ. "Relacion de las Islas Filipinas" (1604). In BR, 12: 175–321.

Cobo, Juan, Philippines, OP. "Father Juan Cobo's Account" (13 July 1589). In *The Chinese in the Philippines, 1750–1770*, edited by Alfonso Felix Jr., 1: 133–42. Manila: Solidaridad Publishing House, 1966.

Dasmariñas, Luiz Perez de. "Letter to Felipe II" (28 June 1597). In BR, 9: 315–25.

Davalos, Melchor. "Letter to Felipe II, Manila" (3 July 1584). In BR, 6: 54–65.

Diaz, Casimiro, OSA. *Conquistas de las Islas Filipinas* (1890). In BR, 42: 117–312.

Jesus, Pablo de, OSF. "Letter to Gregory XIII, Manila" (July 1580). In BR, 34: 316–24.

Manila Synod of 1582: The Draft of its Handbook for Confessors. Translated by Paul A. Dumol. Quezon City: Ateneo de Manila University Press, 2014.

Mentrida, Alfonso de. *Diccionario de la lengua bisaya hiligueina y haraya de la isla de Panay*. Manila: Imp. de D. Manuel y de D. Felis S. Dayot, 1841.

Morga, Antonio de. "Letter to Felipe II" (6 July 1596). In BR, 9: 263–73.

———. *Sucesos de las Islas Filipinas* (1609). In BR, 16: 27–209.

Pinpin, Tomas. *Librong Pagaaralan nang manga Tagalog nang Uicang Castila*. Transcribed and edited by Damon L. Woods. Manila: Univeristy of Santo Tomas Publishing House, 2011.

Plasencia, Juan de, OSF. "Customs of the Tagalogs" (1589). In BR, 7: 173–96.

Salamanca, Juan Cerezo de. "Letters from Juan Cerezo de Salamanca to Felipe IV" (10 August 1634). In BR, 24: 279–94.

Salazar, Domingo de. *Affairs in the Philippine Islands*. In BR, 5: 210–55.

———. "The Chinese and the Parian at Manila." In BR, 7: 212–38.

Sande, Francisco de. "Relation of the Philippine Islands" (7 June 1576). In BR, 4: 21–97.

San Jose, Francisco Blancas de, OP. *Sermones* (1640). Edited by Jose Mario C. Francisco, SJ. Quezon City: Ateneo de Manila University, 1994.

Tello, Francisco. "Ordinances Enacted by the Audiencia de Manila, June 1598–July 1599." In BR, 11: 21–81.

Totanes, Sebastian de. *Arte de la lengua tagala y manual tagalog para la administración de los sacramentos*. Manila: Imprenta de Miguel Sanchez, 1865.

Vera, Santiago de, et al. "Memorial to the Council by Citizens of the Philippine Islands" (26 July 1586). In BR, 6: 157–233.

SECONDARY SOURCES

Books

Bankoff, Greg. *Crime, Society and the State in the Nineteenth Century Philippines*. Quezon City: Ateneo de Manila University, Press, 1996.

Chu, Richard T. *Chinese and Chinese Mestizos of Manila*. Mandaluyong: Anvil Publishing, 2012.

Comenge, Rafael. *Cuestiones Filipinas, primera parte: Los chinos–Estudio social y political*. Manila: Tipo-Litografía de Chofré y Compaña, 1894.

Cushner, Nicholas P., SJ. *Spain in the Philippines: From Conquest to Revolution*. Quezon City: Institute of Philippine Culture, 1971.

De la Costa, Horacio, SJ. *The Jesuits in the Philippines, 1581–1768*. Quezon City: Ateneo de Manila University Press, 2014.

Fradera, Josep M. *Filipinas, La colonia más peculiar: La hacienda pública en la definición de la política colonial, 1762–1868*. Madrid: Consejo Superior en de la Investigaciones Cientificas, 1999.

Foucault, Michel. *The History of Sexuality, Volume 1: An Introduction*. New York: Vintage Books, 1978.

Garcia, J. Neil C. *Philippine Gay Culture: Binabae to Bakla, Silahis to MSM*. Quezon City: University of the Philippines Press, 2008.

Garza, Federico Carvajal. *Butterflies Will Burn: Prosecuting Sodomites in Early Modern Spain and Mexico*. Austin: University of Texas Press, 2003.

Hinsch, Bret. *Passions of the Cut Sleeve: The Male Homosexual Tradition in China*. Berkeley: University of California Press, 1990.

Nagel, Joane. *Race, Ethnicity and Sexuality: Intimate Intersections, Forbidden Frontiers*. Oxford: Oxford University Press, 2003.

Phelan, John Leddy. *The Hispanization of the Philippines: Spanish Aims and Filipino Responses, 1565–1700*. Madison: University of Wisconsin Press, 1967.

Peletz, Michael G. *Gender Pluralism: Southeast Asia since Early Modern Times*. New York: Routledge, 2009.

Rafael, Vicente L. *Contracting Colonialism: Translation and Christian Conversion in Tagalog Society under Early Spanish Rule*. Quezon City: Ateneo de Manila University Press, 2000.

Scott, William Henry. *Barangay: Sixteenth-century Philippine Culture and Society*. Quezon City: Ateneo de Manila University Press, 2015.

Sommer, Matthew H. "Dangerous Males, Vulnerable Males and Polluted Males: The Regulation of Masculinity in Qing Dynasty Law." In *Chinese Femininities / Chinese*

Masculinities: A Reader, edited by Susan Brownell and Jeffrey N. Wasserstrom, 67–88. Berkeley: University of California Press, 2002.

Trexler, Richard C. *Sex and Conquest: Gendered Violence, Political Order and the European Conquest of the Americas*. Cambridge: Polity Press, 1995.

Wickberg, Edgar. *The Chinese in Philippine Life 1850–1898*. Quezon City: Ateneo de Manila University Press, 2000.

Wu, Cuncun. *Homoerotic Sensibilities in Late Imperial China*. New York: Routledge, 2004.

Zaide, Gregorio F. *The Pageant of Philippine History: Political, Economic and Sociocultural*. Vol. 1. Manila: Philippine Education Company, 1979.

Zialcita, Fernando N. *Authentic Though Not Exotic: Essays on Filipino Identity*. Quezon City: Ateneo de Manila University Press, 2005.

Articles

Abásolo, Antonio García. "La imagen española de los chinos en Filipinas." *Revista Española del Pacífico* 21–22 (2008/2009): 67–75.

———. "La Audiencia de Manila y los chinos de Filipinas: Casos de integracion en el delito." In *Homenaje a Alberto de la Hera: Instituto de Investigaciones Jurídicas*, 339–68. Mexico City: Universidad Nacional Autonoma de Mexico, 2008.

Angeles, F. Delors. "The Philippine Inquisition: A Survey." *Philippine Studies* 28, no. 3 (1980): 253–83.

Berco, Cristian. "Producing Patriarchy: Male Sodomy and Gender in Early Modern Spain." *Journal of the History of Sexuality* 17, no. 3 (September 2008): 351–76.

———. "Social Control and Its Limits: Sodomy, Local Sexual Economies, and Inquisitors during Spain's Golden Age." *Sixteenth Century Journal* 36, no. 2 (2005): 331–58.

Brewer, Carolyn. "Baylan, Asog, Transvestism, and Sodomy: Gender, Sexuality and the Sacred in Early Colonial Philippines." *Intersections: Gender, History and Culture in the Asian Context*, no. 2 (May 1999). http://intersections.anu.edu.au/issue2/carolyn2.html.

Cañeque, Alejandro. "The Political and Institutional History of Colonial Spanish America." *History Compass* 11, no. 4 (2013): 280–91.

Chan, Albert, SJ. "Chinese–Philippine Relations in the Late Sixteenth Century to 1603." In *More Tsinoy than We Admit*, edited by Richard T. Chu, 23–53. Quezon City: Vibal Foundation, 2015.

Crewe, Ryan Dominic. "Pacific Purgatory: Spanish Dominicans, Chinese Sangleys, and the Entanglement of Mission and Commerce in Manila, 1580–1620." *Journal of Early Modern History* 19, no. 4 (2015): 337–65.

———. "Transpacifc Mestizo: Religion and Caste in the Worlds of a Moluccan Prisoner of the Mexican Inquisition." *Itinerario* 39, no. 3 (2015): 463–85.

De la Costa, Horacio, SJ. "The Legal Basis of Spanish Imperial Sovereignty." *Philippine Studies* 1, no. 2 (1953): 155–62.

De los Reyes, Guillermo. "'Curas, dones y sodomitas': Discursos de moralidad sexual y prácticas sexuales ilícitas entre sacerdotes en México colonial." *Anuario de Estudios Americanos* 67, no. 1 (January–June 2010): 53–76.dd

Fernandez, André. "The Repression of Sexual Behavior by the Aragonese Inquisition between 1560 and 1700." *Journal of the History of Sexuality* 7, no. 4 (April 1997): 469–501.

Guerrero, Milagros C. "The Chinese in the Philippines, 1570–1770." In *More Tsinoy than We Admit*, edited by Richard T. Chu, 55–83. Quezon City: Vibal Foundation, 2015.

———. "The Political Background." In *More Tsinoy than We Admit*, edited by Richard T. Chu, 113–31. Quezon City: Vibal Foundation, 2015.

Halperin, David M. "How to Do the History of Male Homosexuality." *GLQ: A Journal of Lesbian and Gay Studies* 6, no. 1 (2000): 87–124.

Hart, Donn V. "Homosexuality and Transvestism in the Philippines: The Cebuan Filipino Bayot and Lakin-on." *Behavioral Science Notes* 3, no. 4 (1968): 211–48.

Huang, Martin W. "Male-Male Sexual Bonding and Male Friendship in Late Imperial China." *Journal of the History of Sexuality* 22, no. 2 (May 2013): 312–31.

Keck, David. "Influences of the European Middle Ages in the Philippines." *Philippine Studies* 44, no. 4 (1996): 447–64.

Laven, Mary. "Jesuits and Eunuchs: Representing Masculinity in Late Imperial China." *History and Anthropology* 23, no. 2 (June 2012): 199–214.

Lewis, Laura A. "From Sodomy to Superstition: The Active Pathic and Bodily Transgressions in New Spain." *Ethnohistory* 54, no.1 (2007): 129–57.

Loos, Tamara. "Transnational Histories of Sexualities in Asia." *American Historical Review* 114, no. 5 (2009): 1309–24.

Lynch, Owen. "Spanish Colonial Sovereignty over the Philippine Islands: Legal Origins and Justifications." *Social Science Diliman* 6, no. 2 (December 2010): 79–99.

Nesvig, Martin. "The Complicated Terrain of Latin American Homosexuality." *Hispanic American Historical Review* 81, no. 3 (2001): 689–729.

Reyes, Raquel A.G. "Sodomy in Seventeenth-Century Manila: The Luck of a Mandarin from Taiwan." In *Sexual Diversity in Asia, c. 600–1950*, edited by Raquel Reyes and William G. Clarence-Smith, 127–40. New York: Taylor and Francis, 2012.

Sigal, Pete. "Gender, Male Homosexuality and Power in Colonial Yucatan." *Latin American Perspectives* 29, no.2 (March 2002): 24–40.

Sommer, Matthew H. "The Penetrated Male in Late Imperial China: Judicial Constructions and Social Stigma." *Modern China* 23, no. 2 (April 1997): 140–80.

Tortorici, Zeb. "Against Nature: Sodomy and Homosexuality in Colonial Latin America." *History Compass* 10, no.2 (2012): 61–178.

———. "Heran Todos Putos: Sodomitical Subcultures and Disordered Desire in Early Colonial Mexico." *Ethnohistory* 54, no. 1 (2007): 35–67.

Vitiello, Giovanni. "Exemplary Sodomites: Chivalry and Love in Late Ming Culture." *NAN NÜ* 2 (2000): 207–57.

Unpublished works

Pe, Susan L. "The Dominican Ministry among the Chinese in the Parian, Baybay and Binondo: 1587–1637." MA thesis, Ateneo de Manila University, 1983.

Planta, Ma. Mercedes G. "Prerequisites to a Civilized Life: The American Colonial Public Health System in the Philippines, 1901 to 1927." PhD diss., National University of Singapore, 2008.

UNIT III

FILIPINO SEXUAL
AND GENDER IDENTITIES

Crispulo "Pulong" Luna in native costume (late 1920s).

Pulong was known to be a gender crosser from Paco, Manila during the American occupation. Victoria Studios was where he had his portraits all dressed in female outfits—from an exquisite *baro't saya* to Japanese geisha robes. Pulong became involved with and eventually played "wife" to Juan, a five-years-younger *maestro carpentero*. Photo courtesy of Patricia Callasan-Corre.

This essay was previously published in *Conceiving Sexuality: Approaches to Sex Research in a Postmodern World* (London: Routledge, 1995), 85–96.

MICHAEL L. TAN

From *Bakla* to Gay: Shifting Gender Identities and Sexual Behaviors in the Philippines

THE FIRST REPORT OF HIV INFECTION in the Philippines dates back to 1984. Since then, the cumulative number of reported cases has reached 382 HIV positives and eighty-six AIDS cases as of the end of 1992. Health department officials acknowledge that the small number from 5,000 to 35,000.

Among the cumulative reported cases, self-identified homosexual and bisexual men constitute seven percent of total HIV positives and forty-four percent of total AIDS cases. It is impossible to estimate what the real figures are for the general population or for men who have sex with men (MSMs), but the available statistics do suggest that HIV disease can become a significant problem among MSMs in the Philippines.

HIV prevention programs for MSMs in the Philippines need to be guided by sound research to explore the sexual networks within this population.[1] Unfortunately, other than research on contraceptive prevalence, the Philippines has neven conducted comprehensive surveys on sex and sexuality. The emergence of HIV/AIDS created justification for such surveys, which have been mostly Metro Manila-based. One important survey, commissioned by the US AIDSCOM project (and which I was later asked to analyze [Tan 1990]), was conducted in Metro Manila in 1989 by a marketing research firm among "sentinel populations." One of the surveyed populations consisted of a random sample of 150 young adult males (aged eighteen to twenty-four years), where fifteen percent of respondents said they had had same-sex sexual encounters. The

---

1   Despite its biomedical and behaviorist emphasis, I will use them term MSM because it is internationally accepted among groups working on HIV/AIDS.

figure here comes significantly close to the reported statistic of seventeen percent with another sentinel population: a convenience sample of young male overseas contract workers.

The statistic suggest that there are significant numbers of Filipino MSMs. However, this population is far from being homogeneous, and consists of many subcultures defined by variables such as socio-economic status, age, ethnicity, rural/urban origins, and religious affiliation.

In this paper, my main reference group will be participants in a series of workshops sponsored by The Library Foundation (TLF), a Metro Manila-based group of self-identified gay men. Since 1991, TLF has conducted twelve weekend workshops for about 300 men who have sex with men, addressing HIV prevention in the context of the psychosocial needs of the population. I will cite some information derived from self-administered workshop questionnaires,[2] as well as from interviews and group discussions with the participants both during and after the workshops.

I choose the TLF workshop participants as a reference group because they represent a subculture that is emerging in many developing countries, one whose members self-identify as "gay," and who are beginning to identify with an emerging "gay" community. Passing references to similar groups are found for the *homos* in Indonesia (Oetomo 1991) and the *entendidos* in Brazil (Parker 1985). Such groups remain a minority within the larger population of MSMs but may prove to be crucial as organized responses to the HIV/AIDS epidemic, not just within the MSM population but also in AIDS service organizations in general, where gay men and lesbians have become increasingly active.

Theoretical and methodological premises

The TLF program to reach MSMs in the Philippines works on the premise that this population's risk for HIV emerges from the stigmatization of homosexuality. It is this stigmatization that forces MSMs to circulate within "shadow" sexual networks where sexual encounters are necessarily anonymous and casual. Over the last year and a half, as the program developed, it became clear that this explanation of "anonymous and casual sex" was inadequate. Even among MSMs who had "come out" and self-identify as "gay," comfortably socializing in the few gay establishments

---

2   Data cited in this paper comes from only 210 questionnaires since The Library Foundation revised its forms several times, resulting in difficulties in comparing information.

in Metro Manila, there are still problems with social networking, sexual negotiations, and HIV risk-reduction.

One important issue that emerged during the workshops was the participants' own observation that risk-reduction in sexual behavior is, to a large extent, dependent on specific social settings, particularly "who you are having sex with." In this paper, I will show how these different forms of social interactions relate to sexual identity and how this identity is in turn related to dominant sexual ideologies, including homophobia.

As Dollimore (1991, 28–29) points out, the problem of homophobia is that it is not, as the term phobic suggests, an essentially personal problem. Rather, homophobia, especially in relation to HIV/AIDS, intersects with misogyny, xenophobia, racism and, I would add, discrimination based on class and other socioeconomic status variables. In this paper, I will cite several examples of these intersections not just from outside the MSM population but, more importantly, from within.

An overview

There are a number of Filipino MSM subcultures that are fairly visible to the public. The visible subcultures are all urban-based and consist mainly of people aged below thirty.

1. *Call Boys.* These are male sex workers, whose clientele includes MSMs from different subcultures, as well as middle-aged women (*matronas*). Most call boys self-identify as "straight" and many have wives and children. Many come from urban and rural poor families. The sex workers rarely have fixed incomes except for those who do "macho dancing" or work as waiters. Most call boys are "on call" with various bars and massage parlors, receiving payment only when they have clients. There is also a large number of freelance call boys who cruise the many shopping malls scattered throughout the metropolis.

Call boys are an important segment of the MSM population. In cities outside Metro Manila, there are no gay bars but there are many freelance male sex workers. In Metro Manila itself, there were as of February 1993 at least sixteen gay bars and massage parlors offering male sex workers, as against three exlusively "gay" and six "gay-friend-ly" establishments that do not actively promote male sex workers. Even in these "non-commercial" establishments, there will be a few freelance sex workers, including in some instances waiters of the es-tablishments, offering sex for pay.

2. *Parlorista*. This is a generic term for low-income MSMs, many of whom work in beauty parlors although there are also those working as domestic servants, small market vendors, and as waiters. For the average Filipino, the *parloristas*, who are found throughout the country, represent the entire "homosexual" population, defined as *bakla*, a gender label which I will explain later in this paper. The *parloristas* rarely patronize "gay" establishments and tend to organize their own activities, usually drag beauty pageants, through neighborhood associations.

3. *Gays*. This group has become visible only in the last two decades in Metro Manila. Many self-identify as "gay," "homosexual" or "bisexual," and in contradistinction to the lower-class *bakla/parlorista*. The group is far from being homogeneous, and can basically be divided into those with middle-class origins[3] and those from high-income groups. It is the middle-class group that has been actively organizing the country's gay men's organizations. This gay population remains partly in the shadows, socializing in gay establishments in Metro Manila but keeping its sexual orientation discreet at home and in their workplace. The middle-income groups, far more vulnerable to economic dislocation, tend to remain in the closet even as they become active in gay groups. High-income gay men are more willing to come out, but are essentially apolitical and limit their activities to socializing. The three visible populations have varying linkages with the larger, shadow MSM population consisting of individuals who may self-identify as homosexual but are not "out," as well as others who self-identify as bisexual or heterosexual. Sexual encounters between the "overt" and "covert" sectors of the MSM population are limited to such places as bathhouses, movie houses, shopping malls, or establishments with male sex workers.

Social context: from the outside looking in

The Filipino term most widely used as a gloss for "homosexual" is *bakla*, a contraction of the words *babae* (female) and *lalake* (male). As an adjective,

---

3   "Middle-class" here refers to the petty bourgeoisie including students, white-collar workers and professionals on fixed wage income. The monthly incomes range from US $200 to US $1500 in a country where the average monthly household income in 1991 was US $210 (National Statistics Office 1992).

bakla means uncertainty, indecisiveness. Other, less often used terms carry similar connotations: *binabae* (like a woman) and *syoki* (evolved from the Southern Chinese Hokkien words *syo k'i,* meaning weak-spirited).

As in many other societies, there are no Filipino terms for the different categories of sexual orientation, i.e., "homosexual," "bisexual," or "heterosexual." *Bakla* refers specifically to men who are effeminate, with cross-dressing as a major index feature. It is the concept of effeminacy, of a man with a woman's heart (*pusong babae*), that dominates public discourse, lumping together homosexuals, transvestites, transsexuals, and hermaphrodites. The English term "effeminate" is frequently used, and is defined in Webster's as recently as 1979: "having the qualities generally attributed to women, as weakness, gentleness, delicacy, etc.: unmanly."

The term "homosexual," of recent vintage even in the West, remains ambiguous in the Philippines. It is most often interchanged with *bakla,* with and emphasis on effeminacy and cross-dressing. The "sexual" in "homosexual" seems to have introduced a new element of recognizing sexual acitivity as possibly, but not necessarily, present among the *bakla.*

The public perception of bisexuality is even more enigmatic, mainly because of the difficulty with dissociating effeminacy and homosexuality. Some Filipinos, including many self-identified homosexuals, will declare that bisexuals are "really" homosexuals in the closet. A hybrid term, "macho gay," is sometimes used to refer bisexuals.

Curiously, the term "gay" has also become widely used, mainly as a synonym for homosexual. I should emphasize that "gay" is used like the term "homosexual," which still centers on the *bakla,* the effeminate male or the male with a woman's heart, expanded to include, rather hazily, a sexual persona.

The medicalization and pathologization of homosexuality in the West has been incorporated into Filipino popular perceptions of the *bakla.* Freudian theories that attribute male homosexuality to a dominant mother and absent or weak father continue to be widely invoked, perhaps because they offer a "logical" explanation for the consequences of a subversion of machismo norms. Male sex workers fret about eventually turning *bakla.* Parents explain their sons being *bakla* as resulting from going around with other *bakla. Bakla* is *nakakahawa,* contagious, an interesting conflation of concepts of danger and contagion.

Recent US research into the genetic origins of male homosexuality has had great impact on popular myths. The "gay brain" theory has been especially popular and has been repackaged by the lay public into what I call a "smaller brain" theory.[4]

The reduced or deficient gay brain image fits into other popular myths, such as homosexuality being equated with effeminacy, which is in turn explained as being due to hormonal deficiency and a small brain. The emergence of HIV/AIDS has contributed toward remedicalizing and repathologizing homosexuality, with the discourse centering on the "perversion" of sodomy.

This discussion of the "outsider" perspective is important in contextualizing gender identities among MSMs. We will see how the definition of a *bakla* as a feminized male is ideologically dominant, shaping MSMs' own constructions of gender identity and behavior.

Self-identification: gay or bakla?

I will now discuss native or ethnic perspective starting with the participants in TLF's workshops. The workshop participants were demographically homogeneous: most were aged under thirty (eighty-eight percent), raised in Metro Manila (seventy-eight percent), college-educated or current college students (ninety-four percent), and Roman Catholic (eighty-three percent).

About seventy percent of the workshop participants self-identified as homosexual, twenty-five percent as bisexual; two percent as heterosexual and the remaining four percent having no response or not being sure. The differences in self-ascribed sexual orientation, particularly for "homosexuals" and "bisexuals," are important.

Most TLF participants seem to prefer the label "gay," rather than *bakla,* which is identified with the low-income *parlorista.* Among middle- and high-income MSMs, the social construction of the *bakla* as an effeminate cross-dresser generates an extraordinary amount of cognitive dissonance which in turn affects the process of self-identification. One TLF workshop participant could not have summarized it better than when he described his alarm that he might be "abnormal," the abnormality being defined as a contradiction between his being attracted to other men, and yet never having the desire to cross-dress.

4　　An example comes from a woman writing in a community newspaper, where she urges parents not to beat up their *bakla* sons because (citing "Le Vay, neurobiologist from the Salk Institute") being *bakla* is physiological. The writer's interpretation of Le Vay: "when growing up they got less neutrons in their hypothalamus" (Austria 1993).

Among the few participants who have come out to their family, some describe how their parents accept the disclosure with one request: that they do not cross-dress like a *bakla* (read *parlorista*). The emphasis seems to shift toward status-defined norms and even desexualization. There may, in fact, be underlying messages that "as long as my son does not cross-dress like my hairdresser, he probably will not be having sex with other men."

I must emphasize that many "feminine" behavioral traits and cross-dressing have been adopted by the TLF workshop participants. However, they do distinguish their "feminized" behavior from that of the *parlorista*. Most of the TLF workshop participants consider as unacceptable "routine" daily cross-dressing as the *parlorista* would do. Moreover "feminization" follows class distinctions between the *colegiala* (product of convent schools) and the *palengkera* (a woman market vendor). A person who does not behave like an *Assumptionista* (a graduate of the Assumption, an elite girls' school) is labelled as graduate of Madam Kollerman's, a vocational school that trains beauticians and dressmakers. Being gay seems to be different from being *bakla*.

There is recognition of types within the population, corresponding loosely to the Americans' differentiation of "butch" and "fem" types. Those tending toward masculinity are called "pa-om" while "pa-girl" is used for the more feminine types. "Om" is a phonetic rendition of the abbreviated *hombre*, Spanish for male. The prefix "pa" describes mimicry, loosely translated as "to be like." The linguistic choice here reifies perceptions of a liminal status: neither male nor female, only like-male and like-female. A "real" male remains an *om* (or *hombre*) and a "real" female remains a girl.

Coming out: *Pagladlad ng kapa*

Coming out is described in Filipino gay jargon as *paladlad ng kapa* or unfurling of one's cape. The process is long and difficult. Someone calling himself "Spartan Warrior" (1993) wrote to a clinical psychologist/newspaper columnist expressing his conflicts as he discovers he is attracted to other men. The feelings, he says, are "strange" because "you see, I am cursed with an athletic body . . ." Spartan Warrior says that he intends to remain in the closet: "I cannot do what the *ladlad na bakla* would do externally—act effeminately, dress effeminately, etc." The letter is excruciatingly self-absorbed as Spartan Warrior alternates between expressions of contentment and depression over his situation. Yet, Spartan Warrior probably is typical of Filipino MSMs. It is not suprising that in a gay play produced in 1992 about the problems of "coming out" in the Philippines, the lead character is portrayed by a "butch" type while his alter ego is a drag queen impersonating Diana Ross. This dialectical angst seems to permeate the discourse among MSMs, and is dangerous in the way it becomes a device for self-marginalization: me against the world, including the queens.

Given that effeminacy is the gold standard for coming out as *bakla* or as "a gay" (Filipinos use gay more often as a noun, rather than as an adjective), it should not be surprising that people opt to remain in the closet, or, to tentatively move into self-identification as bisexual. During TLF workshop sessions discussing "gay issues," the issue of bisexuality often emerged with many pariticipants, almost always the more fem types, expressing their view that there was no such thing as a bisexual, i.e., that bisexuals were simply "gays who have not come out."

While it is tempting to dismiss such observations as facetious, we can look back at the statistics for the TLF participants. While twenty-five percent self-identified as bisexual, only nine percent of all the participants reported having sex with both men and women in the past year. Note, too, that this figure of nine percent included a number of participants who self-identified as homosexual.

Self-identification as a bisexual, at least among the TLF workshop participants, may represent an "in process" mode as individuals come to terms with their sexuality. One of TLF's male-to-male helpline counsellors told me, "I get all these calls from men who claim they are bisexual simply because they had sex with a woman eight years ago." Margarita Go-Singco Holmes, a clinical psychologist who writes the newspaper advice column I referred to earlier, says she gets many letters similar to the calls received at TLF's helpline from people asking if they are "gay," always prefaced by a reference to a girlfriend, or to sexual experiences with women a few years back.

The term "defense bisexuality" has been suggested to refer to sexual behavior in societies that stigmatize homosexual roles (Ross 1991, 23). In the same way that many textbooks describe "homosexuality" as a passing stage, I suggest here that self-ascribed bisexuality may in fact represent a transient "heterosexuality" for Filipino MSMs still unravelling their sexuality. It is significant that among the TLF participants, the average age of self-identified bisexuals was significantly lower that that of self-identified homosexuals.

I find it significant that self-ascribed bisexuality would emerge within the TLF group. For self-ascribed bisexuals, if we understand this to be a code for "sexuality-in-progress," attending a three-day live-in workshop publicized as being for MSMs can be daunting, representing a major step in a public unfurling of the cape.

I am not suggesting that "bisexuals," as defined in Western societies along the criterion of sex object choice, do not exist in the Philippines. Neither am I suggesting that the "bisexuals" in the TLF workshops exist only as semantic, self-ascribed categories. The TLF workshop surveys in fact showed very important differences in the sexual behavior of homosexuals and bisexuals. Yet, it is significant that when I cited the survey statistics showing that twenty-five percent of the participants self-identified as bisexual, most ot the TLF members I talked with expressed surprise, and could not identify who the "bisexuals" were. "Bisexual," in the context of the TLF workshop participants, defies existing definitions of homosexual and bisexual, *pa-om* and *pa-girl*, gay and macho gay. These gray areas affect the precesses of coming out and acceptance into the emerging gay community.

Choice of sexual partners: Avoiding the clash of cymbals

It is interesting that many Filipino self-identified gay men will shift from statements such as "There is no such thing as a bisexual—they're all closet gays" to an observation like "most Filipino males are bisexual," in reference to the perception that many "straight" males will have sex with another male.

This takes us into a discussion of sexual object choice. Among *parloristas,* sex between two *bakla,* or two self-identified gay men, is labeled "lesbianism" and is described as a clash of cymbals (*pompyangan*). A *bakla* can have sex only with a "straight man." This "rule" finds support in the Metro Manila survey I mentioned earlier in this paper. One sample of that survey included 200 "overt" gay males, with fifty-seven percent expressing a preference for "straight males" as sex partners, while only eight percent said they prefer "co-homosexuals." All this fits into social contstruction of the *bakla* as feminine.

It is interesting how the *bakla*-as-feminine image emerges in the sex object choice of MSMs who self-identify as "straight." With this subculture of straight "MSMs," the preference is for someone who is "*pa-girl*." There is logical consistency here because a self-identified straight male going to bed with an equally masculine (by his standards) male would forfeit his claims to being straight. "Girl" is again relative. One male sex worker explains: "I cannot do it with someone with a penis larger than mine. *Hindi bagay sa bakla.* It (a larger penis) does not fit a *bakla.*"

It is instructive to look into the following account from a physician who conducted interviews in a bathhouse whose clients are MSMs mainly self-identifying as "straight" or "bisexual."

I had this guy who said he doesn't use condoms. When I asked him why, he answered: *"Straight ako. Hindi naman ako gumagalaw; ako ang gina-galaw. Ako ang sumusubo. "* (I am straight. I do not move; I am moved. I am the one who feeds.)

Two keywords are worth analyzing here. One is the verb *galaw,* to move, which is used in conversational Filipino to refer to sexual inter-course. Usually, it is the man who "moves" a woman, meaning to have sex with a woman. In fact, all the Filipino verbs used to allude to having sex put the male in an active role: *trabaho* (to work); *banat* (to hit); *gamit* (to use). All these terms reflect the male's role as penetrator. Yet in the context of a self-identified straight man who has sex with other men, validation of his sexual identity is grafted on to the concept that it is a *bakla* who initiates sex. The "straight" man is now the one "moved."

The other key word is *subo,* to feed. The straight man's sexual passivity is qualified by his active role in oral sex—he feeds, the *bakla* eats.[5] Perhaps more important for HIV/AIDS programs is that all this discourse, despite its play on the active and passive roles, continues to place the "straight" man having sex with other men in a penetrator role while the *bakla,* consistent with his constructed feminine role, is defined as the one being penetrated whether in oral or anal sex.

It is not clear how much of stereotype corresponds to reality. I have strong doubts about the hegemony of this penetrator/penetrated dichot-omy even in sexual activities between a self-identified straight male and a *bakla.* Nevertheless, the rhetoric is important in that a straight male is de-fined as a "natural" sex object choice for the *bakla* and that this straight male takes a dominant role which includes being the one chased, courted, moved, worked on, fed on, by a *bakla.*

Let us look now at the TLF workshop participants. In contrast to the stereotype, preferences for bisexuals and gay men dominated. At the same

---

5   This is a reversal of the terms described by Fry (1985) and Parker (1991) for Brazil, where the *homem,* by playing the penetrator role, eats, while the *bicha,* the insertee, gives.

time, there were significant numbers indicating preference for "straight" men, either as a sole choice or in combination with "bisexual."

Preferred Male Sex Partners of TLF Workshop Participants

	Homosexuals (n=147)	Bisexuals (n=52)	Total
1. Bisexuals only	28	34	62
2. Gay only	57	3	60
3. Straight only	28	4	32
4. Gay and bisexuals	8	5	13
5. Straight and bisexual	8	5	13
6. Gay, bisexual, or straight	12	1	13
7. Straight and gay	6	0	6

Put briefly, the TLF workshop participants represent an incipient subculture that retains elements of a dominant sexual ideology, particularly the preference for a straight male. At the same time, there are shifts in these preferences, such as a willingness to have gay or bisexual partners sometimes with a provision that they "look straight." It would be useful to remember that a "bisexual" is often perceived as a "straight-looking gay male."

In a focus group discussion where I presented the statistics on preferred choices for sexual partners, the consensus that emerged was that "choices" were made at different levels. A "straight" man may be preferred for a casual sexual encounter, but a "gay" or "bisexual" male, preferably "straight-looking," would be preferred for a lover.

The willingness to go into a "lesbian" relationship is apparently class-bound. For a middle-class, self-identified "gay" person, homosexual or bisexual, a relationship with a *parlorista* would be unthinkable. Here, the rhetoric of the clashing of cymbals would be invoked: a *parlorista* is too "fem" to be a sex partner or even a date. Class definitions of "decency" (*pagkadesente*) are clearly present, intersecting with a fear of being "outed" (*mabuking*, always used in the passive voice) by being seen with a *parlorista*.

The distinction between casual sex partners and lovers is important. This differentiation sets boundaries for a network of dating and steady relationships with people from the same class background even as the boundaries can, and are, easily crossed for casual sex, as they would be with low-income male sex workers or other pick-ups.

Rules extend into roles in oral and anal sex. In the focus group discussion, participants agreed that, with oral sex, alternating or roles (insertor and insertee) occurs more frequently than it does with anal sex. Apparently, the masculine/feminine imagery in anal intercourse is much more powerful, especially as it translates into roles of penetrator and penetrated. Discussions about anal intercourse tend to be protracted, evoking images of male and female roles. It is also interesting how some TLF workshop participants view anal intercourse as representing a relationship of domination and submission.

The implied power relationships in sexual acitivities are crucial. Rules are recognized as being flexible, depending on who the sexual partner is. One participant explained: "You can't just tell your lover, 'Bend over,'" implying that this is possible in other situations, such as with as sex worker. Curiously, during the focus group discussion these was no consensus on when such transgressions are permitted. Some said there are fewer prohibitions in casual sex while other said such "don'ts" were more important in a relationship with lover.

The growing HIV/AIDS threat may provide new rhetoric that will affect gender identity and sexuality, even as such rhetoric draws on existing sexual ideologies. It is here where we find sharp intersections with misogyny, xenophobia, and class discrimination. For example, the popular perception of HIV and sexually-transmitted diseases (STDs) in the Philippines is still that of *sakit ng babae,* or women's disease. It is not surprising, then, to hear Filipino MSMs talking of HIV risk-reduction in terms of avoiding men who have women, especially women sex workers, as partners.

This concept of STDs as women's diseases interfaces with the perception of the *bakla.* As early as 1985, patrons in a bar patronized by high-income gay men complained to me about how the establishment had been invaded by "cheap *parlorista* queens who probably have AIDS." The rationale here was that the *parlorista* (actually, transvestite sex workers) were the only ones willing to have sex with tourists, who by that time were shunned as being potential "AIDS carriers."

In a kind of time warp, it was not until this decade that I began to hear comments from male sex workers expressing their reluctance to have sex with wealthy Filipino clients because such clients had lived in the US and Europe where their *"Kano"* (a generic term for Caucasians) partners were presumed infected with HIV. Such comments conflict with other sex workers' views that it is safer to pick a client who looks *desente* (decent) because such clients are *malinis* (clean).

Synthesis: From epidemiology to epistemology
Social scientists working on HIV/AIDS often reduce their research to an epidemiological framework of asking, as a recent editorial in *The Lancet* did: "How often, and in what ways, and with whom people have sex." Vance (1991, 880) describes this as "the tendency to count acts rather than explore meaning." The biomedical framework drop off four other important questions that need to be asked: "Where, when, why and why not?"

In this paper, I have tried to show how the expanded framework is important in understanding the social context fo HIV transmission in relation to the MSM population in the Philippines. This is, in a sense, and attempt to reconstruct, as cultural history, "a chronicle of intentions, contingencies, and relationships: among people, in a culture, over time." (Fox 1991, 95)

I have given examples to show how the socially-constructed definition of *bakla,* a man with a woman's heart, dominates discourse on male homosexuality and bisexuality. Further complicating sexual ideology are other dominant values such as misogyny, xenophobia, and class discrimination.

I have discussed the impact of this rhetoric on gender and sexuality among a small group of MSMs in the Philippines, and that challenges tradition even as it remains bound to it. The shifts in gender definitions are important, especially in terms of how one comes out of the closet, how one chooses sexual partners, and how one enters (and exits) relationships, whether casual or long-term.

Despite the rhetoric of a community whose members can openly relate to each other, and to the "straight" public as gay men, there are still many problems in social and sexual negotiations. While many Filipino gay men are aware of gender asymmetry in a relationsip between a gay man and a straight man, there tends to be less sensitivity to similar problems between or among self-identified gay men. Among TLF workshop participants, about half of those presently having a lover said they did not know or were unsure if their current lover was having sex with other partners. The problems are inevitable: in an incipient subculture, traditional social and sexual scripts may be insufficient. In the process of transcending gender stereotypes, the emerging "gay" community has to create and ratify a new intersubjectivity.

This intersubjectivity will be an important consideration in HIV prevention programs. The self-esteem and individual change of values that comes with affirmation of one's sexuality may not be enough. In fact, given the middle-class definitions of "being a gay" in the Philippines, this group could easily lapse into creating a moral *cordon sanitaire,* thinking of themselves as "safe," in contradistinction to "the others," whether they be foreigners, women sex workers or the *parlorista/bakla.*

Such dangers may even be amplified among those in a relationship with a lover. At the same time, there may be a danger in over-emphasizing the risks of "anonymous, casual encounters," since high-risk activities may happen more often in the search for a longer lasting relationship, i.e., when one party thinks he has to "prove" his commitment by consenting to unprotected anal intercourse.

Considering that Philippine society continues to be heavily dominated by strong patron-client relationships, it is easy for high-income and middle-class gay men to attempt to reproduce their "values" and sexual ideological framework as they begin to reach out to low-income men who have sex with men, including the *parlorista.* The shifts in gender identity, and in sexual behavior, will continue. Undoubtedly, HIV/AIDS will be a major force in the reshaping of boundaries. The problem is identifying the boundaries as they exist both for the visible populations and for the shadow population—for example, older MSMs; MSMs married to women; MSMs in areas outside Metro Manila. More importantly, we need to better understand the social dynamics involved in the shaping of these boundaries, both as they draw from and resist dominant ideologies.

BIBLIOGRAPHY

Austria, L. T. "Sport Lang." *The Citizen,* January–February 1993, 10.

Dollimore, J. *Sexual Dissidence.* Oxford: Oxford University Press, 1991.

Fox, R. G. "For a Nearly New Culture History." In *Recapturing Anthropology,* edited by R. G. Fox, 93–113. Santa Fe, New Mexico: School of American Research, 1991.

Fry, P. "Male Homosexuality and Spirit Possession in Brazil." *Journal of Homosexuality* 11, no. 3/4 (1985): 137–53.

National Statistics Office, Manila, Philippines. "Preliminary Results from the 1991 Family Income and Expenditures Survey." Typescript, 1992.

Oetomo, D. "Patterns of Bisexuality in Indonesia." In *Bisexuality and HIV/AIDS,* edited by R. A. P. Tielman, M. Carballo, and A. C. Hendriks, 119–26. Buffalo: Prometheus Books, 1991.

Parker, R. G. "Masculinity, Femininity, and Homosexuality: On the Anthropological Interpretation of Sexual Meanings in Brazil." *Journal of Homosexuality* 11, no. 3/4 (1985): 155–63.

———. *Bodies, Pleasures and Passions: Sexual Culture in Contemporary Brazil.* Boston: BeaconPress, 1991.

Ross, M. W. "A Taxonomy of Global Behavior." In *Bisexuality and HIV/AIDS*, edited by R. A. P. Tielman, M. Carballo, and A. C. Hendriks, 21–26. Buffalo: Prometheus Books, 1991.

Spartan Warrior [pseud.]. "An Alternative Lifestyle." *Manila Times*, 1 March 1993, 2.

Tan, M. L. "Synthesis of an AIDS KAP Survey Among Sentinel Groups in Metro Manila." Unpublished document submitted to the Department of Health and the Academy for Educational Development, 1990.

Vance, C. S. "Anthropology Rediscovers Sexuality: A Theoretical Comment." *Social Science and Medicine* 33, no. 8 (1991): 875–84.

Top, A campy rendition of pictures circulating in the media, to highlight the quantum leap from girly to hyper masculine and muscular depictions of gay men then and now. This quantum leap is evident in the profiles and pictures of Filipino gay men who use Planet Romeo, a dating site (*left,* photo from Shutterstock). As discussed in this essay, many of the website users valorize hypermasculinity and harbor discrimination against the effeminate. Illustration commissioned by Ronald Baytan from his friend, Erika Carreon.

RONALD BAYTAN

Crazy Planets: Notes on Filipino "Bisexuals"[1]

THREE YEARS AGO, I stumbled upon a photo with the caption *"Bakla Noon, Bakla Ngayon."* This photo has two frames: the one at the top (*"Noon"* or past) shows effeminate teenage cross-dressing boys ("baklita," young *bakla*) posing in front of the camera as though they were joining a beauty pageant; the bottom frame (*"Ngayon,"* meaning present) show-cases half-naked muscular guys who are clearly older than the "baklita."[2] In terms of temporal continuity, does the photo suggest that these twinky effeminate "baklita" from the past have transformed into these masculine men? What could have prompted the creator of the message to write such caption? The picture begs the question: Why are the masculine-looking and muscular guys labelled as "bakla" as well, especially when the Filipino culture in general equates *kabaklaan* (being *bakla*) with effeminacy? Who then is the *bakla*?

One possible answer to the question is: within the Filipino gay culture, there is a subculture of (supposedly) masculine men who do not necessar-

1 This phrase is from the suicide note of Stella Strada: "It's a crazy planets." I enclose the word "bisexual" in quotation marks and usually spell it as "BI" to emphasize the Filipino specificity of the identity of these "bisexuals" and to denote that BI is not the bisexual that we traditionally know in the LGBTQ community and in the Western world. After all, these BIs usually do not use the full word "bisexual" to name themselves in their PR profiles or in everyday discourse; they use the contracted BI.

2 This picture from Hugot Beki is no longer available online. Nonethe-less, similar pictures appear. Check out these pages: https://sungka.wordpress.com/2015/02/11/1917/ and http://epbites.blogspot.com/2015/02/bakla-noon-bakla-ngayon.html. There are other "Past/Present" *bakla* pictures similar to this one that have circulated online; one picture shows a group of adult *bakla* and their coun-terpart is a small group of three muscular young men. The basic dichotomy for these photographs is effeminate/masculine, denoting that the *bakla* have changed from effeminate to masculine.

ily identify as "bakla," and who usually call themselves BI (or bisexual). Do they consider themselves *bakla*, too? Do the *bakla* call them *bakla*? Should they be labelled as *bakla* or gay? The answer to these questions will depend on many variables, including who is speaking, who is asking the question, what is the context of the articulation, among many other things. To the general gay culture, these BIs are really gay or *bakla*; to the self-named BIs themselves, they most likely know that they are gay in terms of sexual orientation, too, but will insist on self-identifying differently as BIs. Such is the problem that discussions of Filipino"bisexuals" generate, and this is the main concern of my critical project.

Filipino gay men know too well the meaning and power of the words "discreet," "astig" (tough, masculine), "barako" (stud; rough m/animal) and "no trace." Many Filipino gay men know the marketability of (and safety preferred by) "bi," instead of the supposed apt term "gay." They also know the reluctance of many to self-identify as "gay" in dating sites and apps like Planet Romeo—for that would have been tantamount to admitting one has traces of effeminacy. Such facts plague Planet Romeo, all Filipino gay dating sites, and the entire Philippine gay culture. Thus, any study of gay cyber-dating would have yielded similar findings: the BI's revulsion of the effeminate.[3] But we need to ask: why and how? Exactly how do terms like "discreet," "astig," "barako," and more importantly "bi" operate, and how are these categories and ideals constructed and disseminated in Philippine gay culture? Thus, this paper is a modest attempt to offer preliminary theoretical notes on the inviolable link between the *bakla* and the "bisexual" in the Philippines through a study of profiles by Filipino BIs and gays on the dating site and mobile app Planet Romeo. It must be reiterated that the subjects of this study—the BIs—are actually **gay**, and the slippages and distinctions among the local "bi," "gay," "bakla," and the real bisexuals need to be theorized.

Work on cyber identities in the Philippines has been done by Pertierra, Concha, Madula, Montenegro, Benedicto, and Austria (see references). The difference is that this paper specifically addresses the identity of gay men labeling themselves as "bisexual." Focusing on "bisexuality" as a phenomenon in Philippine culture, this paper discusses how Planet Romeo profiles—as

---

3   Fernando Austria's chapter/essay on "Mga Bakla sa Internet," resonating with a previous work by Michael Tan on gay men and MSM ("From Bakla to Gay"), perfectly captures the problem and the fact: "Kadalasan, hindi pipiliin ng baklang Pinoy na nasa Internet ang 'gay.' Ito kasi'y nangangahulugang effeminate or 'yong tinatawag na 'baklang parlorista.' Ang pinipili ay salitang 'bisexual' kahit na walang gusto ang mga baklang ito sa mga babae" (313). (Translation: "More often than not, the baklang Pinoy will not choose 'gay.' The reason is that this denotes being effeminate or 'baklang parlorista.' The preferred term is "bisexual" even if these bakla are not attracted to women.")

invented selves—are suitable sources for theorizing on gay identities in the Philippines. This paper's thesis is thus as follows: the Pinoy BI (and not the practicing or real Pinoy bisexuals) is technically not a bisexual but a variation of the local homosexual *bakla*, a fact known to the gay culture but not quite theorized yet. To add, I submit that the BI's disavowal of the *bakla*, of anything effeminate, borrows its terminology and virulence from the existing heterosexist logic and gender hierarchy firmly entrenched in Philippine culture. I shall discuss three terms associated with being BI in the country: *barako* (fearless stud), *astig* (tough guy), and "discreet." I shall also explain the relationship among the BI, the *bakla*, and the *lalake*—with the end in view of reinforcing the contemporary BI's problematic but inescapable relationship with the *bakla*.

Bakla, gay, and bi in the Philippines

In this section, I shall discuss existing sexual categories and identities related to homosexuality in the Philippines from the twentieth century onwards. I shall give a brief history of the *bakla* and explain how this identity is understood and deployed vis-à-vis its proverbial Other, the *lalake*. I shall also discuss the *bakla*'s connection with Western categories *homosexual* and *gay*. Finally, I shall discuss the *silahis* and how it is related to the *bakla* and to the BI-identified gay men in this study. It is important to discuss these categories first since discussions of BIs necessitate understanding of local gender concepts.

According to Michael Tan, "[b]akla refers specifically to men who are effeminate with cross-dressing as a major index feature" (From Bakla to Gay, 88). The *bakla* belongs to the four genders in the Philippines (*lalake, babae, bakla,* and *tomboy*) which are positioned or arranged hierarchically so that the *lalake* is superior to the *babae* and *babae* is above the *bakla* and so on.[4] Given the centrality of depth (*loob*) in the construction of the Filipino selfhood (Garcia 2009, 120–21), the four genders are defined in accordance to the relationship between the physical exterior or outer self (*labas*) and the inner core (*loob*). The *lalake* is a male individual whose inner core or depth (*loob*) and outward appearance (*labas*) match. He is "male" inside and outside; the same holds true for the *babae* whose feminine interiority matches her female body. The *bakla* possesses a male body yet is female "inside." The supposed misalliance between the *labas* and *loob* accounts for the inferiority

---

4   This section is heavily drawn from and is a simplified version of J. Neil C. Garcia's ideas in *Philippine Gay Culture.* For a more in-depth discussion of the *bakla* and *loob,* please read chapter 1 (61–76) and chapter 2 (116–30) of Garcia's book. Also see Garcia's "LGBT Discourse in the Philippines," 249–52; and his introduction to *Aura,* "Reading Auras: The Gay Theme in Philippine Fiction in English," 9–38.

and "unrealness" of the *bakla* (and the *tomboy*), and has condemned the *bakla* and *tomboy* to their abjection. The *bakla* is twice "unreal": he is not quite *lalake* because he does not possess the qualities of the superior *lalake* and inside him (*loob*) is a female self; nor is he a *babae* because even though his interior or *loob* is female, he is physically male on the outside. It follows then that the *bakla* exists as the Other of the *lalake* who embodies the idealized traits of the male subject—masculinity, strength, courage, virility, and so on, which the *bakla* supposedly lacks. The *lalake* is the "real" man and the *bakla* is his "fake" copy. After all, even the *bakla*'s effeminacy is "a poor copy" (317) and supposedly "inferior to the femininity of 'real women'" (390).

This kind of gender system reeks of sexism and heterosexism. It treats the feminine or the female subject—and everything associated with femininity biologically or culturally—as inferior. It assumes that the *lalake*'s natural sexual object choice is the *babae*. The *bakla*'s sex object choice, given the primacy of the interior (female core) over the exterior, is the *lalake*—and this preference affirms the "normalcy" of the *bakla*'s desire via heterosexist logic. The system cannot take into account the possibility of the *lalake* desiring another *lalake*, or the *babae* desiring another *babae*—sameness as the trajectory of desire is not conceivable in this gender paradigm.

The term *bakla*, however, used to mean something else. Prior to becoming gendered, *bakla* was a word denoting "confusion" or "cowardice." Then, according to Garcia, "during the Spanish colonial period, it slowly became synonymous with the local gender terms for womanish or feminine men except that unlike the words it had come to eclipse—for example, *bayoguin, binabae*, and *asog*—it carried with it the force of macho insult" (Garcia 2016, 250). It must also be noted that before the Spaniards came to the islands, aside from women, effeminate men who dressed as women played the role of healers (*babaylan*) and this cross-gendered figure was not viewed as an outcast but as a vital member of society. Garcia notes: "We can only assume that with the passing of the centuries, and as the status of native women progressively deteriorated, gender-crossing in the traditional sense became more and more difficult to perform, with the gender-crosser herself suffering from the ridicule and scorn which only the Spanish brand of medieval Mediterranean machismo could inflict" (2012, 11).

The American period ushered in the transplantation of Western sexological discourse onto local shores. There was an easy fit between the Western invert and the local *binabae* (or *bakla*) because both—though coming from different regimes of knowledge—involved cross-gender identification. The invert was popularly conceived as a "man trapped in a woman's body." The *bakla* was woman-hearted. The legacy of the American colonial period, unfortunately, is the pathologizing of the *bakla*-cum-homosexual.

Tan avers: "The medicalization and pathologization of homosexuality in the West has been incorporated into Filipino popular perceptions of the *bakla*" (From Bakla to Gay, 89).

It is also unfortunate that the earlier signification of bakla (e.g., cowardice) has spilled over to the sexualized or gendered *bakla*. From the seventies onwards (and perhaps even earlier), the *bakla* and the Philippine gay culture in general have been coming up with newer, sonically similar but morphologically played words like *badaf, bading, badush, vaklush, mokla,* and, most recently this century, *becky,* to denote the same subject.

Despite the homosexualization of the *bakla* and despite the fact that in terms of sexual orientation, the *bakla* is a homosexual, a theoretical distinction needs to be made. Up to now, *bakla* is strictly a gender term denoting an effeminate or cross-dressing male whereas "the homosexual strictly refers to sexual object choice and hence cuts across sexes" (Garcia 2009, 82). In addition, the *bakla's* relationship with his masculine partner is founded on difference. Only the *bakla* is construed to be the "homosexual" in the relationship; whereas in the West, two men who are in a relationship partake of the same homosexual identity (82).

Gay, according to Michael Tan, "has become visible only in the last two decades" [meaning, it has been visible since the 1970s] (From Bakla to Gay, 87). What is good about the deployment of *gay* in the Philippines is that it can refer to both the effeminate homosexuals (like the *bakla*) and the masculine ones who until the gay's arrival had no place in the Filipino sexual imaginary. On the one hand, we can say that the local *bakla* culture has appropriated the Western category to name itself so it is possible to conceive of a gay culture now. On the other hand, because *gay* came from a different epistemic regime, it could refer to other identities in the homosexual spectrum and retain its significations beyond those of the *bakla*. In this paper, I use "gay" to refer to a host of homosexual identities, to both gender-transitive (effeminate ones, *bakla*) and gender-intransitive (masculine gay men) males who desire other men. The *bakla* call themselves gay, but there are gays who may not self-identify as *bakla* or "prefer the label *gay* to *bakla*" (Tan, From Bakla to Gay, 88–89). When I talk about concepts specific to gay men of the *bakla* variety like cross-dressing and effeminacy, I shall use *bakla*. When I talk about the culture as a whole, I generally use "gay culture" since the term "gay" covers both masculine and effeminate individuals.

It needs to be reiterated though: because of the *bakla's* ubiquity in popular media and because of their claiming of the word *gay,* "gay" has also become "mis-associated" with effeminacy. This is further reinforced by stereotypes of gay men circulating in Western and local forms of entertainment. Coupled with effeminacy in the popular imagination, *gay* has become firmly associated with the *bakla*. This is where the divide between the masculine gays and the effeminate ones began. It is no wonder then that even some of the masculine gay men themselves would disavow the term *gay* and instead name themselves BI to distance themselves from the effeminate ones.

Technically, the term "bisexual" refers to an individual whose sexual object choice can be directed towards either of the two sexes. But sexuality—especially how it is imagined, self-professed, performed, and perceived—always defies definitions. Taking off from Tan's studies, the writers of "Being LGBT in Asia" mention: "The bisexual community remains under-represented in the LGBT community in the Philippines, not only because of the stigmatization of bisexuals by both heterosexual and homosexual communities, but also because of the conflicting perceptions among Filipinos on who is bisexual" (18).

In this study, many gay men self-identify as BI, even if they are not bisexual. This phenomenon is not new. Some homosexuals have been using this label to name themselves, and this was mentioned in Tan (From Bakla to Gay, 91). Tan also notes that "'bisexual' may represent an 'in-process mode' as individuals [TLF workshop participants] come to terms with their sexuality" (91).[5]

"Bisexual" as understood in a Western framework or paradigm is different from BI as it circulates in the Filipino gay community. BI in this study is primarily a synonym for gay and *bakla*. It must be emphasized however that gay, *bakla*, and BI are theoretically different from each other, and each of these three is not reducible to the other two. I must also add that bisexuals—who have erotic attraction to and affection for both men and women—do exist in the country and on Planet Romeo; that is why the term "bisexuals" in the country really denotes both (a) bisexuals as in the Western sexological sense and (b) gay men self-identifying as "bisexual."

As Tan's papers demonstrate, the Filipino bisexual shares historical connections with the categories *silahis* and MSM (see Tan's works in the references). While MSM is a 1990s invention and is a convenient category of social workers to reduce the stigma attached to homosexuals by focusing on acts rather than identity, "[s]ilahis is a Tagalog term that is sometimes used, as slang, to refer loosely to bisexuals" (Silahis, 209). "Silahis" is said to have its origins from the phrase "silahis ng araw" (rays of the sun); the idea being that these silahis transform "from day to night" (213), meaning come nighttime they become someone else and revert to their heterosexual or *lalake* selves come daytime. In popular discourse, *silahis* is

---

5   For a typology of bisexuals, please refer to Kristin G. Esterberg, "The Bisexual Menace: Or, Will the Real Bisexual Please Stand Up?" in *Handbook of Lesbian and Gay Studies*, ed. J. Neil Garcia (Mandaluyong: Anvil, 2012), 219.

generally understood as the local term for someone who is involved with both men and women and exhibits masculine behavior; and, at least in the gay community in general, he is considered as someone who is masculine and closeted. In terms of lineage, then, the *silahis* is the proper forefather of the contemporary "bisexual," in so far as *silahis* is the only masculine male homosexual identity that had ever existed before the Pinoy BI became popular. Indeed, because of gender presentation, *silahis* and *bi* are related. They are both antithetical to the *bakla* who is effeminate and desires the *lalake*. Historically, the schism between the BIs and *bakla*/gays this century is reminiscent of the tension between the *silahis* and the *bakla* in the 1970s. I plan to address this lineage further in a different paper.

Filipinos on Planet Romeo
In this section, I shall give an overview of Planet Romeo (PR), explain my methodology, and discuss some quantitative data about the Filipino "bisexual" population on Planet Romeo.

Cyber technology has tremendously affected the way people live on the planet. It has enabled people from diverse cultures to reimagine and recreate the world they live in. Pertierra asserts: "The ease of global communication allows participation in subcultures whose members have easy access to specialized interests. Virtual communities are easily consolidated and developed into subgroups and subcultures" (2010, 58). On the one hand, we can say that websites like PR have endowed the gay subject with agency, or at least a space in which to fashion and refashion his identity. Consider this headline from a BI subject:

OCB
Planet Romeo is my secret world :) im looking for hot encounter :) discreet is a plus.

Gays all over the country have been enabled by websites like PR to express freely their hidden selves and be who they want to be (at least virtually). On a typical afternoon in 2017, Planet Romeo would have the following number of online users:

World - 82078 Users

Philippines - 2688 Users[6]

6   These figures are taken from the website http://www.planetromeo.com as accessed and are valid on the date of its access on 8 April 2017, 3:50 p.m. Please note that this is the number of online users only, not the total users per se. I placed the figures to show that members from the Philippines constitute a sizeable share of the PR population.

Almost half of the users in the country come from Metropolitan Manila, and the men from Makati, Quezon City, and Manila combined constitute more than half of the Metro Manila population. PR Philippines is populated by urban gays, bisexuals, and transgenders from different classes (a sizeable chunk is most likely middle-class), with ages typically ranging from 18 to 50. The majority would be in their mid-20s to early 30s. Since the culture is ageist, it is not common to find men who are clearly in their 40s or 50s declaring their real age (except if they are capitalizing on their "daddy" image).

Members from the Philippines constitute roughly 3 to 4% of the entire PR population in the world. Thus, Planet Romeo profiles—as forms of self-inscription and self-reinvention—are a good source of data for exploring the identity of "bisexuals" and examining their own discourse about their sexuality.

I first embarked on this Planet Romeo (PR) project in 2011 and resurrected the project in 2016. Then and now, various types of phobia and –isms like homophobia, "baklaphobia," transphobia, effeminophobia, racism, regionalism, classism, lookism, and so on, circulate in that gay space. What this BI hatred of the *bakla* or gay on an otherwise gay dating website signifies needs a theoretical discussion. Why is there is so much anger directed at the *bakla*?

It needs to be emphasized this study is not empirical; it is descriptive and more theoretical than anything else. It utilizes nontraditional scholarship in the sense that the data came solely from the profiles, and the use of profiles was limited only to the write-ups: "Headline" (which appears below the picture and basic stats like age, height, weight, location) and "My Own Words" (things members wish to say about themselves). More often than not, the headline was the same as the "My Own Words" write-up. No interviews were conducted with the PR subjects. Many of the Planet Romeo profiles I encountered were short-lived because the members kept changing or deleting their accounts; some got deleted or deactivated because they were inactive for so long. In addition, the members were using handles (aliases) which were not necessarily their real selves (very few reveal their real identity in their profile)—these were invented—and the handles were used precisely to preserve the anonymity of their corporeal/real identities. In "Ephemeral Sexualities," Arnold Concha avers: "The online identities of chatroom goers are textual rather than physical. They go about in the technologically created spaces of the chatrooms, and their fleeting and changeable characteristics do not necessarily resemble those of their physical owners, offline" (2008, 18). Some members also changed their self-identification, sometimes from GAY to BI, or NONE to BI—in the cases I have spotted, it was usually a change to

BI, not to GAY. I deliberately chose for inclusion in this paper profiles that no longer existed online or could no longer be accessed (most likely deleted, and in other cases perhaps deactivated, by the user or by Planet Romeo) to protect the privacy of the members.

The quotes mostly came from the headlines and they were quoted verbatim (unless otherwise stated). Face-to-face contact with them was not necessary, primarily because the interviews would really have no bearing on the "facts" that one could already extract from the profiles alone. It is my contention that by examining carefully extracts from the profile descriptions alone, we can come up with theoretical notes on the "bisexuals." Nonetheless, profile write-ups can only take scholars so far. More empirical-oriented or more in-depth studies of the various identities on Planet Romeo would certainly require one-on-one, face-to-face or online interviews, and would need to take into account the handles, pictures, and other data contained in the profiles.

In addition, this study has an auto-ethnographic dimension because I needed to join Planet Romeo to collect data, get a good feel of this world, and make my observations. I had been logging on to Guys4men for a couple of years until it became Planet Romeo. I logged on almost every day for the entire year of 2016 through April 2017 for data included in this paper. I would normally be able to read fifty profiles per day and make notes on the profiles of subjects, especially those self-identifying as BI. While I must have read more than one thousand profiles, I was able to examine closely at least two hundred fifty profiles from which I selected the data included here. The data are limited to Romeos in Metro Manila. I did not include men from the provinces because of the language barrier and the presence of specific gender identities (e.g., the *bayot* of the Visayan islands) which are beyond the theoretical scope of this paper.

The overarching focus of this paper is the subjects' choice of BI to name themselves; thus, to probe this phenomenon I studied mainly their profile write-up (headlines and personal statement/"My Own Words"). I would also note the other demographic data like age, location, and position (e.g., top, bottom, versa). From the profiles alone, one can get a good grasp of the views of these "bisexuals" on masculinity/effeminacy, gay identities (e.g., bakla and effeminate subjects), their self-concept, their ideal partners, their views about being out and LGBT culture, and their sexual proclivities—and these will be the foci of my analysis later.

Handles or profile names and pictures play an important role in the subjects' construction of their PR self and self-presentation. However, for this study, in order to preserve the anonymity and privacy of the PR members,

I dwelled only on the self-identification of the subjects and their write-ups, I removed their handles from the paper, and I made no reference to their pictures. In addition, despite the possible lies (for PR after all is a site for reinventing the self), embellishments, and "posings" (e.g., pretending to be someone else) on PR in these profiles, the write-ups are still important; while the subjects may lie about themselves, chances are they will lie less about what and who they want. While I am studying these profiles individually, I am more interested in the overall picture that these "bisexual" profiles generate. Surely, when many users keep posting the same lines over and over again (e.g., *bawal effem* [no to effem], *discreet only, no trace for same*), the more than one thousand profiles constitute data in themselves and are enough proof that many BIs at the very least have an "uneasy" relationship with the effeminate homosexuals.

This study cannot claim to be the definitive and exhaustive study of sexualities and the kind of "bisexuality" represented by PR users in the Philippines. The historical conditions and the lives of these BIs are so complex that this paper, especially given its methodology and scope, can only point to certain aspects of their subject position. Some of the things I removed from this paper are the real or practicing bisexuals (those who are truly attracted to both sexes), the chubs, the masseurs and sex workers, the deaf, the trans identities, the Chinese, and people living with HIV/AIDS. At best, this paper aims to offer provisional notes on the self-ascribed "bisexuals" in the country and to broaden the discourse opened up by Michael L. Tan and J. Neil C. Garcia.

Let me now discuss the data and begin with the self-identification of the PR members. Data in 2011 and 2016 bear no difference: there were more self-identified Filipino BIs than gays on PR. Out of ten profiles, normally only six would indicate their sexual orientation; from this 60% population, roughly 70% would be BI; around 20%, GAY; usually 1 to 2%, TRANS. Random checks across 2016 to 2017 revealed this approximation to be true, and never did the number of GAYs exceed that of BIs. In addition, the number of NO RESPONSE for Manila was also high, almost as high as the number of BIs. Sensing the figures to be uncanny, I compared the figures in Makati (Metro Manila) to those in Silom (Bangkok), Bukit Bintang (Kuala Lumpur), and Manhattan (New York City), and I realized that Makati was the only city where the number of bisexuals was higher than that of gays. But how accurate was my observation?

So, to settle the matter once and for all and to give this study's theoretical rumination empirical grounding, I checked the Planet Romeo "Gay

Happiness Index" Project, which was launched in 2015. It was a very use-ful undertaking that determined the satisfaction of gays, bisexuals, and transgenders in various parts of the world. The Philippines ranked 41st; Indonesia and Malaysia (being Muslim countries with anti-homosexual statutes) ranked lower, in 73rd and 77th place respectively; and Thailand clinched the 16th spot, the highest rank for an Asian country.

What is most telling about this study is that it confirmed what I had suspected all along: the Philippines had the highest number of bisexuals in the world, higher than any other country in a study involving 127 countries with 115 thousand participants! This study with its 4, 947 Filipino subjects with a mean age of 29 confirmed my data: the number of Filipinos self-iden-tifying as "bisexual" is simply beyond the normal.[7] It is higher than all the other countries in the world, even beyond the numbers for countries with strong anti-homosexual statutes. Is this scenario statistically possible? Is this Kinsey pushed to the nth power? One cannot simply assume either that the Filipino BIs do not know the meaning of the word "bisexual" because 72.43% of the Filipinos in the PR survey have college degrees.

I mentioned earlier that the number of Filipino Romeos who did not indicate their sexual orientation is very high, almost as high as the BI pop-ulation. Why do the men on PR refuse to identify their sexual preference? In the Planet Romeo Happiness Index, please note that the number of GAYs has significantly become higher, 46% against 50% BIs—still lower com-pared to BIs. Obviously, the numbers for GAY from the Philippines in this international survey came from those Filipino men who did not indicate their sexual orientation in their profiles. Why Filipino men (mostly gays) on Planet Romeo would not articulate their sexual orientation or prefer-ence is very interesting and worth exploring. Nonetheless, at this point, we must remember the most crucial point: even if the number of gays has

---

7   The non-Filipino reader of the survey will have reason to believe the number of BIs (being higher than gays) is accurate because of the item on attraction: "mostly to men and sometimes to women" (45.52) is higher than "attraction only to men" (42.91). But there are other countries in the survey that have similar item results and still have more GAYS than BIs in the sexual orientation item/question. I would also like to be-lieve that some of the BIs answered the attraction question this way either (a) because this was in keeping with their chosen identity as BI somehow (after all, they chose or answered BI in an international survey where "bisexuality" is understood as attraction to both sexes); or, (b) because they considered that when they were much younger they must have had a female crush as well and counted that as part of it.

increased, the BIs still top the numbers game—and that number holds for the entire Planet Romeo, as in literally the entire planet Earth.

In the long run, the most pressing question I believe is the qualitative dimension: Is it possible that there could really be so many "bisexuals" in the entire Philippines? Given all these quantitative data, why do many men self-identify as BI on Planet Romeo? Indeed, at least for this paper, the real question is not *how many*; it is *why this many* and *what are the implications of this phenomenon on how we view sexual identities in the Philippines?*

What readers of the Planet Romeo study will not see is how "bi" is understood, circulated, and internalized in Philippine culture. For once they do, they will understand that **there really is no BI in the world like the Filipino BI in Philippine gay culture**. What we are witnessing is a slippage in the deployment of the concept of "bi" which functions as a universal category in the Planet Romeo study but is utilized quite differently amongst gay men in the Philippines.

The m/animal and the softie
Introducing the astig and the barako
Most of the self-ascribed BIs in the Philippines, including those populating the spaces of Planet Romeo, have a strong preference for the *astig*, *barako*, and *discreet*. Consider the BI profiles below and their ideal mates:

DSB
Discreet guy into clean and safe fun with discreet guys…
NOT into fems, slim, 420, chem, poser, nonsense

OHB
pls discreet and astig hunks only.i don't entertain faggot trans or gay
OUT LOUD
[Note: Astig means "tough" or "masculine"]

IAB
astig.barako.mature.gym goer.for same.no to slim. no to effem.
we all have likes and dislikes, let us learn to accept and RESPECT
[Note: Barako means "stud" or "fearless"]

BDB
Discreet here. Walang bahid. Meet up na Txt nyo na lng ako #
(Discreet here. No trace. Let's meet-up Just text me your #)

These profiles are common on Planet Romeo as far as profiles of self-professed BIs are concerned.[8] The keywords associated with masculinity (*barako, astig, discreet*) exist side by side with their "undesirable" feminine counterparts: *effem, halata*, with *bahid* (trace), and *trans*. Note the tone in these write-ups and the preponderance of the word "no." Note the use of all caps *OUT LOUD* which is a graphic reinforcement of OHB's aversion to sissies and "out" gay men.

Barako and *astig* figure prominently among descriptions of the ideal males of these BI and gay subjects alike. Many BIs describe themselves as *astig* and manly, and whether they truly are is a totally different matter. Note also that even self-professed gays on PR are also looking for the *barako*. Nonetheless, in a very masculinist Philippine gay culture, many self-identified gays on PR also prefer manly ("astig") guys:

OJG
manly to manly

BWG
pakantot here sa astig at laki titi
(Bottom here for manly and big cock)

This preference for the *barako* is usually accompanied by physical features: "gym-goer," "no slim," "no chubs," and "no oldies." Even "malamya" is a physical trait; it pertains to a person's manner of speaking, to something obvious.   Note also that *barako* exists side by side with the rejection of the effeminate ("no") and this preference becomes the justification for respect.[9] Note also the term "no trace" (or *bahid* in Filipino) which is another ideal

8   Please note (a) that the handles of the users have been changed to three letters, to preserve the anonymity of the owners of these profiles and (b) that the extracts from the headlines or personal statements ("my own words") are unedited. The location and age have also been removed to ensure the anonymity of the subjects—even if these profiles are technically no longer available or searchable online. Most of the profile quotes in this paper come from the headlines. PR users tend to be lazy, so it is very common to see the headline repeated verbatim in the "my own words" section. There are loquacious members though who do not only repeat the headline but also add lengthy essays about themselves, write letters to a lost beloved, narrate their sexual adventures, rant about their idiosyncrasies, post journal entries, advertise goods and services, expose posers and thieves, and share lyrics of favorite songs.

9   There is danger in the use of this term "respect" for in many cases "respect for preferences" is used as an excuse for the deep-seated intolerance of and rage directed at the effeminate, most especially the *bakla* and trans.

partner in the BI community, the trace or *bahid* suggesting a "blemish" or a "contamination." I shall discuss the idea of "trace" in detail in another paper.

Let us examine one more profile and examine the fantasy of this BI subject:

TDB

Sino Top dyan na Astig lang at d malamya. wild top sana …discrete ako sigurado yun meet nalang para mag kaalaman!… looking for a fister fun sa di lang halata at barako....yung marunong lang…

(Any top around who is manly and not softie. Wild top preferred… I am discrete for sure let's just meet to find out! … looking for a fister fun with a not obvious guy and manly… only those who know how…)

This BI bottom is looking for a top guy who also knows how to do fisting. Note that he is not just looking for any top—that top must be *astig* (manly and tough, and fearless) and *barako* (a stud, a man who is fearless). In Philippine gay culture and on PR, BI or gay, the ideal male partner still turns out to be the discreet, *barako*, and *astig*. Why?

The *UP Diksiyonaryong Filipino* defines *barako* as (1) "lalaking walang kinakatakutan" (a man who fears nothing); "lalaking matapang" (courageous man); (2) "lalaking hayop na palahian" (a male animal used for breeding; stud) (142). The *barako* is a stud, masculine, oozing with masculine aura and brimming with sexual potency. The male animal (or "manimal") supposedly impregnates and sexually dominates others who submit to his virility and sexual prowess. This is the *barako*—he is not a sissy and he is not a coward.

Astig is defined as "tao na matapang at parang sanggano kumilos" (a person who is brave/fearless and acts rough [akin to a hoodlum]) (84). *Sanggano* is defined as (1) "tao na bulakbol" (a loafer); (2) "tao na walang galang or bastos" (a person who is discourteous or foul-mouthed) (1098). The opposite of the *barako* and the *astig* is the *malamya*. *Lamya* literally means "malambing na pananalita" (speaking softly) (670). *Malamya* is associated with weakness and *kabaklaaan* (being *bakla*), especially since the effeminate ones like the *bakla* are thought to act in a certain way and to speak in a certain curly or soft "un-masculine" manner. Thus, while the so-called true blue male is strong and fearless, his Other is conceived as weak. Note that the ideal partner of TDB must be "discrete" (a misspelling of "discreet," a mistake common on PR Philippines), and being bottom to a femme top is certainly out of the picture. It can also be observed from the data that the bottoms on PR tend to prefer masculine tops.

Both the *barako* and *astig* bring with them physical and emotional qualities men in patriarchal society are supposed to possess, embody, and put into action. And these qualities are associated with and "normally" performed by the (ideal) *lalake*, the "real" man, the heterosexual male, the figure who functions as the proverbial Other of the abjected *bakla*. After all, we must remember one of the former meanings of *bakla* that has been carried over to the sexualization of the word: cowardice. The antithesis of the fearless macho man, to belabor the point, is the "cowardly," soft, woman-hearted *bakla*.

Discreetness, Filipino-style

Planet Romeo is so popular precisely because it is a virtual closet. PR functions as a closet in a culture where many men wrongly associate being out with being loud or being discreet with being closeted. Like *astig, barako,* and *no trace*, another sought-after ideal on PR is the *discreet*, a term which usually functions as a synonym of BI.

Discreet as a term in Philippine gay culture gravitates around the concept of invisibility; the concept of sexuality as a visible sign on the body, as a physically knowable entity; and the concept of "manliness," "realness," and "normality."

As an adjective, *discreet* is defined in the *Oxford English Dictionary* (compact edition) as "showing discernment or judgment in the guidance of one's own speech and action; judicious, prudent, circumspect, cautious; often *esp.* that can be silent when speech would be inconvenient" (V.1: 746, upper left quadrant, meaning 1). The online *Oxford Dictionaries: English* also defines it as "careful and prudent in one's speech or actions, especially in order to keep something confidential or to avoid embarrassment." In American and European PR profiles, one will find the word "discreet"—and it is used properly. In the Philippines, "discreet" has acquired a different meaning.[10]

---

10   In both the Oxford online dictionary and the *Cambridge Guide to English Usage*, the difference between "discreet" and "discrete" is indicated. This gesture from Oxford and Cambridge points to the fact that English language users tend to confuse the two terms. In the Philippine case, similar to the Western speakers, "discreet" is sometimes written as "discrete" for two reasons: one, the user does not know the correct spelling of discreet (after all the two have the same pronunciation); two, the user does not know the difference between the two words. This matter, however, also points to a **class dimension** in the "discreet" problem in the gay community. Educated and non-homophobic *bakla* and gay men would usually poke fun at these effeminophobic BIs and gay men on the basis of their low IQ and lack of education which the inability to use English properly supposedly suggests.

While perceptions of "discreet" may vary across generations or sub-groups in the gay culture, "discreet" as it operates on Philippine Planet Romeo and in contemporary gay culture would usually possess the following features: Someone "discreet" is someone is who is not effeminate (not like the *bakla* who is), someone who is not obvious or "halata" or bears "no trace" (unlike the *bakla* who is undeniably gay), someone who is masculine (unlike the *bakla*), someone who looks and acts "straight" (unlike the *bakla* who is anything but straight), someone who does not cross-dress and is therefore supposedly "decent" (unlike the *bakla* who does), someone who is not out or "ladlad" (not like the *bakla* whose sexuality is supposedly all over his body and needs no coming out).[11] As Austria has correctly pointed out, the use of "discreet" usually co-exists with "bi" (2014, 313–14). In the PR profiles, one would either find the word "bi" coupled with the word "discreet" (e.g., "discreet bi") in the headline or write-up, or see the word "discreet" appearing in profiles where the users self-identify as BI. In short, the "discreet," from this problematic conception, is anything but the *bakla*.[12]

Take note of the slippage in the original English term *discreet* and the local "discreet." Where is the connection between the two? My conjecture is as follows: discretion is normally expected when discussing taboo topics like sex (and this should somehow apply to the use of discreet by white men on PR); and that Filipino "discreet" borrows from its original source the concepts "prudence" and "embarrassment" (and similar meanings). It is a common misconception in the Philippines that the *bakla* are not prudent

---

11   In his work, Austria has captured the sentiments of typical BIs and straight-acting gay men (and *bakla*) in the Philippines: "... dinadagdagan pa ng salitang 'discreet' o 'straight-acting' ang kanilang mga profile. Ito ay para idiin na hindi sila 'gay,' effem, o malamya at mukhang babae sa itsura or kilos." (2014, 314). (Translation: the word 'discreet' or 'straight acting' is added to their profile. This is to emphasize that they are not 'gay,' effem, or malamya, or feminine looking or effeminate.) On another matter, it must be pointed out that perceptions of discreetness may also vary across different types of gay/BI men. To some, discreetness means both "not loud" and "not out"; to some, discreetness may simply mean "not loud" and not necessarily being in the closet for these two clearly are two different things. From this perspective, one can be out (to family and friends) and yet remain not loud. For some, discreetness means having a sense of respectability which the stereotyped *bakla* supposedly does not possess.

12   A few gay men also use "discreet gay" in their profiles. But the coupling of this identity with "discreet" is much more observable among self-identified BIs. After all, to some, if they really think they are "discreet gays," then they would use BI to differentiate the "discreet" from the "not discreet." In addition, I have never encountered the phrase "discreet *bakla*" in my ten years as a PR user; for the two words are popularly conceived as antithetical in Philippine gay culture.

in their actions—they are stereotyped as flamboyant, loud, and vulgar—and therefore their behavior is a cause of embarrassment. "Discreetness" in the country presupposes someone's way of speaking or behavior that is not scandalous or loud and will not cause the subject and his family embarrassment. And this supposed loudness and this lack of tact are part and parcel of the stereotypes hurled at the *bakla*. "Discreetness" in the local case seems to work under the presumption that (a) the *bakla* behavior is not respectable because (b) it does not quite hold as secret something that should be made a secret (one's sexual identity) for the reason that that identity, that "sissy-ness," is just so apparent and obvious in his looks, his actions, and his speech. "Discreetness" therefore brings with it the idea of a "mark" or a "trace." The *bakla* bears, wears, and voices the markings of his identity.

"Discreetness" in the local sense in a way also brings in ideas associated with the older problematic concepts "overt" (obvious) and "covert" (not obvious) because the "discreet" ones are "not obvious."[13] And so, *discreet* is founded on the idea of secrecy (even if it may be an open secret) and fear of disclosure (closetedness). "Discreetness" rests on the desire to keep one's identity a secret (a hidden presence); but the popular conception of the traditional *bakla* is founded on its complete opposite—the refusal of that secrecy (a ubiquitous presence). Therefore, the local usage of discreet brings into it the history of *kabaklaan*, and the local *discreet* (while it bears faint traces, pun intended, of the original) makes full sense only in that context.

The belief that couples being bakla and being effem with vulgarity, unacceptability, and embarrassment, is a product of both the general heteropatriarchal culture and the gay subculture. The general "straight" public has defined for gays what is respectable and acceptable (meaning not flamboyant, not crossdressing, not loud), yet a big chunk of the gay population has also bought this misconception and homophobia. Why should *discreet* be privileged over *halata* (obvious), *no trace* over the obvious and out (*lantad*

---

13   Garcia gives a very good critique of this "overt/covert" dichotomy in *Slip/pages*. The problem with this dichotomy is that it does not make sense as a distinction of homosexual identities because the distinction is based on gender categories, not sexual object choice. Garcia writes: "At the heart of this distinction isn't sexual orientation at all, but rather *kabaklaan* and/or inversion: the covert gay is a *bakla* who hides his effeminate ways, the overt one is the one who flaunts them" (1998, 90). In short, the distinction presupposes a natural, innate effeminacy in the homosexual subject which he either exposes and makes obvious in public (making him "overt") or hides from public view (making him "covert"). Obviously, this distinction cannot take into account the existence of masculine-acting homosexuals because it can only view their masculinity as a put-on since the effeminacy which is supposedly natural to them is just subdued and hidden.

or *ladlad*)? Why should being closeted be equated with discreetness? And why should being in the closet be ideal in the first place?

Consider this BI profile:

TLB
Only interested to: Fit/Muscled/Astig/Manly(Mukhang tambay-totoong manly)/Dads–No bellies/Chubbs/BadBreath/Maputi ang mukha/ Halata Voice Test–Dito malalaman kung **halata**...HORNY NOW!! MY PLACE!!
ME: NoTrace/Fit–Average ... Astig ...
BAWAL ANG MGA OUT NA BAKLA
(Only interested to: Fit/Muscled/Astig/Manly (Looks like a neighbourhood thug-real manly) / Dads–No bellies/Chubbs/BadBreath/ Make up or Fair face /Obvious Voice Test–To find out who's obvious...
HORNY NOW!! MY PLACE!!
ME: NoTrace/Fit–Average ... Astig ...
*** NO TO THE OUT BAKLA***)

The dichotomies that surface in this example are:

Manly / Effeminate
Astig / Malamya
Discreet / Halata (Obvious)
Straight-acting / Bakla
No Trace / Ladlad (Out)

Consider these two more:

KHB
No to feminine o halata. Dicrete astig to astig lang please. Pdeng SOP para malaman ntin sino mas lalaking lalaki sa atin. Pde ring skype or wechat.
(No to feminine or obvious. Discreet astig to astig only please. We can do SOP to determine which one (between) us is more manly. We can do skype or wechat.)

UCB
Yung mga pamintang ISNABERO kala mo kung sinong GWAPO muka nman HIPON! Bawal poser!
(Those SNOBBISH straight-acting men who act as though they're HANDSOME but in truth SHRIMP-looking! No posers!)

What can be gleaned from the three BI profiles are preference for the discreet, preference for self-identifying as discreet, and preference for the masculine.

Note the importance of masculinity and how this is tied up with "maleness" and the notion of the *lalake*. Note the use of the word "lalaki" as the yardstick which in Philippine genders is the opposite of *bakla*. Certainly, sexuality and gender are conflated in this conception. From KHB's profile, one can also see the BI's conception of their identity as *lalake*. I shall discuss the implications of this example in the section on BI/*lalake*.

Halata, malamya, ladlad, and *effem*—all these adjectives point to one figure—the ubiquitous and inexorable *bakla* who is constantly being directly and indirectly maligned in these profiles and on Planet Romeo in general. From the profiles above, what the subjects want is anyone but the *bakla*. Note the all caps, the tone, in TLB's write-up: "BAWAL ANG MGA OUT NA BAKLA."[14] To be *bakla*, then, as constructed on Planet Romeo and in Philippine culture in general, is to be associated with a kind of sexuality that can be intuited and sensed because it is evident all over the body—on a person's "made-up" face and body, in his dressing habits, in his voice, in his gait. And the visible or obvious certainly falls short of the desired ideal, the ideal being the masculine subject. To be *bakla* is to be a menace to the BI population, to become an uneasy target of contempt from/for people who equate closetedness with decency.

Manliness becomes a badge of honor, desirability, and decency. UCB's use of the word *paminta* is telling. Its common translation is "manly" or "straight-acting." *Paminta* literally means "pepper." But this gayspeak word uses punning. The key syllable is "min" which is the equivalent of "men" (lalake). *Pa* as a prefix denotes "acting like." "*Pa-minta*" (or *pa-mhinta* with the effeminate *h*) therefore means someone who is acting masculine, yet, in the gay community, it can also mean someone faking his masculinity.

The local term *pa-min* (or *pa-mhin*) is very interesting because it assumes the gay subject who is *paminta* is already a copy of the lalake to begin with, yet the copy is not a perfect copy, as the "pa" suggests: he is not a man; he is only "like a man." Between *mhin* and *pa-mhin* it is usually the

14 This is a peculiar phrase because the *bakla*'s self-disclosure is *paglaladlad ng kapa*, unfurling of the cape. "Outing" presupposes a "closet," which is a Western trope. So the phrase normally would have been *ladlad* or *ladlad na bakla*. What we see here is the conflation of two distinct discourses, local and Western. A slippage. On second thought, if we go by the traditional conception of *bakla* whose markers are effeminacy and cross-dressing, does a *bakla* still need to come out in the first place if his identity is written all over his body and evident in his actions?

latter which is used in the gay culture for the former is usually reserved for the lalake, the so-called naturally straight guy. On second thought, the term *pa-mhin* already assumes some kind of mimicry, a performance questioning the original. Tan notes in "From Bakla to Gay," "the prefix 'pa' describes mimicry, loosely translated as 'to be like'" (90). Indeed, how can one be original without the copy? And how can masculinity exist without its "pas" or "faux pas" which is the effeminate? To top it all, the very fact that the prefix *pa* is part of the word means that instinctively members of gay culture know that gender is actually a construct and a kind of performance to begin with, and that sexual identity is fluid. The play with gender categories and the mimicry of norms are interesting features of the Philippine gay culture.

The PR website is one big spectacular performance of *pa-mhintahan*, a masculinity always at risk of being found out, a masculinity always under suspicion (note TLB's panic and suggested voice test) not because it is not real but simply because of the investment these subjects have placed on masculinity's immortal and bothersome Other—effeminacy.[15]

I submit: Obsessed with masculinity, the PR users are equally obsessed with effeminacy. There is so much emotional and psychic energy spent and wasted on who's who, as if everyone on the website is hiding something. In the end, it is still the discourse of secrecy and disclosure (that does not always arrive) that permeates and fuels discussions of masculinity. Pictures are not enough to perform one's masculine self. On PR where the mark of desirability is masculinity and musculature, the effeminate becomes the "spectral" other that the masculine cannot get rid of. He represents the margin or border from which the masculine can emerge as a subject. To define the masculine, the effeminate must be incited into discourse (e.g., *no to effem, bawal halata*) and demonized—thus the need to dichotomize the BI and *bakla* as well as the supposedly masculine BI and effeminate gay.

But why is there the obsession with effeminacy?

Simple: because of the tradition of *kabaklaan* from which all forms and modes of homosexuality and transsexuality in the Philippines cannot escape.

The obsession with the body and with beauty—especially among gay cultures—seems to be (if not is) a transcultural phenomenon. What is specific to the Philippines however is the overdetermined context which makes articulations of these ideals possible and which determines the categories individual members from various cultures utilize. *Astig, discreet, barako, no*

---

15   Some ideas in this paper, especially this one, originated from and were developed from my earlier preliminary lecture on Planet Romeo in February 2011: "Romeos in the Metropolis: Notes on Autobiography."

trace, and *malamya* are specific to Philippine culture and can be understood fully only if we to take into account their local habitation. And where are these phobias (effeminophobia, transphobia, and internalized homophobia) coming from, or what concepts are they anchored on?

My modest answer is the hierarchical positioning of genders in the Philippines: boy over girl over babae over bakla over tomboy (Garcia 2009, 248).[16] While we may observe that the preference for the masculine is quite a global phenomenon, we must acknowledge that this tendency is operationalized or routed through the existing oppressive and sexist gender relations in a given country. Abhorring the effeminate and the transgender in the Philippines necessarily involves the discourse of *kabaklaan* (being *bakla*) where the *bakla* and the *tomboy* are considered "fake" and "inferior" versions of the "normal" male (*lalake*) and female (*babae*). We are speaking of decades of persecution of the *bakla*, decades of stereotyping and caricaturing of the *bakla* (and consequently gay) in Philippine mass media—and this is the history that BI subjects were born into and are rebelling against. It is sad though that the rebellion is framed in antagonistic terms (e.g., internalized homophobia, sexism) towards the object of the ridicule. A displacement of the hatred occurs and the *bakla* has unwittingly become the object of the BI's revulsion.

BI and/as bakla, BI and/as lalake

In this section, I shall discuss the contiguities between the BI and the *bakla*, and consequently between the BI and the *lalake*. One of the aims of this project is to show that the "bisexual" and the *bakla* share an inviolable kinship: they are almost one and the same *but not quite*. While we may say at least theoretically that the BI is actually a homophobic *bakla* on the one hand, we can also say that he is not exactly one on the other hand. Theoretically, BI is a *bakla, but not perfectly so*. It is true that many gay men and *bakla* prefer to use the word BI to name themselves when in fact they know themselves to be gay or *bakla*.

But we also need to remember how the terms operate. Consider this excerpt from a BI member's write-up:

IRB

Gwapo nga kayo, baklang bakla naman.... awwww hehe
(You guys are handsome, but so bakla.... awwww hehe)

---

16   This is "Model No. 3: Philippine Conceptions of Gender and Sexuality" in Garcia's *Philippine Gay Culture* (2009, 248).

Look at the condescending attitude of the speaker towards the *bakla* with the word "naman." To add insult to injury, the speaker makes a snide remark with the words "awwww hehe," trivializing and mocking the *bakla* subject.   Note how the speaker establishes distance between the *bakla* ("kayo") and himself. This distance denotes the great divide between the *bakla* and the BIs in the Philippines.

It is a known fact that BI can function as a synonym of *gay* and consequently *bakla* in the Philippines. Gays from all walks of life know this. And the profiles on PR attest to this. There are slippages between gay and BI, and between *bakla* and BI on PR. Let us look at these two profiles where self-identified BIs consider themselves *gay*:

ECB
NO MORE HIDING BUT IT DOESN'T MEAN I HAVE TO TELL EVERYONE THAT I AM **GAY**, STILL ACTING LIKE A STRAIGHT GUY... A NORMAL GUY AHAHA LMAO

XYB
YES! Im BISEXUAL or GAY whatever you want to call me thats okay for me. But take note: "IM MANLY DISCREET/ di halata" [not obvious]. I played basketball and soccer. I even played billiards and surfing.

ECB and XYB both demonstrate the BI men's fear of being labelled as effeminate. They are conscious of the effeminate gay stereotype and insist quite strongly that they are manly. While ECB states he is "a normal guy," XYB demonstrates that he is one by playing basketball and soccer, sports associated with heterosexual men.

Consider this headline from a gay member's profile:

LJG
Cute **bi** here.. Pm ???? ???? kantutin mo ko ???? ???? near north ave.
Only w/place ????
(Cute **bi** here.. Pm ???? ???? Wanna fuck me?????? ...)

While it may be said that the BI and gay (a stand-in for *bakla*) are usually antithetical on Planet Romeo Philippines and gay culture in general, I wish to reiterate nonetheless that what the three profiles above show is the knowledge of the liminality of these concepts: how can one tell them apart when the self-identification as BI does not necessarily mean forsaking one's gayness, that one can have self-knowledge of being both, depending on the

Preceding page, Geraldine Batista Roman was elected as the Representative of the 1st District of Bataan following the 2016 Philippine elections, becoming the first openly transgender woman elected to the Congress of the Philippines. She was named as one of the "100 Leading Global Thinkers of 2016" by the US-based *Foreign Policy* magazine and one of the "13 Inspiring Women of 2016" by *Time* magazine. Photo courtesy of Congresswoman Geraldine Roman.

This spread, clockwise from bottom, The Santo Niño de Cebú is a religious icon of the Child Jesus, believed to be a gift given by Ferdinand Magellan to Rajah Humabon and his chief consort upon their baptism in 1521. Different explanations have been given as to why the statue is black, including being caught in a sixteenth-century conflagration and being painted black by an emotionally-depressed owner during the nineteenth century. Its feast day is held every third Sunday of January, complete with dancing and festivities as in the Ati-Atihan in Iloilo discussed in Alcedo's essay. Filipino gay men are known to be devout devotees of the Santo Niño. Photo courtesy of Mark Blasius. The 4th Migrants Pride held on 18 November 2018 was organized by a coalition of LGBT+ migrant workers mainly from South and Southeast Asia. Among the organizers were Filipino Lesbians Organization (FILO) Hong Kong and Filguys Gabriela Hong Kong. At far right is Nick Delfin of FILO, rallying the marchers to fight for migrant workers' rights and against sexual abuse or discrimination. Migrant Filipino lesbians and tomboys provide a counter-narrative to the Japanese and American-constructed "feminized victim" image of the Filipino overseas workers, as discussed in Kale Bantigue Fajardo's essay. Photo courtesy of Athena Lam. Portrait of a gay man taken during a Pride March in June 2018. Photo courtesy of Chriz Luminario. Pexels.com. Sebastian Castro, a Peruvian-Asian American actor, singer, and YouTube sensation, most widely known for his viral gay-themed music video "Bubble," which garnered over three million views. "Bubble" brought Castro fame across Southeast Asia, most visibly in the Philippines and Thailand. Photo courtesy of Seb Castro. Danton Remoto, chairman emeritus of Ang Ladlad, a lesbian, gay, bisexual, and transgender (LGBT) political party in the Philippines and co-editor (with J. Neil C. Garcia) of *Ladlad: An Anthology of Philippine Gay Writing* (3 vols., 1994–2007). UPD Population Institute scholars Joy Cruz and Ruzzel Brian Mallori speaking at a poster presentation of their paper: "Revisiting Social Acceptance of Homosexuality Among Filipino Youth," February 2008. Photos courtesy of Mark Blasius.

Clockwise from left, Ang Bonggang-Bonggang Batang Beki, written by Rhandee Garlitos and illustrated by Tokwa Peñaflorida, is the first LGBT-themed Philippine children's book. It tells the story of Adel, a boy who stands out from other kids due to his soft-spokenness and love for the color pink. Photo courtesy of Vibal Group, Inc. The comic book character Zsazsa Zaturnnah, created by Carlo Vergara, first appeared in the graphic novel *Ang Kagila-gilalas na Pakikipagsapalaran ni Zsazsa Zaturnnah* (The Amazing Adventures of Zsazsa Zaturnnah) in the year 2002. The character's styling, costume, and superpowers are based on the iconic Philippine superheroine Darna, who transforms from her alter ego—a barrio lass named Narda—after swallowing a white stone and shouting "Darna." In the story of Zsazsa Zaturnnah, the character's alter ego is a gay beautician (*parlorista*) who swallows a melon-sized stone to transform himself. The character quickly became a gay icon. The graphic novel was adapted into a stage musical and a film. Photo courtesy of Visprint, Inc. As pointed out in Brewer's essay, shamans in early Philippine society were mostly women, with some men whose identification with the "feminine," whether in temporary transvestism or a more permanent way of life, was what accorded them spiritual authority. Called *bayog* in Luzon and *asog* in the Visayas, shamans, whether female or male, acted as spiritual mediums who were capable of, among other powers, healing various illnesses or casting spells over others. Reprinted from Fay-Cooper Cole, *The Tinguian: Social, Religious, and Economic Life of a Philippine Tribe* (Chicago: Field Museum of Natural History, 1922), 209. The Golden Gays at a community show in Pasay. Established in the 1970s by LGBT activist Justo Justo, the Home for the Golden Gays is a nonprofit shelter for elderly and homeless gays. However, when Justo died in 2012, the shelter was forced to close. While some of the original residents were taken in by their families, most of them had to live on the streets and work meager jobs despite their old age. Some later decided to live together and put on drag shows to earn a living. Photo © Shirin Bhandari 2016. GALANG Philippines, Inc. and LBTs from Barangay Pansol (who eventually became known as the Lesbian Alliance Movement: Lakas ng Kababaihan Para sa Karapatan), carrying banners reading "May boses ang maralitang lesbiyana" and "Lesbiyanang Lumalaban Brgy. Pansol," attended the 2010 Metro Manila Pride March held along Tomas Morato in Quezon City. Photo courtesy of GALANG Philippines.

Facing page, John Fernandez Raspado, the first Filipino and Southeast Asian man to win the Mr. Gay World 2017 title. He promotes awareness on HIV testing and prevention among gay, bi, and trans men through the Loveyourself PH and CBS Community Based HIV Screening. Being the ninth Mr. Gay World, Raspado serves as a gay ambassador, advancing LGBTQ human rights locally and internationally. Photo courtesy of John Raspado.

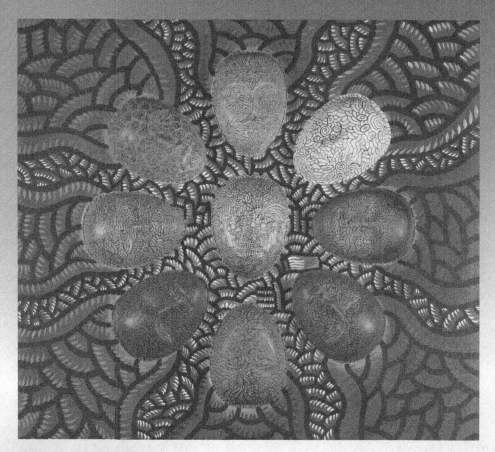

Top to bottom, Faces of Difference by Marconi Calindas. Acrylic and ink on canvas and papier-mâché masks/mixed media. This artwork highlights the artist's take on embracing differences "in this getting-smaller-by-the day world where all human beings live together." The differently colored masks represent the people of different races and genders that make up society, and how they compose a single picture; putting across the message of understanding, of tolerance, and ultimately, of acceptance in the face of differences. Photo courtesy of the artist. Lecture and discussion on the occasion of the 2007 publication of *The Yogyakarta Principles on the Application of International Human Rights Law in Relation to Sexual Orientation and Gender Identity* at the University of the Philippines–Diliman (2008). Participants: Professor Carmen Abubakar, Visiting Professor Mark Blasius, and Professor Sylvia Estrada Claudio, all from the University of the Philippines–Diliman. Event organized by Professor Rosario de Santos del Rosario and sponsored by the UPD Center for International Studies. Dinner among friends in Quezon City, Metro Manila, Philippines. Seated counterclockwise from right: Oscar Atadero, one of the founders of ProGay Philippines (Progressive Organization of Gays in the Philippines) and co-organizer (with Metropolitan Community Church–Manila) of the Philippines' (and Asia's) first LGBT pride march in 1994; seated next to Oscar is J. Neil C. Garcia, contributor to *More Tomboy, More Bakla* and author of *Philippine Gay Culture* (1996), co-editor (with Danton Remoto) of *Ladlad: An Anthology of Philippine Gay Writing* (3 vols., 1994–2007), and Professor of Creative Writing, University of the Philippines–Diliman; Rico C. Barbosa, R.N. of Positive Action Foundation Philippines, Inc. (PAFPI); and author-editor Mark Blasius. Photos courtesy of Mark Blasius.

Clockwise from top left, Young self-identified *baklas* of Tatalon, Metro Manila during an interview with author-editor Mark Blasius, accompanied by a local women's community organizer. Photo courtesy of Dulce Natividad. Global feminist and lesbian activists of the Philippines, Ging Cristobal (OutRight Action International) and Malu Marin (Achieve) with author-editor Mark Blasius. Photo courtesy of Mark Blasius. Bisdak Pride, Inc., taking a selfie before the parade, 24 June 2017. The streets of Cebu City were filled with beautiful colors as members of the LGBTIA+ and allies paraded with their colorful costumes while bannering the rainbow flag. It was the first time that the city had a pride march, and it was entitled "Pabuhagay" which is local language for "outburst." Photo courtesy of Bisdak Pride, Inc. Students commemorating the end of their course "The Politics of Sexuality" with Visiting Professor Mark Blasius, UPD, Spring term 2008. As mentioned in Neil Garcia's essay herein, the University of the Philippines–Diliman is the pioneer university in the country to offer courses on gender and sexuality. Photo courtesy of Mark Blasius. Roxanne Omega Doron, founder of Bisdak Pride, Inc., an LGBT organization in Cebu, with Mark Blasius (left). Photo courtesy of Edmond Cuenca.

Clockwise from top left, Jake Zyrus is an international performer who was once known under the mononym Charice. After initially coming out as a lesbian in 2013, he identified himself as a transgender man in 2017. Since then, he has gone by the name Jake Zyrus. Photo courtesy of Enrique Guadiz Photography. Bernadette Neri, professor from the Departamento ng Filipino at Panitikan ng Pilipinas at the College of Arts and Letters, UP-Diliman and an award-winning author and playwright. She wrote the very first lesbian-themed children's book *Ang Ikaklit sa Aming Hardin* which tackles the story of a young girl with two lesbian moms. Photo courtesy of Bernadette Neri. Annual gay Santacruzan in Marikina. Santacruzan is a religious event held every May. It is a Catholic procession that depicts the journey of Constantine the Great and his mother, Queen Helena, in finding the cross upon which Jesus Christ was crucified. Photo courtesy of Connie Veneracion.

context? What is the difference between BI and the *bakla*/gay when these subjects who identify as BI call themselves gay and these gay-identified individuals also call themselves BI?

Let us examine this bisexual's definition of BI culled from his personal statement:

EBB

Its been six month I already move o since he left me dumb founded.. tss di ka kwalan!!! [You're not my loss] Manigas ka ngayun!!! [The hell with you.] Im open for anything now!! FRIENDS DATE just go with the flow!! Xemp mr. Right padin nmn looking for! [Of course/naturally, I am still looking for Mr Right]

I think I've always been bisexual. I mean, it's somethimg that I've always been interested in. I think everybody kind of fantasizes about the same sex. I think people are born bisexual, and it's just that our parents and society kind of veer us off into this feeling of "Oh, I can't." They say it's taboo. It's ingrained in our heads that it's bad, when it's not bad at all. It's a very beautiful thing.

This is quite a positive personal statement about a man who is moving on and affirming his bisexuality. Yes, following Freud, we all have this bisexual potential. The write-up is quite laudable for it challenges society's dictates and closes with the line about being bisexual as "a very beautiful thing." However, the line "I think everybody kind of fantasizes about the same sex" needs to be examined. If the speaker were truly bisexual, why would he single out "the same sex"? Is he stating this in defense of the same-sex aspect of bisexuality because opposite-sex attraction needs no explanation in a homophoic and erotophobic culture? Why not emphasize the fact that bisexuals can go both ways, for both men and women? What becomes more glaring: There is no mention of women in the profile statement at all. What takes the cake is the first paragraph. The one that broke his heart is a HE; and after getting over him, the one he is looking for is *still* a man: "looking for Mr. Right." Why specifically look for Mr. Right, and not Ms. Right as well? This search for Mr. Right is even reinforced by the certainty and confidence in the "siyempre" (spelled as "xemp") which can mean "of course," "naturally," or "definitely." The clear message here is that his natural and obvious choice is a man. Should he self-identify as gay instead? In a way, the above statement is an interesting performance and performative, for it brings into being his form of "bisexuality," a "bisexuality" firmly entrenched in the Philippine gay/*bakla* imaginary, where its very articulation unwittingly reveals its "subdued" gayness or *kabaklaan*.

Another note: The case of this guy I would argue is not a product of sheer ignorance; after all, he can discourse about society's cruel norms. PR users from the Philippines are mostly educated as the data in the PR Happiness Index indicate that 72.43% have a college degree; it is a deliberate "misuse" of categories which in the Philippines is not quite a misuse after all, at least to the thousands who use this term. More importantly, EBB's profile write-up patently and clearly resonates with the thousands of BI profiles where the BI's claim to his "bisexuality" has nothing to do with any ounce of desire at all for a woman.

My argument is that the invocation of BI necessarily accompanies a kind of estrangement between the *bakla*/gay and the BI—it is a movement away from the effeminate. Why not gay then when gay is not a gender category and does not presuppose effeminacy really? Because homosexuality and gender identity are conflated in this part of the archipelago, and BI occupies that problematic interstice between the two; because gayness in the country has been effeminized and "baklafied," in short, "contaminated" or "tainted," and can no longer claim to have "no trace"; because "gay," due to its coupling with the *bakla* in popular media, has become stereotypically been associated with the effeminate *bakla;* thus, the dichotomy:

Masculine / Effeminate
Bi / Gay
Bi / Bakla
Ideal / Not Ideal
Manly / Effem
No Trace / Contaminated

Thus, ironically, while the masculine ideal for gayness is further reinforced by the global gay culture and the trajectory of gayness in the global market is marked by gender intransitivity, *gay* in the Philippines circulates within and is trapped in a network of relations hounded by the *lalake*/*bakla* dichotomy that assigns femininity to *gay* by virtue of its coupling with the *bakla.* To begin with, the BI subjects in the dating app could choose only between BI and GAY, and not between BAKLA and BI. What this means is that "gay" is understood or utilized by many BIs on PR as a gender-transitive category, not as potentially both gender-transitive (femme) and gender-intransitive (masculine, macho).

How else can we view the relationship between the *bakla* and the BI? Is it simply one of enmity and mutual distrust? Given the headlines/profiles I have already presented, it is obvious that references to the *lalake* abound.

Thus, we need to examine the relationship between the *lalake* and the Pinoy BI as well. Consider these quotes:

MFB

Lalaking lalaki ba hanap mo? E di imsssg mo ko! Isang putok lng solve na 2017 ko.
(Looking for a very manly guy? Then message me! Just one squirt for 2017 and I'll be fine.)

EYB

I JUST WANTED TO EXPLORE MY BEING A MAN.

The bisexual case is an uncanny undoing of the *lalake/bakla* dichotomy currently in place in Philippine society. In breaking the dichotomy through a positing of a "third" entity, the BI actually mimics the *lalake*, and the BI-SEXUAL's endless attempts to act *lalake* expose the very instability and un-realizability of the lalake construct. BI is potentially transgressive because of its being a "proximate" (to use it in the Dollimore-an sense),[17] a copy so close yet so far. The BI's appropriation of the masculine ideal surely has its limits, but it is a threatening copy because if the BI (or the *bakla*) can trans-form himself into the image of the *lalake*, or calls himself or challenges no-tions of *lalake*, who can now tell who is *lalake* indeed? The only sad fact is the actual utilization/practice of the concept/category—because of its mas-culinist orientation—does not successfully deconstruct the concept *lalake* and further perpetuates his privileged status at the expense of the feminine.

To what extent can we theoretically say the BI is a *bakla* and to what extent is it really different from *bakla* and what are the implications of this on our conception or understanding of the BI in the Philippines?

I propose: Pinoy "bisexuality" (among the gay lot) is the quest for the undeconstructed "real" MALE—a pining for the *lalake*. Like the tra-ditional bakla, what the BI desires is a *lalake*, too. There is so much invest-ment in manliness, maleness, masculinity, *astig*, and *barako* that one would ask, who is the object of desire of the bisexual really if not a *lalake* (*but not quite*, for he is desiring a copy of himself)? How different is the *bakla* from the BI who is now so obsessed with *lalake*? Note this headline from a PR member (whose orientation is undisclosed):

17   Read Jonathan Dollimore's discussion of "transgressive reinscription" and the "proximate" in *Sexual Dissidence: Augustine to Wilde, Freud to Focault* (Oxford: Claren-don Press, 1991), 33.

NCE

Pag hanap mo lalaki bakla ka. Pag hanap mo lalaking-lalaki BAKLANG-BAKLA KA!

(If you're looking for a man, you're bakla. If you're looking for a very manly man, you're baklang-bakla!)

From one perspective, Pinoy "bisexuality" may be viewed as a performance of *kabaklaan* insofar as the object of desire turns out to be *lalake* still. Both the *bakla* and the BI are after the same thing, and are involved in the same quest: the desire for the *lalake*. They are also both on the margins because they will perpetually be inferior versions of the *lalake*. The quest for/ to be (the desire to possess and to become) the *lalake* is founded on the existing *bakla* fantasy (because there is no other hermeneutic route in the traditional gender system to account for the BI's desire). Thus, the farther the BI is from the *bakla*, and the closer he gets to becoming a *lalake*, the deeper he is embroiled in the discourse of *kabaklaan* which is premised on the *lalake/bakla* dichotomy and, thus, the closer he is to "performing," to "being" a kind of *bakla* (*but not quite*) by being the *lalake's* proximate. He becomes the very thing he detests.

Yet the paradox still persists: the BI is not the *bakla* and the BI is the *bakla*. To what extent is he not quite the *bakla*?

The trajectory of desire of the traditional *bakla* is difference: he desires what he is not. The traditional *bakla* will not run after another *bakla*: that would have been poisonous (*lason* in gayspeak). Being woman-hearted, the *bakla* wishes to find a partner who is his opposite—same body but different *loob/kalooban* (internal self). On the other hand, the BI desires the same, not his opposite. In fact, to complicate the proposition above, he desires the *lalake* who is both himself and not himself. Take note of the preponderance of the phrase "for same" in the BI profiles, or "____ sa ____" or "tulad" (like "astig sa astig") which denotes sameness. An example would be the assertion of TPB: "At dapat di halata tulad ko" (And he should be not obvious like me).

Whereas the traditional *bakla's* desire is to possess the man, the BI's desire is founded on both *possession of* and *becoming* the man believing himself to be a man (*lalake*) as well. Thus, if we are looking for proof of the implantation of Western homosexual discourse in the country and its ingenious translation or appropriation, the BI's identity is one strong proof: a gesture towards the same, a desire founded on sameness.

Yet from another perspective, we can also view that the BI is an evolved form of *bakla*. After all, who says that the *bakla* should be perpetually effeminate and transvestic? I would like to believe that conceptions of gender and sexuality change through time, and definitions change as well. While the *bakla* may actually have been originally conceived as effeminate and potentially crossdressing, is it not possible for individuals to break the mold? And is it not possible for *bakla* to broaden its significations? Why are masculine gay men now calling themselves *bakla*, too? Should we tell them they are not *bakla* and have no right to claim such a name because *bakla* should mean only woman-hearted, crossdressing, and effeminate males? Should we repeat what has been done to the *silahis* and the masculine homosexuals because the existing critical and popular discourses then (especially in the 1970s) could not put them anywhere (such that even the archaic overt/covert distinctions in the Philippines technically could not even account for them) and they therefore perpetually occupied what Neil Garcia would call an "agonized space" (2009, 97)?

The fact that masculine gays and *bakla* rally forth under the banner "gay" is telling. "Gay" is the term that supposedly includes the masculine-identified and feminine-identified homosexuals. Thus, Pinoy BIs can be considered examples of these masculine-identifying individuals together with the multitudes of masculine gay men who have no problem calling themselves *bakla* and being called *bakla*. Why can't many Pinoy BIs do the same? I used the word "many," because many profiles on PR demonstrate that the three terms—BI, BAKLA, GAY—co-exist and do not necessarily cancel each other out. While there may be gay men who identity as *bakla* and as gay, and BIs who may also self-identify as gay, surely, given all the incessant slippages, there are also men who identify as all three, depending on the context of the self-naming and the parameters used to set the definition. After all, if sexual object choice were the only qualification or criterion, then clearly the bakla and BI would bear no difference. Let me end this section with an extract from a member's "my own words" write-up:

FDB
pag chumuchupa, tumitira ng lalaki, tumitingin sa gwapo,
tumutingin sa bukol ng dibdib at pantalon ng lalaki…
walang nakakaalam pero halos lahat ng tao sa PR na mit mo na…
di ka nga nagbabayad ng sex pero sumusubo ka din at bumubukaka
ano ka? tanga…BAKLA ka…
(If you suck, fuck guys, stare at handsome guys, look at the chest
and crotch of guys…
No one knows but you've meet almost all the guys on PR
You don't pay for sex but suck and open your legs wide
What are you? Dumbass… you're BAKLA …)

This profile perfectly captures the sentiments of many people who are sick and tired of the divide between the *bakla* and the BI as though the *bakla* is a kind of species completely different from the BI. It is also a shout out to some BIs to stop discriminating the others on the basis of their self-identification and their gender presentation. And what I find most interesting here is that this statement comes from someone who self-identifies as BI, which is to say, in his mind, though he may call himself BI, he knows and accepts he is also a *bakla*.

Lastly, if the BI's interest is to break away from the stereotypes hurled at the *bakla*, why not join the fray and show the world a different form of *kabaklaan*? Deconstruct *kabaklaan* from within.

Indeed, questions of who is BI (and who is GAY) in the Philippines eventually lead us to the question *who is bakla*? And arguments will never end because the traditional definition of *kabaklaan*, which differentiates the *bakla* from his Other—the *lalake*—precisely because of his effeminacy, is the force around which self-definitions, sexual practices, public perceptions, community conflicts, and theoretical ruminations gravitate.[18] Because sexuality is a "cultural construction," David Halperin avers: "we must struggle to discern in what we currently regard as our most precious, unique, original, and spontaneous impulses the traces of a previously rehearsed and socially encoded ideological script (1990, 40). And I say: that "script" that has condemned the *bakla* and the BI cannot not change and must be rewritten.

To BI and beyond

SCG
Gustuhin ko man magkaroon ng karelasyon, wala naman ????,
ayaw naman nila ng baklang halata????
(Even if I want to have a relationship, all to no avail???, they are not into bakla who are obviously bakla????)

Baklang halata ako... Halata sa boses at galaw
(I am a bakla who is obvious... Evident in the voice and gestures)

OGB

18   For more on this issue, one can consult chapter one of Martin F. Manalansan's *Global Divas*, 21–44, esp. 25–26; and J. Neil C. Garcia's comment on Manalansan's earlier work in *Philippine Gay Culture*, footnote 77 in chapter 2, 476.

...on dis site' we r all gay ok!!!

The key aim of this paper is to offer notes on the "bisexual" in the Philippines, especially those BIs on the dating website Planet Romeo.

BI is not the bisexual of the West. While it can be used to refer to some men who are literally bisexual (in terms of sexual object choice), the Filipino bisexuals of Planet Romeo are predominantly gay. It is interesting to note that BI is that liminal category that straddles between two different but contiguous realities—the reality of men who engage in both same-sex and opposite sex relations (and this is not my paper's focus), and that of men who engage primarily in same-sex relations but refuse identification with the effeminate *bakla* or gay.

While it is true that there are bisexual Filipino men in the Western sense on PR, the BI in this study is a masculine homosexual identity (or one who least tries to act masculine), and it stands as the masculine counterpart of the effeminate *bakla* and the effeminized (but not necessarily effeminate) gay. This means that in certain segments of the gay culture, especially this lot, "gay" has become construed as effeminate; and the bisexuals' way of distinguishing the masculine ones from the femmes is to invoke the word BI. The ascendancy of masculinity persists: In a way, the BI/BAKLA and the BI/GAY dichotomies are reformulations of the LA-LAKE/BAKLA and LALAKE/BABAE dichotomies which privilege the masculine subject.

It would be easy to say that the bisexual is actually a type of *bakla*. Because he is (as OGB, quoted above, a self-professed BI, would assert). At least to a certain extent. But he is also not completely one either. He may be a *bakla*, but from his perspective he has enough reason to refuse the name because the existing terms associated with *bakla* are unacceptable to him and he feels that these terms do not quite represent him. As we have already shown, there really is no category in the local gender system for someone like him. And he is therefore condemned to exist only via the *bakla* and the *lalake* who are his supposed Others, identities with aspects he possesses and dis/avows. BI represents the conflation between (Western) sexological discourse (identifying people based on sexual object choice) and (local) understandings of gender. Gay should ideally have been the answer to fit both the masculine and effeminate homosexuals; but in the case of these BIs, this is not the ideal route. From the perspective of some of these BIs, gay has been "baklafied," effeminized (and gay- and bakla-identified men stand to lose their marketability in the dating game, as SCG, quoted above, has expressed in his write-up).

The revulsion towards the effeminate is a kind of "displacement" (Dollimore 1991, 54) with the bisexuals directing their anger at the effeminate (*bakla*, girly gays, transgender) who are actually their own kin in the subculture. In short there is internalized homophobia at work here. While it is ironic that the BI subject has chosen a term that supposedly renounces his gayness when the very definition of bisexuality entails gayness, the term of abjection is not operationalized chiefly through the lens of sexual orientation, but gender performance and/or presentation. The problem is not that the *bakla* and so-called effeminate gays desire men—the problem is effeminacy. And what about the effeminate BIs pretending to be masculine? Is it not possible to say that their hatred is borne of their inability to subject their *bakla* self to erasure, that abiding feminine self that could never ever be vanquished?

An important note on the discreet/out (or *ladlad*) dichotomy: this binary opposition (together with its permutations) is what makes the connection between the *bakla* and *silahis* of the past and between the *bakla* and the BIs of the present more pronounced. Through the years, despite the change in terminologies and the renaming of identities, the mark of undesirability has constantly been *lovingly* dedicated to the "obvious."

What we are actually witnessing is a very old theoretical slippage— the conflation of gender (*bakla*) with sexuality (homo, gay), of *bakla* (gender-transitive) with *gay* (supposedly gender-intransitive), two categories construed as the Other of the supposedly superior BI—actualized in new media. The identity politics of Pinoy "bisexuality" is a victim of heteronormative discourse. In the end, it does not destabilize the *lalake/bakla* dichotomy firmly entrenched in Philippine society (and for so long), but promotes it so that the *bakla* and all his "sissy" and "tranny" sisters remain the unwanted Other.

Nevertheless, there are other ways of looking at the bisexuals in the country. BI is the subject's incessant and endless attempt to become the *lalake*, the attempt fuelled by the paradoxical fact that he is one and yet he could never completely be. I would say BI's identity is a **strategic fiction** (to play with Caroline Hau's *Necessary Fictions*) or a **calculated pose**. And the anger for the knowledge of its necessary failure is directed at its proximate, the *bakla*, who historically has been the only subject position he has been allowed to occupy in Philippine society, for the concept of the *lalake* was premised on desiring the opposite which was the *babae*.

The presence of the bisexual all these years therefore is the BI's acceptance and rejection of the categories imposed on him by the traditional social scripts. It exposes the boundaries of the sex-gender system in the country that limits individuals to only four categories: *lalake, babae, bakla,* tomboy. It represents a conscious but uncanny appropriation and translation of Western categories. Filipino bisexuality discussed here is not an undoing of Western sexology but a revelation of the powers of translating, of transplanting discourses onto local shores. It also represents the changing discourses on homosexuality in the Philippines. Clearly, in Garcia's model no. 4: Contemporary Male Homosexual Identities (*Philippine Gay Culture*, 253), the BI would have belonged to the same gender-intransitive models of male homosexuality in the Philippines together with the *silahis*, MSM, and gay.

In addition, despite developments in Western homosexual/queer discourse and their "localization" or habitation in our archipelago, the native/local conceptions of gender still continuously hound and inform the Filipino gay community's conception and deployment of Western sexual categories, reinforcing the impossibility of complete homosexualization of the *bakla* (a point evident in Garcia's work more than two decades ago), or rather that homosexualizing the *bakla* is a continuous never-ending process.

We must also remember that Pinoy "bisexuality" is a performance, a performance implicated in the discourse of *kabaklaan*. While we have shown the relationship between the *bakla* and the BI, we must not forget that the dichotomy BI/*bakla*, BI/gay, *bakla*/gay, masculine/feminine are different in terms of conception and performance, as imagined, as self-percieved, and as lived. What the subjects say they are and who they are, are two different things.

In reality, these BIs and *bakla* will act differently in various situations and will not necessarily be masculine because they call themselves BI or act feminine because they self-identify as gay or *bakla*. There is a camp element to all these performances that we can still pursue in future studies. The exaggeration, excess, and irony in these performances—especially if we take into account the pictures, handles, and other data in the profiles—should be explored. The planet, pun intended, is a global stage of performances.

And in a world fuelled by anonymity, nothing can be ascertained as 100% real. Nothing is ever real or fixed, but fixations are real. For now, at least to me, the only thing that approximates the real, in these calculated fictions, given all the negation and self-immolation on Planet Romeo, is the investment in masculinity, a masculinity that is grounded in the violent history of *kabaklaan* in Philippine culture.

In Philippine society, *kabaklaan*—in certain pockets of Philippine culture—has been stereotyped as low class and limited to certain professions like hairstyling and fashion design. Scholars must explore the role or function of class in the lives of BIs in the Philippines. In Michael Tan's "From Bakla to Gay," one can deduce how class can be a divisive force between the middle/upper-middle-class gay men and the *parlorista*, in matters related to desire with "class definitions of 'decency' (*pagkadesente*)" (94) figuring in the discussion. Neil Garcia also mentions class as a problem in *Philippine Gay Culture* (xvi). In my study, while lack of decency is ascribed to the *parlorista* or *bakla*, I have to gather more data to ascertain the connection between class and the revulsion of the effeminate. For now, what is clear is that many self-identified BIs and even gays coming from different classes— upper, middle, and lower classes—abhor the effeminate *bakla*. To discuss in-depth the ways in which class figures in the practices on PR necessitate a different paper and perhaps a different methodology.

I submit, nonetheless: class figures in this website—regardless of the members' self-identification, regardless of their revulsion of the effeminate—insofar as masculinity functions as capital in the gay culture. Class and the idealization of masculinity work hand in hand in gay/BI cultures. Why do so many profiles contain the phrase "no to money boys"? "Money boy" does not just refer to straight guys or the *lalake* advertising their services on PR; this also refers to so many gays/BIs who use their bodies for economic survival ranging from the outright "bi" masseurs to the men selling their bodies to purchase mobile phones to those who wish to augment their income because their salary is not enough for young men dreaming of a better life. I reiterate: a number of PR subjects use Planet Romeo for financial reasons—and they capitalize on their masculinity and their muscular physique to do this.

Younger men tend to go for older men not only for their maturity but also for the promise of financial stability. Some members—not necessarily CSWs—capitalize on their beauty, youth, and masculinity to attract well-off guys (for purposes like enrollment, travel). A BI member (NHB) states: "Kahit araw-araw kang magpakantot saken sige lang. Tulungan mo lng ako sa tuition ko. Tulog lng di nmn ikaw magbabayad ng buo." (Even if I have to fuck you every day, ok with me. Just help me with my tuition. Just help; you're not paying for the entire amount." This example is framed in terms of *pakimkim*, a form of gratitude, a form of assistance or gift/token one gives to someone for his/her kindness—and NOT outright paid sex work. It brings to the fore a symbiotic and mutually beneficial relationship or friendship between individuals. And this relationship exists in the gay community between members of different economic power. The men (straight, gay, closeted) who flock to the richer gay men's houses come to them for favors both parties benefit from (e.g., they both get something out of it; sexual gratification and material goods) and these men do not and are not viewed as paid sex workers. This phenomenon cuts across sexual identifications (gay, bi, trans), and must be explored by scholars further.

Hunky masculine gay and BI men also use their bodies for money and for PNP/orgies involving chemical use (Partee and Play; note the E in partee). To quote one member (EWG): "Kung kuripot ka, wag ka mag ilusyon na mai-kakama mo ako! Di lahat ng HOT libre! I don't do skype or show dick pics. May bayad yan. You can't have me for free!" (If you're stingy, let go of the il-lusion that you will bed me! Not all HOT guys are free! I don't do skype or show dick pics. That's for pay. You can't have me for free!"). In both profiles above, the guys present themselves as masculine and top. Would these men have ever thought of offering their services had they been effeminate? Would they come off less masculine if they self-identified as bottoms? To their po-tential benefactors, wouldn't a rich effeminate gay man calling himself BI be able to exert tremendous power as well over the terrifyingly beautiful muscu-lar and masculine man of meager means? Indeed, what exists in social media, specifically in gay dating sites like PR, is a form of libidinal economy where we see most clearly how class (capital and economic power), gender (male-ness, manliness, masculinity), and sexuality (homo-, "bisexuality") overlap; where masculinity is prized, where the male body becomes commodity, where money troubles distinctions and roles; and where the definitions of power— as regards who is subjected, who is "subjectivated"—are most volatile.

The BIs of today's generation, I reiterate, already have a group, a commu-nity to belong to. And I would like to add that the community—thanks to social media and the internet—is getting larger and larger. Many BIs and gay men have utilized Twitter to pursue their desires and to find avenues for self-expression: this is called ALTER, which technically is a user's ALTERnative account, an account different from one's primary account. And yet, while most accounts are really created primarily for sexual purposes and some accounts are famous for their sex videos, one can find intelligent discourses on politics and identities in this virtual space. It needs to be added as well that the lure of this alter account is premised upon the politics of in/visibility. Disgruntled with Facebook, Planet Romeo, and Grindr, these "alters" (who are actually gay and some self-identify as BI) nonetheless have continued marking out virtual spaces for themselves and creating a community.[19]

Perhaps it is time that we ask: What exactly constitutes a community and how can we form it and mobilize it towards emancipatory ends? "The time has come to think about sex," Gayle Rubin once boldly announced in 1984 (3). Given all the problems this country and the LGBT community are facing, it is still the right time to think about sex and to pursue "a liberatory body of thought about sexuality" (9). The case of "bisexuals" in

---

19   Please read Jam Pascual's insightful article on this alter world on/of Twitter, "I Will Follow You Into the Dark," *Team Magazine*, issue 8 (2017), 7–83.

the Philippines needs further rethinking especially in light of their perennial problems with the femmes, in light of the great divide hounding the LGBT community, and in light of the AIDS epidemic.[20] Time and again in this latter half of the decade, statistics shows that the highest incidence of HIV infection involves MSM;[21] and these men are the same men who populate the spaces of Planet Romeo and Grindr. It bears noting that "trace" can be used as a trope to explore both the identities and the HIV discourses of these men living with HIV/AIDS.

Another topic that needs to be addressed is the TRANS identity on-line and beyond. When I started the project in 2011, I already spotted a few transgenders landing on the Hot List and I did not encounter a profile write-up containing "no trans"; now, in 2016 and 2017, there are more transgen-ders on the list and some profiles now contain "no trans." I surmise that the growing consciousness among transgenders and the development of the discourse about trans identities have fuelled this trans hatred. In a country where the *bakla* is a ubiquitous presence, the relationship between the trans and the *bakla*—who have the same history and are interchangeable in certain contexts in the Philippines—needs probing. Theoretical/conceptual over-lappings and slippages between the *bakla* and the trans need to be examined. After all, in a very masculinist and effeminophobic Philippine culture, the trans and the *bakla* have so much work to do and so much hate to combat.

While the Pinoy BI may be viewed as actually gay, a masculine gay man, or one who feels he is masculine, there is more to his identity that needs unraveling and exploration. The relationship between *silahis* and BI needs more probing. In addition, more work needs to be done on the married bisexuals as well. The profiles of these men would usually have the words "discreet" and "married with kids." Are these bisexual-identified men really bisexual, and from whose perspective?

We also need to continuously question the notions of being *lalake*. Why should the *lalake* continue to be the only "real" man? The challenges

20   In "Survival Through Pluralism: Emerging Gay Communities in the Philip-pines," Michael L. Tan asked a very important question: "Given that we have diverse communities, is there any basis for unity?" (138). What exactly does "unity" signify and under what circumstances should this remain a goal, if at all?

21   Tina G. Santos, "750 New HIV Cases in December Included 3 Pregnant Women—DOH," *Philippine Daily Inquirer*, 2 February 2017, accessed 27 September 2019, https://newsinfo.inquirer.net/867388/750-new-hiv-cases-in-december-included-3-pregnant-women-doh. The news report states: "Majority of the new cases were trans-mitted sexually with 734 (97.8%), including the 649 (88%) coming from the male-hav-ing-sex-with-male (MSM) sector."

posed by the BI to the *lalake/bakla* dichotomy can be conceptually examined further. We also need to rethink our conceptions of *kabaklaan*. The *bakla* has evolved and we need to think of a plurality of *bakla* subjectivities that can include the BI.[22] This study has only addressed the tip of the iceberg.

To conclude, we must not forget that the BIs who harbor hatred for the effeminate and who valorize hypermasculinity are a peculiar yet important lot in Philippine LGBTQI culture. And I daresay, the impulse to eradicate the effem from the planet is not *primarily* anchored on notions of a global gay culture—it is endemic to the culture. The impulses have long been there. And my conjecture is that the hatred began the moment the *bakla* and *lalake* were created, the moment the gender system abrogated the feminine and its copy the effeminate, assigned non-realness to the *bakla*, and completely forgot about the no-named man who was neither *lalake* nor *bakla*. The Pinoy "bisexual" in this study is one of the excesses in the very rigid sex-gender system in the country. Morphing into a ticking time bomb, it only needed modern technology to explode.

22   Please check the works of Tan, Garcia, Manalansan, Diaz, Benedicto, and Baytan in the references for more perspectives on Philippine gay culture.

Bibliography

Abelove, Henry, Michele Aina Barale, and David Halperin, eds. *The Lesbian and Gay Studies Reader*. New York: Routledge, 1993.

Almario, Virgilio, ed. *UP Diksiyonaryong Filipino*. Rev. ed. Mandaluyong: UP Sentro ng Wikang Filipino and Anvil, 2010.

Anderson, Benedict. *Imagined Communities: Reflections on the Origins and Spread of Nationalism*. Rev. ed. Pasig: Anvil, 2003.

Austria, Fernando A., Jr. "Mga Bakla sa Internet." In *Media at Lipunan*, edited by Rolando B. Tolentino and Josefina M. Santos, 305–20. Quezon City: University of the Philippine Press, 2014.

Baytan, Ronald. "Bading na Bading: Evolving Male Homosexual Identities in Philippines." In *AsiaPacifiQueer: Rethinking Genders and Sexualities*, edited by Fran Martin, Peter A. Jackson, Mark McLelland, and Audrey Yue, 181–96. Champagne: University of Illinois Press, 2008.

Baytan, Ronald. "Romeos in the Metropolis: Notes on AutoBIography." Paper read as part of the Cirilo F. Bautista lecture series of the Department of Literature, De La Salle University, 26 February 2011.

Benedicto, Bobby. "The Haunting of Gay Manila: Global Space-Time and the Specter of *Kabaklaan*." *GLQ: A Journal of Lesbian and Gay Studies* 14.2–3 (2008): 317–38.

Butler, Judith. "Imitation and Gender Insubordination." In *Inside/Out: Lesbian Theories, Gay Theories*, edited by Diana Fuss, 13–31. New York: Routledge, 1991.

Concha, Arnold. "Ephemeral Sexualities." *In Plainspeak: Talking about Sexuality in South and Southeast Asia* 1 (2008).

Dela Cruz, Mikee. "10 Planet Romeo Situations that Highlight Confusion." *Outrage Magazine*, 30 April 2015. Accessed 7 April 2017. http://outragemag.com/10-planetromeo-situations-that-highlight-gay-confusion/.

———. [As Michael David Dela Cruz Tan]. "Victimizing Ourselves." *Outrage Magazine*, November 2012. Accessed 7 April 2017. http://outragemag.com/victimizing-ourselves/.

Diaz, Robert G. "The Limits of Bakla and Gay: My Husband's Lover, Vice Ganda, and Charice Pempengco." *Signs: Journal of Women in Culture and Society* (March 2015): 721–45.

Dollimore, Jonathan. *Sexual Dissidence: Augustine to Wilde, Freud to Foucault*. Oxford: Clarendon Press, 1991.

Esterberg, Kristin G. "The Bisexual Menace: Or, Will the Real Bisexual Please Stand Up?" In *Handbook of Lesbian and Gay Studies*, edited by Diane Richardson and Steven Siedman, 217–27. London: Sage, 2002.

Garcia, J. Neil C. "Reading Auras: The Gay Theme in Philippine Fiction in English." Introduction to *Aura: The Gay Theme in Philippine Fiction in English*, 9–38. Mandaluyong: Anvil, 2012.

———. "LGBT Discourse in the Philippines: A Very Short Report." In *Myth and Writing: Occasional Prose*, 249–52. Quezon City: University of the Philippines Press, 2016.

———. *Philippine Gay Culture: The Last Thirty Years, Binabae to Bakla, Silahis to MSM*. Rev. ed. Hongkong: Hongkong University Press, 2009 [1996].

———. *Slip/pages: Essays in Philippine Gay Criticism (1991–1996)*. Manila: De La Salle University Press, 1998.

———. "Philippine Gay Culture: Reflections on a Study." In *Slip/pages*, 86–108. Paper presented at the Linguistic Society of the Philippines monthly lecture, Philippine Normal University, 26 November 1994.

Halperin, David H. *One Hundred Years of Homosexuality: The New Ancient World and Other Essays on Greek Love*. London: Routledge, 1990.

Hau, Caroline S. *Necessary Fictions: Philippine Literature and the Nation, 1946–1980*. Quezon City: Ateneo de Manila University Press, 2000.

Madula, Rowee D. "www.ang_espasyong_bakla_sa_cyberspace.com: Isang Pagsusuri ng Diskurso ng mga Usapang Bakla sa Cyberspace." *Malay* 22.2 (2010): 85–98.

Manalansan, Martin F. IV. *Global Divas: Filipino Gay Men in the Diaspora*. Philippine ed. Quezon City: Ateneo de Manila University Press, 2006.

Montenegro, Michael R. "Coming to Terms with Sexual Identity: A Study of the Effects of Cybergroup Membership on Selected Bisexual Male Adolescents." MA thesis, De La Salle University, August 2003.

Oxford English Dictionary. Compact ed. Complete text reproduced micrographically. Clarendon: Oxford University Press, 1971.

Oxford English Dictionary Online. S.v. "discreet." Accessed 15 April 2017. https://en.oxforddictionaries.com/definition/discreet.

Pascual, Jam. "I Will Follow You into the Dark." *Team Magazine* 8 (2017): 78–83.

Pertierra, Raul. *The Anthropology of New Media in the Philippines.* Quezon City: Institute of Philippine Culture, Ateneo de Manila University, 2010.

Peters, Pam. *The Cambridge Guide to English Usage.* Cambridge, UK: Cambridge University Press, 2004. ProQuest ebrary. Web. 14 April 2017.

Planet Romeo Foundation. "The Gay Happiness Index." May 2015. Accessed 29 January 2017. https://www.planetromeo.com/en/care/gay happiness index/.

Rubin, Gayle. "Thinking Sex: Notes for a Radical Theory of the Politics of Sexuality." In *The Lesbian and Gay Studies Reader,* edited by Henry Abelove, Michele Barale, and David Halperin, 3–44. New York: Routledge, 1993.

Santos, Tina G. "750 New HIV Cases in December Included 3 Pregnant Women—DOH." *Philippine Daily Inquirer,* 2 February 2017. Accessed 16 April 2017. http://newsinfo.inquirer.net/867388/750-new-hiv-cases-in-december-included-3-pregnant-women-doh.

Sedgwick, Eve Kosofsky. *Epistemology of the Closet.* Berkeley: University of California Press, 1990.

Tan, Michael L. "Walking the Tightrope: Sexual Risk and Male Sex Work in the Philippines." In *Men Who Sell Sex: International Perspectives on Male Prostitution and HIV/AIDS,* edited by Peter Aggleton. Pennsylvania: Temple University Press, 1999.

———. "A Response to Dennis Altman." *Australian Humanities Review* (1996). Accessed April 2017. http://www.australianhumanitiesreview.org/emuse/Globalqueering/tan.html.

———. "AIDS, Medicine and Moral Panic in the Philippines." In *Framing the Sexual Subject: The Politics of Gender, Sexuality, and Power,* edited by Richard Parker, Regina Maria Barbosa, and Peter Aggleton, 143–64. Berkeley: University of California Press, 2000.

———. "From Bakla to Gay: Shifting Gender Identities and Sexual Behaviors in the Philippines." In *Conceiving Sexuality: Approaches to Sex Research in a Postmodern World,* edited by R. Parker and J. Gagnon, 85–96. New York: Routledge, 1994.

———. "Sickness and Sin: Medical and Religious Stigmatization of Homosexuality in the Philippines" (1992). In *Ladlad: An Anthology of Philippine Gay Writiing,* 202–19. Mandaluyong: Anvil, 1994.

———. "*Silahis*: Looking for the Missing Filipino Bisexual Male." In *Bisexualities and AIDS,* edited by Peter Aggleton, 207–26. London: Taylor & Francis, 1998.

———. "Survival Through Pluralism." *Journal of Homosexuality* 40. 3–4 (2001): 117–42. http://dx.doi.org/10.1300/J082v40n03_07.

United Nations Development Program (UNDP) and United States Agency for International Development (USAID). *Being LGBT in Asia: The Philippines Country Report. A Participatory Review and Analysis of the Legal and Social Environment for Lesbian, Gay, Bisexual and Transgender (LGBT) Individuals and Civil Society.* Bangkok: N.p., 2014.

Top, A same-sex couple joins Metro Manila Pride in June 2016. Photo from Shutterstock. *Above*, GALANG Philippines, Inc. held a training on advocacy concepts on 24 October 2012 which was attended by LBTs from their partner communities to strengthen their communication skills. Photo courtesy of GALANG Philippines, Inc.

JENNIFER C. JOSEF
UNIVERSITY OF THE PHILIPPINES–BAGUIO

Pinoy[1] Tomboys, Lesbians, and Transgenders: Their Gender and Sexual Identities and Activism since the 1980s

Introduction

I IDENTIFY AS A LESBIAN-FEMINIST ACTIVIST. I always try to explore lesbian, gay, and transgender (LGT) themes in my research and advocacy work. There was a need to document the experiences and narratives on lesbian/tomboy activism and movement-building in the Philippines. I reluctantly took on the daunting task because I am one of the few qualified individuals who can do the job. My best qualification is that I was there, I witnessed most of the significant events and processes that I am describing in this essay. I am very fortunate to have been part of the dynamic phase of the Philippine women's movement from the 1980s to 1990s and to have been an active participant during the birthing and pioneering phase of lesbian organizing and research on lesbians, tomboys, women-loving women, and transgenders in the Philippines in the early 1990s. When I was doing my course work for my doctoral degree, I wrote a paper on lesbian activism in the Philippines for a class in anthropology. That paper became the basis for this current essay which is my humble contribution to this important collection on Filipino tomboys and *bakla*. The rewrite process triggered sparks of memory, recollection, and retrieval of little nuggets of realization and insights. The information, analyses, and insights I offer in this essay are of events I witnessed firsthand as part of the incipient movement, and as part of my research and advocacy efforts on lesbian, tomboy, bakla, and gay issues.

This essay explores the formation and framing of sexual and gender identities of Filipino lesbians, tomboys, and transgenders, from the 1980s up to 2010s. This essay also explores the processes and factors that helped shape these gender and sexual identities and the political activism of lesbians/tomboys/transgenders.

---

1 "Pinoy" is a colloquial term for "Filipino."

I deliberately limited the focus of my research to lesbians, tomboys, and transgender (female to male) persons. I believe that focusing on tomboys, lesbians, and transgenders is already a complicated and daunting endeavor. I did not want to further complicate this research by including bisexual women, gays (male), and trans women. Moreover, I did not delve into specific gay or bakla themes because many gay/bakla scholars have been doing excellent work on gay and queer studies.

I have taken the position of using the constructs *gender identity* and *sexual identity* whenever applicable instead of the social construct *sexual orientation* as I believe that sexual orientation does not capture the complexities of gender and sexual identities. I avoid using the acronym SOGIE which stands for sexual orientation and gender identity/expression. SOGIE is a buzzword at the United Nations, the European Union, and other international advocacy platforms. However, I use the acronym SOGIE mainly when referring to the anti-discrimination bill pending in the Philippine Congress and when referencing other international instruments where SOGIE is specifically mentioned.

Moreover, I try to avoid using the acronym or "initialism" LGBTIQ+ (which stands for lesbian, gay, bisexual, trans, intersex, queer, etc.) to refer to the ever-increasing variants of non-heteronormative "orientation" and identities. Whenever possible, I use the label *tomboy* (and *bakla* for that matter) and/or its variants in the local vernacular in order to privilege the labels and identities that most of my tomboy and lesbian informants find resonance in and identify with. No matter how inconvenient, I prefer to enumerate all the labels for the various gender and sexual identities in order to provide the proper contexts and integrity to the experiences behind those local labels and identities.

I take the approach of adopting and popularizing the local gender and sexual identity categories such as *tomboy, bakla, bayot* (Cebuano word which means homosexual and/or effeminate), *minamagkit* (from the Bontok word *magmagkit* which means maiden, *minamagkit* therefore means "like a maiden"), and not to uncritically adopt Western concepts and categories (Josef 2018). While *tomboy* is a borrowed label/concept, it was not an uncritical or unmediated borrowing or appropriation. The adoption of local labels helps underscore the importance of the specific local contexts and the likelihood of non-equivalency of local and Western labels, categories, and experiences.

To help me arrive at an understanding of Pinoy non-heteronormative gender and sexual identities, I came up with themes which I think were significant in influencing the framing of Pinoy gender and sexual identities and the forms of lesbian/tomboy/transgender organizing, advocacy, and movement-building work.

I argue that these themes are among the major processes and influences on the gender and sexual identities and activism of Pinoy tomboys, lesbians, and transgenders since the 1980s. For framing gender and sexual identities, the themes include the following: (1) Roman Catholic church and gender and sexual identities; (2) diaspora—LGT migrant workers; (3) gay tourism in the Philippines; (4) advent of hormone therapy, sex reassignment technology, new gender identities and expression, and the required changes in ideologies and laws; and (5) Cyber Information and Communication Technology (ICT) as new platforms and sites for identity-formation.

I consider these themes relevant for various reasons. A majority of our population are Christians, with Catholics comprising the biggest denomination. We are a major migrant worker-sending country and a popular gay tourist destination in Asia. Despite being a low-income country, our population can be considered information-communication tech-savvy, such that we even held the title of being the text (SMS) capital of the world because of the huge volume of text messages Filipinos send daily. Filipinos are active users of social media, with the Philippines ranking as the 7th largest country in Facebook (Visa 2012).

The internet will continue to have a profound impact on the everyday lives and identity-formation of millennials and future generations. Cyber-feminists Flanagan and Booth (2002) consider cyberculture as "a revolutionary social experiment with the potential to create new identities, relationships and cultures" especially for the "always connected" millennial generation. The millennial generation includes those born from 1981 to 1996 or those aged from 22 to 37 in 2018 (Smith and Anderson 2018). Millennials are predicted to account for 72 percent of the workforce in 2025, which makes them the main drivers of the economy as workers and consumers (McCann Truth Central 2016). One in two Filipino millennials, or 50 percent, cannot live without their PCs/laptops (Visa 2012). Data from another research suggests that 75 percent of Filipino millennials view the internet as their main source of information, especially about adulting themes. About 66 percent use the internet to look for products and 79 percent use it for entertainment (Adobo Magazine 2017). Cyber information and communication technology and social media are projected to play significant roles in the development of lesbian/gay/transgender gender and sexual identities.

For the section on lesbian and tomboy activism, I attempted to provide a rudimentary typology and periodization of the activism and movement-building mainly in Metro Manila and a couple of other key cities like Davao in the south and Baguio in northern Philippines. I described some of the pioneer lesbian/tomboy organizations, focusing on the socioeconomic background of the members, the ideologies they espoused, the issues and activities they undertook, and the strategies they employed. The approaches such as mainstreaming, rights-based, legitimation movements (Vaid 1995), and the constructs of "social non-movement" and "quiet encroachment of the ordinary" (Bayat 2010) were useful lenses for viewing some manifestations of activism and movement-building. The more middle-class-identified organizations undertook mainstreaming through visibility campaigns in mass media and legislative reform. The grassroots organizations of urban poor lesbians, bisexuals, and transgenders formed community-based groups that focused on the strategies of mainstreaming and "quiet encroachment of the ordinary" (Bayat 2010). These concepts will later be discussed extensively in the relevant sections of this essay.

Conceptual framework

For the conceptualization of sex/gender and gender/sexual identities, I find affinity with the elucidations of Dowsett (1996) and Connell (2002). Dowsett criticizes what he describes as an increasingly narrow conceptualization of identity limited to distinctions between "sexual orientations" and between "sexes." He describes gender identity framed as either male or female, with transgender and transsexual somehow being accommodated in this dichotomy. Dowsett correctly recognizes that these "taxonomies" are useful as everybody needs labels to identify with, and that these labels enable individuals and categories of people to identify kindred and those who are different from them. More substantively, however, I agree with Dowsett's analysis that these dichotomies do not capture the complexities of gender identities.

Dowsett is also critical of the conceptualization of sexuality as a psychic dimension, i.e., one's homosexuality as an internally experienced desire for one's own sex. This conceptualization of sexuality as psychic resolution, according to Dowsett, barely captures the complexities of sexuality. These complexities include practices and relations, desire, intentions, and meanings. Dowsett recommends the term "sexual subjectivity" as he believes it offers a larger conceptual space to encompass the many ingredients, dimensions, and complexities of sexual identities.

To illuminate the structural character of gender, I turn to R.W. Connell's description of gender as social structure. He argues that gender is not an expression of biology nor a fixed dichotomy. Gender is much more than the either male or female binary. Gender involves relationships, boundaries, practices, identities, and images that are actively created in social processes, come into existence in specific historical and social contexts, shape the lives of people in profound and often contradictory ways, and are subject to historical struggle and change (Connell 2002).

Identities are multifaceted. One does not exist and interact in the world solely as a lesbian, tomboy, or transgender. Lesbians, tomboys, transgenders, and those belonging to other stigmatized non-heteronormative identities suffer from many social inequalities aside from gender and sexual discrimination and oppression.

The social constructs of intersectionality and subjectivity are employed to understand the framing of gender and sexual identities of Pinoy (Filipino) lesbians and transgenders (hooks 1982; Crenshaw 1989; Collins 1990). Intersectionality posits that people experience oppression in various degrees and intensities depending on their positions in society based on race, ethnicity, class, gender, geography, sexual identity, religion, physical appearance, disability, and other subject positions based on their specific personal circumstances such as political ideologies and affiliations, educational background, etc. Race, caste, ethnicity, and other culturally imposed social stratifications increase and compound the layers of discrimination (Pharr 1997). A person may be a lesbian, poor, living in a poor country, belonging to a marginalized ethnic community, and so on. Intersectionality profoundly impacts the lives of lesbians, tomboys, and transgenders, as well their forms of resistance against discrimination, stigma, oppression, homophobia, and so on. The succeeding paragraphs are illustrations of how intersectionality and subjectivities affect the collective lives of Pinoy lesbians, tomboys, and transgender persons.

I surmise that intersectionality is one of the factors why Ladlad—the LGBTQ+ party-list group in the Philippines—has not been successful in landing a Congressional seat. While identity is multidimensional, a voter can only choose one party list. This presents a dilemma as to which of your multiple allegiances corresponding to the various dimensions of your identity should you prioritize to determine your party list choice.

The influence of the Roman Catholic church and other conservative and fundamentalist religious groups on members of Congress has prevented the passage of the anti-discrimination bill. In October 2017, the bill was passed on third and final reading at the House of Representatives and there are high expectations that it could finally be enacted into law under President Rodrigo Duterte's ostensibly LGBT-supportive agenda.

One of the main proponents of the bill is Geraldine Roman, who comes from a traditional political clan and who happens to be a trans woman. She is commended for her work and commitment to the anti-discrimination bill but has been criticized by various political groupings including LGBT organizations for voting on other issues along her class and political party lines. She ran in the last elections under the Liberty Party but has since shifted to the political party of Duterte. She has voted in favor of the re-imposition of the death penalty for drug-related and other crimes. She was absent during the session where Congress voted to slash the 2018 budget of the Commission on Human Rights (CHR) from ₱537 million to ₱1,000.[2] The CHR budget cut is viewed as a punishment for its criticism of the Duterte regime's drug-related extrajudicial killings (EJKs) estimated to account for between 9,000 to 20,000 deaths. Roman has been noticeably silent on the issue of EJKs. She rationalized her pro-Duterte actions as prioritizing the welfare of her constituents in her Congressional district.[3]

Roman is expected to toe the party line with regard to the proposed shift to federalism, which is perceived as a move to eliminate the check and balance mechanisms in government and thus consolidate power in the hands of Duterte. She may be a champion of the anti-discrimination bill but the track record she's building is more along her class interests and family background of traditional politicians engaged in patronage politics with Duterte as the chief patron.

Intersectionality is also a major factor why the sector is factious and deeply divided. Filipinos have never been so deeply divided as we are now. The exchanges on social media have been extraordinarily vicious. Those critical of Duterte and his policies get comments and threats from Digong Duterte Supporters (DDS),[4] such as "*mamatay ka na sana*" (I hope you die), or "*sana ma-rape ka ng drug addict*" (I hope you get raped by a drug addict), or "*sana mamatay ang buong pamilya mo at ma-rape ang mga anak mong babae*" (I hope your entire family dies and that your daughters gets raped).

This extreme polarization under the Duterte presidency extends to Pinoy lesbians/tomboys, bakla/gays, and trans. Some LGBTs have accepted key positions under the Duterte government. There are a good number of gay/bakla, lesbian/tomboy, and transgenders who are Duterte supporters or fanatics. They are pinning their hopes on Duterte enacting the anti-discrimination bill and eventually legalizing same-sex marriage. A few gay and transgender bloggers have come out with blogs supportive of Duterte and virulent towards Duterte critics. Some of these gay and transgender

---

2   The Philippine Senate eventually approved and even increased the CHR's budget to ₱693 million.

3   Marc Jayson Cayabyab, "Transgender Solon Roman on Death Penalty Vote: Politics is Compromise," *Philippine Daily Inquirer*, 8 March 2017, last accessed 7 April 2019, http://newsinfo.inquirer.net/878802/transgender-solon-roman-on-death-penalty-vote-politics-is-compromise/amp.

4   The use of "DDS" is viewed as an attempt to reclaim the acronym originally pertaining to Davao Death Squad. The Davao Death Squad was allegedly responsible for EJKs in Davao City when Rodrigo Duterte was the mayor.

bloggers have been accused of being handsomely paid trolls of Duterte and the sources and propagators of fake news against Duterte critics. In October 2017, there were fights waged on the internet and social media among gay and trans woman personalities who are members of a group they call DDS bloggers.[5]

I had firsthand experience of intersectionality and subjectivities during my fieldwork in 2017 and 2018 in Mountain Province in northern Philippines. Many of my bakla and tomboy key informants in my research welcomed me warmly and trusted me with their stories. We bonded on the basis of our gender and sexual identities. It was only later that we discovered each other's ideologies and political affiliations. As it turned out, some of my bakla/gay, tomboy/lesbian, and transgender key informants are avid Marcos and/or Duterte supporters. My posts on social media reflect my activist background and my ideological leanings. Some of my key informants' posts reveal their pro-Duterte and pro-Marcos standpoint. I believe that a few have unfollowed or blocked me on Facebook upon discovering my ideological leanings. Fortunately, some of them continue to relate with me despite our ideological differences. I remember one incident when one of my key informants who is pro-Marcos and pro-Duterte told me "*sige na nga, para na lang sa mga bakla at tomboy*" (I will do it for the sake of gays and lesbians). I interpreted this as his way of telling me that we may disagree on our politics but we can unite and work together on gay and lesbian issues. Fortunately, we still keep in touch through social media and might eventually become good friends despite our ideological differences.

Our economic class background is a major influence on the types of political organizations and movements we join and the strategies we employ. Lesbians from middle-class backgrounds formed organizations that were mainly involved in rights-based or legitimation movements which undertook a mainstreaming LGBTQ+ agenda. Tomboys and bakla from urban poor communities developed and employed other strategies and programs more appropriate to their gender and sexual identities and the intersections with the other dimensions of their identity such as economic class, and suitable to their specific contexts.

It was 1992 when we started to more formally establish lesbian organizations. Some twenty plus years after, new organizations have sprouted in various areas in the country, but most of the organizations we founded and

---

5   Charmie Joy Pagulong, "Word War Erupts among DDS Bloggers," *Philippine Star*, 11 October 2017, last accessed May 2019, https://www.philstar.com/headlines/2017/10/11/1747978/word-war-erupts-among-dds-bloggers.

the others that existed in the 1990s have all perished. So many changes have happened over the past twenty plus years. There were no social media platforms then. Facebook, Twitter, and Instagram had not yet been invented. There were no e-books and LGBT websites then. This essay is a product of my reflections on my experiences with lesbian organizing and movement-building which we started in the 1990s. I wanted to come up with an initial analysis and hopefully draw some lessons and insights from those experiences.

Processes and influences on gender and sexual identities and activism of Pinoy tomboys, lesbians, and transgenders

Lesbians, gays, tomboys, and transgenders (LGTTs) and the Roman Catholic Church in the Philippines

One major factor affecting the subjectivities of Filipino tomboys, lesbians, and transgender persons is religion. The Roman Catholic Church in the Philippines is the single most powerful institution for socialization in the country. It is able to exert tremendous influence on legislation. For more than a decade it has been successful in blocking legislation on sexual and reproductive health and rights. They have demonized progressive legislation by branding these as "sin bills," including the reproductive health bill (introduced in 1999), the SOGIE anti-discrimination bill (first filed in 2000), and the divorce bill (first introduced in 2005).

Even after the enactment of the reproductive health (RH) law in the country, the Catholic Church, through the Catholic Bishops Conference of the Philippines (CBCP) and other lay organizations, have prevented the implementation of the RH law through a Supreme Court temporary restraining order. They employ various means to cajole, intimidate, and coerce their members and politicians to toe the official line of the Church, lest they be banished to purgatory, or worse, not win in the elections, as the Church machinery would campaign against these politicians.

Relatedly, the passage of the bill on anti-discrimination on the basis of SOGIE has been consistently unsuccessful in the Philippine Congress for almost fifteen years.[6] Fortunately, lesbians/tomboys, gays/bakla, and

6   On 23 September 2017, the House of Representatives of the Philippine Congress unanimously approved the anti-discrimination bill on third and final reading (vote 198-0-0; 198 approved, 0 abstention, 0 disapproved). The Philippine Senate has yet to approve its own version, which is currently pending on second reading. "House Approves Anti-discrimination Bill on 3rd and Final Reading," *CNN Philippines*, 23 September 2017, last accessed December 2018, http://cnnphilippines.com/news/2017/09/20/House-approves-anti-dsicrimination-bill-3rd-and-final-reading.html.

transgender persons' (LGT) groups have had tremendous success enacting anti-discrimination legislation at the local level, e.g., city, municipal, and barangay levels.

The Roman Catholic Church not only enjoys a huge membership but is also able to wield tremendous power through the thousands of educational institutions spread all over the country. Being extremely conservative and homophobic, it exacts a heavy toll on gay and lesbian students in Catholic educational institutions. In the course of lesbian organizing and advocacy work in the 1990s and 2000s, I have come across lesbians who could not reconcile their sexual identity and their religion. There were a number who, after engaging in sex, had to immediately pray the rosary or novena, or go to confession to assuage their guilt. A couple of them were suicidal as they felt extreme guilt over their lesbianism.

The findings of Manalastas (2016) suggest that "sexual orientation appears to be significantly associated with suicide risk, with young Filipino gay and bisexual Filipino men at disproportionately higher risk for suicide ideation than hetero-sexual peers." However, as Manalastas has pointed out, there are limitations in the data and the variables used in the Young Adult and Fertility Study 3 (YAFS 3) con-ducted in 2002, which he analyzed. The research may not have fully captured the normative and minority stressors that could have contributed to the high suicide ideation among gay and bisexual youth. The YAFS is a nationwide survey which started in 1983 and is conducted every ten years.

Gay tourism in the Philippines

Gay tourism in the Philippines became very popular starting in the 1990s. This phenomenon is well documented by Collins (2005) in the case of Malate. Malate was previously dubbed Manila's red-light district. It used to be Metro Manila's center for low-end bars catering to heterosexual prostitu-tion. The purging of heterosexual prostitution in Malate during the first term of Mayor Alfredo Lim paved the way for the "gay gentrification" of the dis-trict. With most of the girlie bars closed, gay expatriates bought and started operating gay bars in Malate. Malate then became the Philippine "gay haven" in the 1990s. Hitherto, the stereotype of the homosexual was limited to the bakla or the effeminate homosexual. This gay gentrification of Malate gave the Filipino heterosexuals and homosexuals a glimpse into the diversity of male homosexuals.

The initial phase of lesbian/tomboy organizing in Metro Manila coin-cided with this. The gay gentrification of Malate and gay tourism are impor-tant, as many middle-class gays (including lesbians) found a safe haven in Malate. They made Malate a gay space, and broke the stereotype of the pe-jorative view of the bakla as *parlorista* and "screaming faggot."

Several lesbian and tomboy convenors of the First National Lesbian Rights Conference 1996 held a press conference at the Blue Café in Remedios Circle, Malate where they also declared December 8 as national lesbian day ("Lesbians Come Out, Come Together in 1st Congress," Francine Medina, *TODAY*, p. 3, 11 December 1996, photography by Bernardino Testa).

Malate also became the site for gay pride marches held yearly by Filipino LGBTs. In fact, it was in one of the bars/cafés in Malate, Blue Café, where we held the press conference for the First National Lesbian Rights Conference (FNLRC) on 9 December 1996. It was also during that press conference that we declared December 8 as National Lesbian Day.

For the lesbians coming from the middle-class and the intelligentsia, the 1990s were exciting years as these were marked by the holding of international/regional lesbian and women's conferences attended by noted lesbian-feminist theoreticians and personalities. These were occasions for fruitful exchanges and networking among foreign and local lesbian-feminists. The Asian Indigenous Women's Conference held in Baguio in 1992 and the Asian Lesbian Network (ALN) Conference held in Quezon City in 1998 are examples of such lesbian and women's events. Among the lesbian-feminist personalities and theoreticians who came to the Philippines in the 1990s who we met were Sheila Jeffreys, Janice Raymond, Pat Hynes, and Jean Grossholtz.[7] I consider Jean Grossholtz to be among the lesbian-feminists who have had significant effects on my personal and professional life. It was Jean Grossholtz who convinced me and my lesbi-

7   Jean Grossholtz was in her sixties when we met her in the Philippines in the 1990s. She is now ninety-two years old and Professor Emeritus of Politics and Women's Studies at Mount Holyoke College in South Hadley in Massachusetts.

an friends in Baguio and in Metro Manila to organize ourselves and form lesbian organizations.

Diaspora: Filipino LGT migrant workers

The concept of diaspora and ethnoscape (Appadurai 1996) are very relevant to the discussion of Filipino tomboys, lesbians, and transgenders. The Philippines is a major sending country for migrant workers and consequently has a large population of diasporic communities, some of whom are believed to be LGBTs.

Filipino overseas migration became more prevalent in the 1920s with the movement of Filipino farmers who migrated to the plantations in Hawaii and California. This was followed by the movement of professionals and highly skilled Filipinos to the US such as doctors, nurses, engineers, etc. There was also a period of boom in overseas migrant work of Filipino men in Middle East countries. Feminization of migration started in the 1980s with a growing proportion of women leaving for overseas migrant work compared to men. In the 1980s, Filipino women left in droves for Japan to work as entertainers. Many Filipinas also left for overseas migrant work as nurses, caregivers, nannies, and domestic helpers in all the continents of the world. It is estimated that 66 percent of the migrant workers were women.

Overseas migrant work provided many Filipino women opportunities to help their families economically and to gain economic autonomy and a certain degree of power. Overseas migrant work enables some women to escape not only poverty but also violent relationships. For some, overseas migrant work also provided them the freedom to explore their sexuality. The exposure to various cultures could also have contributed to more openness to lesbianism/homosexuality.

There are a lot Pinoy tomboys working as domestic helpers, caregivers, nannies, and workers in the service sectors in Asian countries like Singapore and Hong Kong, and in some countries in the Middle East. Migrant work afforded them some degree of economic autonomy and helped them gain tolerance if not acceptance in the family and in the community.

Aside from the phenomenon of feminization of migration, overseas migrant work also provided opportunities for the Filipino bakla and trans woman. Overseas migrant work in Japan in the 1980s and even up to the 1990s opened up lucrative opportunities for the Filipino bakla and trans. The good earnings enabled Pinoy gays/transgenders in Japan to send siblings and cousins, nephews and nieces to school, build concrete homes for their parents, and send monthly allowances to the family.

The bakla and trans women's jobs as dancers, singers, and impersonators afforded them opportunities to cross-dress and engage in other forms of cross-gender behavior, including being in relationships with men who are open to transgender/transsexual partners. Some of these trans women came home for vacations in the Philippines bringing and introducing their Japanese boyfriends.

Migrant work in Japan for many Filipino bakla afforded them the opportunity to be "transformed into women." Some of those who identified as "women" or "trans" underwent female hormone therapy and sex reassignment surgery (SRS). The new term in the literature is *gender confirmation surgery*. One of my informants, who was a veteran *Japayuki beki* (Filipino gay/trans migrant entertainer in Japan), related that the hormone therapy business among Filipino trans entertainers was so lucrative that Filipino dermatologists could afford to periodically go to Japan to administer the hormone therapy (injectable female hormone) and other dermatological procedures to their many Filipino trans clients. The procedures were of course done clandestinely as these Filipino doctors did not have licenses to practice their medical profession in Japan.

Advent of hormone therapy, sex reassignment technology, new gender identities and expression, and the required changes in ideologies and laws
Intersexuality was the initial impetus for the development of sex reassignment technology. However, sex reassignment technology was not confined to intersexed individuals and received greater impetus from transgenders—i.e., people whose biological sex assigned at birth does not match their gender identity—who wanted to avail of the technology. Karkazis (2008) provides a good account of the historical development of the management of intersexuality in the United States. Hugh Hampton Young was one of the first to offer surgical treatments for hermaphroditism in the United States. In the sex determination of his patients, he supplemented his main criterion of gonadal tissue with evidence that included non-physical attributes such as personality traits and sexual desire. Perhaps unintentionally, Young implemented a flexible definition of sex. In 1951, Wilkins invited John Money to join the team at Hopkins. Wilkins, from the early 1950s until his retirement in 1960, oversaw the treatment for intersexuality at Johns Hopkins (Redick 2004; Karkazis 2008).

In the 1950s John Money and the Hampsons came up with protocols which incorporated both biological and psychological variables. This was a radical departure from earlier protocols on hermaphroditism and intersexuality, which was heavy on the "natural" sciences such as genetics and embryology. They introduced the "gender socialization hypothesis" and the concept of "gender role" into the principles and protocols for the medical management of intersexuality. The term gender identity, which specifically refers to the sense of oneself as being male or female, emerged several years later and is credited to the psychoanalyst Robert J. Stoller. Eventually, Money came to use the term gender-identity/role (G-I/R) to refer to what would be distinguished today as gender identity, gender behavior, or role and sexual orientation (Karkazis 2008).

In coming up with reliable treatment protocols in the management of intersexuality, Money, Ehrhardt, and the Hampsons have wittingly or unwittingly produced new discourses and new subject positions. According to Hausman, the introduction of the new terminologies (e.g., gender role and gender identity) in the literature on intersexuality and transsexualism was instrumental in the emergence of the transsexual subject (Hausman 1995).

Previously, only those diagnosed with physiological intersexuality were granted access to sex reassignment technologies. Transsexualism needed a rationale in the absence of a physiological diagnosis requiring surgical and hormonal therapy. Gender offered the rationale. Once gender identity disrupted the idea of sexual difference based entirely on physiology, transsexuals could now claim access to sex change technology. According to Hausman, this is how the constitution of transsexual subjectivity in the demand for sex change was initiated (Hausman 1995).

One of the most famous transgender persons who underwent sex reassignment surgery was Christine Jorgensen. Following the sex reassignment surgery of Christine Jorgensen in Copenhagen in 1952, there was an increased demand for the procedure (Stryker 2008).

Jorgensen came to the Philippines in 1962 as part of her Asian tour. While in the Philippines, she made a cameo appearance in the movie *Kaming mga*

Christine Jorgensen was an American trans woman who was the first person to become widely known in the United States for having sex reassignment surgery in her 20s. Wikimedia Commons.

Talyada (We Who Are Sexy). The movie is described as a comedy with the plot revolving around seven effeminate brothers forcibly enlisted by their father in the military to turn them into "real men." The film was produced by Sampaguita Pictures, one of the three big film companies in the Philippines at that time, and the cast members were popular movie stars. In the movie poster, Christine Jorgensen was described as "the most talked-about international personality today."[8]

On the one hand, Jorgensen's being allowed to come to the Philippines and even participate in a movie dealing with homosexuality or effeminacy could be interpreted as a good thing. On the other hand, the film's plot about conversion therapy negates the presumed openness to transsexualism. The warm welcome extended to Jorgensen and her movie cameo role raise a lot of questions. Could Jorgensen's visit and making a movie in the Philippines be interpreted as indicative of the country's openness to surgical and hormonal procedures for transgenders? Was it merely distraction and entertainment during the 1960s? Was it just a symptom of the Filipino proclivity to cast visiting celebrities such as international singers and beauty pageant winners in local films?

It took another thirty years before Filipino transgenders ventured into hormonal treatment and gender confirmation surgery. In the Philippines, it is believed that transgenders and not intersexed persons are the ones who undergo gender confirmation surgery. Sex hormone therapy became popular among Filipino trans women starting in the 1990s. Trans men increasingly employed hormone therapy only in the 2010s. There is virtually no data on Filipinos undergoing gender confirmation surgery.

It is reported that a common practice of "sex hormone therapy" among gays working in some beauty parlors in Baguio City in the 1990s is the taking of contraceptive pills. Some of the bakla parloristas (gays who work in beauty parlors) who are key informants in a current research in Mountain Province mentioned taking contraceptive pills in the 1990s. The duration of taking the pills ranges from a period of three months to two years. Some of them stopped taking the pills because they observed themselves to be easily irritable and suffered from low libido. A couple of my millennial gay and trans woman key informants from Benguet also report taking contraceptive pills as their means to ingest female hormones. They take these pills without

8   The poster for the film can be viewed at the Internet Movie Database at http://m. imdb.com/title/tt0370830/, and for a reading of the film, see Susan O'Neal Stryker, "*Kaming Mga Talyada* (We Who Are Sexy): The Transsexual Whiteness of Christine Jorgensen in the (Post) Colonial Philippines," in *Transgender Experience: Place, Ethnicity, and Visibility*, ed. Chantal Zabus and David Coad (New York: Taylor and Francis, 2013).

the benefit of any consultation with medical practitioners. They usually consume a month's dosage within a week in order to hasten the anticipated results such as development of breasts. There have been no evidence-based medical studies on the possible side effects of taking these contraceptive pills and hormone replacement drugs on the parloristas and trans women taking them.

There were reports that gender confirmation surgery was available in a well-known private hospital in the Philippines in the late 1990s. This fact, however, was not common knowledge as it was not publicized by the hospital for fear of backlash and reprisals from the Roman Catholic Church hierarchy. Eventually, the hospital reportedly discontinued the provision of such medical surgical procedures. The Philippines has the technology and infrastructure to potentially become the "gender confirmation surgery capital of Asia" but the stronghold of the Catholic Church is a strong deterrent. Consequently, Filipinos have to go to Thailand or the US for the procedure.

The 2000s brought about a more visible sector of trans women (male-to-female or MTF) and trans men (female-to-male or FTM) in the Philippines. This is evident in the increasing number of distinctive and discrete organizations of transgender persons engaged in transsexual activism. Among these are the Society of Transsexual Women of the Philippines (STRAP), Gender and Development Advocates Philippines or GANDA Pilipinas, Trans man Pilipinas, Transpinay of Antipolo Association (TAO), and other organizations of transgender persons in various provinces and regions. I believe that the groups of Pinoy trans women and trans men have the potential to become a very powerful sector in new LGBTIQ+ formations that will emerge in the political landscape.

With a more visible trans men and trans women sector in the Philippines, there is more anecdotal evidence suggesting an increased number of trans women and trans men undergoing sex hormone therapy, and a few cases of gender confirmation surgery. Among the prominent self-identified trans men who have openly admitted plans of undergoing transition are Aiza Seguerra and Charice Pempengco who now prefers to be called Jake Zyrus.

Aiza Seguerra was a child star in the 1990s and is now a popular singer. He identifies as a trans man and now prefers to be called Ice Seguerra. He campaigned for Duterte in the presidential elections and was appointed chairperson of the National Youth Commission. He resigned his position in April 2018. Incidentally, Seguerra's wife, stage actress Liza Diño, also campaigned for Duterte and was appointed chairperson of the Film Development Council of the Philippines.

Jake Zyrus is a Filipino singing sensation formerly known as Charice Pempengco. Charice guested on *Ellen* and *Oprah* and appeared briefly on the TV musical show *Glee*. He had a double mastectomy and is currently undergoing hormone therapy. He disclosed his intention to soon undergo gender confirmation surgery.

Among the more well-known mainstream trans women are Angela King and Geraldine Roman. King's family owns a chain of motels/hotels in the Philippines. Her transition and coming out as a trans woman is supported by her wife Joey Mead, a mass media celebrity, fashion model, and VJ in the Philippines. The couple are still together and have announced that they plan to stay together and remain married. As previously mentioned, Geraldine Roman is Congressional representative of Bataan and is one of the prime movers of the anti-discrimination bill.

The new gender and sexual identities, and the physiological changes on the body made possible by hormone therapy and gender confirmation surgery, require new ideologies and relevant legislation in areas such as family and intimate relations, marriage, social security services, health services, etc. Our social institutions need to undergo changes to be able to catch up with and respond to the changing needs and social contexts brought about by the profound changes in subjectivities, gender and sexual identities, and forms of intimate relationships.

The cases of a number of Filipina transsexuals illustrate how medical technology, such as gender confirmation surgery, come at odds with existing ideologies and social structures such as social institutions and laws. Filipina transsexuals even after having completed gender confirmation surgical procedures are still not allowed to change their sex in their basic papers such as birth certificates and other identification documents. Consequently, they are not allowed to register as female and marry their Filipino or foreign fiancé.

The Philippine Supreme Court (SC) decision denying a petition on "name and gender marker change" (Rommel Silverio versus Republic of the Philippines, G.R. No. 174689: 22 October 2007) made clear its views on gender confirmation surgery vis-à-vis change of gender of an individual. In the SC decision, the court cited that "no law allows the change of entry in the birth certificate as to sex on the ground of sex reassignment" and that "there is no special law in the Philippines governing sex reassignment and its effects."[9] This case had a chilling effect on other Filipino transsexuals who would have wanted to modify their sex and name in their basic papers.

The developments in the US and some European countries legalizing same-sex marriages and civil unions enabled some Filipino trans women to circumvent the bias of Philippine laws against them. Rommel a.k.a. Mely

---

9   To read the entire decision, see http://sc.judiciary.gov.ph/jurisprudence/2007/october2007/174689.htm (last accessed 7 April 2019).

was my professor in social statistics. She completed her gender confirmation surgery several years back. She petitioned Philippine courts to allow her to change her sex and name on her birth certificate, which in turn would enable her to marry her American fiancé. On several occasions, Mely shared with me her frustration regarding the progress or lack of progress of her court case. Her pending court case was overtaken by events in the United States under President Obama. She welcomed the repeal of the Defense of Marriage Act (DOMA) and the enactment of marriage equality, as she was finally allowed to marry her American fiancé.

Marriage law reform in the US and in some parts of Europe was a welcome development for Filipino transsexuals and transgenders as they were able to marry their foreign and Filipino partners in countries where same-sex marriage is allowed. From the standpoint of the LGT movement, it was a lost opportunity to challenge Philippine statutes in these contested areas of marriage and gender/sexual identities. Moreover, these marriages of trans Filipinos in countries where same-sex marriages are allowed are still not considered legal under Philippine laws.

Another case tested the Supreme Court's views on gender and sexual identities and gender confirmation surgery. The court allowed "Jennifer Cagandahan to become Jeff" on account of the rare condition of congenital adrenal hyperplasia, which was considered a "natural" condition (G.R. No. 166676: 12 September 2008). Cagandahan was born with intersex characteristics with female characteristics as initially dominant. Jennifer's male characteristics became dominant upon reaching puberty. According to the court, "respondent here has simply let nature take its course and has not taken unnatural steps to arrest or interfere with what he was born with. And accordingly, he has already ordered his life to that of a male."[10]

To explain the perceived difference in the decision, then SC spokesperson Theodore Te explained that both decisions were consistent, with one case acted favorably on the basis of the "natural course of a medical condition" while the other one was denied because it involved a case of a transsexual who had "surgically altered his reproductive organs to become a woman."

This in effect shows the SC's distinction and different stance on intersex vis-a-vis transsexuals and transgenders. Philippine laws can make accommodations and favorable decisions in cases involving medical/physiological conditions as in the case of intersex persons. It will not, however, accommodate

10   To read the entire decision see http://sc.judiciary.gov.ph/jurisprudence/2008/september2008/166676.htm (last accessed 7 April 2019).

cases of gender realignment of transgenders not based on "natural medical" conditions. This culture lag between sex intervention technology and gender and sexual ideologies is still more complex and controversial, and very difficult to address. Meanwhile, this has adverse consequences on social security and other benefits and privileges being denied to lesbian, gay, and other non-heteronormative intimate relationships.

Information and Communication Technology (ICT) and negotiating gender and sexual identities

Conventional mass media and computer mediated information and communication profoundly affect the processes of forming and negotiating gender and sexual identities. From conventional media such as novels, television, film, and cable television, middle class Filipino LGBTs were exposed to alternative images of lesbians and gays through TV series such as *Will and Grace*, *The Ellen Degeneres Show*, *The L Word*, and via downloaded and pirated DVD copies of lesbian/gay-themed films. The current generation of young adults or what is referred to as the millennial generation are exposed to new and radically different forms of cyber communication technology.

When we started our lesbian organizing in the early 1990s we were closely identified with the women's and feminist movements. Our sources of information were mainly the limited collection of lesbian-feminist books in the libraries of a couple of women's non-government organizations (NGOs). We were hungry for information and materials which could help us make sense of our gender and sexual identities. We discovered that Ateneo de Manila University Katipunan campus then had the most impressive and comprehensive collection of lesbian books and materials. We used to borrow and photocopy the lesbian books from the Ateneo library to make them accessible to the growing number of lesbian-feminists who were starting to come out of the closet.

In the early 1990s, having internet access and being able to send emails was considered "state-of-the art." However, the cost of personal computers and subscription to internet service providers was prohibitive, such that only private businesses and NGOs could afford them. I remember that we even had the rotary dial land phones back then. I had a personal pager. Many NGO offices had pagers. The pager (operated by either Pocketbell or Easy-Call) was one of our most effective means of communication with the lesbians and tomboys we were starting to network with. This was the time when you had to use a landline phone to contact the operator and state your name, the pager number of the person you wish to contact, and your message. Mobile phones were not that common then and the cost of owning a mobile phone was also prohibitive. Back in the early 1990s, access to the internet was relatively limited and there was minimal networking among groups. There were also few search engines and LGBT websites. Social networking sites were not yet fully developed then. All these changed in the 2000s with the growth in infrastructure in telecommunications technology.

The Philippines is among the poorer countries in the Global South but Filipinos are among the most electronic gadget-obsessed and communication technology-savvy people. Studies suggest that approximately 30 percent of the population has internet access. In 2010, there were about 78 million mobile phone users out of a Philippine population of 92.2 million. Moreover, it is common for people who do not own mobile phones to have a SIM card. They borrow the mobile phones of neighbors, relatives, classmates, etc. whenever they need to communicate using a mobile phone. Even in areas without electricity, people resort to regular visits to the trading centers in the *poblacion* or barrio capital in order to recharge their mobile phones. The current figures are presumed to be higher given the advances in communication technology infrastructure coupled with the various promotional packages offered by the rival telecommunication companies.

Despite being a poor country, the Philippines has been heavily influenced by the new information and communication technology. Mobile phones and the internet figure prominently and profoundly in shaping identities and social relationships. This was very evident among Filipino migrant workers and their families in what McKay (2006) calls everyday technologies of translocality, e.g., text messaging, e-mail, phone calls, and cash remittances, and their effects in recreating the local into a new form of transnational place. In a more recent ethnography on Filipinos on Facebook, McKay (2010) explored how social networking technologies like Facebook are transforming everyday lives and relationships especially among Filipino migrants and their families.

The Philippines is also considered the world's leader in text messaging or the "texting capital of the world," with Filipinos sending an average of 200 million mobile phone text messages a month. In 2006, there were about 350–400 million SMS messages sent daily by Filipinos, which is more than the combined SMS messages of all the European countries, the United States, and China.

In 2010, texting (Short Messaging System or SMS) was the preferred channel of communication between teens and their friends. Pew Research Center (2010) findings suggest that a typical teen sends fifty text messages per day, or equivalent to 1,500 text messages per month. The daily SMS volume lessened only after the tremendous popularity of Friendster and eventually of Facebook.

The development of computer-mediated information and communication technology gave rise to the generation of millennials. The typical description of millennials is that they are very tech-savvy, "the always connected generation," or what Prensky (2013) calls the "digital natives." They have grown up with technology, to the point that it pervades their everyday lives, they cannot imagine life without it. Digital content and cyber communication enables their social lives. They cannot remember a world without Google or YouTube. There are about 200 million millennials and they make up more than one-fourth of the population. More than 75 percent of them stated that they cannot live without a computer or mobile phone and 43 percent listed either laptop or mobile phone as the top gadget they cannot live without (Visa 2012).

The prevalence of portable wireless communication devices has dramatically affected communication and interaction patterns (Pew Research Center 2010). Staying connected is important for Filipino millennials. Social networking sites such as Facebook are highly popular in the Philippines. Filipinos hold more than 25 million accounts and the Philippines is ranked the seventh largest country on Facebook (Visa 2012).

In 2010, weekly usage of Facebook and Yahoo is higher than for any other social networking site which is both at 93 percent. The weekly average number of hours spent on these sites are 13.07 hours (on Facebook) and 13.87 hours (on Yahoo). Chatting with friends, commenting on other people's sites/posts and sending a message to friends are the most prominent activities Filipino millennials on social networking websites. One in two Filipino millennials or 50 percent stated they cannot live without their PC/laptops while 37 percent of Filipino millennials say a smartphone is the gadget they cannot live without.[11]

The YAFS 4 findings suggest that in 2013, 6 in 10 of young people aged 15 to 24 are regular internet users. More than 50 percent have social network and email accounts and 78 percent have mobile phones. The average time spent online is 6 hours per week. Some even spend as much as 35 hours online per week. Females, the younger youth, and those from economically better off regions show higher social media consumption vis-à-vis males, older youth, and those from poorer geographic regions. This pattern of internet and information technology use impact on the

---

11   Simon Kemp, "Digital Trends 2019: Every Single Stat you Need to Know about the Internet," *The Next Web*, 31 January 2019, last accessed 7 April 2019, https://thenextweb.com/contributors/2019/01/30/digital-trends-2019-every-single-stat-you-need-to-know-about-the-internet/.

formation of relationships and social networks. One in three Filipino young adults stated they have friends whom they only met online, while 25 percent have friends whom they met through text and have not seen personally.[12]

Data from Google Philippines (Adobo Magazine 2017) reveal that 75 percent of Filipino millennials view the internet as their main source of information. About 66 percent use the internet to look for products and 79 percent use it for entertainment.

Among the key findings of several researches on LGTs and the internet is that LGBTs rely on the internet for the important tasks of identity formation, peer connection, and identification of partners. The data also suggest that the internet provides queer youth with tools to create and refine their queer identities from dating and sexual bonding to politics and activism.

For the Filipino LGBTs, new media and computer mediated communication (CMC) meant more access to LGBT literature, fast and convenient networking with LGBTQs worldwide and engaging in transnational LGBTQ activism and movement-building, and of course meeting prospective friends, partners, and spouses.

Aside from identity formation, the phenomenal and unprecedented growth and widespread access to digital information and communication technology in the form of LGBTQ+ websites and social networking sites profoundly affected LGBT activism and movements and the ideologies related to sexual and gender identity.

Filipino lesbian activism through the years
The following is a rudimentary typology and periodization of lesbian activism and movement-building in the Philippines. This periodization is meant to delineate the forms of lesbian organizations and the ideologies that guided their activism and movement-building. Whenever applicable, notable events surrounding lesbian organizing and activism, especially in Metro Manila and other major cities, are described to provide further contextualization. The organizations mentioned in this paper are the ones I encountered and had some interaction with in the course of my lesbian organizing and advocacy work. This is by no means a complete or comprehensive listing or description of the different types of organizations. In 2015, the website of the

---

12   Demographic Research and Development Foundation, Inc., "Internet, Social Media are Important Part of Young Filipinos' Life—Survey Shows," 6 February 2014, last accessed 12 May 2019, http://www.drdf.org.ph/yafs4/pressrelease/02-06-2014/05.

International Lesbian Gay Transgender and Intersex Association or ILGA listed 96 Philippine LGBT organizations.

The succeeding section provides an overview of the characteristics of the types of lesbian and tomboy formations during specific periods of lesbian organizing and activism:

(1) The early period of formation of lesbian/tomboy organizations in the late 1970s and early 1980s which witnessed the formation of friendship cliques and socio-civic organizations. This first phase (1980s) can be characterized as a period of preparing the ground, planting the seeds, and laying the foundations for a more concerted kind of lesbian organizing and activism.

(2) The second period covering the late 1980s and early 1990s were of two types of formations. There were "secret" or "selectively out" groups in the 1980s and early 1990s and there were also the open and formal organizations which came about in the early 1990s. Both these "secret" and open formal organizations originated from a couple of women's organizations and NGOs. The mid-1990s was the period when lesbian organizations were more linked with women's organizations and the feminist movement/s.

(3) Organizing work among the marginalized sectors such as working-class tomboys and transgenders in the late 1990s. This period can be characterized by grassroots lesbian and tomboy organizing by newly-formed groups allied with the broader national democratic movement.

(4) Emergence of mixed LGBT groups in the mid-1990s and later separate transgender/transsexual organizations in 2010s. The 2000s and 2010s witnessed the emergence of lesbian, gay, trans, and mixed groups in various colleges and universities, and in the towns and municipalities in the different regions in the Philippines. From mixed lesbian and male gay groups, trans women started organizing their separate organizations.

(5) Current grassroots tomboys, lesbians, and trans men organizing in 2010s in indigent communities in Quezon City which employs community organizing along gender/sexual identities and as urban marginals.

What is unique to this latest phase is that it employed the approach of community organizing. It did not employ the conventional approach of sectoral organizing. The organizers went to the residential communities of the tomboys, lesbians, and transgenders and proceeded to employ the strategy of community organizing. Being part of what I consider urban and sexual marginals, the strategies included "social non-movement" and "quiet encroachment of the ordinary" as well as legitimation and mainstreaming strategies.

During this period, there was a growing acknowledgement and more concerted efforts to address intersectionality in the organizing efforts. Instead of focusing exclusively on gender and sexual identities, other dimensions were taken into serious consideration such as socioeconomic class, education, occupation, living conditions, etc. This multidimensionality of oppression is conceptualized as intersectionality. Under intersectionality, people experience oppression in differing forms, degrees, and intensity depending on the various dimensions of their identities such as race, ethnicity, class, gender, sexual identity, and other positionalities. The simultaneous and interconnected influences of dimensions of identity have significant impacts on the everyday lives and on the forms of resistance to discrimination, stigma, oppression, homophobia, and so on (hooks 1982; Crenshaw 1989; Collins 1993).

I find Bayat's (2010) conceptualization of "quiet encroachment of the ordinary" and "social non-movements" relevant to the struggles and strategies of lesbians and tomboys residing in the indigent communities in Quezon City such as Pansol, Balara. Bayat describes the quiet encroachment as a "silent, protracted, and pervasive advancement of ordinary people on the propertied and powerful in a quest for survival and improvement of their lives." For Bayat, this kind of quiet activism involves cumulative encroachment resulting in immediate consequence of redistribution of social goods through the "acquisition of collective consumption (land, shelter, piped water, electricity), public space (street pavements, intersections, street parking places), and opportunities (favorable business conditions, locations, and labels)." Bayat considers this kind of quiet activism as "largely atomized, and prolonged mobilization with episodic collective action—open and fleeting struggles without clear leadership, ideology, or structured organization." It is different from "survival strategies" or "everyday resistance" because the struggles and gains of the grass roots are at the cost not of fellow poor people or themselves (as in survival strategies), but of the state, the rich, and the general public.

As urban marginals employing the strategies of quiet encroachment, the tomboys of Balara encroach on public and privately-owned land, illegally tap electricity and water from the utility companies, encroach on sidewalks as extensions of their houses which they use for mundane activities such as eating or bathing, or use as their place of business, such as retail stores, tire vulcanizing shops, parking spaces of customers in their small business enterprises such as carwash, automotive works, etc. The tomboys can also be considered sexual marginals by virtue of their non-heteronormative and stigmatized gender/sexual identities.

The friendship cliques and socio-civic organizations of lesbians in the late 1970s and early 1980s
Lesbian formations during this period were predominantly friendship cliques engaged in sports and leisure activities such as playing basketball and drinking. The Circle of 'Pre (of Bgy. Pansol in Balara, Quezon City), the Bambang True Friends Association (in Nueva Vizcaya), and the Lucky Guys of La Union (Province of La Union in northern Philippines) fall under this category and period.

Other organizations characteristic of this period took on a sociocivic character engaged in socials, livelihood activities, and other sociocivic programs. These "mainstream" tomboy and transgender groups conducted income-generating projects for their members and engaged in community beautification and re-greening projects and fund raising campaigns for schools and their local communities.

Some of these groups which were active in the 1980s and 1990s include the following: (a) The Group[13] in Davao founded by Andi Consunji; (b) Link Davao Organization Inc.[14] also in Davao; (c) Bambang True Friends Organization[15] in Nueva Vizcaya; (d) The Lucky Guys of La Union;[16] and (e) Lesbind[17] which was an organization of Muslim lesbians in Zamboanga (Josef 1997). Some of these sociocivic groups continued until the 2000s.

13   The Group was mainly a sociocivic group of tomboys and lesbians from the middle class and professionals. It was formed in 1992 and membership was by invitation. In the mid-1990s, the Group had 20 members.

14   Link Davao Organization Inc. was formed in 1992 with members coming from grassroots tomboys and/or lesbians. Many of the members were market vendors. In the mid-1990s, Link counted 150 members but only 15 members actively participated in the organizational activities. Link Davao has a Facebook account at https://www.facebook.com/Link-Davao-Organization-Inc-116366475077397/.

15   Bambang True Friends Association was based in Nueva Vizcaya and in 1997 had 45 members. This was a social group whose members organized parties and basketball games. The members were basically the stereotypical tomboy or butch. During meetings and basketball games, the partners and/or "girlfriends" of the members played "supporting roles," e.g., cooking, serving snacks, and being cheerleaders.

16   Lucky Guys of La Union was based in La Union (northern Philippines) and the tomboy members are predominantly of middle class background.

17   Lesbind was short-lived. It was organization of tomboys who were also part of a labor union being organized in Zamboanga in the 1990s.

From these abovementioned organizations, only Link Davao Organization Inc. has current internet presence mainly through Facebook.

The informal and "secret" lesbian groups and organizations in the late 1980s and the founding of formal and open lesbian organizations in the early 1990s
The second phase (1990s) can be described as a period of birthing pains. The 1990s were interesting times for the women's movement and lesbian activists. While there were splits in the people's and women's movements, these were also times of explorations and growth. The members of these groups came from various women's political organizations and NGOs. Some of the young feminists from the Kalayaan Feminist Collective and the clandestine group of "women with alternative sexuality" from the now defunct Women's Research and Resource Center Inc. (WRRC) are examples of these "not too out" lesbian formations. During this time, the labels for women who love or desire women, at least for those in Metro Manila were limited to *lesbian* or *tomboy* and its variants such as *tibo, t-bird, thunderbird*, etc. I expect that the only familiar term or label outside Metro Manila was *tomboy*. We were not familiar with *queer* or *gender-questioning*. The term "women with alternative sexuality" was conceived by some women from WRRC who at that time were on a journey of exploring their sexuality including having their first relationship with another woman, but could not identify with the label tomboy or lesbian. The original phrase I believe was in Filipino, "babaeng may alternatibong sekswalidad." They used "alternative" sexuality to pertain to the non-heteronormative character of their sexual identities and relationship (personal comm., women who were part of women with alternative sexuality of WRRC, 1993).

Formations during this phase were identified as lesbian-feminist organizations whose members came from various women's organizations. The lesbian-feminist organizations focused on consciousness-raising among their members and the general women's movement, and visibility in mass media.

This period can be characterized as when lesbian organizations were more linked with women's organizations and the feminist movement/s. The Lesbian Collective (TLC),[18] Progressive Lesbians of the Philippines or Prolesb,[19]

18   The Lesbian Collective (TLC) was formed in 1992 in Quezon City. It is considered among the pioneer lesbian organizations in the Philippines. Most of the members were academics or from various women's NGOs and political organizations (POs). Some members of TLC eventually formed other lesbian groups. The author was a founding member of TLC.

19   Prolesb was formed in the 1990s and employed an unusual way of inviting and recruiting members. The main organizer used to go around Metro Manila looking

Womyn Supporting Womyn Committee (WSWC),[20] UP Sappho, Can't Live in the Closet (CLIC), and LesBoND (Lesbians for National Democracy)[21] in Baguio City were among these formal organizations formed in the 1990s. Currently, only LesBoND has internet presence, mainly through Facebook.

From left to right, JJ Josef, Malu Marin, and Ana Marie Dizon, who were then part of the The Lesbian Collective, who for the first time marched as a separate lesbian contingent during the International Women's Day rally on 8 March 1992. This photo was taken in front of the PLDT building near Welcome Rotunda, which is a popular assembly place for rallyists. Photo courtesy of Women's Research and Resource Center (WRRC), Inc.

The Lesbian Collective was the group behind the first time that a lesbian contingent joined the women's groups for the International Women's Day march in 1993. There were only seven of us, in various degrees of being out, scared but exhilarated during this collective coming-out process. We

for hangout places of tomboys/lesbians. She would strike a conversation and hand out calling cards and invitations to butch-looking or tomboy-looking individuals she met. Prolesb's gender-sensitivity training workshops often had over a hundred attendees, usually tomboy/butch street vendors of cigarettes and street food, janitors, students, etc. Prolesb organizing was discontinued when the main organizer had to leave for migrant work.

20   Womyn Supporting Womyn Committee (WSWC) was formed by members of the staff of Women's Education, Development and Productivity Organization (WEDPRO), a women's NGO.

21   LesBoND Baguio replaced the more informal formation Baguio Lesbian Group. LesBoND was formed 1992. The majority of its members come from a middle-class background and self-identify as lesbian-feminists. The members are mostly NGO workers, activists, college students, writers, and from the academe. The author was among the pioneer members of LesBoND. LesBoND is upfront about espousing and being part of the national democratic movement. LesBoND also has a "chapter," LesBoND-EPZA, whose members come from the ranks of workers at the Baguio Export Processing Zone (BEPZ).

were almost not allowed to read our prepared statement. The rally organizers informed us that they could not accommodate the reading of our prepared statement as the program was full. We were asked to read our statement while the march was moving along España Blvd. towards Malacañang. Of course, we did not concede. Our position was either allow us to read the statement on Mendiola Bridge or to not read the statement at all. Some women leaders interceded and we were eventually allowed to read our statement during the program in Mendiola. For us, it was historic as it was the first time that a separate lesbian contingent openly joined a women's march and read a statement near historic Mendiola Bridge in Malacañang.

The butch, tomboys, and the feminist-lesbians/lesbian-feminists in the 1990s
When we started our lesbian organizing in the early 1990s we were closely identified with the women's and feminist movements. I was one of the founding members of three lesbian organizations, namely, Baguio Lesbian Group, the Lesbian Collective (TLC) and Womyn Supporting Womyn Committee (WSWC). The Baguio Lesbian Group started in 1992 but it was later renamed and transformed into LesBoND . The Metro Manila-based Lesbian Collective was formed in 1993. The Womyn Supporting Womyn Committee was also based in Metro Manila and was formed in 1994. WSWC operated the first lesbian hotline counseling service in the Philippines and was the main organizer of the First National Lesbian Rights Conference in 1996 which was attended by more than 200 lesbians coming from various geographic regions and socioeconomic classes.

In this initial and whirlwind phase of organizing and interacting with various women's groups, we tried to soak up all the information we could get to help us understand our lesbianism. We encountered the labels "primary lesbians" vis-a-vis "elective lesbians." The butch and the tomboys who are stereotypically masculine-looking were considered by the feminine-looking lesbians as "primary lesbians," while those who identify as "lesbians" or "lesbian-feminists" or "feminist-lesbians" who are stereotypically feminine-looking referred to themselves as "elective lesbians."

We also learned that there are differences between the "butch" and the "femme," between a tomboy and a lesbian and between a "lesbian-feminist" and a "feminist-lesbian." We were "taught" that the "lesbian-feminist" was first and foremost a feminist but who is also a lesbian, or a woman who loves or desires another woman. On the other hand, a "feminist-lesbian" is a person whose core identity was her being a lesbian, and that she is also a feminist. The difference is in what one considers her core identity, her being a feminist or her being a lesbian. I believe some of us got more confused during these discussions. In several meet-ups and discussions, we were asked to classify ourselves as either tomboy or lesbian. If we identify as lesbians, we were further asked to explain and identify either as a "lesbian-feminist" or a "feminist-lesbian." While we recognize the importance of labels and the process of self-identification, there were also sentiments that were being classified into the "politically correct" and "not politically correct" lesbians. For some of the tomboys or masculine-looking lesbians who were present during this birthing phase of organizing, the initial feeling of exhilaration at meeting other tomboys and lesbians was replaced by feelings of discomfort and confusion and for some feelings of being humiliated by our "lesbian-feminist" sisters.

We were hungry for information. The internet at this time was not well-developed and to a large extent its use was limited to emailing. There were limited websites and virtually no online sources and literature. We frequented the offices and libraries of a few women's NGOs that we knew housed a modest collection of LGBT books.

From these books, we learned that a primary lesbian can be described as a woman who is sexually attracted to another woman. Her lesbianism is believed to be *mainly based on emotional-erotic attractions towards another woman, and not a political choice* (Golden 1987). The primary lesbian is typified as masculine in appearance, demeanor, and mannerisms, i.e., "butch," or what is commonly known in Philippine society as "tomboy."

I have come across several organizations whose members are mainly limited to those who were tomboys, butch, or masculine-looking. Their feminine-looking intimate partners or "girlfriends" are not considered members of the organization. At best, they could be considered auxiliary members. Since they are not full-fledged members, they do not participate in the meetings and decision-making processes of the organizations. Often, their role is limited to cooking and serving food during meetings or serving as cheerleaders during sports events. I saw this in the 1990s and I am aware that this situation continues up to the present. I recognize that these unequal heteronormative gender relations are difficult to dismantle. It would take a long and protracted program of consciousness-raising and providing alternatives to make a dent on this ossified manifestation of patriarchal heteronormative ideology and practice.

The elective lesbian, on the other hand, is somebody who "elects" or decides to become a lesbian. Her lesbianism is deemed to be a *political decision and not merely a consequence of her emotional-erotic attractions* (Golden 1987). During this early phase of lesbian activism and organizing, particularly in Metro Manila, some lesbian-feminists felt that their lesbianism was more "valid" as it was a political choice while the butch or the tomboys were considered by some lesbian-feminists or feminist-lesbians as "un-politicized."

The masculine-looking lesbians and the tomboys within the women's movement felt discriminated against and were painfully aware that the lesbian-feminists looked down on them. Their lesbianism was reduced to their masculine look and demeanor, and the privileging of the perceived "more political" choice of gender and sexual identity of the feminist lesbian vis-a-vis the "less political" basis of the tomboy/butch identity which is same-sex emotional and erotic attraction.

Some feminine-looking lesbian-feminists even articulated that they could not entertain the possibility of being in a relationship with a butch. This is coming from a critique of butch-femme relationship as nothing more than a mimicry of patriarchal heterosexual relationships where unequal gender relations are perpetuated. Vaid (1995) and Kennedy and Davis (1993) view the butch-femme as central "pre-political forms of resistance" during the era when lesbians—in particular, the lesbian community in Buffalo, New York—were just starting to develop solidarity and feminist consciousness. The lesbians had not yet formed political groups at this time. They argue that at this historical juncture, the butch-femme exemplar was an important structure against heteronormativity. Vaid argues that the butch-femme therefore cannot be dismissed simply as an imitation of heterosexual and sexist society. While it may have developed in part from heterosexual models, the butch-femme roles also transformed those models and created an authentic lesbian lifestyle.

The masculine-looking lesbians who were starting lesbian organizing in Metro Manila and who identified as lesbian-feminists were not spared this unfounded criticism of "merely mimicking heterosexual relationships." These masculine-looking lesbian-feminists countered by arguing that they should not be judged by their physical attributes. They explained that gender ideologies and praxis should be assessed in terms of their consciousness and in their everyday interactions in their social and intimate relationships. They added that their "masculine" looks and demeanor should not be judged as indicators of role-playing and unequal heteronormative gender relations.

Of course, we know that deciding to come out as a tomboy, lesbian, or transgender, and deciding to act on emotional-erotic attractions towards the same sex, are always political decisions. I would like to believe that there is now more respect for diversity within the various LGBT organizations. The last thing the lesbian movement needs is discrimination from within.

It was during this period when lesbian-feminist organizations were organized in Metro Manila and in a couple of major cities in other regions. An important context to these political and feminist organizations was the bitter conflicts between the various factions of the broad peoples' movements and between women's groups aligned with the contending factions. We couldn't help but be affected by these conflicts.

After the First National Lesbian Rights Conference in 1996, there were other events held exlusively for lesbians and tomboys and other mixed groups of lesbians, gays, transgenders, trans women, and trans men. There was the Philippines National LGBT conference held in Cavite, Philippines in June 2011. In December 2017, there was the 4th LGBT National Conference held in Cebu City. This was organized by Bisdak Pride, Inc. in cooperation with *Outrage Magazine*. The said conference lists the following organizations as among their partner organizations: Mujer LGBT Organization (Zamboanga City); the Red Ribbon Project, Inc.; SAGE; Iloilo Pride Team; Pinoy Deaf Rainbow; TransDeaf Philippines; Deaf Dykes United; United Lesbians of Davao; ABAKA; ULGA; BUSA; GAIETY; Pink Society; GARBOSA; EventsPortal (Cotabato City); Dumaguete Lesbian; GLOBE-EVSU; KATLO-San Julian; Eastern Visayas Pride; Baybay LGBT; AGILA-ORMOC; League of Pogay in Metro Roxas; Queen of All Queens; and Balay Malingkawasnon.

Organizing work among the marginalized sectors: Grassroots and working-class tomboys and trans men in the late 1990s

In recent years, there have been more concerted efforts towards grassroots lesbian and trans organizing among the marginalized sectors in Metro Manila and in some key cities. Initial efforts at grassroots lesbian organizing include Progressive Lesbians of the Philippines or Prolesb and Lesbians for National Democracy—EPZA ([Baguio] Export Processing Zone) chapter or LesBoND-EPZA. Both groups are believed to have links with the national democratic movement.

Prolesb's members are grassroots (i.e., blue-collar workers or engaged in the informal sector of the economy) tomboys who are mostly into street vending or employed in the food service and janitorial industries. One interesting characteristic of Prolesb is its organizing strategy. The main organizer used to walk around areas with a good concentration of tomboys and transgenders, and give them her calling card and invite them to meetings, assemblies, and gender sensitivity training (GST). The strategy involves the organizer approaching "butch-looking" cigarette vendors, street sweepers, market vendors, or janitors in malls, and inviting them to Prolesb activities. This proved to be initially successful as a few hundred lesbians/tomboys who were first-time attendees would come to their assemblies and training.

Prolesb aimed to "saturate" the tomboys and transgenders with GSTs, with the aim of convincing them to change their gender identification of male to lesbian or woman. Prolesb had links with the Quezon City Gender Office, which was instrumental in the passage of the city ordinance against discrimination on the basis of sexual orientation and gender identity. Prolesb became moribund when the main organizer went abroad for migrant work.

LesBoND-EPZA's members are lesbians, tomboys, and transgenders working for the various firms inside the Baguio Export Processing Zone. Since trade unions are not allowed in export processing zones, lesbian organizing among the workers became an important strategy substituting for union organizing.

Another lesbian group based in Baguio City is the Thunderbirds Association in the Cordilleras and its Suburbs, Inc. (TACSI). The members are predominantly those who identify as tomboy, butch, or transgender who come from several ethnolinguistic groups in the Cordillera. The Thunderbirds became known when their members first played the gongs in the 1980s at a major event in Benguet. This may be interpreted as landmark and transgressive as the dance performed during the *cañao* (generic term for ceremonial feast among the indigenous peoples in the Gran Cordillera Central) is traditionally reserved for males. For the TACSI members, the playing of the gongs was an act of defiance towards Igorot customs and traditions on gender relations. Since then, TACSI members have played gongs on several occasions and worn their trademark "Benguet cowboy" garb of plaid shirts, denim jeans, and leather boots during the annual Baguio Pride marches.

In the early stages of the interactions between lesbian-feminists and the stereotypical tomboys (i.e., masculine-looking and to a certain extent espousing patriarchal views), there was a desire on the part of the lesbian-feminists to "convert" the tomboys. I have misgivings about this "conversion" agenda. I am realistic enough to realize that several GSTs, focus group discussions (FGDs), and consciousness-raising activities, no matter how well-intentioned, would not be enough to make the tomboys change their gender identities and ideologies.

Except for Prolesb and LesBoND-EPZA, it is evident that majority of the lesbian organizations are predominantly middle-class. They all espouse a rights-based or legitimation movement mainly employing mainstreaming strategies. LesBoND-EPZA can be considered an exception as it also openly identifies as aligned with the national democratic liberation movement.

Emergence of mixed LGBT groups in the mid-1990s and later by separate transgender/sexual organizations in 2010s
The HIV-AIDS work in the country during this period gave an impetus to alliances between the various basic sectors and LGBT alliances. I remember attending meetings with individual gay/bakla personalities

and representatives of gay/bakla organizations and HIV-AIDS NGOs. I remember being one of the resource speakers in a forum with Michael Lim Tan held at the Episcopal Church's compound in Quezon City in the 1990s. In the said forum, Tan told the audience and his co-resource speakers, "We gays and lesbians, we have to work together sooner or later. We do not have a choice on this."

Legislative advocacy became part of the thrust of LGBT organizations with the election into office of party-list representatives and other progressive politicians in the Philippine Congress. Ladlad is perhaps the most prominent LGBT advocacy group, being the only LGBT political party joining national elections for party list groups. Unfortunately, Ladlad has not had any success in landing a seat in the Philippine Congress. I believe that this is one glaring example when intersectionality works against us. I believe that one of the major factors affecting Ladlad's failure to land a congressional seat is how the voting for party-list mechanism was designed. The party-list mechanism requires the voter to choose just one party-list. With so many groups competing for votes, one is hard-pressed to choose. For example, which one should I choose from the many party-list groups, immersed as I am in my multifaceted identities and espousing many advocacies: LGBT, women, teachers, indigenous peoples, environmentalists, etc.? Intersectionality engenders multiple allegiances, which in turn is not compatible with the current party-list voting mechanism. Despite this innate flaw of the party-list voting mechanism, other party-list groups have garnered seats; for some, more than one seat in congress. Perhaps Ladlad needs a more thorough and in-depth analysis of their experiences in the elections they have participated in. What lessons can be drawn from these experiences that they could put to use in future elections?

Many of the earlier LGBT groups did not last long enough to become institutionalized, and were unable to access grants from international funding agencies doing work on gender and sexuality issues. Nevertheless, I believe that they paved the way and made it easier for succeeding generations of LGBT NGOs and POs. Equally important is that many of the leaders and members of these earlier LGBT groups continued to work and become leaders in other NGOs.

Utilizing intersectionality in current grassroots tomboy, lesbian and trans men organizing in 2010s which employed the strategies and approaches of community organizing, "social non-movement," "quiet encroachment of the ordinary," as well legitimation and mainstreaming strategies
To help come up with an understanding of lesbian, gay, and transgender movements, I considered the following social constructs: (1)

intersectionality (hooks 1981; Crenshaw 1989; Collins 1990); gay and lesbian rights-based or legitimation movements and mainstreaming strategies (Vaid 1995; Escoffier 1998); and discourse on "social non-movements" and "quiet encroachment of the ordinary" (Bayat 2010).

As I have previously mentioned in another section of this essay, what is unique to this phase of organizing is that it did not employ a conventional sectoral organizing approach. Organizers went to the residential communities where there were great concentrations of tomboys, lesbians and transgenders and employed community organizing strategies. The first community organizers were trained by anthropologist and community organizing expert Jane Austria.

The peopling of Barangay Pansol, Balara, is attributed mainly to migration and connected to the development of the water supply system in the metropolis. *Barangay* is a local term for a village, district, or ward, and is the smallest administrative unit in the Philippines. *Pansol* is a Tagalog or Filipino word which means "water spring" of cold or hot water. Barangay Pansol used to be the site of the housing facilities for employees working in the water filtration plants of the Manila Waterworks and Sewerage System (MWSS). Employees were supposed to vacate the place upon their retirement or termination of their employment. The employees and their families, having established roots in the area, stayed on. Aside from the families of MWSS employees, many migrants also established communities in the area. Because of its strategic location and access to employment opportunities and various social services, the area continues to be a magnet to thousands of migrants from as far away as Visayas and Mindanao. Today, the majority of the residents of Barangay Pansol are indigent and/or informal settlers.

Barangay Pansol is home to many lesbians, tomboys, transgenders, and trans men, who have very different experiences, compared to those belonging to the professional (e.g., doctors and lawyers) and middle classes. They usually have low educational attainment and limited technical skills which could enable them to get gainful employment. Thus, most of them are unemployed or engaged in casual, seasonal employment with below subsistence wages, or engaged in various activities in the informal sector. The middle-class lesbians, on the other hand, have more economic and cultural capital than the urban poor tomboys. Economic survival is less severe for them compared to the tomboys from the lower socioeconomic classes.

Intersectionality, which involves a multidimensional conceptualization of oppression, could not be more evident in the lives of the tomboys and transgenders from Barangay Pansol. In my interactions with them, it is evident that their struggle for economic survival is further exacerbated by their being tomboy or bakla. Their multidimensional identities and the intersection of these identities result in a complex multilayered oppression. Discrimination on the basis of their gender and sexual identities is inextricably linked to their being informal settlers and urban poor. This is the reason why they can be considered "urban and sexual marginals." They belong to the lower socioeconomic classes and at the same time are members of a minoritized group on the basis of their gender and gender identities. The already limited employment opportunities become more inaccessible to them because of the discrimination on account of their butch/mannish appearance and demeanor.

Aside from being urban marginals, I believe that lesbians, tomboys, and transgenders can also be considered sexual marginals. Their cross-gender behavior can be considered gender transgressive and part of the "quiet encroachment of the ordinary" and "social non-movement" approaches. Being "butch" and expressing transgenderism by wearing men's clothes, adopting male demeanor, engaging in cross-gender behavior, among others, help in visibility and showcasing gender/sexual diversity. By fostering their tomboy/transgender identity and living their everyday lives as tomboys, lesbians, or trans, they contribute to making lesbianism, homosexuality, and transgenderism more visible and perhaps eventually accepted and respected as valid choices. These strategies I believe all contribute to an incremental encroachment onto the power base of patriarchal structures.

The stories of Brando and Dush (not their real names) illustrate the struggles of tomboys, lesbians, and trans men as urban and sexual marginals.

Brando's grandfather was an employee of MWSS in the 1930s and 1940s. His family was eligible to live in one of the company's employee housing facilities, which were then mostly located in Barangay Balara Filters. The families of former employees who were evicted from the water agency's housing facilities then encroached on vacant lots in nearby barangays or *purok* (part or smaller sub-division of a barangay) such as Kaingin 1 and Kaingin 2, and eventually expanded to Santa Maria Della Strada, which is adjacent to the posh La Vista Village.

Brando used to do part-time work as a street-sweeper in the barangay. When I spoke with him, he had been out of work for almost a year. He hoped that the barangay councilor who hired him before would win in the upcoming elections so that he could resume his duties as a street-sweeper.

Ako po si Brando, 43 years old, lehitimong taga-Pansol. Mula 9 years old, tibo na. Ganito na. Puro panlalakeng laro. Dito na rin ako nag-aral sa Balara mula elementary hanggang high school. Matagal na kami dito. Matagal na si Tatay (Brandos's grandfather) dito since 1930s. Kaya dito na kami ipinanganak at lumaki. Umalis kami sa Balara Filters noong 1940s noong umalis na si Tatay sa MWSS. Tuwing eleksyon, pinapangako ni Imelda (Marcos) na "sa inyo na yang mga lupang tinitirikan ninyo." Pero 1988 noong binigay sa amin itong lupa, sa mga pioneers o mga unang tao dito sa Pansol. Panahon na iyon ni Cory. May nag-census at surbey (land survey). Kanya-kanyang pa-surbey. Itong sa kabila namin (adjacent property), ang laki nito. Halos isang block iyang pina-surbey niya (neighbor) at binakuran na niya. Tapos binenta rin niya di naglaon. Ang laking pera yan. Kami din naman, sa amin ito. Malaki rin ang napatituluhan namin pero anim na pamilya kaming naghahati-hati dito na nakatira. Magkakapatid, magpipinsan, kasama ang mga tiyahin namin.

I am Brando, forty-three years old, born and raised in Pansol. Tomboy since nine years old. Like this, a tomboy. Always played boys' games. I studied here in Balara from grade school to high school. My grandfather has been here since the 1930s. This is where we were born and where we grew up. We left Balara Filters in the 1940s when Tatay (Brando's grandfather) left the MWSS. Every election, Imelda Marcos would promise us that we would own the lots where our houses were built. But it was only in 1988 when the lots were given to the pioneer residents of Pansol. It was during (President) Cory's time. There was a census and land survey. Everybody undertook land surveys. This adjacent lot is big. Almost a whole block was surveyed and claimed by our neighbor and he built a fence around it. After some time, he sold the lot. Must have been a big amount money. We also got this big piece of lot titled but six families are living and sharing the area. Siblings, cousins, including our aunts.

Dati akong nagtrabaho sa pabrika ng garments sa Taytay mula 1987 to 1993. Nasa packing ako. Okey naman sana kaya lang nagsara. Hindi ako umuuwi sa Balara araw-araw. Kapag alanganing oras na, nakikitulog ako sa mga naging chicks ko na nakatira sa may Valley Golf.

I used to work in a garments factory in Taytay from 1987 to 1993. I worked in the packing department. The work was okay but the factory closed down. I did not go home to Balara daily. If it was late, I would sleep over at the houses of my former girlfriends near Valley Golf (community near the factory).

Maraming tibo doon sa pabrika, Capitol Garment. Ang dami namin doon. Mga libo kami sa pabrika. May pa-liga nga sa basketball doon sa pabrika na puro tibo lang ang players. Iba yung liga para sa mga lalake. Maski boss namin sa packing, tibo rin. Sa bawat department mga 6 hanggang 10 siguro ang mga tibo. Kaso nagsara yung pabrika.

Pagkatapos noon, puro canteen ang napasukan ko. Nagluluto-luto sa canteen. Una sa Angelicum (school), tapos sa canteen sa pabrika sa may Libis. Mag tig-3 years ako sa bawat canteen. Tapos dito na ako sa barangay, street sweeper. Pero pahinga ngayon. Tatakbo naman ulit si Kap (barangay captain) na konsehal naman ngayon. Kaya baka mabalik ako na street sweeper sa barangay. So, ito ngayon, nagluluto-luto rin.

Si Kuya ko nandiyan kasama yung asawa niya. Ako, nakikikain lang kina Kuya at sa mga tiyahin ko. Mga "ex-abroad" (former overseas migrant workers) po kasi ang kuya ko at ang asawa niya. Nag-aaral ngayon yung asawa ni Kuya sa TESDA, housekeeping. Para baka makapag-abroad ulit. Ayaw ko na po lumabas dito, kasi mag-aaply ka sa labas, kailangan din ng panggastos. Baka dito-dito na lang ako. Hintayin ko yung sa barangay.

(Brando, personal communication, January 2013)

There were a lot of tomboys in the factory, Capitol Garment. There were a lot of us. We were about a thousand (tomboys) in the factory. There were even basketball tournaments sponsored by the company with all-lesbian teams. There was a different basketball tournament for the men. Even our boss, the head of the packing section, was also a tomboy. In every department, there must have been six to ten tomboys. Unfortunately, the factory closed down.

After, I was employed mostly in canteens. I was a cook. First, in Angelicum (a private school), then a canteen in a factory in Libis. I stayed for three years in every canteen. Then I became a street sweeper in the barangay. But now, rest period (not currently employed). The barangay captain who hired me is running again in the next elections, this time as a councillor. If he wins, I might be hired back as a street sweeper.

My older brother lives there (pointing to their house) with his wife. I get my meals from my brother and my aunts. My brother's wife is now taking up a housekeeping course at TESDA (Technical Education and Skills Development Authority, government agency providing vocational courses). We hope she can again find work abroad. As for me, I don't want to go out of the community. When you apply outside the community, you will need money. I might just stay here and wait for the barangay, to be re-hired as a street sweeper.

Dush (not his real name) is twenty-four years old, and has resided in Barangay Pansol since 2000. Dush's family was previously from a nearby barangay, which is in front of Miriam College. They were victims of frequent fires in their previous village or barangay. The stories that circulate say that the fires were caused by arson as the owner of the property wanted the informal settlers to leave.

Takot na kami doon. Lagi kasing may sunog. Nalipat kami dito sa Balara kasi yung kuya ko may napulot na wallet ng Amerikanong istudyante sa Ateneo. Kilala namin iyong Amerikanong student kasi lagi iyon dumadaan sa malapit sa tambayan namin sa may Ateneo. Maraming lamang pera yung wallet kasi kaka-withdraw lang niya. Ang kuya ko nakokonsyensya, so isinauli niya yung wallet. Natuwa naman yung Amerikano. Sa condo siya nakatira sa Katipunan. Nong matapos siya ng pag-aaral, lahat ng gamit niya sa condo, iniwan na sa amin. Saka binigyan din kami ng pera para makabili ng lupa dito sa Balara. Nakakuha kami ng bahay at lupa sa Kaingin.

We were afraid there (previous residence). There were frequent fires. We were able to transfer here to Balara because my older brother found the wallet of an American student of Ateneo. We recognized the American because we'd often see him pass by near our hangout place near the Ateneo. There was a lot of money in the wallet as the student had just gotten money from the bank. My older brother returned the money. The American student was pleased. He lived in a condominium in Katipunan. When he graduated he gave us all his things from the condo. He also gave us money that we used to buy a piece of land in Kaingin.

Gusto pa nga nung Amerikano na isama ang kuya ko sa Amerika at pag-aaralin doon. Kaso hindi pumayag ang nanay ko dahil nag-iisa daw na anak niyang lalake tapos aalis pa. Ang nakatira ngayon doon sa bahay na nabili namin, ang kuya ko at ang nanay ko.

The American wanted to bring my brother to the US to study. But my mother did not allow it. My mother said, she would not lose her only son. My mother and brother are the ones living in the house we bought.

Ako nakatira kasama ko iyong girlfriend ko at yung pamilya niya sa Kaingin 2. May sarili kaming kwartong pinagawa. May nagsanla kasi ng lupa doon sa parents ng girlfriend ko na ₱20,000. Nagbigay kami ng ₱10,000. Bale yung kalahati ng pera, kami ng girlfriend ko ang nagbigay, yung kalahati, iyong parents

I am living with my girlfriend and her family here in Kaingin 2. We have our separate room which we had built. Somebody pawned the land (rights to occupy the land as there are no land titles) to the parents of my girlfriend for ₱20,000. Her parents shelled out ₱10,000 while we raised the other

niya. Tapos hindi na natubos. May pinirmahan naman silang dokumento kaya siguro ayos naman iyong transaksyon na yon. Hindi ko lang nakita iyong dokumento dahil ayaw kong makialam. Yung ibang nakatira doon sa area, walang papeles iyong tinitirhan nila. Walang titulo iyong mga iyon, kasi inaangkin iyan ng Marikina. Ang sabi ng Marikina sa kanila daw iyong sa Riverside.

Mula Grade 1, seven years old, tomboy na po ako. Lalake, nagkamali lang sa parte ng katawan na binigay sa akin. Mahilig ako magsayaw at mag-teatro. Doon ako nagsimula. Iyon talaga ang hilig ko, teatro. Ang tagal bago ako nakatapos ng high school dahil sa barkada at sa babae.

Caddie (golf) ako ngayon sa Capitol Golf Club. Marami na rin akong naging trabaho. Una, nasa sales ako, nagbabenta ng mga machine na pang-massage, foot massage, sa Metro World. Tapos naman nun, napunta naman ako sa insurance. Hindi naman ako makabenta kasi hindi pa naman kilala yung kompanya nila. Nagbabahay-bahay lang kami. Mahirap makabenta kasi hindi naman maglalabas ng pera ang tao kung hindi kilala yung kompanya.

Tapos napunta naman ako Demo Power, ang tawag "push girl" kasi ipu-push mo yung produkto. Naka-make-up at saka plunging neckline yung blazer. Asiwa.

₱10,000. The previous "owner" was not able to redeem the lot. They (owner and parents of the girlfriend) signed some documents. But I did not see the document because I did not want to intervene. I guess the papers were in order. The other residents in the area do not have documents or titles to the land they occupy. There are no land titles. The City Government of Marikina is claiming the area called Riverside.

From Grade 1, or seven years old, I was already a tomboy. Male, but there was a mistake in the body parts given to me. I like dancing and theatre. That's where I started. I really love theatre. It took me a long time to finish high school because of my friends and also girls.

I now work as a golf caddie in Capitol Golf Club. I have tried many jobs. Before I was in sales, selling machines for foot massage in Metro World. Then I went into insurance. I was not able to sell (insurance policies) as the company was not yet well known/established. We went house to house. It was difficult to sell because people will not buy if the company is not well-known.

Then I went to Demo Power, we were called "push girls" because we were "pushing" products. We wore make-up and blazers with low necklines. It was awkward.

Ang mga hawak ko noon, mga produkto ng Unilever. Hindi ko rin kinaya kasi eight hours kang nakatayo. Mga 2009 ako doon. Six months lang ang pinakamatagal.

Tapos saleslady na, sa herbal toothpaste na gawa sa Thailand. Depende kung saan ka idedestino, pwede sa Novaliches, sa Cubao, sa SM malls. Pero sa SM ang pwede lang doon yung magaganda. Doon din nagtatrabaho yung girlfriend ko. Nakikita ako ng boss niya kaya inalok ako ng trabaho. Nagpupunta ako sa ibat-ibang grocery. Para kang magnanakaw kasi tinitingnan mo yung mga shelves kung may mga produkto pa. Kaso wala namang sariling merchandiser yung produkto na iyon, nakikiusap lang sa merchandiser ng ibang brand na maglabas at display din ng produkto nila. Umalis din ako doon kasi ang baba ng sahod. Chinese kasi ang may-ari noon. Wala na ngang merchandiser, mababa pa sweldo, eight hours pa trabaho. Yung motorbike ko pinapa-gasolinahan lang nila ng ₱50 tapos mag-iikot ka sa Metro Manila. Wala na ngang pang-kain, talo ka pa sa gasolina. Yung sahod na ₱250 napupunta lang sa gasolina.

Tapos nalaman namin na naghi-hiring sa Capitol (Golf Club). Nag-apply ako kahit wala akong idea kung ano ang ginagawa ng caddie. Ang sabi kailangang matatag ka sa init ng araw. Nagtyaga lang ako. Kasi hindi ako

I was handling products of Unilever. I did not last in that job because you had to stand for eight hours. That was in 2009. I only lasted for six months.

Then I became a (supermarket) saleslady of a herbal toothpaste from Thailand. You will be assigned in different places like Novaliches, Cubao, or SM malls. But in SM, only the good-looking (i.e., pretty and feminine-looking) get assigned. My girlfriend used to work for the toothpaste company. Her boss saw me and offered me a job. My job entailed going to different grocery stores inspecting if there was stock on the grocery shelves. But the toothpaste brand did not have its own merchandiser, we had to resort to asking favors from merchandisers of other products to replenish the stock on the shelves. I left because the wage was too low. The owner was Chinese. Aside from having no merchandiser in the supermarket, the pay was low for eight hours of work. I used my motorbike to get around. They gave me ₱50 for gasoline money to go around Metro Manila. They did not give you food allowance and the gasoline allowance was not even enough. My salary which was ₱250 went to gasoline expenses.

When we learned that Capitol Golf Club was hiring. I applied even though I did not have any idea of what a caddie does. They said you have to be strong and withstand the heat of the sun. I persevered even though I did not undergo

makapag-training masyado. Dati nga ang kita ko nga ₱100 lang. Naghihintay ako maghapon na may kumuha sa akin na caddie para ma-training. Kaso ang mga player (golfer) gusto yung magagandang caddie. Sino ang kukuha sa akin, ganito ang hitsura ko, mukhang lalake, Amazona.

Pero may kumuha din sa akin, kapag wala na kasing golf cart, ako ang "buhat bag." Hindi nila mapagbuhat iyong magagandang babae, kaya ako ang kinukuha. Hanggang na-train na ako. Mag ilang buwan lang yung tambay at ₱100 lang ang kita. Minsan dalawang beses lang ako sa loob ng isang linggo may kita.

Inaral ko na talaga ang pagka-caddie dahil nainis na ako sa pagiging trainee. Natuto na ako. Kapag marunong ka na, alagaan mo ang player mo. Ang kikitain ko sa apat na oras ₱500. Ang standard caddie's fee ₱300 tapos ang tip ₱200. Tapos pinapameryenda pa ako sa tee house. Mahirap din mag-caddie kasi nakasalalay sa iyo yung laro. Kailangan tama ang basa mo sa damo, sa hangin, para tama ang gagamitin nilang pamalo. Kapag mali ang basa mo, mali din ang gagamiting pamalo. Maaapektuhan ang laro.

Sa loob ng isang linggo kumikita ako ng ₱1,500. Kasya naman sa pangangailangan. Mga tatlong beses sa isang linggo ang pagka-caddie. Yung girlfriend ko, caddie din siya, mas

much training. Initially, I would only earn ₱100. I used to wait the whole day until somebody would get me as a caddie. I treated it as a training or learning opportunity. But the golfers preferred the pretty caddies. Who would get me as their caddie with the way I look, an "Amazona" (woman warrior, i.e., masculine woman)?

Eventually, golfers hired me, especially when there were no golf carts left. I carried the heavy golf bags. They could not make the pretty caddies carry the heavy golf bags so they got me instead. Months passed until I had trained myself to be a good caddie. For months, I hung around and only earned ₱100. There were times when I only had earnings for two days for the entire week.

I really trained myself at caddying. I learned. After you have trained and learned, you need to take care of your golfer. You can earn ₱500 for four hours of work. The standard caddie's fee is ₱300, then a ₱200 tip. They even treat me to snacks at the tee house. It is difficult to be a caddie as the game of the golfer depends on the skills of the caddie. You must correctly read the greens, the wind, and the right kind of golf club to use. If you read these wrong, then they will use the wrong club. The game will be affected.

In a week, I now earn ₱1,500. It is enough for our needs. I caddie three times a week. My girlfriend also works as a caddie but she earns more (than me). She has more players so she earns

malaki ang kita nya. Mas marami siyang player kaya mas malaki ang kita niya. May kinalaman ang pagiging feminine niya sa laki ng kita nya. Mas maganda ka, mas kukunin ka ng maraming player.

more. Her being feminine has something to do with her earnings. The prettier you look, the more golfers will hire you.

Minsan nga nakakaabot ng ₱1,300 ang kita, apat na oras lang iyon. Basta marunong kang sumakay sa bastusan, na makipaglandian sa mga player, malaki sila mag-tip. Mas malaki pa ang tip kaysa sa caddie's fee.

There are cases when you can earn as much as ₱1,300 for four hours of work. You have to learn to get used to the lewd jokes and the flirtation. They give generous tips, sometimes the tip is bigger than the caddie's fee.

Plano ko po talaga mag-abroad. May ina-applyan na ako sa may bandang Dubai. Golf course din po, caddie din. Kaso, mababa nga lang ang sweldo, ₱14,000 pero nasa kontrata ₱40,000. Pero kailangan daw magpahaba daw muna ako ng buhok ko. Tapos sa tip ka daw kikita kaso centralized naman ang tip.

My plan is to go abroad. I have applied for a caddie position at a golf course in Dubai. The pay is low, monthly salary is equivalent to ₱14,000 but in the contract the salary is ₱40,000. They said I need to grow my hair long. They also said you earn more from tips but the tips are centralized.

Gusto kong pursigihin ang application na iyon pero nag-aaway pa kami ng girlfriend ko.

I want to pursue my application but my girlfriend and I fight about it.

(Dush, personal communication, January 2013)

The experiences of economic struggle of Brando and Dush are echoed in the life stories of thousands of Pinoy tomboys, lesbians, and transgenders in many poor neighborhoods in the Philippines. Brando, Dush, and a lot of other urban marginals engage in various forms of "quiet encroachment of the ordinary" and social non-movements.

Bayat (2010) describes the quiet encroachment as the "social non-movement of the urban dispossessed." For Bayat, it involves the "discreet and prolonged ways in which the poor struggle to survive and to better their lives by quietly impinging on the propertied and powerful and on society." This involves the "unlawful" appropriation of land for shelter, and then of urban amenities like electricity, water, cable television, etc. They have appropriated the sidewalks for their domestic, business, and leisure activities. These urban marginals, according to Bayat, have transformed the street economy and profoundly altered urban landscapes.

Bayat views these as "social non-movements" because they are limited to "individualistic and quiet encroachment on the public goods and on the power and property of the elite." For Bayat, they do not directly challenge the structure and effect of globalization which have reduced them to being urban marginals. Moreover, Bayat argues that these quiet encroachment strategies are social non-movements because they do not aim to bring about broader political transformation.

These urban marginals, according to Bayat, carry out their activities not as deliberate political acts but rather as driven by the force of necessity to survive and improve life. The notion of "necessity" is invoked to justify the often "unlawful" acts as moral and even "natural" ways to maintain a life with dignity. Illegally tapping water and electricity are therefore rationalized as necessary.

Like in many crowded cities where you can find "urban marginals," the streets, sidewalks, and other open spaces in Barangay Pansol have been appropriated by many community members for residential, domestic, livelihood, and leisure activities. The streets and sidewalks are venues for bathing, washing clothes, parking motor vehicles, and keeping pet dogs and chickens. For livelihood, they have appropriated the streets for vending and for workshops (e.g., vulcanizing, electric appliances repair, motorcycle and bicycle repair), carwashes, pay parking lots, etc. For leisure, the sidewalks can also serve as hangout places and venues for drinking sprees among the residents. Given Filipinos' inexplicable passion for basketball, the streets also serve as spaces for the ubiquitous basketball court.

The lesbians/tomboys and transgenders in Barangay Pansol have long been engaged in "quiet encroachment of the ordinary" both for survival and to "maintain a life of dignity." Barangay Pansol is partly a community of informal settlers who are always in danger of demolition and eviction. Many families in Pansol built their homes on public and private lands, encroaching on public spaces such as roads and sidewalks for their livelihood and recreation and illegally accessing water and electricity. It has become a strategy of the "encroachers" or "urban marginals," such as those in Barangay Pansol, to compel the authorities to extend urban services to their neighborhoods.

These strategies of quiet encroachment of the ordinary employed by some of the Pansol LGBTs are evident in the anecdote of Tess regarding the strategy of illegal tapping of water and electricity. Tess is a tomboy from Pansol. At the time of my conversations with her, she earned a living by accompanying her aunt to Clover Leaf market, known for being a wholesale market. They would wait for trucks from the provinces delivering vegetables and fruits. She worked as a stevedore, hauling the sacks of vegetables and fruits from the trucks to the wholesalers who then later sold to the retailers.

Tess's family is among the pioneer families in the community. Her father was an employee of MWSS. She recalls that illegal tapping of electricity and water was employed by the early residents of Pansol as a strategy to get concessions from utility companies.

Si Tatay ko noon, tinuturuan talaga ng mga leaders ng mga urban poor association kung paano mag-tap sa kuryente at tubig na iligal. Ayaw kasi kaming kabitan ng linya ng tubig at kuryente ng MWSS at Meralco. Kapag nag-illegal tapping ka sa linya ng mayayaman diyan sa La Vista, yung mga homeowners sa La Vista ang magrereklamo sa Meralco at MWSS. Tapos, napu-pwersa ang Meralco at MWSS na kabitan kami ng kuryente at tubig para hindi na kami mag-illegal tapping.

(Tess, personal communication, 20 February 2012)

My father then deliberately taught the leaders of urban poor associations how to illegally tap electricity and water. The utility companies like MWSS and Meralco refuse to provide us with legal connections. When you illegally tap from the electricity and water connections of the wealthy from La Vista (gated village of the rich in Quezon City), the rich homeowners of La Vista will file complaints with Meralco and MWSS. This forces Meralco and MWSS to provide legal water and electrical connections in order for people to stop their illegal tapping activities.

Aside from "social non-movements" and "quiet encroachment of the ordinary" several lesbian and tomboy organizations employ other strategies such as mainstreaming, rights-based legitimation, and liberation movements.

Vaid (1995) deployed the constructs of rights-based legitimation movement vis-à-vis liberation movements in her analysis of the lesbian and gay movements in the US. She describes rights-based movements as aiming for legitimation which employs mainstreaming as its main strategy. Legitimation movements strive for changes in the consciousness of heterosexuals regarding lesbians and gays in order to achieve tolerance and acceptance. In comparison, a liberation movement "seeks nothing less than affirmation, represented in the acknowledgement that queer sexuality is morally equivalent to straight sexuality." The agenda is to implement substantive transformation in social institutions such as government, family, religion, and the economy.

Vaid characterized gay and lesbian movements in the US since the 1950s as a primarily legitimation movement which worked on social acceptance of homosexuals through the mainstreaming strategies of legislative and legal reform, public education and community organizing. For Escoffier (1998) mainstreaming can include the following approaches: institutionalizing the lifestyles in gay and lesbian communities; incorporating gay and lesbian rights into mainstream politics, including having representation in government policy bodies; creating a niche market; increasing representation in commercial mass media; and developing lesbian and gay studies in universities. Escoffier observes that these have all been accomplished in America to various degrees.

Vaid acknowledges that mainstreaming into American political and cultural life had improved the lives of many lesbians, gays, and transgenders as legal and political reforms have allowed them to work, raise families, and contribute to their communities. However, she views the gains of lesbian and gay legitimation movements and mainstreaming strategies as not real freedom but rather as "virtual equality." Escoffier acknowledges that LGBT mainstreaming and its gains have elicited various reactions, from positive to negative. For some, it is considered a form of cooptation. But Escoffier also admits that these mainstreaming strategies have greatly improved the lives of thousands of American lesbians and gays.

For Vaid, the liberties achieved by the legitimation movements are "incomplete, conditional and ultimately revocable just like the advances made by other civil rights movements." Vaid's analyses on rights and liberties achieved over the past seventy years ring true today as the Trump presidency and anti-LGBT forces have been repealing and revoking legislation that advanced LGBTQI+ rights.

Using Vaid's (1995) and Escoffier's (1998) description of rights-based LGBT movement and their enumeration of mainstreaming strategies, we can define a rights-based LGBT movement as a movement that aims for the social acceptance of lesbians, gays, bisexuals and transgenders in society through mainstreaming strategies. Mainstreaming strategies include the following: community organizing; consciousness-raising; institution-building and networking, including holding of conferences and forming both broad and issue-based tactical alliances; public education; visibility campaigns through annual LGBT pride marches and other activities celebrating diversity; increasing representation in commercial mass media; developing LGBT literature and institutionalizing LGBT studies in universities; creating a niche market; legislative and legal reform through enactment of non-discriminatory laws and/or running in elections for national and local positions; and incorporating and institutionalizing gay and lesbian rights into mainstream politics, including having representation in government policy bodies.

In the 2010s, new organizations of tomboys/lesbians, bisexuals, and trans men were founded. One of the more prominent lesbian NGOs which undertook tomboy/lesbian, bisexual, and trans men (LBT) organizing in the 2010s is GALANG (Philippines). GALANG is an NGO doing grassroots organizing in a couple of informal settlers' communities in Quezon City. *Galang* is a Tagalog word which means respect. The founders chose this name to signify their ideal of respect regardless of class, gender, sexual identity, etc. Consistent with their mantra of *galang* (respect) regardless of social identity and status, GALANG can be described as a lesbian NGO adopting an intersectional lens in their organizing and advocacy work. The organization takes into account the economic class, gender, and sexual identities of their target sector which are the urban poor lesbians/tomboys, bisexuals, and trans men.

GALANG can be considered an NGO engaged in a rights-based movement, aiming to address the gender and sexual discrimination and poverty being experienced by LGBTs. The organization employs mainstreaming strategies as evident in their organizing, institutional development, capacity-building and policy advocacy work. GALANG's rights-based and intersectionality politics is evident in their choice of target urban poor communities, and their goals of enacting anti-discrimination ordinances at the community level, and to train LBTs who can be capable of engagement in community development councils.

GALANG employed community organizing strategies in the areas where there were reported to be great concentration of lesbians, transgenders, and trans men. The two pilot areas where GALANG started its grassroots tomboy/lesbian organizing are the barangays of Bagbag and Pansol in Quezon City. Quezon City is one of the most populous cities in the Philippines. Bagbag and Pansol are among the barangays with many informal settlers. These barangays were chosen on the basis of the observation that there is great concentration of LBTs in the community and the existence of anti-discrimination ordinance at the local level.

Barangay Pansol enacted their anti-SOGIE discrimination ordinance on 8 November 2008. This came about through the efforts of gay barangay council members, of which there were four out of the total seven barangay officials.

Barangay Bagbag promulgated their anti-SOGIE discrimination in June 2009. In Bagbag, there are no gay/lesbian members of the barangay council but the gender and development (GAD) focal point of the barangay council is gender-sensitive and pushed for the enactment of an ordinance pertaining to discrimination on the basis of SOGIE. In Bagbag, the barangay anti-discrimination ordinance specifies some forms of the offense such as bullying and insulting LGBTs. The ordinance also specifies the penalty of fine for a first offense which is ₱300. For recidivists, the ordinance says that the penalties will be decided by the barangay council. There are reportedly many incidents of LGBT bullying but there has been no complaint filed with the barangay since its enactment in 2009. The community organizer believes that either the LGBTs in the barangay are not aware of the ordinance or the offended parties just do not bother to file complaints.

GALANG intends to introduce similar anti-discrimination ordinances in all the barangays where they will conduct their organizing work. These two barangays have been consistent awardees for gender-sensitivity and have a long-standing record of partnerships with several women's NGOs. According to Anne Lim, GALANG co-founder and current executive director, they aim to develop the lesbian leaders who would be capable of engagement in barangay development councils, and eventually become members of city development councils.

Before the founding of Lesbian Alliance Movement (LAM) in 2011, there was the Circle of 'Pre (contraction of *pare* or *compadre*) which existed from 2003 to 2011. The Circle of 'Pre is an informal group of tomboys who used to hang out and drink together and sponsor annual basketball games between tomboys and gays or *bekis* (slang for gay/bakla) during the fiesta of Barangay Pansol held every February 12. The Circle of 'Pre was initiated by Brando, who was also instrumental in gathering the lesbians and/or tomboys for a meeting with GALANG in 2009. Brando narrates:

> Bago magkaroon ng LAM, tropa lang kami, painom-inom. Tambay-tambay lang kami, kwentuhan tungkol sa chicks. Kung saan pwedeng tumambay, sa kanto, sa tindahan, sa tabitabi. Tapos binuo ko yung Circle of 'Pre. Informal lang ito, nagkakaroon ng exhibition game tuwing fiesta. Ang kalaban mga bekis (2010s slang for effeminate and/or cross-dressing gays). Laging talo ang mga tomboy. Matatangkad kasi yung mga bekis. Mga spiker yun sa volleyball. So parang iniispike din nila yung bola ng basketball.
>
> (Before there was LAM, we were just a group of friends, always drinking. Hanging out, talking about girls. Wherever we could hang out, in street corners, in the sari-sari stores, sidewalks. Then I formed the Circle of 'Pre. An informal group engaging in exhibition games during fiesta. Our opponents were the gays. The tomboys were always the losers. The gays were tall, and they had spikers in volleyball. So they would spike the basketball just like in volleyball.)

In a conversation with the author on 20 February 2012, Bacbac, a young member of LAM, recalls, "*ang tawag noon sa exhibition game, 'Pa-ek-laban'*" (We called the exhibition game Pa-ek-laban). *Pa-ek* can be interpreted as gimmick, and *laban* means fight or match.

Brando continues, "nagtagal din yung mga exhibition games na yun sa basketball, mga sampung taon din yata, hanggang 2010 yung last game" (The basketball exhibition games lasted long, maybe for almost ten years, the last game was in 2010).

Bacbac related that starting in 2011, the basketball game was now between the tomboys from Pansol and a team from another barangay in Quezon City. The game between the *bekis* and the tomboys was no longer possible because some of the *bekis* in the barangay had left for overseas migrant work. Their opponents in 2011 were a team from nearby Philippine

School of Business Administration (PSBA). The most recent basketball exhibition game at the time of our conversation was held in early March 2012 between the tomboys of Pansol and a team from Libis.

I believe that the Circle of 'Pre, despite its organizational limitations, was important as it was among the few available formations that fostered camaraderie and bonding among the tomboys and transgenders in Barangay Pansol. However, GALANG's organizing efforts in Pansol paved the way for more formal and concerted efforts at rights-based movement building. GALANG was instrumental in the founding of the Lesbian Alliance Movement (LAM) and Lakas ng Kababaihan Para sa Karapatan in Pansol in 2011.

In July 2008, some twenty tomboys from Barangay Pansol attended a meeting/workshop with two community organizers from GALANG. The meeting was facilitated by then Barangay Captain Dominic. Since the founding of LAM in 2011 and until 2012, GALANG estimates that they have touched base with some ninety-two LBTs in Pansol.

The character of intersectionality politics is evident in the attempt of LGBT organizations like LAM and the NGO GALANG to address socio-economic issues—such as housing, public amenities and services, livelihood—as well as other larger issues of social justice, and issues confronting LGBTs such as homophobia, machismo, and patriarchal values.

In 2013, an overwhelming majority of the members of LAM identified as tomboys. Some identified as transgenders (i.e., biologically female but identifying as male). They describe themselves as "physically babae pero sa feelings lalake" (biologically female but male when it comes to feelings). They are now familiar with and use the term lesbian after it was introduced to them by GALANG and a few have also appropriated the label lesbian.

One important strategy according to GALANG is that they do not try to convert the tomboys. As a GALANG/LAM organizer related, "Careful kami sa handling. Hindi binabago ang mga lesbyana o trans men. Hinahayaan ang kanilang identification" (We are careful in our handling. We don't try to convert the lesbians or trans men. We allow whatever their self-identified gender/sexual orientation is).

However, it appears that some GALANG organizers need to be more careful with the gender of nouns and pronouns, to be consistent and respectful of the gender identity and sexual orientation of the members of LAM. In one of my interactions with LAM members, Brando called the attention of one GALANG's community organizers addressing the tomboys of LAM as *ate*, which means older sister. Brando (or Daddy Brando to the young members of LAM) commented, *"ikaw ate ka ng ate. Wala naming ate dito maliban kay..."* (You always call us 'ate' when there is no 'ate' here except for ... [referring to the only feminine-looking member of LAM present during that meeting]). This was Brando's way of asserting their identification as tomboy or transgender. The community organizer immediately apologized to Brando and the other LAM members when she realized her faux pas. Self-identification and labels are very important and if LAM members identify as tomboy or male or transgender, then GALANG organizers should be extra careful with their pronouns as a manifestation of respect or *galang* for the members' self-identified gender and sexual identities.

Two significant issues that GALANG encountered among the LBTs in Barangay Pansol are polygamous relationships as expression of machismo and patriarchal values among the tomboys and trans men, and punitive rape of lesbians. In the cases of punitive rape, the victims did not pursue the case because of the stigma, as well as the emotional and financial costs of filing a case against the perpetrator.

On several occasions, GALANG organizers had to intervene in quarrels between lesbian partners which stemmed from a tomboy having many girlfriends. The tomboys/lesbians and transgenders would reveal that they have many girlfriends because they subscribe to the notion that the measure of being a good tomboy, lesbian, or trans man is the number of girlfriends, i.e., the more girlfriends you have, the better tomboy/lesbian you are. Such appropriation of patriarchal male privilege over women by the tomboy/transgender/trans man indicates treatment of women as objects of possession. The multiple relationships of the tomboy/transgender would contribute to much emotional stress on the part of the girlfriend/partner. Moreover, the conflicts stemming from one party having multiple relationships/partners often resulted in physical and other forms of violence.

GALANG's strength lies in identifying and focusing on the specific sector of lesbians, bisexuals, and trans men that they wanted to work with, which is the (economically) poor LGBTs, and being able to do sustained organizing and mobilization work with these LBTs. GALANG's founding came at an opportune time as it filled a gap as there were virtually no NGOs or POs doing focused and sustained community organizing among grassroots LBTs. I couldn't agree more with GALANG's analyses and choice to focus on grassroots LBTs. GALANG's Facebook page (https://www.facebook.com/galangphilippines/) reveals their bias for the economically disadvantaged LBTs:

> organizing and mobilizing poor LGBTs who comprise the majority of the sector, not only because they are the most vulnerable among us but also because of the belief that without a critical mass of organized Filipino LGBTs, they will continue to suffer from discrimination, with limited access to and control of education, health services, and employment opportunities.

In a way, GALANG found its niche early in its institutional history. I have no doubt that the organization will be able to continue and expand the coverage of its work among the urban poor marginalized LBTs in Metro Manila. For the past years, I believe that it is mainly GALANG that has done any solid grassroots LBT political work in Metro Manila or even in the entire Philippines, and they have received commendations from national and international LGBTQI+ award bodies for their work.

Despite the accomplishments of some discrete lesbian and gay NGOs, I argue that LGBT movement-building efforts in the Philippines are either virtually nonexistent or continue to be narrowly focused on mainstreaming strategies. These mainstreaming strategies are mainly limited to legislative advocacy (lobbying for the passage of the anti-discrimination bill in Congress or in city, municipal, or barangay ordinances), and education and advocacy work among government, law enforcement, and corporate entities. These are all very important and may result in tangible benefits to the LGBT sector but on their own may be very limited if not pursued with liberationist ideologies and strategies.

Conclusion

There are familiar narratives and counternarratives on rights-based political movements vis-à-vis liberationist movements, and on the pragmatic goals and benefits of mainstreaming strategies vis-à-vis the strategic goals and substantive gains that can be achieved through liberationist struggles. Vaid (1995) admits that gay/lesbian movements have resulted in some tangible benefits to the LGBT community. However, she is critical of mainstreaming strategies when not combined with liberationist ideologies and strategies. She argues that more than fifty years of mainstreaming and active campaigning against homophobia and heterosexism has not yielded true equality. She argues that liberationist ideologies and movements are necessary because they aim for the complete affirmation of LGBT sexuality as morally equivalent to heterosexuality. I do not believe that marriage equality has achieved this goal. I agree with Vaid that marriage equality like other civil rights can be won without undermining the moral and sexual hierarchy that enforces LGBT stigmatization and oppression. I also agree with Vaid that civil rights or human rights are often partial, provisional, and revocable, until the underlying religious, moral, and cultural prejudices are eliminated. The lesbian and gay rights movements in the United States have achieved substantive gains over more than seventy years of mainstreaming work.

I also have a suspicion that marriage equality is primarily a middle-class concern. While it is important to have affirmation of one's sexual identity and intimate relationships, I doubt if marriage equality is a major concern among Filipino grassroots tomboys/lesbians, bakla/gays, and transgenders. For the urban poor communities in Metro Manila or the rural poor in my field sites in Mountain Province, marriage equality is the least of their concerns. Livelihood, employment, health, education, and other vital social services are among their significant concerns.

As regards social non-movement strategies of quiet encroachment, Bayat recognizes the importance of the local and everyday life struggles of the "urban marginals." However, he acknowledges the limitations of such strategies to achieve broader political transformation. Bayat recognizes that only the larger national movements have the capacity for such broad and substantive social transformation. The urban and sexual marginals in Barangay Pansol, Balara, in Quezon City, have done a great job employing "quiet encroachment of the ordinary" through appropriating public spaces for residential, domestic, livelihood, and leisure activities. But again, these are "social non-movements." These efforts do not make a substantial dent on exploitative neo-liberal capitalist globalization, and on heterosexism and homophobia.

The challenge for the various tomboy/lesbian, bakla/gay, bisexual, and transgender people's organizations in the Philippines is how to come up with a broad-based movement that strikes a good balance of combining the various ideologies and strategies. This is doubly difficult at this time when the sector is deeply and bitterly divided. How do we justify political accommodation (i.e., push for the enactment of the anti-discrimination bill) but turn a blind eye to wanton disregard for human rights and to drug-related extrajudicial killings (EJKs)? How do we make sense of lesbian/tomboy, gay/bakla, and transgender/transsexual activist-comrades who are effectively complicit and enablers in the drug-related EJKs which have reportedly claimed thousands of lives? Just like before, we continue with our work. But unlike before, it cannot be "business as usual" while we are figuring out our appropriate movement-building ideologies and strategies. We need to figure out appropriate coping and healing processes and strategies to address our current deep divisions during these disquieting times for LGBTQI+ and other minoritized groups globally and nationally.

BIBLIOGRAPHY

Adobo Magazine. "Google Philippines Reveals Filipino Millennials' Search Behavior." 4 September 2017. Last accessed March 2019. https://adobomagazine.com/philippine-news/google-philippines-reveals-filipino-millennials-search-behavior.

Agence France-Presse. "Philippine Police say Facebook Use Spurring Sex Crimes." *ABS-CBN News*, 8 October 2010. Last accessed May 2019. https://news.abs-cbn.com/lifestyle/gadgets-and-tech/10/08/10/philippine-police-say-facebook-use-spurring-sex-crimes.

Appadurai, A. *Modernity at Large: Cultural Dimensions of Globalization*. Minnesota: University of Minnesota Press, 1996.

Bayat, A. (2010). *Life as Politics: How Ordinary People Change the Middle East*. Stanford, California: Stanford University Press, 2010.

Cayabyab, M. J. "Transgender Solon Roman on Death Penalty Vote: Politics is Compromise." *Philippine Daily Inquirer*, 8 March 2017. Last accessed 7 April 2019. http://newsinfo.inquirer.net/878802/transgender-solon-roman-on-death-penalty-vote-politics-is-compromise/amp

CNN Philippines. "House Approves Anti-discrimination Bill on 3rd and Final Reading." 23 September 2017. Last accessed December 2018. http://cnnphilippines.com/news/2017/09/20/House-approves-anti-discrimination-bill-3rd-and-final-reading.html.

Connell, R. W. *Gender*. Cambridge, UK: Polity Press, 2002.

Collins, D. "Identity, Mobility, and Urban Place-Making: Exploring Gay Life in Manila." *Gender and Society* 19, no. 2 (2005): 180–98. http://gas.sagepub.com/cgi/content/abstract/19/2/180.

Collins, P. H. *Black Feminist Thought: Knowledge, Consciousness and the Politics of Empowerment*. New York and London: Routledge, 1990.

Crenshaw, K. "Demarginalizing the Intersection of Race and Sex: A Black Feminist Critique of Antidiscrimination Doctrine, Feminist Theory, and Antiracist Politics." *University of Chicago Legal Forum* (1989). https://chicagounbound.uchicago.edu/uclf/vol1989/iss1/8/.

Demographic Research and Development Foundation, Inc. "Internet, Social Media are Important Part of Young Filipinos' Life—Survey Shows." 6 February 2014. Last accessed March 2019. http://www.drdf.org.ph/yafs4/pressrelease/02-06-2014/05.

Dowsett, G. W. *Practicing Desire: Homosexual Sex in the Era of AIDS*. Stanford, California: Stanford University Press, 1996.

Escoffier, J. *American Homo Community and Perversity*. Berkeley and Los Angeles, California: University of California Press, 1998.

Flanagan, M., and A. Booth. *Reload: Rethinking Women + Cyberculture*. Cambridge, Massachusetts: MIT Press, 2002.

GALANG Philippines website. Last accessed May 2019. https://www.facebook.com/galangphilippines/.

Golden, Carla. "Diversity and Variability in Women's Sexual Identities." In *Lesbian Psychologies: Explorations and Challenges*, edited by Boston Lesbian Psychology Collective. Chicago: University of Illinois Press, 1987.

Hausman, B. *Changing Sex: Transsexualism, Technology, and the Idea of Gender*. Durham and London: Duke University Press, 1995.

hooks, b. *Ain't I a Woman. Black Women and Feminism*. London: Pluto Press, 1982.

Internet Movie Database. "*Kaming Mga Talyada: We Who Are Sexy* (1962)." Last accessed May 2019. https://m.imdb.com/title/tt0370830/.

Josef, J. "*Self-images and Sexual Identities of Womyn-Loving Womyn.*" MA thesis, University of the Philippines Diliman, 1997.

———. "*Bontoc and Northern Kankana-ey Bakla and Tomboy Desires and Identities: Intimate Bodies, Spaces, Histories and Memories.*" PhD diss., University of the Philippines, 2018.

Karkazis, K. *Fixing Sex: Intersex, Medical Authority, and Lived Experience*. Durham and London: Duke University Press, 2008.

Kemp, S. "Digital Trends 2019: Every Single Stat You Need to Know about the Internet." *The Next Web*, 31 January 2019. Last accessed 7 April 2019. https://thenextweb.

com/contributors/2019/01/30/digital-trends-2019-every-single-stat-you-need-to-know-about-the-internet/.

Kennedy, E. L. and M. D. Davis. *Boots of Leather, Slippers of Gold: The History of a Lesbian Community*. New York and London: Routledge, 1993.

Link Davao Organization website. Last accessed May 2019. https://www.facebook.com/Link-Davao-Organization-Inc-116366475077397/.

Manalastas, E. J. "Suicide Ideation and Suicide Attempt among Young Lesbian and Bisexual Filipina Women: Evidence for Disparities in the Philippines." *Asian Women* 32, no. 3 (Autumn 2016): 101–20. https://pages.upd.edu.ph/sites/default/files/ejmanalastas/files/manalastas 2016 lb suicide risk asian women.pdf.

McCann Truth Central. *The Truth about the Youth*. 2016. Last accessed March 2019. https://mccann.com.au/wp-content/uploads/the-truth-about-youth.pdf.

McKay, D. "Translocal Circulation: Place and Subjectivity in an Extended Filipino Community." *Asia Pacific Journal of Anthropology* 7, no. 3 (December 2006).

————. "On the Face of Facebook: Historical Images and Personhood in Filipino Social Networking." *History and Anthropology* 21, no. 4 (2010): 479–98. http://doi.org/10.1080/02757206.2010.522311.

Pagulong, C. J. "Word War Erupts among DDS Bloggers." *Philippine Star*, 11 October 2017. Last accessed May 2019. https://www.philstar.com/headlines/2017/10/11/1747978/word-war-erupts-among-dds-bloggers.

Pew Research Center and Elon University. "Future of the Internet IV Survey." 2010. Last accessed March 2019. http://www.elon.edu/e-web/predictions/expertsurveys/2010survey/default.html.

Pharr, S. *Homophobia: A Weapon of Sexism*. California: Chardon Press, 1997. Last accessed March 2019. https://www.rapereliefshelter.bc.ca/sites/default/files/imce/HomophobiaAWeaponofSexismCondensed.pdf.

Prensky, M. "Digital Natives, Digital Immigrants." In *Cross Currents: Cultures, Communities, Technologies*, edited by K. Blair, R. M. Murphy, and J. Almjeld, 45–51. Boston, Massachusetts: Cengage Learning, 2013.

Redick, A. "American History XY: The Medical Treatment of Intersex, 1916–1955." PhD diss., New York University, 2004. Cited in K. Karkazis, *Fixing Sex: Intersex, Medical Authority, and Lived Experience*. Durham and London: Duke University Press, 2008.

Smith, A. and M. Anderson. "Social Media Use in 2018." Pew Research Center, 1 March 2018. Last accessed April 2019. https://www.pewinternet.org/2018/03/01/social-media-use-in-2018/.

Stryker, S. *Transgender History*. Berkeley, California: Seal Press, 2008.

Tugnet, N., J. C. Goddard, R. M. Vickery, D. Khoosal, and T. R. Terry. "Current Management of Male-to-Female Gender Identity Disorder in the UK." *Postgrad Medical Journal* 83 (October 2007): 638–42. http://www.ncbi.nlm.nih.gov/pmc/articles/PMC2600127/#!po=33.5821.

Vaid, U. *Virtual Equality: The Mainstreaming of Gay and Lesbian Liberation*. New York: Anchor Books, 1995.

Visa. *Connecting with Millennials: A Visa Study*. 2012. Last accessed March 2019. http://www.visa-asia.com/ap/sea/mediacenter/pressrelease/includes/uploads/Visa Gen Y Report 2012 LR.pdf.

Negotiating Sexual and Gender Diversity in Recent Philippine Culture

Foreground, Apparently gay butterfly in Sinulog parade. Photo courtesy of Mark Blasius. *Background,* Sinulog festival in Cebu. Photo courtesy of Wynn Loner U. Uy. Wikimedia Commons.

This essay was previously published in *Journal of Southeast Asian Studies* 38, no. 1 (February 2007): 107–32.

PATRICK ALCEDO

Sacred Camp: Transgendering Faith in a Philippine Festival

Soft shafts of light barely shine through openings of Augusto Fuentes Diangson's two-storey concrete house when he commands Persing, one of his household helpers and a few years younger than him, to start making breakfast. His seven friends, who have come all the way from Manila and Davao City, are about to wake up, and the ten musicians whom he annually hires from the adjacent province of Iloilo have been waiting downstairs for coffee and the usual 'pan de sal' (staple bread roll). For two consecutive days now, *Tay* Augus or *Tay* Gusto, as his close relatives and the local residents of Kalibo, Aklan call him, has been up at five in the morning. He is neither to hear an early Catholic Mass at the nearby Cathedral, as he regularly does, nor to attend to his orchids, which are the envy of his mahjong friends. Preparing for the 2000 Ati-atihan, a week-long street-dancing festival celebrated in the Central Philippines in honor of its unofficial patron saint, the Santo Niño or the Holy Child Jesus, has been the focus of his days.

Tay Augus walks around excitedly, and invites some early guests to have breakfast but hurries to the bedroom. Miniature statues of the Virgin Mary, the crucified Christ, and the ubiquitous Santo Niño emboss its yellow walls. The beautician, Benjie, has been waiting and is already sorting out brushes and make-up ready to transform *Tay* Augus' face similar to past years into a Caucasian- looking Folies Bergère chorus girl. *Tay* Augus, with a height of around 1. 68 meters, sits down, lifts his chin and gazes past into the exposed, bleeding heart of the 'Sacred Heart of Jesus' nailed on his altar wall. He is ready to have himself transformed.

An hour later Ambo, another teenaged male servant of his, appears. He helps *Tay* Augus put on a skimpy bustier and thong. Ambo is tasked to put together a wide array of accoutrements and a set of feather boas and pink plumes that *Tay* Augus' nieces and nephews have sent from faraway

Chicago and San Diego. This is to complete *Tay* Augus' mimicry of the Folies Bergère. By mid-morning, *Tay* Augus will have divested his 80-year old self and taken on a foreign self for the Santo Niño, and for the thousands of devotees who have come to worship and dance.

THE ABOVE AND FOLLOWING VIGNETTES describe the transgendering of *Tay* Augus, an *agi*, a man belonging to what he categorized in English as the "third sex."[1] They recall his participation at the 2000 Ati-atihan festival, an annual carnivalesque, street dancing parade in Kalibo, Aklan on the island of Panay. Every second or third week of January both the local Roman Catholic Church and the municipal government organize this festival to honor the popular Santo Niño or the Holy Child Jesus. The vignettes are portraits as well of the festival life of *Tay* Augus, who, while not secretive about his homosexuality, decided to politely avoid spaces considered in Kalibo to be sites of the *bastos* (lewdness) and *linandi* (flirtatiousness). These sites are almost always associated with the beauty parlors, where lower-middle-class *agi* or the *bakla* hang out.[2] When asked why this was so, he reasoned, "I am a man of the third sex alright, but I have a name to protect, besides I have class and am educated unlike

1   *Tay* is an Akeanon language appellative used to refer to Ta*tay*, which means "father." It is added before a person's name to indicate respect and a significant amount of age difference between the addresser and addressee. Upon the request of *Tay* Augus during my last interview with him in December 2001, his real name is kept. As regards the rest of the individuals interviewed for and quoted in this article, they likewise prefer their real names to pseudonyms.

2   To be called a *bakla* in Kalibo is derogatory, for its semantics is not as fluid as *agi*. For a Kalibonhon, the Akeanon word *agi*, although it could mean "gay" or "homosexual," as does *bakla*, can be an asexualised or a desexualised argot depending on who is speaking and the context in which it is used. The Tagalog *bakla* among Kalibonhons when spoken in the Akeanon language takes on a fixed signified, a negative connotation of male individuals whose sexual preference is towards the same sex, and who usually are uneducated and of lower-middle-class status. *Agi*, on the other hand, is a floating signifier, asymptomatic in its linguistic dynamics; it needs not readily refer to a non-normative sexual behavior, or to being a member of the lower middle class. *Agi* also takes on the qualities of camp. A heterosexual individual when s/he acts playfully, affectedly, and excessively can be jokingly branded as an *agi*, as in the Akeanon banter, "Oh no, there you are *aging* (behaving like an *agi*) again." In this instance, *agi's* fluidity is additionally shown in its versatile nature of filling in different parts of speech: as a noun, an adjective, and an adverb, yet at times also a verb. All translations are mine.

the other *agi* out there."[3] *Tay* Augus here is seen against the background of two opposing poles, on one side, of heteronormative masculinity, and on the other, of the *bakla* who are effeminized men working and/or taking up residence in beauty parlors. He did not fall into either of these worlds, and thus created a third category, an ambiguity that all the more captured the in-between, interstitial character of "camp," and of the Santo Niño Himself.

As evidenced by the awards he received from the provincial government of Aklan for his many years of teaching physical education, Philippine folk dances, and ballet, *Tay* Augus was an outstanding member of his community.[4] He was also known in Kalibo to have participated in the major rituals of the Roman Catholic Church, and hence was considered by parishioners and priests alike to be *Katoliko sarado*, "completely Catholic." His faith was so deeply grounded that his loyalty to the Church was unquestionable. In the eyes of the many Roman Catholics in Kalibo, *Tay* Augus' faith was so exclusively Catholic that no amount of persuasion could have convinced him to change his religion to the growing faiths of Protestantism and Mormonism, or to the very foreign Buddhism and Islam.

Tay Augus carried a strong devotion to the Santo Niño until he lost his battle with colon cancer in 2002. He believed that it was the Santo Niño who saved him in the early 1980s from an appendicitis; it was a near-death experience. Aklan's former provincial governor, a close family relative, helped *Tay* Augus in getting the first flight out of Kalibo so he could be operated on at a government hospital in Manila. *Tay* Augus made a vow that if the Santo Niño were to give him a new lease on life, he would continue his *panaad*, a sacred devotion to the Holy Child Jesus he started in the early 1960s, and would dance for Him for the rest of his life. Given the popularity of the Santo Niño in the way Kalibo residents or Kalibonhons practice Roman Catholicism, and His centrality in their Ati-atihan, the Kalibo community participated in the fulfillment of *Tay* Augus' *panaad*.

3   In December 2001, *Tay* Augus explained predominantly in Akeanon, *Third sex minatuod ako, pero may pangaean ako nga dapat haeungan, may class ana ako ag edukado bukon it piras sa ibang agi una.* I suggest that his choice of the English term 'third sex' to describe his gender and sexuality was a way of separating himself from other *agi* and of marking the education and class membership he claimed.

4   In 1998, *Tay* Augus was awarded, "Most Outstanding Aklanon," the highest possible recognition given by the provincial government of Aklan to its civic members.

The Santo Niño, also known as the Boy King, is a patron of lost causes, and the most popular among Filipinos.[5] Devotion to the Santo Niño is a national phenomenon in the Philippines, and it is said that "if you are not a devotee of the Santo Niño, you are a rare species in the Philippines... Everyone who has ever loved a child, who has ever loved a family, is devoted to the Santo Niño."[6] The Santo Niño is perceived and narrated as a mischievous boy, who surreptitiously leaves His altar at night to play. Yet, devotees such as Tay Augus believe that the Santo Niño is powerful enough to fulfill wishes, such as to be healed from impotency or a debilitating disease. The Santo Niño also grants victory in a governmental election; makes it possible for His adherents to live permanently in countries such as the United States, Australia, and Canada; or enables them to be overseas contract workers in Hong Kong, Singapore, the Middle East, or the United Kingdom in order for them to send remittances back to their families in the province of Aklan. Moreover, since the Santo Niño is still a child, His gender for Kalibonhons remains ambiguous; therefore, participants during Ati-atihan can subvert and make fun of the gender norms the Roman Catholic Church has institutionalized. As a result, at this time of the year, John the Baptist, the official patron saint of Kalibo, is momentarily eclipsed. St. John the Baptist, who baptized

5   For a discussion of the Santo Niño as Boy King, see Sally Ann Ness, *Body, Movement, and Culture: Kinesthetic and Visual Symbolism in a Philippine Community* (Philadelphia: University of Pennsylvania Press, 1992), 58–85. Upon the arrival of Ferdinand Magellan and his men in Cebu, Philippines in 1521, they presented the image of the Santo Niño to the wife of the chieftain, Rajah Humabon, during the baptism of many Cebuanos. Keeping the desire of converting more souls into the Christian faith, Miguel Lopez de Legazpi, together with an Augustinian priest and a maritime team, returned to Cebu in 1565. Unlike Magellan who lost his battle against the Cebuanos and died in the hands of another local chieftain, Lapu- Lapu, de Legazpi succeeded in subduing the nearly 2000 hostile Cebuanos. In the battle remains, de Legazpi found the statue of the Santo Niño, proof that for nearly 40 years the Cebuanos had venerated the Holy Child Jesus unsupervised by Europeans. The relationship of Filipinos with the Santo Niño, therefore, runs deep in their colonial history. This initial contact, dramatized by the 'miraculous' survival of the image, propels the popularity of the Santo Niño in the practice of Philippine Roman Catholicism, especially in the Visayan Islands. For an account of the early development of Christianity in the Philippines, see Barbara Watson Andaya and Yoneo Ishii, "Religious Developments in Southeast Asia, c. 1500–1800," in *The Cambridge History of Southeast Asia*, vol. 1, part 2, ed. Nicholas Tarling (Cambridge: Cambridge University Press, 1992), 185–90.

6   Abe Florendo, ed., *Santo Niño: The Holy Child Devotion in the Philippines* (Manila: Congregacion del Santisimo Nombre del Niño Jesus, 2001), inside back cover.

his cousin Jesus Christ to enable Him to save humankind from their iniquities, was also known to have condemned the incestuous marriage of Herod Antipas with his niece Herodias. A foil to the Santo Niño, St. John the Baptist embodies and safeguards the very heteronormativity the devout *Tay* Augus tweaked, played with, and turned upside down by way of a transgendered performance. St. John the Baptist cannot function as a central figure in the Ati-atihan festival, a carnivalesque event in which societal norms are temporarily broken.

It was the third Sunday of January, the last day of the 2000 Ati-atihan, when I visited *Tay* Augus to participate in and document his festival participation. According to an informal survey conducted by the Kalibo municipal government, 250,000 guests from far and near—even from outside the Philippines—arrived that day at this festival of festivals, the mother of all the Santo Niño festivals in the Visayas, and the most religious, "authentic," and carnivalesque of all the Philippine festivals which venerate the Santo Niño.[7] It was to quadruple Kalibo's population of approximately 65,000, and would fill the streets to the seams with dancing devout bodies. That Sunday was bound to be the most attended of the week-long gathering, understood by faithful participants such as *Tay* Augus, the Kalibo community and the devotees within and beyond the Philippines as the festival which not only honors the Santo Niño, but also respectfully acknowledges the ancestors of the Filipinos: the *ati* or the dark-skinned Negritos.[8] Such gesturing towards a past that was

---

7   Cebu's Sinulog, Iloilo's Dinagyang, Capiz's Halaran, and Bacolod's Maskara are believed to have followed the Ati-atihan's popularity. Based on stories I heard growing up in Kalibo, and interviews with Kalibonhons from years 1999–2001, these Western Visayan festivals have all been borne of Ati-atihan and are its poor and thus inauthentic copycats. These were the same kind of narrative accounts Sally Ann Ness heard when she conducted ethnographic research in Cebu in 1984–1985 (*Body, Movement, and Culture*, 24, 185, 194, 196–97). In the Ati-atihan recently celebrated by the Aklanon community in La Mirada, California in February 2006, banners announcing Ati-atihan as the "Mother of Philippine Festivals" were hung in the ballroom where the festivity was celebrated. Rosalyn Fernandez Cabison, President of the Aklanon Association of Los Angeles, announced that in June 2006, in commemoration of Philippine Independence, an Ati-atihan contingent will lead a parade in downtown Los Angeles ahead of such groups as Sinulog, Dinagyang, and Davao's Kadayawan. She said that for the organizers of this trans-Pacific Philippine Independence Day Celebration Ati-atihan gave birth to these other religious festivals, and thus merits the honor of heading the parade.

8   Due to the tourism development that began in the province of Aklan in the early 1960s, archival and oral historical research shows that Ati-atihan took on carnivalesque elements from much more popular carnival celebrations of Rio de Janeiro and

pure and untouched by modernity and colonialism is articulated in the repetition of 'ati' and the attachment of the verbal affix '-han' in the name, 'Ati-atihan', which gives it the gloss, 'to mimic the *ati*'. Most Ati-atihan participants apply soot on their faces and extremities to appear like the putative first inhabitants of the Philippines. But *Tay* Augus would take paints to whiten himself to distance himself from the 'others'. Later on that day, in his whiteness, he would dance in stark contrast to the darkened rest. This was the kind of difference which he felt would please the Santo Niño even more.

Instead of devoting his mornings to hearing a six o'clock Catholic mass, *Tay* Augus broke that ritual and woke up early to prepare instead for the most important day of the Ati-atihan. For two days, he and his visiting friends from out of town, who similar to him were also *agi*, had been dancing in the streets of Kalibo as Folies Bergère chorus girls. The musicians *Tay* Augus imported from the neighboring Iloilo province had enthusiastically followed behind them. But this day was the 'very day of Ati-atihan,' referred by Kalibonhons as the *kaadlawan it Ati-atihan*. That Sunday, festival participants and Santo Niño devotees alike were to street-dance the route set by the Mayor's Office in close consultation with the Bishop's Office of Kalibo. *Tay* Augus made sure to dress very elaborately to show his *panaad* to the community, especially to the Santo Niño.

According to local accounts, the Santo Niño is a naughty boy, who secretly steps down at night to gallivant around Kalibo's deserted streets to tease and play harmless tricks on the residents. Knowing that the Santo Niño was waiting to have fun that day in exchange for the countless danced petitions to Him, *Tay* Augus launched for the first time his Folies Bergère chorus girl costume made of baby pink feathers and studded with purple rhinestones. He put to rest last year's emerald green brassiere and spandex thong, both shouting with gold sequins. The world premiere of his pink costume, as scanty as last year's, would give *Tay* Augus a dramatic Sunday entrance that would catch the eye of the playful Santo Niño.

New Orleans. This was to turn Ati-atihan, which prior to the 1960s was a local festivity attended only by residents of Kalibo and a few guests, into a national, even global phenomenon in which foreign and Filipino tourists would flock to the streets of Kalibo. My use of "carnivalesque" is informed by Michael Bakhtin, *Rabelais and His World*, trans. Hélène Iswolsky (Bloomington: Indiana University Press, 1968); and, Bakhtin, *Problems of Dostoevsky's Poetics*, ed. and trans. Caryl Emerson, introduction by Wayne C. Booth (Minneapolis and London: University of Minnesota Press, 1984).

Tay Augus mobilized and commanded his own resources and those of his community to carry out his *panaad*, which, since his appendectomy in the early 1980s, had largely defined his Ati-atihan participation. He had pooled together his own savings from his pension as a retired schoolteacher and a former member of the Philippine Constabulary that helped the American soldiers fight the Japanese during World War II; the sales from his inherited land in the nearby town of Bulwang; and the remitted dollars specifically earmarked by his US-citizen nephews and nieces for his festival participation. One hundred thousand pesos (roughly $2,000; the average annual salary of a schoolteacher in Kalibo) was more than enough to cover food, costumes, festival banners, salaries of helpers and professional fees for the musicians and the make-up artist. The public display of his *panaad* turned his transgendering into a communal affair, the embodiment of his own faith in the Santo Niño and that of his family and his Ati-atihan and Kalibo Catholic community as a whole.

Tay Augus would take at least two hours to prepare. Aside from the heavy make-up and the complicated vesting of the different parts of his new costume, a fake bouffant had to be secured on his thinning grey hair to serve as a solid base for his half-meter headdress. Surprisingly all the hustle and bustle did not take a heavy toll on him. When I asked him about his boundless energy, he laughingly credited it as *halin kay Santo Niño*, a gift from the Santo Niño. At around ten in the morning he was already "around and about," fully transformed into a Folies Bergère chorus girl. His younger friends were still in the process of divesting their "old" selves to take on "new" selves for the mischievous Santo Niño and His popular festival.

Ethnography of the particular and notes on agency

Tay Augus' transgendered performance as a feminine, white-skinned dancer during this religious, yet at the same time carnivalesque, festival was an act of cross-dressing, which the Diocese of Kalibo came to consider a necessary element in the Ati-atihan celebration. It was his class, his political affiliations, and his relationships with both the Church and the Santo Niño—an article of faith consistent with his loyalty to the Roman Catholic Church —that principally paved the way for his transgendering as a Folies Bergère chorus girl to become one of Ati-atihan's strongest exploding signifiers. As the Bishop of Kalibo at that time, Monsignor Gabriel Reyes, explained in an interview in 2000, "There will be no Ati-atihan if *Tay* Augus does not come out; he has already become an institution."

My concentrating on *Tay* Augus is an answer to the call of Lila Abu-Lughod to "write against" the homogenizing discourse of culture.[9] The Self, she maintains, is very much determined by the enduring qualities of one's culture, but is also constructed by the shifts and turns of that culture. It is the unique relationship of the individual to the political, economic, and cultural changes—those more challenging to pin down than a generalized understanding of "culture"—that forms his or her own individuality. Incorporating and making central the notions of difference and cultural construction support the assertion that culture is not at all and will never be a complete whole. Abu-Lughod writes in this regard:

> Anthropologists commonly generalize about communities by saying that they are characterized by certain institutions, rules, or ways of doing things. For example, we can and often do say things like "The Bongo-Bongo are polygynous." Yet one could refuse to generalize in this way, instead asking how a particular set of individuals—for instance, a man and his three wives in a Bedouin community in Egypt whom I have known for a decade—live the "institution" that we call polygyny. Stressing the particularity of this marriage and building a picture of it through the participants' discussions, recollections, disagreements, and actions would make several theoretical points.[10]

Ethnographies of the particular emphasize difference and represent the people in the field as individuals who, like the ethnographers momentarily living with them, are also affected by their personal lot in life. This is the kind of subject positioning scholars should strive for, in that it demonstrates the myriad ways of being human from the participant's point of view and not from the generalizations of a community's culture. As a dance ethnographer, I relate my subject position, which is multi-pronged and is both personal and academic, to my being a long time Ati-atihan practitioner, an Aklanon born and raised in Kalibo, and a Santo Niño adherent myself. The many selves I assume form that subject position, a "multiplex identity" shared by Kalibonhons like *Tay* Augus.[11]

---

9   Lila Abu-Lughod, "Writing against Culture," in *Recapturing anthropology: Working in the Present*, ed. Richard G. Fox (Santa Fe, NM: School of American Research Press, 1991), 137–62.

10   Ibid.,153.

11   "Multiplex identity" is a concept taken from Kirin Narayan, "How Native is a 'Native' Anthropologist?," *American Anthropologist* 95, no. 3 (September 1993): 671–86.

The institution of family, which the Philippine Roman Catholic Church feels the need to define at all times as central to Filipino culture, runs parallel with Abu-Lughod's all-encompassing "institution" of polygyny. The highly influential Jaime Cardinal Sin, who died on 21 June 2005 and was the head of the Roman Catholic Church in the Philippines for 18 years by virtue of his being Archbishop of Manila, reminded Filipinos in January 2003 that families should remain hetero-normative if they are to "align" with the "vision of God." A quote from one of the Philippines' national dailies taken from the same address he gave at the Fourth World Meeting of Families in Manila reads: "The family should be the 'focal point of evangelization,' amid incidents of divorce and same sex unions which do not conform to God's 'vision.'"[12] *Tay* Augus reflected—in his weaving together of what I will later describe as webs of signification— an ambivalence to the heterosexual normativity of Philippine culture as homogenized by Cardinal Sin.[13]

A year earlier Cardinal Sin, a Filipino-Chinese and an Aklanon whose roots are in the port town of New Washington, 9 kilometers southeast of where *Tay* Augus lived for most of his life, decided to change his homily at the sixteenth anniversary of the original People Power Movement. He did not revisit the 1986 revolution, where he played a crucial role in ousting Ferdinand Marcos from the presidency due to human rights abuses and corruption, and in catapulting Corazon Aquino to power. Instead, Cardinal Sin heavily criticized a bill filed in Congress that would give equal rights to gays and lesbians. He said, "My goodness, what is happening to our country? Instead of talking about how to solve the problems of poverty, they are talking about the marriage of two male people."[14]

12   "Sin Urges RP Families to Keep 'God's Vision,'" *Philippine Daily Inquirer*, 22 January 2003, http://www.inq7.net/globalnation/sec_new/2003/jan/22-03.htm.

13   The phrase "webs of signification" is highly influenced by the famous line, "that man is an animal suspended in webs of significance he himself has spun," from Clifford Geertz, following Max Weber, in *The Interpretation of Culture* (New York: Basic Books, 1973), 5. My decision to replace "significance" with "signification" is spurred by the need to foreground the active production of the multiplicity of signs spawned by the affective space of Ati-atihan, and to specifically illustrate how *Tay* Augus and his transgendered performance wove together signs in the unnatural process of signification.

14   For a fuller discussion of the 2002 homily in which this quote and the following quotes from Bishop Villegas were taken, see Sol Jose Vanzi, "Same-sex Marriage Unnatural, Unfilipino—Church," *Newsflash*, 26 February 2002, http://www.newsflash.org/2002/02/hl/hl015291.htm.

Manila Auxiliary Bishop Socrates Villegas, in support of Cardinal Sin's stand on homosexuality, said in an interview after the Mass that homosexuality as manifested in same-sex marriage goes "against Filipino sensibilities." Bishop Villegas added, "It is unnatural. It is against our Filipino culture. It is against our Christian faith." Indeed this was a remark that was essentialising, comprehensive in its reach in the way Cardinal Sin similarly resisted heterogeneity in Filipino culture. The admonishment the bill received from the country's two very powerful Roman Catholic leaders, especially from Cardinal Sin, who held a position inferior in power and mandate only to that of the Pope, and by the time of his retirement in 2003 held dominion over close to 68 million Catholic Filipinos, 85 percent of the country's total population, became a most compelling reason why the bill did not go beyond the House of Representatives.[15]

Why did a Santo Niño devotee and a devout Catholic, but a self-confessed *agi*, annually embody a foreign female self at a festival, which was supposed to be Catholic in register and supportive of the homogenous character of Filipino culture? How did he negotiate his faith by working within the bounds of the Church-mandated heteronormative behavior, in a town where 98 percent of the population professes a Roman Catholic faith and therefore supports the maintenance of "family values?"[16] One could encode the transgendered performance of *Tay* Augus, who would volunteer to help the Kalibo Catholic Church organize religious events in rare times when the Cardinal paid his ancestral home a visit, in webs of signification. These are *panaad*, a sacred promise in a form of an embodied prayer, sacred camp, and carnivalesque. Taken together they confirmed for *Tay* Augus the homogeneity of Filipino culture, so adamantly professed by the nation's Roman Catholic leaders. However, they successfully challenged the values and ideas of those same Roman Catholic Church leaders, while also swaying the local church leaders of Kalibo to consider *Tay* Augus' transvestism as emblematic of the Ati-atihan festival. These webs of signification explain how an individual navigated through, with difference and theatrical drama, his hometown's institutions of Roman Catholicism and heterosexuality. His transgendered mimicry should be

15   David Steinberg, *The Philippines: A Singular and Plural Place* (San Francisco: Westview Press, 1994), 93; "Cardinal Sin Retires, Says Vatican Spokesman in Manila," *Philippine Daily Inquirer*, 15 September 2003, http://www.inq7.net/brk/2003/sep/15/brkpol_11-1.htm.

16   Out of the 478,092 residents of Aklan, 420,651 practice Roman Catholicism; *The 2004 Catholic Directory of the Philippines: Containing Status of the Catholic Directory of the Philippines as of January 2004* (Quezon City: Claretian Publications, 2004).

considered a personification of the local and individual practice of Roman Catholicism in Kalibo, which, similar to the demographics of the rest of the Lowland Philippines, overwhelmingly adheres to the Roman Catholic faith.[17] It is in the ambivalence of one's performance, and in the paradox of difference and uniformity–in Tay Augus' fulfillment of his Catholic *panaad* to the Santo Niño through his annual transgendering of the Folies Bergère chorus girl, and therefore through his public performance of his third sex–that an individual's agency is located.[18]

The premises found in the webs of signification are realized by way of a kind of "double sense," an assumption of two bodies, which Tay Augus lived out by using his pedestrian, local body to become a foreign, female body.[19] The two bodies—one as a mimic of the Folies Bergère chorus girls and the other as his quotidian self—mobilized his transgenderism and revealed the double in Tay Augus' corporeality. This very doubleness made it unproblematic for an admiring public and the local Church leadership to regard him as a loyal parishioner, rather than dismiss him as a sacrilegious backslider, remiss in his obligations to the Church.

Like Cardinal Sin, Tay Augus was born and raised in the Aklanon culture, and was of Filipino-Chinese descent; they also shared a similar defining personal history, such as the Japanese occupation (1942–1944) and the Marcos period (1966–86).[20] Cardinal Sin, a well-known bon vivant among Roman Catholic priests and his close friends, was in fact the godson of Tay Augus' mother. During the younger days of the Cardinal, he would visit Tay Augus' ancestral home in Kalibo to pay respect to

17   Homi Bhabha, *The Location of Culture* (London: Routledge, 1994), 85–92; Samuel Weber, "The Sideshow, or: Remarks on a Canny Movement," *Modern Language Notes* 88, no. 6 (1973): 1102–33.

18   Vicente L. Rafael, *Contracting Colonialism: Translation and Christian Conversion in Tagalog Society under Early Spanish Rule* (Durham, NC: Duke University Press, 1993); Rafael, *The Promise of the Foreign: Nationalism and the Technics of Translation in the Spanish Philippines* (Durham, NC: Duke University Press, 2005).

19   Susan Sontag, "Notes on Camp," *Partisan Review* 31, no. 4 (Fall 1964): 520; Moe Meyer, ed., *The Politics and Poetics of Camp* (New York: Routledge, 1994).

20   Both Cardinal Sin and Tay Augus belonged to upper-middle-class families. When I was growing up my late paternal grandparents, Rustico and Leonaria Alcedo, who hailed from Dumaguit, another port town a few miles southeast of New Washington, would tell stories about the Cardinal. His parents owned the biggest retail store in that part of the province, and during the Japanese occupation their ancestral home was razed to the ground. It was also during this time, my grandparents narrated, when they and most probably the Cardinal's family as well evacuated (*nag-ibakwit sa taeon*) to Aklan's hinterlands.

his godmother, *para magbisa*, to touch with his forehead the back of his godmother's right hand. When Cardinal Sin became a priest and received his appointment from the Vatican to be Manila's Cardinal, *Tay* Augus would show the same kind of respect by doing the exact gesture of *bisa* whenever Cardinal Sin visited Aklan.

Why did they see homosexuality in a different light? There is a Filipino 'culture' that exists in the minds of the people and dictates the way they should live their lives in relation to societal norms. Since it is one of the strongest and highly respected gatekeepers of Filipino values, the Roman Catholic Church carefully monitors generalized notions of culture. Articulating, interpreting, and prescribing them to parishioners allows national religious leaders such as Cardinal Sin and Bishop Villegas to remain in positions of power.

As soon as one closely examines, however, the vicissitudes of an individual's life and the local practice of Roman Catholicism, one realizes that there is plenty of mediation and accommodation in expressing one's Roman Catholic faith. In these processes, one understands how an individual like *Tay* Augus can sway past the homogenizing forces of his culture, exemplified by the institution of having a hetero-normative family, while at the same time confirming their power over individuals like him. I consciously limit my comments to the Kalibo community alone. I thus not only foreground the particularities of the local; I also interrogate the ways in which an individual lives this localness through acquiescence and negotiation. Moved by the double bodies of *Tay* Augus and the multiplicity of meanings they generate, I suggest that one can better grasp the culture's fabric of sameness if one takes the time to notice its threads of difference.

Tay Augus' de facto claimed space to perform his difference and veneration to the Santo Niño. He embodied power to dialogue with the overarching institutions of the Roman Catholic Church. Through his dance, which mimicked the foreignness of the Folies Bergère chorus girls, *Tay* Augus displayed the ability of an individual to perform one's difference through the ambiguity of his third sex; in these strategies his agency resided. Being ambivalent, and in a state of constant paradox—neither fish nor fowl, at once mimicking the Folies Bergère chorus girls for his *panaad*, and publicly being an *agi* of strong Catholic faith—makes one slip out from the culture's essentialising clutches; in this particular case, it is from the Church's firmly valued institutions of family and heterosexuality.

Panaad: **Dramatic offering**

To begin the transformation of *Tay* Augus into a Folies Bergère chorus girl, Benjie divides *Tay* Augus' face into sections, and works on one section at a time. After wetting a sponge and rubbing it on a light colored pressed powder, Benjie applies "Kukuryo," an imported foundation from Japan, on *Tay* Augus' entire face, down to his neck, and further to the upper part of his chest that will not be covered by his new brassiere. Similar to previous years and the last two days of *Tay* Augus' street performance, Benjie sets the cosmetic base. He deepens the foundation between *Tay* Augus' eyes and temples; stretching taut with a sponge that section of his face to conceal the many wrinkles there. The cosmetic product gives *Tay* Augus' face a matte finish and a thick layer of make-up, which will withstand the street dancing he will do that day. Above all, its evenness whitens his dusky complexion.

Afterwards Benjie dips the tip of a slim brush, first in the bowl of water, then on a mound of black eyebrow enhancer to pick up color. He unhesitatingly gives *Tay* Augus' eyebrows a shape, clearly defining them. Benjie then goes to work on the eyes. He forms a concave of dark brown shadow on the eyelid's upper portion, carefully making sure that the inward curve left a small circle at the bottom. To make *Tay* Augus' nose narrower, more aquiline than it already is, he lines both sides of the nose ridge with the same off-white make-up. Finishing the eye section, Benjie gently pulls down *Tay* Augus' lower eyelid to saturate it with black eyeliner. The tiniest of brushes is used. Benjie wets it a little to capture the black make-up stored in one of the cosmetic cases.

To contour *Tay* Augus' left eye, Benjie moves the brush from the furthest corner near the temple, to the corner close to the nose ridge, and reverses the movement for the right eye. Cautiously, he confines those left to right movements on the thin skin where the hair edging the eyelid and the conjunctiva meet. *Tay* Augus struggles from the forced dilation; his eyes turn red, and he sheds tears almost instantaneously from the artificial contact. Before his eyes are awash with tears, Benjie quickly extends the eyeliner to the corners of the eyes, securing for *Tay* Augus a feminine "cat's eye look." *Tay* Augus does not stop Benjie from continuing on despite the discomfort.

After Benjie puts on a light blush on *Tay* Augus' cheekbones, and distributes specks of silver glitter on the face, he prepares to glue on the pair of false eyelashes. Benjie removes one of the leaves from the star apple stalk Ambo brought in earlier. Droplets of milky sap ooze out from it, and Benjie expertly lines them on the edge of one of the false eyelashes. He at once fits it over *Tay* Augus' right upper lid, and repeats the same process for the other lid. The sap bonds in seconds the false eyelashes to *Tay* Augus' own lashes, thus extending the natural lashes and erasing his obvious epicanthic fold. *Tay* Augus flutters his eyelashes, now new, longer, and much heavier.

Once again Benjie sweeps a pinkish blush across the hollows of *Tay* Augus' cheeks. His broad strokes reach all the way to the temples. Using a rounded U-tip brush, Benjie dabs dark lipstick on *Tay* Augus' lips, setting them and finally completing the make-up process. *Tay* Augus presses his lips together to even out the freshly applied lipstick. By way of that final gesture, *Tay* Augus corporeally declares his make-up done, and indicates he is now ready to be dressed.

The above description begins to flesh out the first web of signification that is *panaad*, a sacred vow an individual has promised to keep throughout one's lifetime. By 2000, *Tay* Augus had imitated the image of the Folies Bergère chorus girls for close to 40 years. His dedication to the Santo Niño image, seen by the annual transgendering, made his mimicry in his eyes a *panaad*, and as he believed in the eyes of others, of the Kalibo Roman Catholic Church, and of the Santo Niño as well. *Tay* Augus demonstrated what it meant to publicly display one's faith in the Santo Niño through the annual physical labor and at times pain he had to go through. Among the Roman Catholics of Kalibo, for any *panaad* to be legitimately viewed as such, the elements of suffering and transformation should be experienced through one's own body and be rendered visible every year. *Tay* Augus' *panaad* had both these corporeal and temporal elements, essential factors which made residents of Kalibo, like their Bishop in 2000, Monsignor Reyes, consider such transgendering an expression of genuine religious faith. These two elements, which put in motion *Tay* Augus' *panaad*, propelled the local Roman Catholic Church to include him as a defining feature of its Santo Niño festival. *Tay* Augus literally changed the face of the festival and through his *panaad* opened some more the door for transvestism to be part of the Ati-atihan celebration.[21]

21   In spite of the fact that there were other festival participants who transgendered themselves, to my knowledge and according to the Kalibonhons I interviewed for this project, it was only *Tay* Augus who had received the kind of institutional support from the Roman Catholic Church of Kalibo.

One can begin to discern the elements of transformation and temporality in *Tay* Augus' *panaad* from observing Benjie's hands in recreating section by section what seemed to be an already familiar image. By not once hesitating in putting on make-up, not even in the delicate part of marking the eyelids with black eyeliner, it was visibly clear that this was not the first time he was hired to transform *Tay* Augus' face. Benjie had been doing *Tay* Augus' make-up for the past five years, not at his nearby beauty parlor, but always at *Tay* Augus' house, a service requiring extra remuneration which *Tay* Augus and his family did not mind paying. On the third Sunday of January 2000 *Tay* Augus had once more feminized himself through the play of light and dark shadows. His transformed, foreign look recalled yet another imported image from the past and a distant place.

Tay Augus' face and entire body, which was minimally covered by a shimmering bustier and a thong, were a conglomeration of historical and popular images—emanating first from nineteenth-century Bohemian Paris, transported then to the various elsewhere of the Ice Follies skating world, imported next to Manila's Araneta Coliseum via Ice Capades productions, and brought finally by *Tay* Augus to the local streets of Kalibo.[22] Although it cost *Tay* Augus discomfort and trouble to achieve such an overly female look, transgendering himself was necessary to have a dramatic presence in the Ati-atihan. It was also critical in illustrating how sincere he was in keeping the *panaad* he had made 20 years earlier, and for the Ati-atihan and Kalibo Catholic community which had given his *panaad* confirmation.

Tay Augus therefore decided to continue with the make-up process even after he had shed tears from such an unnatural act as having his eyes contoured with black eyeliner. In comparison to the many blessings he had received from the Santo Niño and to the unspeakable sacrifice Jesus Christ had gone through for the sins of mankind, the amount of bodily sacrifice he put into his transgendering, *Tay* Augus explained, was negligible.

22   One of the earliest productions staged by and in the Araneta Coliseum was the Ice Capades extravaganza performed by visiting Ice Follies dancers, who came to Manila in the early 1960s. *Tay* Augus was sent by his parents to Manila in the late 1930s to pursue a bachelor's degree in physical education, but decided to stay to train in ballet and teach physical education at public high schools. He regularly watched these imported productions and recalled how he would save all his earnings as a teacher and ballet dancer for season tickets to Araneta's Ice Capades. In the 1960s *Tay* Augus would take a leave from his work in Manila to go home to Kalibo, where he used such influences in the development of his street dance performance for the Ati-atihan festival.

The holy statues, more than a dozen of them placed on several wooden platforms tiered on his bedroom wall, were constant reminders of those stories of magnanimity. *Tay* Augus was thanking them, particularly the Santo Niño. As any devout Catholic in Kalibo understands, he was also redeeming himself from his sins. And maybe if he danced hard enough and deadened all the discomfort caused by his act of mimicry, he could also ask forgiveness for the transgressions of his neighbors.

Outside Ati-atihan, *Tay* Augus was also known to have had another *panaad* during *Semana Santa* or Holy Week, when he would process his family's life-size image of Mary Magdalene around the streets of Kalibo (see Figure 1). However, his *panaad* was more dramatic during Ati-atihan when his transgendered and later on his dancing body, which he turned into a whitened body, became the very vessel of his *panaad*. He himself had to corporeally transform into a feminized "woman," a Caucasian Other. Such exaggerated transgendering was a *panaad* that gave him necessary pain and joy. For *Tay* Augus these two elements caused the Santo Niño

Figure 1 *Tay* Augus in front of the carriage of Mary Magdalene (*caro ni Santa Maria Magdalena*) during the 2001 Semana Santa in Kalibo, Aklan. Photo courtesy of Patrick Alcedo.

to beam down upon his *panaad* with great delight and amusement. *Tay* Augus found satisfaction in that pain, a paradox which ran throughout his transgendered performance in thanking the Santo Niño for giving him a healthy body to street dance year after year in His honor.

Tay Augus' transformation into a Folies Bergère chorus girl reminded festival participants in the Ati-atihan 2000 of the full extent to which an individual would go in order to fulfill a *panaad*. His gender transformation corporealised the *panaad* of a devotee grateful to the Santo Niño for saving his life and, akin to Mary Magdalene, of a sinner in search and in need of forgiveness. As a Roman Catholic, *Tay* Augus believed that he was doubly a sinner: as a human being with an original sin, which he inherited from Adam and Eve, and as an *agi*, who found himself outside the Church's heterosexual fold. *Tay* Augus moved away from the practice of procreation and therefore became an 'unnatural' member of the Church. I read the *panaad* he observed throughout the year as devout acts of faith of an individual fervently coming to terms with a sin he was born with by virtue of being a Roman Catholic, and of another sin committed by his sexual orientation. According to Roman Catholic doctrine, sin severs one's relationship with the Lord, and it is by doing acts of penance that an individual is once again welcomed to His fold. *Tay* Augus and the members of Kalibo's Catholic Church fulfilled these acts of penance through their local *panaad* practices.

During Ati-atihan *Tay* Augus became a kind of Mary Magdalene. As he would explain, 'We are all sinners, and the Lord knows how to forgive if we submit ourselves to Him.' Even if he did not explicitly express it, his *panaad*, which for him gave joy to the Santo Niño, was his way of negotiating his sexual difference with the Lord Jesus Christ through the young, mischievous Santo Niño. This is a type of gender that is clearly outside the moral rubric of the Roman Catholic Church. Yet, as demonstrated by *Tay* Augus, being an *agi* could be inside the Lord's grace if one professes faith as deeply as Mary Magdalene and becomes consistent with one's *panaad*. The *panaad*, the local practice of Roman Catholicism in Kalibo, and the original sin he shared with the rest of the Roman Catholic world, made it possible for *Tay* Augus to street-dance as an *agi* during the Ati-atihan festival.

Sacred camp: Dressing-up for the Santo Niño

Tay Augus stands up and after a quick search finds his wig lying on a tiny dresser. Facing the cabinet mirror, close to fading photos of the Virgin

Mary and the crucified Christ, he stretches the wig's elastic sides, and fits it all the way to the nape of his neck. Benjie combs *Tay* Augus' front bangs, brushes the side away from his made-up face, and then smoothens the hairs that are out of place. Once again, an immaculate bouffant has been created. *Tay* Augus gives himself a quick smile in the tiny mirror that ends in tiny crows' feet forming between his temple and his eyes. He sits down on his bed, ready for the next part of the dressing-up process.

Ambo takes over. He begins by getting the panty hose *Tay* Augus has worn the past two days. To fit it on *Tay* Augus' right foot, he sits on the hardwood floor. Patiently, he slowly pulls up the translucent pair of stockings. He is careful not to pull it with his nails or else it will ruin the stretchable material. When Ambo successfully fits the stockings up both knees, *Tay* Augus stands up and pulls it all the way up his waist. He then moves over to the piano bench, and from a yellow plastic bag hands the purple bustier he will premier that day to Ambo. Although it is as fully studded with beads and sequins as last year's green bustier, the new purple bustier has its own unique character. Its breast cups do not have the usual curvy, circular look; they follow the kind of rugged edge one finds from a seashell. The breast cups themselves are filled with much glitter, as they are covered with hundreds of diamond- looking beads atop violet sequins. It is easy for Ambo to help *Tay* Augus put on the new purple bustier. Street dancing for the last two days under the sun in last year's green bustier has left round white marks around his breasts and vertical lines on his shoulder top. That sun burnt outline on his torso guides Ambo as he fits the purple bustier on *Tay* Augus, who does not grimace with pain in spite of the contact on his sun-burnt skin.

Tay Augus then takes his thong out from the yellow bag. The thong is the same color as the bustier, made of spandex material and elaborated with strings of beads; it has formed into a knotted ball. Ambo spreads it first and disentangles its beads before fitting it to *Tay* Augus. When Ambo has connected the hooks to hug the sides of *Tay* Augus' waist, the strings of beads cascading from the thong's lower section repeat the breast cups' wavy appearance. Ambo proceeds by retrieving *Tay* Augus' tutu from the wooden closet in front of the wall crowding with holy images. The tutu is made of neon pink boas and imported ostrich feathers his niece bought for him as "eukas" (gifts) when she returned from Chicago the year before. It is not a ballerina's tutu made of tulle; it is not stiff and does not flare out to the sides. Instead it is as limp and droopy as the feathers of a peacock when it does not want to attract its opposite sex. Ambo takes out a safety pin to attach the two sides of the soft feathers.

With Ambo still at his side, *Tay* Augus crowns himself with an almost meter high head- dress of neon pink feather plumes. Affixed to a bejeweled tiara, the plumes arise from it like fountains of pink lights caught in a swirling motion. Once the unwieldy headdress steadies, Ambo sticks three of the same kind of imported plumes on his lower back to represent tails. They fan out as if those of a peacock at the height of its sexual invitation.

Tay Augus steps forward a little and slips into his pink high-heeled sandals with fake purple rhinestones fastened on their outer covering. The rubber sandals are of a lighter shade of pink in comparison to the bright pink plumes and ostrich feather boas. The plumes projecting from his headdress and lower back, and the high-heeled sandals make *Tay* Augus appear much taller. His presence requires space and invites more attention. All of a sudden, this wisp of a man is transformed into a statuesque, larger-than-life Folies Bergère chorus girl.

From a medicine cabinet, *Tay* Augus locates the perfume his nieces from the US gave him, and sprays it generously behind his earlobes and brand new cleavage. *Tay* Augus is to capture the Ati-atihan crowd, which is now growing in the street in front of his house. The local residents of Kalibo especially await his entrance. Similar to last year and the years before that, they are there to cheer for *Tay* Augus. At around nine o'clock, at the time when High Mass will have started at the plaza, they will join his group. *Tay* Augus and his family annually organize this group around his coming out simultaneously as a faithful Santo Niño devotee, and as a flamboyantly transformed Roman Catholic Folies Bergère chorus girl.

The above vignette portrays through the vesting of the different parts of costume on *Tay* Augus' body the second web of signification, which could be called "sacred camp" (see Figure 2). Following Jonathan Z. Smith, the "sacred" is commonly understood to be something that belongs to a special dimension.[23] Religious persons believe it to be imbued with power to transform people's lives. The sacred, Smith argues, however, only comes into being because of the concentrated attention a community gives to it. It is the community's effort that places the sacred at the core of

23   Jonathan Z. Smith, *Imagining Religion: From Babylon to Jonestown* (Chicago: University of Chicago Press, 1982), 55.

Figure 2 *Tay* Augus in the middle of his dance of *cha-cha-cha*, and leading his group in Ati-atihan 2000. Photo courtesy of Eli Africa.

its ritual practices, brings on it sacrality, and, as a result, makes it possess a transcendent quality. Effectively evoked by Susan Sontag, "camp" is an exaggerated play on form, a special kind of ludic behavior, replete with innocence and unintentionality; it is enacted with tender feelings but always with pathetic and theatrical seriousness.[24] Combining these two words, the latter referring to something secular and the former religious, captures the paradox in *Tay* Augus' Ati-atihan participation. For *Tay* Augus, and some members of the Kalibo Catholic community, his transgendering, a profane act in the eyes of the Manila-mandated Roman Catholic Church, was a serious expression of devotion to the playful Santo Niño. *Tay* Augus believed that the only way for him to be sacred was to annually invest energy on using his body as an instrument in becoming a "woman." To speak therefore of sacred camp, as it was performed by *Tay* Augus, is to consider the sum of these paradoxes, and to pay attention to both words as discrete yet related entities.

Through his *panaad* to the Santo Niño, *Tay* Augus together with his community underscored the sacred in his street dancing; neither the Holy Child nor the Roman Catholic Church bestowed sacrality on his performance. Together with the *panaad* during the *Semana Santa*, and the strong bond he had with Kalibo's Catholic Church, it was his Ati-atihan *panaad*

24   Sontag, "Notes on Camp."

which made things sacred. *Tay* Augus energized the omniscience of the Santo Niño and constantly demonstrated that he had to submit to this Supreme Being whom he believed had control over his life. As Smith has observed, nothing is innately sacred, "things are only sacred in relation... These are not substantive categories, but rather situational or relational categories. The ordinary (which remains to the observer's eye, wholly ordinary) becomes significant, becomes sacred, simply by *being there*. It becomes sacred by having our attention directed to it in a special way."[25] In the observer's eye, the people who only see *Tay* Augus inside the Ati-atihan carnival context, his performance may be viewed as that of the "ordinary," one that belonged solely to the festival domain and not the world of the gods and the deities. But for those who knew him well outside the Ati-atihan festival, and were constant witnesses and even partners to his *panaad*, his transgendering was a sacred act of faith. In the end it was *Tay* Augus' devotion to the Santo Niño that convinced the local Church to take his transgendering as a religious offering.

In the words of *Tay* Augus, "it's because it's a religious promise and prayer, and not an act of flirtation." Framing his being a "woman" as an act of prayer negated the profane, as in flirtation, in his performance. *Tay* Augus actively weeded out the elements, which for him were not for the Santo Niño, and only retained those which would delight Him: the doubleness and ambivalence of the performance. It was the choices *Tay* Augus made and the way he harnessed his energy for the Santo Niño that gave religious weight to his transgendering, a gender bending which would otherwise be considered sacrilegious outside the *panaad* context. This sense of the sacred was what finally held together *Tay* Augus' transgendering performance as an expression of his Catholic faith in a mode characterized by Sontag's camp.

Tay Augus openly admitted he was an *agi*. Yet, he also claimed that, "I am not like the other *agi*, since what I am doing is for the Santo Niño." His sacred devotion to the Santo Niño was what set his performance apart from the other *agi* who also dressed up as "women," and who street danced not to stage femininity but to be flirtatious with men. *Tay* Augus took the Holy Child Jesus as a protector of his transgendering, his own couturier if you will, who gave him permission to annually vest the set of bustier and thong in order for him to be more feminine than the "original" chorus girls he saw in Manila in the 1960s. In the sacred lay

25   Jonathan Z. Smith, "The Bare Facts of Ritual," *History of Religions* 20 (August–November 1980): 55. Emphasis in the original.

the possibility of being in the same space and time with the Santo Niño, and with the common public who were devotees as well. Contextualizing his transgendering in that special realm was to suffuse his dressing-up with sacred meanings, and to make his body imitate corporealities, which, even if they were of and from the quotidian, were sensitive to the ways of the sacred. *Tay* Augus, who in relation to his other *panaad*, equating his transgendering through and through with an act of religious faith, was ultimately the person responsible for making his *panaad* the pivot upon which the sacred in his transgendering turned.

Performative double sense

Tay Augus' mimicry worked in two directions. Borrowing Sontag's instructive term, it was this "double sense," which in this case refers to his everyday, female body, which made *Tay* Augus' performance campy as well. He wanted to become a woman, while turning his male, brown body after the image of the white bodies imported from different corners of the figure skating world to perform in such centers of culture as Quezon City and Manila. *Tay* Augus was already 80 years old, when I became witness to and participant in this performance in question. Nonetheless, the amount of foundation and make-up, and the way he wanted his costume tightened to hug his body pointed to his desire to remain youthful and white. At that moment he denied the rust of time, which left wrinkles on his face and sag on his body, corporeal marks no amount of make up and costume could cover. In spite of the make-over of *Tay* Augus, the effort he exerted to become feminine and young, the public, the local Kalibonhons and visitors from out of town, either identified him as *Tay* Augus in his usual Ati-atihan attire, or as an old man masquerading as a nubile "woman."

Tay Augus understood the necessity of going back to his quotidian self after the festival, and of performing only within the festival's immediacy and carnival frame. His transgendering was not to bleed over to the everyday, or else it would elicit pathos, place him in the land of absurdity, and turn itself into a tragedy which would bring shame to him and his family. While his theatrical performance delighted the public, and in the mind of *Tay* Augus and others, the Santo Niño as well, it also gave them a sense of *tristesse*. In *Tay* Augus' case, the public could read his performance as campy, as Janus- faced, with his other face intensely focused on becoming a "woman" for a few days, and the other left with no choice but to accept the inevitability of going back to his old self. They were either torn between relishing or feeling pity for his transgendering's artificiality, an embodied doubleness, which pushed his performance and *panaad* from the onset. *Tay* Augus was distantly exotic and yet utterly familiar, a festival veteran rife with passion in both praising the Santo Niño and staging the "unnatural" act of annually mimicking Folies Bergère chorus girls.

What made *Tay* Augus' performance additionally campy was not only this double sense, but also the innocence strewn across his performance. *Tay* Augus never talked about his performance as being campy, a silence and naiveté that made his street dancing truly as one. As Sontag wrote, "To talk about camp is to betray it." Hence the reading and utterance of camp should be left in the eyes and mouth of the public and not of *Tay* Augus. Although "camp" is a Western idea that evokes all sorts of signifiers, its playful and excessive quality is found in the Akeanon word, *agi*.[26]

Tay Augus reminisced gleefully how, when he first came out in his overly feminized attire, the public literally went berserk: "They all ran up to me in such a frenzied fashion for a photo shoot. I was completely taken by surprise. I could no longer move." He could not forget the white guy, a kano, an "American," *Tay* Augus surmised, who followed him around town taking photos from different angles: "I would see him every year from then on, maybe he was also gay."[27] *Tay* Augus further narrated in Akeanon, "But

---

26   Sontag, "Notes on Camp." In order to arrive to some kind of understanding of "camp" in the world of Akeanon language, another word which could bring out a "campy" feeling or taste is *baduy* (male) or *baday* (female), meaning unfashionable or out of date. Although *baduy* or *baday* has the quality of excess and absence of self-election (actors not intending to be tacky), its negative connotations make it "camp's" partial equivalent. "Camp's" playful quality always places it in a neutral, innocent mode. Indeed "camp" is non-Akeanon, an outsider's concept used in my reading of *Tay* Augus' transgendering. However, "camp's" playful and tender sentiments and affects do exist, still in multiple forms in both the Akeanon language and *Tay* Augus' performance. If I had said to *Tay* Augus for instance that his performance was campy, most probably he would not have understood it, as it was a concept foreign to him. Such epistemological distance, however, does not mean that camp did not exist in *Tay* Augus' transgendering and street dancing.

27   Although *Tay* Augus recounted this incident in Akeanon, he deliberately used the English word "gay." The lexical insertion of the word "gay" demonstrates that such a terminology and its accompanying concept (of a gay individual desiring another gay man) is for *Tay* Augus exclusively applied to American, Caucasian foreigners and not to locals like himself, who self-identified as *agi*. My understanding of *agi* here, and as supported by my ethnographic research and local experience is markedly different from the Tagalog word *bakla*; Fenella Cannel, "The Power of Appearances: Beauty, Mimicry and Transformation," in *Discrepant Histories: Translocal Essays on Filipino Culture*, ed. Vicente L. Rafael (Manila: Anvil Publishing, 1995), 223–58; Cannel "Beauty and the Idea

he never even once introduced himself though. Maybe he was the one responsible for having my photos printed in international travel brochures."

Tay Augus was unaware that it was the campiness of his image which caught the attention of the international media and brought joy to the public. When I was growing up in Kalibo, my mother would bring my siblings and me to the plaza to participate in the Ati-atihan, and *Tay* Augus' promenade and street dance in his "new," "foreign" self would always climax that experience for us. In 2000, after having been educated in Manila and the United States, but still a Santo Niño devotee, I read his performance as campy and sacred at once. For the Kalibo Catholic Church, specifically for the priests who knew *Tay* Augus and were aware of his deep loyalty to the Santo Niño, his transgendered performance was simply read as a sacred devotion. The complexity and multilayeredness of the performance engendered several readings, and one of them is what I offer: sacred camp.

Tay Augus, however, thought the festival participants were attracted to his being markedly different—his transgendering, the comic relief and the carnivalesque atmosphere he provided. Innocence here manifested itself in several ways: his attraction to the Folies Bergère chorus girls was spurred by their foreignness and professionalism, and not by the possibility of camp; and his transgendering was not staged to be campy but to negotiate his being an *agi* and ultimately to reinforce his *panaad*. Given that his gender transformation was committed in the name of his *panaad*, he made sure that he would be more beautiful than the original ice dancers, more sparkling in speckles on the face and costume. He unintentionally corporealised a campy image due to his commitment to his *panaad*, exaggerating every opportunity to be an overly graceful "woman." Even the sweet scent of his imported perfume set him apart from the stench and musk of others' sweating, dancing bodies. To the ongoing music he threw his aging body, an obvious physical limitation not shared by the

of America," in *Power and Intimacy in the Christian Philippines* (Cambridge: Cambridge University Press, 1999), 203–26; Neil Garcia, *Philippine Gay Culture: The Last 30 Years* (Diliman: University of the Philippines Press, 1996); Mark Johnson, *Beauty and Power: Transgendering and Cultural Transformation in the Southern Philippines* (New York: Berg, 1997); Martin F. Manalansan IV, "Speaking of AIDS: Language and the Filipino 'Gay' Experience in America," in *Discrepant Histories*, ed. Vicente L. Rafael, 193–222; Manalansan, *Global Divas: Filipino Gay Men in the Diaspora* (Durham: Duke University Press, 2003); Michael L. Tan, "From *Bakla* to Gay: Shifting Gender Identities and Sexual Behaviors in the Philippines," in *Conceiving Sexuality: Approaches to Sex Research in a Postmodern World*, ed. Richard G. Parker and John H. Gagnon (London: Routledge, 1995), 85–96.

nubile, visiting ice dancers. He swished his tutu-covered hips, and grooved his foundation-layered torso, unmindful of the tropical country's funereal humidity and heat. As a professional performer, *Tay* Augus danced from the beginning to the end of the parade, which he referred to as *prusisyon* (procession) and not *parada* (parade), a lexical choice indicative of his understanding of Ati-atihan participation as a religious procession of *panaad*, similar to the *Semana Santa*, and not exactly synonymous to a secular parade.

The public would be enraptured by his costume, campiness and demonstration of Santo Niño devotion, a sensibility made distinctly peculiar by the excessive image he was projecting and his indefatigable movements. Through the laughter, professionalism, and the outlandish femininity he worked hard to produce, *Tay* Augus believed that the Holy Child would find it in His mischievous Self to be forgiving of his being an *agi*, and once again accepting of his dance of thanks. The public, especially those who were Santo Niño devotees themselves, was aware of that mischief. *Tay* Augus, who knew about the public's awareness, was certain that his becoming this kind of "woman," a delightfully strange being, who desired youthfulness, titillated the Santo Niño. The seriousness and yet innocent play of his sacred devotion, which he staged year after year, qualified his transgendering to belong to the world of camp. By inputting the sacred in his performance, *Tay* Augus, quoting Sontag, made a "good taste of a bad taste." The "good" here paradigmatically substituted by what was sacred, serious in his devotion, and innocent in his act of playful mimicry; and the "bad" by a sexual profane act whose ultimate goal is to *linandi*, to flirt, and not to praise the Santo Niño.

The Santo Niño image

The very image of the Santo Niño mirrors many of *Tay* Augus' campy qualities. As understood in the Kalibo and other Filipino communities, the Santo Niño Himself is campy, in that He embodies Sontag's "double sense" (see Figure 3).[28] Sally Ann Ness in her ethnography of Cebu's

28   There are numerous icons of and devotional practices around the Santo Niño in the Philippines, a plurality which engenders cultural and religious meanings specific to their locales. For instance, in Cebu, devotion to the Santo Niño is manifested in the dance of *sinulog*, which in itself is heterogeneous, and is performed either as a ritual of a candle seller, a street-dancing parade, or a dance-drama, re-enacting a battle between Christians and Muslims. In Ibajay, west of Aklan, devotees venerate the Santo Niño with the same kind of dance-drama called *sayaw*, but their street parade is made unique by their carrying bamboo poles strapped with agricultural and sea products (such as chicken, crabs

Figure 3 The image of the Santo Niño, processed around the town of Kalibo during the Ati-atihan festival of 2001. Photo courtesy of Patrick Alcedo.

Sinulog, a Visayan festival, which pivots as well around the Santo Niño's sacrality, describes the Santo Niño as a "Boy-King."[29] This description of the Santo Niño is consistent with religious stories one hears most often from priests, parishioners and old ladies, who are tasked to clean and decorate His altar every morning with flowers. The Santo Niño is a mischievous boy, who at night secretly steps down from the altar to play. In the morning, the ladies sometimes find *amorsiko* grass, sticking to His robes–proof that He once again had been out in the field. They lightly scold Him and beg Him not to go out again, out of fear that He might not find His way back home to the Cathedral.

and fish) as offerings to the Holy Child. In Tacloban, in Eastern Visayas, a fluvial parade is annually organized to honor the Santo Niño, who the Warays believe helped them in keeping at bay the cholera epidemic of June 1889. In Pakil, Laguna, on the island of Luzon, Tagalog children gently throw petals to the Santo Niño, who is lying on a manger, to ask Him to ward off diseases. Moreover, the Santo Niño statue may appear as dark-skinned as the Negritos, and is dressed up by His owners and communities according to their profession or occupation and by communities to their local history. Thus there are Santo Niños who look like a conquistador, a policeman, a medical doctor, a farmer or a fisherman; Florendo, ed., *Santo Niño*.

29   Ness, *Body, Movement, and Culture*, 58–85.

Yet, the Santo Niño is also a King endowed with the power to answer a myriad of petitions, such as the one asked by a couple who had been childless for a number of years. A husband and his barren wife danced for three days straight in the Ati-atihan, and a year later were blessed with a child. In honor of the Santo Niño, they named their child Niño, and from then on would bring the little boy to Kalibo for the Ati-atihan. When Niño became a toddler, he was placed on top of his father's shoulders and paraded around town as if he was their family's Santo Niño. This is a ritual that children in Kalibo publicly perform with their own fathers during Ati-atihan. As a King, the Santo Niño punishes parishioners who are not remorseful for their sins, and not observant of their religious obligations as Roman Catholics. Their prayers are not heard and they live a dry and bare life. Father Alex Meñez, the priest in charge of my catechism class, would punctuate his Sunday lessons with these kinds of stories and understandings. After class, my grade school classmates and I would genuflect before the Santo Niño's altar with mixed feelings; on the one hand, with delight that He is a young child like us, yet on the other hand, with trepidation that He is powerful enough to chastise us for our misdemeanors.

Father Meñez later explained that the Santo Niño "is innocent, since he is still a child." Thus, Father Meñez reasoned, the Santo Niño is unaware of his sexuality. Given His age and the psychosexual stage He is in, the Santo Niño is asexual, and is therefore able to traverse all at once the worlds of femininity and masculinity. He is only a toddler, and to embody both gender behaviors is expected and considered not only to be innocuous but playful too. In fact, Father Meñez enjoined, if you look at His features, garments, and paraphernalia, double gendering is evident. The Santo Niño has bloomers for his underwear and always wears a red robe, flowing as if caught in mid air, studded with precious and semi-precious stones, outlining His tiny body–vestments, which for Father Meñez are signs of femininity. His gold scepter and crown, and kneecap red boots, however, point to His masculine side. The soft smile, tender facial features, and the long, curly hair, which the old ladies lovingly brush and set prior to an important occasion, make the Santo Niño all the more a transitional figure torn between being a boy and a girl.[30]

Furthermore, the Santo Niño is fond of being dressed up, rather excessively and in different guises at that. One of the rituals during Ati-atihan

30   For an analogous reading of religious figures traversing the boundaries of the feminine and the masculine through vesting of garments, see Marjorie Garber, *Vested Interests: Cross-dressing and Cultural Anxiety* (New York: Routledge, 1992), 210–33.

is either the repair of His old clothes, or giving Him an entirely new set of clothes. Assisted usually by that select group of female parishioners mentioned earlier, the Kalibo Catholic Church every Ati-atihan makes certain the Santo Niño is "presentable" to the public. After removing dirt and soot from the face of the Santo Niño, His red robe is dusted off; if it looks faded and old a new one will be vested on Him. The ladies will complete and even augment the stones on His robes; will whiten and adorn with white lace His undergarments; and will deeply polish His crown, the globe on His left hand, and the scepter on the right hand until they glisten. The Santo Niño will be paraded amidst His devotees in this beautified, immaculately sparkling state, and in His double gendered Self.

Tay Augus in his transgendered self all at once embodied both the sacred and the camp. He was a Catholic of solid faith in the Santo Niño, a local devotee who promised 20 years ago that as long as he could street dance he would continually maintain sensibility toward the foreign image of the Folies Bergère chorus girls. He performed this transgendered self at a time when Kalibo's Roman Catholic Church annually reminds its parishioners to strengthen their devotion to the Santo Niño. It was also a time when the local church allowed them to enter into transgenderism, a gender transformation which otherwise would be deemed transgressive outside the carnivalesque context of Ati-atihan, and, most probably, would even be condemned by the Roman Catholic Church of Manila. By placing in the foreground a unique kind of femaleness in honor of the Santo Niño, and recreating this femaleness year after year within the first web signification of *panaad*, *Tay* Augus vested in an image which was in the realm of the sacred camp. He dressed up in excess and deadened the discomfort that came with his performance–the excessive trouble needed to become a foreign female other.

Tay Augus gathered his resources from both the local (such as the services of Benjie and Ambo, and the skills of the seamstress who patiently beaded his costume) and the global (the US dollars and feather boas from his relatives in Chicago and San Diego) to take on an overly 'female' persona. In his transforming into a chorus girl, *Tay* Augus chose to publicly out himself as an *agi* at the Ati-atihan, where it is the norm for festival participants to extraordinarily dress themselves up to earn religious merit from the Santo Niño. Vesting on a sacred and ludic self was *Tay* Augus' strategic response to fulfilling that religious expectation, but in a manner that was in keeping with his being an *agi*. His exaggerated femininity was of paramount importance to him, as he believed that dressing-up his *panaad* with such fey sensibility brought a tender smile to, and blessings from, the Santo Niño.

As illustrated by *Tay* Augus' dressing-up process, sacred camp follows coinciding designs. While it was colored by his sense of gratitude and loyalty to the Santo Niño, it was also adorned by his transgendering and propensity towards the camp. Similar to the make-up process described earlier and to the actual street dancing he did later, *Tay* Augus' appearance publicly presented a "third sex" capable of deep religious faith. Even though the practice of "third sex" is precolonial, a carry over of an old pattern of gender and sexuality, which is shared by the rest of the Philippines and Southeast Asian countries, *Tay* Augus's brand of "third sex" as vested by sacred camp garbed him into a category entirely of his own making.[31] Both "third sex" and sacred camp enabled him to transform into a transgendered man, who mischievously and yet seriously straddled homosexual camp and Roman Catholic religiosity.

It was the combination of the sacred and the profane, the ambivalence of these designs that set in motion *Tay* Augus' religious faith and transgendering in the religious and carnivalesque world of the Ati-atihan (see Figure 4). In the end, transgendering into a chorus girl in the name of the Santo Niño was his act of restitution for his inability to create his own family, to be part of the Roman Catholic Church's call for procreation. It was an exuberant *panaad*, which could only be fulfilled by his being sacred and playfully campy about it at the same time: an excessive, joyful,

---

31   For discussion of the "third sex" as a continuation of an older pattern in Philippine culture, and as it was encountered during the Spanish colonization in the early part of the sixteenth century, see Carolyn Brewer, "Baylan, Asog, Transvestism, and Sodomy: Gender, Sexuality and the Sacred in Early Colonial Philippines," *Intersections*, no. 2 (May 1999), http://wwwsshe.murdoch.edu.au/intersections/issue2/carolyn2.html. For examining the "third sex" against the grain of other Southeast Asian communities, see among others Leonard Y. Andaya, "The *Bissu*: Study of a Third Gender in Indonesia," in *Other Pasts: Women, Gender and History in Early Modern Southeast Asia*, ed. Barbara Watson Andaya (Honolulu: Center for Southeast Asian Studies University of Hawaii at Manoa, 2000), 27–46; Richard Totman, *The Third Sex: Kathoey–Thailand's Ladyboys* (Chiang Mai: Silkworm Books, 2003); and Megan Sinnott, *Toms and Dees: Transgender Identity and Female Same-sex Relationships in Thailand* (Honolulu: University of Hawaii Press, 2004). My reading of the *agi* as an alternative gender is inspired by Walter L. Williams, *The Spirit and the Flesh: Sexual Diversity in American Indian Culture* (Boston: Beacon Press, 1986); my understanding of gender as performance is informed by Judith Butler, *Gender Trouble: Feminism and the Subversion of Identity* (London: Routledge, 1990).

Figure 4 *Tay* Augus inside Kalibo's St. John the Baptist Cathedral, showing his respect to the Santo Niño, whose statue crowns the altar, at the end of the Ati-atihan 2000. Photo courtesy of Patrick Alcedo.

though at times painful embodiment of faith. The transgendering of faith of *Tay* Augus and the sacrifices and fun which came with it earned him forgiveness for being an *agi*, and by virtue of his being Roman Catholic for the original sin passed on to him by Adam and Eve, who God forever banished from Paradise after eating the forbidden fruit. As demonstrated by his *panaad* and innocent corporealization of camp, *Tay* Augus believed that his annual transgendering ultimately resulted in pleasing the mischievous and yet powerful Holy Child, the Santo Niño.

Conclusion

Father Meñez, the Catechist teacher mentioned earlier, recalled in a 2005 interview in Los Angeles, California that one of his most poignant memories of Ati-atihan is hinged on *Tay* Augus' participation in the early 1980s.

> Before the start of the Sunday procession, before dusk would set in, people in Kalibo—those, who were the *minatuod*, "real" residents [the ones who have always lived around the plaza; most of them neighbors of *Tay* Augus]—would gather in front of the Cathedral. Older ladies, who like *Tay* Augus were regular churchgoers, and some priests would always look for him. Where's Augus; is he here now? If he was not yet around, the bells would not be rung, thus the procession would not start. Every time

he would arrive in his usual Folies Bergère attire, with his whole retinue trailing behind him, these Catholic ladies together with the priests would heave a sigh of relief, and clap admiringly realizing how much he once again spent dressing-up himself. Thank God, he's here now! They would wave their hands to the belfry, commanding the boys up there to now ring the bells. The procession would then start moving forward, with the drums and the xylophones climbing to a steady crescendo.

Born and raised in Kalibo, and therefore one of those "real" residents, Father Meñez said that what made Kalibo's Roman Catholic community support *Tay* Augus' transgendering was the courage and enduring sacrality his transgendered body put into action. In a way, Father Meñez noticed that each time *Tay* Augus became a chorus girl to fulfill his *panaad*, he was saying to the public, "I am all of you." In every family in Kalibo, there is always a son who is an *agi*, or a daughter who is a *tomboy* (lesbian). But families have to be silent about these family members, since they could cause embarrassment and shame when the 'unnaturalness' of their sexuality is publicly known.

Father Meñez was aware that unlike those families *Tay* Augus' family had always been supportive of his "outing" during the Ati-atihan, with his nieces and nephews sending him pieces of his costume from the United States, and his immediate relatives in Kalibo financially contributing to the hiring of the band and food preparation. Every piece of glitter, feather boas and stroke of make-up on *Tay* Augus' body represented an *agi* or a *tomboy* in that circle around the plaza where he spent most of his ordinary and extraordinary life. And every mischief in his dressing-up process and later on his street dancing resonated back to the stories shared inside and outside the Cathedral about how naughty Santo Niño is, and how pleased He becomes when devotees do a "cartwheel" of themselves. Because of *Tay* Augus' transgendering and of what his transgendered body synecdochically signified, other families did not feel the need to go public with their "unnaturalness." In so many ways, this is the reason why *Tay* Augus' transgendering was considered by Kalibonhons to be an exemplary *panaad*. As Father Meñez starkly put it, "During Ati-atihan, *Tay* Augus flaunted his sexual orientation. Kalibo accepted him, and the Church did not say anything against him, because what he did was truly an expression of faith."

Where *Tay* Augus annually changed the colors of his costume, for instance, from predominantly green in 1999 to a saturated pink in 2000, he dressed up consistently following the iconographic image of a Folies Bergère chorus girl. It was his loyalty to this imported image that made Kalibonhons recognize him still as *Tay* Augus, and exclaim, "Thank God, he's here now! The Santo Niño will once again be pleased." Moreover, it was his vesting of the same iconographic image which transformed his transgendering into a *panaad*, with his street performance annually mobilizing synonymous religious meanings. Because of the *panaad* in his transgendering, an act of faith recognized as such by those older ladies and priests, *Tay* Augus became a religious figure who carried the sins of others, a mimicry of Christ's martyrdom. The presence of his transgendered and, in my own reading, sacred campy Self constantly elicited exclamations thanking both God and the Santo Niño, who for Kalibo Catholics are two persons but of one God.

While *Tay* Augus was repenting for his own sins and his community's, he was also asking forgiveness for the "unnaturalness" of the sons and daughters of the Kalibo community. It was a sin he shared with his neighbors; he decided as well not to procreate in a way a "normal" human being should, a hetero-normative value as the Roman Catholic Church declares it in its theological doctrines: "I am an *agi* all right, but I have a sacred promise." From the point of view of *Tay* Augus, of the women who heard countless masses with him, and of the priests who conducted those masses for them, it was his *panaad* that made the Santo Niño look at his appeal for clemency with most favor. *Tay* Augus' extreme mimicry of chorus girls caused him bodily discomfort and cost his family its financial resources. It was an "unnatural" act that the carnivalesque element in the Ati-atihan made "natural," that allowed him to out his own homosexuality, and that enabled him to street dance his and his neighbors' non-normative sexuality and gender. Its campiness brought admiration and laughter to the public, but above all, as *Tay* Augus believed, a smile of mischief and forgiveness to the Santo Niño's tender if not feminine face.

Tay Augus' family made sure that his Ati-atihan *panaad* and performance would define his person even after his death in 2002, and would be the most lasting memory of the Kalibo community about him. When he passed away, his family decided to have an upbeat version of the song "Happy Days Are Here Again" played during the burial procession. This was also to fulfill the promise they made to *Tay* Augus that his death should not be mourned but rather celebrated. Since it was a wish of a dying person, his relatives clearly understood that it had to be granted. The family was able to hire the most coveted Army Band of the Western

Visayas. During that time the Regional Commander of the entire island of Panay was the cousin of the wife of *Tay* Augus' brother. Until the very end, *Tay* Augus embodied the concept of sacred camp, and by way of his authority and family influence allowed the public to embody that paradox at a time of the year when it was supposed to be non-carnival.

A happy refrain was made to partner a most sorrowful event. This unseemly combination produced campy bodies, ambivalent in expressing at once pain or joy. For the first time outside the Ati-atihan context, the carnival moved into the quotidian. *Tay* Augus removed it from Ati-atihan's festival frame to mark his final exit as a person, who because of his *panaad* to the Santo Niño and sexual orientation constantly had to move between the private and the public, the procession and the parade, the ritual and the carnival, and the sacred and the camp. For the last time, *Tay* Augus animated the mischief that the Santo Niño demonstrates in His oral hagiography. Since these narrative accounts are unwritten, unlike the biblical stories re-enacted during the *Semana Santa*, Kalibo Catholics are given the freedom to create them. Kalibonhons keep them alive whenever they share and hear stories about the harmless pranks their Santo Niño has committed, and whenever they themselves perform acts of mischief. *Tay* Augus' extraordinary burial procession and Ati-atihan participation are now part of that organic hagiography. Those sacred yet campy performances will accompany Kalibo Catholics and Ati-atihan participants in their walk down "memory lane" when they remember and decide to mimic *Tay* Augus' everyday and festival lives.

When *Tay* Augus' body reached the cemetery, and before it was entombed, the Army Band stopped playing to give way to a group of military officers in their honorary fusillade. Several shots pierced through the air in recognition of his being a veteran who helped the Americans fight the Japanese during World War II. People present that day, and who paid their last tribute by going to his wake, remembered how *Tay* Augus carried a soft smile, as if he was pleased with how he had lived his life on earth. The late Remedios Cesar, daughter of *Tay* Augus' older sister, described her uncle's life as "good for he had accomplished all the things he wanted." Before he passed away, *Tay* Augus' wish for the longest time had been granted: his application for a US tourist visa was approved. A few months before he died Remedios accompanied him to Chicago, where he visited the shop where his family had bought pieces of his costumes for years. *Tay* Augus was barely able to contain his joy, and decided to buy a set of black feather boas, and a dozen black ostrich feathers for the next year's headdress and tails. He said he had never had black as a motif in Ati-atihan, and he was going to surprise the public with that unlikely choice. A few weeks later, Rosalyn Depositar, sister of the late Remedios Cesar, accompanied *Tay* Augus to Las Vegas, so he could see the "real" Folies Bergère chorus girls.

For the people who really knew *Tay* Augus, the tolling of the church bells, the bands, the firing of the guns and the procession, were a salute to one of Santo Niño's greatest Ati-atihan street dancers, who created for Kalibo an alternative world, where its residents and festival participants could navigate their difference through mischief and the staging of "unnatural" acts. *Tay* Augus was but a strand in the multi-stranded world of Kalibo society. Yet what rings past the particulars of his life was his demonstration of how diverse individuals become in their need to be resilient, and how different they could be in spite of their being considered and wanting to be members of powerful institutions like the Roman Catholic Church.

The people around him that day, who after the reverberating gunshots were covered once again with the lilting tune of "Happy Days Are Here Again," remained in *Tay* Augus' debt for illustrating how it is important to corporealise contradictory premises in order to constantly interact with and negotiate Roman Catholicism and Filipino's institution of heterosexuality. *Tay* Augus wove the webs of signification of *panaad*, sacred camp and carnivalesque into one unforgettable fabric. He vested on and danced away with this fabric with such grace and mischief, giving way to a world where bodies could exist in other forms. For dancing the paradox of the sacred and the camp with such faith inside and outside the carnival context, and for having always prayed to the Santo Niño with a contrite heart, Father Meñez said, he is "certain the Santo Niño was smiling at *Tay* Augus at the entrance to Heaven."

Tay Augus will serve as a steady and graceful partner when Kalibonhons and the Ati-atihan participants decide to transgender their own Catholic faith and to dialogue performatively with their culture's homogeneity. They will have to ensure the sacredness of their *panaad* by transforming themselves through their own dramatic statements of corporeality, make-up, fabric, sequins, feathers and music. Like the remarkable *Tay* Augus of Kalibo, they can empower themselves once a year through sacred camp–the re-ritualisation of the non-quotidian and therefore the sublime. The Ati-atihan festival and their memory of *Tay* Augus teach observers how not to be hemmed in to society's polarization of the masculine and feminine, to momentarily turn off the old tapes of cultural conformity, and to modify and layer the choreography of their everyday lives, so they as Roman Catholics can perform extraordinarily and dance out their individual faith and identity.

The New People's Army (NPA) conducted the rites for same-sex marriage in February 2005. Ka Andres and Ka Jose exchanged their vows before their friends and comrades. Photography by Nico Alconaba, photo courtesy of Philippine Daily Inquirer, that blurred the facial images of Ka Andres and Ka Jose.

This essay was previously published in *Asia-Pacific Social Science Review* 11, no. 2 (2011): 27–42.

Brothers, Lovers, and Revolution: Negotiating Military Masculinity and Homosexual Identity in a Revolutionary Movement in the Philippines

Introduction

IN FEBRUARY 2005, the front page of *The Philippine Daily Inquirer* carried the article entitled "Reds officiate the first gay marriage in NPA" (Pinsoy 2005). It featured a photo of two men kissing with a sequined flag of the Communist Party of the Philippines (CCP) in the background. As a Maoist inspired guerrilla movement, the NPA has waged war against the Philippine government since 1969 under the leadership of the CPP. This piece has immediately piqued my curiosity as it has not only challenged the stereotype of being gay in Philippine Society, but more importantly, it has opened a new dimension of examining how the intersections of gender, sexuality, and militancy are expressed through competing articulations about the masculine/sexual Filipino revolutionary in the heteronormative imaginaries of Philippine Society.

In recent years, there has been an increasing interest in gender and violent conflict in feminist scholarship. However, most of the feminist theorizing on gender and sexuality in situations of war and "soldiering" focus on the problem of "gender inequality," in particular how to integrate women into the army as an attempt to address the issue of gender inequality in the military. Sexuality is often subsumed under gender, with emphasis on sexual exploitation of women within the militaries, or sexual violence against them, mostly focusing on war rape (Zarkov 2006). While undoubtedly important, these studies have largely marginalized the study of men, masculinity, and heteronormativity in feminist scholarship.

The relationship between gender and sexuality has been theoretically problematic for feminist and queer studies. While such studies are now clearly anything but monolithic, a lot of research has come to point out the interface between the two categories, particularly between gender and institutionalized heterosexuality/heteronormativity. Gender has been theorized in a number of ways. One stream addresses gender as a relational concept "built on the presumption of relations between biological males and biological females" (Ingraham 2006,). Another assumes of existence of only two sexes that are "fixed and stable categories," and yet another builds on the "oppositeness" of these categories (Ingraham 2006). In using the term here, I adhere to Joan Scott's (1986) formulation of gender rejecting "fixed and permanent quality of binary opposition" veering away from essentialist theses (40). Not only is gender a product of history which is socially constructed, it is also an organizing principle in society that operates at multiple levels, and a useful category of analysis (Scott 1986). This notion also applies to the analysis of the production of masculinities (Connell 2005). Moving beyond previous conceptions of masculinity in the singular form which primarily deals with power relations of men over women, current research on the field has shown the plurality of masculinities that exist in certain patterns of gender relations in a specific society (Connell 2005; Connell and Messerschmidt 2005) as well as the role of power in constructing ideal masculinities in specific settings. R. W. Connell's (2005) concept of "hegemonic masculinity," wherein one type of masculinity becomes a referent against which other forms are measured at a given times and place has become significant in organization studies, especially in studies of military institutions. Research employing the concept has contributed largely in documenting the consequences and costs of hegemony, uncovering its mechanisms and showing multiplicity of masculinities; and in replacing "categorical models of patriarchy" (Connell and Messerschmidt 2005, 834). While showing how production of masculinities are different cross-culturally, such studies have also shown the ways in which actors "negotiate certain roles and positions, the struggle to maintain continuity or introduce change, the frailty of established boundaries and differences" (Zarkov 2007, 152). In other words, the hegemonic position attained by a certain type of masculinity is never fixed and is always being contested, negotiated, and reconfigured.

Mainstream research on the military shows little interest in gender given that it is a highly gendered institution—governed largely by men who produce and recreate "norms and practices associated with masculinity and heterosexuality" (Kronsell 2005, 281). According to Jeff Hearn (2003), despite the common conception that militarism is tightly linked to what is considered "masculine," there is not a wealth of literature focusing on men, masculinities, and the military, and I would add, even less, if at all, on existing revolutionary armies (xiv). The notion of "military masculinity" seems to bind men's (as well as women's)[1] bodies to one uniform type of masculinity, and focuses more on "male-female axis of opposition" (Kovitz 2003, 10). There is a weakness in such an approach as it might not account for the fractures within "military masculinity" itself. These fractures are masked by a variety of methods employed by the institution; one of which is the ranking system wherein higher ranking officers embody the more "superior" kind of masculinity, thereby debunking the idea of "masculine unity" within the military institution (Kovitz 2003, 9).

In the Philippines, while studies on masculinities in relation to the Philippine military is particular are scant, a number of studies has examined the concept of strength—signifying physical power and military competence—as a core foundation of (hegemonic) masculinity in the army. Hazing, a harsh initiation ceremony that "welcomes" newcomers through harassment, humiliation, and physical abuse, is part of the rite of passage of cadets' transformation to becoming "real men" and true brothers-in-arms (McCoy 1999). Such constructions of military masculinities imply that the male soldier is a real man "inside and out," with heterosexuality as a mandatory requirement. While the Philippines is generally being perceived as "tolerant" of homosexuality as cross-dressing gay men in beauty parlors and in the entertainment industry abound, moral stigma and discrimination remain to be a major problem faced by homosexuals in the Philippines (Garcia 2004). Gay men, who are regarded as feminine and therefore as *not essentially* men, are in fact "discouraged" from entering the Philippine Military as they might not "fit in" with the norms of the military institution (Evangelista 2009). This understanding of the masculine soldier emphasizes the exemplary Filipino male who is strong, brave, alert, and decisive—in binary opposition to the notion of femininity in the Philippines, to which gayness is closely associated, is characterized by weakness, dependence, and the domination of emotion over reason (Israel-Sobritchea 1990).

This paper examines how male homosexuality[2] has come to be negotiated in the context of military masculinity in the New People's Army. I argue for a rethinking of essentialist views of gender and sexuality which fixates the two in rigid, permanent, and ahistorical categories (Ingraham 2006). Heterosexuality has been a taken-for-granted concept, normalized as an infallible standard for sexual relations, with gender embedded and

1   Masculinity is not necessarily attributed only to men.
2   While there are both male and female homosexuals in the NPA, I chose to limit the scope of my study to male homosexuals, mainly because I had difficulty making contact/finding informants within the limited period of my field work.

embodied in fixed social roles—in this case, the "masculine heterosexual soldier." In an attempt to contribute to theorizing the relationship between military masculinity and heteronormativity,[3] I explore the conditions of how the CPP has come to acknowledge and institutionalize same-sex relationships, how this translates into practice within the NPA, and how it affects the lives and affairs of its members. I interrogate the assumptions of the CPP on gender and sexual relations, especially how these have changed in the light of the recognition of same-sex relationships. To do this, I conducted field research from July–August 2008 involving interviews with 12 gay men[4] who formerly served in the NPA as well as two key informants who were part of formulating Party policies on sexual relations, including the founding chair of the Communist Party of the Philippines, Jose Ma. Sison, who currently resides in Utrecht. I also employed documentary research specifically looking the CPP documents on establishing sexual relationships, "On the Proletarian Relationship of the Sexes" [OPRS][5] (Communist Party of the Philippines [CPP] 1998a) with particular interest in Section E (better known as Amendment E)." An accompanying document to this policy is "Some Explanations on the Guidelines for Marriage inside the Party (Ilang Paliwanag sa mga Tuntunin sa Pag-aasawa sa Loob ng Partido)" (Communist Party of the Philippines [CPP] 1998b) explaining the principles on which the policy is based.

"Revolutionizing" gender and sexuality

It is erroneous to conclude that the CPP's gender/sexuality ideology has remained the same since its inception, since it is not separate from the historical development of the organization. During the 1940s–1950s, the People's Army Against Japan (HUKBALAHAP) under the *Partido Komunista ng Pilipinas* (PKP), the precursor of the CPP, enlisted women to join the

---

3   Upon embarking on this research, I became aware if my own limitations as a researcher, sometimes falling into the trap of "thinking straight" or viewing the world through a "heterosexual imaginary" (Ingraham 2006). While I have been educated in the methods of employing feminist and gender-sensitive research, with my own practice in development work mostly focusing on women's organizing, I realized that undertaking a "masculine-sensitive-research" (Curato 2010) was like venturing into an alien territory where my positionality as a woman became my main obstacle. From this standpoint, I was not only to capture the male experience but to map out "the dynamic process of negotiating men's multilayered identity" (Curato 2010, 247).

4   Real names have been concealed to ensure confidentiality and informants' security.

5   Also known as *Hinggil sa Pag-aasawa* (On Marriage), 1998.

armed struggle against the Japanese. The PKP was among the first "major political and military organizations in their countries" that actively recruited women fighters (Lanzona 2008, 3). Among the problems at this time for PKP was how to address the "sex problem" of married men who left their wives at home and took in "forest wives," usually "young single women in the camps." The PKP then came up with a document, *Revolutionary Solution of the Sex Problem*, which allowed these men to have extramarital relations "[c]laiming biological necessity" (Lanzona 2008, 3–4) as a justification. While such policies assigned both men and women "traditional gender roles" (which later became a liability to the HUKBALAHAP), it contributed to placing issues of family, sex, and morality in the organization's agenda, and subjected these to administrative control (Lanzona 2008, 4).

When Jose Ma. Sison (JMS) established the CPP in 1968, the leadership started to codify regulations pertaining to courtship, establishment of relationships, marriage, and divorce. JMS, who had taken part in making the guidelines, said in an interview with me that prior to the codification of the policy in 1972–1974, there was already a harsh "customary law" that regulated these relationships (Jose Ma. Sison, personal communication, 04 July 2008). In contrast to the previous policy in the HUKBALAHAP movement, infidelity (pagkakaliwa) was "punished in the severest way," sometimes even by death. However, JMS, said that the Party eventually learned to deal with such situations. Hence, when the first draft of "On the Relation of Sexes" [ORS] (Communist Party of the Philippines [CPP]1974) came out in 1974 (in English), such acts of infidelity, especially addressing male comrades, were no longer subjected to severe forms of punishment. According to the 1974 ORS draft[6] "[t]he question of the relation of sexes is fundamentally a class question. It is a struggle between two world outlooks—the bourgeois and the proletarian" (CPP 1974).

Using the ORS as a guiding principle, the CPP succeeded in framing personal/sexual relationships within the discourse of "class struggle." Therefore, *proletarian love* became defined as personal relationships that always kept the interest of the revolution a priority—articulated in their mantra of *class love* (political) over *sex love* (personal). As such, party members have appropriated the so-called proletarian love to counter the bourgeois, feudal and largely Catholic views on love and marriage dominant in Philippine society. The ORS set out the basis for creating a 'proletarian relationship' and ultimately for marriage and the creation of a revolutionary family. As a result, all *yunits* (red collectives) were directed

6   A final draft was released in 1977 in Tagalog version.

to intervene in making sure that relationships—from courtship to marriage to raising a family and, in some instances, divorce[7]—are governed by Party rules and guidelines. A main reference for discussing gender/sexual relations of the CPP was the classic work of Frederick Engels, *The Origin of the Family, Private Property and the State* (1972). In looking at women and their relationship with men, the Party adopted Engels' own explanation of the "civilized society founded on private property" giving rise to a "patriarchal class system' that perpetuates male domination over women (Engels 1972, 9). While the ORS (CPP 1974) gives primacy to women exploitation in gender relations within the Party, same-sex relationships are not addressed in the guidelines thereby erasing homosexual partnerships from the Party discourses. Although there were Party members and cadres who were openly gay, according to JMS, they were only "tolerated, respected, and credited" for their contributions to the movement as "cultural workers" of the Party (Jose Ma. Sison, personal communication, 4 July 2008). However, this issue will later be taken up in the Second Great Rectification Movement which is discussed in the succeeding section.

Queering the party
In 1992, the CPP launched the Second Great Rectification Movement which resulted in the split of the Party into "reaffirmists" (RA) and "rejectionists" (RJ), reflecting the ideological schisms that had wracked the organization.[8] Towards the end of the 1990s, the Party declared victory in consolidating ideological, political, and organizational matters, except for the question on sexual/interpersonal relationships. This was seen as directly affecting the "future of the movement" in terms of the social, and literally biological, reproduction of Party cadres. As one key informant explains:

> Before 1992, relationships were handled in distorted way. There was a lot of liberalism[9] among Party cadres, separations, and other sexual indiscretions. No time was invested in deriving lessons from forming and sustaining relationships. Many comrades were having sexual relationships but the guidelines were no longer enforced to help them develop their relationship toward the creation of a revolutionary family. The Party was called upon to enforce such guidelines. A strategic view in establishing sexual relationships

7   The Philippines remains the only country without a divorce law.
8   The RA constitute the present CPP.
9   Referring to a strong sense of individualism which no longer adhered to Party discipline.

was that they should lead to marriage and not be seen as a joke (personal communication, 24 July 2008).

Therefore in 1997, in the initial context of having more "gender sensitivity" in framing sexual relations in the Party, the National Women's Bureau facilitated formal discussions surrounding the issue, providing kits with researched data and documents. They reviewed Engels' (1972) *The Origin of the Family, Private Property and the State* to elevate the issue to a "conceptual level" and to provide theoretical grounding to the notion of a "revolutionary family." Eventually, the discussion led to the topic of homosexuals in the movement. Questions on the scientific basis for homosexuality raised: Were gays and lesbians even entitled to raise revolutionary families when they literally could not reproduce? Would not a proliferation of a "gay culture" lead to decadence and moral degeneration among party cadres? Apart from those questions, there was a prevailing view that the proletarian was one who had firm principles matched with physical strength. Gays were seen to be weepy, emotional, weak, and affectionate (*malambing*)—characteristics seen to be as the complete opposite of a true revolutionary cadre.[10] However, this perception was eventually countered with the argument that the Party aimed to strengthen the ideology and not the physical body. The basis for being a proletarian is not invested in physical strength but in "upholding Marxism-Leninism-Maoism."

Furthermore, the debate on the role of the homosexuals in the revolution occurred within the context of the insurgence of gay rights movement in the Philippines. It should be recalled that homosexuals in the Philippines led the first Gay Pride March in Asia in 1994.[11] Against this backdrop, it was difficult for the Party to ignore the question of homosexuality in the movement. As a result, the Party's leadership has put forth a new set of guidelines for relationships and officially recognized same-sex relations and marriage, stating that the actual participation of gay men and women in the revolution should be considered as a basis for their recognition. Despite resistance with the Party[12] to same-sex relations, a memorandum was eventually issued by the leadership regarding the amendment to the ORS, now popularly referred to

10   Key informant interview on 28 July 2008, Quezon City.
11   "Who are we?" *Pro-Gay Philippines*, accessed 10 October 2008, http://members.tripod.com/progay_philippines/intro.html.
12   From an interview with Reyna, one of my gay informants.

in the movement as *Amendment E*. The OPRS (CPP 1998a)[13] replaced the ORS and became official policy on sexual relations within the Party with Amendment E as a lynchpin for the recognition of same-sex relationships.

Consisting of five sections on courtship, marriage, divorce, disciplinary actions, and recognition of homosexual relations, the OPRS (CPP 1998a) has the following major amendments to the ORS:

a. Pre-marital sex should still be avoided but is no longer subjected to disciplinary action, and will be addressed with criticism, reminders, and education.

b. In granting divorce, the trial period was removed and replaced with careful examination of the basis for divorce presented by one or both parties.

c. There was devolution of power to approve the establishment of relationships and give a couple permission to wed. This is no longer the sole responsibility of higher organs of the Party, but a power granted to the lower committee level, or *seksyon*.

d. Different types of disciplinary actions are applicable to various transgressions of the guidelines which were not made clear in the previous document. Cases that can be tried in the revolutionary courts are also differentiated.

e. *A separate section is added on the recognition and respect for homosexual relationships.* (emphasis added)

The OPRS (CCP 1998a) opens with a statement that in marriage, the Party and the people's revolutionary cause supersedes all other interests. The OPRS has retained much of the substance of the ORS, including the adoption of the concept of *class love* (political) over *sex love* (personal). In *Some Explanations on the Guidelines for Marriage inside the Party* [SEGMP] (CPP. 1998b), a supplementary document of the OPRS, the CPP emphasizes the necessity for all Party and candidate members to study the OPRS since the guidelines will ensure that the interests of the revolution are upheld; secondly, that the rights of individual members are protected; and thirdly, that a healthy proletarian relationship is nurtured by the couple.

The *yunit* plays a big part in Party life—from the making of political and organizational decision to discussing matters such as family problems

13   The ORS was amended in March 1998 during the 10th Plenum of the CPP Central Committee.

and individual concerns. While members are not discouraged to display independence and initiative, they also go by the organizational principle of *democratic centralism*. This principle is based on the notion of the minority acceding to the majority, the lower organs acceding to the higher organs, accountability, and the right of every member to be heard.[14] Hence, in forming relationships and all the issues that occur before, during, and after these are established, the collective is a visible presence. The OPRS states that if a Party member intends to "court" or pursue someone, his/her respective *yunit* must be informed that:

> **Sec. A.2.** In order to court someone, the member or candidate member must have the permission of the *yunit* responsible for overseeing his/ her work. If the person courted is from another *yunit* of the Party, the suitor's *yunit* will inform the other *yunit* of his/her intentions and will ask for permission to initiate the courtship process if the one courted agrees. (CPP 1998a)

The collective is also responsible got scrutinizing whether both *class love* and *sex love* are presented as basis for such relationship before permission is granted. The documents also allows for a Party member to court or accept courtship from someone who is not a Party member who: 1. Can be "processed" to become a candidate member within six months; and 2. is not a traitor or anti-revolutionist or someone who would hold back the Party member from fulfilling one's tasks.

The guidelines strongly forbid any Party member to court or accept courtship from more than one person at a time, and to court or accept courtship from someone already in a relationship or is married. Other provisions include the restriction of New People's Army members or others serving the revolution "full time" from entering a relationship within the first year of service. It also sets a minimum of one year as an engagement period before a couple is allowed to marry. An amended provision pertains to the restrictions on pre-marital sex, aiming to "ensure the protection of women from exploitation and to give the couple time to prepare for the responsibilities of forming a family while waging a revolution" (CPP 1998a, Sec. A. 10).

In the same vein, marriage goes through the same collective intervention as "[it] is a serious thing that should be carefully prepared for by the

14   "Democratic Centralism," *Nation Master*, accessed 24 October 2008, http:// nationmaster.com/encyclopedia/Democratic-centralism.

couple and the responsible *yunit/s* of the Party"(CPP 1998a, Sec. B. 1.). Apart for the *yunit,* sponsors and the chosen officiating CPP cadre have the responsibility to look after the marriage, offering advice to the couple when necessary, such as how to remain loyal to each other and to the revolution, and advice on the "revolutionary way" of bringing up their children (CPP 1998a, Sec. B. 7.). All these rights and responsibilities are inscribed in the marriage contract found in the document.

The last section, *Amendment E* (CPP 1998a), is a very short addendum to the ORS. I have translated its two points below:

> E. On Same-Sex Relations
>   1. The Party recognizes the right of each individual member to choose the sex (*kasarian*).
>   2. The basic principles and guidelines for marriage inside the Party are applicable to their case.

My analysis shows that OPRS (CPP 1998a) very early on brings forward a binary form of categorization, that of the *Proletarian* and the *Bourgeois.* The proletarian viewpoint, which the document claims to represent, portrays the bourgeois mode of thinking about sexual relations, as its categorical other. In SEGMP (CPP 1998b), proletarian love supposedly combines freedom and discipline, rights and responsibilities—constituted by emotions as well as principles. This is opposed to "anarchy" in love present in the bourgeois viewpoint, which is basically the absolute freedom for the individual to do what one wishes. This apparently leads to the violation of others' rights, irresponsibility in getting in and out of relationships, and "loose morality" (CPP 1998b).

The document categorizes individual Party members, whether single, married, or in a relationship, subdivided as "men" and "women," and the *yunit* one might belong to, representing Party authority. While forming relationships is a personal process a Party member might undergo, it is also a collective experience. Whereas these are very explicitly stated in the guidelines, I find another categorization not as candidly expressed—heterosexuality vs homosexuality. This leads me to reflect on assumptions of gender and sexuality underpinning the OPRS. While the document is framed within the Party's conception of proletarian love, it is situated in a larger frame of waging a revolution that rejects bourgeois society, including the culture that informs bourgeois love. However, if we follow the document's arguments for proletarian love we will find that underlying it all is a heteronormative ideology *despite* the inclusion of Section E.

In Section 3 of the SEGMP (CPP 1998b), the heteronormativity of the concept of relationships becomes even more evident, particularly in the following lines: "Love is a natural feeling that grows between a particular *man* and *woman* when they reach a certain age." And in Section 8:

> The essence of marriage is the agreement between a *man* and a *woman* to become a couple inside a monogamous relationship and that this agreement is made formal and recognized in society through the blessing of the state ... [In] the proletarian marriage, a monogamous relationship is strictly enforced for both *man* and *woman* ... the institution of marriage if for the protection of *women* from the exploitation of *men*. (Italics mine)

Furthermore, Sec. B.7.b of the OPRS cites advice on how to "raise and educate the couple's children in a revolutionary way" as among the responsibilities of the sponsors and the collective. The discourse on *marriage-for-family* and *family-within-marriage* is repeatedly emphasized in the document. I noted that within the whole document of the SEGMP, this reference to a man-woman relationship and the creation of a family, or responsibility to children appears 10 times. Thus, while the prospect of marriage and forming a revolutionary family is opened to homosexuals, how same-sex couples figure in this particular construction is unclear.

This now brings me to the peculiar inclusion of *Amendment E* in the guidelines. In the light of such heteronormativity, the amendment does seem "extremely awkward and out of place" (Abinales 2004, 101). If we review the text of *Amendment E,* it briefly contains only two points: the right to choose one's sex (*kasarian),* and the right to marry applicable to their case (homosexuals). The language of *Amendment E* indicates a tendency to create an "other" in the form of homosexual comrades. Section 13 of SEGMP mentions "[t]here is no reason for the Party to refuse membership to an individual who fulfills the requirements just because one has another chosen sex/gender (*naiibang piniling kasarian)." Naiibang piniling kasarian* exactly refers to an "other" kind of sexuality in relation to something that is considered the "normal" kind of sexuality—as *naiiba* comes from the word *iba* which literally translates to "other" or "different." Therefore, labeling homosexuals as those having *naiibang piniling kasarian,* already stresses that homosexuality is out of the framework of what is considered a "normal" *kasarian.* In this sense, the struggle against homophobia, or heterosexism for that matter, is framed within a totalizing discourse of "class struggle." Thus, addressing homosexuality as merely an issue of class oppression obscures the specific experiences of homosexuality in the Philippines.

With the inclusion of same-sex unions in the OPRS, the NPA has become duty-bound by Party directive to "accommodate" openly gay men who joined the revolutionary army. Whereas previously the concept of a red fighter used to be viewed from a masculinist-militarist frame in the NPA expressed as through a discourse of "strength in body and ideology," the formal recognition of gay cadres as stipulated in the OPRS served to undermine this representation. While apparently still heteronormative, the new guidelines have provided gays and lesbians the language and mechanism to assert their right to form unions with the same sex, thereby allowing them to experience proletarian relationships under the supervision of the Party. What does it mean to be a gay red fighter in this context, when the recognition of gay men in the army seemingly creates a refracted image of the strong, principled, brave people's soldier, who now wears lotion to battle? In order to understand the formation of subjectivities, it is necessary to examine how gay identities are created, understood, and experienced, and how these are negotiated within given institutions and ideologies through which actors operate.

The gay red fighters

In examining the social identities of gay men, it is important to see how their gendered identities are substantively constructed in relation to "a range of activities, social organizations and historically specific cultural representations" (Scott 1989, 1068). The presence of gay men in the NPA, as in all military institutions, signifies a contradiction as gay-ness is perceived to be the anti-thesis of the military image. In the Philippine context, the concept of a "gay fighter" seems to be an oxymoron as the term homosexual almost automatically brings to mind the image of a hip-swaying, cross-dressing effeminate male, popularly known as a *bakla*.[15] But what is unique in this case is that CPP/NPA has sanctioned same-sex relations in the organization, which is hardly found in military institutions, if at all. The gay men I interviewed came from a varied range of socio-economic backgrounds. Most had started out as student activists in local universities and later on got recruited to the underground movement and eventually joined the NPA. A few are peasant and urban poor origins, while one is from an indigenous group in Mindanao. The age of the key informants I interviewed ranges from early 20s to mid-40s. During recruitment to the NPA, many were fresh out of college or engaged in activism in their own communities with particular

15   *Bayot, agi,* and *bantut* are comparable terms in other Philippine regions.

local struggles such as militarization in the countryside and demolition of houses in urban poor areas. How NPA gay fighters negotiate their identity in the context of the revolutionary armed struggle shall be discussed in the subsequent sections.

Coming out in the NPA

The process of revealing one's sexual identity entails the ritual of confession by which an individual discloses his/her actions and thoughts, especially in circumstances where they are most difficult to tell (Foucault 1978). Confession is however a double-edged sword. While on the one hand is deemed an exercise of freedom and liberation from constraints that prevent one from actualizing selfhood, it is also subjects one to the acceptance or rejection of a structure or authority that requires such confession, on the other. Seen against this backdrop, the "coming out" process is a defining moment for the affirmation of one's (sexual) selfhood. It refers not only to public disclosure of one's sexuality but also to a complex process of recognizing, accepting, and adopting a sexual identity (Gagne, Tewksbury, and McGaughey 1997). In the Philippines, this process is often referred as *paglaladlad ng kapa*, literally meaning, "unfurling the cape."

Prior to the OPRS document, there seemed to be an unwritten ban on homosexuals (especially gay men) in the NPA. The process of coming out became difficult as gay men were forced to adhere to the traditional concept of military masculinity of the organization. Given this context, confession of one's sexual identity has become a difficult and risky act of gay cadres. One informant, Reyna, who had joined the movement in 1985 until his capture by the state army in the late 90s, narrated how he had been continuously interrogated about his sexuality by comrades. He always denied that he was gay because he feared being stigmatized, and was told repeatedly "to stop being soft-spoken as this would mean acting like a gay. They said that the masses will not accept a gay fighter." He had always referred to his ordeal of concealing his "true feelings" as a thorn that was constantly embedded in his skin.

However, for those who have already come out as gay prior to joining the army, they have been subjected to constant surveillance of their body. Mohan, who joined the NPA in 1992, expressed his disappointment with comrades who told him to look and act like a red fighter, "I was told by some [male] comrades not to sway my hips or be affectionate and that I should act 'manly' with a military figure." Two other informants, Danika and Amihan, who were recruited to the NPA after the policy of recognition of homosexuals had already been implemented, shared that when they were assigned to one NPA camp, some comrades told them upfront "you are gay, you should not be here," or "if only you were not gay, you would be a commander by now." There was an assertion among some of the NPA members that gay people had no place in the armed struggle as they were perceived to be "weaklings" and "cowards."

In some cases, joining the NPA has provided them an avenue to realize their "gay identity." Ariel, for example, who come from a farming village, never admitted he was gay before he enlisted in the NPA because he said his community was "conservative." It is not uncommon in rural communities in the Philippines for gay men to be discriminated. When Ariel first joined the NPA, he pretended that he was "straight": "I used to pretend that I liked girls, but I would cry silently about it when I was alone. But I think they already knew I was gay because of the way I talked and the way I moved ... I was already a girl." With the recognition of homosexuality within the Party, it has opened a space for gay cadres to deal with their "identity crisis." As Ariel aptly puts it: "I became confident enough to admit that I am gay. I learned that my struggle as a gay was part of a bigger struggle of the people." While both coming out and institutional sanction might have opened an opportunity for gay men to assert their identity in the NPA, they have also posed new arenas of struggle.

While many of the informants highly appreciated the CPP's official acceptance of homosexuals, life of gay men in the NPA was a constant act of negotiation. For example, some comrades would ridicule gay fighters by mockingly imitating gay cadres "swaying their hips while fighting." Gay fighters' physical capabilities to carry out military work and combat were always in doubt. In the case of Ariel, he was always questioned whether he was capable of fighting, to which he would retort, "I know how to pull the trigger and use my gun. It is not as if I will be dancing around while fighting is going on!" And indeed, Ariel was able to show his abilities in combat when their camp was raided by the Philippine military. Impressed with Ariel's performance, his comrades told him, "even if you are gay, you really are still useful." Moreover, the ability of gay fighters to bargain for recognition is influenced by their respective backgrounds, such as education, profession, and skills that they capitalize on in the camps (e.g., intelligence work, writing, facilitating educational discussions). Especially for gay cadres with college education, there seems to be more acceptance to their sexuality as they are considered to be assets of the NPA in the larger context of the revolutionary movement.

Entering same-sex relations

While believing in the principle behind the policy that allows same-sex relationships, gay cadres have difficulty dealing with it in the movement. They believe that many comrades are still not ready to accept gay relationships. "Real men" were deemed unprepared to enter serious sexual relationships with gay men, and if they did entertain courtships from gay men, they usually subjected themselves to the process out of "obligation." Hence, only three of the twelve gay men I interviewed experienced going through 'the process' of courtship under the OPRS, but only one was able to form an "official" relationship.

Sekar, a university student who dropped out to join the movement, attempted to court a comrade but he backed out because he felt that the man entertained his courtship simply because "it was a policy." He also felt offended when he was talking to a high ranking comrade about the policy and the latter commented that homosexuality stemmed from bourgeois decadence, "What next? Would we accept marriage to dogs?" Sekar pointedly said:

> I think the process is good in a sense that it opens up a space for same-sex relationships. But I think there is an ideological and political limitation because homosexual experiences have not been extensively documented and summed up, no lessons are derived. It would be better if there is re-examination of Amendment E as I believe that it does not provide full protection for same-sex relationships.

Ameer, from the region that held the same-sex marriage in 2005, tried to go through the process with a male comrade who he had been secretly seeing in order to make their relationship official, but it did not work out:

> When other comrades found out about this, they started to ridicule the guy and kept questioning his sexuality. He was not gay. He was straight. And because of the pressure he felt from other comrades and the distance we had from each other due to the nature of our work, he left the NPA without seeing me again.[16]

16   On this note, an interesting point uncovered in my fieldwork is that homosexuality in the Philippines is not necessarily defined by sexual acts themselves. Hence, a *bakla* might have sex with a "straight" man, but only the *bakla* is considered homosexual (Garcia 2004, 13). It is not necessarily a matter of who is "active" or "passive," as homosexuality has already been defined through gender (the *bakla* being the feminine one). This caught my attention when some of the gay men I interviewed kept referring

This would happen again with another male comrade a few months later. He was also ridiculed. Ameer said that his *yunit* tried to settle the matter but he felt that the relationship was not taken seriously. He recounted hearing one of the *yunit* members say, "Why bother? It's not going to last anyway." On this point, he has this to say about the OPRS:

> I think that the policy is OK as it addresses our human right to be happy in a relationship. But I also think that there is no special protection for homosexuals like what happened to me with my failed relationships. The policy should be holistic. I feel that the treatment of same-sex relationships in my experience is very superficial. The policy that applies to heterosexuals is assumed to apply to us, and it should not be this way.

Similarly, a few of my informants have shared being encouraged to marry the opposite sex despite having openly admitted being gay. "Some comrades viewed that gay relationships are not worth any serious effort" and that "the only productive relationship is a heterosexual one." On the other hand, other informants expressed a more optimistic view of the policy. They regarded it as something that finally afforded them "equality" in terms of recognizing their right to form same-sex relations—something that they have been deprived of by the Catholic Church and the State. The marriage that happened in 2005 generated a lot of excitement for most of them because if seemed like a validation for their hopes that indeed, "it can happen."

The timid guerrilla: Unpacking subjectivities
A dominant discourse in my interviews is the reference to "the woman within." Because their "inside" (*kalooban*) is supposedly "female," gay men are branded as *mahinhin*, connoting physical weakness and inability to fight.[17] Thus, many would question why there were gays in the NPA. This notion has brought with it some ambivalence on how to situate gays in the army, when the inside does not match with the "outside."

At the core of the construction of the Filipino gay man is of one having a male physique and a female heart embodied by the *bakla* (Manalansan

---

to one of the same-sex couple who got married as the "straight husband" and the other one as the "gay wife." Most *baklas* look for a "real man" (i.e., 'straight'), as many of them refer to sexual relations with other *baklas* in "cannibalistic terms," i.e., eating one's own flesh (Manalansan 1995, 200).

17   *Mahuyang* is the equivalent term in the Cebuano language referring to gay men in the NPA, literally meaning weak.

1995). This construction of the *bakla* "primarily centers on two closely related images—the cross-dressing queen and the pseudo-woman" (Manalansan 1995, 197). While *not* all those called *bakla* are effeminate or "cross-dressers," they are generally considered to have the feelings of a woman. Moreover, the concept of *kalooban* (core-ness or what one really is on the inside) greatly informs the (gender) identity of the *bakla* in the Philippines (Garcia 2003)—as a "screaming queen beneath the masculine facade" (Manalansan 1995, 198–99).

Such notion of being a "woman at the core" largely affects how other guerrilla fighters view and interact with gays, and how many of the gay men view themselves.[18] Many times, my informants referred to themselves as being "like a girl in the way I moved and talked" (Ariel), with the "feelings of a woman" (Reyna), and "thinking like a woman" (Danika). In terms of work, most of them are assigned to be medics, instructors, finance officers, and performers (theatre, dance, etc.)—tasks considered "lighter," in the physical sense, and thus, feminine.

This concept of "woman in a man's body" also brings to mind the construction of a *gendered* and *heterosexualized homosexuality*. In the Western sense, homosexuality is "simply a question of sexual orientation regardless of the self-understanding one has of one's gender" (Garcia 2003, 63). But the notion of a woman in a man's body is not simply a matter of orientation. In this context, the desire for other men necessitates the understanding of one having a feminine core. At the same time, since gay men are still physically male, they are thus not allowed to be in close contacts with women as in the case of sleeping and bathing. All this is underpinned by a heterosexualized understanding of gender relations.

Selfhood of gay men is partly constructed by instilling these dominant notions of sexual relations in the Party. As homosexuality intersects with notions of gender, and with concepts of what it means to be a soldier, the subjective identities of gay red fighters emerge. And in some instances, they are able to to use the dominant conception about "gayness" to achieve military gains (e.g., dressing up like a woman to accomplish a mission) and prove their capabilities to comrades in order to gain respect and sense of self-worth.

Embodying military masculinity
The body, more than being a biological entity, is an object and site of power (Foucault 1980). Masculinity and the "male sex role" are closely linked

18   This is also reflects on how almost all of them have chosen feminine code names for the interviews.

to a content-specific image of the "ideal" male body as a "muscular physique that may serve as a symbolic embodiment" of competitiveness, persistence, confidence, and if even superiority. This embodiment of masculinity is closely linked to heterosexuality (Mishkind, Rodin, Silberstein, and Striegel-Moore 2001, 108). In this section, I look at how the body is subjected to discipline—used, transformed, and improved (Foucalt 1977) in accordance with "acceptable" forms of military masculinity. Moreover, I explore the perceived paradoxes inscribed on the (gay) soldier's body as a site for contesting discourses about imagined gender ideals.

The paradox of having a "manly physique" while being a "woman at the core" comes out as a site of tension when gay men interact especially with other men in the NPA. Some of my respondents shared how difficult it was for some comrades to reconcile the perceived incongruence of the muscular male body of a fighter and their "femininity." For instance, Ariel shared that mostly male comrades would wonder how he could carry heavy containers of water from the river to the camp, or the fact that he could carry a heavy rifle. They would ask him, "Why did you become gay when you have a strong body?" On other occasions, while it was easier for male comrades to reconcile the image of gay man in the NPA if they actually dressed like a woman, some gay men were told to be more "manly" in their stance because they were soldiers. We see here many inconsistencies concerning how gay men are viewed in terms of their physique and their gendered meanings. What I find consistent is the imagined paradox between physically male, and emotionally/mentally female. I say it is imagined because these tensions are not inherent in the body of the gay man, but rather shaped according to the meanings inscribed on the body. In this *imagined paradox,* confusion arises on whether one should not be gay if one has a muscular body; or if one is gay, then he should look feminine; or if one is in the army and is gay, one should appear more manly and suppress femininity. It points to the situation that despite official recognition at the institutional level of the CPP-NPA, ambiguities rest at many levels, from the level of formation of subjective identities in the day-to-day negotiations of gay men in the NPA, to the dominant constructs of hegemonic military masculinity of the CPP and the Philippine society. These ambiguities and paradoxes also extend to how the gay man's body is imagined in terms of "discipline" and sexual behavior.

The NPA follows a strict military discipline patterned on Mao Tse-tung's (1969) *The Three Main Rules for Discipline and The Eight Points for Attention* that laid down the rules for combat, treatment of women, barrio folk and their properties, and conduct toward prisoners of war as follows:

A. The Three Main Rules for Discipline
   1. Obey orders in all your actions.
   2. Don't take a single needle or piece of thread from the masses.
   3. Turn in everything captured.

B. Eight Points for Attention
   1. Speak politely.
   2. Pay fairly for what you buy.
   3. Return everything you borrow.
   4. Pay for anything you damage.
   5. Don't hit or swear at people.
   6. Don't damage crops.
   7. Don't take liberties with women.
   8. Don't ill-treat captives.

However, when talking about discipline, my informants almost always refer to regulation of sexual behavior rather than the military code of discipline. While in principle, sexual relations are only one of the domains governed by Party discipline, sexual discipline is most emphasized among (male) heterosexuals. Clearly, the concept of discipline no longer refers to explicit codes of conduct and coercion but on how the object of discipline "makes itself more obedient and more useful" (Foucalt 1977). In this case, sex is a domain of a gay man's life that is subject to heightened scrutiny in the NPA, due to prevailing notion of supposed homosexual promiscuity deemed detrimental to the revolutionary cause and thus must be suppressed. This view is held by some gay cadres themselves, who find that their desires for other men need to be disciplined especially when they are in the army waging a revolution. As Reyna points out, "I understand that we really need to have discipline because it is the nature of gays to have sex whenever and wherever they find the opportunity."

Here, we find a conflation of army discipline and the regulation of sexual behavior, something that may not entirely be specific to gay men alone, but something that definitely becomes more accentuated as a result of being gay. And because if this "expected promiscuity" some gay men also find themselves subjected to sexual violence and aggression—from unwanted touching to demands from sexual favors. In one particular case, Ameer recalled how he was always called the "pretty gay" because of her long hair and feminine body. Sexual favors are considered normal in this situation due to the perception that gay men are by nature promiscuous resulting in such violence. In these instances, many choose to keep quiet about their experiences of violence, while others invoke redress mechanisms through responsible *yunits* within the guerrilla fronts. Despite disciplinary action meted out on some erring (male) comrades, sexual violence remained a reality that many of these gay men faced.

Furthermore, situated in the sexualized concept of discipline is the issue of gay men being "security risks" because of their supposed weakness to temptations when presented with handsome men. Danika shared that he would be told tales of how gay men in the NPA would turn traitor and reveal information to the government forces because they gave in to "temptation." When asked if this was documented, he said he never saw an actual report and that there was no specific event that he knew of. This brings me to reflect on how the internalization of such discourse affects the gay men themselves. Sekar presented a very interesting effect this kind of thinking had on him, "There were times when I was afraid I might cause the capture of my comrades or that if someone did get caught by the military, I might get blamed for it because I am gay." Even the government military seemed to share this idea. For instance, when Reyna was captured after an unsuccessful mission, he was tortured for three days. And during the time of his interrogation, the military would send handsome men to talk to him and to make sexual suggestions if he cooperated. However, Reyna asserted that he never divulged any of the NPA's plans. Despite that, the idea of homosexuals being security risks is still dominant and thus implies monitoring and "disciplining" gay men's sexuality.

In sum, the idea of *discipline* and security risk become highly sexualized because they rest on the ideas of promiscuity, as "the nature of gays." The popular image of male homosexuals as cross-dressers or pseudo-women has resulted in an imagined paradox between having a man's body with a woman residing inside. Ambiguities thus arise in dealing with gay men in the army despite institutional sanction, when the understanding of homosexuality is something left for individual negotiations. One thing that these negotiations can impart is that such ambiguities and contradictions can open a venue for rethinking of constructs that seem to fix what is actually highly fluid.

Conclusion

In negotiating for their place in the New People's Army, gay cadres have challenged hegemonic military masculinity by using resources available to them—various individual skills and capacities, initiating discussions about gay men's place in the NPA, accessing grievance machineries of the Party through their respective *yunits,* and adopting nationalist discourses by situating their struggle for recognition within the larger context of the revolutionary movement. This research shows that hegemonic military masculinity, inextricably linked to heterosexuality, has been constructed in a way that suppresses other existing forms of masculinities in the socio-spatial context of the army. The focus on a normative model of military masculinity not only makes us blind to other masculinities but institutionalizes further a kind of masculinity based on a heterosexual imaginary. The case of gay men in the New People's Army destabilizes a heterosexualized military masculinity which brings forth the heteronormative image of the soldier as a real man patterned on being strong, aggressive, and skilled in the art of war. The enlistment of male homosexuals in the New People's Army produces not just a "new man" but also, with the backdrop of armed struggle, a "new man ready to die"—and even kill—for the revolutionary cause. This "new military man" has claimed a space in the army without adhering to a heterosexual requisite, creating space for alternative masculinities to be explored. My discussion on masculinities in the NPA is not exhaustive, but it provides room to look at possibilities of other existing masculinities along other lines of social relations apart from sexuality. This study highlights the complexities of negotiation: that it is not a linear process, and is carried out on various surfaces of engagement. As gender and sexuality are organizing principles of society, these pervade as ideologies within given gender regimes, permeate institutions and facilitate social (hetero) norms, become lived realities in actual subjective experiences, and inscribe themselves symbolically on (gay men's) bodies. Thus, the space for alternative military masculinities has to be struggled for, in many different levels.

BIBLIOGRAPHY

Abinales, Patricio N. *Love, Sex, and the Filipino Communist or Hinggil sa Pagpipigil ng Panggigigil.* Manila: Anvil Publishing Inc., 2004.

Communist Party of the Philippines. "On the Relation of Sexes (Internal Paper from the Women's Bureau)." In *Love, Sex, and the Filipino Communist or Hinggil sa Pagpipigil ng Panggigigil,* 131–42. Manila: Anvil Publishing, 1974.

————. *On the Proletarian Relationship of the Sexes or Hinggil sa Pag-aasawa: Mga Gabay at Tuntunin sa Pag-aasawa sa Loob ng Partido* 1998a. Retrieved 05 September 2008. http://www.philippinerevolution.net/cgi-bin/cpp/pdocs.pl?id=oprs;page=01.

————. "Some explanations on the guidelines for marriage inside the party." *Communist Party of the Philippines.* Retrieved 5 September 2008. http://www.philippinerevolution.net.

Connell, R. W. *Masculinities*. Cambridge: Polity Press, 2005.

Connell, R. W. and James W. Messerschmidt. "Hegemonic Masculinity: Rethinking the Concept." *Gender and Society* 19, no. 6 (December 2005): 829–59.

Curato, Nicole. "Addressing the Absence of Masculine-sensitive Research Methods: Reflections from Interviewing Military Men." *Philippine Social Science Review* 62, no. 2 (July–December 2010): 245–75. https://journals.upd.edu.ph/index.php/pssr/article/view/2103

Engels, F. *The Origin of the Family, Private Property and the State*. New York: Pathfinder Press, 1972. First published in 1884 in Hottingen-Zurich.

Evangelista, K. "Army: No Policy but Won't Recruit Gays." *Inquirer.net*, 3 March 2009. http://www.newsinfo.inquirer.net/breakingnews/nation/view/20090303-192166/Army-No-policy-but-wont-recruit-gays.

Foucault, Michel. *Discipline and Punish: The Birth of the Prison*. New York: Vintage Books, 1977.

————. *The History of Sexuality: An Introduction*. New York: Vintage Books, 1978.

Gagne, Patricia, Richard Tewksbury, and Deanna McGaughey. "Coming Out and Crossing Over: Identity Formation and Proclamation in a Transgender Community." *Gender and Society* 11, no. 4 (August 1997): 478–508.

Garcia, J. Neil C. *Performing the Self: Occasional Prose*. Quezon City: University of the Philippines Press, 2003.

Hearn, Jeff. Foreword to *Military Masculinities: Identity and the State* by Paul Higate, Jeff Hearn, and Nicholas Laham, xi–xv. Edited by Paul Higate. Westport, Connecticut and London: Praeger Publishers, 2003.

Ingraham, C. "Thinking Straight, Acting Bent: Heteronormativity and Homosexuality." In *Handbook of Gender and Women's Studies*, edited by K. Davis, M. Evans and J. Lorber, 307–21. London: Sage Publications, 2006.

Israel-Sobritchea, C. "The Ideology of Female Domesticity: Its Impact on the Status of Filipino Women." *Review of Women's Studies* 1, no. 1 (1990): 26–41.

Kovitz, Marcia. "The Roots of Military Masculinity." In *Military Masculities: Identity and the State*, edited by Paul Higate, 1–4. Westport, Connecticut and London: Praeger Publishers, 2003.

Kronsell, Annica. "Gendered Practices in Institutions of Hegemonic Masculinity: Reflections from Feminist Standpoint Theory." *International Feminist Journal of Politics* 7, no. 2 (2005): 280–98.

Lanzona, Via. "Sex, Love and the Revolution." *International Institute for Asian Studies* 48 (Summer 2008): 3–5. https://www.iias.asia/sites/default/files/theNewsletter/2019-06/IIAS_NL48_FULL.pdf.

Manalansan, Martin F. I. "Speaking of AIDS: Language and the Filipino 'Gay' Experience in America." In *Discrepant Histories: Translocal Essays on Filipino Cultures*, edited by Vicente L. Rafael, 193–220. Manila: Anvil Publishing, Inc., 1995.

Mao Tse-tung. "On the Reissue of the Three Main Rules of Discipline and Eight Points for Attention." In *Selected Works of Mao Tse-tung*, 155–56. Peking: Foreign Languages Press, 1969. Retrieved 12 December 2011 from http://www.marx2mao.com/Mao/TMR47.html.

McCoy, Alfred W. *Closer than Brothers: Manhood at the Philippine Military Academy*. Manila: Anvil Publishing, Inc., 1999.

Mishkind, Marc E., Judith Rodin, Lisa R. Silberstein, and Ruth H. Striegel-Moore. "The Embodiment of Masculinity: Cultural, Psychological, and Behavioral Dimensions." In *The American Body in Context: An Anthology*, edited by Jessica R. Johnston, 103–20. Wilmington, Delaware: SR Books, 2001.

Ottoson, D. "LGBT World Legal Wrap Up Survey." *International Lesbian and Gay Association*, November 2006. Retrieved 19 October 2008. http://typo3.lsvd.de/fileadmin/pics/Sokumente/Homosexualitaet/World_legal_wrap_up_survey._November2006.pdf.

Pinsoy, R. "Reds Officiate First Gay Marriage in NPA." *Philippine Daily Inquirer*, 7 February 2005.

Scott, Joan Wallach. "Gender: A Useful Category of Historical Analysis." *The American Historical Review*, 91, no. 5 (1986): 1053–75.

Sobritchea, Carolyn Israel. "The Ideology of Female Domesticity: Its Impact on the Status of Filipino Women." *Review of Women's Studies* 1, no. 1 (1990): 26–41.

Zarkov, Dubravka. "Towards a New Theorizing of Women, Gender, and War." In *Handbook of Gender and Women's Studies*, edited by Judith Lorber, Kathy Davis, and Mary Evans, 214–33. London: Sage Publications, 2006.

————. *The Body of War: Media, Ethnicity, and Gender in the Break-up of Yugoslavia*. Durham: Duke University Press, 2007.

The dancers' clothes—denim shorts, boxer briefs, thongs, bandanas that cover the crotch area—signify an affinity with the working class and other subcultures. Images scanned from VCDs, *clockwise from top left, Naked Hunks* (2004); *World Bubble Bath King* (2005); *Asian Hunks* (2004); *World Bubble Bath King* (2005); *Dakota King* (2003); *Dakota King* (2003). Photos courtesy of Rolando B. Tolentino.

This essay was previously published in *The Drama Review (TDR)* 53, no. 2 (2009): 77–89.

ROLANDO B. TOLENTINO

Macho Dancing, the Feminization of Labor, and Neoliberalism in the Philippines

"MACHO DANCING" is the name of the dance performed by male dancers in gay bars, and it is called "macho" to distinguish it from the
vaudeville-like lip-synching and bar performances of transvestites and transsexuals. In other words, macho dancing is performed solely by dancers whose
identification is male heterosexual, the primary object of desire in gay bars in the
Philippines. It is both sensual, using the male dancer's body in the performance,
and sexual, with the performance itself mimicking overt sexual acts. Recently,
dancers have added a form of strip tease: they remove tank tops or vests and the
bottom layers covering the crotch area—denim shorts, boxer briefs, bandana,
swimwear, and tanga or briefs—to display an erect penis (see for example photo on facing page 1); they gyrate to showcase the male performer's body; and
they mimic sexual positions (see fig. 5).[1] Macho dancing has undergone two
phases in its development. The first is the feminine style "snake dancing," a
movement that flows from the feet and legs to the stomach, then to the arms
and chest, on up to the head and back down. It was prevalent when gay bars
first appeared in the Philippines at the height of Ferdinand Marcos's dictatorship (1972–1986). The second phase of macho dancing, in the post-Marcos

1   Taking pictures or videos in gay bars in the Philippines is prohibited. I am thank-
ful to colleague Aristotle Atienza for selecting the images and providing the photo imag-
ing from pirated VCDs. Macho dancing videos are sold through informal channels and
ownership credits are not available.

economically neoliberal period of the 1990s, involves an edgier, jagged, slower, more protracted, and more sexually male style than snake dancing.

I read macho dancing as a symptom of the discursive cultural politics of the Philippines in transition from the Marcos dictatorship that readily inserted the nation-space and its citizens into multinational capitalism, to the present that both intensifies the legacies of labor-export and foreign capital penetration of the Marcos period and perpetuates neoliberalism as a national developmental strategy. The macho dancer's body can also be read as representing the actual shifts in these cultural politics of the nation-state.

Feminization of male labor

Neoliberalism in the Philippines began early on, in the post-independence era that dates from 1946. Many treaties bound the Philippines to the United States. President Diosdado Macapagal pegged the peso to the dollar in 1964, and Marcos's first term saw the 1960s mass exodus of professionals to the United States. Since then, the Philippines has become the largest supplier of immigrant professionals to the United States, particularly nurses, doctors, and medical technologists (Catalan 1996). In the 1970s, Marcos intensified the labor export, creating what are called OFW (Overseas Filipino Workers) and OCW (Overseas Contract Workers)—new labor identities for Filipinos doing flexible and 3-D (dirty, dangerous, and difficult) jobs overseas. The OCW phenomenon is so huge that the Philippines is now the third largest exporter of labor and the second biggest receiver of remittances in the world. One out of ten Filipinos is an OCW, at least one-half of Filipinos have a family member who is an OCW, and therefore, at least half of the population is supported by OCW remittances. Confronted with perennial political and economic crises, post-Marcos national administrations have increased the reliance on OCWs as reliable foreign currency suppliers.

By declaring martial law in 1972, Marcos wanted to both prolong and strengthen his control of the nation. Relying heavily on foreign borrowing and multinational capital to finance his dictatorship, he mobilized the majority of national bodies—the youthful citizenry—and placed them in the service of multinational capital in the homeland and the debt servicing industry in foreign lands. Marcos created economic and export-processing zones free from unions and strikes to service the subcontractual jobs of multinational companies. He also created the government infrastructures that further embedded the OCW in Philippine culture.[2]

Within the nation, young women became multinational laborers, working specifically in the garment and electronics sectors, and in the proliferating sex and entertainment trade. Outside the nation-space, women workers

2   For an economic history of the Marcos period, see Tolentino (1996).

were preferred over men. In 2002, female overseas employment already comprised 69 percent of the total of newly hired OCWs. Initially, the oil boom in the Middle East created jobs for men building desert urbanscapes, but as this situation weakened and other labor-supplying nations joined the field, the demand for Filipino male labor dwindled. These men had to look for jobs elsewhere or take "feminine" jobs. Filipino men did housekeeping in Italy, entertainment work in the hotel and nightclub circuits of Asia, and provided labor for the growing demand in the service sectors. Only in the domain of seafaring did Filipinos continue to dominate, with some 200,000 Filipinos working on international vessels (see Suarez 2001).[3]

This ongoing feminization of male labor is being represented in the Philippines through the proliferation of newer feminized male labor-based identities that have evolved from the Marcos period to the present—the male underwear model, the male "bold" star (a "bomba" or soft-porn movie actor), the male guest-relations officer, transsexual and transvestite Japayuki (an entertainer working in Japan), the male talent show contestant, the male beauty contestant, the male domestic, the male factory worker in economic zones, and, of course, the macho dancer. The masculine qualifiers—"male," "macho," and the Spanish ending "o"—redefine jobs that were early on identified with female labor.

The global trend in economic growth focuses on the service sector, an amalgamation of quasi-industries that include entertainment, medicine, fast food, tourism, education, and other service-oriented endeavors—"quasi" because they do not produce commodities other than the McDonaldized services they provide. These are also "body-positive" because the body of the young worker—the majority of service sector employees are young—should be pleasant-looking, have a pleasing personality, and be able to do 3D jobs. Eighty percent of the gross domestic product of the United States is derived from the service sector; Germany, 70 percent; Hong Kong, 85.3 percent; Japan, 72.2 percent; Singapore and Taiwan, 65.6 percent; and the Philippines, 52.9 percent.[4] The feminization of male labor in the Philippines had taken root as early as the post–World War II period with the introduction

---

3   Furthermore, according to Alex Pabico: "Because one of every five seafarers onboard international ocean-going vessels today is Filipino, the likelihood is that every major maritime disaster in the world would involve a Filipino. The shipping industry is one of the most dangerous in the world, but despite the risks, hundreds of thousands of Filipino seafarers are eager to work abroad, lured by higher wages and the promise of foreign travel [...] Filipino seamen today remit $1 billion back home every year [...]" (2003).

4   See Cleveland (1999); Carrel (2008); Hong Kong General Chamber of Commerce (n.d.); Japan Statistics Bureau (2008); Namatame (2006); SME Toolkit (2008).

A sickly Ferdinand Marcos debunking rumors of his actual health status by flaunting a giant image of a younger robust body. Photo by Sonny Yabao.

of Keynesian economics. This provided the base for the dominance of neo-liberal capitalism in the 1980s and 1990s fostered by Marcos.

The presidential body[5]

Sometime in 1983, soon after the August assassination of opposition leader Benigno Aquino, Marcos convened a press conference in his private office to quell questions about his ill health. A photograph taken by photojournalist Sonny Yabao during the conference foregrounds the relationship between discourse and the presidential body. The picture shows Marcos—appearing harassed and with a bloated face, visible tension lines on the forehead, and shrunken eyes—pointing to an almost life-size photograph of himself smiling, in swimming trunks, and in robust health with firm torso and arms, his eyes hidden by dark sunglasses.[6] The "real" Marcos is covered to the neck by a white barong, his free hand on the table supporting his compact body.

The picture of Marcos in swimming trunks was taken outside. His body seems to be aglow with the available space, extending from his body like the radiant rays in the image of the Sacred Heart of Jesus. In this exterior shot,

5   This section is an abridged version, originally published as "Mattering National Bodies and Sexualities: Corporeal Contest in Marcos and Brocka" (Tolentino 2003). I have adapted and reworked the section to stress the presidential body as context for the appreciation of the macho dancer's and gay client's bodies.

6   A copy of Sonny Yabao's photograph of the "two Marcoses" is reprinted in Jo-Ann Maglipon's "Reprise 1983" (1993, 8).

there are no other figures save Marcos. The real Marcos, on the other hand, is surrounded by a cluttered interior space—bodies of supporters on the left; papers, documents, pens, and two pairs of eyeglasses fore grounded on the table; and a pulley probably used to hoist the flag in the center. In choosing to be photographed in his private office, Marcos exposed the interior operations of the presidency in a state of crisis. The interior space presents the notion of reflexivity in the presidency; operations are laid bare and therefore susceptible to interrogation.

Marcos was so fascinated with his youthful prime that he concocted a presidential apotheosis based on the vitality of his youthful body—the alleged guerrilla leader who earned twenty-eight medals during the Japanese occupation; the exemplar of the all-around athlete in his college days; the "young Turk" in his various political party affiliations; and the young senator who swept the beauty queen off her feet in eleven days of courtship. Though these stories are privately questioned, the wholesale public display Marcos made of his presidential body somehow solidified his hold on national power. This image of a pristine youthful body permitted Marcos to forcefully remain in power, tying a potent political rhetoric to a brute pacification drive in the founding and implementation of the New Society and the New Republic in which people were rendered passive and submissive.[7] In the polemic of modernizing the nation on all fronts, Marcos's vision of Philippine society was equally represented as youthful and innovative, even as it clutched traditional values and institutions.

Whether garbed in formal or informal wear, the presidential body was always at work. The presidential body's personal and family activities were translated into official business; a trip to the airport to welcome his children taking their breaks from schools abroad became a media event. The media also played a role in proliferating the presidential body and extending its official bodily life. The presidential body went beyond the statute of the constitution that limited the presidential term and, to a large extent, even defied the natural impediments of aging and sickness. So long as it appeared to be working toward certain national ideals, the presidential body remained centrally positioned. Like its semblance of sustained national prominence, the presidential body's central positioning created a semblance of national unity.

The kinetic drive to unify and modernize the nation ironically rested on the fragmentation of the presidential body. The body could not possibly

7   Marcos concocted visions of official nation-building. He declared martial law in 1972, then introduced and promulgated "Bagong Lipunan" (the New Society) as the thematic of his rule. In 1981, upon winning another term, he declared himself president of the "Fourth Republic."

be everywhere at all times. Thus the presidential body metonymically functioned through its parts, so as to be in both one place and everywhere. Specifically, it was Marcos's voice and gestures that substituted for his organic body. Media proliferated these body parts—radio disseminated his voice, newspapers his active gestures, and film and television his choate physical and aural presence. Marcos's baritone voice was characterized by its deep enunciation of perfect English, Tagalog, and Ilokano, and his extemporaneous speeches were marked by their forceful delivery. He knew the rhetoric that would get people's attention, and his gestures reiterated authority. Regardless of audience size, Marcos's gestures were wide and animated, similar to actions done in speaking to a huge crowd.

These parts then amounted to a "quasi-corporeal" body,[8] a body whose unity was lost in the efficacy of the parts to represent the entity. On one level, these parts produced "afterimages" of the organic presidential body, resuscitating whatever was left of its unifying substance. On another, their proliferation calls attention to their dispersal and the impossibility of coherence. Thus the organic component of these bodily parts failed the test of time—Marcos began to stutter more frequently, became more incoherent, and his gestures grew frail and even comic. Still widely disseminated today, images of the ailing bodily parts no longer produce the same resonance they had in the past, calling further attention to the breakdown of the entity that was the presidential body.

What is ironic in Marcos's deployment of power through television in 1972 is its disruption through the same media in 1986. While griping to the whole nation about the insurrection led by Juan Ponce Enrile and Fidel V. Ramos, Marcos's image and voice were electronically zapped, replaced by static and TV "snow." Addressing a national broadcast in the company of his complete family, which included small children running around the makeshift news area in the palace, Marcos's image was obliterated by the insurrectionists, who had taken control of the television station. The televisual display of a cohesive presidential family was not enough to unify the nation. Marcos had tried to use the same forceful voice and gestures that characterized his fiery 1972 televised declaration of martial rule, but failed.

A newer image of the presidential body was developing: a "homemaker's" body that maximized the political mileage of her assassinated husband. Corazon Aquino's (1986–1992) public body would be consistently draped in yellow, her favorite color, which in the snap election campaign Imelda

8   "Quasi-corporeality" is a term used by Brian Massumi and Kenneth Dean to denote Reagan's body "*without* an image, [which] has social prestige, not for its inherent qualities or the superior symbolizations and ideations but simply because its kinetic geography is more far-reaching" (1994, 166–67).

Macho dancing engages a variety of everyday objects as props that focus attention on the central feature of the dancers erect penis: fire, grapes, candles, milk. *Clockwise from top left*, images scanned from VCDs: *Star Dancer* (2003); *Macho Valentine* (2005); *Erotic Dudes* (2004); *Macho King* (2003). Photos courtesy of Rolando B. Tolentino.

Marcos said reminded her of "jaundice or a lemon" (in Ellison 1988, 235). Aquino's body would also be initially constructed as a maternal body, giving birth to a clean moral national slate after a dark period of the nation's history.

In subsequent years, the public image of the presidential body has changed. Fidel Ramos (1992–1998) surrounded himself with phallic symbols to remasculinize the presidential body. A cigar in his mouth and the thumbs up symbol of his vision of an industrialized Philippines in 2000 were a phallic reinvestment in the nation's body. Joseph Estrada (1998–2001) conjured the image of the macho defender of the masses. Gloria Macapagal Arroyo's (2001–2010) periodic apologies for her short-tempered outbursts—usually via public scolding of errant officials—her monotone voice, her unapologetic declaration of a state of emergency early in February 2006, and her strong commitment to maintaining the military status quo all contributed to an aggressive image of presidential readiness. But her rule has been questioned repeatedly and dubbed illegitimate—both in terms of her winning office despite massive electoral fraud, and her highly questionable defense of political appointments, government contracts, and national development.

Macho dancing, the first generation

The dissemination of the presidential body as ideal affects the subject-formation of the majority of the nation's citizens. With limited access to

political and economic power, citizens mimic and "make do" with negotiating the ideals imposed by the substance and terms of the presidential
body. The conditions of abject massive poverty—resulting precisely from
the presidential maintenance of national politics through corruption, patronage politics, and elite-centered economics—are the very realities that
allow the presidential body to mobilize national bodies for his own geopolitical purpose ("geobodies"). For example, although relatively well-off
gays cruising economically disenfranchised heterosexual males was commonplace prior to Marcos's ascent to power, what Marcos did via his national development program based on the maximization of young laboring
bodies was to provide the commercial transaction with a quasi-legitimate
venue. The "gay bar" began to operate during the height of Marcos's political regimentation of laboring geobodies, and gay culture moved onto the
public political stage. A further niche enclave of elite gay performance more
intimately tied up with national power was harnessed by Imelda Marcos.

Imelda Marcos promoted and consequently privileged and legitimized
willing gay artists who enjoyed basking in their high-profile status as presidential accessories, especially those who celebrated the virtues of fashion
and beauty, such as designers Pitoy Moreno and Christian Espiritu. She
made gay identity somehow integral to the dispensation of presidential power. Ming Ramos, First Lady to Fidel Ramos, publicly endorsed and promoted the livelihood training program "Isang Gunting, Isang Suklay" (One Pair
of Scissors, One Comb, referring to haircutters and stylists) of Ricky Reyes,
a self-made gay "beautician" and owner of the franchise of hair salons and
host of a television beauty show bearing his name. And President Arroyo
included Ino Sotto's designs in her power wardrobe.

The gay bar both legitimizes the agency of other economically empowered gays in the nation and reconfigures the commercialization of sex, especially among economically disenfranchised male heterosexuals, the love
objects of commercial gay engagements in the Philippines. It is also uncanny that this local modern gay space was formulated at the time of Marcos's own intensified modernization of the nation. Club 690—now Klub
Sais—opened in the 1970s on Retiro Street in Quezon City and was the
first gay bar in the country. Presently, there are some 50 gay bars, concentrated mostly in urban centers throughout the Philippines. There are also
20 gay massage parlors in Metro Manila, another example of the permu-
tation of commercialized sex between gay and straight men. What has become dominant in gay identity in the public sphere is the commercialized
nature of sexual exchange.

The macho dancer has evolved as an aberrant figure of national and sexual geopolitics. As noted above, the snake dancing of the first generation of

A variety of fantasy costumes in an assortment of shows. *Clockwise from top left*, monk, construction worker, military (jacket), Middle Eastern. From *World Bubble Bath King* (2005); *Star Dancer* (2003); *Star Dancer* (2003); and *Private Show* (2003). Photos courtesy of Rolando B. Tolentino.

macho dancing was a feminine routine of slithery bodily movement starting from the toes, moving up to the legs and midsection, then to arms and hands, and the head. Or it could be the reverse: vertical movement beginning with the bopping of the head, fluidly moving down to the feet. Interspersed in this basic movement could be hand and arm gestures of either a crucified posture or circular movements in front of the dancer's midsection. The stomach or gut area is central for providing the strength and fluidity of the vertical movements. The crotch area is the focal point of the performer's display and viewers' attention. The crotch's curvature mimics the hardened yet fluid motions of the dancer's body. The macho dancer, after all, mimics the sexual desire of empowered gays, who in turn mimic the desire on the part of both the nation and the presidential administration for political prestige and cultural legitimacy.

Macho dancing, the second generation

With the toppling of Marcos in 1986, Aquino began the political and economic reworking of the nation to better its standing in the globalizing economy of the period. Her government returned the businesses Marcos appropriated for his administration and cronies, sequestered Marcos's properties, and then sold them to the private sector. She began to develop the laws that would privatize, liberalize, and commercialize the national economy. All these terms remain buzz words of neoliberalism, continuously reiterated by succeeding presidencies.

The political and economic developments honed another variant of macho dancing, a variant that ensured the form's global reception and acceptance into the marketplace. The second generation of macho dancing involves a slower-paced bodily movement, away from corporeal fluidity to the rhythmic fluidity of the dance music. Music choices usually fall into the slow rock category, and include the ballads of Celine Dion, Mariah Carey, and even Tracy Chapman, as well as those by local and East Asian singers.

The ideal is to infuse the dance with a masculine personality, initially presented by the dancer's costume—fitted denim shorts or boxer briefs and sleeveless tops, and what has become standard footwear, cowboy boots—and then in the jagged pacing of the dance steps themselves. The dancer sensually touches his body, from head to knees, while his heels pound the stage floor. Or he uses bars and beams to flaunt his body and tease the audience, or simulates dog styled anal intercourse or the missionary penetration of an imagined partner. What is produced is a campy rendition—a vulgarity in the masculine play, a gay performance of hypermasculinity—of a gay notion of heterosexual masculinity, represented as underclass, a brutish tease, sexually the "upper," and performative. The dancer's role-playing is reinforced by his costume (cowboy, working-class, underwear model-like aesthetic), the movement (macho sex moves), and the music (heterosexual romantic ballads by female singers and go-go dancers singing slow rock).

What is also in play is the construction of gay identity itself: economically of a higher status, a patron of sorts, yet also working within the patriarchal imperatives of the desired male heterosexual. This means that although the gay patron is financially better off, the real phallic power remains to be negotiated based on the terms of the macho dancer. After his dancing sequences, the macho dancer acts as a guest relations officer of the patron—who may be gay but may also be a young woman, usually a female Japayuki or groupie out for a night on the town, but nonetheless, economically empowered— keeping him or her company. The dancer remains in the service of the patron within the bar space, attending to his (or her) every need: offering information on how the club is run and on fellow dancers; on the power structure and what makes for good company, a conversationalist; and serving as temporary boyfriend. His labor also includes placing ice cubes in the guest's drink, keeping a napkin under it, ordering food, and motioning the waiter to bring the patron's bill. This is known as "tabling," where the dancer—usually still in costume—sits with the guest at his or her table.

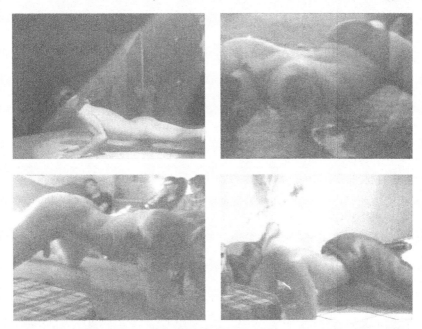

On all fours, the macho dancer moves throughout the stage area, simulating either the missionary or dog-style penetration of an imagined partner. *Clockwise from top left*, images from the scenes of *Private Show* (2003); *Macho King* (2003); *Erotic Dudes* (2004); *Macho Valentine* (2005). Photos courtesy of Rolando B. Tolentino.

The macho dancer can also be requested to service the patron or patrons more privately, within the smaller rooms surrounding the stage area of the gay bar. In this room, the macho dancer dances for the patron for some three songs. During each song, he takes off a piece of clothing until he dances naked. This routine is negotiable, and patrons may request more sexual acts. The "private show," as well as the "table" are performed on a per hour rate; the number of hours is based on the discretion and wallet of the patron, while the quality is at the discretion and skills of the dancer. The dancer is now a privatized laborer within the gay bar. In the first generation of macho dancers, there were no "VIP rooms" for "private shows" by dancers. Thus, services within the bar space were already covertly sexual. This next generation of dancers is housed in bars with private VIP rooms, which can provide for explicit yet publicly concealed sexual acts within the space.

From the open playing field of the stage and audience sections of the first generation of macho dancers, today's dancers can be summoned to perform for the private needs of the more economically empowered gays within the social hierarchy of gays and women in a gay bar, and within the more privatized social spaces of the gay bar. From an economic perspective, macho dancers prefer gay patrons to female patrons because the former tend to be more aggressive in engaging the dancers onstage, and more often solicit the dancers for private show services. Because of its steeper price, the private show is a badge of honor for both patron and dancer, flaunted as they both enter and exit this more exclusive space. The bar takes a cut from all of the dancers' operations within the gay bar space and gets the majority share of profits from drinks in tabled and VIP-room services. It also charges customers a hefty "bar fine" for "take out"—the privilege of leaving with boys for the rest of the night.

What this act does is to create within the gay bar a hierarchy of patrons and dancers, providing for more available services based on a greater capacity to pay and the more open commercialization of sex. This newer practice, together with the requisite details of cowboy boots and dance movements,

In a quick succession of moves between a half standing and kneeling position, the dancer thrusts his body sideways, forward, and backward, twirling and sometimes mimicking a gunfight, gyrating to the tempo of the blaring music. *Clockwise from top left*, scenes from *Dakota King* (2003); *Macho King* (2003); *Macho King* (2003); *Hallow Man Macho Quest*, (2004); *Asian Hunks* (2004); and *5th Best Male Exotic Dance* (2005). Photos courtesy of Rolando B. Tolentino.

is evidence of the state's orchestration in the service sector under neoliberalism. Services and rates are standardized. There is not much discrepancy in gay bars in Metro Manila between tabling a macho dancer and engaging him for a private show. Over time, production and consumption within the gay bar has become standardized, making it more profitable for owners and dancers and creating uniform expectations within the bar, and for commercialized sex in general. What the macho dancer has in common with other, newer masculine identities in the service sector—transvestite entertainer, underwear model, bikini contestant, etc.—is the use of masculinity as a commodity for achieving social mobility. In the bars, the youthful body of the heterosexual male becomes the bearer of capital. The service sector environment as engaged in national development then hones the male body to perform in various sexual ways, to develop a pleasing personality, to maintain and uplift national social ideals in their commercialized sex engagement. The standardization of commercialized desire, sex, social relations, and engagements ensures the efficient and reliable transactions in neoliberalism's service economy, allowing bodies as goods and capital itself to flow more fluidly. By linking heterosexual and gay men, the elite gay patron and the disenfranchised male dancer's relationship becomes the paradigm in the production of desire, as well as its materialization.

After all, elite gays have become a major force in the service sector—as talent managers, trainers, stylists, designers, academics, cosmetic surgeons and dermatologists, media managers, young entrepreneurs, and advertising specialists, among others. Like the burgeoning excess of bodies in the labor force—including the perennial presence of young bodies—youthful male heterosexuals seeking better opportunities for their families ("the sacrificial lamb" mode shared by him and his female counterparts with their OCW geobodies) will always be in steady if not increasing supply, given the limited mobility possible for service sector workers. Within the confines of service sector menial work, the seduction for social mobility is ever-present as an ideal in a nation in perennial crisis.

Body capital as new social mobility
This steady supply of bodies ensures some vertical opening in the usual lateral movement within the service sector. What is appreciated in the disenfranchised male body, as with women, is a colonial and elitist appearance: young, white or fair-skinned, tall or statuesque, nice-looking, with a "pleasing" personality, and a willingness to learn. With the advent of commercial products and services, this look can be modified further to meet the standards and prevailing tastes. The underclass disenfranchised male body has become the new passport for social mobility in the neoliberal age in the Philippines.

"Body capital," or the social privileging of colonial and elite corporeality and sexuality, is the new guarantor of social mobility. During the Spanish colonial period, land ownership was the only means of upward mobility. The American colonial period overtly introduced intellectual capital through the public education system, which made a larger number of colonial subjects eligible for wages and thus mobile. Covertly, the American colonial period, through the same educational apparatus, also introduced the young healthy body, mobilized in physical education classes, and allowed for the display of modern bodies, including women, in exercise, and men, more particularly through body building. Ferdinand and Imelda Marcos introduced the elite gay figure as cultural capital and afforded him legitimacy. Youthful men and

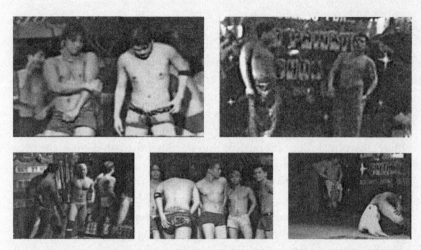

Especially during macho dancing competitions, the presence of all participants is part of the shows beginning and end, allowing audience members to set expectations and make their own final judgment. *Clockwise from top left*, images from *Naked Hunks* (2004); *Private Show* (2003); *Private Show* (2003); *Naked Hunks* (2004); *Hallow Man Macho Quest* (2004). Photos courtesy of Rolando B. Tolentino.

women were mobilized into the workforce, including the entertainment and sex industries. Young male heterosexuals gained access to financial capital and found a space to grapple with and navigate the crisis of the nation in the birth and rise of the gay bar under the Marcos dictatorship. In the hierarchization of power in the gay bar, the macho dancer is equal to the waiters and male domestic help as lowly employees in a structure where the owner—usually a member of the police force or an army man—is the absent landlord, with an OIC (officer-in-charge, a retired or daytime cop) as his surrogate. Under the OIC are the feminine gays of the bar, operating as floor or program managers. But unlike other male employees of the bar, the macho dancer is able to greater utilize his body for extra income and agency.

Philippine neoliberalism introduced, regimented, disseminated, and standardized body capital through beauty pageants, modeling and bikini searches, talent and game shows, and reality television. These have shown the possibility of moving socially upwards using bodily traits that meet the standards of the service sector industries. This body capital is regarded as a desirable resource, uplifting individuals and their impoverished families. It is primarily geared for the underclass and a middle class, who are thereby materially linked with the underclass. The men of the elite class who utilize their bodies for similar acts within the service sector industries do so with a degree of choice that differentiates them from the men of the underclass.

However, given the pervasive conditions of poverty and the overwhelming numbers of the poor, not too many men will have the chance to use their body capital. But the very nature of material bodies, being plastic, malleable, and organic, makes each individual, at least in fantasy, ready to attain middle-class status. Many men will choose to make the attempt in a progressive manner—from working in fast food outlets and malls, to becoming macho dancers and sex workers, to beauty pageant and modeling search contestants with the ultimate goal of making it big in show business. Show business, after all, is also based on the simulation of service sector post-industrial images, of which the dominant strain is the elite, gay, male, macho dancer paradigm.

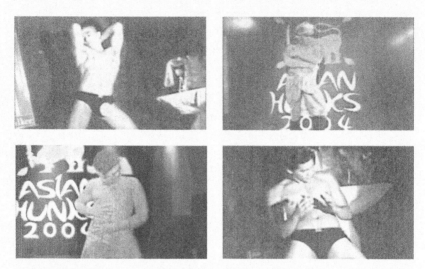

The macho dancer engages in a narcissistic act, indulging in his own eroticized body. To cue the audience response, the dancer sexualizes his body parts as incorporated in a sequence of his dance. *Clockwise from top left*, images from *5th Best Male Exotic Dancer* (2005); *Asian Hunks* (2004); *5th Best Male Exotic Dancer* (2005); *Asian Hunks* (2004). Photos courtesy of Rolando B. Tolentino.

Philippine poverty is feminized through the disenfranchisement of male labor, but what also needs to be foregrounded is the direct effect of poverty on women, especially from the underclass. The stampede tragedy that killed 74 people in the *Wowowee* lunchtime game show in February 2006 illustrates how business is mobilizing underclass bodies in the service sector industries. The underclass becomes part of the production of the service. By becoming contestants on a trivia game show based on what is perceived as underclass knowledge, the underclass itself is enjoined in the production and consumption of the game show. Tens of thousands lined up days in advance at the venue, waiting for the chance to become a contestant on the show that promised to double its cash pot for the first anniversary presentation. When not everyone could be accommodated in the huge venue, a stampede broke out. Of the 74 people who died, only three were men, highlighting the very feminized face of poverty (see Contreras 2006). The desire for social mobility rests on the very women and men who are made to consume the products for collective progress: the winner of the *Pinoy Big Brother* television series—which, like its US counterpart, is based on underclass[9] cellphone voting ("Pinoy" is colloquial for "Filipino")—was Keanna Reeves, an ex-prostitute who turned a new leaf—the most underclass of the reality show finalists. What's more, among the voters are the scavengers of the garbage mountains of Payatas, Quezon City, who spend the few pesos they earn on text messaging that costs one peso per text.

Similar to the middle-class ethos of movie viewing—watching a simulation of romance, action, or horror, and paying to see love, feel loved, or be terrorized—desire is individualized. For viewers of the Keanna Reeves story and the victims and survivors of the Payatas tragedy, the desire is internalized individually, and furthermore, gentrified. In young male heterosexual niches, the desire for economic and social empowerment is sexualized, feeding on a fantasized ideal. On the one hand, the gay elite is the source of the pink peso (a reference to the economic power of gay consumers in the Philippines), especially in the ongoing intensification of the nation's economic and political crises. On the other, the heterosexual male performer is the beneficiary in the pink economy. Both desires are privatized in the imagined agency of individual mobility through each person's use of the other's body, a symbiotic relationship that becomes the modality of the ego-ideal's production of newer body capital: a commercialized masculinity for the male performer, and a viable gay sexuality that can afford to pay for entertainment. The simulated body of empowerment is proliferated among the masses of poor. How can one resist the oasis in the desert, even if it is just a creation of one's own and the desert's delusion? The simulation becomes real, allowing the disenfranchised body to move inch by inch, second by second, at least at a certain disjointed tempo, within the quagmire and vicissitudes of infinite poverty and crisis that is the Philippine nation.

As he performs his nightly grind, the macho dancer becomes both a real and a simulated image of a body desiring and performing social mobility. He realizes his potential, and exercises his individual empowerment, only to return the following night. Desire and performance of social mobility, after all, are only posed in simulation. In gay bars, as in the Philippine nation, real mobility is evasive, restricted, and temporary. Yet every night, the desire and the performance of social mobility are reenacted.

9   The economically disenfranchised underclass represents some 80 percent of the Philippine population.

Bibliography

Carrel, Paul. "German Service Sector Resists Demands for Big Pay Increases." *The International Herald Tribune*, 20 February 2008. Accessed 6 January 2009. https:// www.nytimes.com/2008/02/20/business/worldbusiness/20iht-gcon.4.10243541. html?searchResultPosition=15.

Catalan, Daisy. "The Diversity of Filipinos." In *Remaking America: Contemporary US Immigration*, vol. 4. New Haven, CT: Yale-New Haven Teachers Institute, 1996. http://teachersinstitute.yale.edu/curriculum/units/1996/4/96.04.05.x.html.

Cleveland, Douglas B. "The Role of Services in the Modern US Economy." *US Department of Commerce International Trade Administration, Office of Service Industries.* 1999. Accessed 6 January 2009. http://72.14.235.132/ search?q=cache:09z6zsDWwaAJ:www.trade.gov/td/sif/PDF/ROLSERV199.PDF+ 80+gdp+us+service+economy&hl=en&ct=clnk&cd=2&gl=ph (site discontinued).

Contreras, Volt. "Feminine Face of Poverty: Only 3 Men Died in ULTRA." *Philippine Daily Inquirer*, 9 February 2006. Accessed 12 February 2009. http://news.inq7.net/ nation/index.php?l&story_ id=65582.

Ellison, Katherine W. *Imelda, Steel Butterfly of the Philippines*. New York: McGraw-Hill, 1988.

Hong Kong General Chamber of Commerce. "Welcome and Introduction." Accessed 6 January 2009. http://www.hkcsi.org.hk/ old/about/HKCSI.html.

Japan Statistics Bureau. "Chapter 3, Economy." 2008. Accessed 6 January 2009. http:// www.stat.go.jp/english/data/handbook/pdf/ c03cont.pdf (site discontinued).

Maglipon, Jo-Ann. "Reprise 1983." In *Primed: Selected Stories 1972–1992: Reportage on an Archipelago*. Mandaluyong: Anvil Publishing, Inc., 1993.

Massumi, Brian, and Kenneth Dean. "Postmortem on the Presidential Body, or Where the Rest of Him Went." In *Body Politics: Disease, Desire and the Family*, edited by Michael Ryan and Avery Gordon, 155–73. Boulder: Westview Press, 1994.

Namatame, Akira. "Agent-based Modelling in Services Science." Invited talk, AI-ECON Research Center, National Chengchi University, 2006. Accessed 6 January 2009. http://www.nda.ac.jp/~nama/ (site discontinued).

Pabico, Alex. "Despite the Risks, Filipino Seafarers Toil in the World's Oceans." *Our Latest Report (Philippine Center for Investigative Journalism)*. 2003. Accessed 12 Februrary 2006. http://www.pcij.org/stories/2003/seafarers. html (site discontinued).

SME Toolkit. "Philippines Economic Indicators." http://www.smetoolkit.org/smetoolkit/ en/content/ en/740/Philippines-Economic-Indicators (site discontinued).

Suarez, E.T. "RP Seamen Remit $318M in 4 Months, Last Year's Figure Exceeded." *The Overseas Filipino Workers Online*. 20 September 2001. Accessed 12 February 2006. http://www.theofwonline.com/old/z_rp_seamen.htm.

Tolentino, Rolando B. "Articulations of the Nation-Space: Cinema, Cultural Politics and Transnationalism in the Philippines." PhD diss., University of Southern California, 1996.

———. "Mattering National Bodies and Sexualities: Corporeal Contest in Marcos and Brocka." In *Violence and the Body: Race, Gender, and the State*, edited by Arturo J. Aldama, 113–33. Bloomington: Indiana University Press, 2003.

The 4th Migrants' Pride took place in Hong Kong's Central district, beginning at Edinburgh Place, passing the HSBC headquarters, and ending close to the Landmark. Photo courtesy of Athena Lam.

This essay was previously published in *GLQ: A Journal of Lesbian and Gay Studies* 14, no. 2–3 (June 2008): 403–24.

KALE BANTIGUE FAJARDO

Transportation: Translating Filipino and Filipino American Tomboy Masculinities through Global Migration and Seafaring

A sea of (Filipino/a) global migrants

Recently, the *New York Times* featured a report on the rising numbers of global migrants who collectively send oceanic-size remittances back home to the global south. The *Sunday Magazine* cover includes a photograph of a Filipina nurse—posed as abandoned, forlorn, and castaway—wearing medical scrubs, white shoes in hand, barefoot on a distant shore (Abu Dhabi?), aquamarine waters in the background; while inside the magazine a lengthy article discusses growing waves of migration from the global south to north, specifically focusing on the near constant outflow of Filipino/a migrants as a case study. The isolated and lonesome Filipina nurse on the magazine cover is revealing. She signifies how global migration and labor in general, and Filipino/a global migration and labor in particular, have been feminized.[1] That is, more women than men from the global south, including the Philippines, migrate to and work in the global north. Beyond suggesting the numerical differences in Filipino/a male and female migration patterns, she evokes a specific genealogy of how the Philippines as a nation and Filipino peoples in general have been feminized through US and Japanese colonial, imperialist, capitalist, and misogynist discourses, which consistently inscribe the Philippines as a feminine and hence "weak nation-state," and the country's citizens and workers as exploited people, largely women.[2] Historically, these discourses have circulated through the figure of the Filipina as "prostitute," "mail-order bride," or "DH" (domestic

1 See, for example, Nicole Constable, *Maid to Order in Hong Kong: Stories of Filipina Workers* (Ithaca: Cornell University Press, 1997); and Rhacel Salazar Parreñas, *Servants of Globalization: Women, Migration, and Domestic Work* (Stanford: Stanford University Press, 2001).

2 Neferti X. Tadiar, *Fantasy-Production: Sexual Economies and Other Philippine Consequences for the New World Order* (Hong Kong: Hong Kong University Press, 2004).

helper). The wind-tossed and forsaken Filipina nurse brought to a foreign shore by the powerful tides of economic globalization is therefore a new twist on an entrenched discourse of Philippine and Filipino/a feminization, marginalization, and disempowerment.

Within this social context, in the Philippines and the diaspora, sea-based migration and transportation—also known as seafaring—has emerged as an important economic and cultural space through which Filipinos counter these discourses. Because seafaring is a profession where Filipino men are employed in large numbers, seafaring and seamen provide alternative spaces and figures for Filipino state officials, cultural workers, seamen, and even anthropologists to highlight a more masculine occupation and image of the Philippines and its people.[3]

Although a largely invisible migrant group in the United States, Filipino seamen can be found working on ships docked in every major port around the world. They constitute the largest ethnic/racial/national group in the industry's workforce and currently constitute about twenty-eight percent of the labor in global shipping. Setting a national record in 2006, 260,000 Filipino seamen worked on thousands of container ships and oil tankers, which transport ninety percent of the world's goods and commodities, as well as cruise ships, which transport tourists.[4] Locally (in the Philippines), Filipino seamen as "OFWs" (Overseas Filipino Workers) are significant because they contribute huge sums of foreign currency to the national economy. In 2006 Filipino seamen sent home approximately $2 billion.[5] In the same year, OFWs (land- and sea-based) remitted a record high $12.8 billion. This global-local picture suggests why OFWs in general and Filipino seamen in particular are socially significant in Philippine and diasporic contexts.

3   I use the word *seamen* because it is the term commonly used by seamen, their families, and local people in the Philippines. *Seafarer* and *Overseas Filipino Worker* are terms more widely used by the Philippine government and nongovernmental organizations. On state discourse, see Kale Bantigue Fajardo, "Of Galleons and Globalization," *Mains'l Haul: A Journal of Pacific Maritime History* 38, nos. 1–2 (2002): 61–65; for a literary perspective, see Carlos Cortes, *Longitude* (Quezon City: University of the Philippines Press, 1998).

4   Many Filipino seafarers (men and women) work on cruise ships; my research primarily focuses on Filipino seamen on industrial container ships. For information on multinational cruise corporations, see Ross A. Klein, *Cruise Ship Squeeze: The New Pirates of the Seven Seas* (Gabriola Island, BC: New Society, 2005).

5   Maricel Burgonio, "2006 OFW Remittances Hit Record $12.8 B," *Manila Times*, 16 February 2007, http:// www.manilatimes.net/national/2007/feb/16/yehey/top_stories/20070216top4.html.

For ten years I have been researching how working-class Filipino seamen imagine, experience, and create their masculinities through their everyday practices in global shipping, as well as how the Philippine state and other Filipino subjects imagine and produce Filipino masculinities through the sea and seafaring. From 1997 to 2002, I conducted ethnographic fieldwork with Filipino seamen in Manila and Oakland (primarily at maritime ports), and also with state officials, business people, and seafarer advocates in these two port cities. I gained access to Filipino seamen during fieldwork by accompanying (Catholic) seafarer advocates who were visiting ships, and I also visited ships independently. My encounters and conversations with seamen in ports generally ranged in length from a few minutes to an hour, usually during meals or work breaks.[6] In metropolitan Manila and the provinces, I had longer conversations with seamen who were back from sea; those looking to begin or renew contracts with shipping companies; those still attending maritime schools; and retired seamen. In the summer of 2006, as a passenger-ethnographer, I traveled by container ship from the Port of Oakland to the Port of Hong Kong via the northern Pacific Ocean with stops in Tokyo, Osaka (Japan), and Kiaoshung (Taiwan) to complete follow-up research.

Through this fieldwork I observed a recurring narrative about Filipino seamen used by Philippine state officials, cultural workers, and seamen. This narrative suggests that Filipino seamen are largely heterosexual, geographically and sexually mobile, and heroically nationalistic, while simultaneously being family oriented and usually "macho." Although aspects of this narrative accurately describe some Filipino seamen's experiences, my objective has been to intervene in heteropatriarchal understandings by ethnographically addressing the gaps, contradictions, and contingencies in mainstream representations of Filipino (seamen's) masculinities. These fissures become more intelligible when Filipino seamen's masculinities are engaged through their intimate relationalities—that is, through their close social relationships—with Filipino tomboys.[7] Here, the term

6   The relatively brief duration of conversations is partially due to the fact that while ships are docked in port, seamen are quite busy. Because of mechanization and increased time pressures, working in port is often more fast paced than working at sea (although this depends on the seaman's position).

7   Scott Morgensen uses the phrase "intimate relationalities" to describe the historically close political and cultural relationships between US sexual minority formations and two-spirit (American Indian) formations. See Morgensen's forthcoming book, *Settler Sexuality and the Politics of Indigeneity. Tomboy* is an English word that has been

tomboy broadly refers to male- or masculine-identified females or transgendered subjects on the female-to-male (FTM) spectrum of embodiments, practices, and/ or identities in the Philippines or diaspora who often have sexual and emotional relationships with feminine females who identify as "women." As a result of focusing on seamen's relations with tomboys, dominant state narratives of seamen's watertight masculinities begin to leak, revealing instead the connections and fluidities between conventional and transgender masculinities. The Philippines at this intersection is neither a forlorn and castaway nurse nor a macho seaman, but a contact zone between heterogeneously gendered and situated subjects who come together in dialogue on shore and at sea.[8]

As a researcher who enacts and embodies queer and transgender Filipino (American) tomboy masculinity, I learned that upon meeting and getting to know me, Filipino seamen wanted to share commentaries about tomboys in their past and present lives. Conversations with seamen about tomboys enabled me to address ethnographically the relationships between Filipino seamen's heterosexual masculinities and Filipino tomboy masculinities, which in turn provided me with an opportunity to develop a queer, transgender, and transnational narrative intervention and cultural critique—rather than naturalize and reinforce the (Philippine) state's heteronormative constructions of Filipino (seamen's) masculinities. Thus, what at first glance appears to be a heteronormative phenomenon (Filipino seamen in the global shipping industry), actually contains and reveals nonnormative or queer cultural dynamics, including the affinities between working-class Filipino (sea)men and tomboys, as well as a more expansive and inclusive understanding of Filipino masculinities. In this essay, through queer, immigrant, transgender, and transnational Filipino (American) cultural logics, I argue that differently situated Filipino masculinities—heterosexual male and tomboy— must be understood in relation to, *not* apart from, each other.

"Tagalog-ized" (i.e., the first o is pronounced with an even shorter o sound than the English version). Following the historian Noenoe K. Silva's lead, I do not italicize Tagalog words in this essay. Silva states that she does not italicize Hawai'ian words in order "to resist making the native tongue appear foreign" (*Aloha Betrayed: Native Hawaiian Resistance to American Colonialism* [Durham, NC: Duke University Press, 2004], 13).

8   Omise'eke Natasha Tinsley theorizes oceanic spaces (e.g., black Atlantic) as queer racialized spaces. Tinsley's black queer feminist reading of oceans, ships, and shipmates is in dialogue with the analysis here. See Omise'eke Natasha Tinsley, "Black Atlantic, Queer Atlantic: Queer Imaginings of the Middle Passage," *GLQ: A Journal of Lesbian and Gay Studies* 14, no. 2–3 (June 2008).

Transportation

As a (self-identified) queer, immigrant, and transgender Filipino American tomboy situated on both sides of the Pacific (the Philippines and the United States), I emphasize here a queer, transgender Filipino/American translocal, transnational, and transport(ation)-based cultural interpretation of Filipino seafaring and masculinities. Although migration studies often begin with the arrival of the migrant or immigrant in the "receiving country," the transportation framework I suggest includes examining the spaces in between and across countries/localities/spaces (the Philippines, the United States, the Pacific Ocean), and how movement and geographic positioning re/configure Filipino identities and masculinities. In particular, I examine transportation spaces, places, and movements such as ports, seas, ships, seafaring, migration, and travel, and how mobility reinforces, informs, or disrupts cultural meanings.

This understanding of transportation is partially informed by James Clifford's cultural theorizing in *Routes: Travel and Translation in the Late Twentieth Century*, particularly his idea that "travel [movement] is constitutive of culture." Clifford elaborates on the importance of movement by saying that "thinking historically is a process of locating oneself in space and time. And a location, in [this] perspective . . . is an *itinerary* rather than a bounded site—a series of encounters and translations."[9] Inspired by Clifford's understanding of travel, translations, and itineraries, I foreground cultural encounters and translations in ports and at sea, and suggest how specific embodied practices of mobility and movement—sea-based transportation, migration, and travel—are constitutive of racialized and classed Filipino masculinities. I use the terms *transportation* and *seafaring* to evoke the fact that Filipino seamen are moving through the sea as *sea-based migrant workers*—not as recreational elite travelers, which Clifford acknowledges is what the term *travel* usually connotes. By evoking transportation, I am not suggesting that transportation and seafaring do not involve moments of pleasure or recreation; rather, I do so to acknowledge that the global shipping industry is a (disciplined) site of (largely global south) migrant labor.

In addition to evoking movement across and in between spaces, transportation also calls up gender fluidity and inclusiveness, which the term *transgender* suggests. The "trans" in transgender and transportation evokes movement between and across culturally constructed racialized and classed masculinities and femininities, as well as movement in/through/between

9   James Clifford, *Routes: Travel and Translation in the Twentieth Century* (Cambridge, MA: Harvard University Press, 1997), 11, emphasis mine.

spaces. In other words, transportation as a term and framework highlights the intersections of embodied movement and migration (seafaring) *and* the fluidity of (racialized and classed) gender formations. With this transgender-informed understanding of transportation, I suggest that the non-gender-normative and nonheteronormative formations of Filipino tomboy can be interpreted as expressions and embodiments of transgender Filipino masculinities.

Although many middle-class lesbian activists in the Philippines and diaspora regularly use *tomboy* to describe or evoke Filipina working-class butch lesbians, I suggest that Filipino tomboy formations are akin to other transgender female masculinities rooted and routed through Southeast Asia, such as tombois in Indonesia and toms in Thailand. Anthropologist Megan J. Sinnott, for example, writes that toms in and from Thailand can be understood as "female 'men' " or "transgendered females," while anthropologist Evelyn Blackwood writes that "tomboi is a term used for females acting in the manner of men (*gaya laki-laki*)."[10] In agreement with these ethnographers, I suggest that the Filipino tomboys can also be understood as a form of female masculinity or an embodiment of female manhood or lalaki (the Tagalog word for male/man/guy). With this understanding of transgender masculinities, in addition to being in conversation with interdisciplinary queer studies scholars in the United States, I also seek to be in dialogue with Filipina feminists in the Philippines and diaspora who regularly advance the idea that Filipino tomboys are always lesbians or women.

Moreover, because tomboy is a term and formation that travels and circulates in and between the Philippines, Southeast Asia, and diasporic locations, I intentionally link queer and transgender with tomboy to indicate my transnationally and diasporically situated subject position and interpretive framework. My intention here is not to transport the terms *queer* or *transgender* to the Philippines in a "Western," US American, or global north colonial or imperialist manner but to emphasize the transnational, trans-Pacific, and transport connections and cultural flows between the Philippines and regional, and diasporic, geographies. That is, Filipino/a peoples and ideas flow back and forth between the Philippines and diasporic locations. While it is important to understand the heterogeneity of Philippine/Asian local

10   Megan J. Sinnott, *Toms and Dees: Transgender Identity and Female Same-sex Relationships in Thailand* (Honolulu: University of Hawai'i Press, 2004); Evelyn Blackwood, "*Tombois* in West Sumatra: Constructing Masculinity and Erotic Desire," in *Female Desires: Same-Sex Relations and Transgender Practices across Cultures*, ed. Evelyn Blackwood and Saskia E. Wieringa (New York: Columbia University Press, 1999).

understandings and embodiments of tomboyness, it is also important to understand diasporic and immigrant interpretations and practices of tomboy, where tomboy can also signify FTM transgenderism.

Thus I connect Philippine and diasporic cultural logics and critique through the queer diasporic interpretive lens suggested by Gayatri Gopinath.[11] Gopinath forcefully challenges the dominance of Indian nationalist ideologies, which privilege India as a homeland and marginalize South Asian diasporic communities. Through queer and feminist critical readings of (queer) South Asian public cultures (music, film, novels, activism), Gopinath intervenes in the heteronormative and patriarchal logics of Indian nationalist ideologies rooted in India and routed through South Asian diasporas. Building on Gopinath's framework, I intend *not* to privilege the homeland/nation (Philippines) *or* the diaspora (United States) as the original site of cultural purity or queer authenticity. This analytical and political position is based largely on ethnographic fieldwork, but also personal life experiences, which include regular travel between the United States and the Philippines, as well as substantial residency in both locations.[12] As a (self defined) queer, immigrant, transgender Filipino American tomboy (researcher) who is situated in translocal, transnational, and transport contexts in the Philippines and the United States, I precisely evoke these multiple identity formations (queer, transgender, tomboy, and immigrant), which have different kinds of currency in the Philippines and diaspora (e.g., United States), to emphasize and highlight the complexities of how tomboy as a term, cultural practice, and embodiment circulates, and how tomboy formations are translated and interpreted in different Philippine, diasporic, and immigrant contexts.

The intimate relationalities between Filipino heterosexual (sea)men and Filipino tomboys, as well as the complexities of tomboy formations, became increasingly clear to me through fieldwork in Manila, Oakland, and at sea. As a new ethnographer who lived in the Philippines in the late 1990s, I initially thought that Filipino seamen would speak with me about their lives at sea, the working conditions on ships and in ports, and the politics of Philippine overseas migration policies (since these were my key research areas). Indeed, over the years I have met dozens of Filipino seamen

11   Gayatri Gopinath, *Impossible Desires: Queer Diasporas and South Asian Public Cultures* (Durham, NC: Duke University Press, 2005).

12   I immigrated to the United States in 1973 and have been traveling regularly to the Philippines since then, with trips lasting from ten days to ten months, in the following years: 1977, 1978, 1987, 1988–1989, 1992, 1994, 1996, 1997–1998, 2000, 2005, and 2006.

who have shared stories and social commentaries about life at sea and in port(s). However, I also learned that Filipino seamen wanted to converse with me about transgender Filipino masculinities through the figure of the tomboy. These encounters highlighted how my subject position as tomboy enabled—rather than disabled—certain interactions, exchanges, and conversations with Filipino seamen.

During fieldwork, working-class seamen primarily interacted with me as a Filipino masculine and transgendered subject (tomboy), not as a Filipina feminine subject (woman). As I understand these ethnographic moments, they largely occurred because Filipino seamen understood tomboy to be a working-class embodiment of Filipino masculinity that, for them, was not routed or rooted through/in lesbianism or womanhood. With this shared understanding, we co-navigated conversations by discussing tomboys more generally, and more specifically moved toward seamen's stories, memories, and thoughts about tomboy friends, relatives, and acquaintances. Ethnographic encounters also evoked my own memories as a (young) tomboy in the Philippines, especially memories of Filipino men and tomboys closely interacting with one another.

To further elaborate on these points, this essay analytically moves between different geographic spaces, using what the anthropologist Anna Tsing calls a "patchwork ethnographic [method]" produced in "discrete patches."[13] For Tsing this means ethnographically engaging different geographic sites and scales of cultural contact and interpretive framings, including "the local," "the national," "the regional," "the transnational," and "the global." Here, I evoke and highlight patches or contact zones of encounter and connection, including metropolitan Manila to the San Francisco Bay Area, the Philippines and the United States, and ships in port and at sea.

My approach also dialogues with Clifford's notion of narrative "collage" and Tsing's use of a "portfolio of [writing] methods." Clifford says that he experiments with "travel writing and poetic collage along with formal essays" to "evoke the multiple and uneven practices of research . . . and [the] borders of academic work;" Tsing states that she uses a "portfolio of methods," which results in knowledge that is "variously ethnographic, journalistic, and archival."[14] Informed and inspired by Tsing's and Clifford's interdisciplinary "writing culture" sensibilities, I use multiple methods here to make sense of the intimate relationalities between differently situated Filipino

---

13   Anna Tsing, *Friction: An Ethnography of Global Connection* (Princeton: Princeton University Press, 2005), x.

14   Clifford, *Routes*, 12; Tsing, *Friction*, 3.

masculinities, including ethnographic field- work, discursive analysis, travel reportage, and personal reflection. As a result, the knowledge articulated here is a combination of ethnography, travelogue, and autobiography.

Filipino tomboys: Transnational, trans-Pacific, transport meanings

To understand the full significance of the intimate relation between Filipino heterosexual masculinities and Filipino tomboy masculinities, it is useful to situate and unpack the cultural politics of tomboy cultural meanings in transnational, trans-Pacific, and transport contexts. In Manila and other locations in the Philippines, *tomboy* is a term used to describe a range of gender and sexual practices and identities, including (1) woman-identified lesbianism often transculturated via white US- or European-based notions of gender and sexuality, (2) working-class female-to-male transgender or transsexual embodiments and formations of masculinities where tomboys identify and/or live as lalaki (males/men), and (3) neither "women," "lesbians," or "men" but an entirely different third or fourth gender formation.[15] Cultural interpretations based on the second and third notions do not frequently circulate in scholarly knowledge production, and self-representations by Filipino tomboys are currently limited perhaps because of a lack of economic and educational access (especially in the Philippines). As a result, the first understanding (tomboys as lesbian women) has emerged as a dominant academic and political narrative in the Philippines and in some parts of the diaspora. That is, non-tomboy-authored narratives about tomboys circulate much more widely and have considerable cultural capital.

A significant aspect of how many Filipinos understand tomboy practices and identities in the Philippines and some immigrant communities in North America suggests that being poor or working class is central. This is reflected in popular Philippine discourse where tomboys are often inscribed as poor, working class, unemployed, or working in low-pay service-industry positions as bus conductors, security guards, factory workers, or overseas migrants. While not as visible in popular culture as baklas, poor tomboys can be found in the pages of Manila-based tabloids, as well as in locally made films such as *Tomboy Nora* (1970) and *T-Bird at Ako* (*T-Bird and I*, 1982), both starring the popular Philippine actress Nora Aunor. In an activist example, Information Center Womyn for Womyn (ICWFW), a

---

15   The other gender formation often discussed in Filipino/a contexts is bakla (a Filipino/a male femininity or gay men's formation). See, for example, Martin F. Manalansan IV, *Global Divas: Filipino Gay Men in the Diaspora* (Durham, NC: Duke University Press, 2003), and Bobby Benedicto, "The Haunting of Gay Manila: Global Space-Time and the Specter of Kabaklaan," *GLQ 14*, no. 2–3 (June 2008).

lesbian nongovernmental organization in Manila, conducted a study of what they describe as "working-class lesbians." The organization, which codes tomboys as lesbians rather than as transgender, reports that tomboys in their study were employed in positions such as domestic helper, barber, photocopying clerk, street food vendor, train station security guard, tennis court attendant, retail clerk, library assistant, and massage therapist.[16] In a more literary account, Nice Rodriguez (a Filipino tomboy based in Canada) writes in the short story "Every Full Moon" that the tomboy protagonist "Remy" (a.k.a. "Rambo") works as a bus conductor in metropolitan Manila: "A dangerous job meant for men and butches."[17]

Confirming the precarious economic status of tomboys, the video exposé *Behind the Labels: Garment Workers on US Saipan* (dir. Tia Lessin; 2003) features Filipino tomboy anti-sweatshop activist Chie Abad who worked in a Gap clothing assembly plant for six years in Saipan and who later exposed and organized against the Gap's exploitative employment practices. Abad left the Philippines in the early 1990s to find work in an overseas factory in Saipan. In a personal communication Abad stated, "Many [Filipino] tomboys work abroad as overseas contract workers because they can't find jobs in the Philippines. The Philippines is poor and on top of that tomboys do not want to work in some fields because many companies and government agencies require female employees to wear women's clothing like blouses and skirts."[18] While in Saipan, Abad observed that other tomboys also migrated there for economic reasons. Abad's analysis, which emphasizes a transgender rather than lesbian framework for tomboyness, reveals how the Philippine state's and a multinational corporations' heteronormative gender essentialism attempts to police and enforce Filipina femininity and womanhood, severely limiting tomboy masculine gender expressions and both their and our economic opportunities.

Translating and interpreting tomboy in a US context, Gigi Otálvaro-Hormillosa, a queer performance artist of Colombian and Filipino descent writing from the San Francisco Bay Area, asks, "To what extent does the queer Pinay (Filipina) butch enjoy privilege in the US and in the Philippines, since 'butch' or 'tomboy' status deprives her of power in various

16   Amelia M. de Guzman and Irene R. Chia, *Working Class Lesbians in the Philippines*, 2005, http://www.icwow.org/WCL/WCLenglish.pdf.

17   Nice Rodriguez, *Throw It to the River* (Toronto: Women's Press, 1993), 26.

18   Chie Abad, pers. comm., February 2002.

diasporic settings[?]"[19] Here, Otálvaro-Hormillosa seems to be responding to what she sees as the unequal power relationships between tomboys,
whom she equates with butch lesbians or dykes, and Filipino gay men in
the diaspora. She responds, more specifically, to what she understands as
the "infantilization of the lesbian" through the term *tomboy* as deployed by
anthropologist Martin Manalansan. According to Otálvaro-Hormillosa,
Manalansan inadequately addresses queer Pinays, tomboys, and butches,
and she critiques him for his "brief derogatory mentions" of Filipina lesbians.[20] Through her critique, Otálvaro-Hormillosa attempts to underscore
the power "differences between men and women." That is, she respectively
equates baklas and tomboys with manhood and womanhood/lesbianism
in an immigrant and diasporic context (the United States). Unlike the previously mentioned accounts, Otálvaro-Hormillosa's analysis does not foreground class as a significant marker of tomboyness. Instead, she emphasizes womanness and diasporic or immigrant queer positionality as the clear
central markers of difference in how she deploys and translates tomboy. Although Otálvaro-Hormillosa cites Michael Tan, cautioning, "It is dangerous
to transport Western terms onto sexual practices and identities," she does
precisely that by unequivocally equating tomboyness with lesbianism and
womanhood in her essay. This demonstrates how notions of lesbianism may
get universally transposed.

An alternative reading of Otálvaro-Hormillosa may suggest, however,
that through transculturation she seeks to highlight a (racialized) queer Pi-
nay/Filipina American framework, suggesting that queer Pinays in the diaspora deploy tomboy to refer to *Filipina* butches, lesbians, dykes, and queers
in a US or North American context. In other words, in a diasporic space
Otálvaro-Hormillosa seeks to locally rework, translate, and "Filipina-ize"
terms, ideologies, and formations that regularly circulate globally (womanness and lesbianism). In this different geopolitical location (in the United
States, outside the Philippines), Otálvaro-Hormillosa clearly underscores
a queer lesbian Pinay feminist or "peminist" perspective.[21] This is unlike

19   Gigi Otálvaro-Hormillosa, "Performing Citizenship and 'Temporal Hybridity'
in a Queer Diaspora," *Antithesis* 11 (2000), http://www.devilbunny.org/temporal_
hybridity.htm.

20   My position is that in *Global Divas* Manalansan does not significantly focus
on Filipina tomboys, lesbians, and dykes primarily because it was not within the scope
of his study to address these racialized gender/sexuality formations.

21   Melinda L. de Jésus, ed., *Pinay Power: Peminist Critical Theory: Theorizing the
Filipina/American Experience* (New York: Routledge, 2005).

mainstream Filipina feminist notions in the Philippines, which suggest that tomboys are generally *not* feminist or even anti-feminist. While articulating a clear feminist perspective that highlights gender and power differences in the diaspora, Otálvaro-Hormillosa sidelines class as an axis of difference that intersects with other axes—race, gender, sexuality, nationality, location—in a co-constitutive nexus.

What Filipina feminist analyses published on both sides of the Pacific have in common is that both often use gender essentialist notions of tomboy. That is, queer Pinay feminists in the United States such as Otálvaro-Hormillosa or Filipina lesbian feminists such as those working for ICWFW in Manila suggest that tomboys are unequivocally women or lesbians. This kind of interpretation is reflected, for example, in Amelia M. de Guzman and Irene R. Chia's report on "working-class lesbians" in the Philippines for the ICWFW. De Guzman and Chia conducted lengthy interviews with nine tomboys (my term, not the ICWFW researchers') in Manila. Based on the interviews, their oral history project documents topics such as when tomboys "discovered they were lesbians," their employment histories, their recreational habits, their butch-femme relationships, and their religious practices. Throughout their analysis, de Guzman and Chia primarily use the term *lesbian* to describe the research participants, although admitting that a "unique element that [they] noticed among the participants is their hesitation to say the word lesbian." At another point in their report, de Guzman and Chia write, "All of them said that they like acting like men. They actually want to become men."[22] In my reading of de Guzman and Chia, they seek to advance a Filipina lesbian feminist perspective by applying the term *lesbian* to poor and working-class tomboys who are clearly uncomfortable with lesbian/woman as an identity and in some cases articulate a desire to become men or live as men.

As a result of how being poor or working class intersects with Filipino tomboy formations in common understandings, my own particular embodiment of tomboy masculinity produced unstable readings in "the field." On any given day in Manila (in different settings), Manileños interpreted my subject position in multifarious ways, for example, as "man," "woman," "bakla," or "tomboy." They also identified how these gender/sexual formations intersect with race, nationality, and class background: namely, "Filipino," "balikbayan," "OFW," "Japanese," "Chinese," or "Korean."[23] But significantly,

22   Guzman and Chia, *Working Class Lesbians in the Philippines*, 14, 18.
23   Balikbayan historically refers to Filipinos/as from North America who return to the Philippines. The (Ferdinand) Marcos dictatorship coined this term and promoted tourism with Filipino/a immigrants in Canada and the United States in the 1970s.

when I traveled in and through the port area, if I introduced and represented myself as a student researcher (at the time) originally from Malolos, Bulacan, the town and province in the Philippines where I was born, and conversed in Tagalog, Filipino seamen generally interpreted my personhood as tomboy and interacted with me as a masculine/transgender subject.[24] Tomboy here refers to transgender FTM masculinity that is not woman- or lesbian-identified. Their reactions to my "localness" indicate that the Filipino seamen I encountered also understood tomboy formations in classed ways; namely, that tomboys are often locally situated, poor, or working class. Their reading of me as a (transgender) tomboy and their general understanding of tomboy formations were reinforced if I expressed a working-class sensibility or personal genealogy. For example, if I mentioned that I traveled by jeepney (a form of cheap street-level transportation) from Quezon City to the port or Ermita (a neighborhood in Manila where lots of seamen congregate) rather than by taxi, car, or chauffeur, which from the seamen's perspectives are what middle-class, wealthy, or balikbayan Filipinos might use for local transportation, they interacted with me as a (transgender) tomboy. In other cases, if I revealed my family's humble roots in Malolos, or that one of my male cousins was a seaman, or that a female cousin migrated to Kuwait as an OFW, or that an uncle migrated to "Saudi" (Arabia) and lived and worked there for many years, these personal disclosures marked my genealogy, family, and hence myself as more working class, perhaps middle class, but certainly not elite. This reinforced seamen's understandings of tomboy masculinities, which helped them "locate" my positionality and interact with me in terms of these cultural logics. In contrast, if I introduced other aspects of identity formation, for example, that I was from the United States and was a balikbayan and an academic—three axes of difference that in the Philippines suggest class privilege—working-class seamen were more apt to interact with me as a "woman." If this occurred, I was inspired to contextualize or situate my tomboyness by deepening conversations that highlighted my family's poor and working-class origins. Once I demonstrated an intelligible and locally informed working-class sensibility, my very presence elicited seamen's memories, stories, and thoughts about tomboys.

To illustrate the intimate relationality between working-class Filipino (sea) men and tomboys and our shared spaces of Filipino masculinities,

24   Various readings emerged quickly upon first meeting with Filipinos/as during fieldwork. As Teresita V. Ramos writes, "Filipinos are usually not inhibited about initiating conversations because talking to a stranger is generally not considered intrusive. If thrown together for almost any reason, someone will break the ice. A common conversation opener is *Tagasaan ka?* 'Where are you from?' " (*Intermediate Tagalog: Developing Cultural Awareness through Language* [Honolulu: University of Hawai'i Press, 1981], 38).

the following paragraphs include four examples of commentaries or conversation excerpts that emerged during fieldwork encounters in Manila
and Oakland. The narratives were originally communicated to me in Tagalog but are translated here into English.[25] The seamen's narratives collectively speak to how Filipino heterosexual male masculinities and Filipino transgender tomboy masculinities coexist and are co-produced in
Philippine contexts.[26]

1. In Manila, a Filipino seaman, "Ernesto" (a crew member on the Sea
Star), told me about "Percy," a tomboy he knows through his sister who
lives and works in Hong Kong: "Percy was a big help to me. I had so
many problems in my marriage. I was so depressed one time I was in
Hong Kong. Percy took me out and showed me a good time. We went
out drinking, went to some bars and I tried to forget my wife and my
problems. Percy was the one who reminded me that I should just live
my life. My wife wanted a separation. Percy and I were sitting in a bar
getting really drunk and Percy said, 'Tapos na, Pare' (It's over, compa-
dre/friend). I was sad, but I knew what Percy said was correct, true."

2. In Oakland, a Filipino seaman, "Anthony," remembered his tomboy
cousin, nicknamed "Mel": "Mel's mother died when Mel was young, so
my mother took care of Mel (plus Mel's two brothers and sister). When
the school year started, my mother would buy uniforms and books for
my siblings and me. My mother would also buy Mel and my other cousins these things. Mel was close to my age, so we always played together
when we were young. Mel is a real guy (tunay na lalaki). Now, Mel has
a woman-companion. They've been together a long time. When I have
extra money, I send some to Mel. Mel has a small business at the market, but I know that Mel still needs the help."

3. In Ermita, a retired Filipino captain, "Jonas," recalled a story about
a tomboy he met early on in his career. Now in his late fifties, Jonas re-
members: "The captain, who was a Filipino, brought his 'anak,' a tomboy who was around twenty years of age, on board the ship for part
of our voyage.[27] The captain thought that maybe his anak would meet

25   Tagalog does not have feminine or masculine pronouns. My translations of the
seamen's commentaries reflect the gender-neutral aspects of Tagalog.

26   All names introduced in quotation marks are pseudonyms.

27   Anak is a gender-neutral Tagalog word for child/offspring, and there are no
equivalent Tagalog words for "son" or "daughter." A speaker may say, however, "anak na

a man on board the ship and that this would turn her into a 'real girl.' But none of the men liked the anak. This person was really 'guyish' (or boyish) (lalaking-lalaki). When the captain was not around, the anak would be included as part of the group. We would talk and tell stories or eat together. But when the captain was around, we acted like this person wasn't part of our group. We didn't want to make the captain mad. The captain eventually sent his anak home because he saw that no one wanted this person."

4. And in Oakland, a Filipino seaman, "Ruben," remembered his tomboy cousin "Lou": "We were close in high school. Lou now works at Mega Mall as a security guard. Lou didn't finish college. When I'm on vacation in Manila, I see Lou and we go out drinking with some others from our group. We're still close."

Although these seamen's stories and memories about tomboys were initially unexpected, the regularity of seamen sharing tomboy commentaries begins to reveal how my embodied presence as a Filipino (American) tomboy ethnographer perhaps prompted or encouraged these narratives. That is, it is highly probable that many of the seamen I encountered agreed to talk with me precisely because they had previous experiences with tomboys.[28] The seamen's stories of shared childhood and family experiences and friendships illustrate that in Filipino contexts (particularly among Filipino Christian-based lowlanders) it is culturally sensible and analytically appropriate to analyze Filipino tomboy masculinities in relation to Filipino heterosexual male masculinities, rather than separate them from each other, which frequently happens in feminist accounts.[29] Or, in the case of the (Philippine) state, tomboys are completely ignored or rendered invisible. The seamen's stories and memories speak of overlapping and shared social spaces from and through childhood, youth, kinship/family ties, and friendships where

lalaki" (child that is a male) or "anak na babae" (child that is female) to mark a person's gender. Jonas used the word anak and did not include "na babae" (that is female). So as to not infantilize the tomboy Jonas was referring to, I do not translate anak here as "child." Anak can also refer to adult children.

28   Situated traveling fieldwork emphasizes short-term ethnographic encounters in contact zones and reflexive/situated cultural analysis in contrast to long-term fieldwork in a bounded field site (e.g., village) with hopes of producing "objective ethnography" (the preferred mode in traditional/colonial anthropology).

29   My discussion is most applicable to the largest Philippine lowlander groups (largely Christian-based): Tagalogs, Ilokanos, and Visayans.

different kinds of Filipino masculinities are co-created, co-produced, and co-experienced. The seamen's narratives as a whole strongly suggest that Filipino tomboy masculinities can be—indeed, are—a part of Filipino heterosexual male masculinities and vice versa: that is, some heterosexual Filipino men grow up alongside tomboys, and some tomboys develop meaningful friendships and kinship ties with bio-boys and bio-men.

Seamen's commentaries about friendships and family ties with tomboys also collectively reveal an important component of Filipino masculinities: the ability to connect emotionally and create "oneness" with each other, understood in Tagalog as "pakiisa." In a late-1980s Philippines-based ethnographic study, Jane A. Margold notes the inadequacy of conventional understandings of gender for registering the complexities of Filipino masculinities to the extent that they cannot "account for a masculinity that seeks intimacy and reckons a feeling of trust and oneness with another (including other men) as a highly desirable state (*pakikiisa*, in Tagalog)." Critiquing dominant frameworks that define masculinities through "emotional repression and detachment" and which posit the "Filipino man as macho or patriarchal," Margold emphasizes instead *emotional intimacy* between Filipino men and "more fluid, contingent gender identities."[30] The Ilokano overseas migrant men in Margold's study created and enhanced pakiisa through barkadas (friendship groups), which enabled them to endure oppressive social conditions, where employers referred to them as "'tools,' 'slaves,' and 'dogs,'" and where the threat of (Arab/employer) violence loomed large. Pakiisa as a cultural concept stresses the goal of creating "emotional oneness" through the group, *not* through masculinist individualism, intragroup hierarchies, social competition, and violence that patriarchal European-based notions of dominant masculinities and "male social bonding" have historically reinforced.

In contradistinction, situated in Philippine contexts and cultural logics, pakiisa emphasizes group or collective equality and emotional collaboration, directly suggested in pakiisa's composite parts. As a specialist in Filipino language studies, Teresita V. Ramos, writes, "The prefix 'paki' is roughly equivalent to the English word 'please.' . . . The topic or focus of the *paki*-verb may be any semantic element *other than the actor*, such as the object or goal [e.g. 'isa'/oneness]. . . . [In other words], [t]he actor of a *paki*-verb

---

30 Jane Margold, "Narratives of Masculinity and Transnational Migration: Filipino Workers in the Middle East," in *Bewitching Women, Pious Men: Gender and Body Politics in South East Asia*, ed. Aihwa Ong and Michael G. Peletz (Berkeley: University of California Press, 1995), 279, 283, 274. Margold's *pakikiisa* is a variant of *pakiisa*.

... is always in a non-focus."[31] Since *paki-* refers to a polite request to meet a goal—that is, "please collaborate with me to create a sense of emotional oneness"—and *not* a command, pakiisa suggests that group members value equality and interdependence within the group, which is collectively striving to reach the common goal of isa (emotional oneness). Since the object or goal, not individual actors, is the group's primary focus, pakiisa also suggests that the self or personal ego is subordinate and unimportant; in other words, what takes priority is the group or the overall well-being of the larger unit. Although Margold is specifically referring to Ilokanos, her arguments are applicable to other Filipino lowlanders, such as the Tagalogs and Visayans I encountered during fieldwork. This is particularly the case because pakiisa is defined as a Tagalog word, not Ilokano. In seamen's commentaries, they evoke and remember stories of love, loss, brotherhood, and camaraderie with tomboy cousins, friends, and older relatives, demonstrating how working-class Filipino (sea)men and tomboys co-create masculinities through pakiisa.

Like the working-class Filipino seamen I encountered, I also began to think about moments of pakiisa with other Filipino men and tomboys. Traveling fieldwork encounters with Filipino seamen in Manila, Oakland, and at sea transported me to memories of earlier balikbayan travel where heterogeneous masculinities (straight, tomboy, local, and balikbayan) co-existed. In the following section, I combine ethnographic description, travelogue, and personal reflection to show another example of how heterogeneous Filipino masculinities are co-created. The vignette further demonstrates how tomboy masculinities are interpretable or translatable as transgender formations, and also highlights how heterogeneous masculinities coexist through transportation, seafaring, and immigrant/balikbayan/ OFW travel.

Sunday cockfights (at sea and in Malolos, Bulacan, Philippines)

It is early evening on a Sunday on the *Penang Prince*, after a mostly blue-sky day at sea. The sun is beginning its descent into the always receding horizon, leaking out electric orange light through a few hazy clouds. The *Prince*, a German-flagged container ship en route from Long Beach, California, to Hamburg, Germany, moves through the steel-blue waters. Winds are steady, but not fierce. The *Prince's* regular route is to travel back and forth between Western Europe and Southern California, stopping in ports in the Mediterranean, Red Sea, Indian Ocean, Southeast and East Asia, and then crossing

31   Teresita V. Ramos, *Conversational Tagalog: A Functional-Situational Approach* (Honolulu: University of Hawai'i Press, 1985), 134, emphasis mine. Filipino—largely Tagalog based—is the national language of the Philippines.

the northern Pacific to the US West Coast. I boarded the ship at the Port of Oakland and will disembark at the Port of Hong Kong, our next port of call. I have been a passenger-ethnographer on the *Penang Prince* almost two weeks now. Following the northern Pacific Rim, the *Prince* headed north from the San Francisco Bay Area, up the west coast, and off of the coast of Vancouver, British Columbia, headed west toward Asia, passing through the Gulf of Alaska, the Aleutian Islands, and into the Bering Sea. The *Prince* then traveled toward the south and eventually docked at the Ports of Tokyo, Osaka (Japan), Kiaoshung (Taiwan), and Hong Kong (China). Twenty-one seamen work on board this ship: five Germans (all officers, including the captain), five Filipinos (all officers), and eleven seamen from Kiribati in the South Pacific (all of lower ranks).

The five Filipinos invited me to join them in the officers' recreation room this evening to watch cockfights recorded on a VCD that one of them purchased in Singapore. When I arrive at the gathering, I notice that the second mate has a bottle of Russian vodka and some boxed orange juice, while the chief cook shares small pieces of beef marinated in adobo sauce (soy sauce, garlic, vinegar, and bay leaves) and then baked. My contribution to the group is some Carlsberg beer purchased from the captain's store.

Sunday cockfights remind me of my father's mother, lola (grandmother) Chayong, a small, quiet, and kind woman who in the 1970s ran a food stall at the Malolos Municipal Cockfighting Arena in Bulacan Province. Fortunately for me, my parents'/grandmother's modest home was located directly across from the sabongan (cockfighting arena). As a nine-year-old balikbayan child in 1977, I recall traveling to the Philippines, the cooking frenzy before the cockfights, and then actually watching cockfights with my uncles ("E" and "B") and their tomboy friend ("Jo-Jo"). On Saturday night, my grandmothers, aunts, and older female cousins cooked foods such as bibingka (cassava cake) and ube (sweetened purple yam), and on Sunday morning, they prepped the ingredients for pancit lug-lug, a Central Luzon noodle dish that was my lola's specialty.

All of the action occurred in the kitchen in the morning, but once the cockfights were about to begin, the action moved across the street. On this particular balikbayan trip Titos (uncles) E and B (then in their mid- to late twenties), plus Tito B's tomboy friend, Jo-Jo, who lived in my father's barrio, brought me to watch the cockfights in the upper stands. There, I listened to and observed my uncles and Jo-Jo yelling and placing bets across our section of the arena, the absolute quiet of the place just before the gamecocks clashed, and the crowd's eruption into thunderous cheering and more yelling as one of the gamecocks cut into his opponent's body with a knife attached to an ankle, drawing first blood. Later, some of the losing cocks were butchered near my lola's eatery.

On the ship, the cockfights are much more subdued compared with my childhood immigrant and balikbayan experiences despite the alcohol we have been drinking; there are only six of us, after all. As the VCD plays on the TV screen, the seamen size up the gamecocks, offering commentary on their overall appearance, noting features like feather color, relative size, personality, and demeanor (e.g., "That one's a beauty, that one's ugly. This cock looks mean, that cock looks cowardly"). On board the *Prince*, no one gambles with real money, only fantasy-greenbacks: the third mate bets one million dollars on the large off- white cock, while the electrician prefers the spotted brown one. The second mate bets five million dollars on the indigo-ink-colored cock with the orange-and-white plume feathers; I agree to root for its opponent. We are captivated with each cockfight, which lasts a few minutes or longer. The fights happen in quick succession because we are watching a cockfighting derby where many elite fighting cocks battled each other at Araneta Coliseum in metro Manila several months ago. We produce a similar stillness that happens in live cockfights and the eruption of noise as the gamecocks clash. The Filipino seamen and I are yelling and swearing as the fights develop: "Ang ganda!" (How beautiful!), "Sige!" (Go on!), "Puta!" (Whore!). And when their chosen cocks are slashed or lose: "Naku, patay na ang manok!" (Wow, the chicken is dead!); "Ang bilis!" (How fast [the gamecock lost]!). Excited, the third mate yells at me: "Mas maganda ito kay sa world cup, di ba?!" (This is more beautiful than the World Cup, right?!). (The 2006 World Cup soccer tournament was concluding during the voyage. While the German seamen tracked the tournament through satellite reports, Filipino seamen had little interest in this event.)

What these Sunday cockfights show is that there are clearly spaces where different kinds of masculine subjects—here, Filipino straight men and tomboys—coexist and co-create masculinities in and through transportation and travel, that is, immigrant/balikbayan/OFW mobilities in key masculine social spaces (seafaring and cockfights). This is *not* to say that heterogeneous (including queer and transgender) masculinities are created only through practices of mobility and movement, outside the nation-state/"homeland" and in the diaspora. Indeed, my first experiences of cockfights happened precisely in a "local space" (Malolos). In making this clarification, I aim to dialogue with critiques and concerns raised in Asia where gender and sexuality studies scholars and activists suggest that queer (US) diaspora perspectives have become hegemonic (or even colonial), rendering local/regional queer and Asian cultural formations and geographies "less queer," "more normative," and/or "more traditional."[32] These important knowledge/power critiques situated in Asia are critical to keep in mind as queer studies scholars and activists situated in the United States or global north dialogue and debate with counterparts situated in Asia or the global south. Seamen's narratives illustrate that heterogeneous and queer masculinities are produced in various local, regional, transnational, and global nexuses (e.g., Malolos, Manila, Oakland, Philippines/United States/Southeast Asia/Pacific Rim)—not simply in global north, United States, or diasporic contexts. While I am invested in understanding queer/nonnormative racialized and classed genders and sexualities as they are locally, regionally, transnationally, and globally *rooted in Asia*, I am also committed to showing how heterogeneous masculinities (straight, tomboy, queer, transgender) are also co-produced through transit and transport—*routes in and out of Asia*.

Cross-culturally, cockfights have been largely interpreted as purely "men's spaces" where dominant masculinities are reproduced. This has been especially true in island Southeast Asian studies since Clifford Geertz's watershed essay "Deep Play: Notes on the Balinese Cockfight" has been required anthropological reading in many anthropology departments (and even in gender studies). In and through Geertz's widely acclaimed cultural interpretation, the (Balinese) cockfight has become the signifier par excellence of (Balinese) men and masculinity.[33] This coupling of maleness with masculinity, however, is achieved through essentialist notions that equate biology with gender rather than acknowledge that gender is produced through bodily practices and performances that are fluid, dynamic, and contingent, and not necessarily produced through gendered notions of biology.[34] Although Geertz writes a complex and informative "thick description" of Balinese cockfighting, he narrativizes the cockfights as an absolute men's space, missing the ways that women participate on the sidelines through the selling of food, drinks, and admission tickets.[35] It is also quite probable that with

32   I anecdotally heard about these critiques from US-based queer studies scholars who attended the Sexualities, Genders, and Rights in Asia—1st International Conference of Asia Queer Studies, in Bangkok, Thailand, 7–9 July 2005.

33   Clifford Geertz, "Deep Play: Notes on the Balinese Cockfight," in *The Cockfight: A Casebook*, ed. Alan Dundes (Madison: University of Wisconsin Press, 1994), 99.

34   Judith Butler, *Gender Trouble: Feminism and the Subversion of Identity* (New York: Routledge, 1990).

35   See Scott Guggenheim, "Cock or Bull: Cockfighting, Social Structure, and Political Commentary in the Philippines," in *The Cockfight: A Casebook*, ed. Allan Dundes (Madison: University of Wisconsin Press, 1994), 149, for a brief discussion of Filipinas who work at cockfighting arenas.

this kind of understanding of masculinity/gender, he entirely missed the Indonesian tombois (as well as children) who may have been watching the cockfights with male friends or adult relatives.

In light of these gaps, what at first appears to be a highly normative "heterosexual men's space" (Filipino seamen at sea/watching cockfights) can thus also be read and interpreted through a queer and transgender Filipino (American) framework if the presence of alternative masculinity formations (tomboy) are taken into account. Additionally, if the intimate relations among and between working- class Filipino heterosexual masculinities and Filipino queer female masculinities and the concept of pakiisa are treated seriously, we get an entirely different cultural interpretation or ethnographic description of the scene.

Moreover, watching the cockfights on the ship with the five Filipino seamen evoked my own memories of spending time with other men and tomboys in the Philippines—specifically with my uncles E and B and their tomboy friend Jo-Jo. My own immigrant and balikbayan experiences as a young tomboy participating in Sunday family rituals and watching sabong reflects many of the seamen's stories from port and sea: men and tomboys— young and old—spending time together as friends, family, companions, and neighbors co-creating heterogeneous masculinities.

Avast: To cease hauling; to stop (Conclusion)
Seamen's commentaries about tomboy relatives and friends, as well as my (auto) ethnographic travelogue, articulate clear counternarratives to US and Japanese colonial, imperialist, capitalist, and misogynist discourses that seek to construct the Philippines and Filipino/a peoples as disempowered or feminized victims without agency. Seamen, and now tomboys, provide important masculinist alternatives to the figure of the Filipina DH (domestic helper), prostitute, or mail-order bride, through which to imagine the nation and migrant labor. More important, however, by examining and emphasizing how heterogeneous masculinities (straight, transgender, working class, Filipino and Filipino American) are co-created, co-produced, and clearly contingent, dominant notions of Filipino masculinities are denaturalized and opened up for questioning and challenge. Moreover, the seamen's commentaries, as well as my analysis and autobiographical travelogue of the intimate relations between heterosexual Filipino men and Filipino tomboys, directly contradict Filipina and Filipina American feminist understandings of tomboys as primarily women or lesbians. Interpreting Filipino tomboys as embodiments and formations of transgenderism and FTM manhood, my analytic collage illustrates the importance of addressing the geotemporal

place-moments where differently situated Filipino masculinities intersect, contradict, and reinforce each other.

Finally, through transportation as an essay, theoretical framework, and traveling/migrant practice, I demonstrate there are alternative itineraries and trajectories to queer (*queer* as a verb and noun) in interdisciplinary queer studies. Rather than privileging (queer) sexuality, in this essay I present an alternatively queered itinerary or trajectory routed through the intersections of Filipino/a globalization, migration, immigration, and transportation. This essay also emphasizes how heterogeneous racialized and classed genders and sexualities—routed in and through Manila, Oakland, Malolos, Hong Kong, Southeast Asia, the Pacific Rim, and at sea—are produced through embodied practices of mobility: seafaring, transportation, fieldwork, and travel. Finally, this essay shows how projects, which may initially read as "straight" or normative, can be queered through closer attention to the cultural dynamics of encounter(s) and researchers' positionalities and subjectivities, and by engaging a hybrid interdisciplinary writing style. Through situated traveling fieldwork in ports, ships, and seas, as well as immigrant/balikbayan travel, I have shown that what may appear to be a (hetero)normative cultural moment of gender expression (Filipino men at sea/watching cockfights) reveals other complex cultural dynamics at play: namely, working-class Filipino heterosexual men and tomboys co-creating differently situated masculinities.

Yes, cockfights at sea are more beautiful than the World Cup.

I wish to thank Nancy Chen, Olga Najera Ramirez, Neferti X. Tadiar, ManChui Leung, Martin Manalansan IV, Omise'eke Natasha Tinsley, Jack Halberstam, David Valentine, Scott Morgensen, Karen Ho, and Eithne Luibhéid, who all read drafts and/or parts of this essay and helped strengthen it.

Between the Personal and the Political

The author-editor Richard Chu, and his mother. Photo courtesy of the author.

RICHARD T. CHU

Growing Up Male, Chinese, and Catholic in the Philippines and the Son My Mother Wanted Me to Be

Introduction

FOR SEVERAL YEARS NOW, I have been thinking about writing about my experiences growing up, as the title states, "male," "Catholic," and "Chinese" in the Philippines. The desire to do so became stronger after I wrote "Guilt Trip to China,"[1] which recounts how my travels and studies in China have helped me reshape my understanding of what it means to be "Chinese." For me, being "Chinese" does not only involve my "ethnic" identity, but also other aspects of my being: i.e., sexuality and spirituality. Thus, the impetus to write this essay. However, there is also something to my experience that I wish to share with other people. Having known other Filipino gay Catholics, I am struck by how much of a role religion plays or has played in their struggles with their sexuality. They shared with me their strong guilt about being Catholic and gay, leading them to hide their sexual orientation from their family and friends. On the other hand, I did not feel a strong sense of guilt arising from my religious beliefs. Though at the beginning of my sexual awakening I felt disturbed by my sexual feelings, I did not imagine myself burning in the fires of hell or committing "mortal" sin. Was this because my family was not particularly religious? On the other hand, I had felt some "shame" and another kind of guilt in being gay, and these feelings arose from the pressure to be a filial son to my parents and ancestors.

At the risk of being tagged as self-absorbed, I am employing the autobiographical approach to raise certain questions about a "public" issue. In the words of Ang, the autobiography can be regarded

> as a more or less deliberate, rhetorical construction of a "self" for public, not private purposes: the displayed self is a strategically fabricated

1   See Chu 2001.

405

performance, one which stages a *useful* identity, an identity which can be put to work (1993, 3).

Thus, I hope to use this essay, written in a semi-autobiographical style, to engender discussion on a largely unexplored topic: that of the intersection of religious, ethnic, and sexual identities of the diasporic Chinese.[2] How did and does my being Chinese and Catholic influence my self-perceptions and self-identifications? Where, for example, does Catholicism end and my Confucian heritage begin in terms of dealing with questions of my sexuality and of fulfilling my role as a male in a predominantly female household? Finally, how has my life and experiences as a gay-identified male in the United States, and subsequent visits back to the Philippines, further reshaped my self-identification?

Here, too, lies therefore the "usefulness" of autobiography. For as Ang points out, individualized or autobiographical accounts can help "critique the formalist, post-structuralist tendency to overgeneralize the global currency of so-called nomadic, fragmented and deterritorialized subjectivity" (2001, 24). In this regard, I hope that in recounting my experiences as a gay, Catholic, Chinese, and transnational person, I am able to invite people to re-examine hegemonic discourses of what it means to be male (or female for that matter), "Chinese," and "Catholic."

In the aftermath of the untimely death of my mother, I was pushed even further to write this piece, both as a way to fulfill the objective cited above, and as a tribute to her. Thus, this essay is an exercise that is both academic and personal. I have tried to keep its literary style a balance between "academic" writing and a straight memoir.

Being "Male" and "Chinese": Early childhood and upbringing in Manila

"Your father and I couldn't sleep that night. We were so excited that we finally had a son!"

---

2   This is by no means the first essay to be written on gay Chinese men in the Philippines. In particular, Ronald Baytan has written an essay examining the intersection of sexuality and ethnicity, in which he pointed out that, based on his interviews with ten Filipino-Chinese gay men, for families of these gay men and the Chinese community, being homosexual diminished one's "Chineseness," in that a gay man could not procreate and produce a male heir, which is an essential aspect of being a Chinese man. However, his respondents thought otherwise, i.e., their being gay did not make them less "Chinese" (2000, 397). For other works, see Baytan 1996 and Tan 1997.

So my mother said with a smile on her face and a gleam in her eyes as she reminisced about those moments surrounding my birth. I was born on 26 February 1965, the fifth in line in a family of seven siblings. My deceased parents Chu Tian Hua (a.k.a. Luis Chu) and Agustina Tan Chu were married in 1958. After their marriage, they had in succession four daughters: Nelly who was born in 1959, Julie (1960), Caroline (1961), and Mona (1963). Early in the years of their marriage, my parents and four older sisters lived in a huge compound on Soler Street in Binondo, known as Manila's Chinatown. They stayed there together with my great-grandmother, grandmother, and all the sons, both married and unmarried, of the Chu clan. Whenever a son married, a new room or wing in the compound would be added. The result was a family compound that was a huge wooden edifice constructed in an asymmetric way, with a main wing that had several rooms, large hallways, narrow and steep staircases, and a pedestrian bridge connecting the main structure to a smaller one that housed the families of my father's male cousins.

As was the practice of many Chinese merchants who lived in Manila, our clan built its residence above the family business. On the ground floor of the compound was a large office in which my father, my uncles, and other male relatives worked for my grandfather's lumber business, and at the back, a warehouse. Thus did my mother enter as a shy nineteen-year old into this huge extended family, consisting of not only the male members of the Chu clan but also the female relatives, i.e., her grandmother-in-law, mother-in-law, my father's grandmother, and my uncles' wives.

In her accounts about her life in the Chu compound, my mother seemed to get along with her sisters-in-law, as they helped look out for each other's children. She said that when one of my aunts did not have enough milk to breastfeed her newborn baby, another one breastfed her child. But she also experienced some friction with her in-laws, particularly at times when the young cousins got into fights and each mother would side with her own child or children. Living with her mother-in-law was also difficult, for my mother had not borne a son. "Your grandmother for a time did not treat me well. Whenever I had another daughter, I would overhear her say to others: 'What's wrong with her? How come she can't bear a male child?'"

Pressured to be a good filial daughter-in-law, my mother invoked heaven and earth for a son. She decided to pray to the Buddhist goddess Guanyin (观音),[3] the Buddhist goddess of fertility, and to whom she vowed never to eat

3   This Buddhist goddess, along with Mazu (妈祖), has been venerated by many Fujianese migrants in the Philippines, both in the past and today (Wickberg 2000, 193).

beef again for the rest of her life. She also participated in the fertility ritual dance held in Obando, a town north of Manila and in the province of Bulacan.[4] And lo and behold, the gods and goddesses must have heard her, for soon, my mother conceived and I was born. My grandmother was so excited that, according to my mother, she kept asking: "Is it true? Is it true?" When they went to the hospital for the first time to see my mother, my father ran excitedly up the stairs to the room where she was, leaving behind my grandmother who, with her bound feet,[5] tried as fast as she could to catch up with him.

Thus is the story surrounding my entry into this world. The excitement that accompanied my birth can be understood within the context of the Confucian tradition that gives importance to male children. Sons are expected to produce more (male) descendants to ensure that deceased male relatives are venerated and that the family name is passed on to succeeding generations; and in the case of the eldest son, he is expected to provide his mother with a daughter-in-law who would be like a daughter to his mother.

After succeeding in producing a male heir my parents were encouraged to try their luck again. Two more daughters came out of these attempts: Gina (1967) and Lisa (1970). Just a few months after I was born we moved to an apartment in Pasay City.[6] Seeing that his family was growing bigger, my father decided to strike out on his own. He first worked as an agent for another plywood company. Then, encouraged by my mother, he started a plywood business in 1969. In that same year, we moved to a much bigger house in Pasay City that had enough space to accommodate the family, and to have an office and a warehouse for storing plywood. Thus, in my early years I grew up playing with my sisters, and not my cousins as my older sisters did when the family was still in Binondo. I remember that I enjoyed designing and cutting out paper clothes for paper dolls that my sisters and I played with, and role-playing as beauty pageant contestants. At the age of five I started schooling in Xavier School, an all-boys Catholic Jesuit institution with a Chinese curriculum. There I started playing

For an interesting account of present-day practice of worshipping Mazu among the Chinese in the Philippines, see Ang See and Go 1990, 54–67.

4   Obando, Bulacan is located around 10 miles north of Manila. Typically held from May 17–19, the Obando fertility rites dance is held in honor of Santa Clara, the patron saint of childless women.

5   The practice of binding feet among women of wealthy Chinese families can be traced all the way back to the Song dynasty (960–1280).

6   Pasay City is located south of Manila.

sports like soccer and basketball, and games like *sipa*[7] and "robber-police." As I was naturally adept at these activities, I outgrew playing with my sisters.

Being the only son, was I treated in a special way compared to my sisters? One of my earliest childhood memories was celebrating my *tō-chòe* (Mandarin: duzui度晬),[8] an event that is held when a child turns a year old in the Chinese lunar calendar. I remember being carried by my father and seeing many guests that my parents had invited, sitting around several tables. The event was held one evening on the rooftop of my family's first residence in Pasay City. None of my sisters had such a lavish celebration for their *tō-chòes*. I also had four sets of godparents when I was baptized as a Catholic, while my sisters only had one each.[9] Finally, I slept in my parents' bedroom till I was ten. Thus, it could be said that I was treated in a more special way than my sisters, but this was never a source of envy from my sisters, nor a source of conflict between us.

When I was in preparatory school, my mother would come to Xavier and spend her time reading at the parents' library located beside our playground. During recess time while playing with my classmates, I would occasionally glance in the direction of the library to check and see whether I could see my mother. She would always be there, gazing out of the window and giving me that sweet and reassuring smile of hers. Then I would continue to play. My mother therefore was my source of solace, love, and comfort during my growing-up years. Whenever I needed something from my father, such as his permission to join some school activity or money, I would run to her first. She would then talk to my father on my behalf, and would even cajole him into granting my requests if needed.

It was to her that I asked one day, while we were in our garden and she was watering the plants, whether I was "*bakla*" (Tagalog slang for "sissy").[10] I told her that my classmates had called me that in school. She appeared unperturbed

---

7   Literally, "to kick" in Tagalog. The game consists of two teams alternately kicking to each other a bunch of strings or plastic strips attached to a round piece of metal without letting the gadget hit the ground.

8   For those who can read Chinese and want more information about this practice, see http://taiwanpedia.culture.tw/web/content?ID=11523. Accessed 8 October 2012.

9   Chinese Catholic converts in the Philippines have long used the system of padrinazgo, i.e., acquiring godparents who are prominent members of society in the hope of gaining some benefit from these sponsors. See Wickberg 2000, 191–92; and Chu 2010.

10   For a discussion of how the term is different from "homosexual," and how the term is used in the Philippine context, see Garcia 1996, 52–65. For an interesting essay on the terms used by Chinese Filipinos to refer to gay men, see Baytan 2000a.

by my question, and with that reassuring smile said, "No, you're not *bakla*." With those words, the issue never bothered me again until later in life. But I think that my parents might have been concerned about the possibility of their only son being *bakla*, or at least behaving like one. I remember that, when I was about nine or ten years old, my father admonished me when he heard me say "E-e-e-e." He said that only girls used that expression.

While my mother was the symbol of solace and comfort when I was growing up, my father was the authority figure. He had a tall imposing presence that could immediately put us children in line and make us behave with one look. But I knew that beneath that stern façade was a soft and kind heart. I recall that one day while he was driving, a paraplegic woman was crawling on the grass on the center aisle of the street. My father slowed down and, since he could not stop as this would impede the flow of the traffic, tossed some money at her direction. When I was down with chicken pox he came home one afternoon with an assortment of goodies—from my favorite comic book to a mystery book and some toys—in order to cheer me up. Also, my mother said that when I had asthma attacks as a kid and could not sleep, my father would lift me from bed, lay me on his chest, and rock me to sleep on the rocking chair.

Yet, in spite of all these experiences, my relationship with my father never became really close. Our bonds might have grown stronger had he lived longer. A few months or a year before his untimely death at the age of forty-seven, we were spending more time together. He would bring me along to his business trips, as well as to his other social activities, such as playing golf, watching movies, or eating together at our favorite noodle house in Binondo. He also started training me in the business, teaching me for example how to count deftly with two fingers stacks of plywood, or how to issue receipts. One day when I came home from school my mother told me to see my father in his office. When I went in, he was lying on the couch and one hand was bandaged. My mother told me that he had just been in a fight with a customer. I knelt beside him and he stroked my hair with his other hand. But at that time I remember feeling awkward since I did not really know what to say to comfort him. I was too young to feel any sorrow or sympathy for my father.

Thus were the relationships I developed with my parents. Some theorists on sexuality would say that mine was a classic case of "absentee-father-domineering-mother" to explain why I became gay. They may have a point, for I grew up surrounded by women, and had no real male role model. Furthermore, after my father died, my mother assumed the role of both the father and the mother in the family, which, as I will show later, had a profound impact on our relationship. And yet, I know so many other men who grew up in similar environments but are heterosexual. Also, I know of gay men growing up in totally different environments. But being the only son in a Chinese family, I certainly had to conform to or fulfill the role of being the future *padre de familia*, especially after my father died. I recall one day one of my father's laborers saying to me, "You're now the man of the house." I was only twelve then.

My mother took over the family business and, with some help from my father's unmarried male relatives, did even better than my father. She managed to purchase another delivery truck, employ more workers, and pay off the mortgage of the house, while at the same time raising seven children—the eldest of whom, at the time of my father's death, was only eighteen, and the youngest seven. But being a widow at a young age of thirty-nine gradually took its toll on her health, both psychologically and physically. When my father was alive, she did not have to get involved in running the business. I remember that, just a few days after my father's burial, I woke up in the middle of the night, wanting to go to the bathroom. I was surprised to see that the bathroom light was on. The door was slightly ajar, and peeking through the space, I saw my mother seated on the covered toilet seat, hands clasped tightly, deep in thought, and staring down at the floor. She did not see me, and I quietly went back to bed. Over the years of running the business, she had to face unscrupulous tax collectors, recalcitrant customers and suppliers, and other difficult situations. During the last summer I spent with her before she died, she recounted how she and my sixth uncle had to travel all the way to Cavite[11] one evening when the big truck that was delivering our plywood got stuck in the mud after heavy rains. Efforts to extricate the truck proved futile. Since the delivery had to be executed that day, a smaller truck had to be brought in. The plywood was then transferred onto the smaller truck and delivered to the site. She remembered standing there in the rain having to supervise everything, and at one point, started to feel sorry for herself. She also recounted that on another occasion she had to cancel her plan to attend a relative's birthday party when our delivery truck got stalled somewhere. She had to go where the truck was and fix the problem. Finally, she said that one of the worst experiences she had was facing tax collectors. I remember accompanying her one time to the house of a tax collector in Parañaque. The house looked luxurious, with a grand piano, expensive-looking furniture, and a chandelier in the living room. We went there in order to bring the tax collector a "gift."[12] As my mother reminisced about those times there was no bitterness in her voice, and only a faint smile on her face. But I knew that

11   Cavite is located south of Manila and the Manila Bay.

12   In the Philippines, the government loses hundreds of millions of dollars every year due to graft and corruption, with tax evasion through the practice of gift-giving and bribery posing a serious problem to efficient tax collection and administration.

her experiences of my father's unexpected death (which occurred when she and my father were traveling in Taiwan and my father's ulcer ruptured and he eventually died of internal bleeding, leaving my mother alone in an alien land), of having to raise seven children all by herself, and of the stress of running the family business—all of these caused her to be more fearful, distrustful, and worrisome later in life. She developed hypertension and became a hypochondriac. For instance, during a trip to China with her friends, she suddenly canceled her trip and came back to Manila after suffering from a slight incontinence. Although she continued to travel, she would eschew long-distance travel, citing "health" problems. Whenever her children or grandchildren would go anywhere, or go out late at night, she would always have a reason for dissuading them from going. Gone was the carefree and happy person that my mother was.

My teenage years

Her transformation also affected my relationship with her. Where she used to be the mother who was my source of solace and loving comfort in times of need, her new role as provider became a source of resentment and hurt. For instance, I remember feeling very pained when I told her of my career plans. It happened one night when I was in her room, and I mentioned to her that I wanted to pursue a teaching career. I was hoping for her to support this idea. But she said instead, "Let's see how you can feed a family with a teacher's salary." At that moment I felt a pang of pain, as if she was threatening to disown me should I decide to follow my heart's desire. From that time on my relationship with my mother became strained. I felt like the threat of disinheritance was always hanging over me whenever I harbored thoughts of pursuing an academic career or doing anything that might go against her wishes. Thus when I went to college, I first chose to major in legal management, a course that I thought was a compromise between what she and I wanted. The "legal" side of it allowed me to pursue a career outside of business, but the "management" side of it meant that I might end up being a corporate lawyer. But after taking my first law class in college it was very clear to me that I did not want to be a lawyer. In the end, I majored in interdisciplinary studies, which allowed me to pick and choose any class I want. I graduated with a focus on philosophy and education.

And why this disdain for business? Part of it lies simply in my desire to be an academic. But my attitude toward business—at least the kind of business that my family was engaged in—was largely a result of my experience helping out my mother. During my high school years, my job was to collect money from our customers every Saturday. There was one particular client whom I always dreaded and hated going to because he would have his creditors wait for him in the office the whole morning. No one—not even his secretary—knew exactly what time he would arrive. He would usually arrive late in the morning, but if I wanted him to even consider paying me, I had to be there early, since payments were to be made on a first-come-first-served basis. When he arrived, everyone in the office, from creditors to the employees, became tense. He would walk past the creditors without nary a nod of the head or an acknowledgement, while we anxiously looked at him from our cramped space in the reception area. For the next couple of hours, he would sit in his office, and from where we were, we would hear him shout and say the vilest curse words I had ever heard in Hokkien, mostly to people he was talking to on the phone. Then, when it was my turn to see him, my heart would be thumping. My mother had reminded me that I had to always show my face to him so that he would order his secretary to pay us. I also had to make sure that I said the line she taught me to say to him: "*Lim* (not his real name) *siàn, lí ū hoat (tō) tang kàng gún sa chit khùi bô?* 林先, 汝(你)有法度當降阮捎一氣無?" (simply translated: Mr. Lim, could you help us out?)[13]

Since he was one of our biggest customers and we did not want to lose our business, we therefore had to be nice to him. To his credit, Mr. Lim was never mean to me. Seeing a young teenager might have earned his sympathy, and so more often than not, I would leave the office with a fat check. But sometimes, I would be asked to return another week. This and other unpleasant experiences discouraged me from getting involved in the family business. I must say, however, that my mother let me off the hook quite easily. Every one of my sisters had to help out in the family business while in college. They would have to come home immediately after school and stay in the office. After graduating, they helped out in the family business full-time until they got married. I, on the other hand, stopped helping out in the family business when I was in college. Since I went to Ateneo de Manila, which was quite a distance from home, I lived in the school dormitory and only came home occasionally.

Pursuing an academic career
Thus, ever since college, I was able to pursue my own interests. After graduating in 1986 I joined the Jesuit Volunteers Philippines and spent a year teaching religion at Sacred Heart School for Boys in Cebu City. Then I spent sixteen

---

13   A more literal translation would be: "Mr. Lim, Could you help us take (or find) a breath?" I would like to thank Ganny Tan, McAndrew Chua, Lyonel Ty, Joaquin Sy, and Eric Kaw of Kaisa Para sa Kaunlaran, Inc. for their assistance in transliterating this phrase into Mandarin Chinese.

months at Xiamen University, China, as an exchange student.[14] After returning from China I started teaching at Ateneo. In 1992, I left for the United States to pursue my graduate degrees and a career in teaching.

In a way, all these travels were an escape from my responsibilities as "man of the house." I remember that, in those times when I still lived with my mother, I got upset whenever she berated me for not being able to perform some of the "manly" duties at home, such as fixing the car or the plumbing. I also resented having to be her "driver." On weekends, when I would be home, I would dread hearing the knock on the door of my bedroom at five a.m. It would be my mother asking me to bring her to the Cultural Center Complex or Luneta Park, where she would exercise. On most occasions, I did not mind since I planned on exercising too but there were times when I wanted to sleep longer. Or earlier. Sometimes I had to pick her up from her friend's condo in Binondo, where she played mahjong till around eleven in the evening. I sometimes asked myself, "Why can't she take a taxi, or find some other way to get around?" But to ask those questions was taboo. I could not say "no" to her requests; not when I was supposed to be a filial and dutiful son to my mother. Not when she had been so generous in letting me do what I wanted in terms of my career. Not when she could threaten to disown me.

Money, then became a sticking point in our relationship. As much as possible, I tried to avoid having to ask her for money, especially when it was related to the pursuit of my career interests. I thought that she could easily say, "See, I told you. There's no money in academia." The worst thing that could happen was to find out that she was right, and then have to work in the family business and be under her control. Thus, when I applied to study for master's degree in the United States and got accepted at Stanford University, my mother and I clashed.

"If you were going to take up a course in computer or in business then I would not mind spending the money for your education. But East Asian Studies? What are you going to do with it after?" My mother's voice was already slightly raised after she and I had engaged in a heated debate regarding my decision to study abroad. That meant, for her, spending thirty thousand dollars to put me through the program at Stanford. But pursuing an academic career for me at that time had become an urgent matter. That year was 1992, almost three years after I had returned from my studies in China.

The decision to return to the Philippines halfway through my second year as an exchange student at Xiamen University was spurred by my desire to join the priesthood. While I was interested in becoming an educator, I found being

14   For a fuller account of my experience in China, see Chu 2001.

a Jesuit, with the Society of Jesus's emphasis on education, to be an attractive route toward achieving this goal. The Jesuits would take care of sending me to school for higher education, and of my daily needs. I sincerely thought I was being called to the priestly vocation. But my application to the priesthood was rejected, and I was devastated.

Since priesthood was out of the question, I had to find a way to support myself. Fortunately, I was able to find work immediately. I started teaching in the Chinese Studies Program at Ateneo, and in two years time even became acting director, and then assistant director of the program. However, other faculty members told me that I should be pursuing my advanced degrees, instead of holding an administrative job, which should be left to senior faculty members. Thus, in late 1991 I took the GRE and TOEFL exams, applied to graduate programs in the United States, and a few months later, found myself with the prospect of studying at one of the most prestigious universities in the world.

But my mother was not impressed. "You think money grows on trees? Look for your own sources of money!" With those words, all of my fears about my mother failing to support me seemed to have come true. I walked out of the office and slammed the door. My third sister Caroline, who was there with my mother and I, sought me out in the house and said, "Ricky, that's not the way to behave. You have to understand that mother just wants you to be more practical." For the next few weeks, I did try to look for alternative sources of funding. I approached my school. Almost apologetically, the head of the Faculty Development Fund at Ateneo told me that the university could only provide me with enough cash to purchase a one-way ticket to the United States, with the stipulation that I return to Ateneo upon the completion of my degree. I went to talk to the officers of the Go Family Association.[15] The association oftentimes would extend financial assistance to members for educational purposes. They agreed to provide me with ten thousand pesos (roughly five hundred dollars at that time), in exchange for a photo-op in the Chinese newspapers. Upon hearing this, my mother said that I should forget about asking for money from the association. For some reason unclear to me, she did not want any publicity. Finally, I went to a maternal grand-uncle, a successful doctor and businessman. After listening to my situation, he said, "It seems that your mother is against your studying in the

15   My father's real surname is Go (吳, or Wu in Mandarin), hence we belong to the Go Family Association. As in many Chinese diasporic communities in the world, the practice of purchasing residence certificates of returning Chinese migrants or deceased ones was common among the Chinese in the Philippines. Hence, my grandfather, whose real name was Go Ting-seng, purchased the residence certificate of a certain Chu Ongco in order to enter the Philippines.

US." Hearing those words, I immediately knew what he meant: I did not have to approach him; my mother had the means to support me.

After these attempts at raising money led to almost nothing, my mother finally agreed to finance my studies, with a reminder that I should try to look for a job to help offset some of my expenses. During my first week at Stanford, I applied for and received a research assistantship that paid for my tuition and fees, and provided me with a monthly stipend. Thus, in the end, my mother did not have to shell out a huge sum of money.

For quite some time then I had this love-hate relationship with my mother. It was a "love" relationship because I loved my mother as deeply as a son could, yet, it was a "hate" relationship because I felt for a long time that I was a "failure" in my mother's eyes. I remember asking her one time, "Ma, aren't you proud of my academic achievements?" She gave me this meek and almost embarrassed smile and said, "You may be successful academically, but financially, you're not." Furthermore, I always had this fear that she could simply disown me whenever I pushed the envelope too far. I eventually realized that my mother would never disown her one and only son, that she was just being "strict" with me so that I would be more practical-minded. But this realization did not come until after some time, as I will describe later.

Being gay and Catholic
"Wear this, for you might need it in the United States." These were the words my mother said while she wrapped the gold bracelet around my wrist, a few days before my departure. "You can sell it in case you run out of money," she continued. Of course, she was not being serious, but it was a loving gesture on her part. By that time we had made our peace, and she was supportive of my studies in the United States. She also said, "Maybe you will find a nice Chinese American girl to give it to, and to bring home." Chinese American girl? The irony was not lost on me when after a few months in California, I did meet someone who was Chinese American. The only thing was, he was a Chinese American boy.

The subject of my sexuality first came up a few months before I left for the United States. One day, while we were both in the car, my mother asked me out of the blue, "Are you gay?" Caught offhanded, I muttered, "Why do you ask?" And she said, "My friends think that you are gay because you are still without a girlfriend." I quickly dismissed the topic by saying that her friends' speculations were not true, and that I just did not find the right girl yet. We did not delve into that topic again until a few days later when, finding ourselves alone in her bedroom, she asked me the same question. At that moment, I felt that she was ready for the truth, and that she wanted nothing but the truth. I said yes. There was just a moment of silence, as I waited for her reaction as she lay down there on her bed under the soft glow of the night-lamp. "Are you sure? Can't you change?" I then explained to her how I had come to know I was gay, how I struggled with it, how I felt that, at the age of twenty-seven, I was pretty sure of my sexuality, and that it was not a choice. There was no histrionics or drama that night. At the end of our conversation, I told her that maybe it was better that I had not told her the truth. But she said that she already knew, even if I had not told her.

When did I first know it myself?

While I have heard of other gay men saying that knew they were gay since they were very young, I only felt an attraction for the same sex when I was in seventh grade. I recall having a crush on one classmate named Albert (not his real name). During one recess period, Albert, myself, and other classmates were playing. Albert pushed one of our classmates to the ground and said in a joking way that he would rape him. At that moment I felt something stir inside me, something that I had never felt before. I wished that I was that classmate on the ground instead. After that, throughout high school and during my college years, I had a few crushes. The first great love I had was a classmate from high school, who was straight. When I told Michael (not his real name) how I felt for him, he was "accepting." In reality, he probably did not know what being gay was. I told him that I had this strong sexual and emotional attraction to him, but that he should not worry because I had my feelings under control. So much for control. After Michael fell in love with his female college classmate and started pouring out his grief to me when the girl did not reciprocate his feelings, I could not bear the hurt inside me. Initially I played the role of "best friend" and tried to console him. But deep down inside I was feeling so much jealousy and pain. Finally, I told Michael that I did not want to talk to him anymore.

Sad over my "breakup" with Michael and feeling guilty about my feelings for other men, I went through a period of counseling during my first two years in Ateneo. The counselors were very helpful; they did not make me feel as if being gay was immoral. Then, Manuel came into my life. He and I became very good friends and spent a lot of times together. Then one day, he asked me whether I would be willing to go to bed with him. I was shocked by the question, for Manuel was a "man of the cloth." I resisted the idea for a few days until I gave in to my own desires and curiosity. For the next few years, Manuel and I were to carry on an "off-and-on" relationship. At the beginning I was often wracked with feelings of guilt. Brought up as a Catholic, I felt that it was a sin to be sleeping with Manuel, who was supposed to be celibate. I struggled for a while: I would "break up" with Manuel, only to find myself in his arms again. After countless experiences of agonizing through this moral dilemma, I finally decided that it was pointless to keep on trying to stop seeing Manuel. God knew that I had struggled enough trying to be "good." My need for intimacy was much stronger than any desire to remain an obedient Catholic. Manuel might have also fulfilled the role of being a father figure, for he was older than I was.

Even if my relationship with Manuel did not have any future, I did not regret knowing him. Through our relationship, I learned many lessons, the most important one being a lesson in kindness, compassion, and humility. Once, I asked Manuel how he was able to reconcile his vows with his sexual behavior. He described to me the history of his struggles, of his depression over his sexuality, and how he finally was able to resolve this issue. For him, celibacy was "developmental," in that some priests took more time to be able to accept and live it. Whether his reasoning was right or wrong is not important. My Jesuit educators had taught me that, when it comes to moral issues, only God ultimately can judge someone, especially if that person has gone through a long process of discernment and believes that he or she is living in accordance to God's will. Many people, like myself and Manuel, desire to do the "right" thing or to be a "good" Catholic, but for some reason fall short. And yet, God continues to love us unconditionally. My relationship therefore with Manuel helped me to reconcile my faith and my sexuality.

Furthermore, my family not being too religious may have also played a factor in helping me accept my gayness more easily. My parents were not Catholics, and at home, we practiced a combination of Buddhist and Catholic beliefs. Being partly raised in a Buddhist household may have lessened the pressure and the "guilt" to conform to a heterosexual and Christian identity.

Living and loving in the US
The first person with whom I had a real relationship and who also had an impact in helping me accept my sexuality was Daniel. Daniel was an out-and-out gay man who also went to Stanford. However, he had graduated by the time I started my studies there. We met at a conference in San Francisco. While seated together at the dinner table he told me that he used to be known at Stanford as the "condom man" because, on Valentine's Day, he would dress up like a condom and distribute free condoms on campus. At the time, he ran the Condom Resource Center, a non-profit organization he founded to help educational institutions disseminate information regarding proper condom-use. He was also an officer of the Gay Asian-Pacific Alliance (GAPA) based in San Francisco. Thus, through Daniel, I was introduced to the gay scene in San Francisco. I participated in the city's gay pride parade in 1993, when GAPA had a float shaped like Imelda Marcos's shoe, covered with brightly colored sequins.

Needless to say, Daniel was also out to his family, and he introduced me to them. They were originally from Shanghai, but then emigrated to Argentina, then to New York, and finally to California. It was interesting to listen to him talk to his mother in Spanish and his father in English, while his older relatives spoke Mandarin to each other. They welcomed me with open arms, and I even spent holidays with them. Thus, I got a taste of a "gay family life" that was possible within the context of a loving, accepting, and supportive environment.

With Daniel, I was somehow "forced" to come out to the rest of my own family. When I invited him to visit the Philippines, he said that he would do so only if I introduced him as my boyfriend. Thus, when I went home by myself to visit my family in the summer of 1993, I came out to my sisters. My sisters were okay with the fact that their only brother was gay. Coming out to them made us even closer, for then I felt like I could share with them everything about myself, especially the most important and personal matters. "Who's the female in your relationship?" my sister Julie asked. I had to explain to her that in our relationship, there was no one who assumed a male or female role. Both Daniel and I considered ourselves as "men" and "male" who just happened to be sexually attracted to each other. Some of my high school classmates could not believe that I was gay. "What? *Si* Richard, *nagpapapakain?*" (What, Richard is feeding someone?) Their idea of a gay relationship was an economic relationship, with one person supporting another financially.[16] I had to explain to them I had an "equal" relationship with Daniel.

I have always believed that one should be as true as possible to oneself and to others. Being Daniel's boyfriend for a year and living in California reinforced this belief. Daniel did not hide his sexuality from anyone, at any time. The generally more open society in California also allowed me to explore and deepen other facets of my sexuality. For instance, while at Stanford, I founded a gay and lesbian Catholic group. While doing my doctoral studies at University of Southern California (USC), I was the co-chair of the Lesbian, Gay, Bisexual and Transgender Graduate Students' Association, and helped organize activities aimed at gaining more acceptance and understanding of gay people in the wider society.

But being out in the Philippines is oftentimes a different matter. The general rule-of-thumb seems to be "Don't ask, don't tell." I remember one time

16   In the Philippine context (and in other countries), one of the perceptions of gay men is that they are often in a sexual-economic relationship with heterosexual men. The gay man pays the heterosexual man for sexual favors and provides money to support him, or sometimes his family, which may include a wife and children. For examples of how such practices are carried out in the Philippines, see Johnson 1997, 184–85; and Garcia 1996, 94–95.

when I attended a faculty retreat at Ateneo in 1995. Between 1995 and 1996, I taught again at Ateneo after returning to the Philippines in early 1995 in order to take a break from my graduate studies at USC. The retreat was designed to strengthen the relationship among different departments and programs in the university. At the beginning of the retreat the facilitator asked us to write down on a sheet of paper something about ourselves that very few people or nobody knew. Then, she collected all the pieces of paper and redistributed them, asking each participant to come up to the front and read what was on his/her sheet of paper. Of course, I was aghast when one by one, the "secrets" being read were "I have three cats at home" and "I love to sing while taking a shower." When it came to the person who got my sheet, he read, "Richard wrote, 'Few people know that I am gay.'" I did not feel ashamed at what I had written. Instead, I was more embarrassed for revealing more than I should have. But some of the faculty members took my faux pas well. At the end of the session a few of them came up to me and commended me for being "courageous" in doing what I did. The next day, the news had spread all around campus about what I had done. That experience and my other observations surrounding gay life in the Philippines back then had led me to the conclusion that I could only live comfortably in the United States as a gay person, especially within the context of a long-term relationship. During that time, I thought that Philippine society was not yet ready to accept such relationships.

However, over the course of my visits to the country since I left in 1992, I have seen a number of encouraging developments, among them: the rise in the number of gay-themed films, the flourishing gay scene in Malate and later on in other parts of Manila, the holding of gay-pride parades annually, and the founding of several gay/lesbian organizations. While the Catholic Church is still homophobic, I have many Catholic friends—both lay and religious—who have accepted and loved me for who I am, and support my choices related to my being gay. I also know of a number of gay couples who have been co-habiting.

After Daniel, my next boyfriend was Gianpaolo (not his real name), whom I met when we were both graduate students in California. Gianpaolo came to visit the Philippines twice and met my family. My mother treated him like she would treat any of my friends. I know that for a time, she still wished that I would eventually marry a woman. I recall one time she invited me to have breakfast with my sister Julie's parents-in-law, on the pretext that they wanted to see me. I thought that they were the only ones whom we were meeting. But when we got to the hotel restaurant, I was surprised to see a Chinese man with a young lady sitting beside him. This person turned out to be his daughter. It dawned on me quickly that this was a "set-up" that they had arranged to introduce me to this girl. Mercifully, the breakfast went by quickly, and nothing was said about the matter afterward.

To her credit, my mother never really pushed the issue, although she tried to convince me why I should "change," get married, and raise a family. Among her reasons: that according to the principle of yin-yang (陰陽), two "yins" (masculine forces) make for an unhealthy coupling ("That's why many gays and lesbians don't live long," she said); and that I needed someone to take care of me in my old age. But for every reason she gave I naturally had a rebuttal. Even my sisters chimed in. Seeing that there were so many unhappy heterosexual marriages around, they tried to convince my mother that being married and having children was not the only path to happiness. In time, my mother must have accepted the fact that I would not change, for in the last few years of her life, she never raised the matter again. In the last summer I spent with her, she met my then boyfriend, John, and like a concerned prospective mother-in-law, she immediately made an assessment of his physical condition. "He seems to be weak because he sleeps a lot." Of course, John was simply jet lagged. But that was just like her to always be concerned about her children's well-being and their husbands and children. Whenever I talked to her on the phone, she would, for example, always remind me to take care of myself, to drive carefully, to keep warm at night, to eat right, and to get enough sleep.

Thus, in the last few years of her life, my relationship with my mother greatly improved. This was a result of a couple of events in my life.

Being the son my mother wanted me to be

The first is related to a series of events that began in late 1994. It was Christmas break and Gianpaolo and I had gone to the Philippines for a vacation. During one of my conversations with my family, my mother mentioned in front of her children that she was thinking of closing down the business. The reason for this was that it was not profitable anymore to continue with it. I, however, thought that she was making an indirect warning to me, i.e., that I better decide once and for all whether I wanted to take over the family business or lose it forever. Although she did not say anything to that effect, her words stayed with me even after I returned to the United States. At the time, I was unhappy studying at USC. Gianpaolo was studying at the University of California at Berkeley, which was more than three hundred miles north of Los Angeles. I did not enjoy being apart from him. Furthermore, my pride was hurt when I did not get into more prestigious universities for my doctoral program. Having gone to Stanford, I saw my being at USC as a demotion of my status. So in my first semester at USC I felt miserable. Consequently, when I learned of my mother's plan to close down our family business, I began to grow anxious. Up to that point, although I had been pursuing an academic career, the family business was like a security blanket to me. I had thought to myself that if my career did not work out, there was always the family business to fall back on. Faced with a dilemma, I took a break from my graduate studies and returned to the Philippines to mull things over. However, during my stay there, Gianpaolo broke up with me.

After spending a few months in the Philippines, I finally realized that I really wanted to be an academic, and that USC's program was the best one for me to train as one, given my and my professors' common research interests. More importantly, I realized that my mother was not closing down the business in order to give me an ultimatum. She had long accepted the fact that I would never become a businessman. Her decision to close down the business was based on practical considerations. All of my sisters were married and running the business was not profitable any more. She thought that it was better to close down the business, sell the property, move in with my eldest sister, and retire with the savings she had set aside for herself and from the income arising from the sale of the property.

Having resolved the issue with regard to my career, I returned to the United States in fall of 1996 to resume my studies. When I finished my dissertation and graduated in December 2003, I knew that my mother was very happy. She was also proud when I came out with my first publication, and bought copies of the book in which my essay was published to give to friends. Then, when I was hired as an assistant professor at the University of Massachusetts, Amherst, I could sense that she finally was at peace, for her one remaining unmarried child without a steady source of income was finally on his way to stability and security. I myself felt that I had finally become my "own man"—emotionally, financially, and professionally.

The other "event" that helped in improving my relationship with my mother was the resolution of my guilt for not being "there" for her. Being the only son, I had always felt that her welfare and safety were my responsibility, especially as she grew older. But after she sold our property in Pasay and moved in with my eldest sister Nelly's family in Malate, I felt that she was in very good hands. She lived on the second floor of a residential building that she helped finance, while Nelly and her family lived on the floor above her. In a way, I relegated my filial duties to my eldest sister, who never said anything or complained about her assumed role. No one could have taken better care of my mother than Nelly. But the ties between my mother and I were never broken. Even if I had been living abroad since 1992, whenever I came home I stayed with my mother. She had built an extra room for me in her condo.

Thus, during the last year of her life, my relationship with my mother had never been better. I thought that our family could not be happier, until an unknown assailant's bullet took away her life one fateful evening on 8 November 2004, right outside her residence. It is a tragedy that my sisters and I have to live with and come to terms with for the rest of our lives.

As I look back to the times I shared with my mother and to our relationship over the years, I see that my mother took her role as a mother seriously. To her credit, she did not hold me back from my dreams. Even when her friends were reprimanding her for letting me go away and do things as I pleased, she continued to support my travels abroad, and my decisions with regard to my career. "They told me that I should just drag you home from the United States, let you stay, get married, and raise a family," she said once to me. I know how difficult it is for parents, but especially mothers, to have their children live far away. For my mother, it must have been especially difficult, for she probably had her own dreams of living quietly and contentedly with a son who would take care of her in her aging years, even provide her with a dutiful daughter-in-law, and strong healthy grandchildren whom she could call her own. Over the years, she continued to watch me from the side, silently cheering me on, supporting me, saying "no" if need be, but only because I had to learn some things the hard way.

At her wake, I shared with our family, relatives, and friends the story that my mother had told me when I was a child. It was the story of a mother in ancient China who suddenly heard one day that her long-lost son was being led to execution for a crime he committed. She quickly ran out of the house and to the place where her son was going to be executed. Her son saw her in the crowd. Approaching her, he said, "Mother, why did you not teach me what was right or wrong when I was a kid?"

In my life, the story has been reversed. Earlier on, I mentioned how devastated I was when I asked her whether she was proud of me, especially of my academic achievements, and to which she replied that she would have been prouder if I had been successful financially. I look back now to that moment not with pain or bitterness, but with a better understanding and appreciation of my mother's love for me. Brought up within the context of a Chinese immigrant community in the Philippines, my mother, like many who had experienced the pain and difficulty of growing up amidst financial constraints, just wanted the best for me, for in the Philippines, pursuing an academic career is not the surest way toward financial security.

But my mother did not just want me to be a successful businessman. In my essay "Guilt Trip to China," I wrote that at one point, my mother, distraught over the fact that I wanted to become an academic, had said, "I wish I did not send you to study at Xavier School." She thought that the Jesuits had some undue influence on me, leading me to desire to become, first, a priest, and then later on, an educator. But years later, out of curiosity, I asked my mother why she decided to send me to Xavier School. She said, "Because of the values it teaches." I was surprised at her answer, since I expected something more practical, like its excellent academic standards.

What Xavier had taught me was to be true to myself, and this is an ideal that I have used in pursuing an academic career. I have not regretted following this ideal, and feel happy that I did not compromise myself to meet the expectations of others on what it means to be male, Chinese, and Catholic. To be true to myself and to be happy—this I think is the son my mother wanted me to be.

Bibliography

Ang, Ien. "To Be or Not to Be Chinese: Diaspora, Culture and Postmodern Ethnicity." *Southeast Asian Journal of Social Science* 21, no. 1 (1993): 1–17.

———. *On Not Speaking Chinese: Living between Asia and the West*. London & New York: Routledge, 2001.

Ang See, Teresita and Bon Juan Go. "Religious Syncretism among the Chinese in the Philippines." In *The Chinese in the Philippines: Problems and Perspectives*, edited by Teresita Ang See. Manila: Kaisa Para sa Kaunlaran, 1990.

Baytan, Ronald. "Pua Iyam." In *Ladlad 2: An Anthology of Philippine Gay Writing*, edited by J. Neil C. Garcia and Danton Remoto, 7–14. Manila: Anvil Publishing, Inc., 1996.

———. "Preliminary Notes on the Chinese-Filipino Male Homosexual Identity." In *Intercultural Relations, Cultural Transformation, and Identity: The Ethnic Chinese. Selected Papers Presented at the 1998 ISSCO Conference*, edited by Teresita Ang See, 587–627. Manila: Kaisa Para Sa Kaunlaran, Inc., 2000.

———. "Ethnicity and Language: Exploring Chinese Filipino Male Homosexual Identity." *Culture, Health & Sexuality* 2, no. 4 (October–December 2000a): 391–404.

Chu, Richard T. "Guilt Trip to China." In *Cultural Curiosity: Thirteen Stories About the Search for Chinese Roots*, edited by Josephine M.T. Khu, 128–44. Berkeley: University of California Press, 2001.

———. *Chinese and Chinese Mestizos of Manila: Family, Identity, and Culture 1860s–1930s*. Leiden and Boston: Brill, 2010.

Dy, Ari. *Chinese Buddhism in Catholic Philippines: Syncretism as Identity*. Manila: Anvil Publishing, Inc., 2015.

Garcia, J. Neil. *Philippine Gay Culture: The Last Thirty Years, Binabae to Bakla, Silahis to MSM*. Quezon City: University of the Philippines Press, 1996.

Johnson, Mark. *Beauty and Power: Transgendering and Cultural Transformation in the Southern Philippines*. Oxford and New York: Berg, 1997.

Tan, Michael. "Both Sides Now." In *Primed for Life: Writings on Midlife by 18 Men*, edited by Lorna Kalaw-Tirol, 144–57. Pasig City: Anvil Publishing, Inc., 1997.

Wickberg, Edgar. *The Chinese in Philippine Life: 1850–1898*. 2000. Reprint, Quezon City: Ateneo de Manila University Press, 2002.

Top, Thousands of people join Metro Manila Pride—the longest-running pride march in Southeast Asia—in Manila (June 2016). Photo from Shutterstock. *Above*, the Psychological Association of the Philippines LGBT Special Interest Group organized a roundtable discussion titled "Psychologists Versus Homonegativity: Pacquiao & Beyond" on 20 March 2016. Members of the SIG gathered to brainstorm on how to contribute in addressing the ongoing problem of anti-LGBT stigma in the Philippines. Photo courtesy of Psychological Association of the Philippines LGBT Special Interest Group.

This essay was previously published in *Psychology of Sexualities Review* 7, no. 1 (Spring 2016): 60–72.

ERIC JULIAN MANALASTAS AND BEATRIZ TORRE

LGBT Psychology in the Philippines

MUCH CAN BE DONE WITHIN THE FIELD of psychology to advance the human rights and well-being of lesbian, gay, bisexual, and transgender (LGBT) individuals, families, and communities. The Philippine case is no exception. As a developing country with a long history of colonization under Spanish and US regimes often considered the largest predominantly conservative Roman Catholic nation in Asia, where same-sex marriage, gender identity recognition, sex work, abortion, and even heterosexual divorce remain illegal, the Philippines appears to be an unlikely environment for fostering inclusion, affirmation, and activism for gender and sexual minorities within psychology.

Despite these contextual factors, we will tell a story of the initial gains and successes made within Philippine psychology towards positive engagement of sexual orientation and gender diversity. This paper aims to provide a narrative account, based on our perspectives as insiders, on the progress and developments of an LGBT-inclusive psychology in the Philippines over the past five years. We begin with critical events from 2009 to 2011 in Philippine society that led the Psychological Association of the Philippines (PAP) to adopt a landmark policy resolution on LGBT nondiscrimination, the first of its kind by a professional mental health association in Southeast Asia. A discussion of the on-going initiatives and early results building on this enabling policy platform follows, including the founding of the PAP's LGBT Psychology Special Interest Group and our work in the fourfold areas of research, education, advocacy, and practice. Finally, we conclude with lessons learned thus far as well as reflections on challenges ahead for LGBT psychology in the Philippine context.

The Philippine context: An LGBT- friendly country in Southeast Asia?
The Philippines is one of many archipelagic countries in maritime Southeast Asia. Classified by the World Bank (2015) as a lower-middle-income
economy, a quarter (25.2 percent) of the population of 100.1 million Filipinos currently live below the national poverty threshold (defined as living
on less than PhP 8,778 or GBP 131.51 per month). Filipinos, as a culture,
have experienced a long history of colonial rule under Spain, spanning the
16th to the 19th century, followed by US occupation from 1898 to 1946.
One of the lasting influences of the Spanish regime was in terms of religion
— the Philippines, along with East Timor, remains one of two majority
Roman Catholic countries in Asia, with 80.6 percent of Filipinos belonging to the Roman Catholic Church. Although the Philippine Constitution
guarantees separation of state and church, public debates and legal policies
on a range of social issues are often highly influenced by religious fundamentalism and Roman Catholic morality (Ruiz Austria 2004). Same-sex
marriage, gender identity recognition, sex work, and abortion are all illegal.
Only in 2012 did the Philippine parliament pass a highly contested law for
reproductive health, including access to contraceptives and sexuality education in primary and secondary schools, after more than a decade in the
legislature and a culture war that pitted progressives and the women's movement with the local Roman Catholic bishops' hierarchy. And heterosexual
divorce still remains illegal in the Philippines; the only other country that
does not allow divorce is the ecclesiastical state of the Vatican.

Despite the overall social and sexual conservatism in Filipino culture
(Widmer, Treas, and Newcomb 1998), the Philippines is often considered
one of the more LGBT-friendly countries in Southeast Asia. Despite centuries of colonial rule, same-sex sexual behavior has never been criminalized,
unlike in neighboring Malaysia and Singapore. Indigenous constructions
of gender diversity that blend same-sex sexuality and transgenderism exist
and are widely known (Garcia 2013), such as *bakla* and *bayot*, terms in the
Tagalog and Bisaya languages that may refer to either same-sex attracted
men, especially feminine gay men, or to male-to-female transgender individuals (Nadal and Corpus 2013). Pride events were celebrated as early as
the mid-1990s, and civil society organizing for LGBT rights and equality
is alive and well (UNDP, USAID 2014). Within this backdrop came one
critical event in 2009, when a collective of LGBT Filipinos filed a petition
to run for a seat in the partylist system of the legislature under the banner of
a political party called Ang Ladlad (a Tagalog phrase meaning "those who
are out or openly LGBT"). Their petition was disapproved by the Commission on Elections, who, citing verses from the Catholic Bible as well as

the Quran, declared that Ang Ladlad, being composed of LGBT Filipinos, advocated "immoral doctrines" and represented a threat to "the well-being of the greater number of our people, especially the youth" (Commission on Elections 2009).

Along with other concerned Filipino psychologists, we requested that the Psychological Association of the Philippines (PAP), our national professional organization, issue a public statement concerning the Commission on Elections' ruling, particularly its claim that gender and sexual minorities somehow threaten people's well-being, including the well-being of young people. The PAP refused. Officials from PAP offered regrets, citing the absence of an institutional mechanism to engage in public interest matters despite it being part of the PAP's mission statement. More internal lobbying ensued, and in February 2010, the PAP board formally instituted its Public Interest Committee, patterned after the American Psychological Association's Public Interest Directorate, as a mechanism to address the public on matters of social justice (J. E. G. Saplala, personal communication, 24 March 2010).

At the same time, the Supreme Court of the Philippines had taken on the case of Ang Ladlad. It eventually overturned the ruling of the Commission on Elections, paving the way for the LGBT party's participation in the May 2010 national elections. Although a public statement from PAP became moot at this point, LGBT issues had come to the attention of the Philippines' national psychology organization in a way it never had before. And there was a positive change within PAP's organizational structure highlighting the importance of "psychology in the public interest" (Brewster Smith 1990), which would be instrumental in laying the foundation for LGBT psychology in the Philippines soon thereafter.

Foundations: The PAP (2011) LGBT non-discrimination policy resolution

The PAP's commitment to social justice and LGBT inclusion was tested in February 2011, when a popular morning television talk show called *Umagang Kay Ganda* ran a segment on lesbian and gay children, featuring a Filipino clinical psychologist as a guest expert. Asked how parents should respond to having a lesbian or gay child, this PAP-certified psychologist advised conversion therapy in order to achieve a "happy family life." The PAP received letters and calls from concerned members of the public, including a formal ethics complaint against the psychologist in question, which could not have been possible prior to 2010, the year when the PAP formulated its ethics code.

In response to this critical incident and as a way to address matters related to sexual orientation and gender diversity in a broader, more systematic way, the PAP board directed its Public Interest Committee to come up with a document that would go beyond one incident in the media. In October 2011, the PAP board approved a landmark policy resolution on LGBT non-discrimination. The resolution was published in the *Philippine Journal of Psychology*, the flagship journal of the profession in the country, in December 2011, and widely disseminated to PAP members nationwide, through the organization's official mailing list and website, as well as in print form during subsequent PAP conferences. At the suggestion of LGBT advocates working with communities where (unlike in Philippine psychology as a profession), English is not a primary language used, a translation into Tagalog was drafted and approved in November 2014, and subsequently published online.[1] To date, this policy is the only official document of the PAP available in official bilingual versions, in English and in Tagalog.

The policy statement, the first of its kind by a professional mental health association in Asia, affirms the inherent dignity and equality of individuals who are lesbian, gay, bisexual, and transgender, as well as their right to be free from discrimination on the basis of sexual orientation, gender identity, and gender expression (SOGIE). The policy also affirms that same-gender sexual orientations are a healthy, non-disordered variant of human sexuality, love, and relationships—a position made as early as 1973 by the American Psychiatric Association and supported by a global network of mental health professionals including the American Psychological Association, the British Psychological Society, and the World Health Organization.

This policy statement also laid out a number of action steps to ensure the advancement of LGBT rights and welfare within Philippine psychology. The PAP's commitments are outlined as follows:

1. Oppose discrimination on the basis of actual or perceived sexual orientation, gender identity, and expression;

---

1   Psychological Association of the Philippines, "Pahayag ng Psychological Association of the Philippines Laban sa Diskriminasyon Batay sa Oryentasyong Sekswal, Identidad, at Ekspresyong Pangkasarian," accessed 18 August 2015, http://pap.org.ph/?ctr=page&action=resources.

2. Support the repeal of discriminatory laws and policies and the passage of legislation at the local and national levels that protects the rights and promotes the welfare of people of all sexual orientations and gender identities and expressions;

3. Eliminate anti-LGBT stigma and discrimination in teaching, research, psychological interventions, assessment, and other psychological programs;

4. Encourage psychological research that addresses the needs and concerns of LGBT Filipinos and their families and communities;

5. Disseminate and apply accurate, evidence-based information about sexual orientation and gender identity and expression to design interventions that foster mental health and well-being of LGBT Filipinos.

In order to ensure the organization's commitments to advance LGBT rights and well-being, the PAP formed a partnership with the LGBT Concerns Office of the American Psychological Association's Public Interest Directorate. The APA's LGBT Concerns Office provides technical assistance and support for capacity-building and LGBT mainstreaming within PAP and in the larger Philippine psychology professional community, with the two of us (Eric Manalastas and Beatriz Torre) as coordinators. In 2012, the PAP became the first Asian member of the International Psychology Network for Lesbian, Gay, Bisexual, Transgender, and Intersex Issues (IPsyNET), followed by the Hong Kong Psychological Society in 2013.

Mapping out needs and entry points within Philippine psychology
The policy foundations in place, the two of us in collaboration with like-minded colleagues set out to work towards a particular vision of change—to build a Philippine psychology that advances LGBT human rights and well-being. With previous training and exposure to LGBT psychology (Eric participated in the 1st International LGBT Psychology Summer Institute at the University of Michigan Ann Arbor in 2008, while Beatriz was a participant in the second Institute in 2010), we realized that an important sub-goal to achieve our vision was to build capacity in a larger number of Filipino psychologists to engage LGBT concerns. Specifically, we identified

the following needs in a preliminary scoping of the state of LGBT psychology in the Philippines:

- A visible network of Filipino researchers, practitioners, and psychology professionals engaged in LGBT psychology.

- An organizational structure to coordinate activities among Filipino psychologists and with external stakeholders such as media and the LGBT activist community.

- Locally contextualized, broadly accessible information resources.

To address these needs, we borrowed lessons from initiatives using the framework of gender mainstreaming and development (Daly 2005; Moser and Moser 2005). Adapted to LGBT psychology, mainstreaming here is said to unfold in three stages, beginning with the adoption of SOGIE terminology and the language of LGBT inclusion, followed by putting in place policies related to LGBT inclusion, and finally, implementation. Mainstreaming, as an approach, refers to creating change within existing structures, processes, and practices to achieve a vision, rather than carving out entirely new spaces and perpetuate marginalization. Mainstreaming involves closing the gap between mainstream psychology and LGBT psychology, such that LGBT lives and experiences are understood using the tools and frames of psychological science and practice and at the same time, psychology's theories, evidence base, and professional practice are transformed by knowledge contributions from LGBT voices and perspectives (Goldfried 2001).

To implement the PAP policy, we identified four areas of activity by Filipino psychologists. These activities are: (1) research; (2) education; (3) outreach; and (4) professional practice. First, Filipino psychologists conduct research and produce new scientific knowledge related to human behavior, affect, and cognition (Bernardo 1997). Our flagship peer-reviewed journal, the *Philippine Journal of Psychology*, is published twice a year, in English, by the PAP. Second, Filipino psychologists teach—in higher education, in training contexts, and even in basic education (Teh 2012). Classroom-based as well as non-traditional teaching is an important activity of many Filipino psychologists; for some it may well be their primary professional activity. Third, outreach—which encompasses extension services to the public, policy-related activities such as legislative advocacy, and connecting to media and other platforms for public education (Estrada Claudio 2012). Finally, professional practice—perhaps the quintessential and certainly the most direct form of service conducted by psychologists, especially those coming from subfields like clinical psychology and counseling (Carandang 2012; Tuason et al. 2011).

Using this framework and armed with the PAP policy, we initiated LGBT inclusion efforts across these four interconnected spheres of activity. We discuss some of the initial successes along those four areas.

Research

In terms of knowledge production, we identified the need for more research on Filipino LGBT lives and experiences. Since 2010, we have organized dedicated LGBT programming in the annual conferences of the PAP and of the other national association in psychology, the Pambansang Samahan sa Sikolohiyang Pilipino (PSSP), a smaller but equally active organization dedicated to advancing indigenous and cultural psychology in the Philippines. In the 2010 PAP conference, for example, two symposium sessions carried the phrase *LGBT psychology* for the first time in their titles: "LGBT Psychology 1: Filipino Lesbian and Gay Identities and Relationships" and "LGBT Psychology 2: Issues and Applications" and featured three papers each. In the same year, a symposium titled "Sikolohiyang (Psychology) LGBT" was part of the PSSP conference.

The goal here has been to ensure that LGBT concerns have a visible place in convention programming, where researchers, students, and psychologists can attend and hear empirical work being conducted in the Philippines about Filipino LGBT matters (Ofreneo 2013). Whereas in the past, any paper on an LGBT topic would have been relegated to a generic "gender" or even "sexual behavior" session, now we are strengthening the practice of staking out LGBT-specific spaces and sessions in these research-related events.

Beyond conference programming, we have begun making contributions via peer-reviewed research publications. In December 2013, a special issue of the *Philippine Journal of Psychology* (PJP) dedicated to LGBT psychology was published. In keeping with the spirit of capacity-building, we organized a two-day residential writing workshop for prospective contributors, facilitated by a former PJP editor. After peer review by invited international referees, the issue came out featuring nine original articles by Filipino LGBT psychologists, most of whom were publishing LGBT work for the first time. The issue included a review of Filipino LGBT psychology (Ofreneo 2013) and eight empirical research papers on Filipino sexual prejudice and polyculturalist beliefs (Bernardo 2013), transnegativity in the Philippines (Macapagal 2013), gay children in conflict with the law (Villafuerte 2013), sexual roles among Filipino gay men (Muyargas 2013), coming out stories of Waray youth (Docena 2013), friendships between women and gay men (Torre and Manalastas 2013), dynamics of Filipino lesbian and gay couples (Kintanar 2013), and media-based interventions to reduce homonegativity (Clemente, Billedo, and David 2013). The issue sold out in two months— the second time in PJP history —and is now on its second printing. Plans are now underway to produce a second special issue on LGBT psychology. This is scheduled to come out in 2016.

Education

Psychology is a duly recognized major in universities in the Philippines, according to the Commission on Higher Education (Cue 2015; Teh 2012). As a popular choice among undergraduate students, psychology teaching offers an important site for LGBT inclusion as well as possible exclusion and perpetuation of misinformation about sexual orientation, gender identity, and gender expression.

There are two approaches for making LGBT topics visible in the psychology curriculum: (1) integration into existing courses; and (2) development and delivery of stand-alone courses on LGBT psychology. Initiatives by individual faculty for integration of LGBT topics in psychology courses exist in the Philippines. Teachers in public, state-run universities like the Polytechnic University of the Philippines incorporate LGBT topics in their curriculum. Individual faculty from private, Catholic universities also ensure LGBT inclusion in their courses (e.g., graduate and undergraduate seminars in gender and sexuality at the Ateneo de Manila University, a Jesuit school in Manila). At the De La Salle University Manila, junior faculty have begun to include sexual orientation and gender diversity in courses like introductory psychology and developmental psychology. Though not focusing exclusively on LGBT topics, the courses taught by these Filipino psychologists weave in LGBT concerns and examples in otherwise mainstream psychology content.

A case example of a stand-alone course is an undergraduate special topics elective first designed and taught at the University of the Philippines Diliman entitled LGBT Psychology. This twice-a-week course, which was first offered in 2010 and has been available for nine semesters running, focuses exclusively on LGBT issues in psychology, including topics such as coming out and sexual development, stigma and discrimination, LGBT health, intersectionality, homoparentality, queer politics, faith and religion, and issues in conducting LGBT research (Manalastas 2015). This course has been recently replicated in two other parts of the country, at the University of the Philippines Tacloban and at the University of the Philippines Miag-ao beginning 2014.

Outside formal classroom contexts, we developed a public education module we call LGBT Psych 101. This is a flexible training package, with common core messaging (depathologisation, anti-LGBT stigma, and minority stress), suggested learning activities, and audiovisual support materials that is suitable for delivery to a wide range of public audiences other than psychology classrooms. In May 2013, in partnership with the Ateneo de Manila University's Social Psychology Action Research Laboratory and the University of the Philippines Centre for Women's Studies, we designed and conducted a two-day national facilitators training workshop on conducting LGBT Psych 101. The objective of this activity was to create a pool of talent of Filipino psychologists with the knowledge, skills, and efficacy to run the public education module and "give LGBT psychology away." Eighteen participants from 16 different universities participated, with a commitment to conduct at least two LGBT Psych 101 sessions within six months of the workshop. This strategy led to the immediate delivery of the module for diverse audiences such as the Philippine National Police, the Department of Education, parenting groups, local HIV organizations, school based counsellors, not to mention the 16 academic institutions of the trainees.

Outreach

Outside of research and teaching, psychologists can play a role in broader efforts to promote social change and well-being, an approach sometimes called psychology in the public interest (Brewster Smith 1990). These can include psychology experts sharing knowledge to inform policymakers, engaging media on issues of human behavior, and taking principled and formal stands on pressing social issues where psychological expertise, broadly defined, can contribute in debate and decision-making (Cohen, Lee, and McIlwraith 2012).

As a consequence of its LGBT-affirmative policy, the PAP sent an official letter of support in August 2012, for a proposed ordinance on non-discrimination being debated at the council of Cebu City, the second most populous metropolitan area in the country and an important center of politics, trade, and culture in the southern Philippines. This was the very first time the PAP, as an institution, engaged in legislative advocacy in relation to one of its policy statements. In his sponsorship speech, the main proponent of the bill cited the PAP's policy resolution; the proposed ordinance was passed unanimously shortly thereafter.

Aside from engaging policy and political institutions, attempts have also been made to include LGBT issues in psychological forays into media. Through a column for the online news portal *Interaksyon.com*, Filipino

LGBT psychologists have written a number of popular articles, for example, on lesbian and gay parents (Rosales Parr 2013). One notable use of this online space was to respond to a highly circulated column piece in February 2013, written by one local celebrity-mother on the topic of LGBT children (Bersola-Babao 2013). The writer interviewed a clinical psychologist who, upon being asked for the appropriate response to a child who may be lesbian or gay, remarked: "Arrest the situation. But most parents encourage the situation. Let's be moral in making the child understand the situation. We tell our child, 'Anak, mali ito' [Son/daughter, this is wrong]."

The PAP immediately issued a statement contesting the view that children who are gay or lesbian are somehow inferior, affirming the position of the profession that being gay is non-pathological (PAP 2013). A counterpiece, written by a developmental psychologist and parenting researcher (Peña-Alampay 2013), emphasizing autonomy support and warmth for all children, including LGBT children, was published within days of the original piece.

Professional practice

Professional psychological practice in the Philippines is composed of three streams of interrelated activity: psychological assessment, psychotherapy, and design and delivery of counseling psychological programmes (Cue 2015). A number of individual psychology practitioners have begun to incorporate an LGBT-affirmative lens in their practice, especially in working with clients who are lesbian, gay, bisexual, or transgender. Since the 1990s, Margarita Go-Singco Holmes has pioneered sexuality affirmative clinical practice in Philippine psychology and has written extensively on her experiences, often having been the lone voice in the field for many years (Holmes 1993, 2005). LGBT-affirmative counseling is now being offered by individual practitioners (Ofreneo 2010), while some have presented work on gay-affirmative therapy at the PAP conference (Kintanar and Rodriguez 2011). Some school-based counsellors, for instance, at the University of the East and the Ramon Magsaysay (Cubao) High School, both in Manila, have also been supporting LGBT students via their institutions' guidance and counseling programmes.

Many opportunities to inform and improve psychological practice with LGBT populations exist, especially in contexts where there is a need to transform and redress silences regarding sexual and gender diversity (Nel 2014; Tuason et al. 2011). One important avenue for future work is the development of local practice guidelines for working with LGBT people, akin to what has been established in other countries like the US (American Psychological Association 2012) and the UK (British Psychological Society 2012). Presently, there are no practice guidelines of any sort in Philippine psychology, though there are initiatives to develop a framework in the context of disaster mental health and psychosocial services, which may also serve as a possible entry point for LGBT inclusion in the future (McSherry et al. 2014). The absence of more general clinical practice guidelines in Philippine psychology appears to be one perceived barrier for the development of more population-specific guidelines (A.S. Alianan Jr., personal communication, 6 March 2014), so a more integrationist approach, such as supporting the creation of general guidelines for clinical practice and ensuring LGBT-inclusivity, may be a possible first step.

Another avenue of work in this area is to investigate the prevalence of psychologists engaged in SOCE (sexual orientation change efforts), also known as conversion or reparative therapies (APA Task Force on Appropriate Therapeutic Responses to Sexual Orientation 2009). Little is known about the extent of this unethical practice in the Philippines, though anecdotal reports suggest that some practitioners, especially those from an anti-LGBT faith-based tradition, may be offering some form of it (Estrada Claudio 2012; Holmes 2005).

Strength in numbers

Three years after the PAP's non-discrimination policy, we achieved a milestone in addressing the need for a visible network of Filipino researchers, practitioners, and psychology professionals engaged in LGBT psychology. In January 2014, the PAP approved the creation of the LGBT Psychology Interest Group, the first and only official collective of psychologists and allied mental health professionals in Southeast Asia working for LGBT rights and well-being. This organizational structure, instituted as a permanent arm of the national association, was designed to coordinate activities among Filipino psychologists and with external stakeholders such as media and the LGBT activist community, to fill in the gaps we identified at the beginning of our work in building capacity for Philippine LGBT psychology. And as there is no formal mechanism within PAP for monitoring progress on the commitments outlined in the 2011 policy, the special interest group, since its inception, has also acted in this capacity. Though originally a small circle—we began with ten like-minded Filipino psychologists in our original proposal for formal recognition—we have since grown to more than 50 active members, including affiliates from other Southeast Asian countries like Thailand, Malaysia, and Singapore. After a "coming out party" in March 2014, the special interest group, through a one-day strategic planning exercise, formalized its mission statement:

> We are the Lesbian, Gay, Bisexual, and Transgender (LGBT) Psychology Special Interest Group of the Psychological Association of the Philippines. We build an LGBT-inclusive psychology in the Philippines by developing the capacity of psychologists and allied professionals to engage in research, education, advocacy, and practice for LGBT rights and well-being (Agana 2014, 4).

Under the banner of the special interest group and in partnership with activist colleagues, we have conducted more capacity building activities such as a teachers' workshop on supervising undergraduate LGBT research in January 2015, and a second national facilitators' training workshop on conducting LGBT Psych 101 attended by another 18 participants in April 2015. Aside from internal capacity building, our special interest group has also represented the profession of psychology externally in LGBT community events, such as the 2014 Pride celebration in Quezon City, and in roundtable discussions, fora, and civil society meetings related to LGBT rights advocacy organized by groups like the ASEAN SOGIE Caucus, ISE-AN Hivos, UNDP, and USAID.

Lessons learned so far

Some lessons can be gleaned from our work in the past five years of building LGBT psychology in the Philippines. These insights are necessarily tentative and may not apply directly to the challenge of LGBT inclusion in other countries, especially contexts with highly developed professional psychology associations or extremely hostile, anti-LGBT social climates. Nonetheless the initial gains in the Philippine psychology landscape have lead us to a number of reflections that could serve as suggestions for others interested in initiating similar work. Here we discuss three.

First, assemble a core of like-minded talent. An individual, lone wolf approach is difficult to sustain. Prior to 2009, individual psychologists like Mira Ofreneo (2003) and Margarita Go-Singco Holmes (1993, 2005) had already attempted to begin conversations around homosexuality and Philippine psychology. But given the tendency in mainstream psychology to perceive LGBT issues as peripheral or too specialized (Goldfried 2001), coming together to gather strength in diversity and in numbers greatly benefits the cause of LGBT inclusion within the profession, based on our experience from 2010 onwards. We were conducting informal side meetings for four years during the annual PAP conferences, asking individuals we knew personally to be LGBT or allies to attend, before we were able to gather enough people ready and willing to put their names on a formal request for the institution of the LGBT Psychology Special Interest Group. In hindsight, those meetings and interactions were helpful in building trust and collective readiness that we needed to move forward as a fledgling organization (De Vita, Fleming, and Twombly 2001).

Second, obtain support and legitimacy. Support here refers to the buy-in of the relevant internal authorizing body, in this case, the PAP leadership, while legitimacy refers to recognition and backing by the external community of stakeholders, such as the LGBT activist community and other LGBT psychology collectives (Moore 2013). Both internal and external linkages are critical to achieve the objective of closing the gap between mainstream and LGBT psychologies (Goldfried 2001). One concrete example of an activity we initiated to this end was a half day, no-cost workshop on LGBT psychology for the administrative staff of the PAP in 2013. We ran our LGBT Psych 101 module and invited two prominent LGBT activists to tell their stories, speak about their work, and engage the PAP staff on how the LGBT community would benefit from engagements by psychologists and mental health professionals. The staff, including secretaries and finance officers, expressed appreciation for the learning opportunity, which we later discovered was the very first time they were provided with such a professional development event. Some remarked that it was the first time they met an out transgender woman, and one staff member even took the opportunity to come out as a gay man.

Third, focus on the unique contribution of LGBT psychology to advocacy efforts. In country contexts where mental health professions are marginal and developing (World Health Organization 2009), even local LGBT activist communities may not make the connections between social stigma, LGBT rights, and well-being. LGBT psychologists can provide a language, one based on scientific research, to combat inaccurate social beliefs about LGBT people and to offer another argument—one based on the interplay of enjoyment of rights, health, and well-being—for political projects like nondiscrimination (Morin and Rothblum 1991). This strategy, called "facting" by one LGBT psychologist leader (Pope 2012), is important because psychology, psychiatry, and other mental health professions have long histories of being used as one of three institutional instruments of anti-LGBT stigma, alongside religion and the law. In the Philippines, local activists are now empowered to call upon psychologist voices in addressing persistent beliefs that link sexual orientation and gender diversity to pathology.

Next steps

During the strategic planning exercise of the PAP's LGBT Psychology Special Interest Group, we identified the following strategic objectives for the coming five years (Agana 2014, 7):

- Achieve a critical mass of members nationwide.

- Influence other PAP divisions and interest groups to be more LGBT-inclusive.

- Become the country's foremost provider of evidence-based knowledge resources on LGBT psychology.

- Gain recognition internationally for our contributions to LGBT-affirmative research, education, advocacy, and practice.

These four goals represent our aspirations as a collective in the short term. We hope to increase our numbers, in order to include more voices and perspectives, as well as our reach, to go beyond what is sometimes referred to as "imperial Manila" (the observation that professional activities, opportunities, and resources often center in urban areas, particularly in the nation's capital). Following our approach of mainstreaming, bringing our message of inclusivity to the other divisions and interest groups is an important target, in order to avoid ghettoisation. We also aim to continue giving LGBT psychology away by creating and disseminating scientific evidence on Filipino LGBT lives and experiences towards our vision of equal rights and well-being for LGBT Filipinos. Finally, we wish to share our experiences, challenges, and ongoing lessons as a collective beyond the shores of our archipelago, to provide a model of how LGBT psychology can grow and flourish in a developing, postcolonial nation in the global south.

Many exciting challenges, both internal and external, lie ahead for LGBT psychology in the Philippines. Some of the challenges are the same challenges faced in Philippine psychology in general, including the scarcity of human resources particularly in the very low number of psychologists available to Filipinos, LGBT or otherwise, who need services (estimated to be only 0.14 psychologist per 100,000 citizens in the population; WHO

2009), as well as barriers to health care delivery partly due to Asian cultural values and belief-systems that stigmatize mental health care seeking (David 2010). Capacity building in the four key result areas continues; we want to strengthen, in particular, the practice pillar which so far has received the least attention, especially in the context of increasing state regulation of professional psychology in the Philippines and in the ASEAN (Cue 2015). The spectre of conversion therapy and the complexities of sexual orientation change efforts delivered in the context of faith-based or pastoral counseling locally remain and need to be confronted once and for all. Pressing inter-sectional issues such as gender-based violence especially among sexual and gender-minority women demand attention, and in the absence of feminist organizing in Philippine psychology—there is no PAP division or special in-terest group on the psychology of women or gender—concerned members of our collective have been taking up the cudgels (PAP 2014). Engagement of issues not yet part of our conversations in Philippine psychology and in LGBT rights organizing in the Philippines, such as the experiences of in-tersex people, needs to happen. Finally, with the filing of a comprehensive mental health bill in the Philippine legislature, outreach to the other local mental health professionals such as psychiatrists, social worker, and guid-ance counsellors will be important in the years to come.

Conclusion

LGBT psychology has come to Southeast Asia. Our work in mainstreaming LGBT issues in Philippine psychology—via research, education, advocacy, and practice—are in early development, but the ground work is on-going and there are initial successes to be celebrated. There is much opportunity for psychologists in the Philippines to make our profession truly advancing of the rights and well-being of all Filipinos, across the spectrum of gender identities and sexual orientations.

Acknowledgments

Previous versions of this paper were presented as part of a special sym-posium titled "Toward LGBT-Affirmative Psychology in Asia: Attitudes, Mental Health Issues, and Capacity Building" at the 2013 Annual Con-vention of the American Psychological Association, Hawaii, US, 31 July to 4 August 2013, and as part of a special symposium titled "Equal Human Rights, Well-being, and Sexuality: Initiatives by Southeast Asian Psycholo-gists and Mental Health Professionals Working with LGBT Populations" at the 3rd International Conference on Human Rights and Peace and Conflict in Southeast Asia, Kuala Lumpur, Malaysia, 15–16 October 2014. We acknowledge the support of Clinton Anderson, PhD; Ron Schlittler, MIPP; J. Enrique Saplala, PhD; Ma. Caridad Tarroja, PhD; Ma. Regina Hechanova, PhD; Angela V. Regala, PhD; Allan B. I. Bernardo, PhD; Mira Alexis Ofreneo, PhD; Jay A. Yacat, MA; and the members of the PAP's LGBT Psychology Special Interest Group.

BIBLIOGRAPHY

Agana, T. M. G. III. "Report on the 1st National Strategic Planning Workshop of the LGBT Psychology Special Interest Group of the Psychological Association of the Philippines." Unpublished paper, 2014.

American Psychological Association (APA). "Guidelines for Psychological Practice with Lesbian, Gay, and Bisexual clients." *American Psychologist* 67, no. 1 (2012): 10–42.

American Psychological Association (APA) Task Force on Appropriate Therapeutic Responses to Sexual Orientation. *Report of the Task Force on Appropriate Therapeutic Responses to Sexual Orientation.* Washington, DC: APA, 2009.

Bernardo, A. B. I. "Psychology Research in the Philippines: Observations and Prospects." *Philippine Journal of Psychology* 30, no. 1 (1997): 39–58.

———. "Exploring the Social Cognitive Dimensions of Sexual Prejudice in Filipinos." *Philippine Journal of Psychology* 46, no. 2 (2013): 19–48.

Bersola-Babao, T. "Being Gay." *Philippine Star*, 11 March 2013. http://www.philstar.com/entertainment/2013/ 03/11/918157/being–gay.

Brewster Smith, M. "Psychology in the Public Interest: What Have We Done? What Can We Do?" *American Psychologist* 45, no. 4 (1990): 530–36.

British Psychological Society (BPS). "Guidelines and literature review for psychologists working therapeutically with sexual and gender minority clients." 2012. http://www.bps.org.uk/sites/default/files/ images/rep_92.pdf.

Carandang, M. L. A. "Strengthening Psychology... Serving the Nation (The Practice)." *Philippine Journal of Psychology* 45, no. 2 (2012): 291–97.

Cohen, K. R., C. M. Lee, and R. McIlwraith, R. "The Psychology of Advocacy and the Advocacy of Psychology." *Canadian Psychology* 53, no. 3 (2012): 151–58.

Commission on Elections. "Resolution in the Matter of the Petition for Registration of Ang Ladlad LGBT Party for the Party–list System of Representation in the House of Representatives (SPP no. 09-22)." November 2009. http://www.comelec.gov.ph/?r=Archives/RegularElections/2010NLE/Resolutions/spp09228.

Clemente, J. A. R., C. J. F. Billedo, and C. C. David. "The Role of Broadcast Media in Attitude Change: A Pilot Study on a Campus-based Radio Programme and its LGBT Advocacy." *Philippine Journal of Psychology* 46, no. 2 (2013): 165–79.

Cue, M. P. "Emergence and Development of Philippine Psychology." Plenary paper presented at the 5th ASEAN Regional Union of Psychological Societies Congress, Singapore, March 2015.

Daly, M. "Gender Mainstreaming in Theory and Practice." *Social Politics: International Studies in Gender, State & Society* 12, no. 3 (2005): 433–50.

David, E. J. R. "Cultural Mistrust and Mental Health Help-seeking Attitudes among Filipino Americans." *Asian American Journal of Psychology* 1 no. 1 (2010): 57–66.

De Vita, C. J., C. Fleming, and E. C. Twombly. "Building Non-profit Capacity: A Framework for Addressing the Problem." In C. J. De Vita and C. Fleming, *Building Capacity in Non-profit Organizations*, 5–32. Washington, DC: Urban Institute, 2001.

Docena, P. S. "Developing and Managing One's Sexual Identity: Coming Out Stories of Waray Gay Adolescents." *Philippine Journal of Psychology* 46, no. 2 (2013): 75–103.

Estrada Claudio, S. "Was I Doing Outreach or Was I Standing Outside and Reaching In?" *Philippine Journal of Psychology* 45, no. 2 (2012): 285–90.

Garcia, J. N. C. "Nativism or Universalism: Situating LGBT Discourse in the Philippines." *Kritika Kultura* 20 (2013): 48–68.

Goldfried, M. R. "Integrating Gay, Lesbian, and Bisexual Issues into Mainstream Psychology." *American Psychologist* 56, no. 11 (2001): 977–88.

Holmes, M. G. S. *A Different Love: Being Gay in the Philippines*. Pasig, Philippines: Anvil, 1993.

———. *A Different Love: Being a Gay Man in the Philippines*. Pasig, Philippines: Anvil, 2005.

Hong Kong Psychological Society. *Position Paper for Psychologists Working with Lesbians, Gays, and Bisexual Individuals*. Hong Kong, China: HKPS, 2012.

Kintanar, N. S. M. "Comparing Relationship Satisfaction and Conflict Resolution Tactics of Filipino Gay, Lesbian, and Heterosexual Individuals in Romantic Relationships." *Philippine Journal of Psychology* 46, no. 2 (2013): 133–48.

Kintanar, N. S. and A. A. Rodriguez. "Pink Therapy: A Gay-affirmative and Expressive Art Approach for Group Counseling among Filipino Gay Adolescents." Paper presented at the 48th Annual Convention of the Psychological Association of the Philippines, Iloilo City, August 2011.

Macapagal, R. A. "Further Validation of the Genderism and Transphobia Scale in the Philippines." *Philippine Journal of Psychology*, 46, no. 2 (2013): 49–59.

Manalastas, E. J. "Filipino LGBT Psychology: Moving beyond 'Homosexual' Street Corners to Advancing Contemporary Visions." *Philippine Journal of Psychology* 46, no. 2 (2013): 1–3.

———. "Designing and Delivering an LGBTQ Studies in a Non-Western Country: The Experience of Teaching LGBTQ Psychology in the Philippines." Paper presented at the 2015 Expanding the Circle Summer Institute, San Francisco, June 2015.

McSherry, A., E. J. Manalastas, J. C. Gaillard, and S. N. M. Dalisay. "From Deviant to *Bakla*, Strong to Stronger: Mainstreaming Sexual and Gender Minorities into Disaster Risk Reduction in the Philippines." *Forum for Development Studies* 42, no. 1 (2014): 27–40.

Moore, M. H. *Recognizing Public Value*. Boston, MA: Harvard University Press, 2013.

Morin, S. F., and E. D. Rothblum. "Removing the Stigma: Fifteen Years of Progress." *American Psychologist* 46 (1991): 947–49.

Moser, C. and A. Moser. "Gender Mainstreaming since Beijing: A Review of Success and Limitations in International Institutions." *Gender and Development* 13, no. 2 (2005): 11–22.

Muyargas, M. M. "Exploring Sexual Minority Men and Their Sexual Roles: Understanding Risky Sexual Behaviors through Subjective Norms and Attitudes." *Philippine Journal of Psychology* 46, no. 2 (2013): 105–31.

Nadal, K. L. and M. J. H. Corpus. (2013). "'Tomboys' and 'Baklas': Experiences of Lesbian and Gay Filipino Americans." *Asian American Journal of Psychology* 4, no. 3 (2013): 166–75.

Nel, J. A. "South African Psychology Can and Should Provide Leadership in Advancing Understanding of Sexual and Gender Diversity on the African Continent." *South African Journal of Psychology* 44, no. 2 (2014): 145–48.

Ofreneo, M. A. P. "Tomboys and Lesbians: The Filipino Female Homosexual and Her Identity Development Process." *Philippine Journal of Psychology* 36, no. 1 (2003): 26–52.

———. "Surfacing Issues of Lesbian Women and Their Implications for Counseling." Paper presented at the 47th Annual Convention of the Psychological Association of the Philippines, Iloilo City, August 2010.

———. "Towards an LGBT-inclusive Psychology: Reflecting on a Social Change Agenda for Philippine Psychology." *Philippine Journal of Psychology* 46, no. 2 (2013): 5–17.

Peña-Alampay, L. "Q and A: Parenting Gay Children." *Rappler*, 17 March 2013. http://www.rappler.com/move-ph/23986-parenting-gay-children.

Pope, M. "First We were Sane, Now We are Legal: The Historic Position of Division 44 in LGBT Civil Rights." *Division 44 Newsletter* 28, no. 3 (2012): 14–21.

Prilleltensky, I. "Psychology and the status quo." *American Psychologist* 44 (1989): 795–802.

Psychological Association of the Philippines. "Statement of the Psychological Association of the Philippines on Non-discrimination Based on Sexual Orientation, Gender Identity and Expression." *Philippine Journal of Psychology* 44, no. 2 (2011): 229–30.

———. "PH Psychologists Speak Out on 'Being Gay': 'It's NOT a Disease. It's NOT a Disorder.'" *InterAksyon*, 13 March 2013. http://www.interaksyon.com/article/57043/statement-ph-psychologistsspeak-out-on-being-gay-its-not-a-disease-its-not-a-disorder.

———. "Resolution on Gender-based Violence and Violence against Women (VAW)." *Philippine Journal of Psychology* 47, no. 2 (2014): 153–56.

Psychological Association of the Philippines Scientific and Professional Ethics Committee. "Code of Ethics for Philippine Psychologists." *Philippine Journal of Psychology* 43, no. 2 (2010): 195–217.

Rosales Parr, R. "Is PNoy Right to Worry about Kids Being Raised by Gay Couples? A Psychologist Responds." *InterAksyon*, December 2013. http://www.interaksyon.com/article/76378/commentary-is-pnoy-right-to-worry-about-kids-being-raised-by-gay-couples-a-psychologist-responds.

Ruiz Austria, C. S. "The Church, the State and Women's Bodies in the Context of Religious Fundamentalism in the Philippines." *Reproductive Health Matters* 12, no. 24 (2004): 96–103.

Teh, L. A. "Strengthening the Teaching of Psychology in the Philippines." *Philippine Journal of Psychology* 45, no. 2 (2012): 275–83.

Torre, B. A., and E. J. Manalastas. "Babaeng Bakla: Friendships between Women and Gay Men in the Philippines." *Philippine Journal of Psychology* 46 no. 2 (2013): 149–63.

Tuason, M. T. G., K. T. Galang Fernandez, M. A. D. P. Catipon, L. Trivino-Dey, and M. L. Arellano-Carandang. "Counselling in the Philippines: Past, Present, and Future." *Journal of Counselling and Development* 90, no. 3 (2011): 373–77.

United Nations Development Programme (UNDP) and United States Agency for International Development (USAID). *Being LGBT in Asia: The Philippines Country Report*. Bangkok: United Nations Development Programme, 2014.

Villafuerte, S.L. "Ang Rosas ng Rehab: A Filipino Gay Child in Conflict with the Law Housed in a Youth Centre." *Philippine Journal of Psychology* 46, no. 2 (2013): 61–73.

Widmer, E. D., J. Treas, and R. Newcomb. "Attitudes toward Non-marital Sex in 24 Countries." *Journal of Sex Research* 35, no. 4 (1998): 349–58.

World Bank. "Philippines." Last modified 2015. http://data.worldbank.org/country/Philippines.

World Health Organization (WHO). *Mental Health Systems in Selected Low- and Middle-income Countries: A WHO-AIMS Cross National Analysis*. Geneva: WHO, 2009.

Statement of the Psychological Association of the Philippines on Non-Discrimination Based on Sexual Orientation, Gender Identity, and Expression

LESBIAN, GAY, BISEXUAL, AND TRANSGENDER (LGBT) Filipinos continue to experience stigma, prejudice and discrimination in Philippine society. This stigma is manifested in actions such as: bullying, teasing, and harassment of LGBT children and adolescents in families, schools, and communities; media portrayal of LGBTs as frivolous, untrustworthy, and even dangerous or predatory; denying transgender Filipinos entry into commercial establishments; pigeonholing LGBT Filipinos into particularly limited roles and occupations; or curtailing their rights to participate in the political sphere.

LGBT Filipinos often confront social pressures to hide, suppress or even attempt to change their identities and expressions as conditions for their social acceptance and enjoyment of rights. Although many LGBTs learn to cope with this social stigma, these experiences can cause serious psychological distress, including immediate consequences such as fear, sadness, alienation, anger, and internalized stigma (Hatzenbuehler 2009; Meyer 2003). This anti-LGBT prejudice and discrimination tend to be based on a rhetoric of moral condemnation and are fueled by ignorance or unfounded beliefs associating these gender expressions and sexual orientations with psychopathology or maladjustment.

However, decades of scientific research have led mental health professional organizations worldwide to conclude that lesbian, gay and bisexual orientations are normal variants of human sexuality. These include: the American Psychiatric Association in 1973, the American Psychological Association in 1975, British Psychological Society, the Colombian Society of Psychology, Psychological Society of South Africa, the Australian Psychological Society, and the International Network on Lesbian, Gay and Bisexual Concerns and Transgender Issues in Psychology, among others.

The Psychological Association of the Philippines (PAP) aligns itself with the global initiatives to remove the stigma of mental illness that has long been associated with diverse sexualities and to promote the wellbeing of LGBT people. Moreover, the PAP Code of Ethics (2010) is clear in its stance against discrimination. Filipino

1   Psychological Association of the Philippines, "Statement of the Psychological Association of the Philippines on Non-Discrimination Based on Sexual Orientation, Gender Identity and Expression," *Philippine Journal of Psychology* 44, no. 2 (2011): 229–30.

psychologists are called upon to recognize the unique worth and inherent dignity of all human beings; and to respect the diversity among persons and peoples (Principle I, a and b). This means that Filipino psychologists should not discriminate against or demean persons based on actual or perceived differences in characteristics including gender identity and sexual orientation (Ethical Standard III-A and C; V-B.8).

In order to eliminate stigma, prejudice, discrimination and violence against LGBT, the PAP resolves to support efforts to:

- oppose all public and provate discrimination on the basis of actual or perceived sexual orientation, gender identity, and expression;
- repeal discriminatory laws and policies, and support the passage of legislation at the local and national levels that protect the rights and promote the welfare of people of all sexual orientations and gender identities and expressions;
- eliminate all forms of prejudice and discrimination against LGBTs in teaching, research, psychological interventions, assessment and other psychological programs;
- encourage psychological research that addresses the needs and concerns of LGBT Filipinos and their families and communities; and
- disseminate and apply accurate and evidence-based information about sexual orientation and gender identity and expression to design interventions that foster mental health and wellbeing of LGBT Filipinos.

BIBLIOGRAPHY

American Psychiatric Association. "Position Statement on Homosexuality and Civil Rights." *American Journal of Psychiatry* 131, no. 4 (1973): 497.

Anton, B. S. "Proceedings of the American Psychological Association for the Legislative Year 2008: Minutes of the Annual Meeting of the Council of Representatives, 22–24 February 2008, Washington, DC; 13 and 17 August 2008, Boston, MA; and Minutes of the February, June, August, and December 2008 Meetings of the Board of Directors." *American Psychologist* 64 (2009): 372–453.

Conger, J. J. "Proceedings of the American Psychological Association, Incorporated, for the Year 1974: Minutes of the Annual Meeting of the Council of Representatives." *American Psychologist* 30 (1975): 620–51.

Hatzenbuehler, M. L. "How Does Sexual Minority Stigma 'Get Under the Skin'? A Psychological Mediation Framework." *Psychological Bulletin* 135, no. 5 (2009): 707–30.

International Network for Lesbian, Gay and Bisexual Concerns and Transgender Issues in Psychology. "Sexual Orientation and Mental Health: Toward Global Perspectives on Practice and Policy." Report on the International Meeting on Lesbian, Gay, and Bisexual Concerns in Psychology, San Francisco, CA, 21–23 August 2001. https://www.apa.org/pi/lgbt/resources/international-meeting.pdf.

Meyer, I. H. "Prejudice, Social Stress, and Mental Health in Lesbian, Gay, and Bisexual Populations: Conceptual Issues and Research Evidence." *Psychological Bulletin* 129, no. 5 (2003): 674–97.

Psychological Association of the Philippines Scientific and Professional Ethics Committee. "Code of Ethics for Philippine Psychologists." *Philippine Journal of Psychology* 43 (2010): 195–217.

"Love needs no treatment or repair," according to the LGBTIA campaign to remove homosexuality from classification as a mental illness by Philippine psychology and to dissociate the authority of psychological knowledge and credentials from the practice of so-called conversion or reparative "therapy" used on individuals to make them renounce their same-sex sexual orientation or transgender identity. Photo courtesy of Psychological Association of the Philippines LGBT Special Interest Group.

This essay was previously published in *Philippine Journal of Psychology* 46, no. 2 (2013): 5–17.

MIRA ALEXIS P. OFRENEO

Towards an LGBT-Inclusive Psychology: Reflecting on a Social Change Agenda for Philippine Psychology

O N 8 OCTOBER 2011, the Psychological Association of the Philippines (PAP) approved the Statement on Non-Discrimination Based on Sexual Orientation, Gender Identity, and Expression. This historic document signals the coming out of Philippine psychology as a profession to eliminate the stigma and discrimination against lesbian, gay, bisexual, and transgender or LGBT people. Through the leadership of Eric Manalastas, a collective of LGBT psychologists and allies have come together to make LGBT psychology in the Philippines visible and vibrant. In the past four years alone, several spaces have been created for discussing LGBT issues through symposia and workshops at the conventions of the PAP and the PSSP (Pambansang Samahan sa Sikolohiyang Pilipino). On 9 and 10 May 2013, the first National Facilitators' Training Workshop on Conducting LGBT Psych 101 was held by the PAP with the support of the APA and the Arcus Foundation.

I am part of this collective of Filipino LGBT psychologists who have been promoting the well-being of Filipino LGBT people. And I am also part of the larger collective of Filipino psychologists who are seeking to make a difference in the lives of Filipinos. It is to this larger "we" of Filipino psychologists that I speak to in this paper. In here I reflect on the changes taking place in Philippine psychology as a discipline and as a profession towards an LGBT-inclusive psychology. I map out a vision of change in the professional practice of Filipino psychologists and in the teaching of psychology in the Philippines. And I propose an LGBT psychology research agenda for Filipino psychologists. It is the creation of Filipino LGBT psychological knowledge that is the focus of this paper as I highlight five key ideas for LGBT research in the Philippines. I conclude the paper with a call for affinity to all Filipino psychologists, that we may act always with compassion and care towards people of diverse genders and sexualities.

A vision of change

The vision of change of our small group of Filipino LGBT psychologists is an LGBT-inclusive Philippine psychology. This means that LGBT psychology is not separate from psychology as a discipline and as a profession but is part and parcel of what psychology is about and is for. If psychology as a discipline is the of study tof human thoughts, feelings, and behaviors, then it has to study the cognitions, emotions, and actions of LGBT people. If psychology as a profession upholds the well-being of all human beings, then it has to uphold the well-being of LGBT people.

This vision of change is aligned with the PAP Code of Ethics (2010), which states that "psychologists accept as fundamental the Principle of Respect for the Dignity of Persons and Peoples" (p. 4). This principle includes the values of "respect for the unique worth and inherent dignity of all human beings" and "respect for the diversity among persons and peoples" (p. 4). In accordance with these ethical principles, the PAP issued the Statement of Non-Discrimination concluding that "Filipino psychologists should not discriminate against or demean persons based on actual or perceived differences in characteristics including gender identity and sexual orientation" (PAP 2011, 229–30). Rather, Filipino psychologists are the first to accept and respect human beings who are also lesbian, gay, bisexual, transgender, intersex, queer, *bakla, tomboy, silahis, transpinay,* transman, and all other identity labels signifying the diversity of sexual orientation, gender identity, and expression. (*Bakla* is a term used to refer to gay men and feminine men. *Tomboy* is a term used to refer to lesbians and masculine women. *Silahis* is a term used to refer to bisexual men.)

As Filipino psychologists called upon to uphold the well-being of people of diverse sexual orientations, gender identities, and expressions, the question we ask is, "Do we uphold the well-being of people marginalized because of their gender and sexuality?" And, "How do we uphold the well-being of gender and sexual minorities?" When we imagine a human being, do we imagine a woman? When we think of a person, do we think of a male-to-female transexual? When we talk about men, do we talk about gay men? When we speak about women, do we speak about transwomen? Do we imagine humans as *baklas* and *tomboys*? Or do we only imagine a world of heterosexual, masculine males and heterosexual, feminine females? An LGBT-inclusive psychology recognizes the diversity of being human.

LGBT-affirmative counseling and therapy. An LGBT-inclusive psychology means an LGBT-affirmative counseling practice. When a lesbian student is going through identity issues and seeks help from her guidance counselor, she will not be turned away on the basis of religion or a discriminatory school policy. When a bakla or a transwoman student experiences bullying in school, her gender expression will be validated and she will be protected from violence. When a gay man going through problems with his long-term partner seeks counseling, his relationship problems will not be minimized and he will be adequately helped with his relationship concerns. When we psychologists counsel individuals with gender and sexuality concerns, we have to be able to give affirmation, unconditional love, and acceptance. We need to know about the issues and concerns of LGBT people and gain knowledge and skills that can be useful in counseling and therapy.

There are Filipino psychologists who have been advocating for LGBT-affirmative counseling practice. Rem Moog of the University of the East Caloocan has created a guidance and counseling program to support LGBT students. Venus Dis-aguen of Ramon Magsaysay High School Cubao has asked LGBT students about their issues as LGBT adolescents and has been finding ways to help them. Vangie Castronuevo of De La Salle University Dasmariñas, Niel Kintanar of University of San Carlos Cebu, and I are among the psychologists who have been practicing LGBT-affirmative therapy.

LGBT-inclusive teaching of psychology. An LGBT-inclusive psychology means the LGBT-inclusive teaching of psychology. When we teach psychology subjects, do we include the experiences of people who may not be heterosexual? When we teach general psychology, do we discuss same-sex love and relationships between two men or two women? When we teach developmental psychology, do we talk about the developmental concerns of LGBT people, the unique issues of LGBT adolescents, and the diversity of families including same-sex parents and their children? When we teach social psychology, do we raise the issue of stigma and discrimination on the basis of sexual orientation and gender identity (SOGI)? Do we use textbooks that represent LGBT people, assign readings that tell the stories of LGBT lives, and use research that reflects the diversity of gender and sexuality?

There are Filipino psychologists who have been integrating LGBT into psychology and teaching LGBT psychology in the classroom: Eric Manalastas has been teaching a course on LGBT psychology at the University of the Philippines Diliman. Mira Ofreneo and Nico Canoy have been teaching a gender and sexuality course at the Ateneo de Manila University. Meling Macapagal, Mira Ofreneo, Tina Montiel, and Jopie Nolasco (2013) have written a social psychology textbook for Filipinos that includes a chapter on gender and sexuality.

LGBT-inclusive psychological knowledge. An LGBT-inclusive psychology means LGBT-inclusive psychological knowledge. This implies that when we engage in research, we utilize theories and frameworks that can capture the realities of lesbian, gay, bisexual, and transgender lives. This further implies that, we ask research questions that reflect the psychological issues of LGBT Filipinos. Do we know how LGBT people in the Philippines are able to live happy and meaningful lives despite personal experiences of non-acceptance and a shared experience of discrimination? Do we know how a Filipino transman falls in love and stays in love? Do we know how Filipino gay fathers raise happy children? Do we know how Filipino families accept their gay sons or lesbian daughters? Do we know what makes Filipino lesbian couples happy? Do we know how Filipino LGBT people live their lives in the everyday?

The next section develops an LGBT psychology research agenda and presents five key ideas on how to create LGBT psychological knowledge in the Philippines. Examples of research questions about Filipino LGBT psychological phenomena are presented alongside approaches to doing LGBT research. It is an invitation to reflect on what we need to know about the lives of LGBT people in the Philippines and how we can know what we need to know.

An LGBT psychology research agenda

Clarke, Ellis, Peel, and Riggs (2010), in their introductory textbook to LGBTQ psychology, reflect on the future of the field. They highlight the cultural specificity of the experiences of LGBTQ people and the limitations of Western theories and models of gender and sexuality; the utility of intersectional approaches to capture LGBTQ people's overlapping identities and multiple positions of marginalization; and the application of LGBTQ research in the different areas of psychology. For them, the future direction for LGBTQ psychology is to represent diversity; to go beyond the white, middle-class norm; to imagine an LGBTQ-positive psychology; to promote LGBTQ-specific research and comparative research; and to truly be international in scope by recognizing the cultural specificity of LGBTQ lives.

I resonate with the points raised by Clarke and colleagues in charting an LGBT psychology research agenda, particularly the need to look at LGBT lives in their specific cultural context and the utility of an intersectional lens to understand the complexity of these lives. I elaborate on these two points and offer three of my own: the contribution of positive psychology and focusing on what is positive in the lives of LGBT people; the value of action research and focusing on what is empowering to LGBT communities; and the openness to multiple frameworks and methodologies that can create new theories from Filipino LGBT experiences.

Cultural specificity. Tan (1998) has noted how there is no term in Filipino for sexuality, for homosexual, bisexual, and heterosexual. As we adopt Western terms including lesbian, gay, bisexual, and transgender, we are faced with the confusion and contention in meanings as these terms interface with words found in Filipino such as *bakla, tomboy,* and *silahis.* For instance, the words *lesbian* and *tomboy* have been differentiated in some studies (Josef, 1997; 1999). The same goes with the distinction between *gay* and *bakla* (Tan, 1995a, 1995b). The words we use to refer to diverse genders and sexualities are socially constructed by different groups of people and used in varying contexts.

Some Filipinos believe that the tomboy is the "real" lesbian. This means that a lesbian has to be masculine to be a "real" lesbian. Others believe that tomboys refer to butch women who want to be like men. As such, some Filipino lesbians refuse to identify with tomboys. For them, a lesbian has to be feminine and embody women who love women. And yet some women who love women do not identify as lesbians precisely because they are not tomboys.

Some Filipinos believe that the bakla and gay are the same as both refer to men who like men. Others argue that they are different as bakla refers to feminine or cross-dressing men while gay refers to masculine men who are attracted to men. Still others contend that the bakla is a gay man but that there are other gay men who are not bakla like the discreet, straight-acting, or *pa-min* (masculine) gay men. Still others argue that the bakla is transgender and not gay.

In these examples, we see how we need to deconstruct the meaning of words and understand their implications on how people live their everyday lives. How are these words used in the everyday? When do they mean the same thing and when are they different? Perhaps these labels are constructed in the same way by specific groups of people in particular social contexts and constructed in different ways in others. These are research questions we can ask and we need to ask because language is powerful. In one study, women refused to identify as lesbians even if they had female partners because only the tomboy was seen as the "real" lesbian in their community whereas the feminine female partner was seen as *pumapatol sa tomboy* (condescending to enter a relationship with a tomboy) and retained the identity label of a "girl" (Ofreneo 2000, 2003).

While I raise the issue of contestation in language, I recognize the unique words used in the different dialects and languages in the Philippines

to refer to diverse genders and sexualities. I see the possibility of conflation in meaning in a cultural context that fuses gender and sexuality, where
words such as *bakla* and *tomboy* are used to refer to both gender expression
and sexual orientation. I note the implications of the meaning of words to
identity development and coming out and to how different groups of people will respond to these words used as social identities. Language and the
other facets of culture that shape the lives of LGBT people in the Philippines
need to be understood. For instance, what is the role of the Filipino family, of unique relational patterns, of religion and spirituality, of the Roman
Catholic Church, of our Spanish colonial history, in the lives of LGBT Filipinos? This perhaps requires the use of culturally appropriate frameworks
or the construction of theories developed in our unique cultural context.

Intersectionality. Intersectionality refers to the multidimensionality of
marginalization and how the simultaneous existence of multiple identities
creates unique lived experiences for the marginalized (Crenshaw 1989).
First used in black feminist studies to highlight the intersection of race and
gender in the experience of marginalization of black women, intersectionality has become a framework for understanding the intersection of race, class,
gender, and sexuality, as well as other social identities and social categories.
For instance, butch or masculine lesbians or tomboys report non-hiring,
sexual harassment, and other forms of discrimination at work because they
are immediately stigmatized for their masculinity as compared to femme
or feminine lesbians (Isis International Manila 2010). The intersection of
gender expression with sexual orientation in this example creates a unique
experience for each group of lesbians in the work context.

Intersectionality can be expanded to not only look at experiences of
marginalization but to also examine experiences of agency as well as the
varieties of human experiences in the different life spheres. How does being an urban middle-class educated male shape Filipino gay men's sense of
empowerment in their everyday lives? Does this sense of empowerment
change depending on one's expressed gender? How do tomboy, bakla, and
transgender youth from rural poor communities create spaces to explore
their identities? How does identity exploration vary for youth who identify as bakla compared to those who identify as transgender? An intersectional perspective highlights the multidimensionality of people's identities
and lived experiences.

Positive psychology. I frame the contribution of positive psychology to
an LGBT psychological research agenda within a broader agenda of social
change. That if we are to work towards empowering marginalized LGBT

communities, we need to reframe how we position LGBT people from victims to agents. Positive psychology highlights the strengths rather than the weaknesses of people, their experience of happiness and meaning in life, and the possibility of collective action and social change (Biswas-Diener 2011). Research questions can focus on how LGBT people survive and cope with discrimination; how they are able to live happy and meaningful lives; how they create new models of relationships and find love in a heterosexist world; how they grow up with unconditional love from their parents and families; how they raise children and have families of their own; how they find comfort and solace from peers or find positive LGBT role models to look up to; etc. A positive psychological lens allows us to hear the stories of struggles as well as those of hope and resilience and share the narratives of LGBT people who live empowered lives within a context of marginalization.

Action research. Aligned with an empowerment agenda is engaging in action research. Action research combines research and action by orienting researchers towards research questions that emanate from the realities on the ground (Kagan, Burton, and Siddiquee 2008). It is a commitment to a participatory process where researchers and communities come together from theory to practice (Kagan et al., 2008). Ultimately, the question we are faced with in research is, "So what?" Did we help people with out study? Did we create change? Can our research findings be used to fight social injustice? Can we utilize our results for creating psychosocial interventions? The questions for researchers are, "For whom?" and, "For what end?" Is it possible to ask LGBT people themselves what they need to know, what for them is important, and what would then be meaningful research questions? Is it possible to create an LGBT research agenda together with Filipino LGBT communities? An action research orientation can help us be mindful of our research goals and processes and whether these are truly empowering for LGBT people.

Multiple frameworks and methodologies. Lastly, I speak of an openness to multiple frameworks and methodologies in doing LGBT psychological research. Such an openness to multiple frameworks allows us to utilize both social constructionist frameworks and positivist frameworks when appropriate. It can lead us towards interdisciplinarity so that we can benefit from the theories beyond psychology. If our goal is to do LGBT psychological research that is empowering for Filipino LGBT communities and is sensitive to our unique social and cultural context, perhaps we can develop frameworks that can be empowering and culturally-sensitive. Or theorize from our own realities and experiences.

Where are we in terms of LGBT psychological research?

LGBT psychological research in the Philippines has grown tremendously in the past decade. In the past four years alone, around 20 research papers on various topics within LGBT psychology were presented at the PAP convention from 2010 to 2013. This count is limited to organized symposia and does not include individual paper presentations on LGBT psychological topics. Identity development, coming out, and disclosure has been explored among Filipino lesbians by Vangie Castronuevo of De La Salle University Dasmariñas, among Filipino gay youth by John Kliatchko of Don Bosco, among Filipino male and female bisexuals by Chei Billedo and Eric Manalastas of the University of the Philippines Diliman, among Filipino transgenders by Brenda Alegre of University of Santo Tomas. This set of papers represents an example of practicing specificity, wherein we recognize the unique experience of each specific group rather than the commonality of experiences. Specificity highlights surfacing differences within LGBT communities, without discounting the shared experience of discrimination but rather emphasizing the diversity of issues within LGBT communities (Ofreneo and de Vela 2010). In this case, the diverse meanings of L, G, B, and T identities in the Philippine context.

We see the multiplicity in frameworks used in LGBT studies such as phenomenology to understand the Filipino lesbian closet (Vangie Castronuevo, DLSU Dasmariñas) and bisexual male adolescents (Golda Crisostomo, Letran); intersectionality to understand issues of Filipino lesbian women (Mira Ofreneo, ADMU); an ecological framework within phenomenology to understand young gay men living with HIV (Nico Canoy, DLSU Manila); evolutionary theory to understand mate preferences of Filipino lesbians and gay men (Darren Dumaop, DLSU Dasmariñas); alongside positivist models to predict relationship outness and satisfaction among Filipino gay men and lesbians (Niel Kintanar, USC) and to predict life satisfaction of Filipino LGBT students (Rem Moog, UE Caloocan).

We see the intersection of identities and the possibility of a deeper understanding of the unique lived experiences of LGBT people if framed with an intersectional lens in the case of Filipino Waray gay adolescents (Pierce Docena, UP Tacloban) (Waray refers to the Waray-speaking people of Samar, Leyte, and parts of Eastern Visayas); Filipino gay men playing the *tagasalo* role (Mark Velasco and colleagues; UPD) (*tagasalo* refers to the family member who "carries" or supports the family); Filipino LGBT-identified youth in conflict with the law (Ricky Clores, DLSU Dasmariñas);

and Filipino gay men in their late adulthood (Ronnie Motilla, Miriam College). We see the increasing specificity of research questions going beyond broad experiences of stigma and discrimination to the particularity of issues such as how Filipino gay men meet to create intimate relationships (GT Reyes and colleagues, UPD); work and the contribution to the household of Filipino urban gay and bisexual youth (Eric Manalastas, UPD); advocacy among Filipino LGBT rights activists (Bea Torre and Eric Manalastas, UPD); and the role of broadcast media in LGBT advocacy (Ton Clemente and colleagues, UPD).

Social change in Philippine psychology

LGBT psychology has come out in the Philippines. There is a growing body of knowledge about Filipino LGBT people that is being shared with Filipino psychologists through the numerous symposia and workshops at psychological conventions. There is a growing community of LGBT-identified psychologists. There is a growing alliance with other Filipino psychologists, with the leadership of the PAP and the PSSP, who have shown their support in cases of homophobia among its own professionals and who have issued statements of non-discrimination against LGBT people. There is a growing Philippine psychology for the empowerment of Filipinos marginalized for their gender and sexuality. In the framework of Kagan and Burton (2001) for a critical community psychology, LGBT psychology in the Philippines is engaging in a process of social change as it furthers education, builds a community, develops alliances, and makes psychology useful to people.

We are in the process of making Philippine psychology LGBT-inclusive. Such a psychology of liberation was made possible through the collective action of LGBT-identified psychologists and non-LGBT identified psychologists. it was the political will of individual change agents and the act of solidarity among allies in the profession and the discipline that made the difference. An LGBT-inclusive Philippine psychology is coming together through the work of affinity among Filipino psychologists who share in the wider cause of equality and empowerment for lesbian, gay, bisexual, and transgender people.

A call for affinity

I end this reflection with a call for affinity. This is a call to share "the vision of freedom for people of diverse genders and sexualities" (Ofreneo and de Vela 2010, 213). This is a call for care and compassion as we recognize each other's position of marginalization and carry each other's cause and advocacy. This is a call for an ethics of care that is at the heart of psychology. We do not need to identify as lesbian, gay, bisexual, or transgender to uphold the well-being of LGBT people. We only need to feel an affinity for any group of people that experiences oppression for being different. Affinity politics, rather than identity politics, allows us to work together in wider social movements for social justice and equal rights (Ofreneo and de Vela 2010). We come together because we carry the agenda of the oppressed and the marginalized. We come together because we are allies, partners, and friends.

This is a call for affinity. A call for empathy. And a call to love.

BIBLIOGRAPHY

Biswas-Diener, R., ed. *Positive Psychology as Social Change*. New York: Springer, 2011.

Clarke, V., S. J. Ellis, E. Peel, and D. W. Riggs. *Lesbian, Gay, Bisexual, Trans, and Queer Psychology*. Cambridge: Cambridge University Press, 2010.

Crenshaw, K. W. "Demarginalizing the Intersection of Race and Sex: A Black Feminist Critique of Antidiscrimination Doctrine, Feminist Theory, and Antiracist Politics." *University of Chicago Legal Forum* (1989): 139–67.

Isis International Manila. *Surfacing Lesbian, Bisexual, and Transgendered Women's Issues: Towards Affinity Politics in Feminist Movements (Research Report)*. Manila: Isis International, 2010.

Josef, J. C. "Sexual Identities and Self-images of Woman-loving Women: An Exploratory Study on the Realities of Woman-loving Women in the Philippine Context." Master's thesis, University of the Philippines, Diliman, 1997.

———. "Sexual Identities and Self-images of Women-loving Women." In *Selected Readings on Health and Feminist Research: A Sourcebook*, edited by S. H. Guerrero. Quezon City: University of the Philippines Center for Women's Studies, 1999.

Kagan, C., and M. Burton. *Critical Community Psychology: Praxis for the 21st Century*. IOD Occasional Paper. UK: Manchester Metropolitan University, Interpersonal and Organizational Development Research Group, 2001.

Kagan, C., M. Burton, and A. Siddiquee. "Action Research." In *The SAGE Handbook of Qualitative Research in Psychology*, edited by C. Willing and W. Stainton-Rogers. London: Sage, 2008.

Macapagal, M. E. J., M. A. P. Ofreneo, C. J. Montiel, and J. M. Nolasco. *Social Psychology in the Philippine Context*. Quezon City: Ateneo de Manila University Press, 2013.

Ofreneo, M. A. P. "From Awareness to Acceptance: The Filipino Female Homosexual's Identity Development Process." Master's thesis, Ateneo de Manila University, 2000.

———. "Tomboys and Lesbians: The Filipino Female Homosexual and Her Identity Development Process." *Philippine Journal of Psychology* 36, no. 1 (2003): 26–52.

Ofreneo, M. A. P., and T. C. de Vela. "Spheres of Lesbian, Gay, Bisexual, and Transgender Struggles: A Comparative Feminist Analysis." *Gender, Technology, and Development* 14 (2010): 197–216.

Psychological Association of the Philippines. "Statement of the Psychological Association of the Philippines on Non-discrimination Based on Sexual Orientation, Gender Identity and Expression." *Philippine Journal of Psychology* 44 (2011): 229–30.

Psychological Association of the Philippines Scientific and Professional Ethics Committee. "Code of Ethics for Philippine Psychologists." *Philippine Journal of Psychology* 43 (2010): 195–217.

Tan, M. L. "From *Bakla* to Gay: Shifting Gender Identities and Sexual Behaviors in the Philippines." In *Conceiving Sexuality: Approaches to Sex Research in a Postmodern World*, edited by R. G. Parker and J. H. Gagnon. New York: Routledge, 1995a.

————. "Tita Aida and Emerging Communities of Gay Men: Two Case Studies from Metro Manila, the Philippines." In *Gays and Lesbians in Asia and the Pacific: Social and Human Services*, edited by G. Sullivan and L. W. Leong. New York: Harrington Park Press, 1995b.

————. *Sex and Sexuality*. Policy Research Brief Series 1998-2. Quezon City: University of the Philippines Center for Women's Studies, 1998.

Acknowledgments

THE EDITORS ARE GRATEFUL to many colleagues, friends, and acquaintances who have, over the long germinating period of this book and in many parts of the world, helped us in many different ways bringing our project to fruition. Indeed, it is testimony to the global diasporic reach of Filipina/os and Philippine culture that the ideas motivating, germinating, and producing this collection of essays developed on six continents. This is no small feat considering archipelagic size but not surprising considering the Philippines' internal diversity, the ebbs and flows of its historical experience, and the encounters of generations of Filipinos both near and far from whatever they consider their homeland to be. In such a sense, this book provides a "primer" not only for LGBTIQ studies, but also for the history of what is today called globalization.

Accordingly, we do not prioritize nor otherwise categorize the inspiration or material support for which we express our gratitude, and thus place individuals in simple alphabetical order followed by institutional subjects of our thankfulness. Here are the people: Eufracio Abaya; Patricio (Jojo) Abinales; David B. J. Adams; Ma. Rowena Angeles; Kayle Antonio; Oscar Atadero; Jonas Bagas (LAGABLAB); Rico Barbosa; Jimmy Caro; Behn Cervantes; Guy Claudio; Ging Cristobal; Edmond Cuenca; E. C. Cunanan; Nikos Dacanay; Christopher Datol; Father Louis David; Andrew Donahue; Michael Denneny; Roxanne Omega Doron; Sally Eugenio; Mercy Fabros; Laurindo Garcia; Jennifer C. Josef; Becky Libed; Anne Lim; Martin Manalansan IV; Kristine Mandigma; Virgilio Manzano; Malu Marin; Matinikk (of Tondo—Jef, Roe, and Osang); Society of Homosexual Empowerment of Tondo (SHE)—President Alaia); Zone One (especially Laarmie and Todz Ipong); Dulce Natividad; Fidel Nemenzo; Princess Nemenzo; Ruby Beltran-Palma; Raul Pertierra; Andrea Peterson; Malou Rebullida; Danton Remoto; Mina Roces; Matthew Santamaria; Aida Santos; Anna Leah Sarabia; Rosario de Santos del Rosario; Sass Rogando Sasot; Society of Transexual Women of the Philippines (STRAP— Bemz, Dee, Joy, and Nadine); Teresa Encarnacion Tadem; Michael "Mick" de la Cruz Tan; Michael Tan; Ryan Thoreson;

Shiloah Torrechiva; Cheikh Traore; Angie Umbac; Kim Vance; Tesa de Vela; Gus Vibal; Kate Villaflor; Meredith Weiss; Saskia Wieringa; Chim Zayas; and Sami Zeidan.

Our institutional debt is owed (and hereby paid!) to the City University of New York Graduate Center's MA/PhD Program in Political Science; Council on International Educational Exchange Fulbright Programs; International Association for the Study of Sexuality, Culture and Society; Vibal Foundation; History Department of the University of Massachusetts, Amherst; and Five Colleges Consortium, Inc.

To these individuals and institutions, we offer our gratitude. At the same time, we assume full responsibility for any errors of fact and judgment in the compilation and publication of this book.

Image Credits

WE WISH TO ACKNOWLEDGE several institutions and individuals that have provided images for this anthology. These include the following:

- Archivo General de Indias
- Athena Lam
- Bahay Tsinoy Museum
- Bernadette Neri
- Bernardino Testa
- Bisdak Pride, Inc.
- Dulce Natividad
- Edmond Cuenca
- Enrique Guadiz
- Erika Carreon
- Felix d'Eon
- GALANG Philippines, Inc.
- Rep. Geraldine Roman
- JJ Josef
- Joaine Jan Marquez
- John Raspado
- Marconi Calindas
- Mark Blasius
- PAP LGBT Special Interest Group
- Patricia Callasan-Corre
- Patrick Alcedo
- Philippine Daily Inquirer
- Psychological Association of the Philippines
- Reuters News Agency
- Richard Chu
- Rolando Tolentino
- Sebastian Castro
- Shirin Bhandari and Home for the Golden Gays
- Visprint, Inc.
- Women's Research and Resource Center, Inc.

Contributors

Mark Blasius is Professor Emeritus of Political Science at the Graduate Center of the City University of New York (CUNY), and has also been a visiting professor at the University of the Philippines-Diliman, the University of Amsterdam, the University of Southern California (USC), and Princeton University. He specializes in the areas of contemporary political thought and the politics of gender and sexuality across cultures. He earned a PhD in political philosophy from Princeton University. He is the editor and author of *Sexual Identities, Queer Politics* (Princeton, 2001), co-editor and author of *We Are Everywhere: A Historical Sourcebook of Gay and Lesbian Politics* (Routledge, 1997), author of *Gay and Lesbian Politics: Sexuality and the Emergence of a New Ethic* (Temple, 1994), and has authored various book chapters and articles in such journals as *Political Theory, American Political Science Review, GLQ: A Journal of Lesbian and Gay Studies,* and *Journal of the History of Sexuality.* His writings have been translated into Dutch, French, Japanese, and Spanish. Mark held resident fellowships at the Rockefeller Foundation's Bellagio Center in Italy, the USC Center for Feminist Research, and the USC Center for Multiethnic and Transnational Studies. He received a Fulbright Senior Specialist Award and the CUNY Chancellor's Award for Scholarly Excellence and served on the Boards of Directors of both the CUNY Center for Lesbian and Gay Studies and the International Association for the Study of Sexuality, Culture and Society. Mark is a founding co-chair of the Lesbian and Gay Caucus of the American Political Science Association and served in various capacities for that professional association.

Richard T. Chu is a Five-College associate professor of history at the University of Massachusetts Amherst. He holds a bachelor's degree from Ateneo de Manila University, Philippines, a master's degree from Stanford University, and a doctorate degree in history from the University of Southern California. He was a Fulbright visiting professor at the Ateneo de Manila University for one semester in 2016. His research focuses on Chinese and Chinese mestizo history in the Philippines, centering on themes of empire, ethnicity, nationalism, transnationalism, gender, and race. His published works include *Chinese and Chinese Mestizos of Manila: Family, Identity, and Culture, 1860s–1930s* (Brill 2010; Anvil 2012) and *More Tsinoy Than We Admit* (Vibal, 2015). He is currently working on his next book project entitled *The "Chinaman Question" of the Philippines: A Conundrum in US Imperial Policy, 1899–1908*.

J. Neil C. Garcia teaches creative writing and comparative literature at the University of the Philippines Diliman, where he serves as Director of the university press and a Fellow for Poetry in the Institute of Creative Writing. He is the author of numerous poetry collections and works in literary and cultural criticism. Between 1994 and 2014, he coedited the famous *Ladlad* series of Philippine gay writing. Other important anthologies that he edited are *Aura: the Gay Theme in Philippine Fiction in English* (2012), *Bright Sign, Bright Age: Critical Essays in Philippines Studies* (2017), and the forthcoming *Busilak: New LGBTQ Poetry from the Philippines*. He is the director for the Philippines of Project GlobalGRACE: Global Gender and Cultures of Equality, a world-wide research and arts consortium sponsored by the Research Councils of the United Kingdom and Goldsmiths, University of London. He is currently at work on *Likha*, his seventh poetry book.

Roselle V. Pineda is an activist, researcher, curator, and artist, as well as a professor at the University of the Philippines Department of Art Studies. Her writings have been considered pioneering works in the field of lesbian art history and criticism in the Philippines, and her thesis, "Eloquent Crevices: Lesbian Interventions in (Art) Theory, History, and Production," received a citation for best thesis in 2003. She is an active member of the Congress of Teachers for Nationalism and Democracy (CONTEND-UP) and Concerned Artists of the Philippines (CAP) and the Artistic Curator and founder of Performance Curators Initiatives (PCI) and the community-based arts residency Aurora Artist Residency Program and Space (AARPS).

Carolyn Brewer (now retired and living in Christchurch, New Zealand) is affiliated with the Australian National University as an associate researcher, specializing in the impact of religion on gender and sexuality. She earned her doctoral degree from Murdoch University. Among her published works are *Shamanism, Catholicism and Gender Relations in Colonial Philippines, 1521–1685* (2004) and *Holy Confrontation: Religion, Gender and Sexuality in the Philippines, 1521–1685* (2001). She also contributed to the anthology *More Hispanic Than We Admit 2: Insights into Philippine Cultural History* (2015).

She is editor-in-chief of *Intersections: Gender and Sexuality in Asia and the Pacific*, an electronic journal that has been published since 1998.

Raquel A. G. Reyes is a historian and Philippine current affairs commentator. She obtained her PhD in Southeast Asian history from the School of Oriental and African Studies (SOAS), University of London and was a British Academy postdoctoral fellow. She is the author of *Love, Passion, and Patriotism: Sexuality and the Philippine Propaganda Movement in Europe, 1882–1892*, editor of *Art, Trade and Cultural Mediation in Asia, 1500–1950*, co-editor of *Sexual Diversity in Asia, c. 600 BCE to 1950*, and numerous journal articles on gender and sexuality, history of science, medicine and technology, and early modern global trade and local cultures in Southeast Asia. Her latest work, "Sex in Manila in the late 19th and early 20th centuries," will be published in *The Cambridge World History of Sexualities*.

Joaine Jan A. Marquez earned his master's degree in history from the Ateneo de Manila University. His research interests include the Chinese in Spanish Philippines. He has presented papers at academic conferences, including the Spanish-Filipino Friendship Day Conference at the University of the Philippines Diliman (October 2016), the International Conference on the Chinese in the Philippines at Ateneo de Manila University (January 2017), and the *Binalot* Talks of the UP Archaeological Studies Program (April 2017). He currently lives in Japan where he teaches history at an international school in Yokohama. He taught history in Xavier School, San Juan (Philippines) for six years before teaching internationally in 2018. His first international posting was in Pacific American School (Hsinchu, Taiwan) where he taught a variety of courses, including Modern World History, US History, and 20th-century China and Taiwan.

Michael L. Tan is a veterinarian and a medical anthropologist. He was chancellor of the University of the Philippines Diliman from 2014 to 2020. His research areas include gender and sexuality, health and wellness, culture and ethics, anthrozoology and anthropology, and Southeast Asian studies. He writes a weekly column, "Pinoy Kasi," in the *Philippine Daily Inquirer*.

Ronald Baytan teaches literature, LGBTQ+ studies, and creative writing at De La Salle University. He holds a PhD in English studies from the University of the Philippines Diliman. He is the author of *The Queen Sings the Blues: Poems,1992–2002* (Anvil, 2007) and *The Queen Lives Alone: Personal Essays* (UP Press, 2012).

Jennifer C. Josef earned her MA in sociology from the University of the Philippines Diliman. Her MA thesis, which was the first academic study on Filipino lesbians and tomboys, was a recipient of the Lourdes Lontok-Cruz graduate thesis award conferred by the University of the Philippines Center for Women and Gender Studies. She earned her PhD in anthropology from the University of the Philippines Diliman. Her dissertation, "Bontoc and northern Kankana-ey Bakla and Tomboy Desires and Identities: Intimate Bodies, Spaces, Histories, and Memories," is another pioneering work on gender, sexuality, and LGBTQ+ studies. Her current researches include "Non-prescribed Hormone Therapy among Transgenders in Baguio City and Benguet" and "Sexual Attitudes and Practices of Young Adult Men Having Sex with Men/Boys In Baguio City." Her paper "Vernacular Self-representation in Filipino Gender Identities: The Bontoc Minamagkit" is included in the forthcoming special issue on the Cordillera of the *South East Asia Research* journal of SOAS, University of London. She is currently the chair of the Department of Anthropology, Sociology, and Psychology of the University of the Philippines Baguio.

Patrick Alcedo, holder of the Government of Ontario's Early Researcher Award, is a dance ethnographer specializing in Philippine traditional dances. He earned his doctorate degree in dance history and theory from the University of California, Riverside and is an associate professor in the Department of Dance at York University in Toronto, Canada. In 2014 the Fulbright Association of America awarded him the Selma Jeanne Cohen Fund Scholarship. Writer, director, and producer of five documentary films, his *Dancing Manilenyos* (2018) won a Hollywood International Independent Documentary Film Award.

Kaira Zoe K. Alburo-Cañete is sssistant professor at the University of the Philippines Cebu and currently a PhD candidate at the University of New South Wales in Australia. Her specialization is development studies, focusing on the intersection of gender and environment, particularly in the context of disasters. She was the founding executive director of A2D Project–Research Group for Alternatives to Development—a Cebu-based non-government organization promoting development practices informed by evidence.

Rolando B. Tolentino is faculty of University of the Philippines Film Institute and former dean of the UP College of Mass Communication. He is director of the UP Institute of Creative Writing where he also serves as fellow. He has taught at the Osaka University, National University of Singapore, and University of California, Berkeley. His research interests include Philippine literature, popular culture, cinema and media, and interfacing national and transnational issues. He writes and has published books on fiction and creative non-fiction. He is a member of the Manunuri ng Pelikulang Pilipino (Filipino Film Critics Group), Altermidya (People's Alternative Media Network), and Congress of Teachers and Educators for Nationalism and Democracy (CONTEND-UP).

Kale Bantigue Fajardo completed his MA and PhD in cultural anthropology at the University of California, Santa Cruz. He is a core faculty member of the Department of American Studies and the Asian American Studies Program at the University of Minnesota, Twin Cities. Fajardo is also affiliated with the Department of Gender, Women's and Sexuality Studies and the Department of Asian Studies at Minnesota. He was a Fulbright Scholar in the Philippines (1997–1998). Fajardo's specializations include: maritime/migration/globalization studies; trans masculinities; and oceanic/maritime/archipelagic studies.

Eric Julian Manalastas is founding coordinator of the Psychological Association of the Philippines' LGBT Psychology Special Interest Group. He guest-edited two special issues of the *Philippine Journal of Psychology* in 2013 and in 2016, focusing on LGBT psychology. His research interests are in sexuality, collective action, and LGBT health disparities.

Beatriz Torre is a faculty member of the University of the Philippines Department of Psychology. Her expertise is social psychology, with a particular focus on the LGBT community. She has co-authored several articles with Eric Manalastas.

Mira Alexis P. Ofreneo is the chair of the Department of Psychology of the Ateneo de Manila University, where she earned her PhD in social psychology and master's degree in counseling psychology. She chaired and co-chaired the Psychological Association of the Philippines (PAP) from 2009 to 2013, and is currently the associate editor of the *Philippine Journal of Psychology*. Her doctoral dissertation, "Positioning Theory as a Discursive Approach to Understanding Same-Sex Intimate Violence," was awarded Most Outstanding Dissertation by the PAP in 2012 .

Index

Made in the USA
Monee, IL
23 July 2021